Neuropsychology
and the Hispanic Patient

Neuropsychology and the Hispanic Patient

A Clinical Handbook

Edited by

Marcel O. Pontón
University of California, Los Angeles

José León-Carrión
University of Seville

LEA

LAWRENCE ERLBAUM ASSOCIATES, PUBLISHERS

2001   Mahwah, New Jersey   London

Lawrence Erlbaum Associates, Inc., Publishers
10 Industrial Avenue
Mahwah, NJ 07430

On the cover: Copy of the Rey–Osterrieth Complex Figure by a
63-year-old Latina with 2nd-grade education, diagnosed with possible
Alzheimer's disease. Cover concept by Marcel O. Pontón, Ph.D.
Cover design by Kathryn Houghtaling Lacey.

Library of Congress Cataloging-in-Publication Data

Neuropsychology and the Hispanic patient : a clinical handbook / edited by
Marcel O. Pontón, José León-Carrión.
      p. cm.
      Includes bibliographical references and index.
      ISBN 0–8058–2614–9 (cloth) — ISBN 0–8058–2615–7 (paper)
      1. Clinical neuropsychology—Cross-cultural studies—Handbooks, manuals, etc.
  2. Hispanic Americans—Mental health—Handbooks, manuals, etc. I. Pontón, Marcel O.
  II. León-Carrión, José.
      [DNLM: 1. Nervous System Diseases–diagnosis. 2. Hispanic Americans–psychology.
  3. Nervous System Diseases–therapy. 4. Neuropsychological Tests. WL 141 N49367 2000]
RC386.6.N48 N494 2000
616.89'68073—dc21   00–042221

Printed in the United States of America
10 9 8 7 6 5 4 3 2 1

To Nicole, Gabriel, and Daniel
as they prepare to live during
the Hispanic century in the U.S.
El futuro está en sus manos.

M.O.P.

For all those Hispanic people living
in the States who are giving the best
of themselves every day to make
this nation even greater.

J. L.-C.

Contents

Preface

"Move over John. Make way for Jose, which in 1998 became the most popular baby boy's name in California and Texas."

—Garvey & McDonnell, 1999

U.S. demographics are changing rapidly. Any test developer interested in having an accurate reflection of U.S. demographics in its normative base must of necessity include Hispanics. By 2010, a time when most current neuropsychological tests will need revision, 15% of the U.S. population will be Hispanic. By 2050, one in every four Americans will be Hispanic. Accurate representation of Hispanics in the normative database of our neuropsychological tools is not a political issue but a scientific one. How should test developers proceed with the appropriate representation of Hispanics in their tools? What cultural issues should neuropsychologists take into account in their assessment and treatment of Hispanic patients? This volume, *Neuropsychology and the Hispanic patient: A Clinical Handbook,* attempts to provide practical tools for the clinician working with this population.

In the era of cultural diversity, culture itself has become an obscure variable which defies operationalization. Thus, culture covers a multitude of ambiguities, from unexplained variance in research to variable performance on neuropsychological profiles. But the questions of what exactly is Hispanic culture and how it affects the clinical endeavor deserve objective answers. Otherwise culture could never be taken seriously as a contributing factor to test performance. Since culture falls in the purview of anthropologists and sociologists, their definitions are used to more objectively describe Hispanic culture in the first few chapters. The task of the neuropsychologist with different age groups is addressed in the subsequent chapters. Researchers and clinicians provide guidelines and paradigms to work effectively with this population across the age span. Much remains to be done; however, we are confident that the compilation of this information by leading people in the field will fill a void, stimulate dialogue and continue to encourage neuropsychological research with Hispanic populations in the United States.

Hispanic culture is interacting ever more boldly with the dominant American culture through its tangible products (music, art, cuisine, media, etc.) and through language. In 1999 the glitterati of pop culture in the United States, for instance, included names like Carlos Santana, Jennifer Lopez, Christina Aguilera, Ricky Martin, Enrique Iglesias, and Marc Anthony, among others. Their style, their lyrics, and their music sketched an image of things to come: Rather than assimilation, there appears to be a mixture of two cultures with the emergence of yet a third distinct cultural identity, a *mestizo* culture. Thus, the task of clinical neuropsychologists with this population may be even more complex in the decade to come. How will we assess patients who are "speakin' la lingua loca" by 2010?

Cruz and Teck (1998) gave us plenty of laughs with their *Official Spanglish dictionary*. Little did they know, however, that as the missionaries of old (see chapter 2), their detailed collection of this new *lingua franca* will serve to standardize, disseminate, and operationalize a derided form of language: a form of language used daily in social interactions by an ever growing number of people. What thus far has been perceived as elusive, even inane, may well become the basis for empirical study in the years to come. It will not be long before the first Spanglish test (or "bilingual" for those interested in decorum) will begin to circulate in research and then commercial circles. The issues of test-equivalence or appropriate norms for comparison with the Anglo population will not be as relevant then. Instead, other questions will arise. Questions such as, what is intelligent behavior in a bilingual individual? What is an appropriate measure of vocabulary? What are the effects of acculturation on cognitive performance of native vs. foreign born bilinguals?

While many challenges lie ahead in the nascent field of Hispanic neuropsychology, many more basic questions confront us today. It is our sincere desire to provide some answers to these questions in this volume.

ACKNOWLEDGMENTS

Dr. Pontón extends heartfelt gratitude to Sylvia, whose patience and *cariño* have supported him through this and countless other projects. A word of appreciation to all our contributors is in order. Similarly, we would like to acknowledge Katherine Rankin and Allison Keuning for their clerical assistance. Dr. Lawrence Herrera served as an informal editor. His suggestions and comments were extremely helpful.

REFERENCES

Cruz, B., & Teck, B. (1998). *The official Spanglish dictionary*. New York: Fireside (Simon & Schuster).
Garvey, M., & McDonnell, P. J. (1998, January 8). Jose moves into top spot in name game. *Los Angeles Times*, pp. A1, A16.

1

The Hispanic Population in the United States: An Overview of Sociocultural and Demographic Issues

MARCEL O. PONTÓN
Harbor–UCLA Medical Center

JOSÉ LEÓN-CARRIÓN
Universidad de Sevilla

In order to understand what is neuropsychologically distinctive about Hispanics, there must be a clear definition of who they are and what differentiates them from other ethnic groups in the United States. History, culture, demographics, and language make Hispanics a unique group within the mosaic of U.S. society. Yet, this uniqueness requires an appreciation of their vast diversity. This diversity begins with the most practical of questions: What should this group be called? As noted later, ethnic labels are not inclusive. The history, culture, and demography of the various peoples referred to as Hispanic are kaleidoscopic. A brief review is followed by a consideration of the question of *language* as it relates to assessment. What language do Hispanics speak and how does it affect the clinical interaction? This basic information provides the groundwork for the discussion of the various issues that matter most to clinicians in the subsequent chapters.

DEFINITIONS

This chapter—and the rest of the book—uses the terms *Hispanic/Latino* interchangeably to denote people of various ethnic, racial, national, and cultural backgrounds whose ancestors lived in Spain or Latin America. Stavans (1996) believed that whereas *Hispanic* is used in the context of demographics, education, urban development, drugs, and health, *Latino* is used to refer to artists, musicians, and movie stars. Be that as it may, both terms are widely used and have gained acceptance in the mass media.

Technically, however, people who trace their family background to Belize, the Guyanas, Cape Verde, or the Philippines may be considered Hispanic, given the historical influence of Spain in those countries. Portugal, France, Italy, Spain, and Rumania are European Latin countries; Brazil and Haiti are also Latin American countries even though they do not speak Spanish (Pontón & Ardila, 1999). Thus, having an accurate, universal, and acceptable term to define this population is a challenging task. G. Marin and B. V. Marin (1991) named several other labels that have been used to define this group, including Spanish-speaking, Spanish-surnamed, Latin American, Raza, and Chicano. Additionally, many Hispanics also self-identify with their country/region of origin (e.g., *boricua, tejano, nuevomejicano, español, mejicano, cubano,* etc.), making it even more difficult to have a label that can please everyone in this vastly heterogeneous group (Novas, 1993). The reason is sociocultural in nature, as Stavans (1996) explained, because many Hispanics in the United States have experienced a metamorphosis that includes many losses: citizenship, language, identity, self-esteem, and tradition. Self-definition by country of origin is perhaps an attempt to preserve some of that identity in an environment that demands assimilation.

In this chapter (in fact, throughout the volume), the labels *Hispanic* and/or *Latino* are used with awareness of their simultaneous limitations and appeal.

Difficulties with the labels also point to practical clinical/research limitations for the study of this population group. This task would be easier by an order of magnitude if *Hispanics* fell into neat categories along bidimensional variables. In this ideal scenario, orderly research designs would follow, expanding the knowledge about the cognitive functioning of this population geometrically. The paucity of neuropsychological research on Hispanics, however, suggests an unflattering reality (Cervantes & Acosta, 1992; Cueller, 1998; Echemendia, Harris, Congett, & Diaz, 1997; Flanagan, 1992; Mungas, 1996; Perri, Naplin, & Carpenter, 1995; Pontón, Satz, Herrera, & Ortiz, 1996; Taussig & Pontón, 1996). Adequate neuropsychological investigation of this heterogeneous ethnic group would require massive samples, ample and culturally sensitive personnel, and valid and reliable tests of cognition (Llorente, Pontón, Taussig, & Satz, 1999; Pontón & Ardila, 1999). These requirements are enough to dishearten many an ambitious neuroscientist, especially in this era of minimal resource allocation.

A BRIEF HISTORICAL PERSPECTIVE

Hispanics have a long history and tradition in what is now the United States. Florida was first discovered and named in 1513 by Ponce de León. Consequently, the oldest city in the United States, *San Agustín* (Saint Augustine), Florida, was founded by Spanish settlers in 1565. The Mississippi river was discovered by Alonso Alvarez de Pineda in 1519 while mapping the Gulf of Mexico; García López de Cárdenas, leading a band of Coronado's expedition, discovered the Grand Canyon in 1541. Spanish settlers began immigrating to the Southwest and founded El Paso, Texas, in 1598 and Santa Fe, New Mexico, in 1609. New Mexico counted as many as 20,000 settlers in 1760. In 1769, the mission at San Diego, California, was established and the colonization of California by Spaniards began in earnest (Kanellós, 1994). That same year, 63 men led by Portolá camped near asphalt pits and named the valley they discovered, "El Pueblo de Nuestra Señora La Reina de Los Angeles de Porciuncula." El Pueblo de Los Angeles was founded by Governor Felipe de Neve in 1781, and the first settlers included 11 families (Samora & Simon, 1993). Those families and other Spanish settlers came to be known as *Californios.*

As late as the 1750s, up to half of what is now U.S. territory belonged to the Spanish crown. One century later, in 1848, all of what is now the Western United States belonged to the Viceroyalty of New Spain (Mexico). As De Varona (1996) put it:

FIG. 1.1.   Map of Mexico, 1772, *Intendencias and Provincias de la Nueva España*. From
Las intendencias de la Nueva España (p. 202) by A. Commons, 1993, Mexico City: Universidad Autónoma Nacional de México.

For 335 years Spain, and later Mexico, dominated nearly continuously most of North America. . . . Yet by the end of that period the dominators themselves had been banished from the
continent, their empire in a decline from which it would never recover.

Left behind . . . from Florida to Texas and up and down the Pacific Coast, [are] outposts
that became great cities and . . . European civilization made possible only by Spaniards who
literally blazed trails for faith and country.

Left behind, too, was the new race of people—of mixed Spanish, Indian and African
blood, fundamentally shaped by the institutions of Spanish colonial civilization but sharing
the cultural heritages of all their ancestors. (p. 84)

The Hispanic presence in the history of the United States is pervasive. Commons
(1993) provided a map of the *Intendencias y Provincias Internas de la Nueva España*
[Administration Offices and Internal Provinces of the New Spain], which shows the historical boundaries of the territory claimed by the Spanish Crown in the year 1786. (See
Fig. 1.1). It should be no surprise that Spanish names for the states are still on the map:

California (from a novel of a legendary island of griffins and gold by Ordoñez de Montalvo in 1508), Colorado (from the Spanish word for "reddish"), Florida (blooming with flowers), Montana (mountain), Nevada ("snow-covered"), Oregon (". . . possibly from the word *oreja,* 'ear,' because the Spanish thought the local natives had big ones"; De Varona, 1996, p. 208), Arizona (land of few springs), and New Mexico (Nuevo Mexico). Spanish names of cities are also plentiful: San Diego, Los Angeles, San Francisco, San Luis Obispo, Palo Alto, Sacramento, San Jose, Santa Fe, El Paso, Monterey, and San Antonio, among many others.

Currently, there are four distinct groups of Hispanics in the United States. The first three are those of Mexican, Puerto Rican, and Cuban origin. The fourth, an all-inclusive category of "Other," can be used to describe individuals from Central American, South American, Caribbean, and Spanish backgrounds. Each group has had different historical experiences in the United States.

Mexicans

Mexican identity in the United States is distinct and dates back to the 1700s. The Mexican presence in what is now the U.S. is also marked by conflict with Anglo settlers. It was not until the Treaty of Guadalupe Hidalgo at the end of the war with Mexico (1848) that the United States annexed Texas, New Mexico, Arizona, Nevada, Utah, half of Colorado, and California to its present territory. According to Novas (1993):

> Anglo settlers ousted Mexican grantees from the most desirable lands. This trend continued until the 1930's when a repatriation movement which demanded that Mexican-Americans (regardless of their citizenship) be sent back to Mexico, began gathering significant support. In the 1930's some half a million deportees were sent to Mexico as the collective effort of local government agencies. (p. 84)

Some Mexicans refer to themselves as *Chicano,* which denotes a "person of Mexican heritage born and raised in the U.S. or a person born in Mexico who has become a permanent resident or citizen of the United States" (Galván, 1995, p. 60).

There are people (e.g., in New Mexico) who can trace their roots back to the 1700s, but there is a large contingent that has emigrated in this century directly from Mexico to the United States—particularly between the 1970s and 1990s. These immigrants come mostly from rural areas to find work in agriculture, manufacturing, construction, or service jobs. Their history is marked by racism and discrimination (Dana, 1993).

As noted earlier, the largest contingent of Hispanics in the United States is Mexican, but only recently has this group been growing in political influence, as noted by gains in California, for instance. The 1998 election placed Mexican American politicians in key posts (e.g., lieutenant governor, representatives, leader of the legislature, among others). Given the proximity of Mexico to the United States, it has become a powerful economic ally, with its own influence. In 1998, Mexico was the second largest importer of U.S. goods around the world (behind Canada and ahead of Japan). It is also the third largest exporter of goods to the United States (U.S. Census Bureau, 1998b). Thus, the Mexican presence and cultural influence also comes from a dynamic economic relation.

Puerto Ricans

"An island of . . . farmers and modest sugar, tobacco, and coffee planters, Puerto Rico served as a Spanish outpost, guarding the sea lanes of the Caribbean, as the massive fortifications of San Juan testify to this day" (Carr, 1984, p. 19). When marines landed on July 25, 1898, to make Puerto Rico a U.S. "possession," the island's government was dictated by the U.S. Congress, under colonial administrators.

Puerto Rican culture is made up of an admixture of European, African, Taíno Indian, and American characteristics. There are as many Puerto Ricans in the United States as there are in the *Bella Isla*. Although this group is spread throughout the United States, the great majority of Puerto Ricans live in New York. Thus, the term *Nuyoriqueño*, or *Nuyorican*, has been coined as a designation for those who are part of the largely urban New York Puerto Rican community. In contrast to all other immigrant Hispanic groups, Puerto Ricans are U.S. citizens by birth, a right enacted into law in 1917. In 1952, Puerto Rico approved a constitution, making it a self-governing "commonwealth" of the United States (Wagenheim & Wagenheim, 1994). The people of Puerto Rico decided in 1998 to remain a commonwealth, rejecting the option of statehood or full self-government. Religiously, about 81% of Puerto Ricans describe themselves as Roman Catholic.

Cubans

Because of its proximity to the Florida coast, Cuba historically has been a case in which U.S. interests have collided with those of the island, resulting in blunt U.S. political interventionism. The war with Spain in 1890 was fought with the idea of annexing Cuba to the United States. In the last half of the 19th century, some 10,000 Cubans emigrated to the United States. Interventionism contributed to multiple coup d'etats, the last of which took place with the Castro-led revolution in 1959. The well-known and massive migration of Cubans following the revolution settled mostly in Florida, New Jersey, and New York. This group was made up mostly of middle- to upper-middle-class professionals who were granted political asylum and social benefits. The next massive migration of Cubans (approximately 125,000) took place in 1980 during the Mariel boat lift. In a political move expressing his disdain for U.S. policy toward Cuba, Castro also forced criminals, mentally ill, and other misfit people into the boats leaving the Mariel port. These immigrants came to be known as "Marielitos"; they were mostly working-class people.

The Cuban community has passionate political views about the island's current problems and future solutions. Political activism and participation is very strong. The recent case of Elián González illustrated to the United States the depth of animus Cuban exiles feel against the Castro government. The political ethos of Cuban Americans has been mostly identified with Republican stands (Novas, 1993). The Cuban enclave economy in Miami is prosperous and one of the strongest in the city. It includes banking, business, textiles, food, cigars, and trade (Dana, 1993; De Varona, 1996).

Other

People in this category come from 18 different countries. However, the majority come from Central and South America, as well as the Dominican Republic. In its website, the Census reports large enough numbers of Central and South Americans as a distinct category, separate from "Other" (http://www.census.gov). In the future, there may be enough data available about this group to grant a fifth categorization of Hispanics.

HISPANIC PEOPLES IN THE U.S. TODAY

> The Hispanic experience is unique in U.S. history. Hispanics are at once the oldest and the newest immigrants to the United States. (Kanellós, 1994, p. 21)

The majority of Hispanic peoples living in the United States has historically come from Mexico. This remains true today. The U.S. Census (1998a) indicates that at least 63% of all Hispanics in the United States are from Mexico (see Table 1.1).

With the exception of New York, the Hispanic presence was highest in those states in which Hispanics have lived historically. Thus, in 2000, California will have 10.6 million Hispanic residents, Texas will have 5.9 million, and Florida will have 2.4 million. New York, which boasts a large Caribbean and South American population, will count 2.8 million Hispanics among its residents (according to conservative estimates; U.S. Census Bureau, 1998a). Although the majority of U.S. Hispanics live in California and Texas, 40% of New Mexico's population is Hispanic.

Hispanics are concentrated largely in urban centers. California boasts 4 of the 10 largest Hispanic metropolitan areas in the United States, as can be seen from Table 1.2. It should be noted that these are metropolitan statistical areas, and not only the cities. These data suggest there are some metro areas in the United States with a Hispanic population as large as that of other Latin American cities. The Hispanic population of the Los Angeles/Long Beach metropolitan area (4 million), for instance, is as large as that of Caracas or Bogotá; it is two thirds as large as the total population of El Salvador and about the same size as the total population of Uruguay.

Figure 1.2 presents a map of the distribution, by state, of the Hispanic population in the United States.

Projections from the U.S. Census indicate that Hispanics will grow in numbers and influence in the next century. It can safely be called the "Hispanic Century." By 2050, for instance, 1 in every 4 individuals will be of Hispanic origin. The growth of this population will be significantly higher than that of the non-Hispanic population. Table 1.3 shows the U.S. Census statistics and projections of population growth for the next 50 years. Based on these conservative statistics of population growth, the United States will most likely be the second or third largest Hispanic nation in the world by the year 2050.

From the aforementioned statistics, it can be surmised that U.S. Hispanics are mostly young, largely urbanite, come mostly from Mexico, and are heavily represented in the

TABLE 1.1
Hispanic Population by Country of Origin
(in thousands)

Hispanic Group		*Percentage*
Total Hispanic population	29,703	100%
Mexican	18,795	63%
Puerto Rican	3,152	11%
Cuban	1,258	4%
Central & South American	4,292	14%
Other	2,206	7%

Note: From U.S. Census Bureau.
Internet release date: August 7, 1998.

TABLE 1.2
Hispanic Population by State and County

States with the Largest Hispanic Population by July 1997

State	Ranking	Hispanic Population
California	1	9.9 million
Texas	2	5.7
New York	3	2.6
Florida	4	2.1
Illinois	5	1.2

*States with the Largest Percentage of Hispanics
in Their Population, as of July 1, 1997*

State	Ranking	Hispanic Population
New Mexico	1	40%
California	2	31%
Texas	3	29%
Arizona	4	22%
Nevada	5	15%

*Counties with the Largest Hispanic Population
as of July 1, 1997*

County	Ranking	Hispanic Population
Los Angeles, CA	1	4.0 million
Dade County, FL	2	1.1
Cook County, IL	3	0.87
Harris County, TX	4	0.85
Orange County, CA	5	0.76

Note: U.S. Census Bureau, September 4, 1998.
Public Information Office, release bulletin CB98-160.
http://www.census.gov/population/www/estimates/
statepop.html.

Western United States, New York, and Florida. However, these broad characteristics tell us nothing about the sociocultural background of this population, which is highly heterogeneous. The diverse sociocultural elements of the Hispanic population in the United States may be approached objectively utilizing a three-dimensional model that considers demographics (ethnicity, age, education, SES), language, and acculturation.

Demographic Variables

Ethnicity and Generational History. Ethnicity among Hispanics is quite diverse. Hispanics can be Caucasian, Indian, Black, and any combination thereof. In the words of a Puerto Rican poet, they are "all the colors tied." Moreover, the immigration patterns of different ethnic groups to Latin America from the 1940s to the 1970s (Middle East, Europe, Asia) is also reflected in the groups of Hispanics who have migrated to the United States recently (De Varona, 1996; Llorente et al., 1999). Thus, a Peruvian citizen

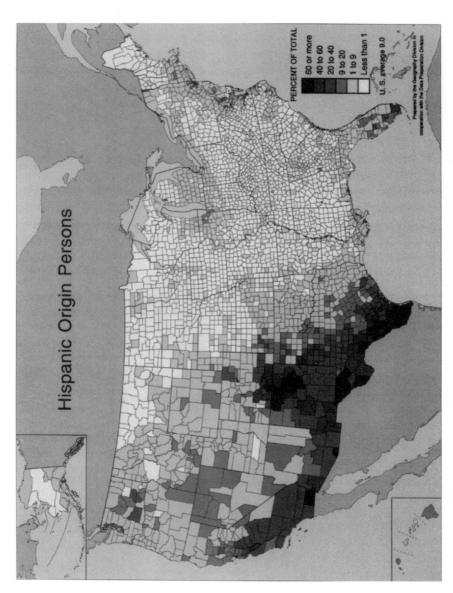

FIG. 1.2.   Distribution of the Hispanic Population in the United States, 1990. *Source:*
Produced by the U.S. Census Bureau. http://www.census.gov/geo/www/mapGallery/
images/hispanic.jpg

TABLE 1.3

Projections of the Hispanic Population in Relation to the U.S. Total Population
Over the Next 50 Years (in thousands)

	July 1, 1998	July 1, 1999	July 1, 2000	July 1, 2005	July 1, 2010
Population	29,566	30,461	31,366	36,057	41,139
(Percent of total)	11.0	11.2	11.4	12.6	13.8
Median age (years)	26.8	26.9	27.0	27.3	27.7
Male population	14,922	15,358	15,799	18,082	20,557
Female population	14,644	15,102	15,566	17,975	20,582

	July 1, 2015	July 1, 2020	July 1, 2025	July 1, 2030
Population	46,705	52,652	58,930	65,570
(Percent of total)	15.1	16.3	17.6	18.9
Median age (years)	28.1	28.8	29.4	29.8
Male population	23,279	26,194	29,276	32,540
Female population	23,426	26,458	29,654	33,031

	July 1, 2035	July 1, 2040	July 1, 2045	July 1, 2050
Population	72,639	80,164	88,125	96,508
(Percent of total)	20.3	21.7	23.1	24.5
Median age (years)	30.1	30.4	30.7	31.0
Male population	36,019	39,731	43,669	47,830
Female population	36,620	40,433	44,456	48,678

of Japanese descent will most likely self-identify as Hispanic culturally and linguistically, but not "ethnically." Moreover, ethnicity in Latin America has been a very dynamic concept; interracial marriages have characterized its societies from the beginning. In today's Mexico, for instance, there are at least 50 ethnic groups, some with preserved Indian languages (Vázquez, 1994). These people obviously form part of the immigrant pool from Mexico to the United States, making it impossible to classify a "Mexican" race.

The U.S. Census Bureau has formally stated that "peoples of Hispanic origins can be of any race," in order to solve its problems of classification. Whereas this definition makes it easy for the government to group together a widely diverse group, it does little to dispel myths and stereotypes about the ethnic characteristics of Hispanics. It is safe to say that ethnicity is not a useful variable for research purposes with this population.

The generational history of Hispanics may be given in many instances by tracing the country of birth at the time of immigration into the United States. However, this is a faulty approach because many Hispanic families in what is now the Southwest have lived in the United States for some 300 years, and have maintained their level of cultural identity intact. For those groups that have immigrated to the United States, there are several categories that can be useful in understanding the generational history of this population (see Table 1.4).

Age and Education. The median age of the U.S. Hispanic population is 26 years, which is much younger than the median age of 35 years for non-Hispanic Whites. A full 41% of the Hispanic population falls under age 21, as compared to 29% of the total non-Hispanic population, reflecting the high birthrate among Latinos. Data from the U.S. Census Bureau (1995) on age distribution of Hispanics reveals a relatively young popula-

TABLE 1.4
Classification of Hispanics by Generational History

Generation	Subjects' Place of Birth	Parents' Place of Birth	Grandparents' Place of Birth
First generation	Latin America		
Second generation	United States	Latin America	
Mixed second generation	United States	United States Latin America	
Third generation	United States	United States	Latin America

TABLE 1.5
Educational Attainment of Hispanics by Country of Origin (1994)

25+ years old	Total	Mexican	Puerto Rican	Cuban	Central & South American	Other
High School graduate	54.7%	48.6%	61.1%	65.2%	63.3%	66.6%
Bachelor's degree or higher	10.3%	7.4%	10.8%	19.7%	14.8%	14.9%

Note. From U.S. Census Bureau (1998b).

tion. Seventeen percent of the total U.S. population of children under age 5 in the year 2000 will be of Hispanic origin. Similarly, 14% of people age 18 to 24 in the United States will be of Hispanic origin in the year 2000. Among Hispanics, those of Mexican origin had the youngest median age (23), and Cubans had the oldest (41).

Educational attainment for Hispanics appears to be relatively low. According to the *Statistical Abstract of the United States: 1998* (U.S. Census Bureau, 1998b), a little more than half of this population (54.7%) had earned a high school diploma, and only 10.3% completed a bachelor's degree or more. This is in stark contrast with the educational attainment for the U.S. population as a whole, which had an 86% and 23.8% completion rate, respectively. However, the actual level of attainment varies according to country of origin, with Central and South American and "Other" showing the highest level of educational attainment. Table 1.5 provides data on the educational attainment of this population by country of origin for subjects age 25 or older.

Reedy (1995) reported a trend suggesting that Hispanic women graduate from high school more often than their male counterparts; however, of those who went to college, more Hispanic men obtained bachelor's degrees than women, particularly in the older groups (age 50 or older). This most likely reflects a cohort effect, as cultural expectations give more importance to men pursuing education (Alduncin-Abitia, 1989).

SES.   The median income of Hispanic households in 1997 was $26,179. Again, this varied according to country of origin, with people from Cuban backgrounds earning the most ($35,616), and Puerto Ricans earning the least ($23,646). Like the rest of the population, household income among Hispanics peaks in the age 45–54 group. Married couples had the highest median income among Hispanic households. Unfortunately, Hispanic married couples have a much higher poverty rate (26%) than do other ethnic groups in the United States (U.S. Census Bureau, 1998b).

The average size of a Hispanic household in the year 2000 will be 3.51 people, as compared to 2.54 for non-Hispanic Whites. Roughly one of every three Hispanic children live with their mother alone, and 71% live with both parents. Forty-two percent of the 6 million Hispanic householders in the United States own their homes, as compared to 64% for the general population. Fifty-five percent of Cubans own their homes, versus 31% of Puerto Ricans (U.S. Census Bureau, 1998b). Los Angeles has the largest number of Hispanic homeowners (U.S. Census Bureau, 1995).

Language

Language as a variable of interest among this population can be understood best along a continuum with monolingualism at its two polarities. Of note, Hispanics may speak Spanish at home, or may have learned it in school, or may not know it all (Dana, 1993; De Varona, 1996). Thus, there appears to be an increasing number of Hispanics with little or no formal training in Spanish. They can perhaps use it socially in conversation but are unable to write with proper grammar and may have difficulties reading as well. The same is true of Hispanics in relation to the English language. Bilingualism can be conceptualized as shown in Fig. 1.3.

Bilingualism can lie anywhere in between these two polarities. It is a matter of degree and depends on the mastery of and relative competence in both languages (Harding & Reiley, 1986). It requires expressive and receptive skills, although a person can understand but not speak well in a second language. Relative competence involves the ability to read, write, speak, and think in either language.

Hispanics may have varying degrees of mastery of either language. The majority of Hispanics born or raised in the United States speak English, and those migrating from Spanish-speaking countries also learn English to a greater or lesser extent. However, Spanish use in the United States is expanding rather than shrinking (Kanellós, 1994). In fact, Spanish ranks first among the top 15 languages other than English spoken at home. More than 54% of those who spoke a language other than English at home reported speaking Spanish. It was nine times more frequent than French, which was in second place. Of the 17.3 million who admitted to speaking Spanish at home, only 48% spoke English, and not very well (i.e., they had some form of bilingualism), according to the Census. Obviously, those who migrated recently or who were less acculturated were more likely to have difficulty with English. Table 1.6 shows data on the five most common foreign languages other than English spoken at home. This does not take into account the number of people who are bilingual but do not speak Spanish at home, or the number of Spanish-speakers who refused to answer the Census questions in English.

The degree of bilingualism of individuals of Hispanic origin in the United States appears to be related to their degree of acculturation (discussed in subsequent chapters) as it relates to research and assessment of this population. The reader is referred to Centeno and Obler's chapter (5) on bilingualism, and Cascallar and Arnold's chapter (4) on second language acquisition for Spanish-speakers.

LANGUAGE

FIG. 1.3. Continuum of language functioning among Hispanics.

TABLE 1.6
Top Five Foreign Languages Spoken at Home in the United States

Language	Number (thousands)
Spanish	17,345
French	1,930
German	1,548
Chinese	1,319
Italian	1,319

Note: From U.S. Census Bureau (1990). The number represents the number of people, not number of households.

CONCLUSIONS

This chapter has provided an overview of foundational issues relevant to this volume. The definition of who a Hispanic person is has been approached from different angles. A rationale for the use of the terms *Hispanic* and *Latino* has been provided, arguing that despite controversies, they have a wide appeal and a historical context. The background of Hispanics in the United States was described from geohistorical and cultural perspectives, and a demographic summary of this population, highlighting population distribution, concentration, projections, and educational attainment was given.

These foundational issues provide a common ground for the neuropsychologist working with this population. Agreement on who Hispanics are allows for discussion to formulate models for sensible solutions to the current problems of research, clinical assessment, and treatment—all of which are considered from conceptual, developmental, and clinical perspectives in the chapters that follow. The hope is to provide clinicians with tools that aid them in delivering effective services to Hispanics.

REFERENCES

Alduncin-Abitia, E. (1989). *Los Volores de los Mexicanos* [Mexican values]. Mexico City: Fomento Cultural Banamex.

Carr, R. (1984). *Puerto Rico: A colonial experiment.* New York: Random House.

Cervantes, R. C., & Acosta, F. X. (1992). Psychological testing for Hispanic Americans. *Applied & Preventive Psychology, 1*(4), 209–219.

Commons, A. (1993). *Las intendencias de la Nueva España.* Mexico City: Universidad Autónoma Nacional de Mexico.

Cueller, I. (1998). Cross-cultural clinical psychological assessment of Hispanic Americans. *Journal of Personality Assessment, 70*(1).

Dana, R. H. (1993). *Multicultural assessment perspectives for professional psychology.* Boston: Allyn & Bacon.

De Varona, F. (1996). *Latino literacy: The complete guide to our Hispanic history and culture.* New York: Henry Holt.

Echemendia, R. J., Harris, J. G., Congett, S. M., & Diaz, M. L. (1997). Neuropsychological training and practices with Hispanics: A national survey. Annual Meeting of the American Psychological Association (1994, Los Angeles, California, US). *Clinical Neuropsychologist, 11*(3), 229–243.

Flanagan, T. A. (1992). Current practices among psychologists in assessing the intellectual functioning of Hispanic adults. *Dissertation Abstracts International, 52*(8-A).

Galván, R. A. (1995). *The dictionary of Chicano Spanish.* Lincolnwood, IL: National Texbook Company.

Harding, E., & Riley, P. (1986). *The bilingual family.* New York: Cambridge University Press.

Kanellós, N. (1994). *The Hispanic almanac: From Columbus to corporate America.* Detroit: Visible Ink Press.

Llorente, A., Pontón, M. O., Taussig, M., & Satz, P. (1999). Patterns of American immigration and their influence on the Acquisition of Neuropsychological norms for minority groups. *Archives of Clinical Neuropsychology, 14*(7), 603–614.

Marin, G., & Marin B. V. (1991). *Research with Hispanic populations.* Newbury Park, CA: Sage.

Mungas, D. (1996). The process of development of valid and reliable neuropsychological assessment measures for English- and Spanish-speaking elderly persons. In D. G.-T. E. Gwen Yeo (Ed.), *Ethnicity and the dementias* (pp. 33–46). Washington, DC: Taylor & Francis.

Novas, H. (1993). *Everything you need to know about Latino history.* New York: Penguin.

Perri, B., Naplin, N. A., & Carpenter, G. A. (1995). A Spanish auditory verbal learning and memory test. *Assessment, 2*(3), 245–253.

Pontón, M. O., & Ardila, A. (1999). The future of neuropsychology with Hispanic populations. *Archives of Clinical Neuropsychology, 14*(7), 565–580.

Pontón, M. O., Satz, P., Herrera, L., & Ortiz, F. (1996). Normative data stratified by age and education for the Neuropsychological Screening Battery for Hispanics (NeSBHIS): Initial report. *Journal of the International Neuropsychological Society, 2*(2), 96–104.

Reedy, M. A. (1995). *Statistical record of Hispanic Americans* (2nd ed.). New York: Gale Research/International Tomson.

Samora, J., & Simon, P. V. (1993). *A history of the Mexican American people.* Notre Dame, IN: University of Notre Dame Press.

Stavans, I. (1996). *The Hispanic condition: Reflections on culture and identity in America.* New York: HarperPerennial.

Taussig, I. M., & Pontón, M. (1996). Issues in neuropsychological assessment for Hispanic older adults: Cultural and linguistic factors. In D. G.-T. E. Gwen Yeo (Ed.), *Ethnicity and the dementias* (pp. 47–58). Washington, DC: Taylor & Francis.

U.S. Census Bureau (1995). Housing in metropolitan areas—Hispanic origin households, *Statistical Brief,* SB/95-4.

U.S. Census Bureau. (1998a, September 4). Public Information Office, release bulletin CB98-158. http://www.census.gov/population/estimates/statepop.html.

U.S. Census Bureau. (1998b, September 29). *Statistical Abstract of the United States: 1998.* http://www.census.gov/prod/3/98pubs/98statab/sasec1.pdf.

Vázquez, J. Z. (1994). *Una historia de México* [A history of Mexico]. Mexico City: Editorial Patria.

Wagenheim, K., & Wagenheim, O. (1994). *The Puerto Ricans: A documentary history.* New York: Praeger.

2

Hispanic Culture in the United States

MARCEL O. PONTÓN
Harbor–UCLA Medical Center

Culture as a measurable construct is a legitimate topic of psychological study and attention (Dana, 1993; Matsumoto, 1996; Ponterotto, Casas, Suzuki, & Alexander, 1995; Rule-Goldberger & Veroff, 1995). Neuropsychology, as part of the larger discipline of psychology, has long considered culture an important element affecting perception (Vygotsky, 1978) and cognitive development, because culture determines what cognitive activities are valued by a society (Ardila, 1995). With the growing diversity of the U.S. population, the practice of psychology, generally, and of neuropsychology, specifically, will have to meet the challenges posed by cultural diversity (Echemendia, Harris, Congett, Diaz, & Puente, 1997; Iijima-Hall, 1997; Llorente, Pontón, Satz, & Taussig, 1999; Yeo & Gallagher-Thompson, 1996). In order to consider culture as a variable impacting the study of brain–behavior relations among Hispanics, however, clinicians and researchers alike must begin with an operational definition of Hispanic culture, so they can understand the ways in which it differs from their own and the ways it impacts data obtained from the patient. This chapter describes *worldview* as the cultural cognitive grid from which behavior derives, and then procedes to define Hispanic culture in the United States following an anthropological paradigm.

WORLDVIEW AS A CULTURAL GRID

Cultures share common ways of understanding reality, or a worldview. *Worldview* is an epistemological map of reality that is shaped by past experiences, language, access to technology, and resources. Worldviews share six universal characteristics: classification, nature of the human universe (person/group), causality, time, space, and relationships (Kearney, 1984). This map evolves with time and with the accumulated knowledge, experience, and resources of a culture. Thus, there is discussion of "western" and "eastern" worldviews and of scientific and cosmic worldviews. To address cultural differences between Hispanic and non-Hispanic Anglo-Americans, the next section outlines differences in their worldviews using the domains of general assumptions about reality and values. This serves as the preface to the discussion of Hispanic culture in the United States. The characterisitics that differentiate a Hispanic worldview from that of its Anglo counterpart within the context of the United States can be broadly conceptualized as follows:

Classification: Anglo-American culture puts things into neat categories, following orderly codes, groupings, or categorizations. Within Hispanic culture, the differences are not so clear. Things are together; they are part of each other. Distinctions are less clear.

Person/Group: Anglo-American culture places emphasis on individuals and their rights. The individual has primary responsibility. Independence and autonomy are encouraged at an early age. Hispanic culture is more family and group oriented. Decisions are made in a way to preserve the rights of the family, even at the expense of some individual rights. Anglo-American culture views nature as an element that can be conquered and predicted by the individual. Hispanic culture sees it as part of a larger, predetermined force that humans must accept with long suffering.

Causality: Scientific laws govern physical and psychological phenomena in the Anglo-American culture. It is a postmodern scientific view of causality. It values objective, rational, linear thinking with an emphasis on quantitative data. God and the supernatural are part of both physical and psychological phenomena to a large portion of the Hispanic culture. Magic Realism (à la García Márquez) impacts many of the phenomena people experience in their psychic and physical lives. The less educated the patients, the likelier they are to conceptualize events as related to special phenomena. In the words of a patient with peripheral neuropathies: "Doctor, the reason I'm having numbness in my feet is because they transfused me with the blood of a bad person. Now I have bad blood circulating in my feet."

Time: Time is linear for the Anglo-American culture, and rigid adherence to it is highly valued. Time has a monetary value, and it is viewed as a commodity (D. W. Sue & D. Sue, 1990). In Hispanic culture, it is viewed from a cyclical perspective. Periods of time, rather than units, are the norm. Thus, some Hispanic patients speak of going back to their country of origin for *una temporada* [a season], as opposed to a time limited vacation. A *temporada* could range from a couple of weeks to a couple of years, depending on the patient's needs.

Space: For Anglo-American culture, individual space and privacy are crucial. The use of space is orderly and maximized; the limits of space use are exact. Physical space and environment can be dominated by the society. For Hispanic culture, individual space is not as important as group space; the use of space grows with needs and the limits are approximate. Society submits to the environment. The best example of these differences can be found in the way people use space in a sporting event. An Anglo-American will expect to sit at a specific seat number in a certain section of the stadium. Throughout Latin America, sporting events are much like movies. People sit on a first-come, first-served basis.

Relation Between Components: This element deals with how people integrate and relate the aforementioned five elements (e.g., relating time to space, classification to causality, individuals to groups, etc.). It provides the guidelines for the different components of the worldview. Table 2.1 provides a summary about the different elements and the assumptions of the Anglo-American worldview, vis-à-vis the Hispanic worldview.

HISPANIC CULTURE: AN ANTHROPOLOGICAL PARADIGM

Culture is defined here as the integrated system of learned patterns of behavior, ideas, and products characteristic of a society (Hiebert, 1983). Culture, in this sense, should be dif-

TABLE 2.1
Anglo and Hispanic Worldviews

Issue	Anglo-American Worldview	Hispanic Worldview
Basic Assumptions	Orderly universe, following physical and scientific laws	Pre-determined universe Cosmic nature of things Different rules for different groups
	Life analyzable in neat categories	Everything is connected Magic realism
	Natural and supenatural dichotomized	No distinction Psychological phenomena is in supernatural category
	Linear time divided into neat segments	Spiraling time; it flows and need not be quantified
	Can validly generalize about others from one's experience	Can't generalize; experience always unique
	Human-centered universe	God- or spirit-centered universe Family centered
	Professional success, money, or possessions are the measure of value	Family relationships are the measure Family prestige is the measure Personal and family respect are the measure
	Unlimited wealth, power, and prestige are available to individuals who pursue them	Limited goods available; amount of goods are getting less
Values	Competition good (need to "get ahead")	Competition bad Cooperation good (want everyone at a similar level)
	Change good (= progress)	Change bad (=destruction of traditions)
	Individual good valued	Family good valued Individualism destructive
	51% democracy	Certain people are "born to rule" Patriarchal/matriarchal decision making

Note: Adapted from Kraft (1996).

ferentiated from *society*. Culture refers to the structured customs of a people, whereas society refers to the people themselves. The United States has a Hispanic culture within its larger society. Every culture and, for the purposes of this chapter, Hispanic culture, has defined structures (Archer, 1988). These structures are social scripts that affect patterns of behavior (Lingefelter, 1992). The relevance of culture to clinical or research endeavors lies in the impact it has on the efficacy of patient participation in treatment or research, on the interaction between the clinician and the Hispanic community, and on the interpretation of test results (Areán & Gallagher-Thompson, 1996; Miranda, Organista, Azocar, Muñoz, & Lieberman, 1996). Therefore, cultural issues should be understood vis-à-vis their impact on neuropsychological assessment and research.

To elucidate culture in a meaningful way for neuropsychologists, Hispanic/Latino culture is described here in terms of its patterns of behavior, its shared ideas, and its cultural "products," or, in the parlance of anthropology, the "material," tangible manifestations

of culture. Only elements deemed relevant to the work of neuropsychologists are covered. Omissions and simplifications are less offensive if read with the caveat that this is a
cursory outline for the purposes of this book.

PATTERNS OF LEARNED BEHAVIORS

There is a large number of structured customs and learned behaviors based on values that
define Hispanic culture (DeMente, 1996; De Varona, 1996; Kanellós, 1994; Padilla,
1995). This section, however, covers only *la familia, respeto, machismo,* and *marianismo,*
as representative and relevant here.

Family

The family is considered the most important institution in the social organization of Hispanics. *La familia* is the greater or extended family, which, in addition to the immediate
nuclear household, includes relatives that are traced on both the maternal and paternal
sides (parents, grandparents, siblings, cousins, and other blood relatives; Kanellós, 1994).
Compadrazgo [godparenthood] is an important supportive institution of la familia. *Compadres* are present at important family events and rites of passage, fomenting the notion of
support in an extended family. Compadres may also help with childrearing responsibilities
and with financial support if necessary.

There are objective data that confirm statistically what is known culturally, namely, that
Latinos in the United States place a high value on the family. Data from the 1997 Current
Population Survey show that married couples with children comprise more than one
third (36%) of Hispanic households. By comparison, less than one quarter (24%) of non-
Hispanic households are made up of married couples with children. The data also show
that children are included in more than half (52%) of the 8.2 million Hispanic house-
holds. Children are found in only one third (33%) of all non-Hispanic households (U.S.
Census Bureau, 1998a, 1998b).

Individually, Hispanic families tend to be larger than those of the general population,
with 3.8 persons versus 3.2 persons for the nation as a whole (Reedy, 1995). Similarly,
25% of all Hispanic households had five or more people living in them in 1992, as compared to 8% for non-Hispanic White households (Valdés & Seoane, 1995). Hispanic
householders are much younger than the population as a whole, with only 11% age 65 or
older (versus 21% for the nation as whole). By the year 2000, approximately 10 million
Hispanic households are expected. In 1993, about 80% of the 6.6 million Hispanic
households were families, as compared to 71% for the nation as a whole. A full two thirds
of Hispanic children live in families with two parents (Reedy, 1995).

The general value supported by this culture is that the needs and welfare of the family
come before those of the individual. The family as a group is the priority. Therefore, parents are obliged to make sacrifices for their children. Older children are expected to show
gratitude and assume responsibility for younger siblings while growing up, and for the parents in their old age. The family defines the ideal roles and behaviors of family members,
with a predilection for the patriarchal system (Kanellós, 1994; Valdés & Seoane, 1995).
However, immigration impacts the traditional view of the family in significant ways.
Approximately 24% of Hispanic households were headed by women in 1992. In fact, it is
women who experience the greatest change in role expectations when they immigrate with

their families (Amaro & Russo, 1987). Many times, it is the wife who can work first and more steadily using her domestic skills; the husband's skills may not adapt as well to a new environment, especially among low skilled immigrants (Comas-Diaz, 1988).

Children are expected to show *respeto* to all elders, which is the mark of successful child-drearing. "However, children's roles have experienced drastic changes. . . . Children often become the social brokers between their parents and the outside world. They . . . know the cultural nuances better than their parents" (Kanellós, 1994, p. 35). Immigrant Hispanic children find showing respect for their parents a challenging task, especially when the parents' status in the new culture may have changed significantly, and they are no longer able to broker assertively between the outside world and the family's needs. Neuropsychologists working with Hispanic families are referred to Falicov's (1998) excellent treatise, *Latino Families in Therapy: A Guide to Multicultural Practice,* for a thorough discussion of clinical and cultural issues impacting immigrant families.

Respect

Hispanics show *respeto* to people for their age, their professional position, their power, and their social status. However, what takes precedence over all other factors is the level of attention to personal relationships (De Mente, 1996). In contrast, North American non-Hispanics show respect to people if they are talented, law abiding, diligent, productive, and successful. The basis for these differences is expectations: for Hispanics, emotional needs come first and material needs come second.

Developing and nurturing respect with Hispanics will therefore require more of a personal, emotional investment, than it would with a non-Hispanic patient. The important criteria for gaining respect are not necessarily a series of accomplishments, but being loyal, generous, and having "soul" or character. In other words, to be *respetuoso*. This concept encompasses the value of dignity (*dignidad*). Latinos can be overly sensitive to the way they are treated. High emphasis is placed on maintaining decency and being treated with courtesy. If dignity is not valued in the doctor–patient relationship, then it will affect the outcome of that interaction negatively, because the patient will most likely feel denigrated. The preservation of dignity is more important for a Hispanic patient than the use of a service. Non-Hispanic clinicians who fail to answer questions in detail, spend little informal time with the patient, assume that their patients are not smart, or talk loud and slowly to them (as if to make themselves understood) are showing disrespect and impacting the dignity of the individual. The needier the situation of the Hispanic patient, the more important their *dignidad* is to them.

Latinos, in general, regard the kind of personal treatment they receive from a health care provider as the crucial test of respect. Hispanics are friendly people for whom *simpatía* is a "social script." *Simpatía* goes beyond its literal translation, which is "to be nice." Simpatía is a mixture of friendly manners with a commitment to avoid or reduce uneasiness or discomfort during social interactions (G. Marín & B. V. Marín, 1991). Some amount of personal interaction is expected in clinician–patient relationships with Hispanics. Paying attention to small details does not take time and can make a difference in the relationship with the patient because it shows concern on behalf of the clinician. The more clinicians nurture their relationship with the Hispanic client, the higher the opportunities for success in the intervention.

A touch of *simpatía* brings the relationship between the clinician and the client closer. It is in this closeness that people open themselves to implementing strategies, directives, and compliance with medication. It is at this point that the clinician can interact with beliefs, values, practices, attitudes, priorities, and fears. Neuropsychologists must come to appreciate that their impact on a patient (whether in research, evaluation, or treatment) does not come from their role in the case, their academic degree, or their language mastery. Rather, it is the quality of the relationship with the client (showing *respeto* for the patient's *dignidad*) that facilitates the effectiveness of the clinician working with this population.

Neuropsychologists working with Hispanic patients will soon recognize that theirs cannot be a surgical, impersonal role limited to an antiseptic administration of tests. In fact, this very notion is the mark of cultural incompetence when working with Hispanics. The major change clinicians must make is to allow time for informal interaction. Non-Hispanic clinicians will benefit from recognizing their own skills, deficits and cultural limitations in working with Latinos. Competence in working with this population increases in the same proportion that clinicians have clearly identified:

- Their limitations in working with this culture.
- The nature of their worldview and how their education, social class, and personal history have shaped their perception of Latino patients.
- The client's values and strengths, which can be used as assets toward the resolution of specific problems.

The clinician must recognize that ignoring these elements can add much error to the already fragile psychometric evaluation of a diverse ethnic group. The results mean false positives (overpathologizing and overdiagnosing of Hispanic patients; Landrine, 1995; Norris, Juarez, & Perkins, 1989).

Illustrations. The following illustrations integrate the issues discussed within a clinical framework.[1] Consider the García family, whose members are very religious, monolingual Spanish-speaking, and come originally from a rural town in Latin America. Ms. García's son, Luis, has a seizure disorder. Luis is a shy 13-year-old that will be held back in school because his frequent seizures kept him from attending classes regularly last year. Adding to Luis' uncertain academic future is the maternal grandmother's unequivocal belief that studying makes Luis' brain "weaker." When Luis is referred by the neurologist for a neuropsychological evaluation, the mother approaches the clinician requesting in no uncertain terms that "a written medical verification" be given to her, stating that Luisito should not go back to school because of his weak brain.

The Pérez family, on the other hand, comes from a large city in Latin America. They are committed Catholics and speak both English and Spanish. Mr. and Mrs. Pérez are the main health decision-makers in the family. They are bringing Francisco to his follow-up appointment. Having accepted the limitations their son will have, their major concern is to help Francisco overcome his poor social adjustment.

When these families come to the clinician's office for the first time, the neuropsychologist can basically take two approaches. One approach is to act as an expert and bluntly confront the family members with the truth of their child's condition while informing them matter of factly about their treatment options. In the case of Mrs. García, the clinician will be unable to do much for the child using this approach. The child's mother will react with resistance, may feel humiliated by the clinician's bluntness, and will quickly try

[1] Dr. America Bracho is credited for this illustration.

to find help elsewhere, even with a *curandero* (herbalist, or witch doctor). In the Pérez case, the parents may accept the information, but may run quickly to another clinician who can treat them with "respect."

A more culturally sensitive approach would be to assume little other than an attitude of respect toward the patient. Clinicians should begin with the phenomenology of the patient and their families. In the García case, for instance, the important link with the family is their notion of the son's "weak brain." Validating the caretaker's impression can lead to openness on behalf of the family. If the clinician and the family accept that Luis' brain is "weak," then both can proceed to make it "stronger." Exploring ways in which both the family and the clinician could work together will follow naturally from such validation, as resistance and confrontation are averted in the best interest of the patient. Using an ethnocentric, assertive, or confrontational style is a sure way to lose a Hispanic patient. *Respeto* and *simpatía* are more important than language skills for the neuropsychologist interested in working with this population.

Machismo

Macho ("male") is one of the many Spanish words that have been well assimilated into the English vocabulary (McKechnie, 1983). *Machismo*, or the "cult of masculinity/manliness" (De Mente, 1996), however, is a poorly understood, little studied concept psychologically. At its core, *machismo* reflects a gender identity issue, dealing with the acquisition of sex-typed preferences, skills, personality attributes, behaviors, and self-concepts early in life (Casas, Waggenheim, Banchero, & Mendoza-Romero, 1995; Mirandé, 1997). It goes beyond treating women in stereotypically dominating ways; it involves men's functioning as providers, protectors, and representatives of their families to the outer world. The man of the family has "obligations and responsibilities to uphold the honor of family members, to deal effectively with the public sphere, and to maintain the integrity of the family unit" (Valdés & Seoane, 1995, p. 168).

The roots of machismo in Latin America can be traced through Spain to the Saracean Moors who ruled southern Spain with varying degrees of control from A.D. 711 to 1492 (García-Pelayo y Gross, 1990). Spanish machismo was based on male superiority combined with a significant degree of chivalry that gave it a romantic aura (De Mente, 1996; Gilmore & Uhl, 1987). It was transferred to the New World, a place where a "manly" self-image, regardless of the suffering involved, was a successful tool in the *Conquista*. Appearing invulnerable to enemies, showing indifference to danger or suffering, abusing alcohol, having an exclusive group of male friends, and bragging about sexual exploits was as common then as it is now among a large proportion of Hispanic males, including those who have migrated to the United States (Mirandé, 1988). The woman's role in this system is to care alone for the household, managing the resources solely provided by the man, and rearing the children to show respect.

Among recent immigrants, the new environment significantly challenges this male gender schema, which in the United States is considered maladaptive. Machismo is associated with high rates of alcohol abuse and alcoholism among low income Hispanics, which has physical, mental, and economic consequences (Panitz, McConchie, Sauber, & Fonseca, 1983). One such consequence is a high rate of head injuries in motor vehicle accidents (Silver & Sporty, 1990). Another is lack of help-seeking behaviors, despite the need for treatment (Casas et al., 1995; Vazquez-Nuttall, Avila-Vivas, & Morales-Barreto, 1984). As can be surmised, this construct will impact neuropsychological treatment and interventions. Head injured male patients who find themselves disabled and incapacitated to return to work, for instance, experience significant emotional turmoil when they can no longer be the provider of the household. Fear and anger for this loss of status can be masked as concrete thinking, personality changes, and rigidity in the clinical presentation of the patient. The patient, however, may be fighting a battle to regain a sense of respect for his status in the family.

The effective clinician should approach the issue of adjustment to role changes, allowing the patient to cathart his feelings and fears about such changes, rather than "encouraging" the patient to assume a new role as his best option. Anger management and conflict resolution will become a key element of the clinicians' treatment, as they guide the patient through education and problem solving to a point where the patient himself identifies the changes "he will allow" in his role as the man of the house. It is counterproductive to force patients to "become independent in meal preparation," for instance, when they never engaged in that activity prior to their injury. Patients enter in conflict with staff and are perceived as dependent or immature when they show resistance to these interventions. The problem is not cognitive, it is cultural. Should the patient's machismo be reinforced? Intervention must begin with an understanding of the patient's cultural framework, respecting his worldview, so that change can take place. The therapeutic point of departure is the patient's, not the clinician's, position (O'Hanlon, 1987).

Marianismo

Although not exactly the counterpart of machismo, *marianismo* is more of an expression of matriarchal rule. Benavides (1992), for instance, argued that instead of machista, Mexican American culture as a subset of Hispanic culture is actually matriarchal, because of its great emphasis on loving and respecting the mother. Motherhood is tied to much of what is good and evil in Hispanic culture. Thus, *madre* is used in the most sublime of prayers and the most vile of insults. The emphasis on motherhood is rooted in the Catholic Church's emphasis on the Virgin Mary.

The Virgin Mary holds a special place in Latin American culture (as she does in many cultures; Pelikan, 1996). Historically, the Virgin Mary was contextualized early into Latin American culture because she was believed to have appeared to several people, was a symbol of protection, and was a central figure in the Catholic Church's teachings. The importance of the Virgin Mary to Hispanic culture has no parallel in Anglo culture, even among Catholics.

In Hispanic culture, exaltation of Mary is public, artistic, communal, and personal. Her apparitions have resulted in the creation of multiple shrines, iconography, and jewelery. Among the most famous apparitions of Mary is that experienced and reported by the Christianized Amerindian Juan Diego (December 12, 1531) at Tepeyac Hill, outside Mexico City. After giving several instructions to Juan Diego, the Virgin's image (dark-haired and brown-skinned) was reportedly imprinted on Juan Diego's cloak. She came to be known as "Our Lady of Guadalupe" (*Nuestra Señora de Guadalupe*) and was soon raised to the status of patron of all Indians (after official recognition from the Vatican), and eventually, patron of all Latin America (in 1910). *La Morenita* [Little Darkling], as Guadalupe is affectionately known, has become the unofficial, private flag of Mexicans (Rodríguez, 1993).

If the Church's incursions failed to make blind disciples of the Indians, La Vírgen de Guadalupe, with her motherly elán, managed to develop tenacious believers. De Mente

(1996) posited that the apparition of Guadalupe was used by the Church to subjugate Indians successfully. This story was repeated countless times with contextual variations throughout Latin America, although they were not officially recognized. *Nuestra Señora de Santa Ana* (El Salvador), *Nuestra Señora de Copacabana* (1538, Bolivia), *Virgen de la Caridad del Cobre* (Cuba), *Virgen del Carmen,* and many others are some examples of the contextualization of the Virgin Mary and the veneration of the Mother of God. To be sure, the idea of "local" Virgins can be found throughout Spain, where *La Virgen de La Macarena* is quite famous. In fact, Spanish regional Virgins can be found in Latin America as a function of the migration patterns of Spaniards (Andalusians, Canarians, etc.) to the New World. Puerto Rico, for instance, has seen aparitions of the *Nuestra Señora de Monserrat* (originally found in Barcelona), *La Virgen del Pilar* (from the Basque country), *Virgen de La Candelaria* (Canary Islands), and *Nuestra Señora del Carmen* (Lady of the sailors), as the commercial ties between Puerto Rico and different cities in Spain expanded (Reichard de Cancio, 1996).

During the wars of independence, the prayers for protection to the Virgin Mary were based on the notion that of all her children in Christendom, the Virgin cared most for her poor and destitute American children (Bidegain, 1992). As Pelikan (1996) pointed out, the Virgin Mary became a woman for all seasons and all reasons.

By virtue of sharing motherhood with the Virgin Mary, Latinas are regarded in the culture as ranking somewhere between angels and saints. This places an undue burden on the mere mortals who find themselves trying to live by the highest possible standards as true paragons of virtue, while ignoring immoral behavior by men (Abitia, 1989). As noted earlier, immigration to a culture where these values are challenged has had an impact on the role and the self-perception of Latinas within their families. This may be a function of economics. Latinas in the United States are more likely to be employed in managerial and professional positions, technical and administrative support, and service occupations (National Association of Hispanic Publications, 1995) than their male counterparts. Raising children and caring for the household are still vital to Latinas. However, their level of dependence on male partners as providers appears to be in decline in this country.

Neuropsychologists working with families in rehabilitation will soon find the family's dependence on the mother/spouse, as well as the multiple expectations for care and nurturance. In cases where the patient is a single male or female, the mother will readily leave her obligations to care for the injured child. If the caregiver is a spouse, her coping skills depend on the degree to which she depended on the husband. If the patient is the mother of the household, then the degree of dysfunction in the family may escalate significantly as the father finds himself in an unfamiliar role of househusband. Other females in the extended family will assist with the care of the young. However, this is an area clamoring for research and deserves much consideration from a scientific perspective as the literature is scarce.

FORM AND MEANING: SHARED IDEAS

This section covers the basic belief systems (religion and fatalism) common to Hispanics residing in the United States. The intent is to describe the phenomenology of these concepts as understood within the Hispanic culture, in order to facilitate clinical interventions.

Religion

Religion, regardless of its form or expression, is central to the Hispanic culture. Religious expression is apparent in the exchanges of everyday life, and is encouraged and maintained through the nurture of families and communities. This section discusses religion as a critical element of Hispanic culture, reflecting its worldview and shaping its approach to interaction with health providers. In an attempt to do justice to this issue, this section provides a historical overview, a brief analysis of the impact of religion on cultural traditions, and a brief set of guidelines for clinicians to understand and appreciate the role of religion in their interactions with the patient.

According to recent surveys, 75% of U.S. Hispanics consider themselves Catholic, 19% Protestant, and 5% other (Jewish, Jehovah's Witness, Mormon, etc.; Kanellós, 1994). The majority of Hispanics are Catholic. However, Catholicism, like the religion of the Mennonite Brethren or the Amish, is not only a denomination, it is a lifestyle. Of note, the largest Catholic contingent in the United States is Hispanic, as well as an increasing proportion of priests going into ministry.

The role of religion and Catholicism in the Hispanic culture would be misunderstood unless it is placed in its proper historical context. Pedro de Arenas was the first priest to set foot on the new continent as part of Columbus' entourage. He celebrated mass in 1492 on the "Isla de Lucaios." With that mass, the expansion of Iberian Christendom began. Pope Sixtus IV referred to Isabella and Ferdinand of Spain as the "Catholic Sovereigns" (*Reyes Católicos*), because they pursued the unification of Spain and Portugal under "one king, one faith, one law" (Wallbank, Taylor, Bailkey, & Jewsbury, 1978). Having gained Papal attention, they also gained the right from him to make Church appointments in Spain. With Columbus' discovery, Isabella and Ferdinand also shaped Christendom in the Indies, extending the royal patronage (power to appoint bishops) to the hand-picked governors of the new lands (Dussel, 1992). These matters received further support when the Spaniard Rodrigo Borgia became Pope Alexander VI in 1492.

With the establishment of the Council of the Indies in 1524, this patronage over the Church was consolidated through the 19th century. Thus, the Church was closely tied to the economic and political efforts of the *Conquistadores*. The Christianization of Latin America began with the Franciscan Order in 1493, and was followed by the Dominicans in 1510, the Augustinians in 1533, and the Jesuits in 1549. It was the period of the "Great Missions" that began in 1519, which assured the hegemony of Spain over the new territories. Thus, Hernán Cortés set out from Cuba to conquer the Aztec empire with an army of soldiers and priests. The conquest and colonization of the Caribbean, Central America, the Inca and Chibcha regions used the same model. With time, however:

> "Warrior Catholicism" began to give way to a settled ruling class, an oligarchy of landowners, sugar mill owners and mine owners: the "patriarchal Catholicism" of the "Lord of the manor" ruling over the *senzala* (slave quarters). The Great Junta of 1548 gave control of the church entirely over to the state, through a system of patronage under which the civil and political powers produced nominees for all church appointments, from the lowliest sacristan to the grandest archbishop. (Dussel, 1992, p. 6)

Church and religion became central elements in the life of the new continent and its people. It was the common meeting place, where the power of the ruling class was justified and the suffering of the oppressed was consoled. To be sure, the Church decried the abuses of slavery and the brutal exploitation of the natives. The work of Dominican Friars in this regard resulted in the *Leyes de Burgos* (1512) designed to protect the rights of native peoples. But it is no secret that the Church played a key role in the economic exploitation of the Indies. In fact, as Fray García de Toledo stated in his *Parecer the Yucay* (published in 1571), "If there is no gold, there is no God in the Indies." In other words, gold is the reason Indians can receive faith and be saved, without it they would be condemned (Rodríguez León, 1992).

The faith of the Amerindians in pre-Colombian times was based on their worldview: intuitive, open to nature and the cosmos, communitarian, and highly symbolic. It reflected the magical-mythical mentality of non-Western religions around the world. Rituals, writings, cremation, and burial customs, as well as the calendars of pre-Columbian America (e.g., the "winged disc" placed on temple door lintels), can be found in the cultures of Egypt, Phoenicia, and Western Asia (Mackenzie, 1923/1996). Hunter societies had shamanism and animism (Northern Patagonia, North America, Araucan Indians). Farmer-potter cultures of Central America and the Andean regions were also animistic and shamanistic, but included the use of hallucinogenic substances as part of their religious ecstasy. Ancient Temple cultures such as the Incas, Mayas, and Aztecs had organized rituals and worshipped the Sun (Schobinger, 1992). Religion was clearly central to the life of the Amerindians well before the introduction of Christianity, as described by an anonymous observer at the time of the *Conquista:*

> [Amerindians] had very large and beautiful buildings for their idols, where they honored them and prayed and sacrificed to them, and there were religious persons dedicated to their service.
> . . . In each province the inhabitants have their own kind of ceremonies, idolatries and sacrifices, for in some places they worship the sun, in others the moon, or the stars, or serpents, or lions and similar wild beasts, of which they have images and statues in their mosques. (De Fuentes, 1963, pp. 174, 176)

Faced with this native religious scenario, the Catholic missionaries from Spain attempted to understand the Indian languages and religion, and offered doctrinal teachings in the form of stories rather than theological abstractions (Rodríguez León, 1992). Another (unofficial) strategy, very much in keeping with the Inquisition, was the burning of things non-Christian. And burn they did. A priest named Landa presided over the burning of all Mayan astronomy books, history, and religious imagery in 1562. This was an irretrievable loss (De Mente, 1996).

But not all was lost. To their credit, the Conquistadors still preserve the linguistic ouvre of their "Great Missionary effort." By edict of Carlos IV (1790), the *Archivo General de Indias* was formed in Seville, Spain, with the intent of organizing all of the papers related to the involvement of Spain in the Americas. The language and grammar of long extinct Indian tribes remain accessible today.

Another cultural element present today comes from this period. Multiple "holy" feasts (up to 84 days a year) served as a venue to attract interest in the Church and to induct people into the symbolism of Christianity. A popular festive activity (originally brought by Marco Polo from China to Europe) involved Spanish friars painting pictures of the spirits and the devil on paper or clay and encouraging native villagers to "kill" the devil, striking at its effigy with a stick. When they "destroyed the evil one," they were rewarded with presents and peanuts that were inside the effigy. This practice is still called by its original name, *Piñata* (http://mexico.ugd.mex/Tradiciones/Posadas/pinatas.html, 1997). This is one example of the many ways in which Catholicism permeates different elements and levels of Hispanic culture.

Lest indigenous peoples be dismissed as passive recipients of things Christian and Spanish, two elements deserve further consideration. First, the zealous proselytism by the Catholic Church was resisted with greater resolve than official accounts would admit. This resistance (passive and otherwise) affected Catholicism as much as it did the native religions. Popular wisdom in Latin America relates the story of the Franciscan priest who makes a convert of the Amerindian and baptizes him. After baptism, he tells him: "Your name will no longer be Chaco, you will now have a Christian name, Juan." As part of his catechism instruction, Juan learns that he should never eat pork meat on Fridays during Lent; he should only eat fish. On Good Friday, the priest sees Juan roasting a pork. He runs frantically toward Juan's hut and confronts him: "Didn't I tell you never to eat pork on Fridays during Lent? You know today is Good Friday. What are you doing?" Juan calmly answered: "Don't worry, Father, his name no longer 'pork.' I baptized him, his name now 'Fish'" (Acevedo, 1995, personal communication). Chaco's answer, although apocryphal, resonated well with the psyche of the new world. A fate worse than poverty was to be a simpleton (*tonto*), and a status better than richness was accomplished by cleverness (*viveza*) (Uslar Pietri, 1991). *Viveza* reversed the injustices of the imposed order by circumventing laws and codes.

A second issue, directly related to this passive resistance, is that the Church simply came to a tacit compromise among religions, resulting in syncretism. *Syncretism,* according to Uslar-Pietri (1991), is another expression of the *mestizo* culture, the mixture of two different races (Indian and Spanish), two vastly different continents (Europe and the Americas) with two independent histories (one written and the other destroyed by the Conquistadors), two worldviews, and two worship systems. The mestizo culture of religion is manifested in syncretistic religious practices that combine myth with mysticism. In practical terms, reverence for *Pachamama* [Mother Earth], for instance, was blended in deep devotion to the Virgin Mary in the Andes. In the Caribbean, homage to Ochún, the goddess of love, was blended with the feast of the *Virgen de la Caridad del Cobre*. Because witchcraft was forbidden by the Catholic Church throughout Latin America, indigenous peoples and African slaves adopted the Catholic saints, but assigned their images to their own gods/deities. It was, therefore, common for the indigenous peoples to appear to be worshipping the Catholic saints during religious feasts, when in fact they were giving homage to their own gods. This was particularly the case throughout the Caribbean (De Varona, 1996). The use of *Santería* (Afro-Caribbean "black magic"), *brujos,* and *curanderos* [witch doctors, shamans] *hechicería* [witchcraft], and other forms of witchcraft is still prevalent among Hispanics, regardless of their country of origin.

Whether syncretistic or orthodox, religion has been central to Hispanics living in the United States. Historically, the largest contingent of Hispanic Catholics in the United States, Mexican Americans, have had a difficult relation with the Church, especially after the Treaty of Guadalupe Hidalgo (1848) when their lands were taken over by Anglo settlers. The new bishops forbade public processions and public expressions of faith throughout the Southwest, affecting their way of practicing religion profoundly. There remains a divide between Anglo and Hispanic Catholics in worship style and emphasis. However, the historical significance of the Catholic Church to Hispanic culture represents a place of continuity (particularly for new immigrants), with the traditions and beliefs of their country of origin.

The clinical relevance of religion to the neuropsychological endeavor lies in the impact of its phenomenology to the rehabilitation process. Supernatural explanations for accidents, symptoms, and everyday problems are pervasive. Belief in the supernatural can directly impact patients' compliance with treatment or progress through therapy, depending on their attributions of causality (Pontón, Gonzalez, & Mares, 1997). Whatever the spectrum of the patient's religiosity, the clinician ought to have an understanding of the elements involved and should approach it respectfully if a successful outcome is desired (Thurman, 1989). The use of religious imagery and support systems in rehabilitation and treatment could enhance the therapeutic or assessment process. For instance, a useful measure of remote and rote memory is to ask Hispanic patients who acknowledge their faith and present with a memory disorder to recite overlearned material, such as a prayer (e.g., the rosary, the *Ave Maria,* the Lord's prayer, the Apostle's creed, etc.). This can be particularly useful with elderly patients who have had little, if any, formal education and who have no familiarity with a formal testing situation. Needless to say, the clinician must have some knowledge (and respect) for such matters if this task is to be meaningful.

Fatalismo

Si naciste pa' martillo, del cielo te caen los clavos. [If you were born a hammer, nails will rain from heaven.] —Rubén Blades, 1984; Pedro Navaja, *Y son del solar . . . Live!* Elektra Entertainment (Warner).

Fatalismo as a cultural phenomenon (not to be confused with the philosophical concept of determinism) is complex and vast in its manifestations. The roots of fatalism are true to its etymology (*fatum:* a prophetic declaration, an oracle, a divine determination). The basic notion behind fatalism is that everything in human lives takes place according to a set, immutable pattern. Humans' reactions to this destiny (*destino*) is to submit in resignation. It is common to hear injured Hispanic patients say: "*Así lo dispuso Dios, que le vamos a hacer*" [This was God's design, there's nothing I can do]. In submission to a predetermined destiny, *fatalismo* retains an element of mystery, as there must be a higher purpose, yet unknown, that explains the present suffering or tragedy.

Fatalism affects the patients' motivation for treatment, their sense of purpose for the future, their understanding of whether the accident or brain insult is part of divine punishment for sins past and present, and their willingness to access resources for future treatment. The wife of a head injured patient came crying once at the lack of support from her injured husband's family. She explained that they felt her husband had been given a spell (*embrujado*) and there was nothing they could or wanted to do until the spell was over. His situation was determined by elements beyond their control, and will persist despite their involvement. Thus, no involvement was a sensible response for them, lest a similar fate befall them for interfering with destiny.

Clinical skill and cultural sensitivity are crucial in guiding patients through their own perceptions of destiny in the recovery process.

CULTURAL "PRODUCTS"

This element deals with the material expression of the culture. This section discusses Hispanic arts and music, literature, media, labor, and political participation in the United States. Given the vastness of this domain, these areas are reviewed for the largest Hispanic groups present in the United States: Mexicans, Puerto Ricans, and Cubans. This information is presented with the intent of familiarizing readers with key aspects of Hispanic culture, because providers of services to this population may want to understand such cultural expressions.

Arts and Music

Mexican Americans. Art in the Mexican culture has been heavily influenced by Catholicism. Architectural religious designs are particularly evident in New Mexico, Texas, Arizona, and California. Mission-type architecture is typical in these regions, and includes churches, altars, and shrines (e.g., to the Virgin de Guadalupe). Some of these buildings are among the oldest of any architectural design in the Southwestern United States. *Nuestra Señora de la Purísima Concepción,* for instance, was built in San Antonio, Texas, in 1755 and the church of San Xavier del Bac was built in Tucson, Arizona, between 1783 and 1797.

Historically, sculpture was mostly religious in nature and included the depiction of saints, angels, and *nacimientos* [nativity scenes]. José Dolores López, Celso Gallegos, and Patrocino Barela are among the best known representatives of this art form. Their carved images in stone and wood can be found in the Museum of International Folk Art, the Taylor Museum, and the National Museum of American Art, respectively.

In terms of fine arts, Mexican American artists were part of the mainstream U.S. art scene from the 1920s to 1950s. The content of this art is regional and individual. Kanellós (1993) identified Octavio Medellín, Antonio García, José Aceves, and Edward Chávez among the most representative from this period. They painted murals dealing with different cultural themes, like the *Aztec Advance* (García in 1929), *McLenna Looking for a Home* (Aceves in 1939), *Xtol: Dance of the Ancient Maya People* (Medellín in 1962), and *Indians of the Plain* (Chávez in 1943), among many others. These murals can be found in different Southwestern states.

Mexican American artists active since the 1960s include Michael Ponce de León, Eugenio Quesada, and Manuel Neri. They have worked with printmaking, drawings of children, and funk art, respectively (Kanellós, 1993).

The *Chicano Art Movement* is prominent in California, Texas, New Mexico, and the Great Lakes region (Valdés & Seoane, 1995). It focuses on issues ranging from the pre-Columbian (conflict with the Spanish settlers) to Chicano conflict with Anglos. Some muralists address issues of social concern on the walls of housing projects, alleys, concrete stairways, grocery stores, pharmacies, and cultural centers in Mexican communities.

Many Mexican artists have influenced American art and many have become known in the United States. The muralist Diego Rivera and his wife Freda Kahlo are notable examples. Kahlo, in fact, was thought to be a feminist heroine since Herrera (1983) published her biography. Lucie-Smith (1993) provided an enlightened discussion of Latin American art, for a clearer understanding of genres, movements, and influences.

If direct contact with the artistic expression of Mexican Americans is desired, it can be found in the museums of Mexican American art, which include the Guadalupe Cultural Arts Center in San Antonio, Texas; the Mexic-Arte Multicultural Works in Austin, Texas; Mexican Fine Arts Center Museum in Chicago, Illinois; the Mexican Museum in San Francisco, California; and Plaza de la Raza in Los Angeles, California.

Although not everyone enjoys regional musical expressions to the same degree, groups of people enjoy particular tunes and styles, thus making them popular. Among the Mexican American community, *Música norteña* has been very popular. It was developed by Mexican Americans from Texas, uses the *corrido* (folktale songs) as its expression, and discusses social themes. *Grupos cumbeiros* provide popular dancing music using cumbia as its rhythm (*La quebradita* has been among the most popular in the 1990s). *Tejano* music (brought to a wider audience by the late singer Selena) and border music are also popular, and incorporate cumbia rhythms as well.

Mexican rock and pop music, which reaches the U.S. Hispanic market via television and radio, are also popular among certain sectors of this community. A complex interplay of generational history, socioeconomic status (SES), acculturation, media and language mastery play a role in musical preferences for these and other musical styles. This is true of other Hispanic groups as well.

Puerto Ricans.   There are plenty of visual and graphic artists who have done excellent work, but their art is not distinctively Puerto Rican or reflective of unique themes relevant to this community. Among the best-known Puerto Rican artists, Olga Albizu excelled at producing paintings for record covers and contributing to the artistic community in New York City. Similarly, Rafael Colón Morales, Arnaldo Roche Rabell, Rafael Ferre, and Ralph Ortiz stand out as visual artists of Puerto Rican origin (Green, 1995).

Jorge Soto is a self-taught artist, who perhaps best represents uniquely Puerto Rican themes in New York City in his art through the *Taller Boricua* [Puerto Rican Workshop] (Kanellós, 1993). The Puerto Rican Culture Institute, Luis Rivera Muñoz Library and Museum, the Institute of Puerto Rican Culture, and the Archivo General de Puerto Rico exhibit distinctively Puerto Rican art. These are all located in San Juan.

Puerto Rican music and songs are festive and usually played at parties where there is dancing. As in much of the Caribbean, Boricua music is polyrhythmic, polyphonic, and blends intricate and complex African percussion with melodic Spanish beats. Whereas there is a rich history of folk music sung by traditional trios, *salsa* music is the most widely popular music (Green, 1995). *Merengue* music and dance are also popular. Puerto Rico is considered a mecca for *salsa,* where new bands must gain acceptance if they are to succeed elsewhere.

Cuban Americans.   As in the case of Puerto Rican art, there is not necessarily a visual art form that is uniquely Cuban American. Luis Cruz Azaceta is a New York-based artist whose work deals with issues of violence. Carlos Alfonso is an artist concerned with Afro-Cuban religious tradition (Kanellós, 1993).

Entertainment is an area where Cuban Americans have found success. Desi Arnaz, César Romero, Andy Garcia, Armand Assante, María Conchita Alonso, Daisy Fuentes, Emilio and Gloria Estefan, Cameron Díaz, and Elizabeth Peña are among some of the best recognized names in U.S. entertainment.

Cuban music is polyrhythmic and polyphonic. It has strong African influence and it has several manifestations: Mambo (known in Cuba as the *son montuno*) is a complex dance tune popularized by Pérez Prado in the 1950s. *Pachanga* is a dance set to a syncopated "ta-tum, ta-tum" beat. *Rumba* is hip-shaking dance with fast syncopated, percussive rhythms, popularized in New York City. *Conga,* named after the narrow drum, is a relatively simple rhythm with a heavy percussive accent on the fourth beat of every measure, popularized by Desi Arnaz. Bugalú is a fusion of the mambo sound with rhythm-and-blues and early rock and roll. *Cha-cha-cha,* which has a punctuating triple beat, was introduced by Cuban musicians as a dance to compete with the more complicated mambo. *Salsa* is certainly an expression of Cuban musicians, which has a call and response structure, placing emphasis on brass, percussion, and marked syncopation

(De Varona, 1996). Cuban-born Celia Cruz is internationally known as the undisputed "Queen of Salsa."

Literature

Literature is an ample area of artistic expression for Hispanics. Literature in Latin America has been a fertile ground because many writers led lives of official diplomatic activity, active revolutionary militancy, imprisonment, exile, or they were at the forefront of public movements (Flores, 1992). Any clinician interested in working with this population will find literature an effective and accessible teacher of customs, history, attitudes, ideals, and hopes of the Hispanic culture. The heterogeneity and diversity of the Hispanic population is forcefully reflected in its literature, thus dispelling group stereotypes.

This section highlights representative authors from the three major Hispanic groups found in the United States along with a brief description of their work or themes of their work. A summary of this nature does not do justice to the ample body of work available. However, it fulfills the intent and scope of this chapter. The serious reader is referred elsewhere (Anderson-Imbert & Florit, 1970; Flores, 1992; Krstovic, 1994; Ryan, 1991; Smith, 1997). An additional list of eight Latin American authors (representing South and Central America as well as Mexico) who have had profound cultural impact in the Hispanic collective psyche is also presented (see Table 2.2).

Media

Spanish-language media in the Southwestern United States precedes any English-language media. It is known that there were at least 16 Spanish-language newspapers in Los Angeles in the 1800s. "For example, in 1858 the editor of *El Clamor Público* denounced the theft of California lands and urged nonconformity to Anglo American culture and domination" (Englekirk & Marín, 1995, p. 912). The Spanish-language press has had a strong role in promoting (since the 1800s) the concept of ethnic identity, the development of social and political associations, and the nurturance of cultural and spiritual ties to all of Latin America. The presence of Spanish-language media in the United States continues to be strong, and its role is the same at the end of the millenium as it was in the mid-1800s. Along with print media, Spanish-language radio and TV enjoy wide popularity among the Hispanic population. Of interest, Spanish-language radio stations have won ratings sweepstakes in New York (1998) and in Los Angeles (1992).

Table 2.3 provides a general listing of the major Spanish-language media outlets as of 1995. It is not exhaustive, or necessarily up to date. It is, however, a compilation of major media outlets according to print, radio, and TV by the three ethnic groups. During the late 1990s several conglomerates of Spanish-language radio stations emerged, including Z-Spanish Radio network (zspanish.com), Eutravision Communications Company (eutravision.com), and Radio Unica Communications Corporation (radiounica.com), among others.

Several publications dealing with Hispanic pop culture have emerged recently. The most notable include *Latina, People En Español, Oye Magazine, Latino Youth, Generation Ñ Magazine,* and *Hispanic Magazine.* Similary, there was a significant growth in the number of web sites and web portals dealing with Hispanic culture and issues. The reader is directed to the limited list at the top of page 34.

TABLE 2.2
List of Latin American Authors

Mexican American Authors	Medium	Representative Work/Themes
Rudolfo Anaya	Novels	Hispanic experiences in the southwest Magic Realism
Fausto Avendaño	Short stories	*El Corrido de California* Historical drama
Ron Arias	Novels	*The Road to Tamazunchale* Magic Realism
Jimmy Santiago Baca	Poetry	Identity issues Hispanic experiences in the Southwest
Raymond Barrios	Short stories	*The Plum Plum Pickers* Migrant workers' issues
Denise Chávez	Novels/playwright	*The Last of the Menu Girls* Adolescent rites of passage
Sandra Cisneros	Short novel	*The House on Mango Street* Adolescent rites of passage
Abelardo Delgado	Poetry	Social themes in the Chicano community
Rolando Hinojosa	Novels	*Klail City Death Trip* Life in Texas
Pat Mora	Poetry, Children's books	*Chants* Hispanic experiences in the Southwest
Estela Portillo Trambley	Playwright	Women in rebellion against male domination
Leroy Quintana	Poetry	*Sangre* *The Reason People Don't Like Mexicans*
Richard Rodríguez	Autobiography	*Hunger and Memory: The Education of Richard Rodríguez* *Days of Obligation: An Argument with My Mexican Father*
Floyd Salas	Novels	*Tatoo the Wicked Cross* Drug culture, political dissent
Luis Omar Salinas	Poetry	Preservation of Mexican identity within the American society
Gary Soto	Poetry	*The Elements of San Joaquin* Chicano experiences in large cities
Luis Valdez	Theater	*El Teatro Campesino* Grassroots theater among farmworkers conveying social themes
José Antonio Villareal	Novels	*El Pocho*
Berenice Zamora	Poetry	*Restless Serpents* Conflicts between men and women

Puerto Rican Authors	Medium	Representative Work/Themes
Jesús Colón	Short stories	*A Puerto Rican in New York, and Other Sketches*
Victor Hernández Cruz	Poetry	Cultural differences
Rosario Ferré	Essays	Feminist themes
Angel Flores	Essayist, Literary Critic	*Spanish American Authors: The Twentieth Century*
Laura Gallego	Poetry	*Celajes*

Continued

TABLE 2.2 (*Continued*)

Puerto Rican Authors	Medium	Representative Work/Themes
Joseph Lizardi	Humor	*El Macho* *Block Party*
René Marqués	Drama	*The Oxcart* *Los soles truncos*
Nicolasa Mohr	Novels, short story	Puerto Rican life in New York City
Evaristo Ribera Chevremont	Poetry	Innovative poetry
Cesáreo Rosa-Nieves	Novels	Criollismo, ensueñismo, noismo
Luis Rafael Sánchez	Playwright, Novels	*The Passion of Antígona Pérez* *Almost the Soul* *Macho Camacho's Beat*
Esmeralda Santiago	Novels	*When I was Puerto Rican*

Cuban American Authors	Medium	Representative Work/Themes
Reinaldo Arenas	Novels	*Singing from the Well* *Farewell to the Sea* Postrevolutionary political issues
Marcelino Arozarena	Poetry	*Canción negra sin color* Afro-Cuban folokore
Lydia Cabrera	Novels	Afro-Cuban folklore; fiction work
Alejo Carpentier	Novels	*The Kingdom of This World* *Explosion in a Cathedral*
Roberto G. Fernández	Novels	*Raining Backwards*
Cristina García	Novels, Journalism	*Dreaming in Cuban*
Nicolás Guillén	Poetry	*Motivos de Son* *West Indies Ltd.*
Oscar Hijuelos	Novel	*The Mambo Kings Play Songs of Love*
Heberto Padilla	Poetry	Political protest
Ricardo Pau-Llosa	Poetry	*Sorting Metaphors*
José Yglesias	Novels, Short stories	Fiction

Other Latin American Writers	Medium	Representative Work/Themes
Miguel Angel Asturias (Guatemala)	Novels	*Señor Presidente* (Nobel, 1967) *Men of Maize*
Rubén Darío (Nicaragua)	Poetry	*Azul* Founder of *modernismo* literary movement
Carlos Fuentes (Mexico)	Novels	*The Death of Artemio Cruz* *Terra Nostra*
Gabriel García Márquez (Colombia)	Novels, Playwright, Journalism	*A Hundred Years of Solitude* (Nobel, 1982) *Love in the Time of Cholera* *Kidnapping*
José Martí (Cuba)	Poetry	Cuban national hero; themes include political activism, patriotism
Gabriela Mistral (Chile)	Poetry	*Desolación* (Nobel, 1945)
Pablo Neruda (Chile)	Poetry	*Canto General a Chile* (Nobel, 1971) Erotic love, social themes
Mario Vargas Llosa (Perú)	Novels, Essays	*The Time of the Hero* *Conversation in the Cathedral* *Aunt Julia and the Scriptwriter*

TABLE 2.3
Hispanic Media in the United States

Media	Medium	City
Mexican American		
Print	La Opinión	Los Angeles, CA
	El Chicano	San Bernardino, CA
	Mexican American Sun	Los Angeles, CA
	El Mundo	Oakland, CA
	Saludos Hispanos	Palm Desert, CA
	El Sol	Phoenix, AZ
Radio	KLAX-FM (97.9)	Los Angeles, CA
	KTNQ-AM (1330)	Los Angeles, CA
	KLOV-FM (107.5)	Los Angeles, CA
	KXKS-AM	Albuquerque, NM
	WIND-AM	Chicago, IL
Television	KDB-59	Albuquerque, NM
	KLUZ-41	Albuquerque, NM
	KHRR-40	Tucson, AZ
	KWHY-22	Los Angeles, CA
	KMEX-34	Los Angeles, CA
	K-52	Los Angeles, CA
	KSTS-48	San Antonio, TX
	KWEX-41	San Antonio, TX
	KINT-26	El Paso, TX
	KTMD-48	Houston, TX
	KGBO-66	Chicago, IL
	KSNS-44	Chicago, IL
Puerto Rican		
Print	El Diario La Prensa	New York, NY
	HISPANIC Magazine	Washington, DC
	Hispanic Business	Santa Barbara, CA
	Hispanic Link Weekly Report	Washington, DC
	Noticias del Mundo	New York, NY
	Vista (Magazine)	Coral Gables, FL
Radio	Radio Caballero Network	New York, NY
	CBS Hispanic Radio Network	New York, NY
	Lotus Hispanic Radio Network	New York, NY
	WHCR-FM (90.3)	New York, NY
	WKDM-AM (1380)	New York, NY
Television	Galavision Network	Los Angeles, CA
	WCIU-TV 26	Chicago, IL
	WNJU	Teterboro, NJ
Cuban American		
Print	Diario Las Américas	Miami, FL
	El Nuevo Herald	Miami, FL
	El Nuevo Patria	Miami, FL
	Linden Lane Magazine	Princeton, NJ
	Mariel (Magazine)	Miami, FL
Radio	WQBA-FM (107.5), AM (1140)	Miami, FL
	WAQ1-AM (710)	Miami, FL
	WRHC-AM (1550)	Miami, FL
Television	WSCV-51	Hialeah, FL
	WLTV-23	Miami, FL

- Lationlink.com
- Latintop.com
- Lati.net
- Terra.com
- Hisp.com
- sipuebla.com

Politics

Political participation by Latinos has increased moderately since 1985 (as can be seen in Table 2.4). Historically, most Cuban Americans elected to public office have been Republican, especially from Florida. Robert Menendez was the first Cuban American elected as a congressperson from the Democratic party (New Jersey). Mexican American and Puerto Rican elected officials have been mostly affiliated with the Democratic party, although there are some notable exceptions. Table 2.4 contains information on the changes in the number of elected officials in the 1992–1996 elections.

Hispanic voter registration and voting has also increased over the past decade. During the 1992 election, for instance, of registered voters, 61.1% of the 55+ age group, 52.7% of 35- to 54-year-olds, and 39% of 34-year-olds and younger cast ballots.

Whereas the total number of Hispanics voting in the presidential and congressional elections has increased from 1980 to 1996, the actual percentage of Hispanic voter participation has experienced a mild decline in 1996. Thus, 30% of Hispanics voted in the 1980 election, as compared to 27% in 1996. Obviously, the latter was a larger number of voters, despite being a lower proportion of the Hispanic population.

Labor Production

Recent figures about Latino participation in the labor force (U.S. Bureau of the Census, 1994) indicate that in 1994 about 78% of males age 16 and older were in the paid labor force, as compared to 74% of non-Hispanic White males. Among females, the rate of labor participation for Latinas is 52% as compared to 59% for non-Latinas. Subgroup

TABLE 2.4
Hispanic Elected Officials: 1985–1994

Year	Region	State Executives/ Legislators	County and Municipal Officials	Judicial and Law Enforcement	Education and School Boards	Total
1985	Total	129	1,316	517	1,185	3,147
1994	Total	199	2,197	651	2,412	5,459
	Northeast	28	42	13	73	156
	Midwest	15	43	8	851	917
	South	61	1,059	410	768	2,298
	West	95	1,053	220	720	2,088

Note: Adapted from U.S. Bureau of the Census (1998). No. 459 Hispanic Public Officials, by Office, 1985 to 1994. *Statistical Abstract of the United States: 1998* (116th ed., p. 286). Washington, DC.

TABLE 2.5
Labor Force Participation by Occupation in 1995

Type of Occupation	Mexican	Puerto Rican	Cuban	Other Hispanic	Total
Managerial/professional	11.7%	19.6%	22.0%	16.0%	14.1%
Tech., sales, admin. support	21.7	29.8	37.5	26.9	24.4
Services	19.5	17.4	14.1	22.6	19.7
Precision production, craft and repair	13.5	10.8	10.4	12.5	12.9
Operators, fabricators and laborers	25.4	21.0	14.3	19.9	23.0
Farming, forestry and fishing	8.3	1.4	1.8	2.1	5.9
Totals (%)	100.0	100.0	100.0	100.0	100.0

Note: U.S. Bureau of the Census (1996). No. 622. Hispanic persons-Civilian labor force participation: 1994 and 1995. *Statistical Abstract of the United States: 1996* (116th ed., p. 398). Washington, DC.

analyses indicate that labor participation ranged from 63% (Cuban males) to 83% (Central American males). Cuban females had a 50% participation, and Central American females had a 58% participation. Table 2.5 provides a description of labor participation according to country of origin and type of occupation.

In contrast, about 11.1% of the Hispanic population was unemployed (March 1994) in comparison to 6.6% of the non-Hispanic population at large in the same period (U.S. Bureau of the Census, 1994).

CONCLUSIONS

The absence of a comprehensive definition of Hispanic culture in the neuropsychological literature makes it necessary to elucidate this issue in a self-contained unit. The vastness of the subject, however, makes it necessary to set and acknowledge the limits of this discussion.

This chapter has attempted to describe broad differences between Anglo-American and Hispanic worldviews. It also defined culture from an anthropological framework. The author contends that Hispanic culture is a relevant element impacting the interaction of the neuropsychologist with this population. An anthropological framework was used to provide an objective definition of culture with three parameters. Hispanic culture was defined in terms of patterns of behavior (*familismo, respeto, simpatía, machismo,* and *marianismo*); shared beliefs (religion and fatalism), and cultural products (art and music, literature, media, politics, and labor participation). There are obvious limitations and dangers related to this discussion, not the least of which are simplification and stereotyping. However, a sincere effort is made to address the major concepts of culture within a responsible framework that provides practical information for the concerned clinician.

Hispanic culture can be explored in more depth through the following sources:

- Boswell, T., & Curtis, J. R. (1983). *The Cuban American experience: Culture, images and perspectives.* Totowa, NJ: Rowman & Allanheld.

- Delgado, R., & Stefancic, H. (1998). *The Latino/a condition: A critical reader.* New York: NYU Press.

- De Varona, F. (1996). *Latino literacy: The complete guide to our Hispanic history and culture.* New York: Henry Holt.

- Kanellós, N. (1996a). *The Hispanic almanac: Second edition*. Detroit: Gale Research.

- Kanellós, N. (1996b). *Hispanic firsts: 500 years of extraordinary achievement*. Detroit: Visible Ink Press.

- Kanellós, N., & Esteva-Fabregat, C. (1993). *The handbook of Hispanic cultures in the United States* (4 vols.). Houston: Arte Público Press.

- Morales Carrion, A. (1984). *Puerto Rico: A political and cultural history*. New York: Norton.

- Novas, H. (1993). *Everything you need to know about Latino history*. New York: Penguin.

- Samora, J., & Simon, P. V. (1993). *A history of the Mexican American people*. South Bend: University of Notre Dame Press.

- Stavans, I. (1996). *The Hispanic condition: Reflections on culture and identity in America*. New York: HarperPerennial.

- Vecoli, R. J. (Ed.). (1995). *Gale encyclopedia of multicultural America* (Vols. 1–2). Detroit: Gale Research.

The challenge of summarizing such a wide topic into a short chapter is accentuated by the dynamic aspects of culture. The constantly evolving process of resistance, acculturation, and new identity of Hispanic peoples in the United States may evolve over the next 10 years into something quite different from what has been outlined herein. Therefore, monitoring the developments in anthropology and sociology with regard to the Hispanic population in this country is a key to effective neuropsychological work with this population.

REFERENCES

Abitia, E. A. (1989). *Los valores de los Mexicanos* [Mexican values]. Mexico City: Fomento Cultural Banamex.

Amaro, H., & Russo, N. F. (1987). Hispanic women and mental health: An overview of contemporary issues in research and practice. Special Issue: Hispanic women and mental health. *Psychology of Women Quarterly, 11*(4), 393–407.

Anderson-Imbert, E., & Florit, E. (1970). *Literatura hispanoamericana: Antología e historia* (2 vols.). New York: Holt, Rinehart & Winston.

Archer, M. S. (1988). *Culture and agency: The place of culture in social theory*. Cambridge: Cambridge University Press.

Ardila, A. (1995). Directions of research in cross-cultural neuropsychology. *Journal of Clinical and Experimental Neuropsychology, 17*(1), 143–150.

Areán, P. A., & Gallagher-Thompson, D. (1996). Issues and recommendations for the recruitment and retention of older ethnic minority adults into clinical research. *Journal of Consulting and Clinical Psychology, 64*(5), 875–880.

Benavides, J. (1992, October 17). Mujeres rule the roosters. *Santa Barbara News Press,* p. B1.

Bidegain, A. M. (1992). The church in the emancipation process (1750–1830). In E. Dussel (Ed.), *The church in Latin America: 1492–1992* (pp. 81–104). Maryknoll, NY: Burns & Oates.

Boswell, T., & Curtis, J. R. (1983). *The Cuban American experience: Culture, images and perspectives*. Totowa, NJ: Rowman & Allanheld.

Casas, J. M., Waggenheim, B. R., Banchero, R., & Mendoza-Romero, J. (1995). Hispanic masculinity: Myth or psychological schema meriting clinical consideration. In A. M. Padilla (Ed.), *Hispanic psychology: Critical issues in theory and research* (pp. 231–244). Thousand Oaks, CA: Sage.

Comas-Diaz, L. (1988). Mainland Puerto Rican women: A sociocultural approach. Special Issue: Women in the community. *Journal of Community Psychology, 16*(1), 21–31.

Dana, R. H. (1993). *Multicultural assessment perspectives for professional psychology.* Boston: Allyn & Bacon.

De Fuentes, P. (1963). The anonymous conquistador. In *The Conquistadors* (pp. 164–181). New York: Orion Press.

Delgado, R., & Stefancic, H. (1998). *The Latino/a condition: A critical reader.* New York: NYU Press.

De Mente, B. (1996). *NTC's dictionary of Mexican culture code words.* Chicago: NTC Publishing Group.

De Varona, F. (1996). *Latino literacy: The complete guide to our Hispanic history and culture.* New York: Henry Holt.

Dussel, E. (1992). General introduction. In E. Dussel (Ed.), *The church in Latin America: 1492–1992* (pp. 1–20). Maryknoll, NY: Burns & Oates.

Echemendia, R. J., Harris, J. G., Congett, S. M., Diaz, M., & Puente, A. (1997). Neuropsychological training and practices with Hispanics: A national Survey. *Clinical Neuropsychologist, 11*(3), 229–243.

Englekirk, A., & Marín, M. (1995). Mexican Americans. In Vecoli, R. J. (Ed.), *Gale encyclopedia of multicultural America* (Vol. 2, pp. 905–989). Detroit: Gale Research.

Falicov, C. J. (1998). *Latino families in therapy: A guide to multicultural practice.* New York: Guilford.

Flores, A. (1992). *Spanish American authors: The twentieth century.* New York: H. W. Wilson.

García-Pelayo y Gross, R. (1990). *El pequeño Larousse ilustrado.* Mexico City: Ediciones Larousse.

Gilmore, D. D., & Uhl, S. C. (1987). Further notes on Andalusian machismo. *Journal of Psychoanalytic Anthropology, 10*(4), 341–360.

Green, D. (1995). Puerto Rican Americans. In R. J. Vecoli (Ed.), *Gale encyclopedia of multicultural America* (Vol. 2, pp. 1129–1143). Detroit: Gale Research.

Herrera, H. (1983). *Frida: A biography of Frida Khalo.* New York: HarperPerennial Library.

Hiebert, P. G. (1983). *Cultural anthropology.* Grand Rapids, MI: Baker Books.

Hillburn, R. (1997, September 20). Luis Miguel's Crossroads. *Los Angeles Times,* pp. F1, F6.

Iijima-Hall, C. (1997). Cultural malpractice: The growing obsolence of psychology with the changing U.S. population. *American Psychologist, 52*(6), 642–651.

Kanellós, N. (1993). *The Hispanic-American almanac: A reference work on Hispanics in the United States.* Detroit: Gale Research.

Kanellós, N. (1994). *The Hispanic almanac: From Columbus to corporate America.* Detroit: Visible Ink Press.

Kanellós, N. (1996a). *The Hispanic almanac* (2nd ed.). Detroit: Gale Research.

Kanellós, N. (1996b). *Hispanic firsts: 500 years of extraordinary achievement.* Detroit: Visible Ink Press.

Kanellós, N., & Esteva-Fabregat, C. (1993). *The handbook of Hispanic cultures in the United States* (4 vols.). Houston: Arte Público Press.

Kearney, M. (1984). *World view.* Noveto, CA: Chandler & Sharp.

Kraft, C. H. (1996). *Anthropology for Christian witness.* Maryknoll, NY: Orbis.

Krstovic, J. (Ed.). (1994). *Hispanic literature criticism* (Vols. 1 & 2). Detroit: Gale Research.

Landrine, H. (1995). Clinical implications of cultural differences: The referential versus the indexical self. In N. Goldberger & J. Veroff (Eds.). *The culture and psychology reader,* (pp. 744–766). New York: New York University Press.

Lingefelter, S. (1992). *Transforming culture.* Grand Rapids, MI: Baker.

Llorente, A., Pontón, M, O., Satz, P., & Taussig, M. (1999). Patterns of American immigration and their impact on the development of norms. *Archives of Clinical Neuropsychology, 14*(7), 603–614.

Lucie-Smith, E. (1993). *Latin American art of the 20th century.* New York: Thames & Hudson.

Mackenzie, D. A. (1996). *Myths of Pre-Columbian America.* New York: Dover. (Original work published 1923)

Marin, G., & Marin B. V. (1991). *Research with Hispanic populations.* Newbury Park, CA: Sage.

Matsumoto, D. R. (1996). *Culture and psychology.* Pacific Grove, CA: Brooks/Cole.

McKechnie, J. L. (Ed.). (1983). *Webster's new universal unabridged dictionary* (2nd ed.). New York: Dorset & Baber.

Miranda, J., Organista, K. C., Azocar, F., Muñoz, R. F., & Lieberman, A. (1996). Recruiting and retaining low income latinos in psychotherapy research. *Journal of Consulting and Clinical Psychology, 64*(5), 868–874.

Mirandé, A. (1988). Que gacho es ser macho: What a drag to be a macho man. *Aztlán, 17,* 63–69.

Mirandé, A. (1997). *Hombres y machos: Masculinity and Latino culture.* Boulder, CO: Westview Press.

Morales Carrion, A. (1984). *Puerto Rico: A political and cultural history.* New York: Norton.

National Association of Hispanic Publications. (1995). *Hispanics-Latinos: Diverse people in a multicultural society.* Washington, DC: National Press Building.

Norris, M. K., Juarez, M. J., & Perkins, M. N. (1989). Adaptation of a screening test for bilingual and bidialectal populations. *Language, Speech, & Hearing Services in Schools, 20*(4), 381–390.

Novas, H. (1993). *Everything you need to know about Latino history.* New York: Penguin.

O'Hanlon, W. H. (1987). *Taproots: Underlying principles of Milton Erickson's therapy and hypnosis.* New York: Norton.

Padilla, A. M. (Ed.). (1995). *Hispanic psychology: Critical issues in theory and research.* Thousand Oaks, CA: Sage.

Panitz, D. R., McConchie, R. D., Sauber, S. R., & Fonseca, J. A. (1983). The role of machismo and the Hispanic family in the etiology and treatment of alcoholism in Hispanic American males. *American Journal of Family Therapy, 11*(1), 31–44.

Pelikan, J. (1996). *Mary through the centuries: Her place in the history of culture.* New Haven, CT: Yale University Press.

Ponterotto, J. G., Casas, J., Suzuki, L. A., & Alexander, C. (Eds.). (1995). *Handbook of multicultural counseling.* Thousand Oaks, CA: Sage.

Pontón, M. O., Gonzalez, J., & Mares, M. (1997) Rehabilitating brain damage in Hispanics. In Jose León-Carrión (Ed.), *Neuropsychological rehabilitation: Fundamentals, innovations and directions* (pp. 513–529). Delray Beach, FL: GR/St. Lucie Press.

Quintanilla, M. (1997, August 7). With Latina, Christy Haubegger aims for women like her—Bilingual, bicultural and underrated. *Los Angeles Times,* pp. E1, E4.

Reedy, M. A. (1995). *Statistical record of Hispanic Americans* (2nd ed.). New York: Gale Research/International Tomson Publishing.

Reichard de Cancio, H. E. (1996). *María en la historia de nuestro Pueblo.* Aguadilla, Puerto Rico: Aguadilla Printing.

Rodríguez, R. (1993). *Days of obligation: An argument with my Mexican father.* New York: Penguin.

Rodríguez-León, M. A. (1992). Invasion and evangelization in the sixteenth century. In E. Dussel (Ed.), *The church in Latin America: 1492–1992* (pp. 43–54). Maryknoll, NY: Burns & Oates.

Rule-Goldberger, & Veroff, J. (Eds.). (1995). *The culture and psychology reader.* New York: New York University Press.

Ryan, B. (Ed.). (1991). *Hispanic writers: A selection of sketches from contemporary authors.* Detroit: Gale Research.

Samora, J., & Simon, P. V. (1993). *A history of the Mexican American people.* Notre Dame, IN: University of Notre Dame Press.

Schobinger, J. (1992). The Amerindian religions. In E. Dussel (Ed.), *The church in Latin America: 1492–1992* (pp. 43–54). Maryknoll, NY: Burns & Oates.

Silver, B. A., & Sporty, L. D. (1990). Behavioral correlates and staff recognition of alcohol use in a university hospital trauma service. *Psychosomatics, 31*(4), 420–425.

Smith, V. (Ed.). (1997). *Encyclopedia of Latin American literature.* Chicago: Fitzroy Dearborn.

Stavans, I. (1996). *The Hispanic condition: Reflections on culture and identity in America.* New York: Harper-Perennial.

Sue, D. W., & Sue, D. (1990). *Counseling the culturally different: Theory and practice* (2nd ed.). New York: Wiley.

Thurman, C. (1989). *The lies we believe.* Nashville, TN: Thomas Nelson Publishers.

Uslar-Pietri, A. (1991). *Medio milenio de Venezuela.* Caracas: Monte Avila Editores.

U.S. Census Bureau. (1994, March). *Current population survey, current population report,* Series P-2-, 438,444,449, 455,465,475.

U.S. Census Bureau. (1998a). *"Married, with Children" more likely to describe Hispanic households, Bureau of the Census says.* Press release CB98-17, issued 2/3/98.

U.S. Census Bureau. (1998b). *http://www.bls.census.gov/cps/pub/1997/int_hisp.html*

Valdés, I. M., & Seoane, M. H. (1995). *Hispanic market handbook.* Detroit: Gale Research.

Vecoli, R. J. (Ed.). (1995). *Gale encyclopedia of multicultural America* (Vols. 1–2). Detroit: Gale Research.

Vazquez-Nuttall, E., Avila-Vivas, Z., & Morales-Barreto, G. (1984). Working with Latin American families. *Family Therapy Collections, 9,* 74–90.

Vygotsky, L. S. (1978). *Mind in society: The development of higher psychological processes.* Cambridge, MA: Harvard University Press.

Wallbank, T. W., Taylor, A. M., Bailkey, N. M., & Jewsbury, G. F. (1978). *Civilization past and present* (5th ed.). New York: Scott Foresman.

Yeo, G., & Gallagher-Thompson, D. (Eds.). (1996). *Ethnicity and the dementias.* Washington, DC: Taylor & Francis.

3

Research and Assessment Issues With Hispanic Populations

Marcel O. Pontón
Harbor–UCLA Medical Center

Practical approaches to assessing and systematically studying Hispanic populations are sorely needed (Artiola i Fortuni & Mullaney, 1998; Cervantes & Acosta, 1992; Eche-mendía, Harris, Congett, & Diaz, 1997; Mitrushina, Boone, & D'Elia, 1999; Mungas, 1996; Pontón & Ardila, 1999). This chapter focuses on the key variables that all neuro-psychologists doing research or performing assessment with Hispanics should integrate into their work. For the development of research, and more specifically for the develop-ment of appropriate norms, a conceptual grid is provided. Each variable within this grid is discussed conceptually both in relation to the background provided in chapter 1 and to its impact on test development. A clinical model for assessing this patient population is also presented. A decision tree based on the key variables of language and acculturation is out-lined to help clinicians make informed decisions in their evaluation of these patients. The chapter ends with a brief review of selected instruments and norms available to evaluate this population.

Acculturation is presented as a significant variable deserving attention in both research and clinical settings. Therefore, a cursory review of this concept is presented to familiarize readers with its meaning and to highlight its relevance to neuropsychology.

ACCULTURATION

Acculturation is defined as the change in cultural patterns that results from the direct and continuous firsthand contact of different cultural groups (Alvidrez, Azocar, & Miranda, 1996; Cuellar, Arnold, & Maldonado, 1995; Marín & Marín, 1991; Mena, Padilla, & Maldonado, 1987). Change in cultural patterns is reciprocal and affects people at the individual and group level (Mena et al., 1987); however, levels of acculturation vary widely for individuals and groups. Acculturation deals with culture change, whereas assimilation deals with the absorption of another culture with the goal of resembling it closely (Cuellar et al., 1995).

The question of how acculturation affects cognitive functioning and by corollary test performance is unclear as of yet (Pontón & Ardila, 1999). However, recent evidence suggests that it may be impacting familiarity with testing situations as well as with the stimuli that reflect the dominant culture's values. Hence, more acculturation results in better performance (Herrera, Pontón, Corona, Gonzalez, & Higareda, 1998). Because this construct belongs to the social psychology/anthropological research arena more than to neuropsychology, there is not a body of research on which to base conclusions concerning its relation to measures of cognition. Moreover, the existing research seems to be complex and equivocal, depending on the dimensions of acculturation they study (i.e., cultural loyalty, ethnic identity, cultural identity, etc.; Keefe, 1992; Miranda & White, 1993; Salgado De Snyder, 1987).

Rather than being an easily quantifiable variable, acculturation can be conceptualized as a unidimensional, bidimensional, or multidimensional construct (Felix-Ortiz, Newcomb, & Myers, 1994). In the latter approach, acculturation can be seen as a cluster of variables, which includes language, values, beliefs, attitudes, gender roles, psychological frame of references, skills, media preferences, leisure activities, observance of holidays, and cultural self-identity. Factor analysis of this construct has identified two elements that account for most of the variance (language and number of years in the United States (Marín & Marín, 1991)). However, it is erroneous to assume that a fully bilingual person with 20 years of residence in the United States has acculturated at the same rate across all domains (Alvidrez et al., 1996; Marín & Marín, 1991; Pontón & Ardila, 1999). Whatever the person's level of acculturation, it must be ascertained objectively so as to be clinically meaningful.

Marín and Marín's (1991) measure of acculturation is the most psychometrically sound, and the most amenable for neuropsychological research (Herrera et al., 1998). The full English and Spanish versions of the same are presented in the appendixes of this chapter.

Along with age, education, gender, and country of origin (see Pontón & León-Carrión, chap. 1 in this book), acculturation helps to solve the puzzle that is cognitive functioning in the Hispanic population. A model to integrate these variables meaningfully is needed for research and clinical endeavors. The model proposed here is a template to develop research with Hispanic populations, particularly in the area of norms development and group comparison. Issues of clinical practice are addressed in a separate section later.

A RESEARCH MODEL FOR UNDERSTANDING COGNITION IN THE HISPANIC POPULATION

The following model takes into account three crucial variables: country of origin, language spoken, and education level. Ethnicity has been obviated for country of origin, because the problems noted previously make it an ineffectual variable. Country of origin, on the other hand, is an easily measured variable, because it can be compared against the Census data for sampling purposes and it provides a standard (albeit loose) of the educational experiences of people who share a common national heritage (Llorente, Pontón, Taussig, & Satz, 1999). Along this dimension, regional differences should also be considered, because a poor rural person from Mexico has more in common with a poor rural person from El Salvador than with an upper-class, highly educated person from Mexico City. For the purposes of research, it would suffice to have rural versus urban differences coded (see Fig. 3.1).

Language spoken is a critical element affecting assessment or research outcomes (Pontón & Ardila, 1999). Its careful categorization is more a science than a clerical task.

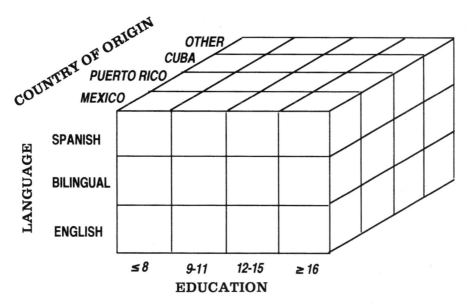

FIG. 3.1.   Model of Hispanic diversity in neuropsychological assessment.

Woodcock and Muñoz-Sandoval (1995) attempted to provide some help in this regard by developing measures of bilingualism and language proficiency. Those are discussed elsewhere in this book. However, making a clear decision about the patients' language use and assessing patients with tools that reflect their actual level of language proficiency will translate into more accurate descriptions of cognitive functioning.

Education has been shown to affect test performance significantly, especially when individuals with educational levels of less than 9 years are evaluated (Heaton, Chelune, Talley, Kay & Curtiss, 1993; Ostrosky-Solis, Ardila, Rosselli, Lopez-Arango, & Uriel-Mendoza (1998); Pontón et al., 1996). As the single most important contributor to test performance, fine differences in education should be taken into account. The current model divides education into four general categories (<8 years, 9–11 years; 12–15 years, and >16 years of education). Although these categories could be somewhat refined (i.e., ≤6, 7–9, 10–11, 12, 13–15, 16–18, 19+), the impractical nature of a research design with such distinctions argues favorably for the parsimony of four educational groups. Previous research has shown that normal subjects with less than 6 years of education perform significantly worse than age peers with 12 years of education or more on a battery assessing neurocognitive functioning (Pontón et al., 1996). An alternative would be to use education as a continuous variable in order to retain the variance. However, recent evidence suggests that education has an asymptotic and possibly curvilinear relation with performance in this population (Ostrosky-Solis, Ardila, Rosselli, Lopez-Arango, & Uriel-Mendoza, 1998). That is to say, test performance increases up to 20 years of education and then it declines. Hence, it is better to use education groups as opposed to categorizing education as a continuous variable.

An illustration can facilitate an understanding of the model at work. Individuals from Puerto Rico could be compared to subjects born in Mexico or the United States (Other Hispanics) in terms of their level of education and language using these factors as either independent or dependent variables. Controlling for language and education will allow accurate descriptions of the patients' performance on the measures taken. If, on the other hand, the researcher is interested in developing appropriate norms for this population on a test or battery, this model would allow stratification along the thorniest variables, using empirically defined parameters. For the latter project, however, it is recommended that in addition, researchers include age groups as they apply to this model. If resources are not an issue, then the final matrix would look like this: Language spoken (3) × Education groups (4) × Age groups (4). Country of origin would be treated as a background variable to match the sample, because there are not equal proportions of subjects reflected in the Census from each country of origin.

The previous model is suggested with the intention of encouraging the research and development of valid and reliable normative data for this population. Assessment is discussed separately in the next section.

ASSESSING THE HISPANIC PATIENT

Assessing cognition of Hispanics has been controversial from the very beginning of mental measurement. Consider the following excerpt from Terman's (1916) book, *The Measurement of Intelligence:*

> M.P. Boy, age 14; mental age 10-8; IQ 77. Has been tested four successive years, IQ being always between 75 and 80. In school nearly eight years and has been promoted to the fifth grade. At 16 was doing poor work in the 6th grade. Good school advantages, as the father has tried conscientiously to give his children a "good education." Perfectly normal in appearance and in play activities and is liked by other children. Seems to be thoroughly dependable both in school and his outside work . . .
>
> It is interesting to note that M.P. and C.P. represent the level of intelligence which is very, very common among Spanish-Indian and Mexican families of the Southwest. . . . Their dullness seems to be racial, or at least inherent in the family stocks from which they come . . .
>
> Children of this group should be segregated in special classes and be given instruction which is concrete and practical. . . . There is no possibility at present of convincing society that they should not be allowed to reproduce, although from a eugenic point of view they constitute a grave problem because of their unusually prolific breeding. (pp. 90–92)

Few psychologists would dare today to make such written statements. Sadly, however, the methodology used to reach conclusions about the actual functioning of this patient population has changed little since Terman's time. The medical-legal arena is a field where these errors abound. Consider the actual case of a neuropsychologist who administered a battery of tests to a Spanish-speaking Latino child. He concluded that the patient had profound cognitive deficits with "some variability." In his deposition, the doctor stated that he could not explain how the child could have obtained an above average scaled score in the Vocabulary subtest of the Wechsler Intelligence Scale for Children (WISC–III) and a markedly impaired standard score on the Peabody Picture Vocabulary Test (PPVT–R). When questioned about his use of an interpreter, the doctor reported using an interpreter for the first session, and then he used his "kitchen Spanish" and the child's "little" English to complete testing over several sessions. The day the child answered questions from the WISC–III Vocabulary subtest, the interpreter was present and "the child was allowed to give some answers in Spanish." Inexperience could be blamed for such disregard of ethical and testing guidelines. Yet, the doctor stated with pride that he had evaluated "hundreds" of Hispanic children using this approach and that he had been in practice for two decades. When asked about the level of confidence in his opinions, he repeatedly cited his experience as the basis for the authority of his conclusions.

This reliance on the atoning power of experience to redeem the sins of unethical methodology is assertively and successfully used by clinicians giving expert legal testimony. But should it continue? Blau (1998) said that reliance on experience alone is now more likely than ever to be ruled inadmissible in forensic cases.

Artiola i Fortuni and Mullaney (1998) argued pointedly that evaluating a patient whose language the clinician does not know is below the standard of practice. However, such evaluations are regularly performed, making this topic highly contentious from an ethical perspective. As a result, it has been formally avoided. Instead of developing a consensus over an explicit set of guidelines, there seems to be a tacit hope and expectation that "a sharp lawyer" would some day make case law by pointing out the ethical breaches involved and by roasting the perpetrators on the stand. This passive position seems prominent among clinicians who notice that colleagues repeatedly disregard ethical guidelines with impunity. Their position seems to assert that until jurisprudence settles the issue, the status quo will persist. Thus, clinicians seem to be waiting for lawyers to set the limits rather than enlightening the legal world about what the standard of practice is in regard to the assessment of Spanish-speaking patients by non-Spanish-speaking clinicians. This widely held position forebodes adversity for the profession.

How then should this issue be confronted? There is the option of preaching loudly that at the nadir of their practice, non-Spanish-speaking neuropsychologists perform these evaluations because they are careless, greedy, insensitive, incompetent, or unethical. However, casting aspersions on the character of colleagues (however unsavory) may open up the horn-blowers themselves to legal actions (e.g., libel) or ethical countercomplaints. Callousness and learned helplessness would inflict lasting wounds to the profession if such a precedent were set. An even less effective, yet equally popular, approach would be to take on a policing role, using a strict interpretation of the current ethical principles. Brave and principled in their intentions, such clinicians could be easily portrayed as rigid or sanctimonious in their arguments to expose offenders. Even worse, they could be counterattacked as wanting to restrict the trade or "corner the market." The prospect of "losing friends and alienating people" is low in most professionals' agenda, regardless of their level of concern about this particular issue.

Short of waiting for adverse case law to dictate the practice or becoming outcasts among peers, there are some ethically sensible and clinically meaningful alternatives, some of which are examined here. They focus on ethical conflicts/issues, language and acculturation barriers, and what measures to use.

ETHICAL CONFLICTS

Current ethical guidelines (American Psychological Association [APA], 1990) give only vague suggestions as to how a non-Spanish-speaking psychologist should proceed with the evaluation of a Spanish-speaking patient (cf. Artiola i Fortuni & Mullaney, 1998; Melendez, chap. 15 in this volume). These are mostly to blame for the current state of affairs. It is critical that the APA formally address the issue of neuropsychological assessment of bilingual and monolingual Spanish-speaking subjects in the United States. Incompetent, misleading, and potentially harmful practices can be stopped and avoided in the future when such guidelines are developed. Current theory suggests a number of workable models in this area (E. C. Lopez, 1997; Sanchez, 1986; see Melendez, chap. 15 in this volume).

Basic methodological practices to which all psychologists adhere apply to the assessment of this population. Consider the following:

1. Seek consultation: If clinicians are about to evaluate a Spanish-speaking or bilingual patient, then they must answer the question of whether they are the most qualified person to see that patient. Seek advice from the regional or local psychological organization. Ethical consultation is encouraged and available for psychologists who request it. Should the clinician refer? Would clinicians be impacting the patient's rights by attempting to offer a service that is actually beyond their area of competence? Consultation should help in answering these crucial questions.

2. Become aware of any limitations in evaluating the patient and communicate those limitations clearly to the client (the patient or referral source). Provide an informed consent about any limitations and the equivocal nature of the results to your client. Results most affected will involve language functioning, intellectual assessment, and the presence and magnitude of psychopathology (both Axis I and Axis II *Diagnostic and Statistical Manual of Mental Disorders,* fourth edition [DSM–IV] pathology).

3. Do not rely on an untrained individual to give a diagnostic impression of the patient (i.e., interpreter). Document the examinee's response to the interpreter as well as the interaction between the examinee and the interpreter in the behavioral observations section of the report. The presence of a third person in a testing situation is clearly disruptive to the testing process and introduces error into the evaluation. Case law in some states (e.g., California) forbids attorneys or third parties to be present in the same room when a patient is examined by a psychologist (Blau, 1998). It simply alters the dynamics of the interaction between patient and clinician. If that third person is an active participant during testing, then there is a much greater likelihood that the standardization assumptions of the tests used will be violated and more error will be introduced. Therefore, this issue must be clearly spelled out in the report, when discussing the meaning of the results obtained. It will be ethical for the non-Spanish-speaking psychologist to communicate these issues to a referring lawyer, before agreeing to take the case.

4. Provide a special discussion in the report of findings that are the most reliable and explain why these are more likely to be accurate. Also indicate which findings are the least reliable and discuss the reasons for this as well.

LANGUAGE AND ACCULTURATION BARRIERS

Effective communication with the patient is crucial if a valid neuropsychological evaluation is desired (Mestre & Royer, 1991; Mungas, 1996; Palmer, Olivarez, Willson, & Fordyce, 1989; Sanchez, 1986; Taussig & Pontón, 1996; Willig, 1988). Thus, ascertaining unequivocally what patients say in response to questions or test items becomes the basis on which diagnostic and treatment decisions are based (Lezak, 1995). It is not only assumed, but crucial, that what clinicians say be just as clearly understood by their patients. The breakdown of effective communication between patient and clinician because of negligence results in errors such as misdiagnosing, overpathologizing (Arroyo, 1996; Cauce & Jacobson, 1980; Malgady, Rogler, & Costantino, 1987; C. W. Stephan & W. G. Stephan, 1986), and producing inadmissible evidence for medical-legal evaluations

(Blau, 1998). Hence, the most important aspect of the evaluation of a Hispanic patient is to decide whether a language barrier is present (see Fig. 3.2).

How can clinicians determine whether a language barrier exists between themselves and their patients? The following suggestions begin with obvious building blocks that provide a foundation from which the clinician can address more ambiguous situations where common sense gives way to clinical decision making:

1. Determine the patient's language of choice: Does the patient speak primarily Spanish or English? Is the patient bilingual? (Please refer to Appendix 3A to address this issue.)

2. Determine your own language proficiency: Are you a native Spanish-speaker? Are you a native English-speaker? Are you a balanced bilingual person (i.e., do you have the same degree of language mastery in English and Spanish)?

3. Determine whether you can evaluate the patient in English.
   a) Use the Woodcock Language Proficiency Test.
   b) Use the G. Marin and B. V. Marin (1991) Acculturation Scale (see Appendix 3B for details).
   c) If you are not a Spanish-speaker, and if the patient is clearly not an English-speaker, then the evaluation should stop, and the patient should be referred. If the patient's English proficiency is low or poor for testing and the clinician is not a native Spanish-speaker, then the patient should be referred as well to an appropriate bilingual (and preferably a bicultural) neuropsychologist.
   d) If the patient can be assessed in English, then the clinician should determine the patient's level of acculturation to confirm that it is high and the evaluation should proceed in English.
   e) If acculturation is moderate or low (as per the Marin scale), then clinicians should state so with clear caveats in the report. A note to the effect that cultural factors may have affected the patient's performance on certain measures of the battery and that the current results are tentative should be included (an example follows).

Sample statement of caveat to use in report with Hispanic patients evaluated via an interpreter.

It should be noted that the above patient was evaluated via an interpreter. The literature suggests that bias and error are introduced into the evaluation when interpreters are used. Additionally, the normative group against which this patient was compared is made up of mostly White, English-speaking subjects whose educational and cultural backgrounds differ greatly from those of the patient. Therefore, the current results are considered highly tentative.

Monolingual Patients

English-Speaking Patients. In this situation, where the patient is monolingual English speaking and has been part of the larger culture since birth, there is no language barrier. The patient should be evaluated in English without any difficulties.

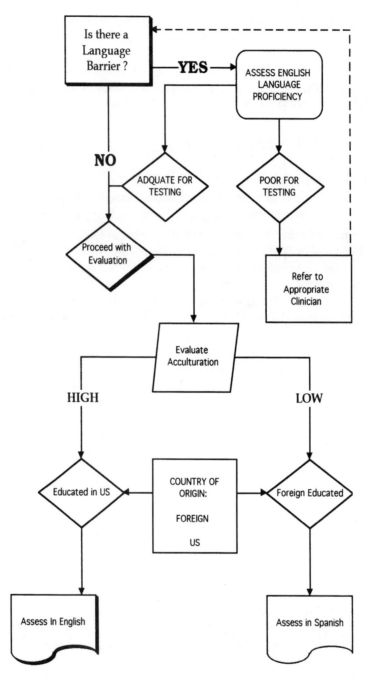

FIG. 3.2.   Decision tree for assessing bilingual Hispanic patients.

Spanish-Speaking Patients. The patient should be evaluated in Spanish by an appropriate bilingual (preferably bicultural) clinician. A non-Spanish-speaking clinician must refer such patients as per the APA guidelines (APA, 1992; Artiola i Fortuni & Mullaney, 1998; Pérez-Arce & Puente, 1996). Interpreters should be used only if there are no appropriate referrals to be made. Clear caveats as to the equivocal nature of the results should be evident in the text of the report and in the conclusions.

Use of Interpreters. As discussed by Melendez later in this book, multiple cautions should accompany the use of interpreters, because they bring much error into the testing session (LaCalle, 1987). The following guidelines are suggested:

1. The best option for clinicians is to refer the patient to a qualified bilingual and bicultural neuropsychologist in the area, if they do not qualify themselves. The use of an interpreter should be a last resource. Blau's (1998) directive is quite appropriate in this regard: "Never agree to be an expert in any area in which you are not an expert" (p. 60). Or, as Artiola i Fortuni and Mullaney (1998) asked: "Can something absurd be ethical?"

2. If there is no qualified bilingual, bicultural clinician in your area who can test the patient, then use an interpreter. However, it is the responsibility of the clinician to (a) verify the interpreter's credentials beforehand; (b) meet with the interpreter before the evaluation and go over the standardized instructions to make sure the interpreter has the adequate vocabulary in the patient's language to translate questions; and (c) make sure interpreters do not become psychologists, and that they do not interfere with the testing by "clarifying" information in either direction.

Bilingual Patients

The bilingual population is one of the most difficult to define and to test (Mestre & Royer, 1991; Ochoa, Powell, & Robles-Piña, 1996). Patients can self-report to be bilingual, yet their degree of mastery of either language can be quite lacking. It is with this group that the largest margin of error rests (see Centeno & Obler, chap. 5 in this book; de Bernard, 1985; Gutierrez-Clellen, 1996; S. Lopez, 1988; Pérez-Arce & Puente, 1996; Sandoval & Duran, 1998).

Regardless of the clinicians' bilingual status, they should determine the patient's actual level of language proficiency, especially if the patient seems to be bilingual.

The elusiveness of bilingualism demands that specific and systematic steps be taken to decrease as much as possible the amount of error from the evaluation. Thus, as soon as a language barrier is suspected, an objective evaluation of the patient's English-language proficiency is needed, particularly if the clinician is not bilingual and is culturally different from the patient.

If the results of this evaluation yield a low score, suggestive of poor English proficiency, then the best option is to refer to an appropriate bilingual, bicultural neuropsychologist. If, however, the objective results indicate the patient's performance on measures of receptive, expressive, and written English language are adequate, then the evaluation could proceed in English.

For bilingual, bicultural clinicians who do not have a language barrier with the patients, they must decide whether to proceed with testing in English or Spanish. Acculturation is the key that facilitates this decision. Using the G. Marin and B. V. Marin (1991) scale, the clinician can determine whether the patient's level of acculturation is

TABLE 3.1
Interpreting the G. Marin and B. V. Marin (1991) Acculturation Scale

Domain	Items	Summative Score	Classification
Language Preference	1–5	≤ 14	LOW
		15–19	MODERATE
		≥ 20	HIGH
Media Preferences	6–8	≤ 8	LOW
		9–11	MODERATE
		≥ 12	HIGH
Ethnic Social Relations Scale	9–12	≤ 11	LOW
		12–15	MODERATE
		≥ 16	HIGH

high or low. The cut-off scores in Table 3.1 should be considered in arriving at this decision.

The values in Table 3.1 will allow clinicians to make informed decisions about the language in which to test the patient. The next element of the formula details the educational background of the patient. Rather than dealing with actual schooling, this variable covers the national context where the individual was educated. As many clinicians will notice, this is a variable of significance, particularly for young patients, because they tend to acculturate faster.

Thus, if the individual has a high level of acculturation to the majority culture in the United States, and was educated in the United States (regardless of country of birth), then this person should be evaluated in English. However, if patients have a "medium" or low level of acculturation, and regardless of their country of birth they were educated in a Spanish-speaking culture, then they should be evaluated in Spanish. For instance, consider a child who is born in Los Angeles from immigrant parents, returns to Mexico after age 8, and lives in Mexico for the next 10 years. When evaluated at age 18 in the United States, this person is seemingly bilingual, but his cultural identity is Mexican, and Spanish is his primary language. This person needs to be evaluated in Spanish. Similarly, an elderly patient who was born to seasonal farm workers in the 1930s in Texas, spoke Spanish at home and lived in Mexico for 30 years beginning in her adolescence needs to be evaluated in Spanish, because it is her primary language.

There are limitations to the aforementioned model, and exceptions can be found to it. However, this model provides directions to maintain the ethical imperatives covering the work of psychologists and neuropsychologists and it offers a workable solution to the problems faced by colleagues in the field.

WHAT MEASURES TO USE

The question most frequently asked about the assessment of this population is not about competency or qualifications to perform the evaluation. Rather, it is very simple: "What good tests in Spanish and norms do you have?"

The answer is obviously more complex than providing a simple list of tests or endorsing a particular battery. First, the reader is referred to various sources from which tests, normative data, and more detailed reviews can be obtained (Mitrushina et al., 1999; Spreen & Strauss, 1998).

However, this volume provides some basic normative data for Hispanics. The following norms are part of the Neuropsychological Screening Battery for Hispanics (NeSBHIS), which is described in detail elsewhere (Pontón et al., 1996; Pontón, Gonzales, Hernandez, Herrera, & Higareda, 2000). The test battery consisted of the following measures: Controlled Word Association Test (F–A–S); Ponton–Satz version of the Boston Naming Test (P–S BNT); the Pin Test; Rey–Osterrieth Complex Figure—copy and 10-minute delay; WHO–UCLA Auditory Verbal Learning Test(AVLT with five learning trials, distraction list, immediate recall, and 20-minute delay recall); Color Trails Test, parts I and 2 (CT1, CT2); Escala de Inteligencia Wechsler para Adultos (EIWA) subtests: Digit Span, Digit Symbol, and Block Design; Ravens Standard Progressive Matrices, total score. The background characteristics of the sample can be found in Table 3.2.

The following norms are divided into groups by years of education. A simple cursory review of the test results speaks to the impact of education on test performance. The following norms can be used with Hispanics from different countries of origin—including Mexico, Central America, Puerto Rico, and Cuba—as they are well represented in the total sample. Given the relatively small size of the cells, it is currently difficult to make finer distinctions (as is suggested in the model presented), further data collection for the NeSBHIS is still underway (Pontón et al., 1998). Other researchers are also encouraged to add to the existing body of normative data. Table 3.3 provides normative data by education groups.

TABLE 3.2
Demographic Characteristics of the Normative Group Used
in the NeSBHIS

Variable	Mean	SD	Range	N
Age	38.4	13.5	16–75	300
Education	10.7	5.1	1–20+	
# Years in U.S.	16.4	14.4	.08–69	

Variable	Count	%
Gender		
Females	180	60
Males	120	40
Language		
Spanish	210	70
Bilingual	90	30
Country of Origin		
Mexico	187	62
Central America	44	15
U.S.	38	12
Other	31	10
Handedness		
Right	283	95
Left	12	4
Ambidextrous	4	1

TABLE 3.3
Normative Data for Education Groups for the NeSBHIS battery

	Years of Education							
	0–6 (n = 81)		7–10 (n = 65)		11–15 (n = 97)		16+ (n = 57)	
	Mean	SD	Mean	SD	Mean	SD	Mean	SD
Memory								
AVLT V	12.26	1.79	12.99	1.75	13.24	1.69	13.63	1.54
AVLT VII	10.70	2.44	11.79	2.11	11.71	2.26	12.21	2.40
AVLT VII	11.11	2.26	11.97	2.23	12.43	2.07	13.19	1.83
REY–O MEM	14.75	6.59	17.81	7.09	18.52	5.95	22.54	4.87
Psychomotor								
DOM Total	83.26	19.45	96.55	18.97	100.60	16.54	103.46	15.89
NDOM Total	67.48	18.27	77.29	18.84	77.36	14.29	81.65	14.39
Language								
MBNT	21.47	3.52	22.79	2.51	23.31	3.44	26.61	2.84
FAS	22.37	10.46	27.74	9.50	30.22	9.58	37.40	9.05
Mental Control								
Dig Span Tot	8.10	1.46	8.82	1.31	9.02	1.73	10.00	1.84
Digit Symbol	34.51	13.22	49.79	11.78	59.47	12.80	64.53	11.20
CT 1	59.68	29.65	47.43	16.44	38.47	12.88	34.68	11.66
CT 2	137.52	51.01	106.08	34.59	88.69	28.51	83.97	23.31
Visuospatial								
Block Design	25.85	9.27	31.85	7.39	35.10	6.55	38.68	5.00
REY–O Copy	26.16	6.55	30.27	4.46	30.86	4.37	32.61	2.87
Reasoning								
Raven's Total	28.48	12.10	38.14	10.43	40.51	9.59	48.16	7.81

People interested in using the battery can obtain the tests from the sources in Table 3.4.

CONCLUSIONS

This chapter has attempted to integrate issues of historical background and demographic characteristics within two conceptual models for the delivery of services to the Hispanic population of the United States. First, it provided a research model that attempts to account for the variables that are unique to this population. Second, it provided a model for the assessment of Hispanic patients, giving clinicians guidelines that avoid ethical pitfalls and maintain the integrity of the assessment process. It ended by providing normative data on a screening battery that can be used clinically and in research with this population (the NeSBHIS; Pontón et al., 1996). These models and data can become useful templates with which the neuropsychological community can properly serve the Hispanic community.

The paucity of ethical guidelines for the assessment of Spanish-speaking Hispanic patients has created a "frontier-climate" in which clinicians believe they can make up the rules as they go. In this ethical vacuum, having done things the same way for a long time is more important than having done them right. Thus, a reference to experience is deemed adequate justification for a variety of inappropriate methods. Not only are practicing psy-

TABLE 3.4
Test Forms for the NeSBHIS Battery

Test	Publisher/Form
Memory	
WHO–UCLA AVLT–Spanish version	See Appendix 3C in this chapter
REY-O CFT	Public Domain
Psychomotor	
PIN Test	P.A.R.
Language	
Pontón-Satz BNT	Author
FAS	Public Domain
Mental Control	
EIWA Digit Span	Psychological Corporation
EIWA Digit Symbol	
Color Trails 1 & 2	P.A.R.
Visuospatial	
EIWA Block Design	Psychological Corporation
REY–O CFT Copy	Public Domain
Reasoning	
Raven's SPM	Psychological Corporation

Note: Spanish-language instructions are available from the author.

chologists experiencing difficulties, but the next generation of clinicians is also benighted (Echemendía et al., 1997). Therefore, it is imperative for the ethics board of the APA to develop specific guidelines for the assessment of patients who speak a different language from the clinician. It is also incumbent on the ABBP/ABCN board to address this issue thoughtfully and expediently. Undoubtedly, this issue concerns ABPP members the most, because by virtue of their certification, these neuropsychologists are usually called on to provide expert testimony.

APPENDIX 3A

Patient's Language of Choice

Language	Domain	Minimum Level of Proficiency
English	Read	6th Grade
	Write	6th Grade
	Speak	Fluent Conversation (Expressive and Receptive)
Spanish	Read	Newspaper (if literate)
	Write	Correspondence (if literate)
	Speak	Fluent Conversation (Expressive and Receptive)

IDIOMA PREFERIDO DEL PACIENTE

Idioma	Capacidad	Criterio Mínimo
Español	Lectura	Leer el Periódico
	Escritura	Escribir cartas
	Lenguaje Hablado	Mantener Conversación fluida
Inglés	Lectura	6to Grado
	Escritura	6to Grado
	Lenguaje Hablado	Mantener Conversación fluida

APPENDIX 3B

Marin Acculturation Scale

ENGLISH VERSION

Name _____   Date _____

PLEASE CIRCLE THE APPROPRIATE NUMBER

1. In general, what language do you speak and read?

1	2	3	4	5
Only Spanish	Spanish better than English	Both equally well	English better than Spanish	Only English

2. What language did you speak as a child?

1	2	3	4	5
Only Spanish	Spanish better than English	Both equally well	English better than Spanish	Only English

3. In general, what language do you speak at home?

1	2	3	4	5
Only Spanish	Spanish better than English	Both equally well	English better than Spanish	Only English

4. In general, what language do you think in?

1	2	3	4	5
Only Spanish	Spanish better than English	Both equally well	English better than Spanish	Only English

5. In general, what language do you use when talking to friends?

1	2	3	4	5
Only Spanish	Spanish better than English	Both equally well	English better than Spanish	Only English

6. In general, what language are the programs you watch on television?

1	2	3	4	5
Only Spanish	Spanish better than English	Both equally well	English better than Spanish	Only English

7. In general, what language are the programs you listen to on the radio?

1	2	3	4	5
Only Spanish	Spanish better than English	Both equally well	English better than Spanish	Only English

8. In general, what language do you prefer to see and listen to movies in, and television and radio programs ?

1	2	3	4	5
Only Spanish	Spanish better than English	Both equally well	English better than Spanish	Only English

9. Your closest friends are:

1	2	3	4	5
Only Latinos	More Latinos than Americans	About half and half	More Americans than Latinos	Only Americans

10. You prefer to go to social gatherings/parties in which there are:

1	2	3	4	5
Only Latinos	More Latinos than Americans	About half and half	More Americans than Latinos	Only Americans

11. The people you visit or who visit you are:

1	2	3	4	5
Only Latinos	More Latinos than Americans	About half and half	More Americans than Latinos	Only Americans

12. If you could choose your sons'/daughters' or younger siblings' friends, they would be:

1	2	3	4	5
Only Latinos	More Latinos than Americans	About half and half	More Americans than Latinos	Only Americans

13. How would you describe yourself?

1	2	3	4	5
Very Latino	More Latino than American	About half and half	More American than Latino	Very American

SPANISH VERSION

Favor de marcar el número apropriado con un circulo

1. Por lo general, ¿qué idioma(s) lee y habla usted?

1	2	3	4	5
Solo Español	Español mejor que Inglés	Ambos por igual	Inglés mejor que Español	Solo Inglés

2. ¿En qué idioma(s) habló usted cuando era niño(a)?

1	2	3	4	5
Solo Español	Español mejor que Inglés	Ambos por igual	Inglés mejor que Español	Solo Inglés

3. Por lo general, ¿qué idioma(s) habla usted en su casa?

1	2	3	4	5
Solo Español	Español mejor que Inglés	Ambos por igual	Inglés mejor que Español	Solo Inglés

4. Por lo general, ¿en qué idioma(s) piensa usted?

1	2	3	4	5
Solo Español	Español mejor que Inglés	Ambos por igual	Inglés mejor que Español	Solo Inglés

5. Por lo general, ¿en qué idioma(s) habla usted con sus amistades?

1	2	3	4	5
Solo Español	Español mejor que Inglés	Ambos por igual	Inglés mejor que Español	Solo Inglés

6. Por lo general, ¿en qué idioma estan los programas de televisión que usted ve?

1	2	3	4	5
Solo Español	Español mejor que Inglés	Ambos por igual	Inglés mejor que Español	Solo Inglés

7. Por lo general, ¿en qué idioma(s) estan los programas de radio que usted escucha?

1	2	3	4	5
Solo Español	Español mejor que Inglés	Ambos por igual	Inglés mejor que Español	Solo Inglés

8. Por lo general, ¿en qué idioma(s) prefiere oir y ver películas, y programas de radio y televisión?

1	2	3	4	5
Solo Español	Español mejor que Inglés	Ambos por igual	Inglés mejor que Español	Solo Inglés

9. Sus amigos y amigas más cercanos son:

1	2	3	4	5
Solo Latinos	Más Latinos que Americanos	Casi mitad y mitad	Más Americanos que Latinos	Solo Americanos

10. Usted prefiere ir a reuniones sociales/fiestas en las cuales las personas son:

1	2	3	4	5
Solo Latinos	Más Latinos que Americanos	Casi mitad y mitad	Más Americanos que Latinos	Solo Americanos

11. Las personas que usted visita o que le visitan a usted son:

1	2	3	4	5
Solo Latinos	Más Latinos que Americanos	Casi mitad y mitad	Más Americanos que Latinos	Solo Americanos

12. Si usted pudiera escoger los amigos (as) de sus hijos (as), quisiera que sean:

1	2	3	4	5
Solo Latinos	Más Latinos que Americanos	Casi mitad y mitad	Más Americanos que Latinos	Solo Americanos

13. ¿C6mo se describiría usted a sí mismo?

1	2	3	4	5
Muy Latino	Más Latino que Americano	Casi mitad y mitad	Más Americano que Latino	Muy Americano

APPENDIX 3C

WHO–UCLA Auditory Verbal Learning Test – Spanish Version

Nombre: _____ Fecha: _____

Lista A	I	II	III	IV	V	Lista B	VI B	VII A	Lista A
BRAZO						BOTA			BRAZO
GATO						MONO			GATO
HACHA						PLATO			HACHA
CAMA						VACA			CAMA
AVION						DEDO			AVION
OREJA						VESTIDO			OREJA
PERRO						ARAÑA			PERRO
MARTILLO						TAZA			MARTILLO
SILLA						ABEJA			SILLA
CARRO						PIE			CARRO
OJO						SOMBRERO			OJO
CABALLO						MOSCA			CABALLO
PUÑAL						OLLA			PUÑAL
RELOJ						RATON			RELOJ
MOTO						MANO			MOTO
RESPUESTAS CORRECTAS									
RESPUESTAS REPETIDAS									
# INTROMISIONES									

Lista A	VIII 20 min	IX Identificación		
BRAZO		espejo	CABALLO	camión
GATO		MARTILLO	pierna	OJO
HACHA		PUÑAL	PERRO	pez
CAMA		vela	mesa	OREJA
AVION		bicicleta	GATO	MOTO

OREJA	
PERRO	
MARTILLO	
SILLA	
CARRO	
OJO	
CABALLO	
PUÑAL	
RELOJ	
MOTO	
RESPUESTAS CORRECTAS	
RESPUESTAS REPETIDAS	
INTROMISIONES	

HACHA	labios	culebra
RELOJ	árbol	butaca
SILLA	BRAZO	bus
AVION	nariz	CAMA
tortuga	sol	CARRO

TOTAL CORRECTO	
TOTAL INTROMISION	

Translated by Marcel Pontón, 1996 (Pontón et al., 1996). See Mitrushina, Boone, and D'Elia (1998) for the English version of the test.

REFERENCES

Alvidrez, J., Axocar, F., & Miranda, J. (1996). Demystifying the concept of ethnicity for psychotherapy researchers. *Journal of Consulting and Clinical Psychology, 64*(5), 903–908.

American Psychological Association: Board of Ethnic Minority Affairs Task Force on the Delivery of Services to Ethnic Minority Populations. (1990). Guidelines for providers of psychological services to ethnic, linguistic, and culturally diverse populations. Washington, DC: Author.

American Psychological Association (1992). Ethical Principles of psychologists and code of conduct. *American Psychologist, 47,* 1597–1611.

Arroyo, J. (1996). Psychotherapist bias with Hispanics: An analog study. *Hispanic Journal of Behavioral Sciences, 18,* 21–28.

Artiola i Fortuny, L., & Mullaney, H. A. (1998). Assessing patients whose language you do not know: Can the absurd be ethical? *Clinical Neuropsychologist, 12,* 113–126.

Blau, T. (1998). *The psychologist as expert witness* (2nd ed.). New York: Wiley.

Cauce, A. M., & Jacobson, L. I. (1980). Implicit and incorrect assumptions concerning the assessment of the Latino in the United States. *American Journal of Community Psychology, 8*(5), 571–586.

Cervantes, R. C., & Acosta, F. X. (1992). Psychological testing for Hispanic Americans. *Applied & Preventive Psychology, 1*(4), 209–219.

Cuellar, I., Arnold, B., & Maldonado, R. (1995). Acculturation rating scale for Mexican Americans-II: A revision of the original ARSMA scale. *Hispanic Journal of Behavioral Sciences, 17*(3), 275–304.

de Bernard, A. E. (1985). Why Jose can't get in the gifted class: The bilingual child and standardized reading tests. *Roeper Review, 8*(2), 80–82.

Echemendía, R. J., Harris, J. G., Congett, S. M., & Diaz, M. L. (1997). Neuropsychological training and practices with Hispanics: A national survey. Annual Meeting of the American Psychological Association (1994, Los Angeles, California, US). *Clinical Neuropsychologist, 11*(3), 229–243.

Felix-Ortiz, M., Newcomb, M. D., & Myers, H. (1994). A multidimensional measure of cultural identity for Latino and Latina adolescents. *Hispanic Journal of Behavioral Sciences, 16*(2), 99–115.

Gutierrez-Clellen, V. F. (1996). Language diversity: Implications for assessment. In K. N. Cole (Ed.), *Assessment of communication and language, Vol. 6. Communication and language intervention series* (pp. 29–56). Baltimore, MD: Paul H. Brookes.

Heaton, R., Chelune, G., Talley, J., Kay, G., & Curtiss, G. (1993). *Wisconsin Card Sorting Test Manual: Revised and expanded*. Odessa, FL: Psychological Assessment Resources.

Herrera, L. P., Pontón, M. O., Corona, M., Gonzalez, J., & Higareda, I. (1998). Acculturation impact on neuropsychological test performance in a Hispanic population. *Archives of Clinical Neuropsychology, 13*(1), 27.

Keefe, S. E. (1992). Ethnic identity: The domain of perceptions of and attachment to ethnic groups and cultures. *Human Organization, 51*(1), 35–44.

LaCalle, J. (1987). Forensic psychological evaluations through an interpreter: Legal and ethical issues. *American Journal of Forensic Psychology, 5*(4), 29–43.

Lezak, M. (1995). *Neuropsychological assessment* (3rd ed.). New York: Oxford University Press.

Llorente, A., Pontón, M. O., Taussig, M., & Satz, P. (1999). Patterns of American immigration and their influence on the Acquisition of Neuropsychological norms for minority groups. *Archives of Clinical Neuropsychology, 14*, 603–614.

Lopez, E. C. (1997). The cognitive assessment of limited English proficiency and bilingual children. In D. P. Flanagan (Ed.), *Contemporary intellectual assessment: Theories, tests, and issues* (pp. 503–516). New York: Guilford Press.

Lopez, S. (1988). The empirical basis of ethnocultural and linguistic bias in mental health evaluations of Hispanics. *American Psychologist, 43*(12), 1095–1097.

Malgady, R. G., Rogler, L. H., & Costantino, G. (1987). Ethnocultural and linguistic bias in mental health evaluation of Hispanics. *American Psychologist, 42*(3), 228–234.

Marin, G., & Marin B. V. (1991). *Research with Hispanic populations*. Newbury Park, CA: Sage.

Mena, F. J., Padilla, A. M., & Maldonado, M. (1987). Acculturative stress and specific coping strategies among inmmigrant and later generation college students. Special Issue: Acculturation research. *Hispanic Journal of Behavioral Sciences, 9*(2), 207–225.

Mestre, J. P., & Royer, J. M. (1991). Cultural and linguistic influences on Latino testing. In G. D. Keller (Ed.), *Assessment and access: Hispanics in higher education. SUNY series, United States Hispanic studies* (pp. 39–66). Albany, NY: State University of New York Press.

Miranda, A. O., & White, P. E. (1993). The relationship between acculturation and level of social interest among Hispanic adults. *Individual Psychology, 49*(1), 76–85.

Mitrushina, M., Boone, K. B., & D'Elia, L. F. (1999). *Handbook of normative data for neuropsychological assessment*. New York: Oxford University Press.

Mungas, D. (1996). The process of development of valid and reliable neuropsychological assessment measures for English- and Spanish-speaking elderly persons. In D. G.-T. E. Gwen Yeo (Ed.), *Ethnicity and the dementias* (pp. 33–46). Washington, DC: Taylor & Francis.

Ochoa, S. H., Powell, M. P., & Robles-Piña, R. (1996). School psychologists' assessment practices with bilingual and limited-English-proficient students. *Journal of Psychoeducational Assessment, 14*(3): 250–275.

Ostrosky-Solis, F., Ardila, A., Rosselli, M., Lopez-Arango, G., & Uriel-Mendoza, V. (1998). Neuropsychological test performance in illiterate subjects. *Archives of Clinical Neuropsychology, 13*(7), 645–660.

Palmer, D. J., Olivarez, A., Willson, V. L., & Fordyce, T. (1989). Ethnicity and language dominance: Influence on the prediction and referred achievement based on intelligence test scores in nonreferred and referred samples. *Learning Disability Quarterly, 12*(4), 261–274.

Pérez-Arce, P., & Puente, A. E. (1996). Neuropsychological assessment of ethnic-minorities: The case of assessing Hispanics living in North America. In R. J. Sbordone (Ed.), *Ecological validity of neuropsychological testing* (pp. 283–300). Delray Beach, FL: GR Press/St Lucie Press.

Pontón, M. O., & Ardila, A. (1999). The future of neuropsychology with Hispanic populations. *Archives of Clinical Neuropsychology, 14*(7), 565–580.

Pontón, M. O., Gonzalez, J. J., Hernandez, I., Herrera, L., & Higareda, I. (2000). Factor Analysis of the Neuropsycholgical Screening Battery for Hispanics (NeSBHIS). *Applied Neuropsychology, 7*(1), 32–39.

Pontón, M. O., Herrera, S., Herrera, L., Gorsuch, R. L., Gonzalez, J. J., Corona, M. E., & the NeSBHIS Research Team. (1998, August). *Continuous Norming for the Neuropsychological Screening Battery for Hispanics–Revised (NeSBHIS–R)*. Paper presented at the 106th annual convention of the American Psychological Association, San Francisco, CA.

Pontón, M. O., Satz, P., Herrera, L., Ortiz, F., Furst, C., & Namerow, N. (1996). Normative data stratified by age and education for the Neuropsychological Screening Battery for Hispanics (NeSBHIS): Initial report. *Journal of the International Neuropsychological Society, 2*(2), 96–104.

Salgado De Snyder, V. N. (1987). The role of ethnic loyalty among Mexican immigrant women. *Hispanic Journal of Behavioral Sciences, 9*(3), 287–289.

Sanchez, M.-E. (1986). Validation of assessment indicators of general patterns of psycholinguistic and cognitive abilities of young Spanish-speaking children. *Dissertation Abstracts International, 47*(6-A), 2059–2060.

Sandoval, J., & Duran, R. P. (1998). Language. In E. Jonathan, H. Sandoval, E. Craig, L. Frisby, et al. (Eds.), *Test interpretation and diversity: Achieving equity in assessment* (pp. 181–211). Washington, DC: American Psychological Association.

Spreen, O., & Strauss, E. (1998). *A compendium of neuropsychological tests* (2nd ed.). New York: Oxford University Press.

Stephan, C. W., & Stephan, W. G. (1986). Habla Ingles? The effects of language translation on simulated juror decisions. *Journal of Applied Social Psychology, 16*(7), 577–589.

Taussig, M., & Ponton, M. O. (1996). Issues in neuropsychological assessment of Hispanic older adults: Cultural and linguistic factors. In G. Yeo & D. Gallagher-Thompson (Eds.), *Ethnicity and the dementias* (pp. 47–58). San Francisco: Taylor & Francis.

Terman, L. M. (1916). *The measurement of intelligence.* San Francisco: Houghton Mifflin.

Willig, A. C. (1988). A case of blaming the victim: The Dunn monograph on bilingual Hispanic children on the U.S. mainland. Special Issue: Achievement testing: Science vs. ideology. *Hispanic Journal of Behavioral Sciences, 10*(3), 219–236.

Woodcock, R. W., & Muñoz-Sandoval, A.F. (1995). *Woodcock-Language Proficiency Battery-Revised, Spanish Form, Supplemental Manual.* Chicago, IL: Riverside Publishing.

Second Language Acquisition

E. C. CASCALLAR
City University of New York

JANE ARNOLD
University of Seville

In order to unravel the intricacies of language and communication, it is necessary to gain an understanding of higher mental abilities and the underlying cognitive processes in human beings. It is assumed that behind all these specific instances of human cognitive activity lies a common cognitive system responsible for individuals' complex patterns of thought, learning, and intelligence. Furthermore, the system capable of the high-level processing found in the human species, is assumed to be a unitary system underlying all cognitive processes (Anderson, 1983).

Central to these issues is the phenomenon of language acquisition as a generalized human experience. Except for a few pathological conditions, the universality of this experience, seems to indicate a shared capacity to acquire language, with biology setting the necessary minimal conditions. In most societies, bilingualism and multilingualism are common, and the various social groups represented by each language interact in various forms. Given the variety of conditions for these multilingual environments, the conditions for language acquisition vary enormously, and combine in complex ways. These conditions could be either as concurrent or sequential acquisition, early in life or at a later stage, in formal education settings or as part of early or later socialization, voluntarily acquired or learned under social pressure, as is many times the case in second language (SL) groups and in numerous other learning situations.

For the purpose of this discussion, some points should be established. First, *language learning* and *language acquisition* are used here interchangeably. Some authors, particularly Krashen (1981) consider this distinction crucial, but given the difficulty of establishing the operational distinction in most instances (McLaughlin, 1984), and the somewhat hazy distinction in cognitive terms, learning and acquisition in this chapter are considered equivalent. Second, the expression *second language acquisition* (SLA) refers to the second language acquired in chronological order, when the first language is already established; however, even this distinction is sometimes difficult to determine under certain acquisition conditions. In addition, second language learners are at various stages of language acquisition and integration along a continuum of bilingualism. Therefore, these learners are often referred to as *bilinguals,* in the sense of possessing various degrees of proficiency in each of the languages (L1 and L2). Furthermore, following several recent views (Ellis, 1994; Kramsch, 1990), the field of second language acquisition is considered to subsume the study of the acquisition of all nonprimary languages. As Freed (1991) suggested, second language acquisition comprises the study of all variables related to the learner and to the learning environment, as well as to all related factors that could affect the process of second language learning. These variables include the learner's cognitive readiness and skills, and other background factors such as first language, learner's personality, learning styles, context for learning, and function of the language.

This chapter examines some of the processing characteristics of second language learners, the cognitive variables that participate in the acquisition of a second language, and other strategic, motivational, and affective variables that explain differences in second language learning.

SYNTACTIC AND SEMANTIC PROCESSING IN SECOND LANGUAGE LEARNERS

In order to reach a better understanding of the cognitive processes involved in second language acquisition and in language comprehension, it is important to determine how these processes relate to the level of proficiency attained in L1 and in L2 by second language learners. It is essential to understand issues of transfer from L1 to L2, and vice versa, both at syntactic and at semantic levels. Furthermore, the development of different levels of language proficiency in the second language learner needs to be explored from a psycholinguistic perspective.

It is important to understand what "being bilingual" is, in terms of the processing of semantic and syntactic information at the level of the individual learner, and to comprehend the process of transfer between languages, including the observation of how the amount and type of transfer may change for different kinds of information (i.e., syntactic and semantic). Various subject characteristics should be examined, among them the degree of bilingualism as determined by the learner's proficiency in each language. According to Cummins' (1979) threshold hypothesis, it is expected that a certain level of bilingualism must be present before certain positive transfer effects can be observed. Information about differential transfer of skills is important for the understanding of the processes involved, and it could also have significant implications for language learning and for language curriculum design. McLaughlin (1990) found evidence to support the interdependence hypothesis, that is, that as expertise develops in one language, it tends to develop also in a second language, supporting the concept of a general language processing capacity that influences bilingual proficiency.

The differential effects of facilitation and interference found at the syntactic and semantic linguistic levels of analysis must be considered. Extensive reviews of this area of research can be found in McLaughlin (1978) and Grosjean (1982). From previous research, it is expected that degree of interference between languages depends on the linguistic level used (i.e., syntactic, phonologic, semantic). It is precisely the differential pattern of interference, and the processing phenomena associated with it, that provide an insight at the level of the conceptual system of the second language learner, and on the representation of both languages in the cognitive system. Previous research reviewed elsewhere (Grosjean, 1982; Paivio & Desrochers, 1980) has examined some of these aspects. The human information-processing approach provides a useful perspective, with the investigation of the effects of context, and of lexical, phonological, and orthographic characteristics of words included in the analysis (McLaughlin, 1995).

The dichotomy between the studies that favor the presence of either one or two lexicons in bilingual subjects is probably due to a confounding with the tasks used to investigate the issue (Grosjean, 1982; Kolers & Gonzalez, 1980). Paradis (1981) proposed a model with two lexicons for bilinguals, where both lexicons are differentially connected to a memory store with language-free mental representations. It is assumed that bilinguals access their two language lexicons during word recognition as a function of the speech mode they are in (Soares & Grosjean, 1984). The fact that this requires a deactivation mechanism led to studies investigating a monitoring system or a language switch (Paradis, 1981). On the other hand, bilinguals are rarely found to deactivate the other language completely when in a "monolingual" speech mode. Various researchers have found evidence for the presence of only partial deactivation: cross-language Stroop tests (Preston & Lambert, 1969), lexical decision tasks (Altenberg & Cairns, 1983), and comprehension tasks in a phoneme monitoring paradigm (Blair & Harris, 1981). Research by Soares and Grosjean (1984) suggests that bilinguals always search both lexicons when confronted with a letter-string that does not correspond to a lexical item (nonword), even when in a "monolingual mode," and that bilinguals always search the base language lexicon first.

Studies that examine reading performance, and the underlying processes in memory among bilinguals, have found that reading may be slower in the second language for reasons that are not necessarily related to knowledge of vocabulary and syntax (Favreau & Segalowitz, 1983). There is evidence that this effect may be due to reduced sensitivity to orthographic, syntactic, and semantic redundancies of the language (Hatch, Polin, & Part, 1974). Additional effects may be due to differences in the automatic and controlled processes used by bilinguals depending on their reading performance and skills (Favreau & Segalowitz, 1983). The effect of context is a very relevant issue in the understanding of language processing in general and of bilingual subjects in particular.

The distinction between automatic and controlled processes is an important one in the study of language, and has direct implications for certain cognitive processes involved in bilingual language processing. Several researchers have argued that cognitive processes may differ in the amount of attention and effort they require (Posner & Snyder, 1975a; Shiffrin & Schneider, 1977). Because of extensive practice and/or exposure, some operations may require only minimal effort and are very fast, whereas others require considerable attention and are relatively slower. The former have been characterized as automatic, and the latter as conscious (Posner & Snyder, 1975b) or effortful (Hasher & Zacks, 1979) processes. This distinction between processes that are automatic and those that are strategic, has important implications for reading in a second language. A complex procedure such as reading involves a number of frequently practiced operations, likely to be fairly automatic (LaBerge, 1975); but many other operations are likely to be under strategic control. For bilinguals, both sets of operations may be different between the first and the second languages, particularly in processes such as word recognition.

Among more recent psycholinguistic models of language acquisition is MacWhinney's (1992) "competition model," which is a powerful and flexible approach to language learning that deals with representational, processing, and learning principles that describe aspects of the process. In addition, McLeod and McLaughlin (1986) and McLaughlin (1990) suggested that improved reading performance in second language learners may originate from a restructuring of language components rather than from automaticity of processing. Another approach to the question of language processing and language learning, which comes from the field of cognitive psychology, is the family of parallel-distributed processing models (Rumelhart, McClelland, & the PDP Research Group, 1986). These types of network models describe knowledge of a language as stored in, and defined by, connections among simple processing units organized into networks. Even if these networks could be described by some set of rules, it is the characteristics of the networks that define the phenomena of language and of language acquisition in particular. The latter is conceptualized as the process of gradual adjusting of connections between the processing units (Rumelhart et al., 1986). The extension of these and other conceptualizations to the process of second language acquisition, as special cases, will likely prove to be useful extensions that will connect the field to current cognitive theories.

SECOND LANGUAGE LEARNING APTITUDE

Any explanation proposed for language learning in general and SLA in particular, has to be able to account for resource and processing aspects of language activity and learning. In order to study the phenomenon of language acquisition, it is essential to reach an understanding of language aptitude, as a measure of *learning potential*. Thorndike (1924) defined intelligence as the "ability to learn," and the measurement of learning potential is currently perceived as a central issue in psychology and education. In addition, with the trend to integrate the assessment of learning potential with the cognitive approach, new perspectives and methods have emerged (Hamers, Sijtsma, & Ruijssenaars, 1993) to investigate language aptitude. Most of the following approaches deal with the phenomenon of second language acquisition in general, some with more emphasis in contexts of formal instruction for the learning process. It is quite evident, however, that in contrasting contextual elements for the acquisition process, it is only a question of degrees that differentiates the participation of the various cognitive variables under different conditions. In focusing first on this *capacity-to-learn* aspect of language acquisition, it is necessary to determine more precisely its relations with other cognitive, motivational, and personality factors. Recently, new interest has emerged in the area of language aptitude assessment, and in cognitive processes that may be involved (Cascallar, 1993, 1995). The role of learning capacity and cognitive participation in measurements of intelligence and performance in various areas, has been an ongoing theme in the learning literature. A recent review of the field of language aptitude (Cascallar, in press) outlines the major contributions to the area, as well as promising new lines of research.

Oller (1981) proposed a single language factor that could account for the variance in a wide range of language measures. In a project that investigated the relation between second language learning aptitude and intelligence, Wesche, Edwards, and Wells (1982) identified three second-order factors: first language verbal knowledge, abstract reasoning ability, and ability to learn new language elements and associations. In addition, a unitary third-order factor was identified, which was interpreted as encompassing general ability or general intelligence. Snow (1989) analyzed a series of cognitive-conative-learning interaction effects, and proposed a way to conceptualize their relations. In a different tradition, Willerman (1979) examined individual differences in educational achievement, and in aptitude and achievement testing, and the roles played by heritability, motivation, educational interventions, and other variables.

Carroll (1962, 1981), from a factor analytic approach, proposed a model that accounts for the individual differences in second language learning. His model identified four components of language aptitude: phonemic coding ability, grammatical sensitivity, inductive language-learning ability, and rote learning activity for language materials. Carroll (1993) also established interesting connections existing between some cognitive processes and the language abilities addressed in his work. Although recognizing the complexity of these relations, he suggested that because various factors of language ability are correlated, these relations could be controlled by complex genetic and environmental interactions, with some cognitive processes underlying common effects found among those factors. Guthke, Heinrich, and Caruso (1986) extended the application of Carroll's factors, by concentrating on inductive learning ability, for which, according to Carroll, no suitable tests had yet been developed. They developed a test using items that tapped recognition of structures, recognition of relations, and ability to map the recognized relations onto another. Positive results suggested that this measure, together with a phonetic test, could be a valuable predictor of second language ability.

Kyllonen and Woltz (1989), and Kyllonen (1993), worked on determinants of success in the acquisition of cognitive skills. They proposed a framework that presents learning success as a function of success in prior learning and of proficiency in four categories of general cognitive factors: (a) general and domain specific knowledge, (b) general and domain specific skills, (c) processing capacity (mainly working memory capacity), and (d) processing speed (retrieval speed, decision speed, etc.). These factors, based on the cognitive architecture suggested by Anderson (1983) in his ACT* theory, determine performance in the three proposed learning phases: knowledge acquisition, skill acquisition, and skill refinement. Some research in the area of language learning and acquisition followed this approach, relating concepts from the psycholinguistic and cognitive research areas to the problem of assessment of language aptitude and abilities, and to interactions with language proficiency. For example, G. Mulder, Wijers, Smid, Brookhuis, and L. Mulder (1989) hypothesized that differences in cognitive abilities arise from three different sources: differences in elementary cognitive processes, differences in strategic aspects of thought, and knowledge aspects of thought. G. Mulder et al. also called for approaches emphasizing fast process research and electrophysiological measures.

Guttmann (1986) studied fluctuations of learning capability, and found cortical potential shifts correlated with increased learning performance. Using certain linguistic tasks, he suggested the possibility of inducing a state of learning readiness and offered potential applications. Gathercole and Baddeley (1993) linked vocabulary acquisition, phonological working memory, the role of the central executive system in speech production, and language comprehension. O'Mara, Lett, and Alexander (1990) reviewed applications of the field in areas of the prediction of success in second language learning when considering intensive language programs for adult learners. Similarly, Gardner (1991) examined the role of attitudes, motivation, and personality, and Oxford (1990) reviewed the role of learning styles and learning strategies.

Several studies reviewed by Wells (1985) and Skehan (1989) examined the interrelations between first language development, second language aptitude, and achievement in a second language. Results suggested (Skehan, 1989) that in addition to the language ability factor, social class, parent level of education, and vocabulary, adequately predict aptitude levels. It could be hypothesized that some of the research currently in progress could help to tie together basic cognitive processes (which might also have a hereditary component) to issues like vocabulary and level of education. Skehan (1989) pointed out the finding that aptitude seems more strongly related to first language development than to achievement in the second language, because of the different learning situations that produce the latter. He noted that the underlying language learning capacities of the student may not "be exploited in language teaching classrooms" (p. 32), and explained that this effect may be due to the decontextualized nature of second language learning in some situations. Skehan went on to analyze and critique the current state of research, and suggested future investigations to determine the nature of the abilities involved in language aptitude. He also covered many relevant areas of language achievement, including motivation, learning strategies, and important aptitude-treatment interactions. Both Ellis (1994) and Skehan (1989) suggested that language aptitude is still the best single predictor of achievement in a second language.

Having examined some general cognitive and linguistic characteristics that are involved in human language processing, and in second language learning, it is now possible to address some specific sociocultural, affective, motivational, and personality variables that also participate in second language learning. These variables can also be said to be particularly sensitive to group differences reflecting varied social and cultural interactions, values, and power relations. In this context, some specific issues related to Hispanic second language learners in the United States are addressed. Of course, these considerations, necessarily generic, will only reflect a somewhat stereotypical description of the Hispanic population, which has a great and varied wealth of traditions and cultural backgrounds. Therefore, it will focus on the Hispanic experience as seen in some of the more marginal groups, not fully integrated into mainstream society due to a variety of reasons.

Sociocultural Variables

During the 1970s and 1980s, much of the research in second language acquisition was concerned with the phenomenon of variability in language learning. This work was channeled in two directions: studies to discover, on the one hand, why successful language learners have learned and, on the other, why unsuccessful language learners have not learned. In a pedagogical context, the first trend is particularly important, because it provides examples of behavior learners can model; one of the offshoots has been the growth of interest in language learning strategies. However, the present discussion concentrates mainly on some of the social and psychological factors that raise barriers to the acquisition of a second language, focusing especially on Hispanic learners of English in the United States.

Hispanics who are either immigrants from a Spanish-speaking country or members of a primarily Spanish-speaking community within the United States are learners of a second language (as opposed to a foreign language), because they live in a country other than their own, one where the target language (TL) is spoken, and where they may or may not be involved in formal learning but will have the possibility of accessing extensive daily contact with the TL through contact with native speakers, television, radio, newspapers, and so on. This situation might seem ideal; the goal of many foreign language learners is precisely to have the opportunity to live in a country where the language they are learning is spoken. However, not all Hispanics in the United States, especially those who have entered in contact with English as late adolescents or adults, learn the language well.

Sociocultural variables provide some insight into the reasons why people who are adequately exposed might not acquire English. It could be said that culture is so important, that if people did not have a culture, they would have to invent one. People's identity—

values, beliefs, biases, perceptions, attitudes—in large part depends on their culture and on the experiences they have within it. Hispanic immigrants in the United States are learning not just the English language, they are also acquiring a new culture. The intimate relation between the two is undeniable and can lead to a vicious circle situation: To be integrated into a culture, people must speak its language; but to learn to speak the language, to some degree they need to be integrated into the culture in order to have the opportunity to participate in the necessary interaction with speakers of the language. Reactions to learning English will of course vary greatly, but it cannot be assumed that SLA is a painless process or is limited to mastering lexical and syntactic information and not influenced by cultural factors.

Hofstede (1991) referred to culture as the "software of the mind," a sort of mental programming of the members of a social group that conditions their behavior, including many "ordinary and menial things in life: greeting, eating, showing or not showing emotions, keeping a certain physical distance from others, making love or maintaining body hygiene" (p. 5).

For successful language acquisition to occur, a learner "must be both able and willing to adopt various aspects of behavior, including verbal behaviour, which characterizes members of the other linguistic-cultural group" (Lambert, 1967, p. 102). The importance of sociocultural factors for language learning is seen in the acculturation model (Schumann, 1978, 1986) which is very relevant for the Hispanic immigrant communities. Schumann (1986) defined acculturation as the "social and psychological integration of the learner with the target language (TL) group" (p. 379). He proposed that this combination of social and affective factors is a significant causal variable in SLA, because learners will learn the language to the degree that they acculturate. The acculturation framework involves the notion of distance from the TL group. The greater the distance, socially or psychologically, the more persistent will be the nonstandard fossilized or "pidginized" forms in the learners' speech. The *actual* social distance may not be as important as what Acton (1979) termed *perceived* social distance, which measures what learners conceive of as the social distance, because people's perception is what defines their reality.

Social distance, in the case at hand, is caused by a number of societal factors that inhibit the approximation of the English- and Spanish-speaking populations. One of the most important factors is dominance. A dominant group does not usually acquire the language of a culturally inferior group. Also a group such as the Hispanic population in the United States would not be in a good position for acquiring the language, being in a situation of "political, cultural, technological and economic" subordination in relation to the TL group (Schumann, 1986, p. 381). These factors of subordination will tend to keep learners at a distance from their possible linguistic models, limiting the interaction necessary for successful SLA. They may also create demotivation if the learners perceive themselves as not having access to upward social mobility.

Similarly, enclosure and cohesiveness of the SL group, the degree to which they have and keep to their own speech community's activities for schooling, work, and socializing, will limit the development of linguistic proficiency. Thus, groups of Hispanics in many areas of the United States can easily turn to other Spanish-speakers in their communities for solutions to everyday problems without having to recur to the use of English. The fact that the Hispanic population is numerically quite important in several sectors of the United States may inhibit the need for linguistic proficiency in English of Spanish-speakers in these areas. Discussion of these and other factors involved in establishing social distance can be found in Schumann (1986).

Berry (1980) identified acculturation with adaptation, and described the language shift that takes place in the nondominant group, as well as the conditions under which the traditional language is maintained or reinstated. He also referred to the alternative options of bilingualism or linguistic merging. Other influences mentioned in his work are cognitive style effects, personality factors, identity issues, and attitudes toward acculturation modes. Olmedo (1980) and Olmedo and Padilla (1978) presented useful quantitative models of acculturation. Olmedo recommended multivariate approaches to address complex issues such as cognition and language in the context of acculturation effects. Methodologies such as covariance structures and structural equation modeling, he suggested, could be of great utility in the study of acculturation. Padilla's (1980) model of acculturation clearly identified cultural awareness and ethnic loyalty as the two essential elements. Furthermore, he postulated that a critical dimension to assess the level of acculturative change is precisely "language familiarity and usage."

Integration Patterns

The aforementioned factors condition the integration patterns of Hispanics. The three main patterns are *assimilation,* where the SL group abandons its own lifestyles and values in order to take on those of the TL group; *adaptation,* where the SL group keeps its own cultural patterns to some extent in order to use them in intra-group experiences; and *preservation,* where the SL group rejects the TL group's lifestyle and values and preserves its own as much as possible (Schumann, 1986, p. 381). There are obvious advantages to assimilation for SL development, although too extreme an acceptance of this pattern can be counterproductive.

For all-around well-being, adaptation may be the healthiest option. However, for reasons already discussed, large sectors of the Hispanic population can best be characterized by the pattern of preservation, which is that of greatest social distance from the TL group and the least favorable for SLA. Nevertheless, social distance depends to some degree on class origin. Schumann (1976) referred to a study of untutored acquisition of English by six native speakers of Spanish, and the social distance was shown to be affected substantially by social class. With Hispanic worker immigrants, the profile would be subordination, high enclosure and cohesiveness, and an integration pattern somewhere between preservation and assimilation. As Schumann (1976) recognized, "American society in general expects them to assimilate as it does all immigrants, but it does not necessarily make the assimilation easy" (p. 400).

Upper-middle-class Hispanic professional immigrants would be nondominant rather than subordinate in relation to the English-speaking mainstream, and they are highly acculturative with much less tendency to enclosure and cohesiveness. With their reduced social distance from the TL group, greater linguistic proficiency is to be expected. However, in both cases the Hispanics, as opposed to non-Western immigrants, exhibit relative congruence, which referes to the degree to which the two cultures are similar. This factor can eventually make the move from preservation to assimilation easier, as can the matter of attitudes. If both groups have a positive attitude toward each other, then there will be greater opportunity for contact and, therefore, language acquisition. Gardner (1985) researched the question of attitudes and motivation among language learners for several decades in the context of the study of French in Canada, affirming that attitudes toward the speakers of the TL and, especially, to learning the language itself, seem to "account for a significant and meaningful proportion of the variance in L2 achievement" (Gardner, 1985, p. 50), because they lead to motivation, which directly influences learning.

Social Identity

In a study of SLA among immigrant women in Canada, Peirce (1995) proposed that the distinction often found in SLA studies between the individual and the social is actually artificial. She stated that a comprehensive theory of social identity is needed in order to integrate the language learner and the context, because language is the means for the development of social organization and also for the construction of individuals' sense of self. She was concerned with the manner in which SL learners are limited in their opportunities to practice the TL with native speakers because of unequal power situations, which in a sense rob them of their voices. However, as change is part of her framework, Peirce stressed the importance of providing the second language learner with means for challenging a situation of social marginalization and claiming the right to speak. The way to do this is not simple or straightforward. If the learner has access to programs of formal instruction, these should be designed to teach much more than the language or to teach the language through materials that also provide sociocultural information that will empower the learner in contacts with English-speakers. Levine, Baxter, and McNulty (1987) presented some very helpful activities for integrating language learning and culture learning.

Affective Variables

Many aspects of second language acquisition are intimately related to emotions. Self-esteem, hopes for success, ego permeability, anxiety, and other affect-related factors can have a decisive effect on language learning. In much of the research on SLA, the cognitive side of the learning process has been stressed, yet even more than in many other areas of learning, the acquisition of a second language, especially among postpuberty individuals, is significantly influenced by affect.

In dealing with the social factors of language learning, there is concern with Hispanics as a group relating to English-speakers in the United States. However, there is also a set of psychological factors of learners as individuals that influences the acculturation process and language learning, and psychological distance from the TL group can also keep the learner from receiving the necessary interaction for successful learning to occur.

In a pioneer study, Stengal (1939) pointed out that difficulties in language learning may be the result of language shock. Adult learners fear that their words in the TL do not reflect their ideas adequately. Moreover, the use of a language they do not fully control robs them of a source of narcissistic gratification they might receive when using their own language. Stengal also noted that language shock may involve adult learners' fear of appearing comic, as if they were dressing up in fancy clothes. However, just as a child enjoys dressing up, the SL is a source of play and pleasure for the young learner; this carefree state of mind is an asset in language learning. "The adult will learn the new language more easily, the more of these infantile characteristics he has preserved" (Stengal, 1939, p. 478).

Another variable leading to blockage in language learning is *culture shock,* which can be defined as anxiety resulting from the disorientation encountered on entering a new culture. In their classic study of this condition, Larsen and Smalley (1972) pointed out how great amounts of energy are used up in dealing with culture shock: "New problems mean new demands on one's supply of energy. New climate, the new foods, the new people all mean that the alien must muster up every bit of available energy and put it to use in new ways" (Larsen & Smalley, 1972, p. 41). In the measure that Hispanics in the United States are located in an area where they can be part of a Spanish-speaking enclave, many of the effects of culture shock may be mitigated. However, some of the symptoms—"from mild irritability to deep psychological panic and crisis" (Brown, 1993, p. 170)—are generally present at least for a certain time. Because the essential characteristics of good mental health are often undermined by the confrontation with a new culture, what might appear to be symptoms of mental health disorders may actually have its origins in culture shock. Indeed, Clarke (1976) compared SLA with schizophrenia. The learner is in a double-bind situation. Individuals do not learn the language if they do not have contact with speakers of the language; yet, if they try to establish this contact without knowing the language, then this can lead to not being understood, to painful embarrassment, or even to rejection by the TL speakers. In the second language learners' mind, they could seem to be in a no-win situation. In this state of things, the individual "in attempting to find a cause for his disorientation, may reject himself, his own culture, the organization for which he is working and the people of the host country" (Schumann, 1986, p. 383)—a highly unfavorable situation for language learning.

It is important to keep in mind that failure to learn a second language, especially in an untutored setting, quite probably is only partially dependent on aptitude or intelligence, in the sense already described. It may not even have to do with the individual's ability to cope with stressful situations in general. However, being surrounded by a culture that forces individuals to define reality in unfamiliar terms can be extremely disconcerting and conducive to an inability to acquire the language of the new culture or, indeed, to function normally in a number of situations. Clarke (1976) presented a theoretical framework in which he contended that the most important difficulties facing foreigners in the United States as they attempt to learn English have to do with what he termed a "clash of consciousness," which is closely related to culture shock and has to do with the "degree of difference in modernization between their society and the U.S." (Clarke, 1976, p. 383). This point of view stresses the fact that people's consciousness is determined by the attitudes, experiences, and opinions that constitute reality for them.

The more extreme culture shock may not last long if the individual develops a repertoire of ways of coping with the new environment, but more subtle problems may persist, producing what Larsen and Smalley (1972) called *culture stress*. Culture stress has to do with questions of identity, as individuals have no fixed reference group to relate to, neither the native one left behind nor the local one to which they do not yet belong. In the case of Hispanic immigrants, however, many of the native points of reference have been transferred to the linguistic and cultural ghettos in the United States, and so the lack of integration with the local English-speaking reference group may have less impact.

Culture shock and stress, however, can in many cases induce a sense of rejection in language learners, above all, rejection of the TL speakers who are perceived as the cause of their disorientation. At some point, they might also reject themselves, feeling incapable of adapting to the country and learning the language. Furthermore, they may reject their own culture, a situation that might be very damaging if they do not accept the new culture in its place. This might lead to *anomie*, a sort of no man's—or no woman's—land without strong, supportive ties to the native culture or to the SL culture. Support systems in general are extremely important in the intellectually and, above all, emotionally challenging situation of acquiring a second language and a second culture. For a useful review of stress and coping mechanisms in Hispanic populations, see Cervantes and Castro (1985). This source provides useful models for the full understanding of the stress-mediation-coping process, and the authors emphasize the role of cultural factors, among which language and second language acquisition should definitely be included.

Brown (1993) considered it possible to divide acculturation into four stages. The first is a state of excitement about the new culture. The second stage would be culture shock, which appears as cultural differences intrude into images of self and security. The third stage, culture stress, is a tentative move toward recovery. Some problems persist but slow progress is made, as the individual begins to accept more aspects of the new culture. Stage four represents assimilation or adaptation to the new culture and acceptance of the self within it. The third stage is a key moment for language acquisition, in that the discomfort of the situation has diminished somewhat but there is still enough tension produced by the need to resolve many things to provide the language learner with the will to continue.

Motivation

All theorists of SLA indicate the crucial importance of a further affective variable: *motivation*, which is a cluster of factors that provide direction and energy to behavior (Hilgard, 1963). Motivation involves the learner's reasons for attempting to acquire the second language, but precisely what creates motivation is the crux of the matter. In the early work of Gardner and Lambert (1972), motivation was seen to be divided into two very general orientations: integrative and instrumental. The former refers to a desire to learn the language in order to relate to and even become part of the TL culture and the latter has to do with practical reasons for language learning, such as getting a promotion. One type of motivation is not necessarily more effective than the other; what is important is the degree of energizing and the firmness of the direction it provides. And that will depend on many other variables within the learner.

This basic early model for language learning motivation has been elaborated further by Gardner (1985) and by other SLA researchers. Another fruitful distinction is extrinsic and intrinsic motivation. Extrinsic motivation comes from the desire to get a reward or avoid punishment; the focus is on something external to the learning activity itself. With intrinsic motivation, the learning experience is its own reward. Deci and Ryan (1985) considered that "intrinsic motivation is in evidence whenever students' natural curiosity and interest energize their learning" (p. 245). This distinction is perhaps seen more clearly in an instructional learning setting and is less easily amenable to manipulation in natural language acquisition. However, should the individual be involved in classroom learning, it is recommended that intrinsic motivation be encouraged by insuring that the course is challenging yet accessible, varied, stimulating, and geared to the learner interests. Deci (1992, p. 60) stated that studies of sociocontextual influences confirm that the optimal situation for the development of intrinsic motivation is the "convergence of autonomy support, competence-promoting feedback and interpersonal involvement." Those dealing with Hispanic learners should attempt to facilitate their intrinsic motivation for learning English by providing an environment and activities designed to encourage this convergence.

Dornyei (1994) pointed out that in addition to the affective aspects of motivation, educational psychology has put forth cognitive theories of motivation in which it is seen to be a function of a person's thought processes. He described three major cognitive conceptual systems referred to by Weiner (1992), all of which are relevant to Hispanic language learners in the United States: attribution theory, learned helplessness, and self-efficacy.

In their discussion of extending the motivational framework for SLA, Oxford and Shearin (1994) considered other contributions from general psychology, such as the concept of need hierarchies. Whereas FL (foreign language) learners might not register needs on the lowest levels, the SL learners' needs "would be negotiated in the target language from the very lowest levels of the hierarchy; even physiological, physical safety, and physical security needs might not be assured without the use of the target language" (Oxford & Shearin 1994, p. 17).

Somatic Markers and Neurobiological Participation

Damasio's (1994) concept of somatic markers could provide one explanation for success or failure in language learning: "Somatic markers are a special instance of feelings generated from secondary emotions. Those emotions and feelings have been connected, by learning, to predicted future outcomes of certain scenarios. When a negative somatic marker is juxtaposed to a particular future outcome, the combination functions as an alarm bell. When a positive somatic marker is juxtaposed instead, it becomes a beacon of incentive" (Damasio, 1994, p. 174). Thus, the language learning situation may be paired with a positive somatic response in learners whose previous experiences have been pleasant. In this case, they will seek more potential pleasure through language learning.

Schumann and his associates (Jacobs & Schumann, 1992; Pulvermüller & Schumann, 1994; Schumann, 1994) presented neurobiological explanations for second language acquisition and have done much to further the development of a neurobiological framework for understanding language acquisition. Schumann (1994) argued for the importance of affect in SLA, citing current research on the neurobiological level, which shows that in the brain affect and cognition are distinguishable but inseparable. The limbic system, for example, is actively involved in the affective side of learning. The amygdala in the temporal lobe assesses the emotional significance and motivational relevance of stimuli; this appraisal then influences attention and memory (Mishkin & Appenzeller, 1987). Schumann (1997) discussed extensively the neurobiological level of language learning.

On the neurobiological and psychological levels, there is an explanation for the construct used in SLA studies of the affective filter (Krashen, 1981), which, at least on a metaphorical level gives one reason for the variability in language learning. The filter operates in the following way: If motivation is lacking, anxiety is high, and self-esteem is low, then the filter will be up and input will not become intake (i.e., input will not be processed so as to produce learning). Thus, there are convincing reasons for all those dealing with SL learners—be they teachers, social workers, medical practitioners, or others—to remain sensitive to the influence of affect on language learning.

Clearly, many of the obstacles for successful language acquisition have to do with affective factors of one type or another. Their elimination is not easy, but there are some possible partial solutions. Facilitators dealing with Hispanics who have not successfully acquired English might approach problems caused by language and culture shock and stress by first of all discussing the problems, in groups, if possible. Learners' awareness that they are not alone in their feelings of isolation and incapacity can itself be helpful. Some of the stress can be relieved if learners realize they are going through a normal process, difficult though it may be. It is useful to discuss cultural differences and explain aspects of the target culture that tend to be problematic for Hispanics, although Scarcella and Oxford (1992) also stressed the importance of finding similarities "so that students feel more at home and less in a state of culture shock" (p. 188).

Donahue and Parsons (1982) proposed the use of role play to overcome "cultural fatigue," which Szanston (1966, p. 48) defined as "the physical and emotional exhaustion that almost invariably results from the infinite series of minute adjustments" that are necessary in order to adopt to living in a different cultural environment. Through role play, the facilitator can give learners an opportunity to express their feelings of negativity, to find ways to deal with current problems, and to work out anticipated future situations. For example, if a learner has had an unsuccessful conversation leading to feelings of humiliation, then the conversation could be reconstructed in a way that is nonthreatening and more conducive to protecting self-esteem and encouraging language learning.

Writing can also be a very useful tool. Depending on the learners' degree of preparation for writing, written tasks can be given to help them work out their negative feelings. Journal writing as a means of developing reflection can provide an outlet for problems. Other possibilities might be relaxation and visualization exercises and different types of physical activity such as cross-lateral movement. According to Hannaford (1995), the latter can reduce anxiety and integrate brain functions to maximize learning.

Possibly the most useful solution is the presence of a surrogate family. Larsen and Smalley (1972) stressed the importance for the learner of "a small community of sympathetic people who will help him in the difficult period when he is a linguistic and cultural child-adult" (p. 46). This community—teachers, employers, fellow workers, friends— can provide learners with a sense of identity and help them cope with their environment, as well as provide them with an important source of linguistic input.

CONCLUSIONS

This chapter has presented a series of comments about second language acquisition aimed at introducing this very broad and diversified area to those involved with neuropsychological issues and the Hispanic community. A multidisciplinary approach is called for to increase neuropsychologists' understanding of such a complex process.

It would be helpful for the neuropsychologist dealing with the Hispanic population to take into account the factors mentioned in order to have a clearer idea of how aspects related to the acquisition process may be influencing their Hispanic patients, especially those who are still struggling with the onerous task of learning to function in a different culture, for which task the understanding and production of a new language is essential.

Among those factors that have been considered are the processing at different linguistic levels (syntactic, semantic, phonological) and the differential effects of facilitation and interference, the influence of language aptitude on variance in acquisition, and the sociocultural variables that influence the acquisition process, conditioning the integration patterns of the learners and their social identity. Affective factors are also of undeniable importance for acquisition, because they can either restrict or favor the cognitive processes in operation. Current research indicates there seems to be clear neurobiological justification for incorporating aspects of the affective domain into language learning models.

It is to be hoped that further investigation in neurobiology and neuropsychology many contribute to the extensive work being done in other disciplines to provide ever more accurate conceptions of the language acquisition process.

REFERENCES

Acton, W. (1979). *Second language learning and perception of difference in attitude.* Unpublished doctoral dissertation, University of Michigan, Ann Arbor.

Altenberg, E., & Cairns, H. (1983). The effects of phonotactic constraints on lexical processing in bilingual and monolingual subjects. *Journal of Verbal Learning and Verbal Behavior, 22,* 174–188.

Anderson, J. R. (1983). *The architecture of cognition.* Cambridge, MA: Harvard University Press.

Berry, J. W. (1980). Acculturation as varieties of adaptation. In A. M. Padilla (Ed.), *Acculturation: Theory, models and some new findings* (pp. 9–25). Boulder, CO: Westview.

Blair, D., & Harris, R. (1981). A test of interlingual interaction in comprehension by bilinguals. *Journal of Psycholinguistic Research, 10,* 457–467.

Brown, H. D. (1993). *Principles of language learning and teaching.* Englewood Cliffs, NJ: Prentice-Hall Regents.

Carroll, J. B. (1962). The prediction of success in intensive foreign language training. In R. Glaser (Ed.), *Training research and education* (pp. 87–136). Pittsburgh, PA: University of Pittsburgh Press.

Carroll, J. B. (1981). Twenty-five years of research on foreign language aptitude. In K. C. Diller (Ed.), *Individual differences and universals in language learning aptitude.* Rowley, MA: Newbury House.

Carroll, J. B. (1993). *Human cognitive abilities.* Cambridge, England: Cambridge University Press.

Cascallar, E. C. (1993, August). *A new cognitive approach for the assessment of language aptitude.* Paper presented at the 15th Language Testing Research Colloquium, Arnhem, The Netherlands.

Cascallar, E. C. (1995). Introduction. *Language Testing, 12,* 259–63.

Cascallar, E. C. (In press). The assessment of second language learning aptitude. In *Encyclopedia of language and education* (Vol. 7). Dordrecht, The Netherlands: Kluwer Academic.

Cervantes, R. C., & Castro, F. G. (1985). Stress, coping, and Mexican American mental health: A systematic review. *Hispanic Journal of Behavioral Sciences, 7,* 1–73.

Clarke, M. (1976). Second language acquisition as a clash of consciousness. *Language Learning, 26,* 377–390.

Cummins, J. (1979). Linguistic interdependence and the educational development of bilingual children. *Bilingual Education Paper Series, 3,* (2). Los Angeles: National Dissemination Center, California State University—Los Angeles.

Damasio, A. R. (1994). *Descartes' error: Emotion, reason and the human brain.* New York: Avon.

Deci, E. L. (1992). The relation of interest to the motivation of behavior: A self-determination theory perspective. In K. Renninger, S. Hidi, & A. Krapp (Eds.), *The role of interest in learning and development.* Hillsdale, NJ: Lawrence Erlbaum Associates.

Deci, E. L., & Ryan, R. M. (1985). *Intrinsic motivation and self-determination in human behavior.* New York: Plenum.

Donahue, M., & Parsons, A. (1982). The use of roleplay to overcome cultural fatigue. *TESOL Quarterly, 16,* 359–365.

Dornyei, Z. (1994). Motivation and motivating in the foreign language classroom. *Modern Language Journal, 78,* 273–284.

Ellis, R. (1994). *The study of second language acquisition.* Oxford, England: Oxford University Press.

Favreau, M., & Segalowitz, N. (1983). Automatic and controlled processes in the first- and second-language reading of fluent bilinguals. *Memory & Cognition, 11,* 565–574.

Freed, B. F. (1991). Current realities and future prospects in foreign language acquisition research. In B. F. Freed (Ed.), *Foreign language acquisition research and the classroom* (pp. 3–27). Lexington, MA: Heath.

Gardner, R. C. (1985). *Social psychology and second language learning: The role attitudes and motivation.* London: Edward Arnold.

Gardner, R. C. (1991). Second language learning in adults: Correlates of proficiency. *Applied Language Learning, 2,* 1–28.

Gardner, R. C., & Lambert, W. (1972). *Attitudes and motivation in second language learning.* Rowley, MA: Newbury House.

Gathercole, S. E., & Baddeley, A. D. (1993). *Working memory and language.* Hillsdale, NJ: Lawrence Erlbaum Associates.

Grosjean, F. (1982). *Life with two languages: An introduction to bilingualism.* Cambridge, MA: Harvard University Press.

Guthke, J., Heinrich, A., & Caruso, M. (1986). The diagnostic program of "Syntactical Rule and Vocabulary Acquisition": A contribution to the psychodiagnosis of foreign language learning ability. In F. Klix & H.

Hagendorf (Eds.), *Human memory and cognitive capabilities: Mechanisms and performances—Part B* (pp. 903–911). Amsterdam: Elsevier Science.

Guttmann, G. (1986). Fluctuations of learning capability. In F. Klix & H. Hagendorf (Eds.), *Human memory and cognitive capabilities: Mechanisms and performances—Part B* (pp. 639–648). Amsterdam: Elsevier Science.

Hamers, J.H.M., Sijtsma, K., & Ruijssenaars, A.J.J.M. (Eds.). (1993). *Learning potential assessment: Theoretical, methodological and practical issues.* Amsterdam: Swets & Zeitlinger B. V.

Hannaford, C. (1995). *Smart moves: Why learning is not all in your head.* Arlington, VA: Great Ocean Publishers.

Hasher, L., & Zacks, R. T. (1979). Automatic and effortful processes in memory. *Journal of Experimental Psychology: General, 108,* 356–388.

Hatch, E., Polin, P., & Part, S. (1974). Acoustic scanning and syntactic processing: Three reading experiments with first and second language learners. *Journal of Reading Behavior, 6,* 275–285.

Hilgard, E. (1963). Motivation in learning theory. In S. Koch (Ed.), *Psychology: A study of science* (Vol. 5). New York: McGraw-Hill.

Hofstede, G. (1991). *Cultures and organizations. Intercultural cooperation and its importance for survival.* London: Harper Collins.

Jacobs, B., & Schumann, J. H. (1992). Language acquisition and the neurosciences: Towards a more integrative perspective. *Applied Linguistics, 13,* 282–301.

Kolers, P., & Gonzalez, E. (1980). Memory for words, synonyms, and translations. *Journal of Experimental Psychology: Human Learning and Memory, 6,* 53–65.

Kramsch, C. (1990). What is foreign language learning research? In B. VanPatten & J. F. Lee (Eds.), *Second language acquisition—foreign language learning* (pp. 27–33). Clevedon, UK: Multilingual Matters.

Krashen, S. (1981). *Second language acquisition and second language learning.* Oxford, England: Pergamon Press.

Kyllonen, P. C. (1993). Aptitude testing inspired by information processing: A test of the four-sources model. *Journal of General Psychology, 120,* 375–405.

Kyllonen, P. C., & Woltz, D. J. (1989). Role of cognitive factors in the acquisition of cognitive skill. In R. Kanfer, P. L. Ackerman, & R. Cudeck (Eds.), *Abilities, motivation, and methodology: The Minnesota Symposium on Learning and Individual Differences* (pp. 239–80). Hillsdale, NJ: Lawrence Erlbaum Associates.

LaBerge, D. (1975). Acquisition of automatic processing in perceptual and associative learning. In P.M.A. Rabbitt & S. Dornic (Eds.), *Attention and performance, Vol. 5.* New York: Academic Press.

Lambert, W. (1967). A social psychology of bilingualism. *Journal of Social Issues, 23,* 91–109.

Larsen, D., & Smalley, W. (1972). *Becoming bilingual: A guide to language learning.* New Canaan, CT: Practical Anthropology.

Levine, D., Baxter, J., & McNulty, P. (1987). *The culture puzzle: Cross-cultural communication for English as a second language.* Englewood Cliffs, NJ: Prentice-Hall Regents.

MacWhinney, B. (1992). Transfer and competition in second language learning. In R. Harris (Ed.), *Cognitive processing in bilinguals* (pp. 371–390). Amsterdam: Elsevier Science.

McLaughlin, B. (1978). *Second language acquisition in childhood.* Hillsdale, NJ: Lawrence Erlbaum Associates.

McLaughlin, B. (1984). *Second-language acquisition in childhood: Vol. 1. Preschool children* (2nd ed.). Hillsdale, NJ: Lawrence Erlbaum Associates.

McLaughlin, B. (1990). Restructuring. *Applied Linguistics, 11,* 1–16.

McLaughlin, B. (1995). Aptitude from an information-processing perspective. *Language Testing, 12,* 370–387.

McLeod, B., & McLaughlin, B. (1986). Restructuring or automaticity?: Reading in a second language. *Language Learning, 36,* 109–123.

Mishkin, M., & Appenzeller, T. (1987). The anatomy of memory. *Scientific American, 256,* 80–89.

Mulder, G., Wijers, A., Smid, H., Brookhuis, K., & Mulder, L. (1989). Individual differences in computational mechanisms: A psychophysiological analysis. In R. Kanfer, P. L. Ackerman, & R. Cudeck (Eds.), *Abilities, motivation, and methodology: The Minnesota Symposium on Learning and Individual Differences* (pp. 391–434). Hillsdale, NJ: Lawrence Erlbaum Associates.

Oller, J. W., Jr. (1981). Language as intelligence? *Language Learning, 31,* 465–92.

Olmedo, E. L. (1980). Quantitative models of acculturation: An overview. In A. M. Padilla (Ed.), *Acculturation: Theory, models and some new findings* (pp. 27–45). Boulder, CO: Westview.

Olmedo, E. L., & Padilla, A. M. (1978). Empirical and construct validation of a measure of acculturation for Mexican Americans. *Journal of Social Psychology, 105,* 179–187.

O'Mara, F. E., Lett, J. A., & Alexander, E. E. (1994). The prediction of language learning success at DLIFLC

(LSCP Report II). In U.S. Department of Defense Report, *The Language Skill Change Project*. Monterey, CA: Defense Language Institute Foreign Language Center.

Oxford, R. L. (1990). Styles, strategies, and aptitude: Connections for language learning. In T. S. Parry & C. W. Stansfield (Eds.), *Language aptitude revisited* (pp. 67–125). Englewood Cliffs, NJ: Prentice-Hall Regents.

Oxford, R., & Shearin, J. (1994). Language learning and motivation: Expanding the theoretical framework. *Modern Language Journal, 78,* 12–28.

Padilla, A. M. (1980). The role of cultural awareness and ethnic loyalty in acculturation. In A. M. Padilla (Ed.), *Acculturation: Theory, models and some new findings* (pp. 47–84). Boulder, CO: Westview.

Paivio, A., & Desrochers, A. (1980). A dual-coding approach to bilingual memory. *Canadian Journal of Psychology, 34,* 388–399.

Paradis, M. (1981). Contributions of neurolinguistics to the theory of bilingualism. In R. K. Herbert (Ed.), *Applications of linguistic theory in the human sciences*. Michigan State University, Department of Linguistics.

Peirce, B. N. (1995). Social identity, investment, and language learning. *TESOL Quarterly, 29,* 9–31.

Posner, M. I., & Snyder, C.R.R. (1975a). Attention and cognitive control. In R. L. Solso (Ed.), *Information processing and cognition: The Loyola Symposium*. Hillsdale, NJ: Lawrence Erlbaum Associates.

Posner, M. I., & Snyder, C.R.R. (1975b). Facilitation and inhibition in the processing of signals. In P.M.A. Rabbitt & S. Dornic (Eds.), *Attention and performance, Vol. 5*. New York: Academic Press.

Preston, M., & Lambert, W. (1969). Interlingual interference in a bilingual version of the Stroop Color-Word Task. *Journal of Verbal Learning and Verbal Behavior, 8,* 295–301.

Pulvermüller, F., & Schumann, J. H. (1994). Neurobiological mechanisms of language acquisition. *Language Learning, 44,* 681–734.

Rumelhart, D. E., McClelland, J. L., & the PDP Research Group (1986). *Parallel distributed processing: Explorations in the microstructure of cognition* (Vol. 1). Cambridge, MA: Bradford Books.

Scarcella, R., & Oxford, R. (1992). *The tapestry of language learning: The individual in the communicative classroom*. Boston: Heinle & Heinle.

Schumann, J. H. (1976). The pidginization hypothesis. *Language Learning, 26,* 391–408.

Schumann, J. H. (1978). *The pidginization process: A model for second language acquisition*. Rowley, MA: Newbury House.

Schumann, J. H. (1986). Research on the acculturation model for second language acquisition. *Journal of Multilingual and Multicultural Development, 7,* 379–392.

Schumann, J. H. (1994). Where is cognition?: Emotion and cognition in second language acquisition. *Studies in Second Language Acquisition, 16,* 231–242.

Schumann, J. H. (1997). *The neuropsychology of affect in language*. New York: Blackwell.

Shiffrin, R. M., & Schneider, W. (1977). Controlled and automatic human information processing: II. Perceptual learning, automatic attending, and a general theory. *Psychological Review, 84,* 127–190.

Skehan, P. (1989). *Individual differences in second-language learning*. London: Edward Arnold.

Snow, R. E. (1989). Cognitive-conative aptitude interactions in learning. In R. Kanfer, P. L. Ackerman, & R. Cudeck (Eds.), *Abilities, motivation, and methodology: The Minnesota Symposium on Learning and Individual Differences* (pp. 435–74). Hillsdale, NJ: Lawrence Erlbaum Associates.

Soares, C., & Grosjean, F. (1984). Bilinguals in a monolingual and a bilingual speech mode: The effect on lexical access. *Memory & Cognition, 12,* 380–386.

Stengal, E. (1939). On learning a new language. *International Journal of Psychoanalysis, 2,* 471–479.

Szanston, D. (1966). Cultural confrontation in the Phillipines. In R. Textor (Ed.), *Cultural frontiers of the Peace Corps* (pp. 35–61). Boston: MIT Press.

Thorndike, E. L. (1924). *An Introduction to the theory of mental and social measurement*. New York: Wiley.

Weiner, B. (1992). Motivation. In *Encyclopedia of educational research* (6th ed., Vol. 3, pp. 860–865). New York: Macmillan.

Wells, C. G. (1985). *Language development in pre-school years*. Cambridge, England: Cambridge University Press.

Wesche, M. B., Edwards, H., & Wells, W. (1982). Foreign language aptitude and intelligence. *Applied Psycholinguistics, 3,* 127–40.

Willerman, L. (1979). *The psychology of individual and group differences*. San Francisco, CA: Freeman.

Principles of Bilingualism

José G. Centeno
St. John's University

Loraine K. Obler
City University of New York Graduate School

Spanish coexists with other languages in prominent situations of bilingualism throughout the world. Silva-Corvalan (1995) reported that, as a majority language, Spanish is found in several Latin American countries along with indigenous languages (e.g., Ecuador, Peru, and Colombia), with Portuguese (e.g., Uruguay), and with English (e.g., Puerto Rico). As a minority language, it coexists with English in the United States, with Basque in the Basque Country in Europe; with Arabic, French, and indigenous languages in Africa; and with indigenous languages in the Philippines.

The interaction between Spanish and English in the United States provides an interesting and important bilingualism context. Although having a minority presence relative to English in most parts of the United States, Spanish has a great vitality resulting from the constant influx of new Spanish monolingual speakers and a growing institutional support by newspapers, magazines, television, and radio programs (Torres, 1997). New arrivals from such places as Puerto Rico, the Dominican Republic, Mexico, and many countries in both Central and South America add momentum to the increasing trends seen in the U.S. Hispanic population. The growing Hispanic community in the United States—having expanded to 9% (22 million) of the total population in 1990 up from 6% (14 million) in 1980 (U.S. Bureau of the Census, 1990)—has shown great interest in being proficient in English, despite a loyalty to their Spanish as a home language, which supports their desire to be bilingual (Garcia, Evangelista, Martinez, Disla, & Paulino, 1988; Torres, 1997; Zentella, 1990).

The interplay seen when two languages are in contact comprises a multidimensional process with factors operating at both individual and societal levels and with repercussions on the use and survival of each of the two languages. At the individual level, the speakers' motivation to use their languages and the communicative demands requiring their use of those languages, and, at the societal level, the social and linguistic impact of official language policies have direct consequences on the strength and maintenance of the languages employed by a bilingual person and a bilingual community.

This chapter summarizes sociolinguistic, cognitive, neurolinguistic, and neuropsychological aspects of bilingualism relevant to neuropsychological intervention with the Hispanic bilingual. When possible, the focus is on Spanish-speaking bilinguals. Elsewhere, it is useful to speak about what is known about bilingual populations more generally. The chapter starts by defining bilingualism. Then, the discussion continues with the factors contributing to language use in bilingual communities, followed by the ways in which bilingualism may interact with cognitive skills. Next, the poststroke language performance seen in bilinguals is addressed and the variables that have been implicated to explain it are discussed. The chapter concludes with the future directions that bilingualism research should take to enhance clinical work in this population.

DEFINITION

In its narrowest sense, *bilingualism* refers to the alternate use of two languages by the same individual (Mackey, 1962; Weinreich, 1953). Yet, given the different modalities in which language performance can be assessed (i.e., reading, listening, writing, and speaking), the different linguistic levels (i.e., vocabulary, sentence comprehension and production, etc.), and the different contexts of language use (i.e., formal vs. informal, with a bilingual or monolingual interlocutor, etc.), proficiency in each language has to be described along these three dimensions: language modality, linguistic level, and context. The degree of ability in the assessed areas will place performance in the first (L1) and the second language (L2) along a continuum ranging from minimal to native or near-native proficiency.

The complexity involved in describing bilingualism is evident in the range and limitations of its numerous definitions proposed in the literature to characterize language balance or dominance. For instance, Fishman, Cooper, and Ma (1971) argued that identifying a bilingual speaker as *balanced* raises theoretical issues because rarely will anyone be equally competent in all communicative situations. Leaning toward a functional specialization of language, Fishman (1965) supported the notion that most bilingual individuals will use their two languages for different purposes and functions. For example, a bilingual person might be required to use one language at home and another one at work.

Another definition categorizes bilingual speakers based on their mastery of skills in both languages. Some bilingual speakers have been considered to be *semilingual* in both languages when their language skills in each language, such as vocabulary repertory and correctnes of language use, are not comparable to those of monolingual speakers of each language (Skutnabb-Kangas, 1981). Because this label might lead to abuse, it must be used with caution since limitations in either of a bilingual's languages may be the result of a lack of stimulation in L1, unavailable in their new country to the same extent as in their country of origin, and socioeconomic circumstances isolating the bilingual immigrant group from an intensive exposure to L2 in their new country (Baetens Beardsmore, 1986).

Other terminology includes *receptive bilingualism* (Baetens Beardsmore, 1986), referring to an adequate understanding of a second language in either spoken or written form without necessarily being able to speak or write it; *incipient bilingualism* (Diebold, 1961), describing the initial prelingual stages in second language acquisition; and *additive* and *subtractive bilingualism* (Lambert, 1977), arguing for an enriching or competing impact of bilingual experiences.

The multidimensional nature of bilingualism, reflected in the discussion of the factors interacting in its definition, makes its measurement a daunting task. A review of the proposed assessment procedures for bilingualism and biculturalism would be beyond the scope of this chapter. Refer to some exhaustive discussions on assessing bilinguality and biculturalism available in the literature (Baetens Beardsmore, 1986; Hamers & Blanc, 1989; Macnamara, 1967, 1969).

Generally speaking, assessing bilingualism requires evaluating the degree of proficiency or ability demonstrated by bilingual speakers in each of their languages. Assessment procedures employed for this purpose are intended to measure bilingual individuals' language competence (inner, mental representation, or knowledge of the language) and/or their language performance (actual use of the language). Findings involving "performance" measures are considered to provide insights into the possible "competence" available to each bilingual speaker. For instance, in a task of learning and recall of pictorial material in two languages, Ervin-Tripp (1973) showed that pictures were easier to name in a bilingual's more fluent language and were recalled more significantly in that language regardless of the language of learning. Similarly, a test of word detection ability when given a nonsense letter sequence (e.g., DANSONODEND), in either French or English, provided evidence that correlated to the extent of bilingualism in three groups of subjects with differing degrees of French–English bilingualism (Lambert, Havelka, & Gardner, 1959).

Macnamara (1969, p. 84) argued that assessment procedures such as those already discribed only confirm what can already be assumed from the bilingual subject's case history—namely, the greater the contact with two languages, the greater the likelihood of balance and the smaller the effect of dominance. Nonetheless, efforts to develop formal assessment protocols of language proficiency in bilinguals should be encouraged because they would objectify skills that, at times, can be contradictory. Dornic (1978, 1979) argued that the discrepancy between competence and performance can be blurred when a speaker who shows a great command in both languages is under stress, fatigue, or emotionally uncomfortable. These factors will bring out a hidden imbalance that might well be masked by good pronunciation and an apparent accuracy under normal circumstances.

In terms of language performance, the major concern in a clinical setting is to evaluate a bilingual speaker's language dominance or balance in order to determine the language(s) to be used during the diagnostic process and intervention programs. A second concern is to determine the extent to which lack of full proficiency in a language can falsely mimic or exaggerate neuropsychological deficits. The bilingual speech/language pathologist, the language and communication specialist on an interdisciplinary rehabilitation team, can provide important information regarding language dominance. The bilingual speech/language pathologist is involved in the determination of language dominance using both formal (tests) and informal (conversational language samples) assessment tools and the analysis of findings to differentiate any language deficits from second language acquisition issues, language loss, limited language stimulation, and language disabilities (Centeno, 1997). In this process, the bilingual speech/language clinician heavily relies on the collection of a full language history to obtain important details on factors such as the language development contexts (i.e., home, school, community), age of language acquisition, countries of residence, and modalities of language use (speaking, writing) and exposure (listening, reading) in the bilingual client (Obler, Centeno, & Eng, 1995; see Paradis, 1987). This information may also be employed by other members on the clinical team to evaluate the amount and frequency of language stimulation and use in the bilingual, since the onset of the speaker's bilingual experiences, with important linguistic implications in neuropsychological intervention.

LANGUAGE CHOICE IN BILINGUAL COMMUNITIES

If both clinician and client are bilingual and from the same culture, then subtle issues around language choice during testing and rehabilitation are unlikely to occur. If not, however, it behooves clinicians to at least be aware of the cultural factors reflected by language choice so they can implement clinical procedures in an unbiased and respectful manner.

The dynamics of language use in a bilingual community depend on a complex process in which the speaker, the listener, and the conversational setting interact under the influence of cultural, social, and political variables. At the level of the individual speaker, several accounts have been proposed to explain language choice by bilinguals. One argument proposes that a bilingual interaction involves a linguistic adjustment (accommodation) between the speaker and the listener (Giles, Bourhis, & Taylor, 1977; Giles & Smith, 1979) such that bilingual speakers will decrease (convergence) or increase (divergence) the distance with their listeners by using the language in which the listeners feel the most comfortable. Another proposal, chiefly addressing the dynamics of language choice by investigating the factors needed to answer the question "who speaks what to whom and when?," advances the tenet that bilingual communication is dictated by the specific "domains" in which each language is used (Fishman, 1965). In particular, family, religion, education, friendship, and employment were identified to be the five chief domains that anchored the selection of either Spanish or English by Spanish–English Puerto Rican bilinguals in New York City (Fishman et al., 1971). However, later investigations in a similar population suggested that domains are not rigid or impenetrable to either of the languages spoken by the bilingual person. Instead, both languages can be used because the communicative context might involve monolingual speakers of both languages or bilingual speakers switching between languages (Zentella, 1997).

Language use by bilingual speakers is also dependent on the individual's cultural identity. Language, an important component of culture along with customs, values, food, clothing, beliefs, and art (Hamers & Blanc, 1989; Leeds-Hurwitz, 1993), is "the main tool for the internalization of culture" by an individual (Hamers & Blanc, 1989, p. 116). Often, viewed in the context of the development of bilinguality, the interaction between language use and cultural affinity is an important phenomenon to consider in bilingualism because the degree of cultural identification has an impact on language valorization and use. For instance, Matute-Bianchi's (1991) findings demonstrate that the degree of fluency in Spanish and English exhibited by high school students of Mexican descent in California depended on the extent of their assimilation to the United States. Those students fluent in English, mostly U.S. born, often did not have a strong identity with the Mexican culture. Similarly, Torres (1997) reported that the majority of Puerto Rican bilingual students in the community of Brentwood, Long Island, albeit supporting the use of Spanish for affective reasons toward their family and culture, rated English as their best language and did not identify Spanish "as the language or even a language of the United States" (p. 29).

Societal language attitudes also have an impact on language maintenance in a bilingual community. Because bilingualism often occurs in social contexts involving social groups not having the same political and economic power, the minority language is seen as lacking prestige and as not associated with academic achievement and economic progress (Appel & Muysken, 1987; Grosjean, 1982). In fact, Giles et al. (1977) claimed that pressure by the majority group frequently forces minority individuals to encourage their young to learn the majority language. Likewise, Grosjean (1982) suggested that children of a stigmatized minority may decide not to use their native language with their older relatives so as not to be differentiated from the children of the majority group. Indeed, history has shown that approval of bilingualism by mainstream social groups does not often occur until it has been enforced by governmental policies such as Canada's Official Language Act of 1968–1969, which granted equal status to both English and French at the level of the federal government.

In brief, the language patterns exhibited by bilingual speakers are related to the characteristics of the conversational setting, bilingual individuals' idiosyncrasies toward their two languages, and the bilingual group's cultural norms reflecting, and shaped by, larger political, socioeconomic, and sociocultural forces (Appel & Muysken, 1987; Hamers & Blanc, 1989; Zentella, 1997). When looking at the trends in language use and maintenance in a bilingual community, it is not only necessary to look at the individual's motivation and social networks, but also at the social and political backdrop supporting each language.

The preceding interaction between language and nonlinguistic elements illustrates that clinical intervention with bilingual Hispanics requires a wholistic approach considering their pre-morbid social, economic, cultural, and linguistic background. The Hispanic population in the United States differs from the rest of the U.S. population in terms of average age, family size, income, education, occupation, and health care utilization (Langdon, 1992). A greater number of Hispanics (26%) live below the poverty level relative to non-Hispanics (12%) (U.S. Bureau of the Census, 1990), a result that can be attributed to the high incidence of low paying jobs, high unemployment, and limited education among Hispanics in the United States (Langdon, 1992). In addition to the previous factors, the various U.S. Hispanic subgroups also differ among one another in terms of the Spanish dialect they speak and the cultural norms in their communities. In fact, the variety of Spanish that each group speaks is the most distinctive marker of its individuality, particularly in terms of vocabulary, pronunciation, and some grammatical constructions (Zentella, 1997).

Thus, clinicians should ensure that the diagnostic findings represent true deficits and not behaviors resulting from the socioeconomic, cultural, and linguistic environment of each Hispanic community. Determining whether a clinical deficit exists in a bilingual Hispanic person, especially in language-mediated skills, should be consistently confirmed by a wholistic intake obtained from the family and diagnostic observations from both formal and informal testing (Kayser, 1995; Reyes, 1997), particularly, because verbal tasks (as compared to spatial and visuoperceptual tasks) are precisely those tasks where performance is found to be the most directly dependent on a person's sociocultural level (Ostrosky-Solis et al., 1985).

BILINGUALISM AND COGNITIVE SKILLS

The neuropsychologist's goal is to evaluate the cognitive abilities of a client. If that client is not a fluent speaker of the language of the test, then the results will be biased. Recall that European immigrants to the United States were given the new "intelligence" tests in the early 1900s, and many failed. For example, using a translated version of Alfred Binet's intelligence test in English to assess the intelligence of Jewish immigrants through an interpreter, Goddard (1917) reported that 25 out of 30 adult immigrants were "feeble-minded" due to their restricted vocabulary. These negative attitudes toward immigrants also influenced the work with bilingual children. Smith (1939, cited in Hakuta, 1986; Romaine, 1995), relying on language norms obtained for Caucasian monolingual English-speaking children, argued that bilingual children of various native language backgrounds (e.g., Portuguese, Korean, and Filipino) showed inferior performance apparently resulting from the use of two languages.

The hostility to immigrants permitted the logical problems in using assessment measures to evaluate them to go unnoticed for a long time. Early studies of bilingualism have widely been criticized for critical methodological limitations, including the inclusion of bilingual subjects without consideration to the different degrees of bilingualism, the comparison of bilingual subjects with monolingual speakers without considering their socioeconomic status, and testing the cognitive abilities of bilingual subjects in their weaker language (Hamers & Blanc, 1989; Romaine, 1995).

An initial effort to systematically control for the aforementioned variables in bilingualism research was reported by Peal and Lambert (1962). In contrast to the previous investigations, mainly conducted to study the negative effects of bilingualism, Peal and Lambert's research was done with a positive attitude toward bilingualism in Canada and was supported by the Official Languages Act of 1968–1969, which provided equal status to English and French at the federal government level (Hakuta, 1986; Romaine, 1995). In their study, Peal and Lambert were careful to control for socioeconomic backgrounds and degree of bilingualism because they used middle-class subjects equally proficient in both French and English. Their findings revealed that bilingual children performed better than monolingual children in both verbal and nonverbal intelligence measures. In particular, bilinguals excelled in tests involving mental or symbolic flexibility and the reorganization of visual patterns.

After Peal and Lambert, a large number of investigations have strongly supported the benefits of bilingualism on cognitive development, particularly at the level of a higher language creativity and reorganization of information, and nonverbal, perceptual tasks (see Hamers & Blanc, 1989, for a comprehensive list). In an attempt to explain this interaction between bilingualism and cognitive gains, Diaz and Klingler (1991) advanced the notion that exposure to two languages, such as in simultaneous, additive situations, gives children a unique advantage to the "objectification of language" (p. 188), an enriched approach that would foster the use of language as a tool of thought. Theoretical efforts in this direction are the next step to follow because they would weave the increasing amount of data that has emerged on the impact of bilingualism on language and cognitive gains into coherent models of cognitive processes that characterize different types of bilinguals and multilinguals (Bialystok & Cummins, 1991).

In sum, bilingual status alone may have modest positive effects on performance on cognitive tasks heavily dependent on linguistic knowledge. On such tasks, the examiner may consider if a client's abilities are being overestimated. In many more instances, however, the neuropsychologist must consider whether the client's cognitive abilities are being underestimated due to a lack of full linguistic proficiency in the language of testing or rehabilitation. Because language is critical for the understanding and execution of many neuropsychological tasks, neuropsychologists may remain frustrated if they are unable to determine whether a client's poor performance is due to language proficiency issues or true neuropsychological deficits. Fortunately, today's neuropsychologists seek the use of more sophisticated methods and have more culturally sensitive attitudes than their predecessors in the early 1900s. This may distinguish true deficits from social, cultural, economic, and language differences.

POLYGLOT APHASIA

The languages known by a polyglot[1] are not always recovered to the same extent or at the same rate. Overall, parallel deficits and restitution of these speakers' languages, involving similar aphasic impairments and a simultaneous rate of recovery, are the most frequently seen patterns after neurological damage in a multilingual brain (Albert & Obler, 1978; Charlton, 1964; Paradis, 1977). Yet, in his review of the literature on aphasia in bilinguals and polyglots, Paradis (1977, 1989) identified as many as nine unequal language recovery patterns, including parallel restitution. For example, other possible recovery patterns can be described as differential, when the languages are not equally impaired or do not recover at the same rate; successive, when one language does not begin to reappear until another has been maximally recovered; antagonistic, when one language regresses as the other one progresses; selective, when patients do not regain the use of one or more of their premorbid languages; and mixed, when the patient blends languages while speaking.

Some of the aforementioned clinical profiles have been documented in bilingual speakers for whom Spanish was one of their languages. Silverberg and Gordon (1979) reported a case of differential recovery in a 26-year-old Spanish- and Hebrew-speaking female who suffered a left-sided embolic infarction. Born and raised in Chile in an exclusively Spanish-speaking family and community, she learned Hebrew after migrating to Israel at age 23. She learned Hebrew formally in an intensive language program and used it at work in Israel while continuing to use her Spanish with friends and relatives. Three days after the onset of the disturbance, her oral expression was telegraphic and nonfluent in Spanish (L1) with word-finding deficits, and fluent with literal and verbal paraphasias in Hebrew (L2). Comprehension was similarly impaired in both languages. Later, 1 month after the brain damage, examination revealed progress in both languages, with Spanish still preserving some of its earlier nonfluent quality and Hebrew showing no aphasic deficit. Comprehension was intact in both languages.

Wulfeck, Juarez, Bates, and Kilborn (1986) provided evidence on successive recovery in a bilingual 70-year-old male showing aphasic symptoms secondary to a left CVA in the left inferior frontal gyrus. This patient, who acquired Spanish in Puerto Rico where he was born, used Spanish at home and socially, and learned English as part of the school curriculum. After migrating to the United States at age 20, his language environment included both Spanish and English in and outside his home, as revealed by the language history questionnaire. Shortly after the stroke, this patient could only produce fragments of Spanish, although he could understand simple commands in both Spanish and English. A few weeks later, English began to appear in his speaking and his Spanish continued to improve. Posteriorly, 6 months post-onset, he was nonfluent in either language, yet fluency was better for Spanish than for English.

---

[1] Bilinguals are often included in the term polyglot (Albert & Obler, 1978, p. 95).

LANGUAGE LOCALIZATION AND PROCESSING
IN BILINGUAL SPEAKERS

Several accounts have been advanced to explain nonparallel recovery in polyglots. However, no single factor has been able to explain the different cases of unequal language restitution reported in the polyglot aphasia literature. As early as the 1800s, Ribot (1882) and Pitres (1895) suggested two separate proposals. Ribot's rule stated that the first learned language should be less impaired and should recover first in aphasia, whereas Pitres' rule argued that the most familiar or most recently used language emerges first in polyglot aphasia. Of the two arguments, a survey of reported cases of polyglot aphasia revealed that Pitres' principle could explain recovery at significantly more than chance frequency, and Ribot's, particularly in the nonelderly patients (i.e., those individuals under age 60), could not (Obler & Albert, 1977).

Other early arguments supported the interaction between age of acquisition and the degree of language practice (Freud, 1953), negative or positive feelings associated with each language (Krapf, 1955), a reliance on the language involving the least expressive effort (Charlton, 1964), and a variety of other factors (see Paradis, 1989, for a comprehensive review).

In terms of pyscholinguistic accounts, the compound-coordinate dichotomy in bilingualism, first articulated by Ervin and Osgood (1954), describes the psychological representation of vocabulary items in bilinguals to consist of a single (compound) or two (coordinate) sets of processes, meanings, and responses as a result of a mixed or separate acquisition contexts, respectively. That is, social environments encouraging the continual and concurrent use of two languages stimulate compound bilingualism, whereas those social contexts encouraging the distinctive and separate use of one of a bilingual speaker's two languages enhance coordinate bilingualism (Ervin & Osgood, 1954; Lambert & Fillenbaum, 1959).

The compound–coordinate description of language representation in bilingualism has been modified. There is evidence supporting Albert and Obler's (1978) argument that bilingual speakers might lie along a compound–coordinate continuum, or part of the language system might be coordinate. Specifically, based on the more frequent occurrence of word blending from different languages in the same utterances (lexical mixing) by her German–French–English polyglot subject, Perecman (1984) argued that coordination is more likely to happen at the lexical (vocabulary) level than at any other level of linguistic structure (i.e., phonological [sounds in words], morphological [word endings], or syntactic [word order]). Consonant with Obler and Albert (1978), Perecman used these observations to suggest that the vocabulary of languages might be more closely tied across languages than other aspects of the grammar. That is, polyglot speakers might be able to "compound" their languages in one linguistic context (i.e., vocabulary) and "coordinate" them in another (e.g., word order).

Another model of the organization of the bilingual brain proposed the involvement of cortical areas in a "switch mechanism" responsible for controlling the selective use of either language by the bilingual speaker (Albert & Obler, 1978; Paradis, 1977). Damage to this area would result in an inappropriate switch between languages with polyglot speakers, for instance, being able to use only one of their languages or erratically fluctuating between languages. Although the actual cortical localization of the switch is far from settled (see Paradis, 1977), Obler and Albert (1978) suggested that, for the switch mechanism to operate and be turned off or on, it must be triggered by a monitor system operating continuously throughout language processing.

Other explanatory efforts of nonparallel recovery have involved experimental studies looking at the possible differences that might exist in the polyglot's cortical language localization. Ojemann and Whitaker (1978) employed a cortical electrical stimulation technique to investigate naming disruption in two bilingual speakers. Their findings showed that languages may be somewhat differentially represented in the brain because subjects, in addition to experiencing similar naming impairment for both languages for some cortical areas, exhibited disruption in only one language in other areas. They also observed that the nondominant language occupied a larger cortical area than the dominant language and the right hemisphere was involved in naming in one of their two subjects. Rapport, Tan, and Whitaker (1983) observed that language functions were differentially localized along the left perisylvian area in Chinese–English bilinguals under the effect of cortical electrical stimulation. Fedio et al.'s (1992) findings supported the more diffuse localization of the nondominant language reported by Ojemann and Whitaker. Kim, Relkin, Lee, and Hirsch (1997) reported differential localization of two languages in Broca's, but not in Wernicke's, area.

Language-specific and acquisitional factors have been held responsible for the differential language localization patterns (see Genesee, 1988, and Vaid, 1983, for a comprehensive review). Regarding language-specific variables, such as the direction and the type of the script, investigations have not clearly specified whether the results obtained stem from bilingualism or from actual cross-linguistic differences that could be found in unilingual speakers of the languages in question (e.g., Chinese vs. English). In terms of acquisitional factors, studies have looked at the manner (formal [school] vs. informal [social environment]), and stage (initial [nonproficient] vs. late [proficient]) of second language acquisition, and age. Reports tend to agree that formal language instruction, with its emphasis on language-rule learning, as compared to informal language exposure relying on meaning rather than structure (Krashen, 1977), encourages left hemispheric localization. Yet, results are far from conclusive regarding the impact of initial or late second language exposure on a differential hemispheric specialization. Studies pertaining to the impact of age on second language acquisition point in the direction of a greater right hemisphere involvement the later the second language is acquired. Finally, keep in mind that the contradictions seen in the language lateralization research in bilinguals might stem from methodological issues, including subject selection criteria, language and stimulus selection, testing procedures, and data analysis (Obler, Zatorre, Galloway, & Vaid, 1982).

CONCLUSIONS

The preceding discussion has illustrated that bilingualism is a multidimensional phenomenon under the influence of variables extrinsic and intrinsic to the speaker. Language performance in Hispanic bilinguals, like all bilingual speakers, is subject to sociolinguistic, cognitive, neuropsychological, and neurolinguistic factors that may be important in providing neuropsychological services. A clinician's diagnostic and therapeutic arsenal has to be sensitive to the possible social, linguistic, cognitive, and neuropsychological/neurolinguistic elements that might be responsible for the patient's postlesion abilities and subsequent progress. Research that would facilitate the development of assessment and intervention procedures employing culturally, linguistically, and cognitively realistic protocols to service this population should be encouraged. For instance, regarding language skills, the Bilingual Aphasia Test (BAT) (Paradis, 1987) evaluates the same linguistic areas in the two languages known by a bilingual speaker. The BAT exists in 45 languages and 61 language pairs, thus allowing the comparison of poststroke integrity between the two languages of a bilingual aphasic.

Much research is still needed. In particular, further investigation is needed on the cognitive and psycholinguistic processes operating in the bilingual brain, the mechanisms of language recovery in bilingual aphasics, and the language–culture–cognition interaction in bilingualism. These research efforts should be incorporated in the development of unbiased and realistic diagnostic instruments and therapeutic programs to service the bilingual individual.

REFERENCES

Albert, M., & Obler, L. K. (1978). *The bilingual brain*. New York: Academic Press.

Appel, R., & Muysken, P. (1987). *Language contact and bilingualism*. London: Edward Arnold.

Baetens Beardsmore, H. (1986). *Bilingualism: Basic principles* (2nd ed.). San Diego: College-Hill.

Bialystok, E., & Cummins, J. (1991). Language, cognition, and education of bilingual children. In E. Bialystok (Ed.), *Language processing in bilingual children* (pp. 222–232). Cambridge, England: Cambridge University Press.

Charlton, M. H. (1964). Aphasia in bilingual and polyglot patients—A neurological and psychological study. *Journal of Speech and Hearing Disorders, 29*, 307–311.

Centeno, J. (1997, November). *The bilingual speech/language pathologist in the multilingual and multicultural classroom: A clinician and an advocate*. Paper presented at the meeting of the Council for Exceptional Children, New York, NY.

Diaz, R. M., & Klingler, C. (1991). Towards an explanatory model of the interaction between bilingualism and cognitive development. In E. Bialystok (Ed.), *Language processing in bilingual children* (pp. 167–192). Cambridge, England: Cambridge University Press.

Diebold, A.R. (1961). Incipient bilingualism. *Language, 37*, 97–112.

Dornic, S. (1978). The bilingual's performance: Language dominance, stress, and individual differences. In D. Gerver & H. Sinaiko (Eds.), *Language, interpretation and communication* (pp. 198–215). New York: Plenum.

Dornic, S. (1979). Information processing in bilinguals: Some selected issues. *Psychological Research, 40*, 329–348.

Ervin, S. M., & Osgood, C. E. (1954). Psycholinguistics: A survey of theory and research problems. In C. Osgood & T. Sebeok (Eds.), *Psycholinguistics* (pp. 75–110). Baltimore: Waverly.

Ervin-Tripp, S. (1973). Learning and recall in bilinguals. In A. Dil (Ed.), *Language acquisition and communicative choice* (pp. 139–146). Stanford, CA: Stanford University.

Fedio, P., August, A., Myatt, C., Kertzman, C, Miletich, R., Snyder, P., Satz, S., & Kafta, C. (1992, February). *Functional localization of languages in a bilingual patient with intracarotid amytal, subdural electrical stimulation, and positron emission tomography*. Paper presented at International Neuropsychological Society meeting, San Diego, CA.

Fishman, J. A. (1965). Who speaks what to whom and when? *Linguistics, 2*, 67–88.

Fishman, J. A., Cooper, R., & Ma, R. (Eds.). (1971). *Bilingualism in the barrio*. Bloomington: Indiana University.

Freud, S. (1953). *On aphasia* (E. Stengel, Ed. and Trans.). New York: International Universities Press. (Original work published 1891)

Garcia, O., Evangelista, I., Martinez, M., Disla, C., & Paulino, B. (1988). Spanish language use and attitudes: A study of two New York City communities. *Language in Society, 17*, 474–512.

Genesee, F. (1988). Neuropsychology and second language acquisition. In L. M. Beebe (Ed.), *Issues in second language acquisition: Multiple perspectives* (pp. 79–112). New York: Newbury House.

Giles, H., Bourhis, R. Y., & Taylor, D. M. (1977). Towards a theory of language in ethnic group relations. In H. Giles (Ed.), *Language, ethnicity, and intergroup relations* (pp. 307–349). London: Academic.

Giles, H., & Smith, P. (1979). Accommodation theory: Optimal levels of convergence. In H. Giles & R. N. St. Clair (Eds.), *Language and social psychology* (pp. 177–192). Oxford: Blackwell.

Goddard, H. H. (1917). Mental tests and the immigrant. *Journal of Delinquency, 2,* 243–277.

Grosjean, F. (1982). *Life with two languages: An introduction to bilingualism.* Cambridge, MA: Harvard University Press.

Hakuta, K. (1986). *Mirror of language: The debate on bilingualism.* New York: Basic Books.

Hamers, J. F., & Blanc, M.H.A. (1989). *Bilinguality and bilingualism.* Cambridge, England: Cambridge University Press.

Kayser, H. (1995). Bilingualism, myths, and language impairments. In H. Kayser (Ed.), *Bilingual speech-language pathology: An Hispanic focus* (pp. 185–206). San Diego: Singular.

Kim, K. H., Relkin, N. R., Lee, K. M., & Hirsch, J. (1997). Distinct cortical areas associated with native and second languages. *Nature, 388,* 171–174.

Krapf, E. E. (1955). The choice of language in polyglot psychoanalysis. *Psychoanalytic Quarterly, 24,* 343–357.

Krashen, S. D. (1977). The monitor model for adult second language performance. In M. Burt, H. Dulay, & M. Finocchiaro (Eds.), *Viewpoints on English as a second language* (pp. 77–93). New York: Regents.

Lambert, W. E. (1977). The effects of bilingualism on the individual: Cognitive and sociocultural consequences. In P. A. Hornby (Ed.), *Bilingualism: Psychological, social, and education implications* (pp. 15–28). New York: Academic.

Lambert, W. E., & Fillenbaum, S. (1959). A pilot study of aphasia among bilinguals. *Canadian Journal of Psychology, 13,* 28–34.

Lambert, W. E., Havelka, J., & Gardner, R. (1959). Linguistic manifestations of bilingualism. *American Journal of Psychology, 72,* 77–82.

Langdon, H. W. (1992). The Hispanic population: Facts and figures. In H. W. Langdon (Ed.), *Hispanic children and adults with communication disorders* (pp. 20–56). Gaithersburg, MD: Aspen.

Leeds-Hurwitz, W. (1993). *Semiotics and communication: Signs, codes, and cultures.* Hillsdale, NJ: Lawrence Erlbaum Associates.

Mackey, W. F. (1962). The description of bilingualism. *Canadian Journal of Linguistics, 7,* 51–85.

Macnamara, J. (1967). The bilingual's linguistic performance: A psychological overview. *Journal of Social Issues, 23,* 59–77.

Macnamara, J. (1969). How can one measure the extent of a person's bilingual proficiency? In L. G. Kelly (Ed.), *Description and measurement of bilingualism* (pp. 80–98). Toronto: University of Toronto.

Matute-Bianchi, M. (1991). Situational ethnicity and patterns of school performance among immigrant Mexican-descent students. In M. Gibson & J. Ogbu (Eds.), *Minority status and schooling* (pp. 48–58). New York: Garland.

Obler, L. K., & Albert, M. (1977). Influence of aging on recovery from aphasia in polyglots. *Brain and Language, 4,* 460–463.

Obler, L. K., & Albert, M. (1978). A monitor system for bilingual language processing. In M. Paradis (Ed.), *Aspects of bilingualism* (pp. 67–81). Columbia, SC: Hornbeam.

Obler, L. K., Centeno, J., & Eng, N. (1995). Bilingual and polyglot aphasia. In L. Menn, M. O'Connor, L. K. Obler, & A. Holland (Eds.), *Non-fluent aphasia in a multilingual world* (pp. 132–143). Amsterdam: John Benjamins.

Obler, L. K., Zatorre, R. J., Galloway, L., & Vaid, J. (1982). Cerebral lateralization in bilinguals: Methodological issues. *Brain and Language, 15,* 40–54.

Ojemann, G. A., & Whitaker, H. A. (1978). The bilingual brain. *Archives of Neurology, 35,* 409–412.

Ostrosky-Solis, F., Canseco, E., Quintanar, L., Navarro, E., Meneses, S., & Ardila, A. (1985). Sociocultural effects in neuropsychological assessment. *International Journal of Neuroscience, 27,* 53–66.

Paradis, M. (1977). Bilingualism and aphasia. In H. Whitaker & H. A. Whitaker (Eds.), *Studies in neurolinguistics* (Vol. 3, pp. 131–150). New York: Academic.

Paradis, M. (1987). *The assessment of bilingual aphasia.* Hillsdale, NJ: Lawrence Erlbaum Associates.

Paradis, M. (1989). Bilingual and polyglot aphasia. In F. Boller & J. Graiman (Eds.), *Handbook of neuropsychology* (Vol. 2, pp. 117–140). New York: Elsevier.

Peal, E., & Lambert, W. E. (1962). Relation of bilingualism to intelligence. *Psychological Monographs, 76,* 1–23.

Perecman, E. (1984). Spontaneous translation and language mixing in a polyglot aphasic. *Brain and Language, 23,* 43–63.

Pitres, A. (1895). Etude sur l'aphasie [Study on aphasia]. *Revue de Médicine, 15,* 873–899.

Rapport, R. L., Tan, C. T., & Whitaker, H. A. (1983). Language function and dysfunction among Chinese- and English-speaking polyglots: Cortical stimulation, Wada testing, and clinical studies. *Brain and Language, 18,* 342–366.

Reyes, B. (1997). Neurogenic communication disorders in bilingual adults: Management considerations. Newsletter of the Division of Communication Disorders and Sciences in Culturally and Linguistically Diverse Populations, *American Speech-Language-Hearing Association, 3,* 8–10.

Ribot, T. (1882). *Diseases of memory: An essay in the positive psychology.* London: Paul. (Original work published 1881 as *Les maladies de la memoire,* Paris: G. Baillere)

Romaine, S. (1995). *Bilingualism* (2nd ed.). Oxford, England: Blackwell.

Silva-Corvalan, C. (Ed.). (1995). *Spanish in four continents: Studies in language in contact and bilingualism.* Washington, DC: Georgetown University.

Silverberg, R., & Gordon, H. W. (1979). Differential aphasia in two bilingual individuals. *Neurology, 29,* 51–55.

Skutnabb-Kangas, T. (1981). *Bilingualism or not: The education of minorities.* Clevedon: Multilingual Matters.

Torres, L. (1997). *Puerto Rican discourse: A sociolinguistic study of a New York suburb.* Hillsdale, NJ: Lawrence Erlbaum Associates.

U.S. Bureau of the Census. (1990). *The Hispanic population in the United States.* Current Population Reports. Washington, DC: U.S. Government Printing Office.

Vaid, J. (1983). Bilingualism and brain lateralization. In S. J. Segalowitz, *Language functions and brain organization* (pp. 315–340). New York: Academic.

Weinreich, U. (1953). *Languages in contact.* The Hague: Mouton.

Wulfeck, B. B., Juarez, L., Bates, E. A., & Kilborn, K. (1986). Sentence interpretation strategies in healthy and aphasic bilingual adults. In J. Vaid (Ed.), *Language processing in bilinguals.* Hillsdale, NJ: Lawrence Erlbaum Associates.

Zentella, A. C. (1990). Lexical leveling in four New York City Spanish dialects: Linguistic and social factors. *Hispania, 73,* 1094–1105.

Zentella, A. C. (1997). *Growing up bilingual.* Malden, MA: Blackwell.

6

Acquired Language Disorders

ALFREDO ARDILA
Instituto Colombiano de Neuropsicologia

Language disturbances are correlated with the idiosyncrasies of each language. The Spanish language, as any other language, holds its own phonological, lexical, grammatical, semantic, and pragmatic particularities. Furthermore, reading and writing in Spanish requires following some specific rules. This chapter analyzes oral and written language disturbances in Spanish associated with brain pathology. Oral language disturbances and written language impairments are considered.

PHONOLOGY

The Spanish language spoken in Latin America has 17 consonantic, five vocalic, and two semivocalic phonemes (Table 6.1). The voiced lateral palatal (phonologically, /l̷/; written as a double L, e.g., *caballo*, "horse") is found only in some regions, especially the Andean areas, but in general this phoneme is dropping out of the language. The phoneme /x/ (voiced, velar fricative) is lowering articulatorily into the glottal region. The voiced oral stop phonemes /b/, /d/, and /g/ have weakly articulated fricative allophones in intervocalic position that are slowly vocalizing to the point of not being fully recognized as fricatives, but often only as highly sonorant approximations. There are five simple vowel phonemes at cardinal points: /a/, /e/, /i/, /o/, and /u/.

The two semivocalic phonemes are [y] and [w]. However, they function as semiconsonant when they are the nontonic left member of diphthongs, such as [tyene] and [kwatro], whereas they function as semivowels when they are the nontonic right member of diphthongs such as [peyne] and [kawsa]. The [y] and the [w] function as full consonants when they occur alone with no contiguous consonant such as [yeso].

The question of phonological disorders observed in Spanish-speaking aphasics was approached by Ardila, Montañes, Caro, Delgado, and Buckingham (1989). They reported several types of phonological changes observed in Spanish-speaking aphasics (Table 6.2). Vocalic changes were found to be particularly unusual in Spanish. They were observed with a frequency below 10% in motor (Broca and conduction) aphasias, and in about one fourth of the cases in Wernicke and anomic aphasia. Voiced/voiceless changes in oral stops are also infrequent. They represent less that 5% of literal changes in motor aphasias, and about 10% in Wernicke and anomic aphasia. Most of the literal paraphasias

TABLE 6.1
Phonological System of the Spanish Spoken in Latin America

	Labials		Dentals		Alveolars		Palatals		Velars	
	Vl	Vd	Vl	Vd	Vl	Vd	Vl	Vd	Vl	Vd
Stops	p	b	t	d					k	g
Affricates							t̑			
Nasals		m				n		ɲ		
Flap								r		
Trill								r̄		
Fricatives	f				s				x	
Laterals						l		ĺ		

Note: Vl = voiceless; Vd = voiced.

TABLE 6.2
Characteristics of Literal Paraphasias in Spanish-Speaking Aphasics
(Percentage of Different Types of Changes and Mechanisms Utilized)

	Broca	Conduction	Wernicke	Anomia
Type of Change				
Manner of articulation	46	57	35	32
Place of articulation	13	11	9	22
Manner and place of articulation	28	23	19	16
Voiced/voiceless (oral stops)	4	4	8	8
Vocalic changes	9	5	29	22
Mechanisms Utilized				
Substitution	62	52	72	78
Deletion	20	25	12	2
Reduplicative substitution	8	15	8	10
Addition	5	4	6	5
Reduplicative addition	2	3	1	0
Exchange	1	1	1	5

Note: Adapted from Ardila et al. (1989).

in Spanish language are due to errors in place of articulation, manner of articulation, or both. Usually, phonological errors in aphasia result from phoneme substitutions. In motor aphasias, phonological errors in about one fourth of the cases are due to phoneme deletions. Phoneme exchanges are extremely unusual, and are found in only 5% of the cases with anomic aphasia.

It is interesting to note the extremely low frequency of vocalic changes in Spanish-speaking aphasics. This is most likely the result of the Spanish vocalic system. The Spanish vocalic system is quite simple (only five vowels) and vowels are extremely important and salient. Syllabic clusters are formed around the vowels. Vowels are not usually simplified in spontaneous language. Further, when learning to write, children almost never present errors in writing vowels, but consonants (Ardila, Rosselli, & Ostrosky, 1996; Bravo-Valdivieso, 1982, 1988). Consequently, it is not surprising that in aphasia syndromes, most of the errors found are also consonantic errors.

Ardila and Rosselli (1992) analyzed the errors in repetitive language in a large sample of Spanish-speaking aphasic patients. The three subtests in the repetition sections (words,

TABLE 6.3

Percentage of Correct Repetition in Different Groups of Aphasic Patients
in Three Repetition Subsets

	Extrasylvian Motor	Broca	Conduction	Wernicke	Anomic
Words	98.0	46.0	63.0	74.0	100.00
High Probability Sentences	95.0	50.0	53.7	45.0	71.2
Low Probability Sentences	67.5	45.0	21.2	22.5	52.5

Note: Adapted from Ardila & Rosselli, (1992). Results in the three subtests of the repetition sections (words, high probability sentences, and low probability sentences of the Boston Diagnostic Aphasia Examination; Goodglass & Kaplan, 1979) are presented.

high probability sentences, and low probability sentences) of the Spanish version of the Boston Diagnostic Aphasia Examination (Goodglass & Kaplan, 1979) were used (Table 6.3). It was found that in extrasylvian (transcortical) motor aphasia associated with left prefrontal damage (dynamic aphasia), some errors were observed in the repetition of low probability sentences. These errors resulted from omissions and changes in word order in sentences. In long sentences, extrasylvian (transcortical) motor aphasia patients often omitted some elements to make the sentences simpler and more normal. Errors in Broca aphasia were due to literal paraphasias (anticipations, substitutions, and deletions) in word repetition, and to the omission of words in sentence repetition. Sentence repetition was agrammatical with evident deletion of grammatical connectors. Interestingly, in Broca aphasia, the percentage of repetition errors were similar in the three conditions (words, high probability and low probability sentences). Literal errors, self-corrections, and approximations to the target word were evident in conduction aphasia individuals. A significant difference between high probability and low probability sentence repetition scores was observed in conduction aphasia. Broca aphasia patients scored better in word repetition and high probability sentence repetition tasks than in the low probability conditions, whereas conduction aphasics scored up to 50% lower than Broca aphasia patients. In Wernicke aphasia, literal paraphasias were evident in the repetition of words and sentences. Repetition of sentences was much harder than the repetition of words, likely due to limitations in verbal memory. In anomic aphasia, errors were observed only with sentence repetition, particularly with long sentences. Errors were due to the omission of words and to verbal paraphasias.

Thus, it is clear that repetition errors are usually associated with perysilvian aphasias. In all aphasic groups, however, including extrasylvian (transcortical) motor aphasia, some errors can be observed. Repetition errors in aphasia are not only quantitatively but also qualitatively different, and depending on the specific repetition task, errors may be evident or unnoticed in a particular aphasia group. Different mechanisms underlying repetition deficits in aphasia may be assumed.

PARAPHASIAS

There are different types of paraphasias in the Spanish language. These include the literal or phonemic paraphasias, and verbal paraphasias (formal morphemic and semantic). They are discussed in detail next:

1. Literal (or phonemic) paraphasias result from an inappropriate phoneme sequence. Literal errors can be due to omissions, additions, displacements or substitutions of phonemes (Ardila, Rosselli, & Pinzón, 1989; Blumstein, 1988; Buckingham, 1989a, 1989b; Lecours, 1975).

2. A verbal paraphasia can be defined as the erroneous use of a word belonging to an inventory of the language in place of another word that also belongs to one of the language inventories (Lecóurs, Trepagnier, Naesser, & Lavelle-Huynh, 1983; Ryalls, Valdois, & Lecours, 1988). Different subtypes of verbal paraphasias can be distinguished.

a. *Formal verbal paraphasia* is a transformation in which the substituting word and the substituted word are similar in terms of their form, not their meaning (Blanken, 1990; Lecours & Rouillon, 1976). Formal verbal paraphasias might be considered as well as a particular type of phonemic paraphasias (Lecours et al., 1983).

b. *Morphemic verbal paraphasia* refers to an inappropriate word that has been assembled using morphemes belonging to the language inventory (Lecours, 1975; Lecours & Lhermitte, 1972). The resulting word may be acceptable from the point of view of the language, but it is unacceptable for the current context. These innovations (creation of a new word by combining existing morphemes in a new way) are particularly observed in Wernicke aphasia (Liederman, Kohn, Wolf, & Goodglass, 1983).

c. *Semantic verbal paraphasia* designates the aphasic transformation in which the substituting and the substituted words are close in meaning but not in phonology. Different types of semantic verbal paraphasias can be distinguished: (1) the substituting and the substituted words belong to the same semantic field; (2) they are antonymous; (3) the target word is replaced by a superordinate; as a matter of fact, aphasic language frequently recurs to words with a high level of generality but low content; and (4) there is an environmental proximity between the substituting and the substituted words (Ryalls et al., 1988).

Besides these three types of verbal paraphasias (formal morphemic, and semantic), at times a patient can introduce a word, given the context, that does not seem phonologically or semantically related to what appears to be required. This type of error has been designated as unrelated verbal paraphasia (Buckingham, 1989a, 1989b; Green, 1969). Aphasic substitutions can appear among linguistic units more complex than words; this type of substitution is known as syntagmatic paraphasia.

Some additional types of language deviations may be mentioned. Object description and instrument function are often observed in aphasic language. The anaphor is a word that has an antecedent occurring before or after its referent (Buckingham, 1981a). Aphasics often use anaphors for which a referent is nonexisting (indefinite anaphors) (e.g., "I read it." That is, if previously some word such as book, letter, or newspaper has not been mentioned, "it" will be an indefinite anaphor). Neologisms can be observed in aphasic language. Buckingham and Kertesz (1976) defined neologism as a phonological form for which it is impossible to recover with any reasonable degree of certainty some single item or items in the vocabulary of the patient's language as it presumably existed before the onset of the disease. In other words, it is not possible to identify the target word; however, it is almost always possible to identify its grammatical category based on its position and inflection. A neologism may be due to a double error: A lexical selection error, which, before it reaches phonetic materialization, is subsequently distorted phonemically (Buckingham, 1981b). Some examples of paraphasias in Spanish are presented in Table 6.4.

TABLE 6.4
Some Examples of Paraphasias Observed in Spanish-Speaking Aphasics

Type of Paraphasia	Example
Literal or Phonemic Paraphasias	
Omissions	perder → peder
Additions	camino → carmino
Displacement	tortuga → toturga
Substitutions	mesa → tesa
Verbal Paraphasias	
Formal verbal	cajetilla → carretilla
Morphologic verbal	nochemente
Semantic Verbal Paraphasias	
Same semantic field	nariz → oreja
antonyms	salir → entrar
Superordinate	caballo → animal
Proximity	papel → lápiz
Unrelated Verbal Paraphasias	casa → nariz
Syntagmatic Paraphasias	el acuario del pez → la jaula del león
Circumlocutions	
Object description	moneda → redonda, pequeña
Instrumental function	reloj → para la hora
Neologisms	camisa → surinja

Ardila and Rosselli (1993) analyzed the frequency of different types of paraphasias in Spanish-speaking aphasics. A sample of right-handed, monolingual Spanish-speaking aphasic patients with left hemisphere damage was selected. Paraphasias were scored and analyzed for the Picture Description (Plate #1, The Cookie Theft), Repetition (Words, High and Low Probability Sentences), and Naming (Responsive Naming, Confrontation, and Body Part Naming) subtests of the Boston Diagnostic Aphasia Examination, Spanish version (Goodglass & Kaplan, 1979). Unfortunately, frequency of different paraphasias are not readily available in other languages, and in consequence, it is difficult to know how these results compare with other languages (e.g., English).

Literal paraphasias are strongly associated with perisylvian aphasia syndromes. Frequency of literal paraphasias in other groups are very low. In the extrasylvian (transcortical) motor aphasia (dynamic aphasia), only some formal verbal paraphasias are present. In Broca aphasia patients, the frequency of literal paraphasias is very high due to phoneme omissions and substitutions. Although these patients present some other types of paraphasias, their frequency is low, and appear only in some individuals. In conduction aphasia syndrome, the frequency of literal paraphasias is particularly high. These patients present substitutions, but also omissions, additions, and displacements.

All the language deviation types are observed in Wernicke aphasia patients. Literal paraphasias and neologisms clearly predominate. In literal paraphasias, substitutions predominate. The total number of verbal paraphasias and literal paraphasias are roughly similar in frequency. Patients with anomia usually present semantic verbal paraphasias, due to substitutions within the same semantic field. Occasionally, superordinate words are used. Unrelated verbal paraphasias and literal paraphasias resulting from phoneme substitutions are infrequent.

The ratio of "literal paraphasias/verbal paraphasias" has been calculated for the different aphasic groups. This ratio is about 5 for Broca patients and close to 10 for conduction aphasia, implying a neat predominance of literal over verbal paraphasias. However, in Wernicke aphasia, this ratio is close to 1; that is, the amount of literal and verbal paraphasias is roughly equivalent. In extrasylvian (transcortical) motor aphasia, paraphasias are virtually absent; however, some verbal paraphasias were disclosed sporadically; literal paraphasia are not observed. In anomic patients, a noticeable amount of verbal semantic paraphasias is usually observed. Literal paraphasias are virtually absent, and the ratio of "literal paraphasias/verbal paraphasias" approaches to zero.

In summary, despite the fact that some language deviations clearly tend to predominate in specific forms of aphasia, this relation is far from being simple. However, much more cross-linguistic comparisons are obviously required.

GRAMMAR

A few research studies have analyzed the grammatical impairments associated with aphasia in Spanish (Benedet, Christiansen, & Goodglass, 1998; Ostrosky-Solis, Marcos-Ortega, Ardila, Rosselli, & Palacios, 1999; Reznik, Dubrovsky, & Maldonado, 1995). This research and the clinical experience of the author reveal the following:

1. The most sensitive sign of agrammatism in Spanish language is the omission of articles. This defect can be observed in naming tasks. When naming in Spanish, usually an article (definite or indefinite) is included. Patients with even very slight agrammatism tend omit the article when naming.

2. Spanish is a language with highly flexible word order. In cases of aphasia associated with agrammatism, however, this flexibility not only in language production but also in language understanding seems to be impaired.

3. Morphological errors are more frequent in Spanish than in English, as a result of the morphological complexity.

Analyzing the question of agrammatism in Spanish, Reznik et al. (1995) reported the case of a 55-year-old right-handed woman who presented an extensive right parieto-temporal cortical-subcortical infarction, with extension to the occipital lobe, discrete mass effect, and no frontal lobe enlargement. Severe aphasia and anarthria were initially observed and a diagnosis of crossed aphasia was proposed. Three months after onset, the patient's language had improved. The diagnosis of Broca aphasia was given, and grammatical analysis of oral language was performed. In the data analyzed, 535 words occurred, of which 51.03% were open-class words and 48.97% were closed-class words (grammatical formatives). This is similar to what is found in normal speech. Two types of defects were observed, however: (a) frequent omissions of clitic pronouns, and (b) a mild problem in the production of canonical word order at the sentence level.

Undoubtedly, this is an extremely unusual case, and in no sense can it be considered as representative of agrammatism in Spanish. The patient suffered an extensive posterior infarction in the right hemisphere. Three months after the cerebrovascular accident (CVA) onset, language recovery was virtually total. Indeed, the patient did not present any evident agrammatism (open-class words and grammatical formatives distribution was similar to that found in normal speech). Moreover, word order in Spanish language is extremely flexible, and the frequent productions of noncanonical sentences cannot be considered agrammatic. Only the omissions of clitic pronouns may be interpreted as agrammatism. It seems to represent an extremely selective form of agrammatism, and in no sense can be considered as the usual agrammatism found in Broca aphasia (Benson & Ardila, 1996).

On another study of agrammatism, Ostrosky-Solis et al. (1999) approached only the question of word order in Broca aphasia. Ten right-handed Spanish-speaking patients with Broca aphasia were selected using as diagnostic criteria the Western Aphasia Battery–Spanish version (Kertesz, Pascual-Leone, & Pascual-Leone, 1990). The Spanish Syntactic Comprehension Test developed by Marcos and Ostrosky (1995) was used. This is a standardized instrument used to assess the syntactic comprehension in Spanish language. A forced election task is used in which the subject listened to the 190 different reversible sentences and was asked to select, by pointing, one of four options presented on a plate. Each option contains a pair of animals performing a specific action, and only one option is correct. The four options corresponded to: (a) correct action and correct animal; (b) same action but performed by the inverse animal; (c) different action performed by the same animal action but performed by the inverse animal; and (d) same action performed by different pair of animals. Four pairs of animals (*lion-tiger, camel-horse, duck-rooster, rabbit-skunk*) and five different transitive verbs (*hit, kick, bite, pull,* and *pick*) are used, based on pragmatic knowledge that both animals are equally able to perform the action. In the Spanish Syntactic Comprehension Test, the effects of different factors are studied: sentence type, presence and absence of the preposition, and the use of the definite/indefinite article. Included in the test are 38 different types of sentences and five examples of each type of sentence.

Ostrosky-Solis et al. (1999) concluded that unlike normal Spanish-speaking subjects, patients with Broca aphasia do not use structural strategies in active sentences, such as the canonical order of the sentence; they do not use superficial signs, such as articles; and they cannot process passive sentences. Syntax complexity and canonical order do not affect subject performance—as long as the preposition "a" (to) is present, the subjects perform at the same level in sentences in which the order was canonical as those in which it was not. The authors proposed that in Broca aphasia there is morphology processing; however, patients do not process all the morphology because in passive sentences that contain two signs "por" (by) and the verbal termination "-ado," the results are at the chance level. Apparently, the preposition "a" (to) is resistant to brain damage because it is the strongest source of information in Spanish.

Benedet et al. (1998) compared six agrammatic Spanish-speaking Broca's aphasics with seven English-speaking Broca's aphasics. They used the Morphosyntax Battery developed in English by Goodglass, Christiansen, and Gallagher (1993), and a translated version in Spanish. When comparing the Spanish-speaking agrammatic patients to their English-speaking counterparts, they found that the relative difficulty of various grammatical constructions in both production and comprehension were strikingly similar, with two exceptions: (a) The Spanish speakers were better at producing subject/verb agreement, and (b) they were worse at comprehending both active and passive sentences. The authors proposed that the better production of subject/verb agreement could be accounted for by the higher cue validity of agreement in Spanish. The difficulty in comprehending active sentences was explained by the lower cue validity of word order in Spanish. And the great disparity between the two groups of patients in understanding passive voices was related to the lower frequency of the passive voice in Spanish. This study clearly illustrates the similarities and differences in agrammatism in different languages, despite comparing two relatively close languages, such a Spanish and English.

AGRAPHIA

Spanish possesses a phonologically transparent reading system, but a less transparent writing system. However, many words potentially can be written in different ways (orthographic rules) (e.g., the spoken word /muxer/ (woman) might be written "mujer" or "muger"; the first one corresponds to the accepted spelling), but read in only one way (e.g., "mujer"—as any word or pseudoword—can be read in only one way, as /muxer/). In other words, in Spanish there is some homophonic heterography, whereas homographic heterophony is absent (Table 6.5).

Two different types of errors can be made when writing in Spanish: (a) In *homophone errors* (usually referred in Spanish as *orthographic* errors; e.g., the word "mujer" is written as "muger"—both are read exactly the same and both phonologically represent the spoken word, /muxer/), the phonographemic conversion is correct, but it is not performed according to the accepted Spanish orthographic rules. (b) *Nonhomophone errors* (usually referred to in Spanish as "writing errors") are due to some letter additions, letter omissions, and letter substitution that change the written representation of the spoken word

TABLE 6.5
Phoneme–Grapheme Correspondence in Spanish Language

Phoneme	Grapheme
/b/	b, v
/s/	c (before e, i), s, z
/tʃ/	ch
/d/	d
/f/	f
/g/	g (before a, o, u) and gu (before e, i)
/i/	i, y (as a conjuction and in diphthongs)
/x/	j, g (before e, i)
/k/	c (before a, o, u) and qu (before e, i)
/l/	l
/ĺ/ or /j/	ll
/m/	m
/n/	n
/ɲ/	ñ
/p/	p
/r/	r
/ř/	rr, r (at the beginning of a word)
/t/	t
/k/ + /s/	x
/j/	y
–	h
/a/	a
/e/	e
/i/	i
/o/	o
/u/	u

(e.g., if the word /muxer/ were written as "muer"—"j" omission—it no longer corresponds to a phonographemic conversion of the spoken word /muxer/). The first type of error (homophone or orthographic) is very frequently observed in Spanish-speaking subjects, particularly in children and individuals of low educational levels. The second type (non-homophone) is extremely unusual, except in brain damaged individuals. The majority of Spanish-speaking people consider only the second type of error (nonhomophone) to be a real writing error, because graphophonemic reading results in a pseudoword. From the Spanish-language perspective, a word containing a homophone (orthographic) error is not a nonsense pseudoword. Homophone errors do not involve the substitution of a phoneme (in such a case, the error would be a nonhomophone error), but the substitution (or addition, or omission) of a letter that in a particular position results in a string of letters that are phonologically equivalent to the target word.

Ardila et al. (1996) analyzed writing errors made in Spanish. Two different general population groups were selected: third-grade children and adult individuals with a high level of education. Thus, an attempt was made to find out how normal people write in Spanish. The experimental group (14 brain damaged patients) was divided in three subgroups: (a) Broca aphasics, (b) Wernicke aphasics, and (c) right hemisphere damaged patients. The Boston Diagnostic Aphasia Examination, Spanish version (Goodglass & Kaplan, 1979), was administered to the patients with left hemisphere damage. According to the results obtained from this test battery, patients were classified as Broca and Wernicke aphasics.

A 95-word writing test was designed. Words were dictated to the subjects. Words were randomly mixed and orally dictated.

Two different types of errors were analyzed:

1. *Nonhomophone errors.* The frequency of letter substitutions, letter additions, letter omissions, letter interchanges, morpheme omissions, morpheme substitutions, and neologisms (non recognizable words) was calculated.

2. *Homophone errors.* Each word in the writing test was designed to elicit one specific type of orthographic error. Seven different types of orthographic (homophone) errors were distinguished. When a word presented several homophone errors (or a homophone error other than the intended one), all errors were counted.

Finally, correlations between word frequency and number of errors were calculated in the different subgroups.

Among Wernicke aphasics, letter substitution errors were observed frequently. Letter additions and letter omissions were also found. Morpheme substitutions were higher and morpheme omissions were lower than among Broca aphasia patients. Right hemisphere damaged patients presented a very low number of nonhomophone errors, especially letter substitutions, and letter omissions and additions were even less frequent in this group.

The percentage of normal subjects and brain damaged patients presenting with different types of homophone (orthographic) errors in the writing test was calculated. In all groups, a significant amount of homophone errors was observed. In Broca aphasics, the amount of homophone errors was similar to the amount observed in normal adults. The amount of homophone errors in patients with right hemisphere damage was roughly equivalent to the amount of these errors observed in third-grade schoolchildren. In Wernicke aphasics, the amount was even higher. However, homophone errors were made by each of the groups.

The previous results strongly suggest that normal Spanish-speakers with high levels of education can present a certain degree of dysorthography. Less than 10% of normal adults wrote the 95-word list without making any errors. Dysorthography was significantly increased in cases of brain damage, but only in right hemisphere damaged patients and in Wernicke aphasics. Evidently, in cases of Wernicke aphasia, as a consequence of language comprehension impairment, the patient writes real words as nonsense pseudowords, performing a direct phonographemic conversion. Thus, it can be posited that language comprehension defects in Spanish are at least partially responsible for the increased number of homophone errors found in this group of patients. Therefore, it might be proposed that dysorthography in the Spanish language is especially associated with right hemisphere pathology (Ardila, 1984).

Of interest, when making orthographic decisions, Spanish-speakers quite often have to write down the word in order to see "how it looks." The increased number of homophone errors found in cases of right hemisphere pathology gives credence to the hypothesis that orthographic knowledge for Spanish-speakers represents a visuoperceptual ability. The spelling of a word is an artificial (and nonsense) task when writing in Spanish. This also holds true for other languages with phonological writing systems (e.g., Italian, Russian, etc.).

In addition to the educational level and, no doubt, the subject's reading habits, orthographic ability in the Spanish language has been proposed to be associated with two additional factors: (a) It has been pointed out that reading-disabled individuals often misuse orthography as a long-term dyslexic sequel (Bravo-Valdivieso, 1982, 1988). (b) It has been emphasized that orthography knowledge in the Spanish language may reflect a kind of "metalinguistic knowledge," or "language insight" (R. Avila, 1982, personal communication). Orthography in Spanish clearly depends on the origins and evolution of words.

The number of homophone errors was not significantly associated with word frequency even though a tendency in this direction was quite evident. Homophone and nonhomophone errors were negatively, albeit nonsignificantly, correlated with word frequency.

Current psycholinguistic models of agraphias have been developed in English and partially in French, two languages with particularly irregular (from a phonological point of view) writing systems. The English reading/writing system does not represent a purely phonological system. It might be described as a compromise between the phonological and logographic principles (Sampson, 1985). Reading and writing of words is achieved partially by following specific grapheme/phoneme correspondence principles and partially following a visual "gestalt" recognition that is not necessarily analyzed into individual letters. It is reasonable that two different reading/writing systems have been proposed in the English language. Unfortunately, very few reports of alexia and agraphia in non-Indo-European languages are currently available (e.g., Al Alaoui-Faris et al., 1994).

Agraphia in the Spanish language is not easy to interpret using the current psycholinguistic models (Bub & Chertkow, 1988; Roeltgen, 1985). In Spanish, dysorthography might correspond to the lexical agraphia (dysgraphia) syndrome that includes difficulties for spelling irregular and ambiguous words with a preserved ability to spell regular words. The ability to write decreases, whereas the orthographic ambiguity of the target words increases. Usually these individuals tend to present a "regularization" in writing: The target word is written in such a way that can be phonologically correct, despite being orthographically incorrect (Beauvois & Drouesn, 1981; Berhmann & Bub, 1992; Hartfield & Patterson, 1983; Roeltgen, 1985; Roeltgen, Sevush, & Heilman, 1983; Shallice, 1981). If so, it has to be concluded that normal, highly educated Spanish-speakers can present a certain degree of lexical dysgraphia. Also, the severity of this "near-normal" lexical dysgraphia increases in cases of brain pathology, especially right hemisphere damage. Furthermore, in cases of brain pathology, lexical agraphia is not associated with aphasia.

Based on the aforementioned observations, it is evident that the concept of lexical (or surface) agraphia seems confusing when applied to Spanish writing.

Phonological agraphia is understood as the preserved ability to write familiar words, both regular and irregular; the inability to spell nonwords; the ability to use legitimate words, even if low frequency words that contain unusual spelling patterns are used; and the overt inability to write legitimate pseudowords under dictation. This type of agraphia has been described for English-speakers (Baxter & Warrington, 1985; Bub & Kertesz, 1982; Hartfield, 1985). The critical issue revolves around word frequency. Patients with phonological agraphia perform best when writing high frequency words, and worst when writing low frequency words (or nonwords). Even though this tendency has been pointed out in English using individual case analyses, it has not been corroborated in a large series of brain damaged patients. Analyzing both writing and orthographic errors, no statistically significant association with word frequency was observed in Spanish, even though a trend in this direction was found.

Alexander, Friedman, Loverso, and Fischer (1992) (based on their own cases and cases previously reported in literature) concluded that phonological agraphia can be produced by lesions in a wide range of perisylvian cortical regions that share a role in central phonological processing. In the patient sample, writing errors were primarily observed in cases of aphasia associated with left hemisphere pathology.

ALEXIA

Different strategies to represent spoken language have been developed in human history. A major division has been established between logographic and phonographic writing systems (Sampson, 1985). *Logographic* systems are those based on meaningful units (morphemes, words); *phonographic* systems are those based on phonological (sound) units. Under normal conditions, logographic reading is not required to read Spanish. The longest units that must be read as a whole are syllables composed of three letters (in letter combinations such as GUI and GUA).

It should be noted that during written-word recognition tasks in Spanish (lexical decision), both a word frequency and a wordlength effect are observed. It is remarkable that correlation with the number of syllables (phonological length) is higher than correlation with the number of letters in the word (Ardila, Rosselli, & Lecours, 1993). As a result, it seems reasonable to assume that the "reading unit" in Spanish may be the syllable, whereas the "reading unit" in English likely corresponds to the morpheme.

Wordlength and morphological complexity represent additional factors that should be taken into consideration when comparing English and Spanish reading tasks. Words in Spanish are, on average, longer than those in English. Similarly, Spanish word morphology is more complex. To a significant extent, English represents a monosyllabic language. To read short words in a direct way is obviously easier than to read longer words with a complex derivational system.

The reading unit (likely, the syllable) is usually meaningless in Spanish. In polysyllabic words (most words in the Spanish language), the word meaning is attained only after sequencing a string of syllables. This process evidently requires a phonological mediation. Conversely, in English the reading unit (likely, the morpheme) would be meaningful, and therefore, the reading system could be interpreted (at least partially) as a logographic system (Sampson, 1985).

Departing from these theoretical considerations and from direct clinical experience, it has been proposed that semantic paralexias, and consequently deep alexia, should be rather infrequent in Spanish (Ardila, 1991; Ardila, Rosselli et al., 1989). As a matter of fact, deep alexia is not expected to be found in Spanish-language reading, unless some logographic reading is present (e.g., when reading highly frequent logograms) (Ardila, 1991). This point of view, however, can be challenged (e.g., Valle-Arroyo, 1996), and recently four cases of semantic paralexias and deep alexia have been reported in Spanish-speaking aphasics (Dalmás, 1991; Diaz, 1995; Ferreres & Miravalles, 1995; Ruiz, Ansaldo, & Lecours, 1994). When comparing these four available cases of semantic paralexias and deep alexia in Spanish, which have been reported only recently, some common characteristics emerge:

1. The semantic paralexias were reported in all these patients only after a significant amount of time had elapsed since onset of their brain damage.

2. All of the patients had a high level of education. One of the patients was a research scientist (Diaz, 1995).

3. All the patients presented a motor-type aphasia.

4. After analyzing the samples of errors reported about each patient, it is evident that a large percentage of errors (and in some cases, most of the errors) can be classified as verbal morphological paralexias.

Landis, Regard, Graves, and Goodglass (1983) found, in an unselected sample of English-speaking aphasics, that over 50% presented one or several semantic paralexias in reading words. It is interesting to note that among their patients with semantic paralexias, some were of the fluent and others of the nonfluent type and even some patients presented a right visual field defect. No doubt, semantic paralexias in the English language can be observed in a quite heterogeneous group of aphasics, despite the fact that they are more frequently found in nonfluent, than in fluent, aphasics (Coltheart, Patterson, & Marshall, 1980). Landis et al. (1983) concluded that although semantic paralexias are produced in a lower rate by "common aphasics" than by "deep alexics," the fact that about half of unselected aphasics presented at least one paralexia indicates that semantic paralexias is actually a common phenomenon in English-speaking aphasics.

According to Coltheart (1982), if a language lacked homophones and alternative spellings of a single sound were impossible, then surface dyslexia could not exist. An example of this regularity could be found in the Italian language. Coltheart concluded that "none of the symptoms of surface dyslexia can be observed in Italian dyslexics" (p. 160). However, differences in reading strategy have to be taken into consideration.

Ardila, Rosselli, and Pinzón (1989) studied the reading errors in a sample of Spanish-speaking patients with left hemisphere pathology. Using standard classification criteria, patients were classified into five different groups: Extrasylvian (transcortical) motor aphasia (dynamic aphasia), Broca aphasia, conduction aphasia, Wernicke aphasia, and alexia without agraphia (left occipital damage). It was observed that literal substitutions repre-

TABLE 6.6

Percentage of Various Types of Reading Errors Observed in Different Groups
of Spanish-speaking Aphasic Patients

	Extrasylvian Motor	Broca	Conduction	Wernicke	Alexia w/o Agraphia
Literal substitutions	13	19	34	30	23
Literal omissions	27	30	10	13	2
Literal additions	7	7	10	5	7
Anticipations	0	18	10	3	0
Perseverations	0	24	5	3	14
Literal reading (letter-by-letter)	0	0	10	6	23
Word omissions	0	0	0	5	2
Neologisms (incomprehensible)	0	0	5	21	8
Pseudowords to meaningful words	53	2	10	8	4
Morphological Paralexias	0	0	6	6	17

Note: Adapted from Ardila, Rosselli, and Pinzón (1989). The reading test included 20 letters, 12 syllables, 13 words, 11 pseudowords, and 5 sentences.

sented the most frequent type of reading error, accounting for about one third of the total number of errors. In extrasylvian motor (dynamic) aphasia, there was a tendency to read pseudowords as real words. In Broca aphasia, literal omissions, anticipation, and perseveration errors predominated. The highest frequency of literal paralexias was found in conduction aphasia. In Wernicke's aphasia, all types of errors were found, especially literal substitutions and neologisms (reading words were incomprehensible). In alexia without agraphia (pure alexia), letter-by-letter reading and literal substitutions predominated. A significant amount of verbal morphological paralexias was observed in this group of patients with left occipital damage (Table 6.6).

Of note, when appropriate opportunities are provided (i.e., when frequently exposed to written language) to illiterate individuals, they usually learn to correctly recognize ("read") a great deal of written words, particularly logograms. Goldblum and Matute (1986) studied the impairments in this ability to "read" common words in a sample of brain damaged illiterate subjects. In cases of left, but not right, hemisphere pathology, this ability to "read" common words was impaired. Furthermore, in cases of "alexia" in illiterate individuals, a significant number of semantic paralexias was observed. However, semantic paralexias (semantic errors when recognizing words; e.g., instead of "reading" a particular beer brand, they "read" a different beer brand) are also frequently observed in normal non-brain-damaged illiterates. This type of semantic "paralexias" are also observed in literate Spanish-speaking aphasics (Ardila, 1991).

It seems reasonable to conclude that reading in the Spanish language takes place via the use of a graphophonemic strategy. This, however, does not prelude that eventually some other additional strategies can also be developed—for instance, when reading high frequency logograms, or when special reading training is provided. Table 6.7 presents some examples of writing and reading errors observed in Spanish-speaking alexics.

TABLE 6.7
Some Examples of Writing and Reading Errors in Spanish Language

Type of error	Example
Writing Errors	
Homophone (orthographic)	mujer → muger
Nonhomophone (writing)	
Letter additions	mujer → murjer
Letter omissions	mujer → muer
Letter substitution	mujer → mufer
Letter interchanges	mujer → jumer
Reading Errors	
Literal substitutions	MUJER → /muter/
Literal omissions	MUJER → /muer/
Literal additions	MUJER → /muexer/
Anticipations	MUJER → /murer/
Perseverations	MUJER → /mumer/
Literal reading	MUJER → /eme/, /u/, /xota/, /e/, /ere/
Word omissions	LA CASA ES GRANDE → /la kasa grande/
Neologisms (incomprehensible)	MUJER → /turina/
Pseudowords to meaningful words	TLA → la
Morphological paralexias	CAFETERIA → /kafetal/

In summary, even though semantic paralexias are actually a common phenomenon in English-speaking aphasics (Landis et al., 1983), they represent quite a rare and unusual phenomenon in the Spanish language. Most probably it is restricted to a very limited subsample of aphasic individuals: highly educated (and even eventually multilingual) patients with a motor type of aphasia, and after lengthy language therapy process. Semantic paralexias may be found in quite a diverse and heterogeneous group of aphasics in English-speaking aphasics. Of course, this is an area of relevance to U.S. Hispanics who may be bilingual, but whose primary language is Spanish.

Reading and writing can illustrate the enormous complexity of brain organization of any cognitive process. Supposedly, reading is based on certain fundamental abilities (e.g., complex shape perception, cross-modal learning, etc.) already in existence 5,000 years ago, and of course, present also in illiterate individuals. The human brain might be specialized ("wired") not for reading or writing per se, but for certain basic abilities (information-processing levels) required to read and to write, albeit not exclusively for either task. It does not seem reasonable to assume that some brain areas are specialized for reading or writing, in the same manner that it is unreasonable to assume that some brain areas are specialized for using computers. Basic cognitive abilities (information-processing levels) required to read and to write in Chinese, English, and Spanish do not seem to be completely coincidental.

CONCLUSIONS

An attempt has been made to summarize the main research studies dealing with aphasia, alexia, and agraphia that can be found in Spanish-speakers. As with any language, Spanish holds its own phonological, lexical, grammatical, semantic, and pragmatic particularities.

Given those particularities, a language disorder in Spanish must be understood within the following parameters:

1. Phonological errors are significantly found more frequently in vowels than in consonants. This is particularly true in cases of motor (Broca and conduction) aphasias. Errors in writing and reading in normal and reading-disabled children, are also significantly more frequent in vowels than in consonants. No doubt, this is related with the salience of vowels in Spanish.

2. Agrammatism in Spanish has certain idiosyncrasies related with the enormous flexibility of the word order, and the use of some prepositions to mark who is the agent and who is the patient in a sentence.

3. Literal paraphasias are about 10 times more frequent than verbal paraphasias in conduction aphasia. In Broca aphasia, they are about five times more frequent, whereas in Wernicke aphasia the amount of literal and verbal paraphasias is roughly equivalent. In patients with anomia, a very significant amount of verbal, especially semantic, paraphasias is observed, and literal paraphasias are virtually absent. It is difficult to know how these results can be applicable to other languages, as a consequence of the absence of cross-linguistic comparisons in aphasia. This is an area of special relevance for researchers interested in learning about language deficiencies among monolingual and bilingual Hispanics in the United States.

4. Two different writing errors are observed in the Spanish language: *homophone* (orthographic) and *nonhomophone* errors. Homophone errors are quite frequent even in normal individuals, but they increase in cases of brain pathology. Dysorthography seems to be most evident in cases of right hemisphere pathology.

5. Reading errors in Spanish include letter substitutions, anticipations, literal reading, reading of pseudowords as meaningful words, literal omissions, and literal additions. Morphological errors and letter-by-letter reading are frequently found in cases of left occipital damage associated with alexia without agraphia syndrome. Patients with prefrontal damage tend to read pseudowords as meaningful words. Neologistic reading is correlated with Wernicke aphasia.

6. Cognitive models of reading and writing developed in English do not seem to apply well to Spanish, even though some similarities can be found. This has a direct impact on the assessment task of neuropsychologists. Clearly, Spanish-language measures with a theoretical understanding of the previous issues must be developed to assess the ever-growing number of Spanish-speakers in the United States.

REFERENCES

Al Alaoui-Faris, M., Benbeland, F., Alaoui, C., Tahiri, L., Jiddane, M., Amarti, A., & Chkili, T. (1994). Alexia sans agraphie en langue Arabe: Etude neurolinguistique et IRM [Alexia without agraphia in Arab language: A neurolinguistic and MRI study]. *Revue Neurologique, 150,* 771–775.

Alexander, M. P., Friedman, R. B., Loverso, F., & Fischer, R. S. (1992). Lesion localization in phonological agraphia. *Brain and Language, 43,* 83–95.

Ardila, A. (1984). Right hemisphere participation in language. In A. Ardila & F. Ostrosky-Sols (Eds.) *The right hemisphere: Neurology and neuropsychology* (pp. 99–110). London: Gordon & Breach Science.

Ardila, A. (1991). Errors resembling semantic paralexias in Spanish-speaking aphasics. *Brain and Language, 41,* 437–455.

Ardila, A., Montañes, P., Caro, C., Delgado, F., & Buckingham, H. W. (1989). Phonological transformations in Spanish-speaking aphasics. *Journal of Psycholinguistic Research, 18,* 163–180.

Ardila, A., & Rosselli, M. (1992). Repetition in aphasia. *Journal of Neurolinguistics, 7,* 1–11.

Ardila, A., & Rosselli, M. (1993). Language deviations in aphasia: A frequency analysis. *Brain and Language, 44,* 165–180.

Ardila, A., Rosselli, M., & Lecours, A. R. (1993). Decision lexical en sujetos hispanoparlantes: efecto de la frecuencia y la longitud [Lexical decision in Spanish-speaking subjects: Frequency and length effects]. Montevideo (Uruguay): III Congreso Latinoamericano de Neuropsicología.

Ardila, A., Rosselli, M., & Ostrosky, F. (1996). Agraphia in Spanish-language. *Aphasiology, 10,* 723–739.

Ardila, A., Rosselli, M., & Pinzón, O. (1989). Alexia and agraphia in Spanish speakers: CAT correlations and inter-linguistic analysis. In A. Ardila & F. Ostrosky (Eds.), *Brain organization of language and cognitive processes* (pp. 147–175). New York: Plenum.

Avila, R. (1982). Personal communication to AA. Mexico, D.F.

Baxter, D. M., & Warrington, E. K. (1985). Category specific phonological dysgraphia. *Neuropsychologia, 23,* 653–666.

Beauvois, M. F., & Drouesn, J. (1981). Lexical or orthographic agraphia. *Brain, 104,* 21–49.

Benedet, M. J., Christiansen, J. A., & Goodglass, H. A. (1998). Cross-linguistic study of grammatical morphology in Spanish- and English-speaking agrammatic patients. *Cortex, 34*(3), 309–336.

Benson, D. F., & Ardila, A. (1996). *Aphasia: A clinical perspective.* New York: Oxford University Press.

Berhmann, M., & Bub, D. (1992). Surface dyslexia and dysgraphia: Dual routes, single lexicon. *Cognitive Neuropsychology, 9,* 209–252.

Blanken, G. (1990). Formal paraphasias: A single case study. *Brain and Language, 38,* 534–554.

Blumstein, S. E. (1988). Approaches to speech production deficits in aphasia. In F. Boller, J. Grafman, G. Rizzolati, & H. Goodglass (Eds.), *Handbook of neuropsychology* (Vol 1, pp. 349–365). Amsterdam: Elsevier.

Bub, D., & Chertkow, H. (1988). Agraphia. In F. Boller, F. Grafman, G. Rizzolatti, & H. Goodglass (Eds.), *Handbook of Neuropsychology* (Vol. 1, pp. 393–414). Amsterdam: Elsevier.

Bub, D., & Kertesz, A. (1982). Evidence for lexicographic processing in a patient with preserved written over oral single word naming. *Brain, 105,* 697–711.

Buckingham, H. W. (1981a). Lexical and semantic aspects of aphasia. In M. T. Sarno (Ed.), *Acquired aphasia* (pp. 269–307). New York: Academic Press.

Buckingham, H. W. (1981b). Where do neologisms come from? In J. Brown (Ed.), *Jargonaphasia* (pp. 57–75). New York: Academic Press.

Buckingham, H. W. (1989a). Mechanisms underlying aphasic transformations. In A. Ardila & F. Ostrosky (Eds.), *Brain organization of language and cognitive processes* (pp. 123–145). New York: Plenum.

Buckingham, H. W. (1989b). Phonological paraphasia. In C. Code (Ed.), *The characteristics of aphasia* (pp. 77–116). London: Taylor & Francis.

Buckingham, H. W., & Kertesz, A. (1976). *Neologistic jargon aphasia.* Amsterdam: Zwets and Zeitlinger.

Bravo-Valdivieso, L. (1982). Dislexia, maduración e integración de funciones cerebrales [Dyslexia, maturation and brain function integration]. *Avances en Psicologia Clínica Latinoamericana, 1,* 111–127.

Bravo-Valdivieso, L. (1988). Las dislexias: investigación en Latinoamerica [Dyslexias: Research in Latin America]. In A. Ardila & F. Ostrosky-Sols (Eds.), *Lenguaje oral y escrito* [Oral and written language] (pp. 172–193). Mexico: Trillas.

Coltheart, M. (1982). The psycholinguistic analysis of acquired dyslexia: Some illustrations. *Philosophical Transactions of the Royal Society of London, B298,* 151–164.

Coltheart, M., Patterson, K., & Marshall, J. (Eds.). (1980). *Deep dyslexia.* London: Routledge & Kegan Paul.

Dalmás, F. (1991). Personal communication, Montevideo (Uruguay).

Diaz, A. R. (1995). *Afasia motora aferente: Estudio de un caso* [Afferent motor aphasia: A case study]. Puebla (Mexico): Benemrita Universidad Autnoma de Puebla.

Ferreres, A. R., & Miravalles, G. (1995). The production of semantic paralexias in Spanish-speaking aphasics. *Brain and Language, 49,* 153–162.

Goodglass, H., & Kaplan, E. (1979). *Evaluación de las afasias y de trastornos similares* [Assessment of aphasia and related disorders]. Buenos Aires: Editorial Médica Panamericana.

Goodglass, H., Christiansen, J. A., & Gallagher, R. (1993). Comparison of morphology and syntax in free narrative and structured tests: Fluent vs. nonfluent aphasics. *Cortex, 29,* 377–407.

Goldblum, M. C., & Matute, E. (1986). Are illiterate people deep dyslexics? *Journal of Neurolinguistics, 2,* 103–114.

Green, E. (1969). Phonological and grammatical aspects of jargon in an aphasic patient. *Language and Speech, 12,* 103–118.

Hartfield, M. F. (1985). Visual and phonological factors in acquired agraphia. *Neuropsychologia, 23,* 13–29.

Hartfield, F. M., & Patterson, K. (1983). Phonological spelling. *Quarterly Journal of Experimental Psychology, 35,* 451–458.

Kertesz, A., Pascual-Leone, P., & Pascual-Leone, G. (1990). *Bateria de las afasias Wertern* [The Wertern Aphasia Battery]. Valencia (Spain): Nau Libres.

Landis, T., Regard, M., Graves, R., & Goodglass, H. (1983). Semantic paralexia: A release of right hemispheric function from left control. *Neuropsychologia, 21,* 359–364.

Lecours, A. R. (1975). Methods for the description of aphasic transformation of language. In E. H. Lenneberg & E. Lenneberg (Eds.), *Foundations of language development* (Vol. 2, pp. 75–92). New York: Academic Press.

Lecours, A. R., & Lhermitte, F. (1972). Recherches sur le langage des aphasiques: 4. Analyse d'un corpus de nologismes (notion de paraphasie monmique). *Enchephale, 61,* 295–315.

Lecours, A. R., & Rouillon, F. (1976). Neurolinguistic analysis of jargonaphasia and jargonagraphia. In H. Whitaker & H. Whitaker (Eds.), *Studies in neurolinguistics* (Vol. 2, pp. 221–241). New York: Academic Press.

Lecours, A. R., Trepagnier, C., Naesser, C. J., & Lavelle-Huynh, G. (1983). The interaction between linguistics and aphasiology. In A. R. Lecours, F. Lhermitte, & B. Bryans (Eds.), *Aphasiology* (pp. 170–193). London: Bailliere Tindall.

Liederman, J., Kohn, S., Wolf, M., & Goodglass, H. (1983). Lexical creativity during instances of word-finding difficulty: Broca's versus Wernicke's aphasia. *Brain and Language, 20,* 21–32.

Marcos, J., & Ostrosky, F. (1995). Estrategias para la asignación de papeles temáticos en la interpretación de enunciados en español [Strategies for the assignment of thematic roles in the interpretation of Spanish statements]. In D. Pool (Ed.), *Estudios en linguistica formal* (pp. 75–102). Mexico, D.F.: El Colegio de México.

Ostrosky-Solis, F., Marcos-Ortega, J., Ardila, A., Rosselli, M., & Palacios, S. (1999). Syntactic comprehension in Broca's aphasic Spanish-speaking patients: Null effects of word order. *Aphasiology, 13,* 553–571.

Reznik, M., Dubrovsky, S., & Maldonado, S. (1995). Agrammatism in Spanish: A case study. *Brain and Language, 51,* 355–358.

Roeltgen, D. (1985). Agraphia. In K. M. Heilman & E. Valenstein (Eds.), *Clinical neuropsychology* (2nd ed., pp. 63–90). New York: Oxford University Press.

Roeltgen, D., Sevush, S., & Heilman, K. M. (1983). Phonological agraphia, writing by the lexical-semantic route. *Neurology, 33,* 755–765.

Ruiz, A., & Ansaldo, A. I., & Lecours, A. R. (1994). Two cases of deep dyslexia in unilingual Hispanophone aphasics. *Brain and Language, 46,* 245–257.

Ryalls, J., Valdois, S., & Lecours, A. R. (1988). Paraphasia and jargon. In F. Boller, J. Grafman, G. Rizzolati, & H. Goodglass (Eds.), *Handbook of neuropsychology* (Vol. 1, pp. 227–236). Amsterdam: Elsevier.

Sampson, G. (1985). *Writing systems.* Stanford, CA: Stanford University Press.

Shallice, T. (1981). Phonological agraphia and lexical route in writing. *Brain, 104,* 412–429.

Valle-Arroyo, F. (1996). Dual-route models in Spanish: Developmental and neuropsychological data. In M. Carreiras, J. E. Garcia-Albea, & N. Sebastian-Galles (Eds.), *Language processing in Spanish* (pp. 89–118). Mahwah, NJ: Lawrence Erlbaum Associates.

Pediatric Assessment

José J. Gonzalez
Los Angeles Unified School District
USC School of Medicine

The application of neuropsychological theory and methods to clinically evaluate Spanish-speaking adults is still under much debate and scrutiny. However, if minimal progress has been made to create more appropriate assessment procedures for Hispanic adults, the field of neuropsychological assessment of Spanish-speaking children is even less developed. Myriads of issues have led to concern about the use of standardized tests with Hispanic children. As our knowledge base with this group increases, the expectations for standardized instruments have become more stringent and more complex (Cummins, 1989; Figueroa, 1989; Hartlage & Williams, 1997; Lopez, 1997). Cultural plurality has posed a challenge to the assessment of cognitive skills from the early days of testing. Between 1901 and 1910, over nine million immigrants entered the United States. Today, an estimated 9% of Hispanic children living in the United States were born abroad (U.S. Census Bureau, 1997). In addition, 32 million Americans (13%) speak a language other than English at home. The largest percentage (17.3%) speaks Spanish at home. The creation of new tests (i.e. Batería–R, WLPB–R, EIWN) has not proved sufficient to meet the assessment and diagnostic needs of a multicultural ethnic group because new tests cannot preclude poor interpretation. In many cases clinicians choose the wrong test and make inappropriate interpretations of the data (Shepard, 1989). Interpretations have often been simplistic and culturally bound, showing a lack of appreciation for cultural differences and traditions (Armour-Thomas, 1992; Cummins, 1984; Dana, 1996; Hamayan & Damico, 1991; Kayser, 1987). The issues pertaining to the use of interpreters, acculturation factors, and cultural nuances have been discussed elsewhere in the book, this chapter focuses on providing a comprehensive guide to what instruments are available, what their psychometric properties are, relevant research on the instruments, and a clinical framework to use in the assessment of bilingual children. The idea is to give readers a set of tools, from which they can choose in order to create a comprehensive neuropsychological battery to assess Hispanic children.

Before any discussion about assessing Hispanic children, be aware of key issues: (a) Latino/Hispanic children are a highly heterogenous group and (b) Latino/Hispanic parents play a unique role in the assessment process (i.e., Pontón & Ardila, 1999). Hispanics are an unusually multicultural group, characterized by individuals with diverse values, religious beliefs, and socioeconomic and educational backgrounds. Most remarkably, its language unifies this heterogeneous group: Spanish. However, although a Mexican individual can read and understand a newspaper from Chile, and a Chilean can do the same with a newspaper from Spain, when it comes to colloquial expressions that pertain to social life, the simililarities end. These variations impact assessment, because the arena of evaluation involves social/functional domains. In addition, when assessing any child, the examiner must consider the background and experiences of the parent. Hispanic parents play a crucial role in the assessment process because of their expectations of the doctor and patient relationship, their level of sophisticiation, and their ability to navigate through the educational system. Taking into account the inherent diversity within this group, this discussion attempts to make sense of the materials available to assess these children.

The utility of standardized tests for minority children or non-English-speaking children has been questioned on numerous occasions (i.e., Figueroa, 1990; Lam, 1993). Standardized tests have come under greater scrutiny because of their use or misuse rather than because of their content. The controversy of the misuse of testing with Hispanics has been well documented (Sandoval, Frisby, Geisinger, Scheuneman, & Grenier, 1998).

Many assessors today make the faulty assumption that once bilingual children can speak English, they can complete cognitive tasks, especially higher order tasks and also complete academic tasks in English. Second language acquisition is a lengthy, developmental process whereby students whose native language is not English acquire listening, speaking, reading, and writing skills in English from over 5 to 10 years (Cummins, 1984). In order to understand, evaluate, and serve this increasing popualtion of monolingual Spanish and bilingual children with limited English proficiency, psychologists need to understand second language acquistion. Not only is it necessary that the psychologists assess children's native langauge (Spanish), but they must also assess the children's secondary language (English) and how these two languages interplay and co-develop.

As a result, the psychologists need to take into account language proficiency. But, how do psychologists decide in which language to assess the bilingual child? Obviously, they would like to have the time and resources to assess both languages, if possible, yet this is not always plausible. The information gathered by the bilingual neuropsychological, testing a bilingual child, involves many facets of the evaluation: developmental history gathering, assessment of formalized/standardized scores, qualitative assessment of language output, and quantity and quality of schooling. Finally, based on all this information, the student is assessed in a formal setting with standardized tests. What is deemed the dominant language is assessed first. Then, depending on the fluency and level of the child's secondary language, it will also need to be assessed, either formally or informally, again depending on the level and fluency.

This chapter provides a description of each major test used with bilingual Hispnaic children. Hence, language, cognitive functioning, and academic performance tests are reviewed. For each test, data assessing test bias through content validity, construct validity, and predictive validity are provided.

THE PSYCHOMETRIC APPROACH

The term *bias,* or *statistical bias,* is defined as constant or systematic error, in contrast to chance or random error, in the estimation of some value. In the context of this chapter, bias refers to psychological testing, in particular to the estimation of a score on a psychological test. Detailed methods for evaluating item bias are not reviewed and the reader is referred to other work for further review of that topic (Hambleton, Clauser, Mazor, & Jones, 1993; Kadlec, 1999; Kazdin, 1998).

Although there are many psychometric issues to be judged in selecting an instrument for use with Hispanic/Latino children, only a few are discussed here. Assuming the intended purpose for a test has been clarified, the next step is to consider the content of each test. After assessing the content of each test, the technical properties of the test must be evaluated. Finally, a number of more practical concerns are required to decide which test is to be used. This chapter hopes to provide some assistance in this process. Due to the abundance of available tests (whether they be commercially available, translated, or used locally), only a brief overview of the most commonly used tests is given.

A thorough evaluation of tests consists of assessing technical information, such as the normative data, reliability, and validity. The representativeness of the standardization sample should be evaluated. The reliability of the test should be assessed in relation to the intended uses and decisions made. In other words, the consistency of measurement (stability) should be evaluated and deemed acceptable (i.e. .80 or higher). In addition, the validity or the extent that a test measures what it reports it is measuring is extremely important. The appropriateness with which inferences can be made on the basis of the test results is essential in clinical practice. Three basic aspects of validity are content, criterion, and construct validity. Unless the test is reliable and valid, the tests can not be used to make individual assessment and diagnostic classifications, and placement decisions cannot be made.

Although this chapter provides some assistance in evaluating tests, questions related to the cross-cultural use of identical/equivalent tests, equivalence of translated tests, and bias in inferences and interpretation of scores still need to be addressed and answered within this population.

LANGUAGE FUNCTIONING

For decades, clinicians have and continue to ignore language when assessing a bilingual child. This practice is unethical. Research touts language as the cornerstone of cognitive development and general ability (Crawford & Parker, 1989; Hartlage & Williams, 1997). Therefore, the practices of only using nonverbal measures, translating a test not normed or standardized for Spanish-speakers, and using interpreters to express nuances to others, avoids the direct assessment of language functioning. By not assessing language (correctly), only a partial and fairly limited neuropsychological picture of the child can be obtained. This section presents a guide to assessing bilingual children.

How do you decide in which language to assess the bilingual child? Obviously, clinicians would like to have the time and resources to assess both languages (Spanish/English), if possible. But, if they cannot, then the following will serve as a guide. First, language in the classroom or in the learning environment (see Fig. 7.1) must be assessed. What is the language of instruction? Is it Spanish, English, or both? What language is spoken at recess/nutrition and lunch among peers? Second, what language is the child exposed to at home? The parents' language, media exposure, and language spoken among other adults and among siblings must be assessed. Third, the language the student prefers in informal settings and among siblings must be assessed. Finally, the student is assessed in a formal setting with standardized tests (discussed later). Given all this infor-

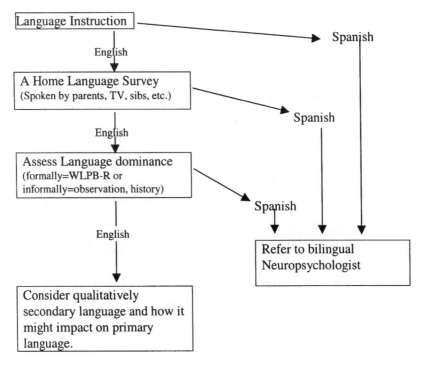

FIG. 7.1   Language assessment flow chart.

mation, hopefully it becomes clear that bilingual neuropsychological testing of children involves many facets of evaluation: thorough developmental history gathering, assessment of formalized/standardized scores, qualitative assessment of language output (Do children use a place holder for a word not known or do they use the languages interchangeably ["code switching"]?) (The latter is more indicative of a greater degree of bilingualism than the prior.), and quantity and quality of schooling. In any case, the bottom line is what language is assessed first (i.e., language dominance). Then, some idea of their secondary language needs to be assessed, both formally and/or informally.

The following tests measure language functioning in the bilingual child, which clinicians can use to proceed appropriately in their assessment of this population. Decisions of which tests to use should follow the decision tree of Fig. 7.1.

Woodcock Language Proficiency Battery–Revised

The Woodcock Language Proficiency Battery–Revised (WLPB–R; Woodcock, 1991) measures oral language, reading and written language abilities and achievement. The battery also provides an overall measure of English-language competence (Broad English Ability) and also evaluates the individual's oral language, reading, and written language strengths and weaknesses (intra-English discrepancies).

The WLPB–R standardization sample was selected from the Woodcock-Johnson Psycho-Educational Battery–Revised normative data. The final WLPB–R sample was randomly selected and controlled for community/subject variables (e.g. race, household income). The WLPB–R sample consisted of 705 preschool children (ages 2 to 5 and not enrolled in kindergarten), 3,245 school-age subjects (kindergarten through Grade 12), 916 college/university subjects, and 1,493 adult nonschool English-speaking subjects.

Reliability

Internal Consistency Reliability. WLPB–R reliabilities generally are in the high .80s and low .90s for the tests and in the mid-.90s for the clusters, with only one subtest (Listening Comprehension) falling below .70 (Listening Comprehension, .664) at age 13.

Alternate-Forms Reliability. The sample for the alternate-forms reliability of the Handwriting scale included Grade 3, Grade 7, college, and adults. Reliability correlations were .78, .72, .78, and .74, respectively.

Interrater Reliability. Interrater reliabilities were obtained for the WLPB–R Writing Samples, Writing Fluency, and Handwriting subtests. The sample for the Writing Sample subtest was selected from the original Grade 2, Grade 9, and Grade 16 subjects from which an intercorrelation of about .90 was observed. Two years later, after scoring rules and criteria had been improved, a sample of Grade 3, high school, and college subjects produced an intercorrelation of about .98. Finally, a third study consisted of a sample of learning disabled subjects and showed an intercorrelation of .93. The Writing Fluency subtest and the Handwriting subtest sample consisted of Grade 3, Grade 7, college, and adult subjects and showed an intercorrelation of about .98 and .78, respectively.

Validity

Content Validity. Items included in the various tests were selected using item validity studies as well as expert opinion.

Concurrent Validity. Several concurrent validity studies are reported in the manual. A preschool study (30–43 months) showed relatively low correlations on the WLPB–R Dictation test, which is not a measure of oral language, with the criterion measures and relatively high correlation of the Broad English Ability cluster with all criterion measures. The WLPB–R Memory for Sentences test shows the highest correlation with the Stanford–Binet IV Memory for Sentences test (.647). Similarly, the WLPB–R Picture Vocabulary test showed the highest correlations with the Stanford–Binet IV Vocabulary (.712) and Verbal Reasoning (.733) tests.

Woodcock Language Proficiency Battery–Revised, Spanish

The Spanish Form of the Woodcock Language Proficiency Battery–Revised (WLPB–R, Spanish; Woodcock & Muñoz-Sandoval, 1995) measures oral language, reading and written language abilities and achievement. The battery also provides an overall measure of Spanish-language competence (Amplia habilidad en Español) and also evaluates the individual's oral language, reading, and written language strengths and weaknesses (discrepancias intra-español).

Two new interpretation features have been added to the Spanish WLPB–R that are not provided in the English edition. First, there is a rating of language proficiency level based on predicted performance in instructional situations requiring cognitive-academic language proficiency. Second, there is the Comparative Language Index/Indice de comparacion de idiomas (CLI) that allows for direct comparison of Spanish and English language proficiencies in a single index.

Both forms of the WLPB–R measure the same abilities and contain parallel tests and clusters. The translation process involved approximately 30 examiners in 5 Spanish-speaking countries and a board of consulting editors. The item data were Rasch-calibrated separately for each of the five regions. Extensive renorming, additions, and revisions were added to the Spanish WLPB–R from the Spanish WLPB.

The Spanish WLPB–R sample consisted of approximately 2,000 Spanish-speaking subjects from Costa Rica, Mexico, Peru, Puerto Rico, and Spain and 1,325 bilingual subjects were tested in the United States (Arizona, California, Florida, New York, and Texas).

The tasks underlying each Spanish test are rescaled according to the empirical difficulty of counterpart tasks in English. Two thousand native Spanish-speaking subjects participated in the calibration-equating data procedures. As a result, the Spanish test scores have been calibrated, so that the English norms can be used with the Spanish test. The English and Spanish test versions' scores are then acquired from one set of norms (English).

Reliability

The manual does not summarize reliability results; instead, they list two tables. One table lists reliability coefficients for each WLPB–R, Spanish subtest that were generally in the .80s and .90s. Remaining reliability coefficients were in the .70s with four subtests falling below .70 (Correccion de textos "Proofing": .51; age 6). The second table listed WLPB–R, Spanish cluster reliability coefficients that were generally in the .90s. Only three cluster reliability coefficients were in the .80s, Amplia habilidad en lenguaje escrito (Broad Written Skills) at .88 (age 13), Destrezas basicas en escritura (Basic Written Skills) at .86 (age 6), and Expresion escrita (Written Expression) at .89 (age 13).

Validity

The manual refers the reader to Chapter 7 of the WLPB–R, English Examiner's Manual. Then the manual states that the WLPB–R English and Spanish batteries are parallel in content and structure and therefore the English WLPB–R results are generalizable to the Spanish WLPB–R. The manual also lists validity studies that are unique to the Spanish WLPB–R. The first is a concurrent validity study with 70 kindergarten limited-English-proficient students that found a correlation between the WLPB–R Oral Language/Lenguaje oral cluster with the Language Rating Scale, Language Rating Scale (PreLAS), and the Woodcock–Muñoz Language Survey English and Spanish Forms (W–MLS). A second concurrent validity study looked at 120 Grade 2 limited-English-proficient students and found that the WLPB–R Oral Language was correlated with the Oral Language Proficiency Test I (IDEA; .678), the Language Rating Scale (LRS; .407), and the Language Assessment Scales (LAS; .468). The intercorrelations between the IDEA, the LRS, and the LAS were .209, .260, and .172, respectively. Therefore, the manual concludes that the WLPB–R Oral Language is more comprehensive, measuring the content of the other three tests. However, the other three tests do not measure the same content among themselves.

Conclusion

A reliability and validity summary is provided by the manual: The reliability and validity characteristics of both forms of the WLPB–R meet basic technical requirements for both individual placement and programming decisions and are especially suited to meet certain assessment needs in bilingual education. Yet, the data/studies provided in the manual do not clearly support this statement for the Spanish form of the WLPB–R. At the present time, more studies are needed on the WLPB-R Spanish test to demonstrate its reliability and validity with bilingual/monolingual Spanish-speaking children.

Yet, the wide age range and breadth of coverage are important advantages (strengths) underlying use of the Spanish and English forms of the WLPB–R for clinical purposes or for research on language abilities with subjects from the preschool to geriatric level.

Peabody Picture Vocabulary Test-III

The PPVT–III is an individually administered test of hearing vocabulary, available in two separate forms (Dunn & Dunn, 1997). Due to its recent release, their is limited research on it. Thus, the PPVT–R (the previous verison) is reviewed here. Due to research studies reporting on items that were biased culturally, sexually, regionally, and racially, only 144 of the original 300 stimulus words were retained from the PPVT to the PPVT–R. The PPVT–R test plates attempted careful sex and ethnic balance on the plates containing humans. Final plate selection included 54% male figures, 46% female figures, 68% Anglo figures, 13% Black, 6% Indian or Mexican, 5% Oriental, 8% indefinite classification (Dunn & Dunn, 1981). The subject's task is to select the picture considered to illustrate best the meaning of a stimulus word presented orally by the examiner. The test is designed for persons age 2½ through 40 who can see and hear reasonably well, and understand standard English to some degree. The PPVT–R was standardized and normed nationally between 1976 and 1980 on a sample of 5,028 persons (4,200 children and adolescents, and 828 adults).

The standardization for ages 2½ through 18 years was based on the 1970 U.S. Census and contained chronological and sex balance. A total of 200 persons were included within each of 21 age groups (100 male, 100 female). Geographic representation was comprised of four regions of the United States as defined by the 1970 Census (Northeast, South, North, Central, and West). Alaska, Hawaii, plus U.S. territories were excluded. Occupation of the major wage earner in the family was used to ensure appropriate socioeconomic representation in the standardization sample. Ethnic representation was similar to that of the U.S. population based also on the 1970 Census. Hispanic children included Mexican, Puerto Rican, Cuban, and other Spanish heritage. The category "other" included Indian, Japanese, Chinese, Filipino, and all other races not classified as Black, White, or Hispanic. Subjects were selected from three types of communities—cities, suburbs or small towns, and rural areas—to match the total U.S. population by community size for persons under age 19. Standardization for ages 19 through 40 years was comprised of approximately 200 adults in each of four age groups with equal male and female representation. Geographic representation included the four regions previously discussed, except that the North Central and Western regions were overrepresented, and the Northeast and Southern regions were underrepresented. Occupational representation was the same as the younger sample; however, ethnic and community representation data were not gathered.

Reliability

Coefficients of internal consistency included split-half reliabilities on Form L and M for children and youth (ages 2½ through 18). The range was from .67 to .88 on Form L (median .80), and from .61 to .86 on Form M (median .81). Thus, the split-half reliabilities for Forms L and M are quite similar. Specifically, on Form L, a .67 reliability was noted for the 2-6 through 2-11 age group (all others were above .70) and on Form M, a .61 reliability was noted for the 7-0 through 7-11 age group (all others were above .70).

The median split-half reliability for the adult standardization sample was .82; however, only Form L was administered.

Immediate retest alternate form raw score reliability coefficients for ages 2½ through 18 ranged from .71 to .89, with a median of .79. Delayed retest raw score reliabilities (minimum 9 days and maximum 31 days) ranged from .52 to .90, with a median value of .78, and coefficients for standard scores ranged from .54 to .90, with a median of .77. Overall, based on median values, the reliabilities dropped very little from immediate retesting to delayed retesting. In general, the revised PPVT is a slightly more reliable measure than the original PPVT. The overall reliability of the PPVT–R appear to be satisfactory. The characteristics of the items within each form are quite consistent and comparable. Alternate forms are closely parallel, and the scores remain relatively stable for periods of up to 1 month (Dunn & Dunn, 1981).

Validity

Content Validity.   A complete search was made of *Webster's New Collegiate Dictionary* (1953) for all words whose meanings could be depicted by a picture. This dictionary was assumed to represent the content universe for hearing vocabulary, with the restriction that words that could not be illustrated were omitted.

Construct Validity.   Words were generally included when they fit the curve for hearing vocabulary established by using the Rasch–Wright latent trait model. On the other hand, conventional percentage passing data for each age were available for each item. Items with too steep or flat an item characteristic curve tended to be those not fitting the Rasch–Wright latent trait curve for hearing. The fundamental rule for including items was that, for each successive age group, the percentage of subjects responding correctly to the item must increase gradually. This criterion was fulfilled.

Criterion-Related Validity.   No predictive validity data were available when the manual was published for the PPVT–R. Except for the results of the study equating the original and revised editions, there are also no concurrent validity data.

Validity studies have shown that these scales correlate well with other vocabulary tests and with many individual tests of verbal intelligence. The manual refers the reader to the PPVT–R Technical Supplement (Robertson & Eisenberg, 1981).

Test de Vocabulario en Imagenes Peabody

The Test de Vocabulario en Imagenes Peabody (TVIP; Dunn, Padilla, Lugo, & Dunn, 1986) is a Spanish-language, Hispanic-American adaptation of the PPVT–R, which measures an individual's receptive or hearing vocabulary of single Spanish words spoken by the examiner. Overall, some features are unique to the Spanish-language adaptation, but most of its content was retained from the PPVT and PPVT–R editions. The TVIP is unique in that the stimulus words are in standard, universal Spanish, which is used to some degree in all countries where Spanish is spoken. The TVIP drawings are free of obvious "Americanisms" and include a balance of age, ethnic group, and sex. There is a wide age range of 2½ to 18 years and the norms were developed from testing monolingual, Spanish-speaking students in Latin America. The manual describes how the Latin American sample allows for a consistent frame of reference rather than shifting bilingual subjects in the United States who heavily rely on a mix of English and Spanish while growing up.

Finally, separate norms for Puerto Rico and Mexico are provided, in addition to composite norms from both places.

The TVIP should be viewed as an achievement test, because it shows the extent of Spanish vocabulary acquisition of the subject. It may also be seen as a screening test of scholastic aptitude (verbal ability or verbal intelligence); however, it should be considered as such only when Spanish is the primary language spoken in the home and community into which the subject was born, has grown up, resides, and when Spanish is, and has been, the primary language of instruction at school. The TVIP can also be used as one element in a comprehensive test battery of cognitive processes. In general, the TVIP can be used in educational, clinical, or research settings as a measure of achievement, to establish rapport, to identify the language of instruction, to monitor Spanish-language growth/retention, for pre-school testing, to test handicapped children, to measure scholastic aptitude of school-age children, to test at the college or university level, to conduct research, or to complete a test battery.

Prior to the TVIP, some Spanish translations (most nonstandardized) included U.S. Puerto Rican, Cuban, and Mexican versions that relied on norms from the English-language editions. Thereafter, the TVIP was developed. Initially, Spanish instructors in Hawaii translated the 350 English edition words (175 Form L & 175 Form M) into Castilian. Castilian was chosen because it was considered universal. This list of 350 words was then evaluated and edited by psychologists in Mexico. As a result, some words that were specific to the Mexican language were substituted for the universal Castilian words. Field testing was then conducted in the federal district of Mexico (metropolitan area). Translations of Forms L and M of the PPVT–R were administered in late summer 1981 in counterbalanced order to a small sample of 323 children (156 male, 167 female). A final 175 items were selected from the original 350 items and were then rank ordered according to the level of difficulty.

The Mexican testing program was developed and standardization took place between September 1981 and November 1982. The 175 items were administered to 1,219 children, ages 2-6 through 15-11, from public schools in Mexico City and surrounding communities (598 male, 621 female). To the degree possible, schools and subjects were randomly selected; however, social economic status, rural areas, and private schools were not included. The Puerto Rican testing program subsequently reviewed the 175 words used by the Mexican testing program and omitted eight of the items because they were not believed to be of common usage of the Puerto Rican dialect. The remaining 167 items were administered to a school-age sample of 1,488 subjects (747 male, 741 female), which were selected from three large, representative public schools and two private schools from a metropolitan area, and from three public schools in a small town. The pre-school sample was drawn primarily from nurseries and homes in the San Juan metropolitan area, which included low-income homes in public housing projects. As much as possible, the subjects were randomly selected and the sampling plan was structured to take into account age, sex, size of community, type of school (public or private), and socioeconomic status of the home. The Puerto Rican standardization process took place from September 1982 through February 1983.

Instead of testing a separate sample for item calibration, test data from both standardization samples were used. Items were calibrated using the Rasch-Wright one-parameter latent-trait model (Wright & Stone, 1980), which allowed for more precise calibration of item difficulty estimates, making the test equally sensitive over the full range of younger to older groups. In addition, use of the Rasch–Wright item difficulty estimates permitted identification of items showing significant discrepancies between Puerto Rican and Mexican standardization samples so that these items could be considered for possible elimination. As a result of using both the Rasch–Wright item calibration and traditional item analysis procedures, 42 items were eliminated from the initial pool of 175 items, in addition to the 8 items dropped before the Puerto Rican administration. Therefore, the final edition of the TVIP contains 125 items. Overall, there was a slight superiority of the Mexican sample between ages 3½ and 6 years, apparently the result of over sampling of children from higher socioeconomic areas at these ages. Also, differences between the Mexico and Puerto Rican norms and those developed for the combined sample are slight. Therefore, the manual therefore recommends the combined set of norms for general use.

Validity

The TVIP claims to measure directly the extent of hearing vocabulary of a subject in standard Spanish. More indirectly, for a subject who has spoken Spanish in the home, school, and community since birth, it claims to be a good screening measure of verbal ability or scholastic aptitude, and therefore a predictor of school success.

Content Validity.   The manual focuses on how the TVIP stimulus words can be traced directly to their English counterparts in the PPVT–R (Dunn & Dunn, 1981), which in turn was built on the foundation of stimulus words used in the original PPVT (Dunn, 1959). The manual further outlines how the original PPVT words were based upon an exhaustive search of the 1953 edition of *Webster's New Collegiate Dictionary,* and how all 125 TVIP stimulus words (except *deciduo*), which are comprised of a "universal Spanish," can be found in both the *New Revised Velasquez Spanish and English Dictionary* (Velasquez, 1985) and in the ultimate authority, *Diccionario de la Lengua Española* (1970). Therefore, the manual concludes that the 125 stimulus words retained for the TVIP can be regarded as a sample from the complete Spanish vocabulary, with the proviso that words that cannot be illustrated are excluded.

Construct Validity.   The manual defines the TVIP as a measure of scholastic aptitude and therefore refers to professional literature on intelligence testing when discussing construct validity. Binet and Simon, Terman and Merrill, Wechsler, and Elliott are quoted and referenced in support of the vocabulary test as a valuable single test of an intelligence scale, and high correlations between vocabulary subtest scores and Full Scale IQ scores. Finally, the manual highlights the TVIP as a measure of receptive language, unlike IQ vocabulary subtests that tend to also include measures of expressive vocabulary; however, the concluding statement is that both tap the subject's comprehension of spoken words —it is primarily the mode of expression that varies. Also, the manual states that the percentage of subjects who responded correctly to an item increased with age, which is referred to as indirect but not conclusive evidence of construct validity.

Concurrent Validity.   The manual states that little research had been conducted at the time the manual was published (1986), which provided direct statistical evidence of the TVIP's concurrent validity; therefore, indirect evidence is presented from PPVT research. The justification for including PPVT research when discussing TVIP concurrent validity is that both the Hispanic-American adaptation and the English-American edition of the test measure hearing recognition of single spoken words and that the Spanish items are simply translations of the English stimulus words. The manual concludes that because both tests measure the same attribute, the evidence from earlier American research would seem to hold for the Spanish version. High correlations are presented between the PPVT and other measures of vocabulary (median of .71), such as the Full-Range Picture Vocabulary Test (Ammons & Ammons, 1948) and the Van Alstyne Picture Vocabulary Test (1949)—both correlations of .86 (Dunn & Dunn, 1981). Moreover, the English-language PPVT correlates moderately well with other individual tests of intelligence, especially those that measure verbal ability. Median correlations with the Stanford–Binet and Wechsler scales have generally been found to be in the .62 to .72 range. In one study, the Mexican TVIP standardization subjects were also given the Kaufman Assessment Battery for Children–Spanish (K-ABC–S: Gomez-Palacio, Rangel, & Padilla, 1985) as part of the standardization program, which showed that the TVIP had a much stronger relationship with the K-ABC–S Achievement Scale than with the K-ABC–S Mental Processing and Nonverbal scales.

Reliability

The manual states that it is important to present reliability separate from validity; however, they never present a discussion of reliability. The manual states that to date (when manual was published, 1986), the evidence indicates that the reliability of the Spanish and English versions of the PPVT are quite similar. One standardization was mentioned, which was done in Barcelona, Spain (Muñoz Amilibia, 1969), and the other in Xalapa, Mexico (Simon & Joiner, 1976). Both of these studies, however, were based on the PPVT.

Conclusion

The PPVT and TVIP are both technically sound instruments, even though the TVIP lacks extensive reliability data. Both tests have extensive norms and varying degrees of sophistication for the differences in regional dialect. In addition, the TVIP has separate norms for separate Hispanic populations. As a result, both tests are extremely useful clinically for a measure of receptive language. However, the TVIP does need an update for this century with new norms. It should also be noted that there have been some concerns regarding its translation and validation methods and application with Puerto Rican and Mexican American children (Prewitt Diaz, 1988).

Prueba del Desarrollo Inicial del Lenguaje

This is an individual test of Spanish-language proficiency (form and content) for children between the ages of 3 and 7 (Hresko, Reid, & Hammill, 1982). Thirty-eight items provide data on both receptive and expressive language. The manual categorizes each item in terms of receptive or expressive mode and form or content. Some items can be responded to with a gesture and others with an oral response. Items include pictures on cards, responses of the child's experience, and repetition of a sentence with correct order and grammar. This instrument was derived/translated from the Test of Early Language Development, which is in its third edition (Hresko, Reid, & Hammill, 1999).

Validity and Reliability

Content and Concurrent Validity, Reliability, mean scores of age increases, and relation with IQ tests were based on the original English-language version of the PDIL (Test of Early Language Development), but not the Spanish-language version.

Conclusion

The test identifies children with special needs in language development, documents progress in linguistic development, serves as a valid, reliable, and normed research tool, and guides diagnostic/prescriptive instruction. However, almost all of the people depicted would be classified by any observer as Anglo-Saxons. The few non-White figures have darker skin and seem to be Black; one is obviously Asian. Two might be identified as Hispanic, and the dress of one suggests East Indian or Samoan decent. Cultural inappropriateness is also discussed as one scene on a stimulus card shows a birthday party with children gathered around a birthday cake. The gifts in the background are a bike, a train, and a kite. The author comments on how a "piñata" may be more relevant for a Hispanic child's interpretation of a birthday party. Additional items that show cultural bias, according to the author, are men in neckties, a mansion, a child washing a car, and a figure of a cockroach. The author urged for modified picture stimuli on the Spanish-language version.

Although the PDIL provides a very useful profile (test results can be recorded according to the number of correct responses expected of children from different ages, categorized by the receptive and expressive modes and by the content and form criteria), the interpretive statistics, the insufficient translation methods, and the cultural biases, question its utility with Spanish-language children.

Spanish Version of the Test for Auditory Comprehension of Language (TACL)

Normative data for the Spanish version of the Test for Auditory Comprehension of Language (TACL) are presented (Wilcox & McGuinn-Aasby, 1988). The latest version of the TACL (Test of Auditory Comprehension of Language–Third Edition; Carrow-Woolfolk, 1999) was published in 1999. The TACL is used to assess the receptive spoken language skills of English- and Spanish-speaking children. However, most previous reports of the performance of Spanish-speaking children on the English versions of the TACL have included a variety of Mexican-American subjects and hence have led to different normative results.

The data for the Spanish version of the TACL were collected from 60 Mexican children who resided in either Tampico or Ciudad Medero, Mexico. The age range was from 4 to 4½, 6 to 6½, and 8-6 to 8-11. Ten subjects (5 male, 5 female) were from a high socioeconomic status, private school settings, were rated by their teachers as "normal" in academic skills, and were taught in English only since age 5 (conversed primarily in Spanish outside of classtime). Preschoolers (age 4) were selected from the same private school setting; however, these children did not have as much English-language exposure. All children from this private school setting were considered primarily monolingual. The remaining 30 children were from a low socioeconomic setting (same sex and age as high-SES children) and were selected from a government orphanage and had not been exposed to formal English. There was no formal testing; however, there were reports of developmental or educational delays. The authors mentioned a "richer" educational environment, but they did not comment on generalizability limitations (e.g., quality of life).

Results show that the acquisition of a second language did not interfere with comprehension abilities in the first language, which does not support the concept of second language interference. The data could support bilingualism as beneficial to first language learning; however, the authors highlighted the learning advantages available to the bilingual students. Bilingual, high SES children performed at a level greater than their mono-lingual/low SES peers and did not vary greatly from the original English-speaking TACL norming group.

Validity and Reliability

Content and Concurrent Validity, Reliability, and relation with other language tests were based on the original English-language version of the TACL (Test for Auditory Comprehension of Language), but not the Spanish-language version.

Conclusion

The test identifies children with special needs in language development, documents progress in auditory-linguistic development, and can guide diagnostic/prescriptive in-struction. However, due to the small sample size and limited studies, it is not clear if it is a valid, reliable, and well-normed instrument.

Focus is placed on the different subgroups and importance of considering the entire environment in the language acquisition process. Examples are given that compare the U.S. bilingual students to Mexican bilingual students. For instance, the Mexican bilingual students were in the high SES bracket in this study; however, U.S. bilingual students are typically in the lower SES bracket. The authors suggest using the low-SES children in this study as a source of interpretable TACL norms (as a beginning comparison group), based on their disadvantaged monolingual status. Finally, the performance of the high SES chil-dren is considered the upper range of Spanish speakers' performance on the TACL.

Dos Amigos: Verbal Language Scales

This version (Crithchlow, 1996) is a criterion-referenced test, as opposed to the previous (1972) norm-referenced version. It is meant to be used as a screening tool to assess lan-guage dominance and is widely used in the Southwestern United States. It utilizes the examinee's antonym understanding as a means to sample English- and Spanish-language development and conceptualization. Children are given a word and they are supposed to give the opposite or antonym of the word. Correct scores are tallied and then compared to a cut-off score. If the items correct are equal or greater than the score, then that child is considered dominant in that language. The test was normed on 1,167 5- to 13½-year-olds in the Southwestern United States.

Validity and Reliability

The manual includes a short description of the field-testing done to develop the instru-ment. In addition, there is one clinical pilot study cited. It states that the Dos Amigos had a "positive relationship" with English reading-instructional level, as measured by the Gilmore Oral Reading Test. The manual provides limited to no reliability and validity information.

Conclusion

Although the test is supposed to determine language domiance, it sometimes finds that a child meets criteria/cut-off in both languages. Does that mean they are fully bilingual? It is not clear. The test is extremely quick administration time (5–10 minutes), yet it is not known if psychometric properties are good. In addition, construct validity has not been determined. It does not appear to be a comprehensive measure of language functioning.

COGNITIVE FUNCTIONING

Intelligence tests are among the most frequently administered of all tests by neuro-psychologists (Lezak, 1995; Mitrushina, Boone, & D'Elia, 1999), who spend most of their time engaged in testing activities (Echemendia, Harris, Congett, Diaz, & Puente, 1997; Gifford 1991; Putnam & DeLuca, 1990). Even though neuropsychologists some-times become removed from intelligence testing, it is an essential part of the overall neu-ropsychological evaluation and interpretation. The IQ test, or general mental functioning evaluation, is the essential or crux of brain functioning and interpretation. Because IQ tests represent a multiplicity of cognitive functions assessed (see, e.g., Leckliter, Mata-razza, & Silverstein, 1985), it is a useful starting point in evaluating tests and assessment techniques available for Hispanic, Spanish-speaking children.

A brief review of several intelligence tests is provided: Woodcock–Johnson Psycho-Educational Battery (Batería–R), McCarthy Scales of Children's Abilities, Kaufman Assessment Battery for Children, Leiter–R, and the Wechsler Intelligence Scales for Children. These tests are also the major tests available in English (possibly excluding the Stanford–Binet). Rather than providing a meta-analytic review of the literature, only clin-ical issues pertinent to the goal of this chapter will be reviewed.

McCarthy Scales of Children's Abilities

The McCarthy Scales of Children's Abilities (McCarthy Scales/MSCA; McCarthy, 1972) is an individually administered measure of general intellectual ability for children from age 2½ to 8½. Instructions for the McCarthy Scales are provided in English and are made up of 18 separate subtests that are reduced to six scales: Verbal, Perceptual-Performance, Quantitative, General Cognitive, Memory, and Motor. A final General Cognitive Index (GCI) is obtained from the McCarthy Scales, which includes the Verbal, Perceptual-Per-formance, and Quantitative scales; these three scales do not overlap in content. The GCI has a mean of 100 and a standard deviation of 16, and the mean and standard deviation of the five remaining scales is 50 and 10, respectively.

The standardization of the McCarthy Scales was compiled from a nationwide sample and looked at age, sex, ethnicity, geographic region, father's occupation, and urban ver-sus rural residence. The ethnic composition of the children in this sample was 83.5% White and 16.4% ethnic minority. Examiners were asked to select either White or non-White subjects (Blacks, American Indians, Orientals, and Filipinos; McCarthy, 1972). However, Valencia (1988) stated that of the total minority sample (n = 170), 91% were Black children; he further estimated that less than 1% were Mexican American and Puerto Rican children.

Validity

Concurrent validity of the McCarthy scales has been found to be acceptable with the Stanford–Binet (4th edition; Karr, Carvajal, & Palmer, 1992), WPPSI–R (Karr, Carvajal, Elser, & Bays, 1993), K-ABC (Zucker & Copeland, 1988), and WISC–R and Woodcock–Johnson Tests of Cognitive Ability (Reilly, Drudge, Rosen, Loew, & Fischer, 1985), although correlations range from .75 to .88. As evidenced from the wide range of corre-lations, there is some concern as well about the McCarthy scales construct validity. Although the standardization on data yielded five factors generally throughout the scale,

Verbal, Motor, General Cognitive, Memory, and Perceptual-Performance, later studies have not replicated these earlier findings (Purvis & Bolen, 1984).

Reliability

Statistical information from the original McCarthy standardization (1972) shows an average GCI reliability coefficient of .93. Averages for the other scales range from .79 to .88 with the Motor Scale reliability coefficients below .70 for 6½ and 8½ age groups. Stability coefficients showed .90 for the General Cognitive Scale, .75 to .89 correlations for the remaining four scales, and .69 for the Motor Scale at ages 7½ and 8½. The Predictive Validity of the GCI and several other Indexes correlated significantly with most achievement scores; however, due to a small sample (n = 31), these results should be interpreted with caution.

Hispanic Findings

Additional statistical information was reviewed, for the purposes of this chapter, with a focus on Hispanic-Latino populations. Valencia (1990) looks at a number of minority-related studies on the McCarthy Scales and states that research with this instrument has increased about 200% since Kaufman's (1982) review. Salient findings from Valencia's review are discussed later.

Puerto Rican Children. Valencia (1988) reported that the available literature on the psychometric properties of the McCarthy with Puerto Rican children is too limited to provide recommendations and therefore states that any interpretations and generalizations of this research should be made with extreme care.

Valencia (1988) cited one study that reports mean performance data from English-speaking Puerto Rican children. This study found that the Perceptual-Performance and Motor scale means for the Puerto Rican children in this sample were similar to McCarthy standardization means (47.3 and 49.7, respectively). However, performance on Quantitative and Memory scales and the GCI were approximately 1 standard deviation below the McCarthy norming means. Similarly, the Verbal scale was about 1.3 standard deviation below the original McCarthy standardization mean.

A separate study looked at concurrent validity of the McCarthy scales with an English-speaking sample of Puerto Rican children and found that the McCarthy scores were correlated with WISC–R combination scores (Information and Comprehension): GCI (.68), Verbal (.67), Perceptual-Performance (.49), Quantitative (.61), Memory (.67), and Motor (.35) (Valencia, 1988). This study concluded that higher McCarthy Verbal scale scores were more highly correlated with the identified WISC–R subtests.

Reliability coefficients from a Spanish translation and administration of the McCarthy with Puerto Rican children showed the following: GCI (.94), Verbal (.79), Perceptual-Performance (.84), Memory (.63), and Motor (.64) (Shellenberger, 1982). Predictive Validity of the same study reported a strong correlation between GCI and Achievement (.77). Most importantly, however, it was reported that the Verbal scale was not the best predictor of achievement for this sample and the Perceptual-Performance and Quantitative scales were the best predictors (Valencia, 1988).

Mexican-American Children. Valencia recommended the McCarthy scales for psychoeducational assessment with English-speaking Mexican American children (especially preschoolers), while maintaining extreme caution with interpretations of the Verbal scale. Specifically, according to five studies reviewed by Valencia (1988), mean McCarthy performance was 99.9. Perceptual-Performance, Quantitative, and Memory scale means were at or above 50 (53.2, 51.3, & 49.6, respectively) with the Verbal scale mean falling 0.3 standard deviation below the original McCarthy standardization mean of 50 (45.1).

Moreover, construct validity showed three similar factors for Mexican American and White children: Verbal, Motor, and Perceptual-Performance. Concurrent validity was .77 between the McCarthy and the WPPSI FSIQ with the majority of the correlations falling between the high .70s and the low .80s. Predictive validity showed significant correlations between the McCarthy GCI and the CTBS Total Reading, with the McCarthy showing stronger prediction for reading than for mathematics. Also, the McCarthy Verbal scale indicted a .43 correlation with reading achievement. Finally, content validity showed item bias was restricted to the 46 Verbal scale items. Reliability coefficients ranged from .73 to .94 and the stability coefficient was .86 over a one-year test-retest period with all other scales ranging from .86 to .92.

Valencia and Cruz (1981) developed a Spanish translation of the McCarthy scales for research purposes. Valencia (1988) further stated that the McCarthy has undergone translation, norming, and validity research in Mexico in a cooperative effort between Mexican and American test developers. Additionally, Kaufman (1975) translated a short-form version of the McCarthy that Valencia (1988) felt may have some assessment utility as a screening test that leads to in-depth assessment, as long as the results are interpreted with utmost care.

A focus on Valencia's (1988) review of Spanish-speaking children who were assessed with the "Spanish McCarthy" shows a mean GCI of 92.7, which is about .5 standard deviation lower than the original McCarthy norm. Moreover, mean performances on the Verbal (M = 41.8), Quantitative (M = 46.4), and memory (M = 44.3) scales were about .8, .3, and .6 standard deviation below the norms, respectively. However, the mean score on the Perceptual-Performance Scale (M = 52.3) was near the original McCarthy standardization mean of 50. A study evaluating content validity in the McCarthy scales with Spanish-speaking preschool children demonstrated that 17 items were biased against this group (Valencia & Rankin, 1985). Twelve (71%) of these items were clustered in both the Verbal Memory I and the Numerical Memory II subtests. Finally, a GCI stability coefficient of .79 was reported for a different sample of Spanish-speaking children (Valencia, 1983). Overall, given the results of previous studies, Valencia (1988) concluded that the administration of the MSCA Perceptual-Performance subtests may be of some use.

In terms of the issue of factor structure, several studies have looked at the McCarthy scales in a sample of children outside of the United States. Trueman, Lynch, and Branthwaite (1984) found that a UK version of the McCarthy given to normal children age 4¼ generated a factor solution support of four factors: GCI, Perceptual-Performance, Verbal, and Motor indices. However, no support was found for the Memory or Quantitative indices. In a study carried out in Spain, Forns Santacana and Gomez Benito (1990) demonstrated varied construct validity with the McCarthy scales in a Spanish-speaking population. The study (Forns Santacana & Gomez Benito, 1990) performed on 4¼-year-olds yielded a two-factor structure of verbal and perceptual-performance factors, with undifferentiated quantitative and memory factors along with little to no support for a motor factor. In addition, Gomez Benito and Forns Santacana (1996) examined the construct validity of the McCarthy with 7-year-old Spanish children. In this study, the content of the five factors found was not only different from the one found for the 4¼-year-olds, but also it was very different from the previous studies in that they only found one factor. Overall, we see that different factor solutions were found than the original norming sample.

Conclusions

Whereas Valencia (1988) reported a 200% increase in studies focusing on the McCarthy since 1982, it appears from the literature review conducted for this chapter that McCarthy studies focusing primarily on Spanish-speaking populations is limited. Future research is needed to support some of Valencia's conclusions. Reviews of the literature indicate that the McCarthy scales show most promising results for English-speaking Mexican American preschool samples; however, caution should still be exercised with Verbal scale interpretations. Moreover, until valid and reliable clinical versions of the McCarthy Spanish translations (Mexican and Puerto Rican versions) are available, the McCarthy scales are not recommended for clinical assessment with Spanish-speaking children in general. Similarly, the McCarthy scales should be avoided or used with extreme caution with bilingual children regardless of their dominant language until further research is conducted with this population. What appears to be lacking is a large sample size of Hispanic (monolingual/bilingual) subjects with appropriate psychometric properties. As a result, one must be extremely cautious in interpreting the results of the McCarthy scales in Hispanic/Latino children. Therefore, there has been support of the strong interference language and parental schooling background has on GCI scores beyond SES and other family variables (Valencia, Hendersen, & Rankin, 1985).

Wechsler Intelligence Scales for Children

In general, there appear to be large inconsistencies in the factor structure of the WISC (Wechsler, 1949, 1951, 1967) in different populations, in particular among Spanish-speaking subjects. Studies conducted in the United States have shown significant discrepancies between the Wechsler Intelligence Scales for Children–Revised (WISC–R) Verbal and the Performance IQs when administered to Hispanic resident children who reside in the U.S. (Munford & Muñoz, 1980; Pontón, 1989). Such discrepancies often resulted in the misdiagnosis of children into special education placement, such as educable mentally retarded (Herrans & Rodriguez, 1992; Reynolds, 1992). As a result, translated versions of the WISC–R were developed.

Escala de Inteligencia Wechsler para Niños–Revisada (WISC-RM)

The WISC–R was translated and published for use in Mexico and Latin America; however, these translations relied on U.S. norms for scoring and interpretation. Moreover, research in Mexico City has suggested that the use of the Wechsler norms (U.S.) in order to diagnostically classify children's care is likely to underestimate the academic potential of Mexican children (Gomez-Palacio, Ransel-Hinojosa, & Padilla, 1982).

The WISC–RM was translated and adapted for Mexican citizens; for instance, WISC–R items that were found to be inappropriate when the standardization data were analyzed were changed, dropped, or modified. Specifically, on the Information, Vocabulary, and Comprehension subtests, revisions were made that were more representative of Mexican culture (Padilla, Roll, & Gomez-Palacio, 1982). The WISC–RM was normed in Mexico City on 1,100 male and female subjects (ages 6–16) from public elementary and secondary public schools in Mexico City.

Validity.   Support for the construct validity of the WISC–RM is provided by Rousey (1990). She compared factor structures between the WISC–R and the WISC–RM. The sample consisted of 300 children from Mexico and 1,281 children (613 Latino and 668 Anglo) from the U.S. On the performance factor, a .98 coefficient of congruence was obtained between the Latino and Mexican samples, and .90 between the Mexican and the Anglo samples. The verbal factor coefficient of congruence was .96 between the Latino and Mexican samples, and .95 between the Mexican and Anglo samples. Moreover, .93 and .96 congruence coefficients were obtained for the distractibility factor between the Latino and Mexican sample, and between the Mexican and Anglo samples, respectively.

Reliability.   Rousey (1990) concluded that the WISC–RM has adequate reliability and is factorially similar to the WISC–R. Data regarding predictive validity are still lacking (Rousey, 1990). Rousey further makes comments that the WISC–RM measures the same dimensions in different groups, but she provided no empirical support on whether these abilities are measured equally well or how predictive they are in the different cultures. Although Rousey reported no WISC–RM data on the prediction of external criteria such as academic performance, her study did show support of factorial similarity between the WISC–R and WISC–RM.

Fletcher (1989) compared the performance of 90 fifth-grade students in Mexico City on the WISC–RM and the Pruebas de Habilidad Cognoscitiva (Spanish version of the Woodcock Johnson Tests of Cognitive Ability: Batería) and found a 5.1-point full-scale difference with the low achieving sample receiving higher WISC–RM scores. Fletcher stated that the difference corresponds to the U.S. English full-scale discrepancies that showed higher scores on the WISC–R Full Scale when compared to the Woodcock Johnson Tests of Cognitive Ability. Fletcher (1989) concluded that the WISC–RM may create a "false positive" or "false negative" identification of a bilingual or Spanish monolingual Hispanic student. Because the Batería and the WISC–RM are widely used to determine special education eligibility (Fletcher, 1989), psychometric research would benefit from future research which compared the Batería–R, the WISC–RM, and the EIWN–R.

Escala de Inteligencia Wechsler para Niños (EIWN)

The EIWN (Wechsler, 1951) is a Puerto Rican translation and adaptation of the Wechsler Intelligence Scale for Children (WISC; Wechsler, 1949). The WISC was translated in 1955 by the Department of Public Instruction of Puerto Rico to assess children from age 6 to 16. Some order and content was changed, yet separate Puerto Rican norms were not provided. Nevertheless, the need for separate norms is supported by the discrepancy in mean IQs between Hispanic children (mean IQ = 88) and American children (mean IQ = 100) (Wilen & van Maanen Seeting, 1986). Roca (1955) validated the translation in three different studies; however, because the samples for these studies were inadequate, he suggested that the EIWN should be revised and validated.

Escala de Inteligencia Wechsler para Niños–Revisada (EIWN–R)/Experimental Version

In 1977, the WISC–R was translated into Spanish (Martin, 1977) and norms were based on students tested in Dade County, Florida, which consisted of a predominantly Spanish-speaking Cuban sample (Prewitt-Diaz & Rodriguez, 1986). Prewitt-Diaz and Rodriguez (1986) warn against use of the EIWN–R because of its experimental nature. For instance, it is not considered a fully developed intelligence scale because the test was published without norms for a representative sample of Hispanic children. The EIWN–R sample was identified according to Hispanic surnames alone and no other measures of ethnicity.

Puerto Rican psychologists were not satisfied with the U.S. "Florida" translation of the WISC–R and were also not comfortable using the WISC–RM (Mexican translation) because of cultural differences between Mexican and Puerto Rican cultures (Herrans & Rodriguez, 1992). Moreover, researchers were interested in asking questions specific to Puerto Rican populations. As a result, Prewitt-Diaz and Rodriguez (1986) tested fourth- and fifth-grade students in Puerto Rico ($N = 51$) with the EIWN–R (experimental version) and concluded that with minor modifications, the EWIN-R was ready for the standardized norming with Puerto Rican children.

Escala de Inteligencia Wechsler para Niños–Revisada de Puerto Rico (EIWN–R de Puerto Rico)

According the to the EIWN–R de Puerto Rico Manual (Herrans & Rodriguez, 1992), the EIWN–R (experimental version) underwent revisions to correct for culturally loaded items/subtests. For example, in making the EIWN–R more appropriate for a Puerto Rican sample, inappropriate direct translations (e.g. content and grammar) were corrected and/or eliminated/substituted. New responses were created for 8 of the 12 subtests and pilot studies were conducted to evaluate the new "corrected" instrument. Overall, Object Assembly, Mazes, Symbol Search, and Digit Span were not altered. Information and Similarities subtests resulted in the greatest change (43% and 47% respectively), which various authors have identified as highly correlated with the "G" factor of verbal intelligence (e.g. Herrans & Rodriguez, 1992; Sattler, 1982). Finally, back-translation procedures were initiated and the norming process began in 1986.

Testing for the EIWN–R de Puerto Rico occurred between 1986–1987 and 1989–90, and the norming sample consisted of 2,200 subjects from Puerto Rican schools between the ages of 6 and 17-11.

Validity. Internal Validity for all norm ages (6–16) were .92 (Verbal IQ), .88 (Performance IQ), and .94 (Total IQ). Verbal subscale fluctuation ranged from .67 to .83 and Performance subscale fluctuation was between .62 and .84. Although the internal validity appears to be adequate, the verbal fluctuations were fairly large.

Reliability. Subtest reliabilities were taken from a group of 150 students who were tested on two occasions and ranged from .53 to .91. Reliability for Verbal, Performance, and Total IQs were .91, .77, and .90 respectively. The manual highlights elevated scores of 3.50, 3.07, and 3.84 points, respectively, on Verbal, Performance, and Total IQs between first second test administrations. Therefore, it is recommended that this increase in score, which may be a practice effect, must be considered with subjects who repeat the EIWN–R within a short time interval (e.g., two weeks).

Conclusions. There has been a lot of work on the Wechsler Intelligence Scales for Children from the initial WISC–RM. Although the EIWN–R is an improvement on its predecessors, it continues to be an almost "direct" translation of the WISC–R. Also, the reliability figures appear to vary drastically on retest (although more data needs to be gathered at larger intervals). At the present moment, the EIWN–R is a test fraught with problems with generalizability to the different Hispanic/Latino groups in the United

States and its reliability over time. Several studies have found that the WISC test has underestimated cognitive ability of bilingual children in comparison to the K-ABC (Flanagan, 1995) and the Leiter (Lewis & Lorentz, 1994). In fact, some cities/areas have developed their own local norms and standardization adaptations for the EIWN–R in New York (OREA, 1991) and the WISC–R in Chicago (Tamayo, 1990).

At the time of publication, the development of the WISC–III Spanish version was stopped. If it is ever completed, it hopes to be the logical next step in developing an appropriate, psychometrically sound test for Spanish-speaking or bilingual Latino children. Early results from the WISC–III English version show continued bias with this population (Weiss, Prifitera, & Roid, 1993).

Woodcock–Johnson Psycho-Educational Battery

Batería Woodcock Psycho-Educativa en Español (Batería)

The Batería Woodcock Psycho-Educativa en Español (Batería; Woodcock, 1982) is the Spanish version of the Woodcock–Johnson Psycho-Educational Battery (Woodcock & Johnson, 1977, 1989) and is comprised of 10 tests of cognitive ability and 7 tests of achievement. The general Spanish norms are based on a sample of 802 students from urban areas in Costa Rica, Mexico, Peru, Puerto Rico, and Spain, with cluster score reliabilities across grade levels in the .90s for Oral Language, Written Language and Broad Language and in the .80s and .90s for Reading. Cluster reliabilities across grade levels for the Broad Cognitive Ability Full Scale are in the .90s and are in the high .80s to low .90s in Mathematics (Fletcher, 1989). The Batería sampled students from both public and private schools from six urbanized areas throughout the Spanish-speaking world.

Batería Woodcock–Muñoz Pruebas de Habilidad Cognitiva–Revisada (Batería–R)

The Batería Woodcock-Muñoz Pruebas de Habilidad Cognitiva–Revisada (Batería–R; Woodcock & Muñoz, 1996) is the Spanish version of the Woodcock–Johnson Tests of Cognitive Ability (WJ–R; Woodcock & Johnson, 1989). The original normative data for the WJ–R were gathered from 6,359 subjects in over 100 geographically diverse U.S. communities and was comprised of White, Black, Native American, Asian Pacific, and Hispanic ethnic groups. The age range was from age 2 to over 90. After the WJ–R was developed, a Spanish version began to be developed utilizing diverse techniques from back translation to language experts reviewing items (see Woodcock & Muñoz-Sandoval, 1996, for more details). The Batería–R was then tested on 3,911 subjects in the calibration-equating study to match subtests/items from the Spanish version to the already existing English version. The subjects came from seven different countries: Argentina, Costa Rica, Mexico (4 sites), Peru, Puerto Rico (2 sites), Spain, and five states in the United States (Arizona; California; Florida, 2 sites; New York, 2 sites; and Texas, 2 sites). Out of all the subjects, 2,586 were from outside of the United States and 1,325 were from the United States. All were monolingual Spanish-speakers, or nearly so, and 98.3% spoke Spanish as a first language. The tasks underlying each test in the Batería–R were scaled, or equated, to their empirical difficulty in English. As a result, the norms, originally published for the WJ–R, are used for calculating the Batería–R scores.

Validity.   Concurrent validity correlations of the Batería–R Oral Language cognitive factor and several other commonly used measures of language ability were investigated

(Woodcock & Muñoz-Sandoval, 1996). In one study in Arizona, 70 Limited English Proficient kindergartners were given the Batería–R and other language measures (Language Assessment Scales, Language Rating Scale, and Woodcock–Muñoz Language Survey (W–M LS; Woodcock & Muñoz, 1993). The validity coefficients ranged from .75 to .95. In a similar study, using the same instruments (plus the IDEA Oral Language Proficiency Test I), 120 Limited English Proficiency second-graders in Texas were administered most of the tests. The validity coefficients between the Oral Language factor (Batería–R) and other measures varied from .15/.32 with the Pronunciation subtest (LAS and LRS, respectively) and .93 with the Broad Spanish Ability (W–M LS).

Reliability. Reliabilities for the general cognitive factors reported in the manual, for the calibration data (Woodcock & Muñoz-Sandoval, 1996) are generally in the high .80s to .90s. However, some individual subtest have much lower reliabilities, such as the Palabras Incompletas (Incomplete Words) subtest, which yielded reliabilities of .53 (age 9) and .49 (age 13). Similarly, this was seen in the English version, which also yielded low reliabilities of .64 (age 9) and .60 (age 13). In addition, Comprensión de Oraciones (Listening Comprehension) yielded a reliability coefficient of .61 (ages 30–39). All other reliabilities were mostly in the low .70s to .90s, as stated by the manual (Woodcock & Muñoz-Sandoval, 1996).

Conclusions. The best feature that the Batería–R has is its comparison with the WJ–R. It allows direct comparison of Spanish and English oral language proficiencies via a single score on the Comparative Language Index/Índice de comparación de idiomas (CLI; Woodcock & Muñoz-Sandoval, 1996). In addition, an individual child's subtest and cluster scores can be compared in both languages. Along with the CLI, the Batería–R provides the examiner with a gradation system in which to place the child's language performance from: negligible–very limited–limited–fluent–advanced. These categories are obtained from the Cognitive Academic Language Proficiency (CALP; Cummins, 1984) level classification system. The parallel English and Spanish versions allow examiners to track individuals over time and see changes in their cognitive/language (neuropsychological) functioning. This is ideal for longitudinal testing and bilingual setting, in which language development is changing over time. Another advantage of the Batería–R is that it applies a more advanced and enhanced fit with the Horn–Cattell theory of cognitive functioning than the previous Batería (for more detailed information, see chapter 8 in this book).

The Leiter International Performance Scale–Revised

The original Leiter scale, developed in 1940, was criticized for poor normative data and outdated illustrations, so it was redesigned/restandardized in 1993 under a 3-year federally funded research project. The goal of the Leiter–R (Roid, 1997) was to develop a battery of nonverbal assessments useful in estimating intellectual (fluid reasoning) capabilities of children and adolescents from ages 2–40. According to Roid (1996), nonverbal intelligence excludes the abilities to perceive, manipulate, and reason with words or numbers, or with printed material and stories. Instead, nonverbal intelligence is assessed with pictures, figural illustrations, and coded symbols, in an attempt to provide "culture fair" testing. The Leiter–R measures four cognitive domains: Reasoning, Visualization, Attention, and Memory. New Attention and Memory domains were added to differentiate children with ADHD, LD, and TBI. Also, new "Growth Scores" are available for all domains and special scoring options are provided for neuropsychological evaluations. Composite scores include Full Scale IQ Score, Brief IQ Screening Score, Brief ADHD Screening Score, Brief GIFTED Screening Score, Reasoning Score, Visualization Score, Attention Score, Memory Score.

The Leiter–R sample consisted of 1,754 normal and 692 clinical/atypical children and adolescents. Clinical classification included speech impaired, hearing impaired, motor impaired, traumatic brain injury, cognitive delay, attention deficit disorder, gifted, Learning Disabled-VIQ high, Learning Disabled-PIQ high, ESL Spanish (72), and ESL Asian (28). The racial composition of the Leiter–R sample included Caucasian, Black, Hispanic, Asian, and other ethnic groups. Social Economic Status was determined by education (e.g. < HS Graduate; High School/GED; 1 Yr. College). The sample ranged from ages 2–18 and the gender breakdown was 881 male and 873 female subjects. (Madsen, Roid, & Miller, 1996).

Validity

Content-Related Validity.   Preliminary content validity for the Leiter–R was established by a combination of factor verification (to establish consistency with intelligence theory), expert review, and empirical studies of internal consistency (Roid, 1996). Preliminary norming of the 10 Visualization and Reasoning subtests of the Leiter–R was conducted on a sample of 1,272 representing 80% of the normal subjects in the normative sample. Based on the "brief IQ four subscale estimator" ($M = 100$, $SD = 15$; proved to have a consistent, unidimensional "g" factor across age groups), normal children, $n = 1,372$, median 101 and ESL-Hispanic, $n = 45$, median 95. Overall, the pattern of medians between normal and clinical samples provide criterion-related evidence of the Leiter–R validity, and is similar to patterns found with Wechsler Performance IQ values in various research studies in the literature (Roid, 1996). Specifically, preliminary analyses of the Attention and Memory subtests show that the Leiter–R profile of subtests exhibits differentiation between learning disabled and normal subjects and between ADHD and normal subjects. There is no mention of differentiation within the Hispanic sample.

Concurrent Validity.   Correlations of .83 were found between the Brief IQ estimator from the Leiter–R and the WISC–III Full Scale IQ ($n = 93$, $p < .001$), and the original Leiter IQ score ($n = 103$, $p < .001$). The most highly correlated subtest was Sequential Order, which was correlated .72 with WISC–III Performance IQ. Studies of correlations with other batteries such as Stanford–Binet, Woodcock–Johnson, WRAML, and TOMAL are not yet completed.

Construct Validity.   In a factor analysis study (Gidley, Bos, & Roid, 1996), the Leiter–R subtests fit the underlying hierarchical "g" model used to design the Leiter–R, with the exception that adolescents appear to show greater differentiations in abilities compared to young children. The Gridley et al. study and that of Bay (1996) showed that the four subtests of Figure Ground, Form Completion, Repeated Patterns, and Sequential Order provide a unidimensional "g" factor, with factorial invariance, across the full age range of 2 to 21. This "g" factor accounted for 54% to 75% of the four subtests for the age 2 to 21 group.

Several studies (Armenteros & Roid, 1996; Flemmer & Roid, 1996; Grant, Roid, & Fallow, 1996; McLellan & Walton, 1996; Mellott & McLellan, 1996) have shown the Leiter–R to have few significant differences between Anglo and Hispanic samples matched for parental education levels. Madsen et al. (1996) examined item bias of the Visualization and Reasoning subtests and found that the 10 subtests were free from differential item functioning between Anglo and Hispanic samples. Blair (1996) looked at four of the picture-oriented Visualization and Reasoning subtests for matched samples of Anglo and ESL-Hispanic subjects and found only two items with positive partial correlations which were subsequently removed from the final published version of the Leiter–R.

Both the Tryout edition and the Standardization edition of the Leiter–R have shown highly significant age effects on items and subtests showing that the Leiter–R follows the expected pattern of maturation across cross-sectional age groupings.

Reliability

A tryout edition of the Leiter–R (Madsen et al., 1996) was administered to 550 children from a representative sample of SES and ethnic backgrounds from ages 2 to 21. Reliabilities for each of the final versions of the 17 subtests ranged from .75 to .96, with most in the high .80s to .90s. Seventeen out of the original 23 subtests were retained and many items were redesigned for the Standardization Edition, which consists of 20 subtests. Preliminary internal consistency reliability estimates for Visualization and Reasoning subtests range from .70 to .95 for ages 2 to 6 and from .60 to .95 for ages 7 to 18+, with an overall .80s and .90s average for ages 2 through 18+. Preliminary internal consistency reliability estimates for the Attention and Memory subtests ranged from .50 to .92 with overall averages in the .70s and .80s. Interim validity information of the Visualization and Reasoning domains show a correlation of .83 with the old edition of the Leiter, and correlation of .83 with the WISC–III.

Studies with Hispanic Populations

Armenteros and Roid (1996) compared Hispanic and Anglo nonverbal ability among preschoolers using the Leiter–R. Subjects were selected from the Leiter–R standardization sample (a stratified random sampling plan based on the 1993 U.S. Census). A total of 320 Anglo-non-Hispanic, and 63 Hispanic children from age 3 to age 5 composed the ethnic-contrast sample. No significant differences were found on the 7 nonverbal subtests of the Leiter–R "Visualization and Reasoning" battery between Anglo and Hispanic subjects.

All of the four key subtests that from a brief IQ screening index had differences of less than one fourth SD in effect size. These differences are much smaller in magnitude than those found on traditional, verbal IQ batteries. Preliminary internal consistency reliability estimates for the 7 visualization and reasoning subtests in the preschool sample range from .71 to .95 for ages 2 to 5.

In a study by Flemmer and Roid (1996), subjects were obtained from the standardization of the Leiter–R from stratified random sampling plan based on the 1993 U.S. Census. A total of 258 Anglo-non-Hispanic and 62 Hispanic adolescents from age 11 to 21 composed the ethnic contrast sample. Subjects were administered the Visualization and Reasoning battery of the Leiter–R. Results showed a small effect size of .107; nonsignificant differences resulted in 7 of the 10 subtest. The subfactor on which the Hispanic and Anglo adolescents differed most was "spatial ability" as measured by Paper Folding and Figure Rotation, which are rather abstract, visual subtests. The other subtest was Form Completion. Flemmer and Roid (1996) stated that these subtests should be used cautiously with Hispanic adolescents until further studies (with larger sample size) can be completed to verify the effect.

Flemmer and Roid (1996) also stated that three of the four key subtests that form a brief IQ screening index (Repeated Patterns, Sequential Order and Figure Ground) all had differences of less than one third SD in effect size. Flemmer and Roid (1996) concluded that overall, the Leiter–R shows promise for cultural fair assessment. Preliminary internal consistency reliability estimates for the Visualization and Reasoning subtests range from .70 to .95 for ages 2 through 8 and .60 to .94 for ages 9 through 18+, with an average overall in the .80 to .90 range.

Conclusions

Some authors strongly suggest the use of nonverbal measures of intelligence with limited English proficient Hispanic children/adolescents (e.g., Wilen & van Maanen Seeting, 1986) whereas others caution against their use (e.g. Cervantes & Acosta, 1992). Cervantes and Acosta (1992), for example, stated that relying on nonverbal measures of intelligence limits the interpretation of the individual's general cognitive abilities, especially when the nonverbal measures are not administered in the client's language of choice. The issues addressed by the aforementioned authors are equally important; for example, nonverbal measures should always be supplemented by additional measures (e.g. verbal) in a battery when interpreting general cognitive functioning. Most importantly, when relying solely on performance measures as opposed to performance and verbal measures (e.g., Wechsler Intelligence Scales), general cognitive intelligence interpretations cannot be provided.

Kaufman Assessment Battery for Children

The Kaufman Assessment Battery for Children (K-ABC; Kaufman & Kaufman, 1983) includes intelligence and achievement measures and provides Spanish directions for sample and teaching items on the Mental Processing Subtests. Also, correct Spanish responses are provided for all subtests except Reading/Decoding and Reading/Understanding.

The K-ABC Manual, national standardization program (1981), included 2,000 children, in 24 states, from ages 2½ to 12½. The following race or ethnic group categories, derived from the U.S. Census classifications, were used: White, Black, Hispanic, and Other. Approximately 157 Hispanics were included in the standardization sample (n = 30, age 2-6 through 4-11; n = 128, ages 5-0 through 12-5). No separate norms are available for the Spanish instructions/responses. There is a Spanish K-ABC (Kaufman, Kaufman, & Padilla, 1984), which provides Mexican norms, but is not readily available within the United States; therefore, it is not described.

Validity

Wilson, Reynolds, Chatman, and Kaufman (1983) found no significant differences between female and male correlations, or between ethnic group correlations (e.g., Blacks, Hispanics, or Whites). Wilson et al. (1985) found correlations of about .60 for preschool level subtest (e.g. Magic Window, Face Recognition, Expressive Vocabulary) and higher relations for subtests that spanned wide age ranges (.65–.90).

Concurrent Validity values range from .40 to .76 and (median of .60) for the Mental Processing Composite. A .70 correlation was cited between the K-ABC Mental Processing Composite and the WISC–R Full Scale IQ (Kaufman & Kaufman, 1983). However, cited correlations between K-ABC Simultaneous Processing and Nonverbal standard scores were higher (upper .60s) with the WISC–R Full Scale IQ than the correlation between the K-ABC Sequential Processing standard score and the WISC–R Full Scale IQ (.47).

Reliability

The preschool level Mental Processing subtest mean values ranged from .72 (Magic Window) to .88 (Number Recall). At the school age level, the range was from .71 (Gestalt Closure) to .85 (Matrix Analogies) (Kaufman & Kaufman, 1983).

Studies with Hispanic Populations

For preschool children, the means were 5 to 7 points higher than the means for school-age children. Specifically, there was a 5-point superiority on the Mental Processing Composite as compared to the Achievement Scale, indicative of better performance on problem-solving tasks than on subtests that depend more heavily on verbal skills and acquired factual information (Kaufman & Kaufman, 1983).

In an attempt to investigate cultural bias, Valencia, Rankin, and Livingston (1995) examined content (item) bias on the K-ABC Mental Processing Scales and the Achievement Scale. Their sample consisted of 100 Mexican American and 100 White fifth- and sixth-grade boys and girls (all English speaking and from similar SES backgrounds) in a central California city. Their findings showed a difference between the White and Mexican American children to be on Riddles (the largest on the Achievement subtest comparisons). In addition, the Mexican American group performed the lowest on the Riddles Achievement subtest. Also, the Riddles subtest, compared to the other four Achievement subtests, contained the highest percentage of biased items (88.9%). In sum, the authors perceive the solutions to the Riddles items to be very dependent on vocabulary understanding, which is a major aspect of English-language development. From the 26 Faces and Places subtest items, the majority (15) were found to be biased. The authors grouped the Faces and Places subtest items into three categories (School Setting, Out of School Setting, Combined), from which they estimated that two thirds of the 15 biased items came from the "out of school" category. Valencia et al. (1995) stated that the "out of school" category addresses topics related to postcards, movies, television, magazines, and travel, and then suggested that learning opportunities in the "out of school" category tend to be linked to SES (e.g., children who had greater opportunities to travel, read educational magazines like *National Geographic*, and view educational television), which may have had increased exposure learning opportunities to many items on the Faces and Places subtest. Valencia and colleagues (1995) further stated that it is likely that some of the Mexican American children tended to have less of the enrichment opportunities due to their lower SES background, therefore items clustering in the "out of school" category may have been more difficult for them.

In summary, Valencia and colleagues (1995) urged extreme caution in using the K-ABC MPC as a predictor of academic achievement. Furthermore, they suggested that school psychologists and other assessment professionals refrain from using the K-ABC with this population.

ACADEMIC PERFORMANCE

Batería-R

The total sample (3,911) for this test of the Batería–R (Woodcock & Muñoz-Sandoval, 1996) was drawn from the United States (1,325: Arizona, California, Florida, New York,

& Texas) as well as international (Costa Rica, Mexico, Peru, Puerto Rico, Spain) geographic regions of which 2,000 were native Spanish-speakers. Subjects were selected if they were monolingual Spanish "or nearly so," as based on the informant's opinion and an optional Language Use Survey; however, the Language Use Survey was not completed for all subjects. Spanish was reported as the first language learned by 98.3% of the U.S. sample and English by 1.7% (386 did not respond). They explained that the "Calculo" (Calculation) subtest from the Batería–R APR shows identical item content and task requirements whether administered in English or Spanish; therefore, direct WJ–R Test of Achievement norms were applied with this subtest. The remaining tests had different item content in the Spanish-language form; therefore, research was conducted to calibrate new items and scores. For example, Spanish norms were equated to English norms.

Validity

The manual refers the reader to the examiner's manual for WJ–R Test of Achievement validity studies because the two batteries are described as parallel in content and structure. Woodcock and Muñoz-Sandoval (1996) stated that the WJ–R results are generalizable to the Batería–R APR. The manual explains that there is only one concurrent validity study unique to the Batería–R. This research took place in Texas (n = 120) in which Grade 2 limited-English-proficient students were administered several tests from the Batería–R (COG & APR) and the Woodcok–Muñoz Language Survey, Spanish Form. Results that are relevant to the Batería–R APR include the correlations between Amplia lectura and the WM-LS Lectura-Escritura (.92) and between Amplio lenguaje escrito and the WM-LS Lectura-Escritura (.95). The high correlations reported between these two pairs of measures is due, in part, to common content.

Reliability

Based on the Spanish calibration data, there is a range of .51 to .98. Lowest reliabilities with age 2 on the Standard Battery are .62 for "Estudios Sociales" (Social Studies) with all others above .70. Lowest reliabilities on the Supplementary Battery were at age 6 for "Correccion de textos" (Proofing) = .51, "Fluidez en la redaccion" (Writing Fluency) = .62, and at age 18 for "Puntuacion y Mayusculas" (Punctuation & Capitalization) = .66.

Conclusions

The best feature that the Batería–R has is its comparison with the WJ–R. It allows direct comparison of Spanish and English academic proficiencies over time via a comparative. In addition, an individual child's subtest and cluster scores can be compared in both languages. Although the manual states that English and Spanish versions are parallel and can allow examiners to track individuals over time and see changes in their academic/language functioning, it has not been shown by any extensive study of the topic. In fact, it is hard to believe that academic standards are the same across the different states and across the different countries, where similar education goals may be achieved at different grade levels. Further study should focus on what children learn and can perform at the same grade in the different respective countries (U.S., Costa Rica, Peru, Spain, etc.), so that those subgroups can be compared.

K-ABC Achievement Scales

Achievement subtests ranged from .77 (Faces & Places) at the preschool level to .92 (Reading/Decoding) for the K-ABC Achievement Scales (Kaufman & Kaufman, 1983).

All mean coefficients were .85 and above for Achievement subtests, except for preschool ages on Faces & Places and Riddles. Test–Retest Reliability on Achievement ranged from .95 to .97 for all age groups.

Only one study comparing the Woodcock–Johnson Tests of Cognitive Abilities and the K-ABC was identified by the manual that had a limited sample number ($n = 25$). The results are tentative, however; they showed a .69 correlation between the K-ABC Achievement Scale and the WJ Broad Cognitive Ability deviation IQ and a .41 correlation for the Mental Processing Composite (Kaufman & Kaufman, 1983). When corrected for the considerable range restriction on the K-ABC variables, these coefficients improved to .84 and .55, respectively. Overall, the mean Woodcock-Johnson deviation IQ and K-ABC Mental Processing Composite were very similar, differing by less than one standard score point.

At the school-age level a mean of about 98 was reported for the Mental Processing and Nonverbal Scales, which is very close to the normative mean of 100; however, the Achievement mean (92) on Achievement is about half a standard deviation below the normative mean. Mean standard scores on all Achievement subtests were similar to the one half standard deviation discrepancy that was described by the global Achievement Scale. Overall, compared to Whites on the WISC–R and K-ABC, there is a heavier discrepancy on the Achievement Scale of about 9-point superiority (Whites over Hispanics) on this scale across the entire K-ABC age range.

Valenica et al. (1995) presented a stronger argument that relates to segregation. They stated that segregation is strongly correlated with poor academic achievement and that in their study, perhaps the White students in the White segregated school were being provided with greater opportunities to learn curricular material of the type that is tested on the K-ABC Achievement Scale.

CONCLUSIONS

Many psychologists today assume that a child that can speak English can complete cognitive tasks, and also complete academic tasks in English. However, hopefully this book has convinced psychologists/assessors that this is not the case. Second language acquisition is a lengthy, develomental process whereby students whose native language is not English acquire listening, speaking, reading, and writing skills in English over a long time. In order to effectively assess and serve this increasing popualtion of monolingual Spanish and bilingual children, psychologists need to understand second language acquistion. In addition, psychologists must take into account both the child's native langauge (Spanish) and their secondary language (English) and assess the interplay and develpoment of both.

As a result, the psychologist needs to take into account language proficiency, the ease in which second language is acquired, differentiate between second language acquisition and handicapping conditions, and loss of language or regression in language development in one or both languages. So, again, how do psychologists decide in which language to assess the bilingual child? Obviously, we would like to have the time and resources to assess both languages if possible, yet this is not always plausible. First, language in the learning environment must be assessed. What is the language of instruction? Second, what language is the child exposed to at home? Third, what language does the student prefer in informal settings? Information gathered by the bilingual neuropsychological testing of children involves many facets of evaluation: developmental history gathering, assessment of formalized/standardized scores, qualitative assessment of language output, and quantity and quality of schooling. Finally, based on all this information, the student is assessed in a formal setting with standardized tests. What is deemed the dominant language will be assessed first. Then, depending on the fluency and level of the child's secondary language, it will also need to be assessed, either formally or informally. Finally, when the psychologist compares the child's performance to others or to a given standard, the psychologist must take into account language development and realize that the child's scores will probably be lower than the norms. For example, a child who immigrates to the United States at age 10 (Grade 5) and is assessed in 2 years at age 12 (Grade 7) cannot be expected to perform at the same level as a 12-year-old Spanish or English student or at the same level as a seventh-grade Spanish or English student. Because the student has had less exposure to Spanish and not enough exposure to English, he or she will perform below monolingual peers, yet one needs to be careful not to interpret this as a disability but as part of multi-language development.

Now that some of the major instruments available have been reviewed, this chapter may be used as a guide to utilizing and interpreting test information gathered from a bilingual child. Teasing apart the separate languages and the interaction of bilingual language processing is the challenge of future research. Greater understanding of language (bilingual) processing is needed. In addtion, better tests that are strictly developed for this population are also necessary. Clinicians have relied too long on translated tests or adaptations of already existing monolingual tests, in particuar those in English. As the amount of bilingual children in this country increase, further theoretical and empirical work will be necessary to pursue these questions of what is really going on in the bilingual mind and how it changes over time. Not only does test development need to be more sensitive to the needs of the bilingual child (clinicians cannot sum up two monolingual tests [Spanish + English] and expect to understand bilingualism), but there must be an understanding of the development of bilingualism. As a result, clinicians will be more aware of the dynamic nature of bilingualism. Possibly, imaging studies will provide the future of this understanding of the bilingual mind and its development. Until then, there continue to be slow strides and advances in the field.

ACKNOWLEDGMENT

Special thanks go to Marta Elena Corona-LoMonaco, University of Southern California, for preparation of this chapter.

REFERENCES

Ammons, R. B., & Ammons, H. S. (1948). *The Fullrange picture vocabulary test*. New Orleans, LA: Author.

Armenteros, E., & Roid, G. H. (1996, August). *Nonverbal abilities of Hispanic and speech-impaired preschoolers: A case study.* Paper presented at the meeting of the American Psychological Association, Toronto, Ontario, Canada.

Armour-Thomas, E. (1992). Intellectual assessment of children from culturally diverse backgorunds. *School Psychology review, 21*(4), 552–565.

Bay, M. (1996). *Factor structure of the Leiter–R standardization edition across age groups.* Unpublished doctoral dissertation, George Fox University.

Blair, R. J. (1996). *Item bias analysis of the Leiter–R for English as a Second Language populations.* Unpublished doctoral dissertation, George Fox University.

Carrow-Woolfolk, E. (1999). *Test of Auditory Comprehension of Language–Third Edition*. Austin, TX: Pro-Ed.

Cervantes, R. C., & Acosta, F. X. (1992). Psychological testing for Hispanic Americans. *Applied and Preventive Psychology, 1*(4), 209–219.

Crawford, J. & Parker, D. M. (1989). *Developments in clinical and experimental neuropsychology*. New York: Plenum.

Critchlow, D. E. (1996). *Dos amigos: Verbal language scales (An English–Spanish aptitude test)*. Novato, CA: Academic Therapy Publications.

Cummins, J. (1984). *Bilingualism and special education: Issues in assessment and pedagogy*. San Diego, CA: College Hill Press.

Cummins, J. (1989). A theoretical framework for bilingual special education. *Exceptional Children, 56*(2), 111–119.

Dana, R. H. (1996). Impact of the use of standard psychological assessment on the diagnosis and treatment of ethnic minorities. In J. F. Aponte & R. Y. Rivers (Eds.), *Psychological interventions and cultural diversity* (pp. 57–73). Boston, MA: Allyn & Bacon.

Dunn, L. M. (1959). *Peabody Picture Vocabulary Test*. Circle Pines, MN: American Guidance Service.

Dunn, L. M., & Dunn, L. M. (1981). *Peabody Picture Vocabulary Test–Revised*. Circle Pines, MN: American Guidance Service.

Dunn, L. M., & Dunn, L. M. (1997). *Peabody Picture Vocabulary Test* (3rd ed.). Circle Pines, MN: American Guidance Service.

Dunn, L. M., Padilla, E. R., Lugo, D. E., & Dunn, L. M. (1986). *Test de Vocabulario en Imagenes Peabody: Adaptacion Hispanoamericana* [Peabody Picture Vocabulary Test: Hispanic American Adaptation]. Circle Pines, MN: American Guidance Service.

Echemendia, R. J., Harris, J. G., Congett, S. M., Diaz, M. L., & Puente, A. E. (1997). Neuropsychological training and practices with Hispanics: A national survey. *Clinical Neuropsychologist, 11*(3), 229–243.

Figueroa, R. A. (1989). Psychological testing of linguistic-minority students: Knowledge gaps and regulations, *Exceptional Children, 56*(2), 145–152.

Figueroa, R. A. (1990). Assessment of linguistic minority children. In C. R. Reynolds & R. W. Kamphaus (Eds.), *Handbook of psychological and educational assessment of children: Intelligence and achievement* (pp. 671–696). New York: Guilford.

Flanagan, R. (1995). The utility of the Kaufman Assessment Battery for Children (K-ABC) and the Wechsler Intelligence scales for linguistically different children: Clinical considerations. *Psychology in the Schools, 32*(1), 5–11.

Flemmer, D., & Roid, G. H. (1996, August). *Nonverbal intellectual assessment of Hispanic and speech-impaired adolescents*. Paper presented at the meeting of the American Psychological Association, Toronto, Ontario, Canada.

Fletcher, T. (1989). A comparison of the Mexican version of the Wechsler Intelligence Scale for Children–Revised and the Woodcock Psycho-Educational Battery in Spanish. *Journal of Psychoeducational Assessment, 7*, 56–65.

Forns Santacana, M., & Gomez Benito, J. (1990). Factor structure of the McCarthy Scales. *Psychology in the Schools, 27*(2), 111–115.

Gifford, R. (1991). *Applied psychology: Variety and opportunity*. Boston, MA: Allyn & Bacon.

Gomez Benito, J., & Forns Santacana, M. (1996). Factor structure of the McCarthy Scales in 7-year-old Spanish children. *Psychology in the Schools, 33*(3), 231–238.

Gomez-Palacio, M., Rangel, E., & Padilla, E. (1985). *Kaufman Bateria de Evaluacion intelectual: Manual de aplicacion y calificacion* [Kaufman Assessment Battery for Children: Interpretive Manual]. Mexico City: Direccion General de Educacion Especial.

Gomez-Palacio, M., Ransel-Hinojosa, E., & Padilla, E. (1982). *Estandarizacion de la bateria de pruebas SOMPA in Mexico D.F.: Informe sobre teoria y resultados* [Standardization of the SOMPA battery of tests in Mexico City: Report on the theory and results]. Mexico City: Secretaira de Educacion Publica.

Grant, G., Roid, G. H., & Fallow, G. (1996, April). *Fairness of intellectual assessment for children with speech impairments*. Paper presented at the meeting of the Western Psychological Association, San Jose, CA.

Gridley, B. Bos, J. S., & Roid, G. H. (1996). *Factor structure of a new nonverbal cognitive battery: The Leiter International Performance Scale–Revised*. Paper presented at the meeting of the American Psychological Association, Toronto, Canada.

Hamayan, E. V., & Damico, J. S. (1991). *Limiting bias in the assessment of bilingual students*. Austin, TX: Pro-Ed.

Hambleton, R. K., Clauser, B. E., Mazor, K. M., & Jones, R. W. (1993). Advances in the detection of differentially functioning test items. *European Journal of Psychological Assessment, 9*(1), 1–18.

Hartlage, L. C., & Williams, B. L. (1997). Pediatric neuropsychology. In A. M. Horton, Jr., D. Wedding, & J. Webster (Eds.), *The neuropsychology handbook: Vol. 2 Treatment issues and special populations* (2nd ed., pp. 211–235). New York: Springer.

Herrans, L. L., & Rodriguez, J. M. (1992). *Escala de Inteligencia Wechsler para Ninos-Revisada* [Wechsler Intelligence Scale for Children–Revised]. San Diego, CA: The Psychological Corporation.

Hresko, W. P., Reid, D. K., & Hammill, D. D. (1982). Test review: Prueba del desarrollo inicial del lenguaje [Test of Early Language Development]. *The Reading Teacher, 428*–431.

Hresko, W. P., Reid, D. K., & Hammill, D. D. (1999). *Test of Early Language Development–Third Edition.* Austin, TX: Pro-Ed.

Kadlec, H. (1999). Statistical properties of d' and betaestimates of signal detection theory. *Psychological Methods, 4*(1), 22–43.

Karr, S. K., Carvajal, H. H., Elser, D., & Bays, K. (1993). Concurrent validity of the WPPSI–R and the McCarthy Scales of Children's Abilities. *Psychological Reports, 72,* 940–942.

Karr, S. K., Carvajal, H., & Palmer, B. L. (1992). Comparison of Kaufman's short form of the McCarthy Scales of Children's Abilities and the Stanford-Binet Intelligence Scales–Fourth Edition. *Perceptual and Motor Skills, 74*(3), 1120–1122.

Kaufman, A. S. (1975). Factor structures of the McCarthy Scales at 5 age levels between 2½ and 8½. *Educational and Psychological Measurement, 35*(3), 641–656.

Kaufman, A. S. (1982). An integrated review of almost a decade of research on the McCarthy Scales. In T. R. Kratochwill (Ed.), *Advances in school psychology* (Vol. 2, pp. 119–169). Hillsdale, NJ: Lawrence Erlbaum Associates.

Kaufman, A. S., & Kaufman, N. L. (1983). *Kaufman Assessment Battery for Children: Interpretive manual.* Circle Pines, MN: American Guidance Service.

Kaufman, A. S., Kaufman, N. L., & Padilla, E. R. (1984). *Batería Kaufman de Evaluación para Ninos: Manual para el examinador* [Kaufman Assessment Battery for Children: Examiner's Manual]. Circle Pines, MN: American Guidance Service.

Kayser, H. G. (1987). A study of three Mexican American children labeled language disordered. *NABE Journal, 12,* 1–22.

Kazdin, A. E. (1998). *Research design in clincial psychology* (3rd ed.). Boston, MA: Allyn & Bacon.

Lam, T. C. (1993). Testability: A critical issue in testing language minority students with standardized achievement tests. *Measurement and Evaluation in Counseling Development 26*(3), 179–191.

Leckliter, I. N., Matarazzo, J. D., & Silverstein, A. B. (1986). A literature review of factor analytic studies of the WAIS–R. *Journal of Clinical Psychology, 42*(2), 332–342.

Lewis, C. D., & Lorentz, S. (1994). Comparison of the Leiter International Performance Scale and the Wechsler intelligence scales. *Psychological Reports, 74,* 521–522.

Lezak, M. D. (1995). *Neuropsychological Assessment* (3rd ed.). New York: Oxford University Press.

Lopez, E. C. (1997). The cognitive assessment of limited English proficiency and bilingual children. In D. P. Flanagan & J. L. Genshaft (Eds.), *Contemporary intellectual assessment: Theories, tests, and issues* (pp. 503–516). New York: Guilford.

Madsen, D. H., Roid, G. H., & Miller, L. J. (1996, August). *Nonverbal intellectual assessment: Restandardization of a new measure — The Leiter International Performance Scale–Revised.* Paper presented at the meeting of the American Psychological Association, Toronto, Ontario, Canada.

Martin, P. C. (1977). *A Spanish translation, adaptation, and standardization of the Wechsler Intelligence Scale for Children–Revised.* Unpublished doctoral dissertation, University of Miami.

McCarthy, D. (1972). *Manual for the McCarthy Scales of Children's Abilities.* Cleveland, OH: The Psychological Corporation.

McLellan, M. J. & Walton, M. J. (1996, August). *Concurrent validation of the Leiter–R and WISC–III with Navajo children.* Paper presented at the meeting of the American Psychological Association, Toronto, Ontario, Canada.

Mellott, M. J., & McLellan, M. J. (1996, April). *Using nonverbal cognitive scales with Navajo children.* Paper presented at the meeting of the Western Psychological Association, San Jose, CA.

Mitrushina, M. N., Boone, K. B., & D'Elia, L. F. (1999). *Handbook of normative data for neuropsychological assessment.* New York: Oxford University Press.

Munford, P. R., & Muñoz, A. (1980). A comparison of the WISC and WISC–R on Hispanic children. *Journal of Clinical Psychology, 36*(2), 452–458.

Muñoz Amilibia, M. D. (1969). Adaptation and norms of the Peabody Picture Vocabulary Test in Spain. *Revista de Psicologia General y Aplicada, 24,* 677–688.

OREA. (1991). *New York City norms for the Escala de Inteligencia Wechsler para Niños–Revisada*. New York: NYC Board of Education.

Padilla, E. R., Roll, S., & Gomez-Palacio, M. G. (1982). The performance of Mexican children and adolescents on the WISC–R. *Interamerican Journal of Psychology, 16*(2), 122–128.

Pontón, M. O. (1989). *Meta-analysis of the Wechsler scales for Hispanics*. Unpublished doctoral dissertation, Fuller University.

Pontón, M. O., & Ardila, A. (1999). The future of neuropsychology with Hispanic populations in the United States. *Archives of Clinical Neuropsycholgy, 14*(7), 565–580.

Prewitt Diaz, J. O. (1988). Assessment of Puerto Rican children in bilingual education programs in the United States: A critique of Lloyd M. Dunn's monograph. *Hispanic Journal of Behavioral Sciences, 10*(3), 237–252.

Prewitt Diaz, J. O., & Rodriguez, M. D. (1986). Reliability of an experimental version in Spanish of the WISC–R with Puerto Rican children 9-5 to 13-1 years of age. *Psychological Reports, 58,* 271–275.

Purvis, M. A., & Bolen, L. M. (1984). Factor structure of the McCarthy Scales for males and females. *Journal of Clinical Psychology, 40*(1), 108–114.

Putnam, S. H., & DeLuca, J. W. (1990). The TCN professional practice survey: I. General practices of neuropsychologists in primary employment and private practice settings. *Clinical Neuropsychologist, 43*(3), 199–243.

Reilly, T. P., Drudge, O. W., Rosen, J. C., Loew, D. E., & Fischer, M. (1985). Concurrent and predictive validity of the WISC-R, McCarthy Scales, Woodcock–Johnson, and academic achievement. *Psychology in the Schools, 22,* 380–382.

Reynolds, C. R. (1992). Two key concepts in the diagnosis of learning disabilities and the habilitation of learning. *Learning Disabilities Quarterly, 15*(1), 2–12.

Richardson, K. (1995). The development of intelligence. In V. Lee & P. Das Pranja (Eds.), *Children's cognitive and language development* (pp. 149–187). Buckingham, England: The Open University.

Robertson, J. R., & Eisenberg, J. L. (1981). *Technical supplement to the Peabody Picture Vocabulary Test–Revised*. Circle Pines, MN: American Guidance Service.

Roca, P. (1955). Problems of adapting intelligence scales from one culture to another. *The High School Journal, 18*(4), 124–131.

Roid, G. H. (1996, August). *The Leiter International Performance Scale–Revised: Preliminary report on validity*. Paper presented at the meeting of the American Psychological Association, Toronto, Ontario, Canada.

Roid, G. H. (1997). *Leiter International Performance Scale–Revised*. Wood Dale, IL: Stoelting Co.

Rousey, A. (1990). Factor structure of the WISC-R Mexicano. *Educational and Psychological Measurement, 50,* 351–357.

Sandoval, J. H., Frisby, C. L., Geisinger, K. F., Sheuneman, J. D., & Grenier, J. R. (Eds.). (1998). *Test interpretation and diversity: Achieving equity in assessment*. Washington, DC: American Psychological Association.

Sattler, J. M. (1992). *Assessment of children: Revised and updated* (3rd ed.). San Diego, CA: Jerome M. Sattler.

Shellenberger, S. (1982). Assessment of Puerto Rican children: A cross-cultural study with the Spanish McCarthy Scales of Children's Abilities. *Bilingual Review, 9,* 109–119.

Shepard, L. A. (1989). Identification of mild handicaps. In R. L. Linn (Ed.), *Educational measurement* (3rd ed., pp. 545–572). New York: Macmillan.

Simon, A. J., & Joiner, L. M. (1976). A Mexican version of the Peabody Picture Vocabulary Test. *Journal of Educational Measurement, 13*(2), 137–143.

Tamayo, J. M. (1990). A validated translation into Spanish of the WISC–R vocabulary subtest words. *Educational and Psychological Measurement, 50,* 915–921.

Trueman, M., Lynch, A., & Branthwaite, A. (1984). A factor analytic study of the McCarthy Scales of Children's Abilities. *British Journal of Educational Psychology, 54*(3), 331–335.

U.S. Census Bureau of Statistics. (1997). *Findings on questions on race and Hispanic origin tested in the 1996 National Content Survey*. Washington, DC: U.S. Government Printing Office.

Valencia, R. R. (1983). Stability of the McCarthy Scales of Children's Abilities over a one-year period for Mexican-American children. *Psychology in the Schools, 20,* 29–34.

Valencia, R. R. (1988). The McCarthy scales and Hispanic children: A review of psychometric research. *Hispanic Journal of Behavioral Sciences, 10*(2), 81–104.

Valencia, R. R., & Cruz, J. (1981). *Mexican American mothers' estimations of their preschool children's cognitive performance (Report No. 90-c-1777)*. Washington, DC: Administration for Children, Youth, and Families, Office of Human Development Services, U.S. Department of Health, Education, and Welfare.

Valencia, R. R., Henderson, R. W., & Rankin, R. J. (1985). Family status, family constellation, and home environmental variables as predictors of cognitive performance of Mexican-American children. *Journal of Educational Psychology, 77,* 323–331.

Valencia, R. R., & Rankin, R. J. (1985). Evidence of content bias on the McCarthy Scales with Mexican-American children: Implications for test translation and non-biased assessment. *Journal of Educational Psychology, 77,* 197–207.

Valencia, R. R., Rankin, R. J., & Livingston, R. (1995). K-ABC content bias: Comparisons between Mexican American and White children. *Psychology in the Schools, 32,* 153–169.

Velazquez de la Cadena, M. (1985). *New revised Velazquez Spanish and English dictionary.* Piscataway, NJ: New Century Publishers.

Wechsler, D. (1949). *Wechsler Intelligence Scale for Children.* New York: The Psychological Corporation.

Wechsler, D. (1951). *Escala de Inteligencia Wechsler para Ninos* [Wechsler Intelligence Scale for Children]. New York: Psychological Corporation.

Wechsler, D. (1967). *WPPSI Manual.* New York: The Psychological Corporation.

Weiss, L. G., Prifitera, A., & Roid, G. H. (1993). The WISC-III and the fairness of predicting achievement across ethnic and gender groups. In B. A. Bracken & R. S. McCallum (Eds.), *Wechsler Intelligence Scale for Children: Third Edition. Journal of Psychoeducational Assessment. Advances in psychoeducational assessment* (pp. 35–42). Brandon, VT: Clinical Psychology.

Wilcox, K. A., & McGuinn-Aasby, S. (1988). The performance of monolingual and bilingual Mexican children on the TACL. *Language, Speech, and Hearing Services in the Schools, 19,* 34–40.

Wilen, D. K., & van Maanen Seeting, C. (1986). Assessment of limited English proficient Hispanic students. *School Psychology Review, 15*(1), 59–75.

Wilson, V. L., Reynolds, C. R., Chatman, S. P., & Kaufman, A. S. (1985). Confirmatory factor analysis of simultaneous, sequential, and achievement factors on the K-ABC at 11 age levels ranging from 2½ to 12½ years. *Journal of School Psychology, 23*(3), 261–269.

Woodcock, R. W. (1982). *Batería Woodcock Psicho-educativa en Español.* Chicago: Riverside.

Woodcock, R. W. (1991). *Woodcock Language Proficiency Battery–Revised.* Chicago: Riverside.

Woodcock, R. W., & Johnson, M. B. (1977). *Woodcock–Johnson Psycho-Educational Battery.* Chicago: Riverside.

Woodcock, R. W., & Johnson, M. B. (1989). *Woodcock–Johnson Psycho-Educational Battery–Revised.* Chicago: Riverside.

Woodcock, R. W., & Muñoz-Sandoval, A. F. (1993). *Woodcock Language Proficiency Battery–Revised, Spanish Form, supplemental manual.* Chicago: Riverside.

Woodcock, R. W., & Muñoz-Sandoval, A. F. (1996). *Batería Woodcock–Muñoz: Pruebas de aprovechamiento–Revisada.* Chicago: Riverside.

Wright, B. D., & Stone, M. H. (1980). *Best test design.* Chicago, IL: MESA Press.

Zucker, S., & Copeland, E. P. (1988). K-ABC and McCarthy scale performance among "at-risk" and normal preschoolers. *Psychology-in-the-Schools, 25*(1), 5–10.

The Batería-R in Neuropsychological Assessment

RICHARD W. WOODCOCK
ANA F. MUÑOZ-SANDOVAL
Measurement/Learning/Consultants, LLC

> *One distinguishing characteristic of neuropsychological assessment is its emphasis on the identification and measurement of psychological deficits. . . . Neuropsychological assessment is also concerned with the documentation and description of preserved functions— the patient's behavioral competencies and strengths. (Lezak, 1995, p. 97)*

This chapter provides the neuropsychologist with an overview of the Batería–R and its related English-language batteries. Although the Batería–R does not cover all aspects required for a comprehensive neuropsychological evaluation, it does provide more coverage for the assessment and description of deficits and preserved neurocognitive functions than any other single source.

The chapter is organized into two parts. Part 1 provides an overview of the Batería–R and Part 2 presents illustrative cases. The first section of Part 1 provides basic information about the system of tests, including coverage, special features, and interpretation. The second section identifies two issues related to the development and use of tests with Hispanic/Latino patients in the United States and describes how these issues were addressed in the Batería–R. The third section presents the contemporary model of multiple cognitive abilities, called Gf-Gc theory, that underlies the Batería–R. In the fourth section, the tests of the Batería–R are related to both Gf-Gc theory and the following classification, which is similar to some traditional classifications in human neuropsychology:

Attention
Visual Perception/Processing
Auditory Perception/Processing
Memory and Learning
Language
Reasoning and Problem Solving
Academic Achievement

The final section of Part 1 includes practical information for using the Batería–R with monolingual and bilingual Hispanic/Latino patients.

Part 2 presents two illustrative cases. The first case is a 22-year-old female who sustained a severe closed head injury in an automobile accident. The second case is an 8-year-old male with a language and learning disability.

PART 1: OVERVIEW OF THE BATERÍA-R

Description

The Batería–R is comprised of two separate, but co-normed, batteries: Batería Woodcock–Muñoz: Pruebas de habilidad cognitiva–Revisada (Batería–R COG) (Woodcock & Muñoz-Sandoval, 1996c), and Batería Woodcock–Muñoz: Pruebas de aprovechamiento–Revisada (Batería–R APR) (Woodcock & Muñoz-Sandoval, 1996a). Two English-language batteries are direct counterparts to the Batería–R: Woodcock–Johnson Tests of Cognitive Ability–Revised (WJ–R COG) (Woodcock & Johnson, 1989b), and the Woodcock–Johnson Tests of Achievement–Revised (WJ–R ACH) (Woodcock & Johnson, 1989a).

The pair of batteries in either language provides the neuropsychologist with a wide age range and comprehensive set of individually administered tests. Each pair of batteries provides a total of 39 tests that measures cognitive abilities, oral language, and academic achievement. All tests in the Batería–R and the WJ–R are parallel in content and organization. However, the item content is different in the tests that assess oral language, reading, and writing. As a result, scores of Spanish- or English-language abilities from the two batteries can be compared directly without concern that the subject's experience with a test in one language will enhance performance on the counterpart test in the other language.

Norms for the Batería–R are *equated* to the WJ–R norms. This was accomplished by capitalizing on certain advantages of item response theory (IRT), in particular the Rasch model, to equate and scale the *tasks* underlying each Batería–R test to their empirical difficulties in English (Woodcock & Muñoz-Sandoval, 1993, 1994). Normative data are based on 6,359 subjects, from age 24 months to over 90 years and include special norms for college and university students.

The interpretation plan for the Batería–R includes a full array of derived scores and profiles for reporting and displaying results. The functional level indices that derive from Rasch scaling are particularly useful in neuropsychological settings for describing the degree of deficit or preserved functions demonstrated by the patient in comparison to the general population. The *Woodcock Scoring and Interpretive Program* (Schrank & Woodcock, 1999) is a computer program that can score and generate narrative reports for any combination of tests from the Spanish-language Batería–R and the English-language WJ–R. The breadth of coverage and wide age range of the Batería–R make it particularly suited for use as a neuropsychological instrument with Hispanic/Latino patients, either as the primary battery or as a resource of supplemental measures.

In summary, several features of the Batería–R enhance its usefulness as a neuropsychological instrument:

The wide age range of application spans from 2 to 90+ years.

All tests are normed and used across almost the entire life span.

All major areas of cognitive functioning and academic achievement can be assessed.

The wide range of item difficulty within each test allows the documentation of strengths and superior performance as well as deficits.

Ease of administration includes page-by-page directions for all tests in easel test books.

Critical auditory stimuli tests (e.g., auditory memory span, phonological processing, and listening comprehension) are presented by recorded audiotape.

Selective testing principle allows any single test or combination of tests to be selected for use and interpreted by the norms.

Special college and university level norms are provided.

Computerized scoring and narrative report program available.

Test and Cluster Descriptions.   The 39 tests included in the Batería–R and in the WJ–R are listed in Table 8.1. The name of each test is provided both in Spanish and English.

Although many neuropsychologists evaluate performance at the level of the individual test or subtest, clusters of tests often provide the most valid way to describe deficits and preserved functions for broad abilities (e.g., short-term memory, reading ability). A cluster is a combination of two or more tests that measures different narrow aspects of a broad complex ability. Cluster interpretation minimizes the danger of generalizing from a single, narrow behavior to a broad, multifaceted ability. Cluster interpretation also tends to be more reliable than interpretation of individual tests or subtests. The Batería–R and the WJ–R provide 16 cognitive and 11 achievement clusters. Table 8.2 lists these cognitive and achievement clusters and the tests each comprise.

Further Information.   For further descriptive and technical information about the Batería–R and WJ–R, refer to the examiner's manuals accompanying those batteries and to the underlying technical manual (McGrew, Werder, & Woodcock, 1991). Other sources of information and reviews include the following:

Theoretical Foundations of the WJ–R Measures of Cognitive Ability (Woodcock, 1990). This journal article reports the results from several joint factor analysis studies with the WJ–R and other intelligence batteries.

Assessing Adult and Adolescent Intelligence (Kaufman, 1990, pp. 599–605). This section of Kaufman's book presents a description and the author's evaluation of the WJ–R COG.

Test Review of the Woodcock–Johnson Psycho-Educational Battery–Revised (McGhee & Buckhalt, 1993). A review of the WJ–R appearing in the *Journal of Psychoeducational Assessment.*

Use and Interpretation of the Woodcock–Johnson Psycho-Educational Battery–Revised (Hessler, 1993). A book that describes clinical applications of the WJ–R and includes several case studies.

Clinical Interpretation of the Woodcock–Johnson Tests of Cognitive Ability–Revised (McGrew, 1994a). The second edition of a book that bridges research and practice with the WJ–R.

Woodcock–Johnson Tests of Cognitive Ability–Revised (McGrew, 1994b). An encyclopedia article.

Review of the Woodcock–Johnson Psycho-Educational Battery–Revised (Cummings, 1994). A review found in the Buros *Supplement to the Eleventh Mental Measurements Yearbook.*

TABLE 8.1
The 39 Batería–R and WJ–R Tests

Test	Batería–R	WJ–R
Cognitive Battery		
1	Memoria para nombres	Memory for Names
2	Memoria para frases	Memory for Sentences
3	Pareo visual	Visual Matching
4	Palabras incompletas	Incomplete Words
5	Integración visual	Visual Closure
6	Vocabulario sobre dibujos	Picture Vocabulary
7	Análisis-Síntesis	Analysis-Synthesis
8	Aprendizaje visual-auditivo	Visual-Auditory Learning
9	Memoria para palabras	Memory for Words
10	Tachar	Cross Out
11	Integración de sonidos	Sound Blending
12	Reconocimiento de dibujos	Picture Recognition
13	Vocabulario oral	Oral Vocabulary
14	Formación de conceptos	Concept Formation
15	Memoria diferida–Memoria para nombres	Delayed Recall–Memory for Names
16	Memoria diferida–Aprendizaje visual-auditivo	Delayed Recall–Visual-Auditory Learning
17	Inversión de números	Numbers Reversed
18	Configuración de sonidos	Sound Patterns
19	Relaciones espaciales	Spatial Relations
20	Comprensión de oraciones	Listening Comprehension
21	Analogías verbales	Verbal Analogies
Achievement Battery		
22	Identificación de letras y palabras	Letter-Word Identification
23	Comprensión de textos	Passage Comprehension
24	Cálculo	Calculation
25	Problemas aplicados	Applied Problems
26	Dictado	Dictation
27	Muestras de redacción	Writing Samples
28	Ciencia	Science
29	Estudios sociales	Social Studies
30	Humanidades	Humanities
31	Análisis de palabras	Word Attack
32	Vocabulario de lectura	Reading Vocabulary
33	Conceptos cuantitativos	Quantitative Concepts
34	Corrección de textos	Proofing
35	Fluidez en la redacción	Writing Fluency
P	Puntuación y Mayúsculas	P Punctuation
O	Ortografía	S Spelling
C	Concordancia	U Usage
E	Escritura	H Handwriting

TABLE 8.2

TABLE 8.2
A Description of the Batería–R and WJ–R Clusters

Cluster Name	Cluster Composition
Cognitive Clusters	
Habilidad cognitiva amplia (BCA)	
Broad Cognitive Ability (BCA)	
Escala de desarrollo temprano	Tests 1, 2, 4, 5, and 6
Early Development Scale	
Escala estándar	Tests 1 to 7
Standard Scale	
Escala extendida	Tests 1 to 14
Extended Scale	
Cognitive Factors	
Recuperación a largo plazo (Glr)	Tests 1 and 8
Long-Term Retrieval	
Memoria a corto plazo (Gsm)	Tests 2 and 9
Short-Term Memory	
Rapidez en el procesamiento (Gs)	Tests 3 and 10
Processing Speed	
Procesamiento auditivo (Ga)	Tests 4 and 11
Auditory Processing	
Procesamiento visual (Gv)	Tests 5 and 12
Visual Processing	
Comprensión-Conocimiento (Gc)	Tests 6 and 13
Comprehension-Knowledge	
Procesamiento fluido (Gf)	Tests 7 and 14
Fluid Processing	
Scholastic Aptitude	
Aptitud en lectura	Tests 2, 3, 11, and 13
Reading Aptitude	
Aptitud en matemáticas	Tests 3, 7, 13, and 14
Mathematics Aptitude	
Aptitud en lenguaje escrito	Tests 3, 8, 11, and 13
Written Language Aptitude	
Aptitud en conocimiento	Tests 2, 5, 11, and 14
Knowledge Aptitude	
Oral Language	
Lenguaje oral	Tests 2, 6, 13, 20, and 21
Oral Language	
Aptitude en lenguaje oral	Tests 12, 14, 17, and 18
Oral Language Aptitude	
Academic Achievement Clusters	
Amplia lectura	Tests 22 and 23
Broad Reading	
Destrezas básicas en lectura	Tests 22 and 31
Basic Reading Skills	
Comprensión de lectura	Tests 23 and 32
Reading Comprehension	
Amplias matemáticas	Tests 24 and 25
Broad Mathematics	

Continued

TABLE 8.2 (*Continued*)

Cluster Name	Cluster Composition
Destrezas básicas en matemáticas Basic Mathematics Skills	Tests 24 and 33
Razonamiento en matemáticas Mathematics Reasoning	Test 25
Amplio lenguaje escrito Broad Written Language	Tests 26 and 27
Destrezas básicas en escritura Basic Writing Skills	Tests 26 and 34
Expresión escrita Written Expression	Tests 27 and 35
Amplio conocimiento Broad Knowledge	Tests 28, 29, and 30
Destrezas Skills	Tests 22, 25, and 26

Review of the Woodcock–Johnson Psycho-Educational Battery–Revised (Lee & Stefany, 1994). A review found in the Buros *Supplement to the Eleventh Mental Measurements Yearbook.*

The Woodcock–Johnson Tests of Cognitive Ability–Revised (Woodcock, 1997). A chapter in a book devoted to contemporary theories and tests used for intellectual assessment.

Issues Related to the Development and Norming of Tests for Use With Hispanic/Latino Patients

Translating . . . tests and questionnaires prepared in one language and culture for use in other languages and cultures has been a long-standing practice. Unfortunately, there is considerable technical evidence which suggests that the quality of test translations vary considerably and too often the translations are not very good, thus reducing the validity of any results produced with the translated tests and questionnaires. (Hambleton, 1993, p. 57)

Among the issues that must be considered by developers of a Spanish-language test, especially if it is to be used in the United States, are problems of translation/adaptation and of norming. This section describes how those issues have been addressed during the development of the Batería–R.

Translation/Adaptation. During test development, special attention was directed toward designing items and test instructions that would be deemed appropriate across the Spanish-speaking world. Professionals from several regions of the Spanish-speaking world were involved cooperatively in developing the item banks and in the preparation and review of test instructions.

A frequent experience reported by those who have been involved in the translation of a test into Spanish is as follows: The test goes through its first translation, perhaps by someone of Mexican background. This translation is then passed to a different translator, perhaps of Puerto Rican background, for review and edits. The edited version is passed on again for review and edits, perhaps to a translator of South American origin. Typically, at each stage, many "errors" will be noted and the comment made that "this is not good

Spanish," or "this is not the way *we* would say that." Experiences of this kind reinforce the myth that no single translation will be acceptable to Spanish-speakers from different regions of the Spanish-speaking world. This myth is based on the assumption that there are major differences in the Spanish language used in different regions of the world.

There are fewer differences in Spanish spoken across the Spanish-speaking world than there are in English spoken just within the United States, and even fewer differences if the comparison extends to other English-speaking countries (e.g., England and Australia). A Spanish-speaker can go to any other place in the Spanish-speaking world and immediately communicate fully and clearly. There are, of course, pronunciation differences from one part of the Spanish-speaking world to another, but these are minor compared to the differences in English pronunciations just within the United States. Standard written Spanish has even fewer, if any, differences from region to region. It is also noteworthy that television programming in any Spanish-speaking country utilizes a mixture of programs originating from throughout the Spanish-speaking world.

A source of difference from one part of the Spanish-speaking world to another (as in the English-speaking world) is the vocabulary for some common objects. Some of this vocabulary may be an important component in certain test items. The plan for developing an acceptable test translation, therefore, should include procedures for identifying and accommodating these regional differences in common vocabulary. Appropriate accommodations may include the provision of alternate terminology for some test directions, answer keys that include acceptable variant answers, and even the exclusion of particular items from the translated test.

A critical goal of test translation is to communicate the exact intent of the instructions and scoring keys. This often involves manipulating subtle nuances of language. Toward approximating this goal, a strategy of "consensus translation" (Woodcock & Muñoz-Sandoval, 1992) has been adopted. Three principles underlie the consensus translation approach.

1. Whenever possible, a translator should be someone whose native language is Spanish. Many persons, for whom a second language has been acquired, will not be sufficiently sensitive to the unique patterns of a language to produce a translation that sounds natural to a native speaker.

2. The initial translation of items and directions should involve several Spanish-speaking professionals, preferably representing different regions of the world. The output from each translator should be reviewed by at least two other translators. The "corrections" suggested by subsequent reviewers are not (and this is important!) accepted automatically. The suggestions are passed back and forth among the reviewers and original translators until a consensus is achieved.

3. During the course of data gathering, which will ideally take place in several Spanish-speaking countries, each data-gatherer has an additional responsibility to provide a critique of the test translation and scoring keys. These critiques are, in turn, reviewed and evaluated by the earlier participants in the consensus translation effort.

The frequently suggested "back translation" procedure in which a test is translated into Spanish and then translated back into English by another translator to be checked against the original English text, has not been as effective as the consensus translation approach. On the surface, back translation appears eminently logical. Some advocates of back translation may assume, perhaps from lack of personal translating experience, that the major task is to translate the words. Such exact translations are usually impossible to achieve. A more realistic goal is to seek an adaptation of the test with an "equivalent" translation that has accommodated the nuances in both languages.

Norming. "Why not base your norms on data from a sample of Spanish-speaking children and adults residing in the United States?" "Isn't this the group to which test performance should be compared?" These question are asked frequently. The test norms, no matter what the source, are valid only to the extent that they provide meaningful information with which to compare an individual's test performance. For the information to be meaningful, the data must be drawn carefully from a sample of a relevant population that is expected to remain somewhat stable over time. For a population to be relevant, it must be a group (e.g., the general population of the United States) with familiar characteristics to test users. If the nature of the sampled population is not well-defined, or if it is in a state of flux, then the obtained norms cannot be relied on and, at best, may have been valid only at the time they were collected.

At this time, it would be difficult, if not impossible, to assemble a norming sample of Spanish-speaking subjects in the United States that would be accepted by the majority of professionals as representative enough for their purposes. Details regarding the distribution and location of the Spanish-speaking subpopulation are limited, and the composition of this subpopulation is constantly changing. In contrast, the general population of the United States, a group that is both describable and relatively stable over time, is the standard reference for norms on tests used in the United States. There are advantages, therefore, in providing a system of norms that allows comparison to the general population of the United States. Through calibration and equating research, it is possible to relate performance on tests in the Spanish language to the distribution of like abilities in the general U.S. population (Woodcock & Muñoz-Sandoval, 1993, 1994).

Certain tests in the Batería–R (e.g., Pareo visual/Visual Matching, Formación de conceptos/Concept Formation, Cálculo/Calculation) have identical item content and task requirements whether presented with Spanish-language or English-language instructions. With such tests, the WJ–R norms are used directly. The remaining tests have different item content in their Spanish-language form. It has been necessary, therefore, to collect research data for the purpose of calibrating new items and equating scores on the Spanish tests to the WJ–R norms (Woodcock & Muñoz-Sandoval, 1996b, 1996d).

Because language is highly developmental and some tests are used to evaluate an individual's language level, the subjects included in the test calibration and norming samples should reflect the general normal course of development in Spanish. Data from subjects who are not in the general stream of normal language development present an unreliable sequence and pattern of language proficiency. Many children developing language in a bilingual setting are probably not developing vocabulary and other language skills in the same general progression as their monolingual counterparts in either language.

The sample chosen to calibrate and equate the Spanish-language items was drawn from both inside and outside the United States. Calibration-equating data for each test were typically obtained from approximately 2,000 native Spanish-speaking subjects. The subjects sought for inclusion in this study were to be monolingual Spanish, or nearly so. Altogether, 3,911 different subjects were administered one or more of the calibration-equating tests. The Spanish-language ability of these subjects ranged from age 2 to university graduate students. Of these subjects, 116 were tested in Costa Rica, 1,512 in Mexico, 196 in Peru, 634 in Puerto Rico, 128 in Spain, and 1,325 in the United States. The subjects tested in the United States were drawn from five states: 68 from Arizona, 357 from

TABLE 8.3
U.S. Spanish Calibration Sample: Country of Birth

Country	n
United States	331
Mexico	254
Cuba	98
Nicaragua	92
Dominican Republic	85
Puerto Rico	61
Honduras	58
Colombia	31
Venezuela	24
Peru	20
Spain	13
Ecuador	12
Guatemala	12
El Salvador	12
Argentina, Chile, Costa Rica, Panama, Paraguay, Bahamas, Brazil, Bolivia	8 or less, each country
Not reported	198
Total	1,325

California, 476 from Florida, 191 from New York, and 233 from Texas. Table 8.3 presents data regarding country of birth for the subjects tested in the United States.

The concept of "Equated U.S. Norms," that is, Spanish norms *equated* to English norms, first appeared as a feature of the *Batería Woodcock de proficiencia en el idioma* (Woodcock, 1981). An important outcome of this procedure is that the tasks underlying each Spanish test are rescaled according to the empirical difficulty of counterpart tasks in English. The preparation of U.S. Equated Norms for the Batería–R was accomplished by the application of Rasch model technology (Rasch, 1960; Wright & Linacre, 1991; Wright & Stone, 1979). Briefly stated, a bank of English items was developed, Rasch-calibrated, and normed, all as part of the development and norming of the WJ–R. Following that, a similar bank of Spanish items was developed and Rasch-calibrated. Included in the bank of Spanish items was a subset of items drawn from the English item bank, translated into Spanish, and used as an equating link between the two banks of items. The difficulty scale underlying the Spanish item bank was then rescaled, through the intermediate subset of parallel equating items, to the difficulty scale underlying the English bank.

Gf-Gc Theory

Effective use of any test battery is enhanced by understanding the theory on which it is based. The Batería–R is an operational representation of a particular theory of cognitive processing—the Horn-Cattell *Gf-Gc theory*. At an American Psychological Association meeting in 1941, Cattell proposed two types of intelligence that he called *fluid* and *crystallized*. Since 1941, Gf-Gc theory has grown and emerged as a major conceptualization of multiple intelligences. Eight to 10 broad abilities have been consistently identified through factor analysis and replicated in the work of Cattell, Horn, and others (Horn, 1988, 1991, 1998; Horn & Noll, 1997; Woodcock, 1994, 1998a). Another prominent empirically derived theory of multiple cognitive abilities is Carroll's *three-stratum theory*

(Carroll, 1993, 1997, 1998). Both theories have evolved from the statistical and logical analyses of hundreds of data sets involving many published and unpublished batteries of cognitive tests. Stratum two of Carroll's three-stratum theory and the set of second-order factors described by Gf-Gc theory are quite similar in detail and number. For the purpose of this chapter, the discussion of cognitive ability is oriented toward Gf-Gc theory.

The Batería–R assesses the nine Gf-Gc broad abilities listed in Table 8.4. Included in the table is a brief definition of each ability and a statement of some possible implications for a patient with deficits. One of the factors, Reading/Writing (Grw), has not yet been well-defined in the literature but has been recognized by several investigators (Carroll, 1993; Horn, 1988; McGrew et al., 1991; Woodcock, 1998a). The Grw factor appears to represent a common factor underlying both reading and writing.

An important feature of Gf-Gc theory is the distinction between broad abilities and the narrower aspects of each ability. Each of the broad abilities can be measured by a variety of tasks, each of which could measure a different narrow aspect of the broad ability. These narrow abilities are called *first-order factors* in Gf-Gc theory and *first-stratum factors* in Carroll's three-stratum theory. McGrew (1997) classified the individual tests in several major cognitive batteries according to their likely first-order narrow ability factor or factors.

Why should a practicing neuropsychologist expend time studying new models of cognitive abilities and, in particular, Gf-Gc theory? One reason is that these models are based on the best of current research into the structure of intellect and provide new insights about the nature of cognitive ability. A second reason is that the Gf-Gc organization offers an empirically derived classification of cognitive abilities that is characterized by a high level of functional independence among the categories. Traditional classifications used in neuropsychology have evolved out of clinical practice and broadly defined areas of special interest. As a result, the classifications sometimes overlap and, at other times, they may be a mix of two or three distinctly different types of functions as defined by current cognitive science. Toward the goal of urging the integration of Gf-Gc theory into current neuropsychological thought, the next section discusses the measurement of deficits and preserved functions in the context of a traditional organization but cross-referenced to Gf-Gc categories and labels.

Application of the Batería–R to Areas of Neuropsychological Assessment

The Batería–R provides measures across a wide spectrum of functions. For some functions, the available tests are observed to measure aspects of a process from basic to more complex. When this is obvious, the tests are ordered along this dimension in the discussion. Note that several tests appear in more than one category of functions.

Attention (Gs, Gsm).   In the past several decades, *attention* has evolved from its conceptualization as a unitary construct to a complex and multidimensional construct (Mirsky, 1996). The Batería–R does not measure all of the important aspects of this construct; however three aspects—*selective attention, sustained attention,* and *attentional capacity*—are measured by the six tests listed in Table 8.5. These three aspects of attention are labeled *focus/execute, sustain,* and *encode* by Mirsky. Two of the Batería–R tests, Visual Matching (Gs) and Cross Out (Gs), are speed tests that measure selective and sustained attention. Each of these two tests have a 3-minute time limit. A third test, Writing Fluency (a mixed measure of Gs and Grw), probably measures sustained attention only. That test has a 7-minute time limit.

TABLE 8.4
A Description of Nine Gf-Gc Broad Abilities

Gf-Gc Ability	Description	Implications of Deficits
Rapidez en el procesamiento (Gs) Processing Speed	The ability to rapidly perform automatic or very simple cognitive tasks.	Gs deficits are characterized by slowness in executing easy cognitive tasks.
Procesamiento visual (Gv) Visual Processing	Spatial orientation and the ability to analyze and synthesize visual stimuli.	Gv deficits may result in poor spatial orientation, misperception of object–space relations, difficulty with art, and difficulty with using maps.
Procesamiento auditivo (Ga) Auditory Processing	The ability to analyze and synthesize auditory stimuli.	Ga deficits may be characterized by speech discrimination problems, poor phonological knowledge, and failure in recognizing sounds.
Memoria a corto plazo (Gsm) Short-Term Memory	The ability to hold information in immediate awareness and then use it within a few seconds.	Gsm deficits may result in difficulty in remembering just imparted instructions or information.
Recuperación a largo plazo (Glr) Long-term Retrieval	The ability to store information and retrieve it later through association.	Glr deficits may result in difficulty in recalling relevant information, and in learning and retrieving names.
Comprensión-Conocimiento (Gc) Comprehension-Knowledge	The breadth and depth of knowledge, including verbal communication, information, and reasoning when using previously learned procedures.	Gc deficits are characterized by lack of information, language skills, and knowledge of procedures.
Razonamiento fluido (Gf) Fluid Reasoning	The ability to reason, form concepts, and solve problems that include unfamiliar information or procedures. Manifested in the reorganization, transformation, and extrapolation of information.	Gf deficits may be characterized by difficulty in generalizing rules, forming concepts, and seeing implications.
Lectura/Escritura (Grw) Reading/Writing	An ability associated with both reading and writing, probably including basic reading and writing skills, and the skills required for comprehension/expression.	Grw deficits are reflected in difficulty with reading and writing tasks.
Habilidad cuantitativa (Gq) Quantitative Ability	The ability to comprehend quantitative concepts and relationships and to manipulate numerical symbols.	Gq deficits are reflected in difficulty with numerical tasks.

Three other tests are measures of attentional capacity. Memory for Words (Gsm) and Numbers Reversed (Gsm) are clean measures of short-term memory, whereas Memory for Sentences (Gsm, Gc) is a factorially mixed measure. There are probably no strong measures of another type of attention (i.e., divided or shifting) in the Batería–R.

Visual Perception/Processing (Gv). Visual skills are part of everyday life that enable individuals to receive, process, integrate, and synthesize information that is seen. Table

TABLE 8.5
Batería–R/WJ–R Tests of Attention

Test	Gf/Gc Factor	Description
Selective and Sustained Attention		
3 Pareo visual / Visual Matching	Gs	Measures the ability to quickly locate and circle the two identical numbers in a row of six numbers: Task proceeds in difficulty from single-digit numbers to triple-digit numbers and has a 3-minute time limit.
10 Tachar / Cross Out	Gs	Measures the ability to quickly scan and compare visual information: Subject must mark the 5 drawings in a row of 20 drawings that are identical to the first drawing in the row; examinee is given a 3-minute time limit to complete as many rows of items as possible.
Sustained Attention		
35 Fluidez en la redacción / Writing Fluency	Gs, Grw	Measures the examinee's skill in formulating and writing simple sentences quickly. This subtest has a 7-minute time limit.
Attentional Capacity		
9 Memoria para palabras / Memory for Words	Gsm	Measures the ability to repeat lists of unrelated words in the correct sequence; words are presented by audiotape.
2 Memoria para frases / Memory for Sentences	Gsm, Gc	Measures the ability to remember and repeat simple words, phrases, and sentences presented auditorily by a tape player.
17 Inversión de números / Numbers Reversed	Gsm	Measures the ability to repeat a series of random numbers backward; number sequences are presented by audiotape. A measure of "working memory."

TABLE 8.6
Batería–R/WJ–R Tests of Visual Perception/Processing

Test	Gf/Gc Factor	Description
5 Integración visual / Visual Closure	Gv	Measures the ability to name a drawing or picture of a simple object that is altered or obscured in one of several ways.
19 Relaciones espaciales / Spatial Relations	Gv	Measures the ability to visually match, mentally rotate, and combine shapes; subject must select, from a series of shapes, the component parts composing a given whole shape.
12 Reconocimiento de dibujos / Picture Recognition	Gv	Measures the ability to recognize a subset of previously presented pictures within a larger set of pictures. A measure of visual memory.

8.6 lists the three Batería–R tests of visuospatial processing: Visual Closure (Gv), Spatial Relations (Gv), and Picture Recognition (Gv). Picture Recognition may be interpreted also as a measure of *visual memory.*

Auditory Perception/Processing (Ga).   Auditory processing involves the ability to perceive, discriminate, process, and synthesize both speech and nonspeech sounds. The three Batería–R tests listed in Table 8.7 measure aspects of auditory functioning. The first two tests, Incomplete Words (Ga) and Sound Blending (Ga), are measures of *phonologi-*

TABLE 8.7
Batería–R/WJ–R Tests of Auditory Perception/Processing

	Test	Gf/Gc Factor	Description
4	Palabras incompletas Incomplete Words	Ga	An audiotape subtest that measures auditory closure: After hearing a recorded word with one or more phonemes missing, subject names the complete word.
11	Integración de sonidos Sound Blending	Ga	Measures the ability to integrate and then say whole words after hearing parts (syllables and/or phonemes) of the word; audiotape presents word parts in their proper order for each item.
18	Configuración de sonidos Sound Patterns	Ga	Measures the ability to indicate whether pairs of complex sound patterns are the same or different: Patterns may differ in pitch, rhythm, or sound content; sound patterns are presented by an audiotape.

cal awareness or *phonemic knowledge*. The third test, Sound Patterns (Ga), is a non-language auditory task measuring sensitivity to differences in timing, pitch, or content between a pair of complex sound patterns.

Memory and Learning (Gsm, Glr, and Gc).   Memory and learning tests constitute the broadest category of tests in a traditional neuropsychological classification. Three of the Gf-Gc broad abilities (Gsm, Glr, Gc) fall within this category.

The clinical assessment of memory deficits typically involves evaluation of the ability to actively learn and remember new material presented in both auditory and visual modalities. The adequacy of both *short-term memory* (immediate recall) and *long-term retention* (delayed recall) are typically assessed. Indices of remote memory may also be helpful with persons of advanced age and other clinical populations. Eleven of the Batería–R tests are presented in Table 8.8 as good measures of some aspect of memory or learning. Tests of auditory short-term memory include Memory for Words (Gsm), Memory for Sentences (a mixed measure of Gsm and Gc), and Numbers Reversed (Gsm). Numbers Reversed may also be interpreted as a measure of *working memory*. Picture Recognition (Gv) is included in Table 8.8 as an indicator of immediate visual recall.

The next four tests in Table 8.8 are classified as measures of *new learning, long-term retrieval*, or *associational memory*. Memory for Names (Glr) is an auditory-visual association learning task and Visual-Auditory Learning (Glr) is a visual-auditory association learning task. Both tests require learning new material with corrective feedback provided whenever the examinee makes an error. There are delayed recall versions of these two tests that are based on the ability to recall the newly learned associations from 1 to 8 days later: Delayed Recall–Memory for Names (Glr) and Delayed Recall–Visual-Auditory Learning (Glr). The Batería–R/WJ–R Tests of Memory and Learning are among the few clinical memory tests that include standardized and normed delay procedures extending more than 24 hours after initial administration.

Two other tests in the Batería–R are not listed in Table 8.8, but they can be characterized as new learning tasks: Analysis-Synthesis (Gf) and Concept Formation (Gf).

Some neuropsychologists include tests of learned information (sometimes called *long-term memory* or *remote memory*) among their assessment procedures. The three Batería–R tests of knowledge may serve this purpose: Science (Gc), Social Studies (Gc), and Humanities (Gc).

TABLE 8.8
Batería–R/WJ–R Tests of Memory and Learning

Test	Gf/Gc Factor	Description
Short-Term Memory		
9 Memoria para palabras Memory for Words	Gsm	Measures the ability to repeat lists of unrelated words in the correct sequence; words are presented by audiotape.
2 Memoria para frases Memory for Sentences	Gsm	Measures the ability to remember and repeat simple words, phrases, and sentences presented auditorily by a tape player.
17 Inversión de números Numbers Reversed	Gsm	Measures the ability to repeat a series of random numbers backward; number sequences are presented by audiotape. A measure of "working memory."
12 Reconocimiento de dibujos Picture Recognition	Gv	Measures the ability to recognize a subset of previously presented pictures within a larger set of pictures. A measure of visual memory.
Long-Term Retrieval		
1 Memoria para nombres Memory for Names	Glr	Measures the ability to learn associations between unfamiliar auditory and visual stimuli (an auditory-visual association task): Task requires learning the names of a series of space creatures.
8 Aprendizaje visual-auditivo Visual-Auditory Learning	Glr	Measures the ability to associate new visual symbols (rebuses) with familiar words in oral language and to translate a series of symbols presented as a reading passage (a visual-auditory association task).
15 Memoria diferida–Memoria para nombres Delayed Recall–Memory for Names	Glr	Measures the ability to recall (after 1 to 8 days) the space creatures presented in Memory for Names.
16 Memoria diferida–Aprendizaje visual-auditivo Delayed Recall–Visual-Auditory Learning	Glr	Measures the ability to recall (after 1 to 8 days) the symbols (rebuses) presented in Visual-Auditory Learning.
Remote Memory		
28 Ciencia Science	Gc	Measures the subject's knowledge in various areas of the biological and physical sciences.
29 Estudios sociales Social Studies	Gc	Measures the subject's knowledge of history, geography, government, economics, and other aspects of social studies.
30 Humanidades Humanities	Gc	Measures the subject's knowledge in various areas of art, music, and literature.

Language (Gc). The ability to communicate through language is typically assessed through examination of both receptive and expressive language. The three broad divisions of language are oral language, reading, and writing. The Batería–R tests of oral language are discussed in this section. Reading and writing are generally considered skills that are learned primarily through formal schooling. Therefore, those tests are described in the section on academic achievement.

The spectrum of oral language tasks included in the Batería–R range from requiring the naming of pictures to verbal reasoning. The five oral language tests, listed in Table

TABLE 8.9
Batería–R/WJ–R Tests of Language

	Test	Gf/Gc Factor	Description
6	Vocabulario sobre dibujos Picture Vocabulary	Gc	Measures the ability to name familiar and unfamiliar pictured objects.
13	Vocabulario oral Oral Vocabulary	Gc	Measures knowledge of word meanings. In Part A: Synonyms, the examinee must say a word similar in meaning to the word presented. In Part B: Antonyms, the examinee must say a word that is opposite in meaning to the word presented.
2	Memoria para frases Memory for Sentences	Gc, Gsm	Measures the ability to remember and repeat simple words, phrases, and sentences presented auditorily by a tape player.
20	Comprensión de oraciones Listening Comprehension	Gc	Measures the ability to listen to a short tape-recorded passage and to verbally supply the single word missing at the end of the passage.
21	Analogías verbales Verbal Analogies	Gc, Gf	Measures the ability to complete phrases with words that indicate appropriate analogies; although the vocabulary remains relatively simple, the relations among the words become increasingly complex.

8.9, include Picture Vocabulary (Gc), Oral Vocabulary (Gc), Memory for Sentences (a mixed measure of Gc and Gsm), Listening Comprehension (Gc), and Verbal Analogies (a mixed measure of Gc and Gf).

The front cover of the *Batería–R Test Record* provides a structured Language Use Survey used to record information about five aspects of the examinee's language history and use. The questions address the first language learned by the examinee and to what extent different languages are used by the examinee and others at home, in informal social situations, and in the classroom. This additional information may be useful to the neuropsychologist for Hispanic/Latino patients.

Reasoning and Problem-Solving (Gf).   Problem solving, or the ability to arrive at solutions in novel and unpracticed situations, involves a complex set of cognitive processes. Abstract thinking and adequate concept formation are required to formulate flexible ideas and strategies and to apply them across a variety of situations.

Table 8.10 lists the seven tests in the Batería–R that measure aspects of reasoning. Two tests are strong measures of abstract reasoning: Analysis-Synthesis (Gf) and Concept Formation (Gf). Three other tests that measure reasoning or types of problem solving include Verbal Analogies (Gf mixed with Gc), Spatial Relations (Gv), and Numbers Reversed (Gsm).

Some discussions of tests that measure reasoning (e.g., Carroll, 1993) include quantitative reasoning. The two Batería–R tests that may be considered measures of quantitative reasoning are Calculation (Gq) and Applied Problems (Gq). These two tests are listed again as measures of academic achievement.

Academic Achievement.   The Batería–R provides a number of tests that measure learned skills associated with formal schooling. Four tests of reading (see Table 8.11) measure the ability to identify letters and words in isolation to the comprehension of writ-

TABLE 8.10
Batería–R/WJ–R Tests of Reasoning and Problem Solving

	Test	Gf/Gc Factor	Description
7	Análisis-Síntesis Analysis-Synthesis	Gf	Measures the ability to analyze the components of an incomplete logic puzzle and to determine and name the missing components.
14	Formación de conceptos Concept Formation	Gf	Measures the ability to identify and state the rule for a concept about a set of colored geometric figures when shown instances and noninstances of the concept.
21	Analogías verbales Verbal Analogies	Gf, Gc	Measures the ability to complete phrases with words that indicate appropriate analogies; although the vocabulary remains relatively simple, the relation among the words become increasingly complex.
19	Relaciones espaciales Spatial Relations	Gv	Measures the ability to visually match and combine shapes; subject must select, from a series of shapes, the component parts composing a given whole shape.
17	Inversión de números Numbers Reversed	Gsm	Measures the ability to repeat a series of random numbers backward; number sequences are presented by audiotape.
24	Cálculo Calculation	Gq	Measures the subject's skill in performing mathematical calculation ranging from simple addition to calculus; subject is not required to make any decisions about what operations to use or what data to include.
25	Problemas aplicados Applied Problems	Gq	Measures the subject's skill in analyzing and solving practical problems in mathematics; subject must decide not only the appropriate mathematical operations to use but also which of the data to include in the calculation.

ten text. The tests are Letter-Word Identification (Grw), Word Attack (Grw mixed with Ga), Reading Vocabulary (Grw mixed with Gc), and Passage Comprehension (Grw).

The four tests of writing ability include Dictation (Grw), Proofing (Grw), Writing Fluency (Grw mixed with Gs), and Writing Samples (Grw). They are listed in Table 8.12.

The tests of mathematics are listed in Table 8.13 and include Calculation (Gq), Applied Problems (Gq), and Quantitative Concepts (Gq mixed with Gc).

Three of the Batería–R tests measure knowledge in the major content areas. They are listed in Table 8.14 and include Science (Gc), Social Studies (Gc), and Humanities (Gc). These three tests have been described earlier as possible measures of remote memory.

Handwriting. The Batería–R includes a normed scale of handwriting legibility. A patient's quality of handwriting may provide useful information about fine-motor hand coordination. This may be particularly useful if premorbid samples of the patient's handwriting are also available for evaluation. Although this procedure is usually applied to the written output from the Writing Samples test, the scale can be applied to any handwritten product.

Using the Batería–R

Learning to Use the Batería–R. Competent administration and interpretation of any portion of the Batería–R require careful study and practice, as with any clinical instrument. The test procedures have been designed so that experienced clinical testers can

TABLE 8.11
Batería–R/WJ–R Tests of Reading Achievement

	Test	Gf/Gc Factor	Description
22	Identificación de letras y palabras Letter-Word Identification	Grw	Measures the examinee's reading skills in identifying isolated letters and words. It is not necessary that the examinee know the meaning of any word correctly identified.
31	Análisis de palabras Word Attack	Grw, Ga	Measures the examinee's ability in applying phonic and structural analysis skills to the pronunciation of phonically regular words.
32	Vocabulario de lectura Reading Vocabulary	Grw, Gc	Measures the examinee's skill in reading words and supplying appropriate meanings. In Part A: Synonyms, the examinee must state a word similar in meaning to the word presented. In Part B: Antonyms, the examinee must state a word that is opposite in meaning to the word presented.
23	Comprensión de textos Passage Comprehension	Grw	Measures the examinee's skill in reading a short passage and identifying a missing key word. In this modified cloze procedure, the examinee must exercise a variety of comprehension and vocabulary skills.

TABLE 8.12
Batería–R/WJ–R Tests of Writing Ability

	Test	Gf/Gc Factor	Description
26	Dictado Dictation	Grw	Measures the examinee's skill in providing written responses to a variety of questions requiring knowledge of letter forms, spelling, punctuation, capitalization, and word usage.
34	Corrección de textos Proofing	Grw	Measures the examinee's skill in identifying a mistake in a typewritten passage and indicating how to correct the mistake. The error in the passage may be incorrect punctuation or capitalization, inappropriate word usage, or a misspelling.
35	Fluidez en la redacción Writing Fluency	Grw, Gs	Measures the examinee's skill in formulating and writing simple sentences quickly. This subtest has a 7-minute time limit.
27	Muestras de redacción Writing Samples	Grw	Measures the examinee's skill in writing responses to a variety of demands. The examinee must phrase and present written sentences that are evaluated with respect to the quality of expression. The examinee is not penalized for errors in the basic mechanics of writing, such as spelling or punctuation.

become proficient in administering the Batería–R through self-study, practice, and observation. Each of the two examiner's manuals contains a chapter entitled "Examiner Training and Practice Exercises." Those chapters provide a guide to examiner training, including a suggested learning sequence with examiner review and practice exercises.

Interpretation. The range of interpretive information available for each test and cluster in the Batería–R includes information regarding test behavior and errors, developmental status (age equivalents, grade equivalents), degree of proficiency, and comparison

TABLE 8.13
Batería–R/WJ–R Tests of Mathematics Achievement

	Test	Gf/Gc Factor	Description
24	Cálculo Calculation	Gq	Measures the examinee's skill in performing mathematical calculation ranging from simple addition to calculus; examinee is not required to make any decisions about what operations to use or what data to include.
25	Problemas aplicados Applied Problems	Gq	Measures the examinee's skill in analyzing and solving practical problems in mathematics; examinee must decide not only the appropriate mathematical operations to use but also which of the data to include in the calculation.
33	Conceptos cuantitativos Quantitative Concepts	Gq, Gc	Measures the examinee's knowledge of mathematical concepts and vocabulary. No calculation skills are required.

TABLE 8.14
Batería–R/WJ–R Tests of Curricular Knowledge

	Test	Gf/Gc Factor	Description
28	Ciencia Science	Gc	Measures the examinee's knowledge in various areas of the biological and physical sciences.
29	Estudios sociales Social Studies	Gc	Measures the examinee's knowledge of history, geography, government, economics, and other aspects of social studies.
30	Humanidades Humanities	Gc	Measures the examinee's knowledge in various areas of art, music, and literature.

with age or grade peers (percentile ranks, standard scores). The examiner's manuals for the Batería–R COG and Batería–R APR explain the derivation and use of the several interpretation options.

Table 8.15 presents a suggested modification for the verbal labels used in Table 2-2 of the supplemental manuals for the Batería–R. The terminology in those tables is oriented toward reporting levels of language functioning. Table 8.15 provides a parallel set of labels oriented toward reporting levels of deficit or preserved function in neuropsychological reports.

Spanish-Speaking Ancillary Examiners. There is a major need to assess cognitive abilities and academic achievement in Hispanic/Latino patients with tests such as the Batería–R. Unfortunately, qualified Spanish-speaking examiners may be unavailable in some clinical settings. It is both practical and proper, however, to prepare a Spanish-speaker to assist in the assessment process following appropriate training and under supervision. Chapter 4 in the *Batería–R Supplemental Manuals* (Woodcock & Muñoz-Sandoval, 1996b, 1996d) describes a *primary and ancillary examiner team* approach that facilitates obtaining assessments in the Spanish language when a regularly qualified Spanish-speaking examiner is not available.

For the purposes of ancillary examiner training, as described in the supplemental manuals, it is assumed that the *primary examiner* is English-speaking and qualified to use the WJ–R. The *ancillary examiner* is preferably a native Spanish-speaker who will be trained to administer the Batería–R. The trained ancillary examiner will administer the test and

TABLE 8.15
Functional Level/Deficit Descriptions

Functional Level	Patient Will Find Demands of Related Age Level Tasks	RPI	W Difference
Advanced	Very Easy	96/90 to 100/90	+10 and above
Adequate	Manageable	75/90 to 96/90	−10 to +10
Mildly Impaired	Very Difficult	25/90 to 75/90	−30 to −10
Moderately Impaired	Extremely Difficult	4/90 to 25/90	−50 to −30
Severely Impaired	Impossible	0/90 to 4/90	−50 and below

compute raw scores under the supervision of the primary examiner. The primary examiner will continue to be responsible for the calculation of derived scores and the interpretation of test results.

The chapter describing ancillary examiner training includes detailed directions for conducting the training, practice exercises, and a checklist to use while observing the ancillary examiner administer practice tests.

PART 2: ILLUSTRATIVE CASES

Two cases are presented to illustrate the use of the Batería–R in neuropsychological assessment. Each case is based on an actual evaluation, although identifying characteristics and additional details are changed to protect confidentiality. The reports are abbreviated, therefore the reasons for referral, medical history, test results, and conclusions are presented in a summarized form. Substantial background history, behavioral and qualitative observations, recommendations, and test results from other neuropsychological instruments have not been included. The table of scores presented for each case is a modified version of the table produced by the scoring and reporting program (Schrank & Woodcock, 1997).

Case 1: Traumatic Brain Injury in a 22-Year-Old Female

Reason for Referral

María M. was referred for neuropsychological evaluation after having sustained a severe closed head injury in an automobile accident 8 months prior to this evaluation. She was admitted to the hospital comatose with a Glasgow Coma Scale score of 7. She demonstrated impaired consciousness for approximately 40 hours after the accident. CT scans revealed a right frontal cerebral contusion. Subsequent to the accident, María developed frontal migraine headaches with visual anomalies. At the time of this evaluation, María presented with complaints of poor concentration, generalized feelings of apathy, mood swings, and depression. She reported that she is easily fatigued by tasks that she previously accomplished without difficulty.

Background Information

María is a 22-year-old Hispanic woman. She was raised in Monterey, Mexico, and has a high school education. She has lived in the United States about 5 years and has worked as a stock clerk in a retail store. She was administered the *Woodcock–Muñoz Language Survey* in Spanish and in English. The results indicate that she has limited to fluent proficiency in oral and written Spanish, but very limited proficiency in English.

Tests Administered

María was administered a set of tests from the *Batería Woodcock–Muñoz: Pruebas de habilidad cognitiva–Revisada* and the *Batería Woodcock–Muñoz: Pruebas de aprovechamiento–Revisada*. The *Pruebas de habilidad cognitiva* measure overall intellectual functioning and specific cognitive abilities. The *Pruebas de aprovechamiento* measure various aspects of scholastic achievement.

Test Results and Interpretation

María's cognitive functions were examined in a variety of areas (see Table 8.16). Test results are described primarily in terms of comparison to age peers (*percentile rank*) and relative proficiency (descriptive terms, such as *within normal limits* or *mildly impaired,* corresponding to the quality of María's performance on criterion tasks of given difficulty).

General Cognitive and Intellectual Functioning.   María's Broad Cognitive Ability, an overall measure of intellectual functioning, ranks at the 15th percentile for her age. Her global capacity to understand and cope with the surrounding world appears mildly impaired to within normal limits. She may have greater difficulty in endeavors requiring the specific abilities (discussed later) in which she demonstrates relative weakness.

Attention.   María's ability to sustain and focus attention over brief periods of time is mildly impaired; she ranks at the 11th percentile for her age. She is likely to find age-appropriate tasks very difficult when asked to sustain attention over time and resist distraction.

Visual Perception/Processing.   María's ability to visually process information is mildly impaired and ranks at the 4th percentile for her age. This weakness in visual processing is consistent with expectations based on her right frontal cerebral contusion and suggests that she will find most adult nonverbal, visual tasks to be very difficult. In line with her relative strengths, she may attempt to verbally mediate many nonverbal tasks to compensate for her impairment.

Auditory Perception/Processing.   María's ability to perceive and process auditory information is mildly impaired to within normal limits. She ranks at the 30th percentile in this ability for her age. She is likely to find tasks requiring the perception of speech and nonspeech sounds to be fairly manageable.

Language.   María's ability to communicate was examined for both expressive and receptive language. Test findings suggest that her Spanish-language expression and comprehension abilities are mildly impaired to within normal limits. Expressive language was clinically observed to be fluent and well-articulated, with no evidence of word-finding difficulties. Test performance on naming tasks, which tend to be sensitive to language impairment of any type, ranked at the 23rd percentile for age and was mildly impaired to within normal limits. María's ability to repeat words and sentences is mild to moderately impaired (10th and 14th percentiles, respectively), presumably due to problems with short-term memory rather than language difficulties.

TABLE 8.16
Table of Batería–R Scores for Case 1, María

Cluster/Test	Age Equivalent	Relative Proficiency Index	Percentile Rank	Standard Score
BCA (Ext)	12–8	73/90	15	85
L-T RETRV (Glr)	11–4	85/90	36	95
S-T MEM (Gsm)	8–0	29/90	8	79
PROC SPEED (Gs)	12–1	58/90	11	81
AUD PROC (Ga)	11–10	81/90	30	92
VIS PROC (Gv)	9–0	61/90	4	74
COMP-KNOW (Gc)	17–9	77/90	30	92
FLUID REAS (Gf)	25	91/90	54	101
BROAD READING (Grw)	15–2	68/90	26	90
BROAD MATH (Gq)	12–2	29/90	11	82
Memory Names	5–11	61/90	9	80
Memory Sents	8–3	34/90	14	84
Visual Matching	12–7	55/90	19	87
Inc Words	9–5	75/90	19	87
Visual Closure	15–3	82/90	29	92
Picture Vocab	16–8	71/90	23	89
Analysis-Synth	21	90/90	50	100
V-A Learning	25	96/90	76	111
Memory Words	7–7	25/90	10	81
Cross Out	11–6	63/90	9	80
Sound Blending	13–10	85/90	42	97
Picture Recog	5–11	34/90	2	68
Oral Vocab	18–8	82/90	39	96
Concept Form	28	93/90	59	103
Sound Patterns	19	90/90	50	100
Spatial Rels	13–0	73/90	24	90
Verbal Anlgs	16–6	77/90	34	94
L-W Ident	15–1	63/90	28	91
Passage Comp	15–5	71/90	25	90
Calculation	10–9	9/90	4	74
Applied Probs	15–3	61/90	27	91
Dictation	11–5	32/90	9	80
Writing Fluency	9–1	12/90	1	67

Memory and Learning.   Three dimensions of María's memory were assessed: short-term acquisition and retention; long-term storage and retrieval of newly learned material; and recall of older remote memories, including those that were learned long ago. María demonstrates mild to moderate impairment in the encoding and acquisition of new material. Her performance on measures of short-term memory ranks at the 8th percentile for her age. She will find many adult-level tasks requiring short-term memory very to extremely difficult. Once new material is effectively learned, María demonstrates adequate associational memory skills, ranking at the 36th percentile for her age in this area. However, her ability to access old knowledge directly appears to be somewhat inefficient so that she will find many tasks drawing on remote memory to be difficult. María also demonstrated a mild impairment and falls at the 2nd percentile for age on a measure of visual memory. This suggests that there may be a clinically meaningful weakness in her memory for visual material relative to her memory for verbal material. This finding is also consistent with expectations based on her right hemisphere cerebral contusion. When new learning stimuli are auditory and a visual association response is required (i.e., the Memory for Names test), the task is very difficult for María and she falls at the 9th percentile. However, when stimuli are visual and María must respond with an auditory association (i.e., the Visual-Auditory Learning Test), the task is easy for her and she falls at the 76th percentile. This observation may have clinical and programmatic implications.

Reasoning and Problem Solving. María's ability to think abstractly, form concepts, and reason through novel problems falls entirely within normal limits, ranking at the 54th percentile for her age. This may represent a significant relative strength for her. On tasks (e.g., verbal analogies) in which she must rely on previously acquired knowledge in order to solve abstract problems, she may experience some difficulty.

Academic Achievement. María's skills in reading, writing, and mathematics were examined. When compared to other adults at her age level, María's functioning in reading is mildly impaired to within normal limits (26th percentile for age). Her functioning in mathematics is mildly to moderately impaired (11th percentile for age). On mathematical tasks, she demonstrated a relative weakness in rote written calculations (4th percentile for age) compared to problems requiring the application of mathematical concepts (27th percentile for age). María's functioning with Spanish written language tasks is mildly to moderately impaired and she ranks between the 1st and 9th percentiles for her age. No evidence of a specific reading disability or mathematics disability was evident, although María may find the performance demands of adult-level tasks in reading to be difficult, in math to be very to extremely difficult, and in writing to be very to extremely difficult. In the absence of any report of premorbid problems with written calculations or written language, it is possible that María's current difficulties may be related to the visual processing difficulties described earlier.

Summary and Conclusions

María is a 22-year-old female who sustained a severe traumatic brain injury eight months ago. She is currently functioning in the low average range of overall cognitive ability, but she demonstrates mild to moderate impairment on measures of focused and sustained attention, visual processing and memory, encoding and short-term memory, written mathematics, and written language. Given her uncomplicated developmental and academic history, these findings are commensurate with expectations based on her recent medical history of traumatic brain injury and right frontal cerebral contusion.

Case 2: Language and Learning Disability in an 8-Year-Old Male

Reason for Referral

Carlos S. was referred for neuropsychological evaluation to assess his cognitive and intellectual strengths and weaknesses and to assist in intervention planning. His parents complain that he is demonstrating numerous academic difficulties, his grades are poor, and it is difficult for him to effectively communicate his needs. They also report that he demonstrates excessive inattentiveness and anxiety. These problems were initially observed by his first-grade teacher and now may cause him to be held back in the second grade.

Background Information

Carlos is an 8-year, 9-month-old Hispanic child. He was born and raised in Miami, Florida, and he is currently in the second grade in a public school bilingual program. He repeated first grade at the request of his parents because he seemed immature and had not learned to read. He lives with his mother, father, and two younger sisters. Spanish is the principal language used in the home. Prior to this evaluation, the school had administered the *Woodcock–Muñoz Language Survey* in Spanish and in English. The results indicate that he has limited oral language proficiency in both Spanish and English and negligible reading–writing proficiency in both Spanish and English. There is no known family history of neurologic or psychiatric problems, although Carlos' father reports that he received tutoring when he was Carlos' age.

Tests Administered

Carlos was administered a set of tests from the *Batería Woodcock–Muñoz: Pruebas de habilidad cognitiva–Revisada* and the *Batería Woodcock–Muñoz: Pruebas de aprovechamiento–Revisada*. The *Pruebas de habilidad cognitiva* measure overall intellectual functioning and specific cognitive abilities. The *Pruebas de aprovechamiento* measure various aspects of scholastic achievement.

Test Results and Interpretation

Carlos's cognitive functions were examined in a variety of areas (see Table 8.17). Test results are described primarily in terms of comparison to age peers (*percentile rank*) and relative proficiency (descriptive terms such as *within normal limits* or *mildly impaired* corresponding to the quality of Carlos' performance on criterion tasks of given difficulty).

General Cognitive and Intellectual Functioning.   Carlos's Broad Cognitive Ability, an overall measure of intellectual functioning, ranks at the 4th percentile for his age. His global capacity to understand and cope with the surrounding world appears mildly impaired, and he can be expected to find many age-appropriate cognitive tasks at school and home to be very difficult. His functioning in specific cognitive areas is described later.

Attention.   Carlos's ability to sustain and focus attention over brief periods of time is mildly impaired to within normal limits and he ranks at the 12th percentile for his age. He is likely to find age-level tasks difficult when asked to sustain attention over time and resist distraction. His attentional capacity, or the amount of information he can hold in conscious awareness at any given time, ranks at the 5th percentile for his age and is mildly to moderately impaired. Accordingly, he may become overwhelmed when even age-appropriate amounts of material and complex instructions are presented or taught to him.

Visual Perception/Processing.   Carlos' ability to visually process information is within normal limits and ranks at the 62nd percentile for his age. He is likely to find the cognitive demands of age-level tasks involving visual processing to be manageable. His ability to process nonverbal information represents an intracognitive strength that may have value in intervention planning.

Auditory Perception/Processing.   Carlos' ability to perceive and process auditory information is mildly impaired, ranking at the 10th percentile for his age. He is likely to

TABLE 8.17
Table of Batería–R Scores for Case 2, Carlos

Cluster/Test	Age Equivalent	Relative Proficiency Index	Percentile Rank	Standard Score
BCA (Ext)	6–5	63/90	4	73
L-T RETRV (Glr)	6–1	75/90	12	82
S-T MEM (Gsm)	4–4	25/90	5	75
PROC SPEED (Gs)	7–4	71/90	12	82
AUD PROC (Ga)	6–0	58/90	10	80
VIS PROC (Gv)	9–0	92/90	62	105
COMP-KNOW (Gc)	6–9	61/90	12	82
FLUID REAS (Gf)	6–4	47/90	11	82
BROAD READING (Grw)	6–5	1/90	1	61
BROAD KNOWLEDGE (Gc)	6–10	63/90	16	85
Memory Names	6–4	82/90	26	90
Memory Sents	3–8	7/90	1	66
Visual Matching	7–5	61/90	12	82
Inc Words	5–9	63/90	9	80
Visual Closure	8–3	88/90	43	97
Picture Vocab	7–2	75/90	23	89
Analysis-Synth	7–3	75/90	26	91
V-A Learning	6–2	66/90	6	76
Memory Words	6–4	66/90	25	90
Cross Out	7–5	81/90	21	88
Sound Blending	6–3	53/90	15	84
Picture Recog	10–3	93/90	74	110
Oral Vocab	6–4	42/90	5	76
Concept Form	5–4	23/90	7	78
Listening Comp	7–0	73/90	23	89
L-W Ident	6–8	2/90	2	68
Passage Comp	6–3	1/90	1	59
Science	6–9	55/90	16	85
Social Studies	7–5	71/90	23	89
Humanities	6–8	66/90	19	87

	Actual	Predicted	Significance	
DISCREPANCIES Aptitude/Ach:	SS	SS	PR	SD
BROAD READING	61	79	3	–1.86*
BROAD KNOWLEDGE	85	81	65	0.37

*Significant

find tasks requiring the perception of speech and nonspeech sounds to be very difficult. It is possible that some of his difficulties with attention may be related to his central auditory processing difficulties.

Language.   Carlos' ability to communicate was examined for both expressive and receptive language. Test findings suggest that his Spanish-language expression and comprehension abilities are generally mildly impaired. Expressive language was clinically observed to be adequately articulated but with less coherence and goal-directedness than is normally expected in an 8-year-old. Carlos sometimes lost his train of thought and demonstrated occasional word-finding difficulties. Carlos' word knowledge was mildly impaired, ranking at the 5th percentile for his age. Test performance on naming tasks, which tend to be sensitive to language impairment of any type, ranked at the 23rd percentile for age and was mildly impaired to within normal limits. Listening comprehension was also mildly impaired to within normal limits. Carlos' ability to repeat words and sentences is mildly to moderately impaired (25th and 1st percentiles, respectively). Taken together, these findings suggest that Carlos will experience more difficulty with verbal than nonverbal cognitive tasks.

Memory and Learning.   Three dimensions of Carlos' memory were assessed: short-term acquisition and retention; long-term storage and retrieval of newly learned material; and recall of older remote memories, including those that were learned long ago. Carlos demonstrates mild to moderate impairment in the encoding and acquisition of new material. His performance on measures of short-term memory ranks at the 5th percentile for his age. He will find many age-level tasks requiring short-term memory very to extremely difficult, and he may be overwhelmed by being presented too much information to learn at a time. He is likely to learn at a slower rate and need more practice and repetition than his peers. Once new material is effectively encoded, Carlos demonstrates somewhat more adequate memory, with his long-term associational memory skills ranking at the 12th percentile for his age and falling in the mildly impaired to within normal limits range of expectations. His ability to directly recall old knowledge appears to be mildly impaired so that he will find many tasks drawing on remote memory to be very difficult. Carlos demonstrates a strength in his memory for visual material relative to his memory for verbal material, performing within normal limits and ranking at the 74th percentile for age on a measure of visual memory. When new learning stimuli are auditory and a visual association response is required (i.e., the Memory for Names test), the task is manageable for Carlos and he ranks at the 26th percentile for age. However, when stimuli are visual and Carlos must respond with an auditory association (i.e., the Visual-Auditory Learning Test), the task is very difficult for him and he ranks at the 6th percentile. This observation may have clinical and programmatic implications, especially for reading instruction.

Reasoning and Problem-Solving.   Carlos' ability to think abstractly, form concepts, and reason through novel problems is mildly impaired, and ranks at the 11th percentile for his age. He was somewhat better able to analyze a problem and identify a missing element (26th percentile) than to analyze a problem and deduce a governing rule or principle (7th percentile).

Academic Achievement.   Carlos' skills in reading Spanish were examined. When compared to other children his age, Carlos' broad reading skills are severely impaired, falling at the 1st percentile for his age. His word attack skills rank at the 2nd percentile for age, and his reading comprehension ranks at the 1st percentile for age. An aptitude/achievement evaluation indicates that Carlos has a significant discrepancy between reading aptitude and reading achievement. These results, and Carlos' history, support a diagnosis of reading disability and suggest that Carlos should be given appropriate educational services.

Summary and Conclusions

Carlos is an 8-year-old male who was referred for poor school performance, communication difficulties, and attention and anxiety problems. He is currently functioning in a low and mildly impaired range of overall cognitive ability, but he demonstrates a significant strength in his ability to process visual information relative to verbal information. His attentional processes are characterized by considerable variability, ranging from within normal limits to moderate impairment. Given his parents' presenting complaint that he has difficulties with attention, he may benefit from trials with an attention-facilitating medication. He demonstrates mild impairment in central auditory processing, including the perception and integration of speech sounds, as well as language expression and comprehension. These findings are also consistent with his parents' presenting complaints and suggest the possible presence of a mixed expressive/receptive language disorder, which may be corroborated by an audiological and speech/language evaluation. Carlos' learning ability is characterized by mild to moderately impaired short-term memory, mildly impaired long-term retrieval, and mildly impaired remote memory. His problems with learning and memory are most prominent when verbal responses are required, and he is likely to require more time and effort than most children his age to learn new material. His ability to think abstractly is mildly impaired. Finally, Carlos demonstrates severe impairment in his reading skills and is likely to find most age-level reading tasks to be impossible. A clinically significant dyslexia is evident, which is likely accompanied by a contributing language disorder. Given his mild impairment in auditory processing, a reading instruction program emphasizing phonics instruction may be inappropriate for Carlos. Special education services for learning disability and language disorder are indicated.

In a continuing effort to investigate the validity of the WJ–R and Batería–R in clinical neuropsychology, a data pool of neurological and psychiatric patients has been collected. Two research reports (Dean & Woodcock, 1999; Woodcock, 1998b) document results from a sample of 1,315 patients, ages 5 to 81 years. Descriptive statistics are presented for 31 clinical groups, including 9 samples with known lesion localization. In addition, the second report includes information about the forthcoming *Dean-Woodcock Neuropsychological Assessment System* (D-WNAS; Dean & Woodcock, in press). In addition to the cognitive and achievement batteries, the D-WNAS includes a sensory motor battery, structured interview, and mental status exam.

CONCLUSIONS

The Batería–R comprises a set of Spanish-language tests that can assess many of the deficits and preserved functions of concern to the neuropsychologist. Its wide age range and breadth of coverage allow the battery to be used as either a core battery or as a source of supplemental information. The battery comes out of an empirical tradition, based on factor analytic studies of human cognitive processes, and is based on Horn–Cattell Gf-Gc theory. This chapter describes the main features of both the Spanish-language and English-language batteries. Issues related to the translation/adaptation and norming of a battery of Spanish-language tests are presented and the way in which those issues were addressed with the Batería–R are described. A brief description of Horn–Cattell Gf-Gc theory is presented and the organization of abilities provided by that theory is recommended for attention by the field of neuropsychology. A major section of this chapter describes the application of Batería–R tests to several aspects of neuropsychological assessment. These applications are presented in the context of both Gf-Gc theory and a traditional classification of cognitive abilities familiar to all neuropsychologists. Some suggestions are presented for learning to use the Batería–R and also for training ancillary examiners to aid in some assessment activities.

The procedures followed in developing and standardizing the Batería–R COG and Batería–R APR have produced instruments that can be used with confidence for a variety of clinical purposes and for research with subjects from the preschool to the geriatric level.

ACKNOWLEDGMENTS

John Wasserman, formerly of Riverside Publishing, has provided significant guidance in the preparation of this chapter. His contribution is gratefully acknowledged.

Appreciation is expressed to Joseph D. Eubanks of San Antonio, Texas, for providing some of the clinical case information reported here.

REFERENCES

Carroll, J. B. (1993). *Human cognitive abilities: A survey of factor-analytic studies.* New York: Cambridge University Press.

Carroll, J. B. (1997). The three-stratum theory of cognitive abilities. In D. P. Flanagan, J. L. Genshaft, & P. L. Harrison (Eds.), *Contemporary intellectual assessment: Theories, tests, and issues* (pp. 122–130). New York: Guilford.

Carroll, J. B. (1998). Human cognitive abilities: A critique. In J. J. McArdle & R. W. Woodcock (Eds.), *Human cognitive abilities in theory and practice* (pp. 52–53). Hillsdale, NJ: Lawrence Erlbaum Associates.

Cummings, J. A. (1994). Review of the Woodcock–Johnson Psycho-Educational Battery–Revised. In L. L. Murphy (Ed.), *Supplement to the eleventh mental measurements yearbook* (pp. 283–287). Lincoln: Buros, University of Nebraska Press.

Dean, R. S., & Woodcock, R. W. (1999). *The WJ-R and Batería-R in neuropsychological assessment: Research report number 3.* Itasca, IL: Riverside Publishing.

Dean, R. S., & Woodcock, R. W. (in press). *Dean-Woodcock Neuropsychological Assessment System.* Itasca, IL: Riverside Publishing.

Hambleton, R. K. (1993). Translating achievement tests for use in cross-national studies. *European Journal of Psychological Assessment, 9,* 57–58.

Hessler, G. L. (1993). *Use and interpretation of the Woodcock–Johnson Psycho-Educational Battery–Revised.* Itasca, IL: Riverside.

Horn, J. L. (1988). Thinking about human abilities. In J. R. Nesselroade & R. B. Cattell (Eds.), *Handbook of multivariate psychology* (Rev. ed., pp. 645–685). New York: Academic Press.

Horn, J. L. (1991). Measurement of intellectual capabilities: A review of theory. In K. S. McGrew, J. K. Werder, & R. W. Woodcock, *WJ–R technical manual* (pp. 197–232). Itasca, IL: Riverside.

Horn, J. L. (1998). A basis for research on age differences in cognitive capabilities. In J. J. McArdle & R. W. Woodcock (Eds.), *Human cognitive abilities in theory and practice* (pp. 57–91). Hillsdale, NJ: Lawrence Erlbaum Associates.

Horn, J. L., & Noll, J. (1997). Human cognitive abilities: Gf-Gc theory. In D. P. Flanagan, J. L. Genshaft, & P. L. Harrison (Eds.), *Contemporary intellectual assessment: Theories, tests, and issues* (pp. 53–91). New York: Guilford.

Kaufman, A. S. (1990). *Assessing adolescent and adult intelligence.* Boston: Allyn & Bacon.

Lee, S. W., & Stefany, E. F. (1994). Review of the Woodcock–Johnson Psycho-Educational Battery–Revised. In L. L. Murphy (Ed.), *Supplement to the eleventh mental measurements yearbook* (pp. 287–288). Lincoln: Buros, University of Nebraska Press.

Lezak, M. D. (1995). *Neuropsychological assessment* (3rd ed.). New York: Oxford University Press.

McGhee, R. L., & Buckhalt, J. A. (1993). Test review of the Woodcock–Johnson Psycho-Educational Battery–Revised. *Journal of Psychoeducational Assessment* [Monograph Series: WJ–R monograph], 136–149.

McGrew, K. S. (1994a). *Clinical interpretation of the Woodcock–Johnson Tests of Cognitive Ability–Revised.* Boston: Allyn & Bacon.

McGrew, K. S. (1994b). Woodcock–Johnson Tests of Cognitive Ability–Revised. In J. R. Sternberg (Ed.), *Encyclopedia of human intelligence* (pp. 1152–1158). New York: Macmillan.

McGrew, K. S. (1997). Analysis of the major intelligence batteries according to a proposed comprehensive Gf-Gc framework. In D. P. Flanagan, J. L. Genshaft, & P. L. Harrison (Eds.), *Contemporary intellectual assessment: Theories, tests, and issues* (pp. 151–179). New York: Guilford.

McGrew, K. S., Werder, J. K., & Woodcock, R. W. (1991). *WJ–R technical manual: A reference on theory and current research.* Itasca, IL: Riverside.

Mirsky, A. F. (1996). Disorders of attention: A neuropsychological perspective. In G. R. Lyon & N. A. Krasnegor (Eds.), *Attention, memory, and executive function* (pp. 71–96). Baltimore: Paul H. Brooks.

Rasch, G. (1960). *Probabilistic models for some intelligence and attainment tests.* Copenhagen, Denmark: Danish Institute for Educational Research.

Schrank, F. A., & Woodcock, R. W. (1997). *Woodcock Scoring and Interpretive Program.* Itasca, IL: Riverside.

Woodcock, R. W. (1981). *Batería Woodcock de proficiencia en el idioma* [Woodcock Language Proficiency Battery]. Itasca, IL: Riverside.

Woodcock, R. W. (1990). Theoretical foundations of the WJ–R measures of cognitive ability. *Journal of Psychoeducational Assessment, 8,* 231–258.

Woodcock, R. W. (1994). Measures of fluid and crystallized theory of intelligence. In J. R. Sternberg (Ed.), *Encyclopedia of human intelligence* (pp. 452–456). New York: Macmillan.

Woodcock, R. W. (1997). The Woodcock–Johnson Tests of Cognitive Ability–Revised. In D. P. Flanagan, J. L. Genshaft, & P. L. Harrison (Eds.), *Contemporary intellectual assessment: Theories, tests, and issues* (pp. 230–246). New York: Guilford.

Woodcock, R. W. (1998a). Extending Gf-Gc theory into practice. In J. J. McArdle & R. W. Woodcock (Eds.), *Human cognitive abilities in theory and practice* (pp. 137–156). Hillsdale, NJ: Lawrence Erlbaum Associates.

Woodcock, R. W. (1998b). *The WJ-R and Batería-R in neuropsychological assessment: Research report number 1.* Itasca, IL: Riverside Publishing.

Woodcock, R. W., & Johnson, M. B. (1989a). *Woodcock–Johnson Tests of Achievement–Revised.* Itasca, IL: Riverside Publishing.

Woodcock, R. W., & Johnson, M. B. (1989b). *Woodcock–Johnson Tests of Cognitive Ability–Revised.* Itasca, IL: Riverside.

Woodcock, R. W., & Muñoz-Sandoval, A. F. (1992). *Test translation guidelines: A "consensus translation" approach.* Unpublished Manuscript. (Available from Measurement/Learning/Consultants, PO Box 161, Tolovana Park, OR 97145)

Woodcock, R. W., & Muñoz-Sandoval, A. F. (1993). An IRT approach to cross-language test equating and interpretation. *European Journal of Psychological Assessment, 9*(3), 233–241.

Woodcock, R. W., & Muñoz-Sandoval, A. F. (1994). Cross-language test equating. *Rasch Measurement Transactions, 7*(4), 329.

Woodcock, R. W., & Muñoz-Sandoval, A. F. (1996a). *Batería Woodcock–Muñoz: Pruebas de aprovechamiento–Revisada.* Itasca, IL: Riverside.

Woodcock, R. W., & Muñoz-Sandoval, A. F. (1996b). *Batería Woodcock–Muñoz: Pruebas de aprovechamiento–Revisada, Supplemental Manual.* Itasca, IL: Riverside.

Woodcock, R. W., & Muñoz-Sandoval, A. F. (1996c). *Batería Woodcock–Muñoz: Pruebas de habilidad cognitiva–Revisada.* Itasca, IL: Riverside.

Woodcock, R. W., & Muñoz-Sandoval, A. F. (1996d). *Batería Woodcock–Muñoz: Pruebas de habilidad cognitiva–Revisada, Supplemental Manual.* Itasca, IL: Riverside.

Wright, B. D., & Linacre, J. M. (1991). *BIGSTEPS: Rasch-model computer program.* Chicago: MESA Press.

Wright, B. D., & Stone, M. H. (1979). *Best test design.* Chicago: MESA Press.

Diagnosing Learning Disabilities in Bilingual Urban Students: A Neuropsychological Framework

MANUEL A. SEDÓ
Boston Public Schools, Boston, MA

The nonstigmatizing term *Learning Disabilities* (LDs) was created to describe a cluster of "specific" central nervous system dysfunctions that would help explain the disappointing academic performance of otherwise competent children not responding to traditional teaching methods. Named by Samuel Kirk in 1963, LDs were recognized as an official handicapping condition 5 years later and became the basis of a legal educational mandate in the early 1970s. A quarter of a century later, 10.24% of all U.S. children from age 6 to 17 (and up to 25% of all children in some urban areas) are attending special education programs—and slightly over half of them (5.2 million children) are described as "learning disabled" (Reschly, 1995). At this time, the diagnosis of LDs is *seven times more frequent* than either the diagnosis of mental retardation or the diagnosis of emotional disturbance (U.S. Department of Education, 1994).

Hispanic overrepresentation in special education has been a concern since the 1970s. Tucker (1980), after studying school districts of the southwest, suggested that "LD designation has provided a convenient alternative placement for disproportionately large numbers of minority students" (p. 95). Examining data on four school districts, Reschly (1995) observed that children of all racial groups who qualified for subsidized school lunches had much higher rates of placement in special education, averaging 19% as opposed to 5% to 9% among their more advantaged peers. Reschly concluded that "poverty circumstances are a plausible explanation for the special education overrepresentation, although additional studies are needed of the nature and magnitude of the relation of poverty to disability diagnosis and special education placement" (p. 16).

Rueda (1989) discussed the inadequacy of assessment instruments, the controversy on the definition of learning disabilities, and the difficulty in translating assessment data into practical suggestions for educational intervention. Hispanic professionals often agree that special education is often used "as a substitute for much needed school programs that are nonexistent" and that regular programs should be able to accomodate a broader range of students with different learning styles and learning levels, reserving special programs only "for those who have not been able to progress, despite repeated attempts to modify the regular curriculum" (Langdon, 1992, p. 52).

This chapter considers learning disabilities as differential learning styles of children, making suggestions about their detection and description.

LD'S FOUR "CLUSTERS"

In the 1990s, LDs were generally considered to include a number of tactile, motor, visual, auditory and linguistic processing differences impacting the reception, retention, and analysis of incoming information; the ability to access past experiences from long-term memory; the mental control of the subject; and the planning, execution, and monitoring of future-oriented problem-solving strategies.

It is important to realize that the success of LDs was never due to the precision of the knowledge about them. The concept of LDs has changed with the times, as it can be easily seen from the diagnostic terms that have been used during the past 30 years: from the "perceptual-motor problems" studied in the 1960s, to the "linguistic processing difficulties" of the 1970s and 1980s, to the "attention deficits" and "cognitive organization problems" more often described in the 1990s.

Educational research on LDs has led to a series of groupings, or "typologies," of LDs (Bakker, 1990; Barkley, 1981; Boder, 1973; Mattis, French, & Rapin, 1975). One of the latest counts included up to 42 classification systems covering three large pages written in small print (Lyon, 1996, pp. 411–413). In general, most of these classifications revolve around the presence of "verbal" and "nonverbal" problems, and are often divided into three or four basic forms of dysfunction.

First Group: Low-Language Students (Esprit de Finesse)

The first major group of LDs is often thought to include those relating to the linguistic functioning of the dominant hemisphere of the brain (the left hemisphere in most right-handed subjects) and characterized by the presence of difficulties in the areas of language comprehension and language production. Low language LD students may be characterized by a slowness of auditory perception and may have a specific difficulty "processing brief components of information which enter the nervous system in rapid succession" (Tallal, Miller, & Fitch, 1996). This student may have limited auditory discrimination, slow language development, and limited memory for language; may have difficulty using verbal mediation for problem solving or using self-directed talk for self-control; may have difficulty abstracting verbal concepts from concrete situations ("how are an apple and a banana alike?") or comprehending and reading "little words" (conjunctions, prepositions, articles, etc.) that evoke no precise visual associations. They may also have difficulty retrieving words from long-term memory, producing sentences with complex syntactic structure; and—most relevant to reading—may have difficulty analyzing sentences into words, words into syllables, and syllables into sounds. As Witkin (1967) suggested, they may be more attentive to the context and to the interpersonal situation than to the contents of a message; they may pay much more attention to their teacher as a person than to the contents of her words. At the younger developmental levels, teachers can often attract their undivided attention by using what Luria (1961, 1980) liked to call a *motor echo*, or *echopraxia* (i.e., locking step with them by just imitating any of their minor facial or body movements). They are better lookers than listeners (it is possible to catch them by pointing to one thing and talking about another), and their visual scores are systematically higher than their auditory scores.

At perceptual tasks, low language students are always more perceptive of contours than of details. It is often instructive to compare their performance at the puzzles of the "horse" and the "car" of the traditional Wechsler Intelligence Scale for Children (WISC) battery—because the horse is all contours and has no details and the car has plenty of inner details and very little contour. They may react to too many aspects of the immediate situation, and thus they may have extreme difficulty solving visual tests of embedded figures or "figure ground" where "alternative" facets of a total picture should be perceived. In sharp contrast, their interpersonal, perceptual, and artistic abilities may be particularly high: As Levine (1994) liked to say, it is sometimes difficult to decide whether a particular brain is "disabled" or whether it is "highly specialized" for something else (p. 5). The low language level field sensitivity of contextually bound subjects was first described in the 18th century by Blaise Pascal (see 1989), who considered it a distinctive "cognitive style" and called it "Esprit de finesse." Esprit de finesse (according to Pascal) could become a virtual "Learning Disability" in "perceptual people who can only be perceptual," that is, in lookers who cannot become listeners or verbalizers, immediate situational reactors who are unable to use abstract concepts, master linguistic conventions or follow the rules of propositional reasoning.

At the learning style level, this sort of low language level field sensitivity is often presented as *the* characteristic learning style of many Hispanic people, particularly those in the less educated or more disadvantaged groups (see Christiansen & Livermore, 1970; S. A. Cohen, 1967; Gerken, 1978; Lesser, Fifer, & Clark, 1965; Marmorale & Brown, 1973; M. N. Meeker & R. Meeker, 1973; Oakland, 1983; Shellenberger, 1977; Taylor, Ziegler, & Partenio, 1984; Weiss, Prifitera, & Roid, 1993). This was also the profile most often found in disabled Hispanic students (Garcia & Yates, 1986; Gutkin, 1979) and in gifted Hispanic students (Ortiz & Vollof, 1987). Erenberg, Mattis, and French (1978) found it in 63% of their Hispanic referrals at a New York Hospital.

The physical and social basis of this low language learning style is now beyond doubt. Testing for field sensitivity and for logical reasoning during periods of transitory "hemispheric supression" after Electro Convulsive Therapy (Cohen, Berent, & Silverman, 1973) showed the differential functioning style of the "context bound" right hemisphere and the "abstract-logical" left hemisphere. On the other hand, esprit de finesse, or *field sensitivity,* is considered a basic cognitive characteristic of people in traditional countries (Witkin & Berry, 1975; Witkin & Goodenough, 1981). In the 16th century, 200 years before Blaise Pascal, the Spanish explorer Cabeza de Vaca observed and described this style among the natives of Texas, Arizona, New Mexico, and Mexico who "do not wrap themselves in a robe of words the way we do." Nevertheless, *field sensitivity* does not appear to be a durable characteristic, particularly in areas undergoing quick economic changes or in immigrant populations living in a more developed society. Four hundred years after Cabeza de Vaca, Ramirez and Ramirez (1974) and Ramirez and Price-Williams (1974) documented changes to a less field sensitive learning style in immigrants having lived a series of years in the United States, or in a still more acculturated population of children of immigrants.

The school psychologist should be ready to encounter this context-bound learning style in a very large number of students. In early childhood, context-bound children will learn the colors "orange" and "coffee" (that describe actual objects) much more easily than the abstract colors red, blue, and yellow.

Second Group: Abstract Thinkers

A second major group of LDs includes the learning problems that relate to the functioning of the nondominant hemisphere of the brain (the right hemisphere in most right-handed subjects) and impacts the ability to adjust to the environment in direct experiential terms rather than in linguistic terms. *Low Visual* students may have a specific difficulty using the quick magnocellular perceptual system (in the occipital visual brain) that provides individuals with global three-dimensional perceptual images; and must rely on the slow parvocellular system (in the temporal lobes) that provides individuals with detailed fragmented analysis of the perceptual field (Chase, 1996). Due to the low level of visual and interpersonal feedback received, low visual students tend to have a characteristically sober or taciturn expression; can be extremely self-reliant; are persistent in the face of failure; may feel invigorated rather than frustrated by spatial puzzles (where they often undo their own good but poorly perceived good responses); and may become quite argumentative about the quality of their own responses—responses that they can barely judge in realistic terms. They may have little situational or interpersonal perception, may often react to absent events rather than to present stimuli, and may live in a state of continuous "stream of verbal consciousness." Very characteristically, they build impersistent and fragmented visual images, and have unusually low visual memory; actually, they tend to replace spatial images with "verbal analogs" of the configuration and of its details, demonstrating Jaynes' (1976) early assertion that "language is an organ of perception, not simply a means of communication" (p. 50). They may also have weaker and slower left hands (Denckla, 1973, 1985; Sedo, 1995a, 1995b), may start their drawings from the right end of the field or draw from the bottom up, working their way up from details to contours; and they may break the "matrix" of the model in strikingly incongruous ways. At the lower developmental levels, they use little visual exploration, replace images with words, and may have slow or impaired constructional skills; they may use "motor" as well as "verbal" mediation, drawing images in the air, touching their own face while assembling the puzzle of a face, or touching their own face and limbs when they draw the image of a human body. On two occasions, visually disabled students have been observed drawing a bisected square (a square that is vertically split in two) as a V, perhaps drawing the "shape" of the exploratory movement of their eyes rather than the model explored. More frequently, they would draw the bisected square as two vertical rectangles. The slowness of their drawing is also as impressive as the anomalies of their reproductions. A competent 15-year-old may look 12 times at the model to draw a 12-line transparent Necker cube: Some other complex models would take up to 45 eye movements. Visual disability can be validly measured with tests of Gestalt Closure, tests of Spatial Memory, and tests of Graphic performance, but can also be observed rather than measured. By the way, visual disability is probably rather unusual in Hispanic populations: Erenberg et al. (1976) found it in only 5% of Hispanic ghetto children, that is, in just one fourth the proportion expected. The progress of low functioning visual students may be slow: forty percent may be nongainers when using Budoff's Learning Potential Assessment Device (Hausman, 1988) and barely 20% reacted to stimulant medication.

Students with visuospatial disorders may become efficient talkers, outstanding reasoners, and even better and more conceptual readers than the other students (Badian, 1986; Denckla, Rudel, & Broman, 1981); may often live in a parallel "verbal" world, or may have brilliant literary talents; and may often become highly successful students, betrayed perhaps by their poor handwriting, low spelling skills, and hate of mathematics. They may often have difficulty telling time or understanding fractions, they operate step-by-step losing all awareness of the "size of the ballpark," and may make unbelievable mistakes based on the wrong use of verbalizations ("six times seven is thirty five"; or "one third plus one third is two sixths"). At the lower developmental level, they may have difficulty operating in columns or understanding fractions.

Their functioning style is often characteristic. Interpersonal difficulties are frequently present, unless offset by emotional dependency on present or ideal models. Deeply entrenched preprogrammed attitudes are also frequent: some students may specialize in creating hostile reactions in others, and some others may specialize on becoming full-time professional clowns. In one or the other case, they "know" the reaction they are getting without having to "read" it on somebody's face—which is the one thing they cannot do. Their lack of facial expression is often a deadly giveaway: it goes with their lack of immediate reactivity, extremely low visual memory, and strong verbal skills. "Low visual, high conceptual thinkers" were first described by Pascal (1989) as people having a particular *Esprit de Geometrie* (it would more accurately be called *Esprit d'Abstraction*), characterized by the ability to use precise, rigorous propositional thinking. Pascal also described the possibility of this cognitive style becoming an anomaly (virtually, a learning disability) in subjects with low visual skills who may become high reasoners but are extremely poor observers.

Visuospatial disorder ("organicity") was (like Freud's repetition compulsion) a child of World War I. After the seminal contribution of Goldstein (1939), Strauss and Lehtinen (1947) and their colleagues applied to education the insights obtained from psychopathology. The 1960s saw the peak of a perceptual-motor school and the appearance of the well-known Visual-Motor Tests of Frostig, Lefever, and Whittlesey (1964) and Beery (1967/1997). At this time, visual disabilities have become definitely unfashionable, and meaning rather than images has become the basic concern of diagnosticians. This second group of learning disabilities is often ignored or bypassed by experienced speech and language pathologists, special teachers, and clinical therapists taken in by the reasonable verbal facade of the student and unable to explain the inconsistencies in the student's academic work and interpersonal and social skills.

Third Group: Low Sequencers

A third major group of LDs includes the learning problems that relate to the activation of the oblique axis of the brain, going from the brain stem to the frontal lobes, and have to do with to the development of attention, endurance, executive effort, sequencing of events, and planning and monitoring of sequential problem-solving behaviors. Students having problems in this area tend to present a combination of motor, attentional, spatial, and verbal difficulties, and their performance may often be insightful but unreliable. *Low sequencers* may have a specific difficulty in organizing rapid sequential motor output (Tallal et al., 1996) and are often described as "low automatizers" (Broverman & Klaiber, 1966). They may have difficulty focusing attention, exerting mental effort, executing rapid sequential movements, developing behavioral routines, learning seriated materials, planning for sequential behaviors, or following a rigorous line of reasoning. At the lower ages, they are often recognized at subtle motor signs (skipping words or lines, transposing letters in writing and sounds in oral language, dyslexia with dyslalia; they may have difficulty with even easy tongue-twisters, and may attack letters from unusual angles). They may have oral-motor–related reading problems that prevent the organized sequential blending of strings of sounds or oral movements, perhaps related to the presence of an early oral motor sequencing (oral disarthric) difficulty. These children love to hear that the problem is not in their minds, but in their mouths; that their basic problem is probably that they think too fast and not systematically enough. The basic objective of the school should be to show them how to learn to think more slowly and systematically.

Low sequencing is rarely diagnosed in urban Hispanic students, and its different components (attention span, memory, executive effort, sequencing ability, frontal lobe control) are also rarely considered in psychological diagnosis, which is much too often focused on only Verbal and Performance scores. A hidden measure of sequencing is, of course, the old ACID factor of the Wechsler battery, including the subtests of Arithmetic, Coding, Information, and Digit Span (Nichols, Inglis, Lawson, & MacKay, 1988); this factor measures fluid executive capacity rather than "crystallized verbal knowledge."

Low sequencing can also be recognized without difficulty in disadvantaged students. After all, lack of exposure to educational experience should explain the lack of mastery at sequential mental routines: if individuals do not know the days of the week or the months of the year, they cannot be expected to say what day was it 3 days ago or what month will it be 3 months from now. Slowness in processing is often explained in the name of academic understimulation.

Since the 1970s, research has looked at two ways out of this dilemma:

1. One solution involves the measurement of "executive effort" in situations unrelated to "acquired knowledge," thus more or less independent from past learning. Sedó (1997) developed tasks of continuous performance (Sequential Planning, Five Digit Test, Visual Trail Making) requiring a minimum of past knowledge and a maximum of mental effort, aimed at detecting the "low automatizer" at the inability to perceive and perform organized sequences or at the slowness in performing easy repetitive tasks.

2. A second possible solution involves the measurement of "executive effort" and "acquired knowledge" at parallel curriculum-related series (Sedó, 1997). This is the equivalent of putting together the Information subtest of the WISC battery and the Mental Control subtest of the Wechsler memory scales. For instance, naming three things you ride on, three things you wear, or three members of the family may define conceptual knowledge at a given level; knowing the days of the week, what day was it yesterday, and the letters of the alphabet may define sequencing at exactly the same curricular level. But the child may develop ability to do the sequential items one year after thay have already developed the conceptual skill. Naming three sports or three cities are higher level crystallized knowledge, whereas reciting the alphabet skipping every other letter (A-C-E-G . . .) or reciting months and numbers together (January 1, February 2, March 3 . . .) are third-grade level sequencing. (Trying a three-term sequence such as January-1-Monday, February-2-Tuesday, March-3-Wednesday, etc., would top fifth-grade level sequencing.) After exploring these parallel and complementary series of *crystallized knowledge* and *fluid sequencing,* it is quite possible to compare them: an academically backward student may have a weakness in both conceptual knowledge and sequential operations areas or may have a problem just in sequencing. He may be characterized by a lack of executive effort. In disabled urban children, "acquired knowledge" (Information) is one or more grades above "executive effort" (Mental Control). Subjects cannot perform sequences at their own expected level of knowledge, and are relatively unable to mobilize the executive effort required to manipulate acquired information.

The use of "executive effort" as a measure of "processing power" fits well with some ideas formulated around the 1960s (e.g., the theories of "fluid" and "crystallized" intelligence) that are now finally being converted in test: Horn and Cattell (1966) distinguished between "crystallized" abilities (Columbus reached America in 1492) and "fluid" abilities (how much is 14.92 divided by 2?). Miller, Galanter, and Pribram (1960) distinguished between "posterior" functions based on perception, comprehension, and memory; and "frontal" functions related to the active production and implementation of action plans.

There is a general lack of emphasis on motor testing of executive skills: Motor sequencing measures ("the lowly motor end of executive skills," as Denckla would call it) have for years been connected with executive control of sequential movement.

Finally, some authors emphasize "speed" of processing as a measurable, closely related aspect of the traditional g factor often limited to the measurement of reasoning. This is an important aspect of the functioning of the learning disabled student, who has been occasionally described as an "inactive learner" (Torgesen & Licht, 1983).

Fourth Group: Body Awareness and Control (Immature or Clumsy Students)

There is a fourth strand of LDs that often underlies one or another or all of the three basic learning disability styles (verbal, nonverbal, frontal) already described. LDs often go accompanied by other more general difficulties in standing balance and time estimation (related to cerebellar-vestibular function); bimanual, binocular, and binaural integration (related to callosal disconnection), and difficulties in body awareness and in intersensory integration (related to the functioning of the parietal lobes). The more global and involved cases of LDs are often found to be related to serious difficulties in body awareness and may involve basic problems in right–left organization, body awareness, finger agnosia, dysgraphia, and dyscalculia. Parietal students often appear to be unable to understand the sensations of their own body, mouth, or hand; and they are unable to understand and prefigure the planning of movements necessary to explore and recognize shapes and write signs; or they are unable to understand the world beyond their skins; or they are unable to create an inner world of cognitive representations. They are often unable to do the spatial rotation of blocks in their inner minds or to understand the series of the 10 basic numbers (corresponding to the 10 fingers in both hands). This student is sure to present sizable word finding problems and constructional reversals, and auditory-to-visual integration so necessary to read (Geschwind, 1965). This student may often be a total mystery to the traditional clinician who relies on psychodynamic explanations, and to the traditional educator relying on curriculum-based measurements in the absence of neuropsychological insights.

At this time, it is obvious that "neurodevelopmental soft signs" (believed to be more likely to be present in disadvantaged slow learners) are nearly universally present on students with learning problems (Denckla, 1985). It is also obvious that "hard signs" (tactile imperception at the Tactile Performance Test of the Halstead-Reitan battery, past-pointing at Baranyi's test, left-hand dyspraxia in students with right brain dysfunction or disconnection, unexpected manual speed at students relying on automatic responses, etc.) can be used to obtain a better description of the learning strategies of LD students.

CONCLUSIONS

Looking at the current panorama of school services and educational philosophies, the school psychologist working with urban Hispanic children often feels at the starting point of a long road. Of 100 children defined as disabled in the third grade, 74% were still considered disabled in the ninth grade; and most of the 20% to 25% of children who may make appreciable gains in reading will be those suffering from the least severe forms of disability (Francis, Fletcher, Rourke, & York, 1992). It is still not possible to distinguish learning style from learning disability, environmental deprivation from individual competence. In spite of the current emphasis on special education, special education may not have to be called special and special students may not have to be segregated. Perhaps tutoring and help in language, space organization, movement, and reading should not be called special at all, but be made more available to more children. Indeed, it may well be that there is much to learn.

The role of neuropsychological knowledge to understand the academic difficulties of children is clear. Children with neurological problems have always had learning problems; and the relation of brain to mental function may perhaps help understand those learning problems. Neuropsychology provides a new form of observation and description of child behavior, in spatial and verbal terms (right–left axis of the brain), receptive and productive terms (posterior–frontal axis), and automatic and conscious terms (vertical axis). There is the hope that "theories of neuropsychology might well apply across cultures to a greater degree than do our current theories of psychopathology" (Parsons, 1972, p. 50). Teachers of learning disordered disadvantaged students might be able to learn from neuropsychology the fine art of re-analyzing school tasks (reading and math) to help the children's brains do what they do best: that is, finding wonderfully mysterious ways to associate one bit of knowledge to another.

APPENDIX 9A

Two Validity Checks

1. BILINGUAL VERBAL OPPOSITES

This bilingual checklist of Verbal Opposites will help determine whether the difference between English and Spanish levels in subjects may invalidate the verbal testing done. (A large difference between the English and the Spanish score would invite a serious doubt about the use of monolingual measures in the weaker language.)

This multilingual checklist is accessible to most mainstream psychologists, who can easily produce one-word utterances in Spanish and recognize one-word utterances provided by the subject. Of course, this checklist can be also administered with the help of a trained interpreter.

This Validity Check will probably discriminate between a language-processing problem and a language barrier, although both may look very much the same to many non-Spanish–speaking professionals.

After administering this bilingual checklist, there should be little, if any, difficulty in determining what kind of complementary help may be needed in testing subjects. Although many Hispanic students are routinely defined as limited-English–proficient (LEP) students (Bakker, 1990), Dulay and Burt (1980) found that one third of the Hispanic students identified as such in a sample of California districts *were actually more fluent in English than they were in Spanish,* and that in one district, almost 40% of the Hispanic low English proficiency students *were able to speak no Spanish at all.*

Validity Checklist

Directions. Say to the student: *I am going to say a word, and you will tell me the word that means just the opposite. For instance: if I say "big" you will say ("small" or "little") because it ("small or little") is exactly the opposite of "big." If I say "good" you will say . . . ("bad") because "bad" is exactly the opposite of "good."*

Directions in Spanish: *Voy a decirte una palabra y tu me dices la palabra que significa exactamente lo contrario. Cuando yo diga "grande"* *tu tienes que decir . . . ("pequeño" o "chiquito") porque "pequeño" o "chiquito" es exactamente lo contrario de "grande"; cuando yo diga "bueno" tú tienes que decir . . . ("malo") porque "malo" es exactamente lo contrario de "bueno."*

At the end of the list or after four consecutive mistakes you may want to say: *Now we are going to try it in Spanish.* When the Spanish list was the one initially administered, you may want to say: *Ahora vamos a tratar en inglés.*

Verbal Opposites

A. big (small, little)
B. good (bad)

  1. up (down)
  2. hot (cold)
  3. front (back)
  4. early (late, night)
  5. near (far)

(2nd grade)

[*Very good. That was easy.*]

  6. asleep (awake)
  7. absent (present, here, in)
  8. lost (found, won)
  9. difficult (easy)
  10. after (before, now)

(5th grade)

[*Let's try something more difficult.*]

  11. heavy (light)
  12. vertical (horizontal)
  13. public (private)
  14. bless (curse, damn)
  15. reject (accept)

(10th grade)

[*Now let's make it real difficult.*]

  16. deep (shallow, high)
  17. create (destroy)
  18. gradual (sudden)
  19. superfluous (necessary)
  20. intermittent (continuous)

(College level)

[*And now, let's try it in Spanish.*]

English Score: _____

A. grande (pequeño, chiquito)
B. bueno (malo)

  1. arriba (abajo, debajo)
  2. caliente (frío)
  3. delante (detrás, atrás, p'atrás)
  4. temprano (tarde, de noche)
  5. cerca (lejos, distante, remoto)

[*Muy bien. Qué fácil.*]

  6. dormido (despierto)
  7. ausente (presente, aquí)
  8. perdido (hallado, encontrado, aparecido, ganado)
  9. dificil (fácil)
  10. después (antes, ahora, ahorita)

[*Vamos a probar algo mas difícil.*]

  11. pesado (liviano, ligero)
  12. vertical (horizontal)
  13. público (privado)
  14. bendecir (maldecir, condenar)
  15. rechazar (aceptar, admitir, recibir, acoger)

[*Ahora vamos a probar palabras mucho más dificiles.*]

  16. profundo (superficial, llano; elevado, encimado)
  17. crear (destruir)
  18. gradual (repentino)
  19. superfluo (necesario)
  20. intermitente (continuo)

[*Ahora vamos a tratar en ingles.*]

Spanish Score: _____

2. KIDDY WORDS: DEVELOPMENTAL NAMING SAMPLES

Validity checks are particularly important in younger children, who may have had much less exposure to the second language. For this reason, the language level of preschoolers may deserve very special attention.

Apart from the final levels obtained in each language, the psychologist may want to pay attention to two factors: (a) language bifurcation (first described by Anastasi & De Jesus in 1953), which may be present in a number of subjects having learned independent lexicons at home and in the schools; (b) the style of miscues, which may suggest a characteristic approach to naming. Younger children may mimic their responses or define objects by their usages ("to write, to cut"). Some miscues (semantic approximations) may suggest a temporal search for items in the same category ("spoon" for "knife," "brush" for "comb"), a frontal search for phonological approximations ("marshmallow" for "mushroom," "tirejas" for "tijeras," etc), or an endless search for circumlocutions, quite often observed in learning-disordered children.

On the other hand, visual misperceptions (like "orange" for "wheel") may suggest an entirely different problem, centered on spatial perception rather than on language processing.

Developmental Naming Samples

ENGLISH FORM:	SPANISH FORM:
This is a BOY	*Esto es un NIÑO*
this is a GIRL	*Esto es una NIÑA*
This is a [DOG]	*Esto es un [PERRO]*

1. car	1. carro, máquina, coche	25. letter,envlp	25. sobre, carta
2. chair, seat	2. silla	26. money	26. dinero, chavos
3. fork	3. tenedor	27. flag	26. bandera
4. key	4. llave	(4)	(4)
5. book (Bible)	5. libro	28. bag, suitcase	28. maleta, bulto
6. clock	6. reloj	29. bag, purse	29. monedero, cartera
7. telephone	7. teléfono	30. whistle	30. pito, silbato
8. house	8. casa	31. plug	31. enchufe
9. tree, bush	9. árbol, mata	32. arrow	32. flecha
(2)	(2)	33. watering can	33. regadera
10. comb	10. peine (-illa)	34. screw	34. tornillo
11. pencil	11. lápiz	35. (pad)lock	35. candado
12. knife	12. cuchillo	36. helicopter	36. helicóptero
13. hammer	13. martillo	(5)	(5)
14. scissors	14. tijeras	37. mask	37. careta, máscara
15. table	15. mesa	38. wrench	38. llave (inglesa)
16. wheel	16. goma, llanta, goma	39. snail	39. caracol
17. boat	17. barco	40. mushroom	40. seta, hongo
18. plane	18. airplane, jet	41. thermometer	41. termómetro
(3)	(3)	42. racquet	42. raqueta
19. butterfly	19. mariposa	43. globe	43. bola del mdo, esfera
20. leaf	20. hoja	44. anchor	44. áncora
21. hanger	21. gancho, percha, colgador	45. propeller	45. helice, ventilador, abanico
22. broom	22. escoba	(6)	(6)
23. (tooth)brush	23. cepillo (de dents)		
24. ladder	24. escalera		

After administering the test in one language, say:

Ahora vamos a ver en español.   OR: *Now let's try it in English.*

TOTAL ENGLISH: _____   SPANISH: _____

Underline the response given by the child.
Write down any depart from the expectation.

Cross out the numbers of the items failed.
Discontinue after *eight consecutive failures.* THEN:
Circle the number of the last item succeeded.
AND: *Subtract* the number of items failed.

When patchy performances are observed in both languages (language bifurcation), an *EITHER/OR SCORE* may provide a more sensible estimate of the student's actual fund of words.

EITHER/OR: _____

APPENDIX 9B

Verbal-Conceptual Fund

Once the language dominance has been established, the psychologist may want to establish the basic strength of the subject as measured in academic terms. This may constitute a basic developmental benchmark that will allow the psychologist to compare the child's relative deficits in other areas (Appendix 9C). OREA (1989), when testing urban Hispanic students in Spanish, observed a particular weakness of their short- and long-term memory and a difficulty in their effort for conceptualization. Sedó (1999) defined four areas of relative difficulty in the learning style of learning-disordered Hispanic students: (a) sequential operations are far less developed than contextualized conceptual knowledge; (b) contextual visual analysis is much higher than decontextualized auditory analysis and is tied much less to the surrounding environment and much more to the active inner world of the subject; (c) evidently, self-directed sequential movement is well under global environment-related movement; and (d) syntactically complex sentences of increasing lengths may be repeated with much more difficulty than easy declarative sentences, and may be one of the most constant markers found in learning-disabled children.

This initial developmental measure of school-related knowledge may throw light on the possible existence of an academic weakness, the existence of an environmental under-stimulation, or unrelated weaknesses observed in other than contextually related academic knowledge.

VERBAL-CONCEPTUAL FUND
Administered in: Spanish/English

Developmental Norms

(K)	(*)	1. Name three things you eat	(Gr. 1)	(*)	6. Name three things you ride on
		2. Name three things you drink			7. Three things you wear
		3. Name three colors			8. Three things that write
		4. Name three animals			9. Three things people read
		5. Name three fruits			10. Three people in a family

(*) Introductory items for students over the age of 7. If the student succeeds all the introductory items, go on administering the test from the third grade level on. In case of failure to any item, go down one grade level and administer the test item by item from that point on. Discontinue testing when successive failures represent one whole grade and one more item.

(Gr. 2) (*) 11. Name three tools
        12. Three musical instruments
        13. Three different rooms in a house
        14. Three pieces of furniture
        15. Three public holidays [do not accept Saturdays and Sundays]

(Gr. 3)   16. Name three kinds of (geometric) shapes
        17. Name three sports
        18. Name three insects [accept spiders and centipedes as insects]
        19. Name three cities [write down any mistakes made]
        20. Name three organs inside your body

(Gr. 4)   21. Name three states [write down any mistakes]
        22. Name three planets
        23. Name three countries [write down any mistakes]
        24. Name three oceans [write down any mistakes]
        25. Name three fish

(Gr. 5)   26. Name three metals
        27. Name three reptiles
        28. Name three continents
        29. Name three forms of energy
        30. Name three means of communication

APPENDIX 9C

Three Mental Sequencing Checklists

The three following checklists reflect some of the more basic weakness actually found in the learning-disordered Hispanic student.

The lower performance of learning-disordered children and dyslexic children at these sequential tasks may be particularly dramatic, and reflects an operational difficulty rather than a simple problem in conceptual knowledge.

The three sequential tasks include the automatized sequencing of mental routines, the context-free sequential analysis of sounds in oral words, and the repetition of organized motor sequences.

The first task (Automatic Series) can be presented in just about any language without any loss in its validity, although slight allowances may have to be made. Hispanic subjects tend to recite the days of the week beginning with Sunday, or may add a few letters (ch, ll, ñ) in their complete recitation of the alphabet.

1. AUTOMATIZED SERIES
Form of administration: administered in English; translated to Spanish.

Developmental Norms

(Nursery) (*) 1. What is your name?
        2. And your family name?

(PK)   3. Mom is a woman, Dad is a . . .   (man)
        4. A hat goes on your head, shoes go on your . . .   (feet)

| | | 5. An elephant is big, a mouse is . . . | (small, little) |
| | | 6. A stove is hot, an icecream is . . . | (cold) |

(K)   (*)   7. I want you to tell me your address. In what street do you live?
              8. At what number?
              9. (Show three fingers: move them in sequence to cue the student.)
                 When I eat I use a knife, a fork and a . . .   (spoon)
             10. (Show three fingers: move them in sequence to cue the student.)
                 The flag is red, white and . . .   (blue) (**)
             11. (Show three fingers: move them in sequence to cue the student.)
                 We eat breakfast, lunch and . . .   (dinner)
             12. (Show five fingers; move them in sequence to cue the student.)
                 The five vowels are A E I . . .   (O U)

(Gr. 1) (*) 13. Tell me the days of the week: Monday, Tuesday . . . (Wd Th Fr Sat Sun) (***)
             14. What day of the week is it today?
             15. If today is (. . .) what day was it yesterday?   (. . .)
             16. What day will it be tomorrow?   (. . .)
             17. And the day after tomorrow?   (. . .)
             18. When is your birthday?   (day and month)
         (*) 19. Tell me the letters of the alphabet: ABC . . .   (DEFG)
         (*) 20.   (HIJKLMNOP)
         (*) 21.   (QRSTUVWXYZ) (***)
             22. Which letter is the fourth letter of the alphabet?   (D)

(Gr. 2)   23. And the seventh letter?   (G)
             24. In what year were you born?
             25. What day is it today?   (month and number)
             26. What month was it last month?   (. . .)
             27. And what month will it be two months from now?   (. . .)
             28. Tell me the days backwards: Sunday, Saturday . . . (Fri, Thu, Wed, Tue, Mon)
             29. Tell me the months of the year: January, February . . . (***)
                                            (Mch Ap May Jn Jl Aug Spt Oct Nov Dec)
         (*) 30. Tell me the four seasons of the year (in any order)
             31. What letter comes two letters before M?   (K)
             32. And two letters after M?   (O)
         (*) 33. Tell me the days and their numbers: Monday 1, Tuesday 2 . . .
                                                (Wd 3, Th 4, Fr 5, Sat 6, Sun 7)
         (*) 34. Tell me the letters and the numbers: A1 B2 C3 . . .
                                                (D4 E5 F6 GG7 H8 I9 J10)

(Gr. 3)   35. What is the third letter before M?   (J)
             36. What is the sixth letter after M?   (S)
             37. What month was it three months ago?   (. . .)
             38. What month will it be six months from now?   (. . .)

(*) Introductory items for students over the age of 7. If the student succeeds all the introductory items, go on administering the test from the third grade level on. In case of failure to any item, go down one grade level and administer the test item by item from that point on. Discontinue testing when successive failures represent one whole grade and one more item.

(**) In countries without a three-colored flag, use: "I am going to be here three days: yesterday, today, and . . ." (tomorrow).

(***) When testing bilingual students, present those items in both languages: Very many students who are Spanish-dominant are likely to have learned the days of the week, the letters in the alphabet, and the months of the year as a school task; that is, in their nondominant language.

39. Tell me the months and their numbers: January 1, February 2 . . .
    (Mch 3 Ap 4 May 5 Jn 6 Jl 7 Aug 8 Spt 9 Oct 10 Nov 11 Dec 12)
40. Tell me the alphabet skipping every other letter: A-C-E . . .
    (Demonstrate by touching a finger when you produce a letter)
    (G I K M O Q S U W Y)

(Gr. 4) 41. Tell me the alphabet skipping two letters at a time: A—D—G . . .
    (Demonstrate) (J—M—P—S—V—Y)
42. Tell me the alphabet skipping three letters at a time: A—E—I . . .
    (Demonstrate).   (M—Q—U—Y)
43. What day is New Year's Day?
44. Tell me the months backwards from December: December, November . . .
    (Oct Sept Aug Jl Jn May Apr Mch Feb Jan)
45. Tell me the four directions: North . . .   (South, East, West)

(Gr. 5) 46. Tell me the months backwards and the numbers forwards: December 1,
    November 2 . . .
    (Oct 3 Spt 4 Aug 5 Jl 6 Jn 7 May 8 Apr 9 Mch 10 Feb 11 Jan 12)
47. Starting with K1, tell me the letters and the numbers: K1 L2 . . .
    (M3 N4 O5 P6 Q7 R8 S9 T10 U11 V12 W13 X14 Y15 Z16)
48. Tell me the months forwards and backwards: January–December,
    February–November . . .   (Mch–Oct Ap–Spt May–Aug Jn–Jl)
49. Tell me the months, the numbers, and the days like this: January-1-Monday,
    February-2-Tuesday . . .   (Mch-3-Wd Ap-4-Th May-5-Fr Jn-6-Sat Jl-7-Sun)
50. Tell me the months and two numbers: January 1–2, February 3–4, March . . .

2. PHONOLOGICAL ANALYSIS ("HIDDEN WORDS")

This task of mental deletion was first developed in 1964 by the British psychologist D. J. Bruce. The first American equivalents appeared in the following years (Liberman et al., 1974; Rosner, 1975), but the task has remained strangely unfamiliar to most educators and psychologists, and commercial forms are only now becoming available to the English-speaking diagnostician.

This Spanish adaptation of the task is particularly valid as a predictor of reading in the Spanish language; after all, Spanish decoding is achieved only through the syllabic and literal analysis of the words and through the final blending of the sounds obtained, which are exactly the tasks measured by this test.

This measure (context-free rather than semantically organized) may contrast sharply with the fund of academic knowledge calculated in Appendix 9B, and may differ enormously from the level of visual analysis obtained at any Developmental task of Visual-Motor integration already administered.

Hidden Words
(Spanish form)

Developmental Norms

(PK)   1. (Show four fingers) Di: *Juan bebe agua fresca.*
    (Hide the corresponding finger.) Sin decir "fresca."   (JUAN BEBE AGUA)
    * 2. (Hide the corresponding fingers.) Sin decir "agua fesca"   (JUAN BEBE)
    3. (Show five fingers) Di: *Juan come mucho pan blanco.*
    (Hide the corresponding fingers.) Sin decir: blanco.
    (JUAN COME MUCHO PAN)

4. (Hide the corresponding fingers.) Sin decir "pan blanco."

(JUAN COME MUCHO)

* 5. (Hide the corresponding fingers.) Sin decir "mucho pan blanco."

(JUAN COME)

* 6. (Show three fingers. Move each of them as you say:)
Di: *Uno, dos, tres.* Ahora di uno, dos, tres sin decir "uno."   (DOS-TRES)
(Hide the corresponding finger.)

7. Di uno, dos, tres sin decir "dos." (Hide the corresponding finger.)

(UNO-TRES)

8. Di uno, dos, tres sin decir "tres." (Hide the corresponding finger.) (UNO-DOS)

* 9. (Show two fingers. Move each finger as you say:) Di *Juan Rey.*
(Use the student's first and last name.)
(Hide the corresponding finger) Di *Juan Rey* sin decir "Rey."   (JUAN)

10. Di *Juan Rey.*
(Hide the corresponding finger) Ahora di Juan Rey sin decir "Juan."   (REY)

(K)   11. Di *Puerto Rico.* Ahora di Puerto Rico sin decir "Rico."   (PUERTO)

12. Di *barbacoa.* Ahora di barbacoa sin decir "coa."   (BARBA)

(*) 13. Di *bendito.* Ahora di bendito sin decir "to."   (VENDI)

14. Di *comedia.* Ahora di comedia sin decir "co."   (MEDIA)

15. Di *bonita.* Ahora di bonita sin decir "ni."   (BOTA)

16. Di *camisa.* Ahora di camisa sin decir "mi."   (CASA)

17. Di *órgano.* Ahora di órgano sin decir "ga."   (HORNO)

18. Di *religión.* Ahora di religion sin decir "li."   (REGION)

19. Di *trabajo.* Ahora di trabajo sin decir "ba."   (TRAJO)

(*) 20. Di *culebra.* Ahora di culebra sin decir "le."   (CUBRA)

(Segments component words, prefixes, and syllables.)

(Gr. 1) (*)   (Show four fingers. Point to each of them as you say: "Ce-U-Be-A, CUBA.")

21. Di *cuba.* Ahora di cuba sin decir la "ca."   (UVA)

22. Di *nave.* Ahora di nave sin decir la "ene."   (AVE)

(*) 23. Di *salió.* Ahora di pared sin decir la "o."   (SALI)

24. Di *cruce.* Ahora di cruce sin decir la "e."   (CRUZ)

(*) 25. Di *lechón.* Ahora otra vez sin decir la "che."   (LEON)

26. Di *cabida.* Ahora otra vez sin decir la "be."   (CAIDA)

(*) 27. Di *piano.* Ahora otra vez sin decir la "a."   (PINO)

28. Di *juego.* Ahora otra vez sin decir la "e."   (JUGO)

(*) 29. Di *careta.* Ahora otra vez sin decir la "e."   (CARTA)

30. Di *aroma.* Ahora otra vez sin decir la "o."   (ARMA)

(Segments initial, final, and medial sounds.)

(Gr. 2) (*) 31. Di *plazo.* Ahora otra vez sin decir la "p."   (LAZO)

32. Di *cabra.* Ahora otra vez sin decir la "b."   (CARA)

(*) 33. Di *cerveza.* Ahora otra vez sin decir la "ve."   (CEREZA)

34. Di *adicción.* Ahora ortra vez sin decir el sonido "k."

(Segments first element of a consonant blend.)

(Gr. 3)   35. Di *flecha.* Ahora otra vez sin decir la "ele."   (FECHA)

36. Di *cable.* Ahora otra vez sin decir la "ele."   (CABE)

(*) Introductory items for older students over the age of 7. If the student succeeds all the introductory items, go on administering the test item by item from the third grade level on. In case of failure to any introductory item, go down one more grade level and administer the test item by item from that point on. Discontinue testing when successive failures represent one whole grade and one more item.

37. Di *magro*. Ahora otra vez sin decir la "erre."   (MAGO)
38. Di *bucle*. Ahora otra vez sin decir la "ele."   (BUQUE)
39. Di *desplegar*. Ahora otra vez sin decir la "l."   (DESPEGAR)
40. Di *complete*. Ahora otra vez sin decir la "ele."   (COMPETE)
   (Segments the second element of a consonant blend.)

(Gr. 4)   41. Di *inspecto*. Ahora otra vez sin decir la "pe."   (INSECTO)
   (Segments third element of a multiple cluster.)
42. Di *pinto*. Ahora, en lugar del sonito p di el sonito q.   (QUINTO)
43. Di *grato*. Ahora, en lugar del sonido a, di el sonido i.   (GRITO)
44. Di *paz*. Ahora, en vez del sonido a di el sonido e.   (PEZ)
45. Di *clima*. Ahora, en lugar del sonido cl, di el sonido pr.   (PRIMA)
46. DI *claro*. Ahora, en el lughar del sonido cl, di el sonido f.   (FARO)
47. Di *pluma*. Ahora, en lugar del sonido pl di el sonido br.   (BRUMA)

3. SEQUENTIAL MOVEMENT

Sequential movement is very rarely explored in batteries for learning-disordered children. Acevedo et al. (1972) observed low sequential movement in all their dyslexic Uruguayan students, and a strong relation appeared (Hurwitz et al., 1972) between motor sequencing and learning disabilities. Kosslyn and Klein (1993) suggested that actions, like sentences in a language, must be produced by a generative system. Early tests of sequential movement were developed by Stamback (1964), Deutsch and Schumer (1970), and McCarthy (1975).

Denckla (1996) considered that our limited use of "lowly motor tasks" represents a relative neglect of the motoric border of Executive Functions. We may also regret the lack of sequential motor exploration of the skills as a more culture-free approach to the study of the skills of linguistically and culturally different students. Sizable correlations were found (Sedó, 1987) between the motor sequencing and the academic achievement of first-, third-, and fifth-graders.

Sequential Echopraxias

Introductory Items

Sit facing the student and say: *Do exactly as I do*. Tap on the table with a one-second interval.

Scoring. 2 points for correct reproduction of the auditory sequence after the first presentation of the item; 0 for failure.

Items may be presented twice, but success at the second attempt is not scored.

Items marked (*) are introductory items to

be used with students aged 7 or older. If the student succeeds all the introductory items, go on administering every item from the third grade level on. In case of failure to any introductory item, go down to the beginning of the previous grade and administer all items from that point on. Discontinue testing when the number of successive failures represents one whole grade and one more item.

Developmental Norms

(Nursery)	(*) 1. 1		(PK)	(*) 7. 2 2
	2. 2			8. 1 3
	3. 1 1			9. 3 1
	4. 1 2			
	5. 2 1		(K)	(*) 10. 2 3
	6. 3			11. 3 2

*Introductory items for older students over the age of 7.

(Gr. 1)	(*) 12. 1 2 2		20. 3 1 2 1
	13. 2 1 2	(Gr. 4)	21. 1 3 2 3
	14. 2 2 1		22. 3 1 3 2
(Gr. 2)	(*) 15. 2 3 1		23. 3 2 2 3
	16. 3 1 3	(Gr. 5)	24. 3 2 2 1 3
	17. 3 3 1		25. 2 3 2 2 3
(Gr. 3)	18. 1 2 3 1		26. 3 2 2 3 2
	19. 2 1 2 3		

(Adapted from: Sedó, M. A. *Low-Language Non-Reading Instruments to predict Academic Achievement.* Chestnut Hill, MA: Boston College School of Arts and Sciences, unpublished doctoral dissertation, 1987.)

APPENDIX 9D

Ten Tasks of Spanish Reading

This decoding checklist will help the mainstream neuropsychologist recognize the ten basic decoding levels present in the letter-by-letter reading made by Spanish readers reading in their language. The initial 4 segments present all the basic difficulties of *syllable decoding.* The following 3 segments (5 to 7) cover the awareness of all *basic letter signs and the recognition and decoding of frequent and less frequent combinations of letters.* The final 3 segments (8 to 10) explore the neglected signs of *letter-by-letter dyslexic reading:* misreading of tonic and graphic accents, misreading of the soft and hard sounds of *g,* misreading of the tonic and silent *u*s, and slow reading of longer words. The presence of these signs may suggest a surface dyslexia disguised by the phonological simplicity of the Spanish reading mechanics.

1.   ma pa se tu ni lo de
        A O U I E
        i u a e o

2.   el le al la se es
        yo no se ir   si, ya se   yo no lo ví
        el se va ya   yo no se si él se va
        él es un as o no lo es

3.   del pon les van por sin con
        sin ver sin dar por mas con tal
        los sol las sal nos son des sed res ser
        ten pon más pan ven sal del bar

4.   soy voy hoy hay pie rey sea buey sois seis
        salió leamos marea no peleo
        más miel veis cuan ruin aun no se fue

5.   n l s m b d r t ll g c
        ñ x k f ch h y z w j v
        baño rifa tiñe fijo hizo viejo daño vicio voz
        cace caño queme raro buho buche
        bla bra cle dri flo fru glo gru pla pri
        plan tres tras tren clan clin cruz

6.   f y p b d q u n doy dan dio
        daba dada nado nabo dedo bebo pode
        rodaba robada rodada robaba

7.   oíais oía reía huía reía roían reíais
        caos caso asco saco digno atlas capta luzca
        rumbo capto gozne diezmo trasgo pizca chusma
        buitre suegra ciudad cuidad pulcro brusco
        excluyo constreñir transversal inmunizar
        exclaustrar inextricable inexpugnable
        drástico, gástrico y diagnóstico

8. ( )   lean leal osan osar
         oran oral oras tonel toser tosen

   (')   ésta está río rió deje dejé pillo pilló
         lleve llevé amen amén rey reí
         público publico publicó   tráfico trafico traficó
         rótulo rotulo rotuló módulo modulo moduló

9. (G)   gama gema goma gima
         agota agita paga page
   (GU) aguce guise riegue guasa guiasen seguían
   (")   desagüe reguero lengüeta
         laguito yegüita roguemos

10.   Tú eres un otorrinolaringólogo
         la inimitable perfectibilidad
         incuestionablemente desasosegado
         y encareciéndoseles desproporcionadamente
         antidesconceptualizacionalísticamente subcompartimentalizatorio

                                        Total time: _____ (40 sec.)

Scoring Form

	Partial achvt.	Total achvt.	
1. __/10 letter vowel signs (high and low case)	1	2	
Easy syllables	1 ( )	2 ( )	
2. VC-CV without reversals	1	2	
3. CVC without reversals	1	2	
4. CVV–CVVC–VVC	1	2	(_/10)

5. Consonant contrasts		1 (9)	2 (19)	
6. Reversible signs		1	2	
7. Less frequent oral motor combinations: VW CC		1	2	
8. Stress: vowel blends, tonic, graphic		1	2	
9. Two sounds of g and of gu; diaesis		1	2	(_/20)

10. Exploring and blending longer words

Era un otorrinolaringólogo	0	1 (_) 2	__	__	(Total: 6 sec)
La inim. perfect.	0	1 (_) 2	__	__	(Total: 10 sec)
Incuest. desasoseg.	0	1 (_) 2	__	__	(Total: 18 sec)
Y encar. desprop.	0	1 (_) 2	__	__	(Total: 28 sec)
Antidesc. subcompart.	0	1 (_) 2	__	__	(Total: 40 sec)

PUNTAJE TOTAL (1 to 30) _____

SOME OBSERVED MISCUES:

Letter/number	__		
e/a/o	__		
b/d	__		
d/b	__		
h/ch	__		
l/ll	__		
c/qu	__		
s/c/z	__		
Other reversals	__	Observed:	_____
Transpositions:	__	Observed:	_____
Delays	__	Observed:	_____

APPENDIX 9E

Is It Possible for Some Students to Read Better English Than Spanish?

Spanish is a phonetic language; the knowledge of just 26 individual sign-to-sound correspondences ensures the automatic decoding of all possible sounds and the blending of all possible words. Syllable recognition and letter decoding form the basis of all there is to know about Spanish decoding; full phonological decoding is often achieved at the end of the first grade level and may show little, if any, progress afterward. English, on the other hand, uses an unpredictable reading code, in which letters and groups of letters may be sounded in different contradictory ways. Progress in English decoding does not stop in the elementary school years, but develops unceasingly all through the school career of the student. For these reasons, it is easy to conclude that Spanish reading is actually the easier of the two reading systems, and that the phonology of Spanish should probably be used as an easy introduction to the more difficult and unpredictable phonology of English. After all, most readers of Spanish can easily achieve the reading and writing of Spanish, based on the strict correspondence of signs and sounds in reading and writing. Even the surface dyslexic (that is, the letter-by-letter phonological reader) may be able to achieve the nearly correct reading of all Spanish words, and hide forever a basic dyslexic style.

For these reasons, the bilingual specialist may have difficulty accepting two seemingly logical but incongruent sets of data that may disprove their basic evaluation of the relative difficulties of the Spanish and English reading tasks. There is, after all, a moment in the career of the child where letter-by-letter reading (the basic characteristic of Spanish reading) may not be completely achieved; and there are precise kinds of learners (spatially disabled, highly conceptual readers) for whom English reading may often present a much easier task than Spanish reading. This paradox must be carefully explained since it may be difficult to believe.

Sedó (1994) described the precise student who must find English much easier than Spanish: the student who is still unable to develop the sign-to-sound correspondence of simple letter signs and the simple blending of signs into words. He baptized this syndrome as a *Sudden Affinity for English Reading,* and the student as a S.A.F.E.R. child. Whenever the identification of letters cannot be achieved, English may automatically become much easier than Spanish and can be used to convey to the Spanish-speaking students a linguistic awareness of word meanings and language structures that Spanish will never be able to convey through the impossible task of decoding and blending. Azcoaga (1988) emphasized the difference between direct semantic recognition and phonological letter-by-letter decoding of words. For subjects unable to do the letter-by-letter decoding, Spanish reading stops very close to the first-grade level, whereas English can be easily taught at the 2nd- or 3rd-grade level (Theroux, 1994). Mothers and teachers may be surprised when the nonreading child is suddenly exposed to the English of English sight-words, even in the absence of previous English knowledge. Teachers of English in Latin American capitals have already discovered that when a child is exposed to both English and Spanish reading, English is the first language acquired. The lack of Spanish reading is often the first sign of a latent dyslexia that is more obvious in Spanish than in English; the student may have a basic difficulty in creating letter-by-letter associations and doing letter-after-letter blendings. It is even possible to read English before learning oral English by learning the new meanings one word at a time rather than one letter at a time. "Barking to the words" is (whether we may want it or not) much easier than analyzing words.

A second phenomenon may also be observed: the baffling experience of students who, against all possible expectations, will find English inexplicably easier than Spanish and will become attached to their second language to the point of abandoning their primary language. This phenomanon was described as a *Sudden Affinity for English,* and the students as S.A.F.E. students. This fact has never been explained in terms of any particular learning style or individual predisposition. In fact, most English words are monosyllabic and much shorter than most Spanish words. English words are much more often invariant, more directly juxtaposed than Spanish words, and are much less prone to be inflected or derived. English may offer to the high-conceptual/low-visual reader the experience of avoiding the slow blending of sounds and the direct exposure to one new concept for each new syllable of English text. When a student has quickly adopted English as their second language or done too well in it, the psychologist should always suspect the presence of a high-conceptual/low-visual learning style that the student has only learned to use to his or her own advantage.

The presence of S.A.F.E.R. and S.A.F.E. students has never been considered or researched in the past. The existence of S.A.F.E. and S.A.F.E.R. children is not always easy to accept by linguistis, as it may present a new challenge that they are not ready to accept.

REFERENCES

Acevedo de Mendilaharsu, S., López de Cayaffa, C., Delfino de Cultelli, Bermúdez, A., Laguardia de Pérez, G., Rodríguez de Bordoli, L., & Mendilaharsu, C. (1972). Estudio de la dislexia de Evolución [A study of developmental dyslexia]. *Acta Neurológica Latinoamericana, 18,* 299–317.

Anastasi, A., & De Jesus, C. (1953). Language development and non-verbal IQ of Puerto Rican preschool children in New York City. *Journal of Abnormal Psychology, 48,* 357–366.

Azcoaga, J. E. (1988). Procesos neurofisiológicos que operan en la transcodificación verbográfica [Neurophysiological processes in visual-verbal transcoding]. In A. Ardila & F. Ostrosky-Solis (Eds.), *Lenguaje oral y escrito.* Mexico: Editorial Trillas.

Badian, N. (1986). Nonverbal disorders of learning: The reverse of dyslexia? *Annals of Dyslexia, 36,* 253–259.

Baker, K. (1990). Bilingual education's 20 year failure to provide civil rights protection for language-minority students. In A. Barona & E. E. García (Eds.), *Children at risk: Poverty, minority status, and other issues in educational equity.*

Bakker, D. (1990). *Neuropsychological treatment of dyslexia.* Oxford: Oxford University Press.

Barkley, R. (1981). Learning disabilities. In E. J. Mash & L. G. Terdal (Eds.), *Behavioral assessment of childhood disorders.* New York: Guilford.

Beery, K. E. (1997). *The VMI Developmental Test of Visual–Motor Integration* (4th ed.). Parsippanny, NJ: Modern Curriculum Press. (First appeared in 1967)

Boder, E. (1973). Developmental dyslexia: A diagnostic approach based on three atypical reading–spelling patterns. *Developmental Medicine and Child Neurology, 15,* 663–687.

Broverman, D. M., Broverman, I. K., & Klaiber, E. (1966). The ability to automatize and the automatization cognitive style: A validation study. *Journal of Perceptual and Motor Skills, 23,* 419–437.

Bruce, L. J. (1964). The analysis of word sounds by young children. *British Journal of Educational Psychology, 34,* 158–170.

Carbonell de Grompone, M. A. (1974). Children who spell better than they read. *Academic Therapy, 9,* 281–288.

Carbonell de Grompone, M. A. (1975). Colonialismo y Dislexia. In J. B. de Quirós (Ed.), *El lenguaje lectoescrito y sus problemas.* Buenos Aires: Editorial Médica Panamericana.

Chase, C. H. (1996). A visual deficit model of developmental dyslexia. In C. H. Chase, G. D. Rosen, & G. F. Sherman (Eds.), *Developmental dyslexia: Neural, cognitive, and genetic mechanisms.* Baltimore: York Press.

Christiansen, T., & Livermore, G. A. (1970). A comparison of Anglo American and Spanish American children on the WISC. *Journal of Social Psychology, 30,* 15–41.

Cohen, B. D., Berent, S., & Silverman, A. J. (1973). Field-dependence and lateralization of function in the human brain. *Archives of General Psychiatry, 28,* 165–167.

Cohen, S. A. (1967). *Teach them all to read: Theories, methods and materials in teaching the Disadvantaged.* New York: Random House.

Denckla, M. B. (1973). Development of speed in repetitive and successive finger-movements in normal children. *Developmental Medicine and Child Neurology, 15,* 635–645.

Denckla, M. B. (1977). The neurological basis of learning disability. In F. G. Roswell & G. Natchez (Eds.), *Reading disability: A human approach to learning* (3rd ed., rev. & expanded). New York: Basic Books.

Denckla, M. B. (1985). Motor coordination in dyslexic children: Theoretical and clinical implications. In F. H. Duffy & N. Gescwind (Eds.), *Dyslexia: A neuroscientific approach to clinical evaluation.* Boston: Little, Brown.

Denckla, M. B. (1996). A theory and model of executive function: A neuropsychological perspective. In G. R. Lyon & N. A. Krasnegor (Eds.), *Attention, memory and executive function.* Baltimore: Paul H. Brookes.

Denckla, M. B., Rudel, R., & Broman, M. (1981). Tests that discriminate between dyslexic and other learning-disabled boys. *Brain and Language, 13,* 118–129.

Deutsch, C. P., & Schumer, F. (1970). *Brain-damaged children: A modality-oriented exploration of performance.* New York: Brunner/Mazel.

Dulay, H., & Burt, M. (1980). The relative proficiency of limited English proficiency students. In J. E. Alatis (Ed.), *Georgetown University roundtable on language and linguistics.* Washington, DC: Georgetown University Press.

Erenberg, G., Mattis, S., & French, J. H. (1978). *Four hundred children referred to an urban ghetto developmental disabilities clinic: Computer assisted analysis of demographic, social, psychological and medical data.* New York: Montefiore Hospital (mimeo).

Ferreiro, E., & Teberosky, A. (1979). *Literacy before schooling*. Portsmouth, NH: Heinemann.

Francis, D. J., Fletcher, J. M., Rourke, B. P., & York, M. J. (1992). A five-factor model for motor, psychomotor, and visual-spatial tests used in the neuropsychological assessment of children. *Journal of Clinical and Experimental Neuropsychology, 14,* 625–637.

Frostig, M., Lefever, D., & Whittlesey, J. (1964). *The Marianne Frostig Developmental Test of Visual Perception.* Chicago: Follett.

Garcia, S. B., & Yates, J. R. (1986). Policy issues associated with serving bilingual exceptional children. In A. C. Willig & H. F. Greenberg (Eds.), *Bilingualism and learning disabilities: Policy and practice for teachers and administrators* (pp. 113–134). New York: American Library Publishing.

Gerken, K. (1978). Performance of Mexican American children on intelligence tests. *Exceptional Children, 44,* 438–443.

Geschwind, N. (1965). Disconnection syndromes in animals and man, Parts I and II. *Brain, 88,* 237–294, 585–644.

Goldstein, K. (1939). *The organism.* New York: American Book.

Gutkin, T. B. (1979). Bannatyne patterns of Caucasian and Mexican-American learning disabled children. *Psychology in the Schools, 16,* 178–183.

Hausman, R. M. (1988). The use of Budoff's learning assessment techniques with a Mexican-American, moderately handicapped student. In R. L. Jones (Ed.), *Psychoeducational assessment of minority group children : A casebook.* Berkeley, CA: Cobb and Henry.

Horn, J. L., & Cattell, R. B. (1966). Refinement and test of the theory of fluid and crystallized intelligence. *Journal of Educational Psychology, 57,* 253–270.

Hurwitz, I., Bibace, R. M., Wolff, P. H., & Robotham, B. M. (1972). Neuropsychological function of normal boys, delinquent boys and boys with learning disabilities. *Perceptual and Motor Skills, 35,* 387–394.

Jaynes, J. (1976). *The origins of consciousness in the breakdown of the bicameral mind.* Boston, MA: Houghton-Mifflin.

Kaplan, E., Goodglass, H., & Weintraub, S. (1983). *Boston Naming test.* Philadelphia, PA: Lea & Febiger.

Kosslyn, S. M., & Klein, O. (1993). *Wet mind: The new cognitive neuroscience.* New York: Free Press.

Langdon, H. W. (1992). *Hispanic children and adults with communication disorders: Assessment and intervention.* Gaithersburg, MD: Aspen Publishers.

Lesser, G. S., Fifer, G., & Clark, D. H. (1965). Mental abilities of children from different social-class and cultural groups. *Monograph of the Society for Research in Child Development,* No. 102.

Levine, M. D. (1994). *Educational care: A system for understanding and helping children with learning problems at home and in school.* Cambridge, MA: Educators Publishing Service.

Levine, M. D., Brooks, R., & Shonkoff, J. P. (1980). *A pediatric approach to learning disorders.* New York: Wiley.

Liberman, I. Y., Shankweiler, D., Liberman, A. M., Fowler, C., & Fischer, F. W. (1974). Reading and the awareness of linguistic segments. *Journal of Experimental Child Psychology, 18,* 201–212.

Luria, A. R. (1961). *The role of speech in the regulation of normal and abnormal behavior.* New York: Liveright.

Luria, A. R. (1980). *Higher cortical functions in man* (2nd ed.). New York: Basic Books.

Lyon, G. R. (1996). Learning disabilities. In E. J. Mash & R. A. Barkley (Eds.), *Child psychopathology.* New York: Guilford.

Marmorale, A., & Brown, F. (1973). *Mental health in the primary grades.* New York: Behavioral Books.

Mattis, S., French, J. H., & Rapin, I. (1975). Dyslexia in children and young adults: Three independent neuropsychological syndromes. *Developmental Medicine and Child Neurology, 17,* 150–163.

McCarthy, D. (1975). *McCarthy scales of children's abilities.* New York: Psychological Corporation.

Meeker, M. N., & Meeker, R. (1973). Strategies for assessing intellecrtual patterns in Black, Anglo and Mexican American—or any other children—and implications for education. *Journal of School Psychology, 11,* 341–350.

Miller, G. A., Gallanter, E., & Pribram, K. H. (1960). *Plans and the structure of behavior.* New York: Holt, Reinhardt, & Winston.

Nichols, E, G., Inglis, J., Lawson, J. S. & MacKay, I. (1988). A cross-validation study of patterns of cognitive ability in children with learning difficulties, as described by factorially defined WISC-R Verbal and Performance IQs. *Journal of Learning Disabilities, 21,* 504–508.

Oakland, T. (1983). Concurrent predictive validity estimates for the WISC-R and ELPs by racial-ethnic and SES groups. *School Psychology Review, 12,* 57–61.

O.R.E.A. (1989). *Preliminary report—New York City norms for the EIWN–R.* New York: Board of Education, Office of Research, Evaluation and Assessment.

Ortiz, V., & Volloff, W. (1987). Identification of gifted and accelerated Hispanic students. *Journal for the Education of the Gifted, 11,* 45–55.

Parsons, O. A. (1972). Clinical neuropsychology. In C. D. Spielberger (Ed.), *Current topics in clinical and community psychology* (pp. 1–60). New York: Academic Press.

Pascal, B. (1989). *Pensees—Extraits* [Thoughts—Excerpts]. Paris, France: Librairie Larousse. (Original work published 1669–1670)

Peal, E., & Lambert, W. (1962). The relationship of bilingualism to intelligence. *Psychological Monographs, 76,* 1–23.

Ramirez, M., & Price-Williams, D. (1974). Cognitive styles of three ethnic groups in the United States. *Journal of Cross-Cultural Psychology, 5.*

Ramirez, M., III, & Ramirez, C. (1974). *Cultural democracy, bicognitive development and education.* New York: Academic.

Reschly, D. J. (1995, January 21). *IQ and special education: History, current status, and alternatives.* Paper presented at a workshop of the Board on Testing and Assessment, La Jolla, CA.

Rosner, J. (1975). *Helping children overcome learning difficulties.* New York: Walker & Co.

Rourke, B. P. (1995). Introduction: The NLD Syndrome and the white matter model. In B. P. Rourke (Ed.), *Syndrome of nonverbal learning disabilities: Neurodevelopmental manifestations.* New York: Guilford.

Rourke, B. P. (1998). Significance of verbal-performance discrepancies for subtypes of children with learning disabilities: Opportunities for the WISC–III. In A. Prifitera & D. H. Saklofske (Eds.), *WISC–III clinical use and interpretation: Scientist- practitioner perspectives.* San Diego, CA: Academic Press.

Rueda, R. (1989). Defining mild disabilities with language-minority children. *Exceptional Children, 56,* 121–128.

Sedó, M. A. (1994, July). S.A.F.E.R. students: Sudden affinity for English reading in some bilingual Spanish students. Poster presented to the 12th International Congress of Cross-Cultural Psychology, Pamplona, Spain.

Sedó, M. A. (1995a, July). *Hiperlateralización: un signo olvidado de problems para el aprendizaje?* Workshop presented at the 25th Congreso Interamericano de Psicología, San Juan, Puerto Rico.

Sedó, M. A. (1995b, May). *"48 DRAWINGS": Dual (concept and spatial) aspects of graphic performance.* Poster presented at the 9th annual Science Fair of the Massachusetts Neurological Society, Cambridge, MA.

Sedó, M. A. (1997). *Dislexia en inglés y en español* [Dyslexia in English and in Spanish]. Paper presented at the 5th meeting of the Latin American Neuropsychological Society (S.L.A.N.), Guadalajara, Mexico.

Sedó, M. A. (1999). *Motor and mental problems of Hispanic special children.* Paper presented to the 27th Meeting of the Interamerican Psychological Society, Caracas, Venezuela.

Semel, E., Wiig, E. H., & Secord, W. A. (1996). *Clinical evaluation of language fundamentals—Third edition (CELF–3) Spanish edition.* San Antonio, TX: Psychological Corporation

Shellenberger, S. (1977). *A cross-cultural investigation of the Spanish version of the McCarthy Scales of Children's Abilities for Puerto Rican children.* Unpublished doctoral dissertation, University of Georgia.

Sparrow, S. S., Balla, D. A., & Cichetti, D. V. (1984). *Vineland Adaptive Behavior Scales, interview edition.* Circle Pines, MN: American Guidance Service.

Spreen, O., & Strauss, E. (1998). *A compendium of neuropsychological tests: Administration, norms and commentary* (2nd ed.). New York, Oxford University Press.

Stamback. (1964). Trois épreuves de rhythme [Three rhythmic tests]. In R. Zazzo (Ed.), *Manual pour l'examen psychologique de l'enfant* (Vol. 2). Neuchatel and Paris: Delachaux et Niestlé.

Strauss, A. A., & Lehtinen, L. E. (1947). *Psychopathology and education of the brain injured child.* New York: Grune & Stratton.

Taleporos, E. (1989). *Preliminary report: New York City norms for the EIWN–R.* New York: New York City Board of Education.

Tallal, P., Miller, S., & Fitch, R. H. (1996). Neurobiological basis of speech: A case for the preeminence of temporal processing. In C. H. Chase, G. D. Rosen, & G. F. Sherman (Eds)., *Developmental dyslexia: Neural, cognitive, and genetic mechanisms.* Baltimore, MD: York Press.

Taylor, R. L., Ziegler, E. W., & Partenio, I. (1984). An investigation of WISC–R Verbal-Performance differences as a function of ethnic status. *Psychology in the Schools, 21,* 437–441.

Theroux, P. (1994). *Translating LA: A tour of the Rainbow City.* New York: W. W. Norton.

Torgesen, J. K., & Licht, B. (1983). The learning disabled child as an inactive learner: Retrospects and prospects. In J. D. McKinney & L. Feagass (Eds.), *Topics in learning disabilities* (Vol. 1, pp. 33–32). Rockville, MD: Aspen Press.

Tucker, J. (1980). Ethnic proportions in classes for the learning disabled: Issues in non-biased assessment. *Journal of Special Education, 14,* 93–105.

U.S. Bureau of the Census. (1999). *Statistical abstract of the United States, 1999* (119th ed.). Washington, DC: U.S. Government Printing Office.

U.S. Department of Education. (1994). *Sixteenth annual report to Congress on the implementation of the Individual with Disabilities Education Act.* Washington, DC: Office of Special Education Programs.

Wechsler, D. (1993). *Manual. Escala de inteligencia Wechsler para niños–revisada* (manual) Wechsler Intelligence Scale for Children–Revised]. Adapted and normated for Puerto Rico by L. L. Herrans & J. M. Rodriguez. San Antonio, TX: Psychological Corp.

Wechsler, D. (1999). *Wechsler Abreviated Scale of Intelligence.* San Antonio, TX: Psychological Corporation.

Weiss, L. G., Prifitera, A., & Roid, G. H. (1993). The WISC–III and the fairness of predicting achievement across ethnic and gender groups. In B. A. Bracken & R. S. McCallum (Eds.), *Journal of psychoeducational assessment monograph series, advances in psychoeducational Assessment: Wechsler Intelligence Scale for Children* (3rd ed., pp. 35–42). Germantown, TN: Psychoeducational Corporation.

Witkin, H. A., & Goodenough, D. R. (1981). *Cognitive styles: Essence and origins.* International Universities Press.

Woodcock, R. W., & Dean, R. (1998). The WJ-R and Bateria-R in Neuropsychological assessment. Workshop given at the 28th Annual Conference of the National Academy of Neuropsychology.

10

Organic Behavioral Problems and Social Skills in Children

CARMEN G. ARMENGOL-DE LA MIYAR
Northeastern University

Hispanic families of children with behavioral problems face many issues, particularly when the problems are organic in nature. Language barriers (for immigrants to the United States), minority status, financial limitations and concomitantly living in disadvantaged (often high crime) neighborhoods, lack of understanding by service providers (including school personnel) of the impact of cognitive limitations on behavioral regulation, and limited community support and advocacy systems, are some of those issues. Individually, each presents a formidable challenge; in combination they assume catastrophic proportions. Two cases, Raúl and Francisco, illustrate these issues.

Both Raúl and Francisco present with organic behavioral disorders. *Organic* is a term that, in the context of clinical psychology, has been used to denote brain damage. Organic disorders, or disorders of the central nervous system, are contrasted with *functional* disorders (e.g., anxiety and depression), although the biological substrate of neurodevelopmental disorders previously considered functional is being increasingly acknowledged (e.g., schizophrenia). The definition of *organic* used in this chapter follows the thinking expressed by Lishman (1998), and encompasses structural, chemical, hormonal, and metabolic influences on the central nervous system.

This chapter aims to place behavioral and social skill disorders in children in the context of neuropsychological functioning. For Hispanic children and their families, consideration must also be given to cultural tenets. Hispanics, although in many ways a heterogeneous population, share general values (interpersonal relatedness, strong family ties), beliefs, and childrearing practices (e.g., fostering adherence to convention, respect for authority, demonstrating respect and dignity in relations to others, greater physical closeness, etc.). Those cultural factors, modified by acculturation stage and socioeconomic status, will determine how an individual family will view the causes of behavior and disability, and which interventions will be valued and implemented (Zúñiga, 1992).

Neuropsychology seeks to study the relation between mind and brain, that is, it attempts to link actions, thoughts, and emotions to their physical substrate. In its more applied aspect, neuropsychology is "concerned with the behavioral expression of brain dysfunction. Its rapid evolution in recent years reflects a growing sensitivity among clinicians to the practical problems of identification, assessment, care, and treatment of brain

damaged patients" (Lezak, 1995, p. 7). It is argued that a neuropsychological understanding must inform the diagnosis and treatment of behavioral and social disabilities, in
order to enhance the effectiveness of interventions. As the purpose of this book is also to
make an understanding of human neuropsychology relevant to populations loosely
referred to as Hispanic, sociocultural factors relevant to the treatment of organically based
behavioral disorders are also addressed.

EPIDEMIOLOGY OF ORGANIC BEHAVIORAL
AND SOCIAL DISORDERS

Estimates of the prevalence of behavioral disorders in children vary widely. Wood and
Zabel's (1978) review of prevalence studies yielded two distinct groups: those reporting
low incidence (2%–3%), and those reporting high figures (over 25%). Analyses of factors
leading to these discrepancies reveal that who the raters are and what people are asked to
rate largely account for them. When raters are asked to determine the presence of behavioral problems in the classroom, as opposed to emotional disturbance, a much higher
incidence is obtained. When teachers and individuals who care for the children on a day-
to-day basis are doing the rating, higher incidences are obtained than when school administrators do the reporting. This, according to Rosenberg, Wilson, Maheady, and Sindelar
(1997), reflects short-term (i.e., teachers') versus long-term (i.e., administrators') management concerns of the raters.

The *Disagnostic and Statistical Manual of Mental Disorders* (*DSM–IV;* 1994) offers
epidemiological data on various childhood disorders; most pertinent to this chapter are
Attention Deficit Hyperactivity Disorder, Disruptive Behavior Disorders, Tic Disorders,
and Pervasive Developmental Disorders. Table 10.1 offers a summary of prevalence figures for disorders listed under these categories.

Quay (1979) proposed five behavioral patterns resulting from factor analytic studies of
observations of children using the Behavior Problem Checklist. These purport to offer
greater face validity than more traditional or medically oriented approaches (Rosenberg
et al., 1997). The five categories are hyperactivity, aggression, juvenile delinquency, social
withdrawal, and severe (e.g., pervasive) behavior disorders. Only the fifth factor (which
includes Autism, Asperger's, and Early Onset Schizophrenia among other disorders) is
classified as low incidence. All others are considered highly prevalent.

Although there is merit in operationally clustering behavioral disorders so as to maximize interrater consistency, the question remains as to whether it adds much to the
understanding of behavior disorders. It might be argued that by carefully considering all
factors that could result in certain dysfunctional behavioral constellations, a more informed and hopefully a more successful approach to their treatment can be attained.

The problem with the *DSM–IV* and other classifications is that typically they fail to
examine comorbidity of behavioral and medical disorders (e.g., attention deficit hyperactivity disorder, ADHD, and head injury). Furthermore, they fail to differentiate the various neuropsychological profiles and specific neuropathologies underlying the diagnoses,
which would provide a better insight into the problem and would also serve to guide
treatments.

The discussion of social skills and behavioral disorders in children centers around their
presence in clearly established neuropsychological conditions. Those conditions include
acquired conditions such as traumatic head injury, seizure disorders, and developmental

TABLE 10.1
Prevalence of Most Common Behavioral Disorders per *DSM–IV*

Autistic Disorder	2–5 per 10,000
Attention Deficit Hyperactivity Disorder	3–5 per 100
Conduct Disorder	6–16 per 100 (males:females = 9:2)
Oppositional Defiant Disorder	2–16 per 100
Tourette's Disorder	4–5 per 10,000

learning disorders (including the less established, but currently of great interest, disorders, such as Asperger's syndrome and Nonverbal Learning Disabilities).

The contribution of traumatic head injury to behavioral disorders is not factored in separately in epidemiological studies of behavior disorders. Nonetheless, head injuries are common in childhood; in fact, according to Rivara and Mueller (1987), they constitute the most important cause of childhood disease, disability, and death. Figures from the United Kingdom indicate that one in six children from age 5 to 14 will die from trauma to the head (H.R.M. Hayes & Jackson, 1989). Figures for the United States are higher; up to 50% of all deaths in childhood and adolescence are due to head injury (Fenichel, 1988). Mild head traumas tend to be the most common form of head injury (89%, according to Kraus et al., 1987).

Studies of psychiatric sequelae of head injury have shown that problems are common (up to 60% at 2½ years postinjury) in severely head-injured children (Brown et al., 1981). Eide and Tysnes (1992) found that multifocal bilateral lesions were more likely to be associated with greater social and adjustment problems. In a developing brain, insults have more opportunity to affect behavior, as they can impair the consolidation of skills being learned, or the development of new skills (Fletcher, Miner, & Ewing-Cobbs, 1987; Ewing-Cobbs, Fletcher, & Levin, 1986). Learning deficits often lead to maladaptive behavior; this is because previously attained strategies to cope with social, environmental, and emotional factors that had been developed have been disrupted. The ability to learn behavioral consequences or attend to warning stimuli can also be impaired, thus what would appear to be a straightforward stimulus–consequence learning situation may no longer be so (Middleton, 1989).

Convulsive disorders are considered a "disorder of childhood," because the majority of affected individuals develop symptoms before age 20 (Spreen, Risser, & Edgell, 1995). Prevalence in children varies depending on how inclusive the definition of the disorder is; a more restrictive definition (those in whom the disorder is active, and who are receiving treatment) results in a 10.5 per 1,000 figure (Cowan, Bodensteiner, Leviton, & Doherty, 1989). Behavioral and emotional disorders in these children are higher than in unaffected populations. Mood disturbances, motor restlessness, lack of drive, isolation, and lack of social integration are among the types of difficulties a child can experience. Many factors must be considered, in addition to the effect of the convulsive disorder itself, when explaining those, such as the etiology of the seizures, type and severity of seizures, degree of concomitant cognitive involvement, developmental stage of a child, and reactions to anticonvulsants (Baron, Fennell, & Voeller, 1995; Lewis, 1994).

In sum, behavioral and social problems in children are quite frequent. Neurological insult resulting from head trauma, prenatal and perinatal accidents (anoxia, infections, etc.), and other organismic disorders impacting the brain has not customarily been incorporated in the discussion and treatment of behavioral disorders. Ways in which neurocognitive problems impact on behavior must be considered here within a developmental framework.

A CONCEPTUAL FRAMEWORK OF DEVELOPMENTAL BRAIN–BEHAVIOR RELATIONSHIPS

The consequences of brain insult or dysfunction are varied, depending on the site, etiology, severity of the dysfunction, and age and maturation of the child. Other organismic factors further determine behavior (e.g., nutrition). A critical issue to consider when dealing with children is the fact that their brains are in the process of maturing, and disruptions in cognitive functioning and behavior may not be evident until later (Dennis, 1988; Dinklage, 1994; Luria, 1973). A boy whose case is reviewed later presented with nocturnal bedwetting at age 10; this obviously did not become a "problem" until this behavior no longer was considered developmentally appropriate.

In order to better understand the functioning of a disordered system, it is necessary to have a model that describes the system in its intact form. One such developmental model of mind/brain functioning has been proposed by Luria (1973).

As Spreen et al. (1995, chap. 4) have indicated, whereas there are several theories of cognitive development on which to draw, little has been done to provide an explicit theoretical model relating neural and cognitive development. One possible exception is the work of Diamond and her colleagues (1990), who investigated the relation between early maturation of the frontal lobes and performance on Piagetian tasks requiring inhibitory control and memory, and other neuropsychological tasks (e.g., the dissociation between knowing and doing). However, Diamond tended not to place her work in the context of a more overarching theory of neuropsychological development. Luria's model, although dated, provides a broad model for relating ontogenetic development of brain–behavior relations. His model is briefly reviewed here to provide a framework within which pediatric organic behavioral dysfunction can be discussed and to provide a basis for meaningful interventions.

Luria divided cognitive functions into three primary brain units: (a) a unit to regulate cortical tone, waking, and mental states; (b) a unit to obtain, process, and store information; and (c) a unit for programming, regulating, and verifying activity (including mental activity).

Luria saw all units as acting interdependently and simultaneously. He also referred to three principles of brain organization: vertical (from brainstem to frontal cortex), hierarchical (from greater to lesser modal specificity), and lateralized at the level of secondary and tertiary levels of integration. He used those principles to explain the impact of disruption to one brain area on the functioning of another and to the developmental stage of the organism.

The first unit, the regulation of tone and waking, is of paramount importance to consider when assessing the impact of brain dysfunction on behavior. A child who is having difficulty with the regulation of this unit may exhibit a number of difficulties. Fatigue, variability, irritability, apathy, and impaired attention are common manifestations of disruptions to this system. Understanding whether and how this functional unit is disrupted will have significant repercussions on the way behavioral problems are addressed.

For instance, it is commonly observed among traumatically brain injured children that as they fatigue, they are more easily overwhelmed (overstimulated) by chatter, loud or persistent music, or stimulation from ongoing simultaneous activities. It is not uncommon that as the level of distress caused by the overload rises, children are less able to modulate their behavior, and more likely to act in unacceptable ways (e.g., throwing a plate of food, striking out, yelling). It is also not uncommon for the child at that point (i.e., after the child is already overstimulated) to be removed from the environment as punishment (e.g., time-out). The agitated behavior often ceases as the aversive event (overstimulation) ends. Disruptions in the child's normal sleep–wake cycle are also an important clue to problems that can be expected.

Behavioral interventions that do not take into account organismic variables may do the right thing (i.e., withdrawing a brain injured child from an overstimulating environment) for the wrong reasons (i.e., to decrease the frequency of agitated or aggressive behavior) and have success. Other variables not addressed, such as self-concept and self-efficacy, are often adversely affected. A more appropriate intervention, one that takes into account that a brain-injured child is prone to fatigue, is to avoid placing that child in noisy and busy environments and/or to offer periodic quiet times (or even naps) to allow for "down times" so the system can rest.

Unfortunately, it is not uncommon to observe in various settings behavioral interventions that are not appropriate for the child because they assume a level of information processing and storage/retrieval not present in the child (i.e., failed to take into account Luria's second functional unit).

One example of mismatched behavioral plans involved an adolescent named "David." David had been the victim of a drowning accident. Previously, he was reportedly quite bright, inquisitive, and an excellent student. This youngster was now being treated at a long-term neurobehavioral rehabilitation facility. In addition to having significant attentional, memory, and reasoning problems, David was unwilling to participate in therapeutic activities, and was agitated (pacing nonstop). A token economy approach was attempted, whereby he was able to earn points for participating in scheduled daily activities. This failed to interest or motivate David. Searching for more appropriate contingencies, the behavior specialist discovered the patient was always talking about his father, and looked forward to receiving telephone calls from him. The behaviorist therefore paired the phone call with completion of physical therapy, as his daily participation in this activity was a priority.

Whereas this reinforcer seemed to have an impact on David's willingness to participate in therapy, an unforeseen complication was his inability to remember that he had received his phone call. He became very insistent with staff that a phone call had to be placed to his father, and threw temper tantrums when told he had already had his call. To deal with his increased agitation, the consulting neurologist placed him on Inderal, and his pacing decreased. David's compliance with treatment, however, did not change, and all he was interested in doing was watching television in his bedroom or sleeping. Removal of the television, the next step, clearly did not help.

What was required, and what proved ultimately effective, was an intervention that took into account David's memory disorder. In this case, audiotapes were obtained from his father instructing David to attend each individual therapy. In addition, each phone call between David and his father was recorded (with permission), and played back in the event that David forgot that he already had his phone call. His father stated the date and time for each taped conversation.

When a problem with the second functional unit (i.e., reception, processing, and storage of information) unfolds developmentally and affects specific modalities, the nature of this disorder is sometimes poorly understood or may be misdiagnosed altogether. For instance, a child that has slow processing speed for certain academic subjects may be seen as uninterested or unmotivated; reinforcement strategies geared at increasing processing efficiency in those children are bound to fail. On the other hand, an acute onset of difficulties (e.g., following an accident) may be more readily identified. For example, if, following a bicycle accident, a girl who is previously functioning at age level presents with significant memory or language comprehension problems, it is unlikely that she will be expected to read a text and retell it from memory.

Malfunction of the third functional unit—particularly as it involves planning, execution, and evaluation of motor programs and mental activity—is often the most perplexing. It is hard for care providers and parents to understand, and difficult to address. A child with damage to this unit may show difficulties in one or more of these areas: self-monitoring, planning and organization, ability to learn from errors, refraining from impulsive responding, taking another's perspective, and coordination of thought and action (i.e., self-commands providing a directive to behavior). These are often referred to as metacognitive behaviors. The inability to inhibit a response effectively can be very confusing to others, especially when the child can state that the response is incorrect and promises not to engage in it (cf. Diamond, 1995; Gerstadt, Hong, & Diamond, 1994, for discussion of the speech–action disconnection in young children).

A glaring example of this disconnection between thought and action and failure to self-regulate occurred during the evaluation of a 7-year-old child who had sustained a concussion at age 4. This very bright and inquisitive boy was having a hard time maintaining focus on tasks, and reinforcers had to be used (a token economy approach with frequent cash-ins) for virtually every response he was required to provide. This child did not lack initiative and the ability to problem solve (e.g., he took the initiative to make himself a cup of hot tea), and he did not have memory problems. Later, when sitting next to a lit lamp while waiting to engage in computerized tests of attention, he put his finger on the light bulb, promptly withdrawing it while exclaiming "It's hot." Not long after the examiner reinforced this awareness by telling him not to touch the light bulb, he proceeded to place his finger on it again. This lack of mindfulness regarding potentially dangerous situations (caused by his inability to inhibit his response) was of significant concern to his parents, but hard for them to formulate clearly and to convey to school personnel. In actuality, this disconnection between "knowing" and "doing" has been extensively described by Teuber (see Walsh, 1994), and more recently, their developmental dissociation has been demonstrated by Diamond (1995) using the Wisconsin Card Sorting Test.

The previous discussion underscores the importance of a good neuropsychological understanding of the children in designing and implementing interventions to deal with their behavioral and socioemotional difficulties. The Process Approach (Kaplan, 1983, 1988), based in an ontogenetic understanding of brain–behavior relations, emphasizes a hierarchical and developmental analysis of a child's performance, rather than a computation of impairment levels. It is only through an understanding of cognitive processes underlying behavior and cognitive performance in a child that an adequate level of therapeutic intervention can be prescribed. This parsing out of observed behavior into inter-related functions permits a more meaningful analysis of the effect of interventions and outcome. Kaplan's assessment approach shares many theoretical commonalties with Luria's neuropsychological formulations, in particular the underlying onotogenetic premises, and the focus on dissociable cognitive functional systems. A major difference is that Kaplan emphasized quantification of qualitative data.

Sohlberg and Mateer (1989) summarized the characteristics of Kaplan's Process-Specific approach as follows:

1. It must provide a systematic and comprehensive review of functional cognitive systems.
2. It must be structured according to current cognitive and neuropsychological theory and seek to investigate major areas of cognitive function in terms of relevant components.
3. It must use available tests and clinical techniques that lend themselves to this process analysis approach. (p. 69)

Using the process approach as the basis of therapy, they proposed six basic rehabilitation principles:

1. A theoretically motivated model defines each cognitive process area.
2. Therapy tasks are administered repetitively.
3. Goals and objectives are hierarchically organized.
4. Remediation involves data-based and directed treatment.
5. The use of generalization probes provides measurements of treatment success.
6. Ultimate measures of success must be improvements in level of vocational ability and independent living. (Sohlberg & Mateer, 1989, p. 32)

Utilizing such a model for therapeutic interventions is more conducive to success than "cookbook" interventions, particularly because with these populations, a systematic trial-and-error approach is the only meaningful way to proceed.

CASE EXAMPLES

Francisco

Francisco was 8 years old and living in Puerto Rico when he was struck by a car while riding his bicycle, sustaining severe head and bodily injuries. He was unconscious for a month, and required extensive physical rehabilitation. Close supervision for about a year following his injury was necessary, because he was very depressed and attempted to commit suicide by throwing himself against a window (he lived in a fifth-floor apartment). As he became older, he had further minor pedestrian accidents, which his mother suspects were suicide attempts. Francisco later befriended young adolescents who had trouble with the law, and was arrested several times for theft and possession of illegal substances. On every occasion, his mother was able to successfully argue for his release on the grounds of incompetence. Meanwhile, she kept seeking services for her son; when options seemed exhausted in Puerto Rico, she searched for them on the mainland. She finally spoke with a bilingual therapist at a hospital, who told her that her son could benefit from further rehabilitation. Finally, the last time he was arrested, the judge ordered him to seek treatment outside Puerto Rico. He was 15 when he arrived in Connecticut.

The family went to live in an inner-city area with a large concentration of Latinos, where a relative of his mother resided. Francisco and his three younger siblings (a boy and two girls) were enrolled in a bilingual program at school. The move represented a great adjustment for the family. The mother, in particular, felt isolated and experienced significant distress; she was disconnected from her social supports in Puerto Rico, and the demands her son's level of supervision placed on her kept her further confined to the home.

Because of his disinhibited behavior, Francisco was placed on 1:1 supervision at school and was prevented from riding the school bus. Other difficulties that developed included his running away and molesting his sisters (his parents placed a lock that could only be opened from the outside, which caused protective services to become involved). The mother had tried to recontact the person she had spoken to earlier about rehabilitation, but she no longer worked at that hospital. She was very overwhelmed with the ongoing difficulties, and quite worried that her son would be killed due to his poor judgment when he was on his own. (His younger brother was entrusted with going out with him to play basketball; the boy was displeased with this burden being placed on him.) Self-endangering behaviors included counting money (the provenance of which was not always clear) in front of individuals of ill repute, and hitching rides when he ran away (at times ending up in neighboring states).

A bilingual school psychologist had earlier recommended residential placement, but the recommendation was ignored. The school was providing counseling services twice a week; they had failed to acknowledge that he required residential placement, and did not even include behavioral problems in the individual education plan (IEP). The mother, who did not speak English, was overwhelmed and, being unfamiliar with the system, was not the most effective advocate for him.

At the request of Protective Services, this author was asked to conduct a review of Francisco's case and to perform a neuropsychological evaluation. Residual deficits included severe dysarthria and left upper extremity paresis. Sleep regulation was poor (he recounted nightmares with a very anxious content, which included running in fright) and he tended to ingest large amounts of sugar, almost compulsively, as described by his father (he ate bowlfulls of sugar and candies nonstop, but was not overweight). Francisco was polite and appeared socially thoughtful (he used overlearned courtesies). Mental status examination, however, revealed concreteness of thought, difficulty with purposeful inhibition of automatized behavior (e.g., on tasks such as Luria's Go–No Go), and limited mental manipulation abilities. Strong recommendations were made to seek residential placement (relief staff was provided at home for the family). The mother was given phone numbers of a local community counseling agency and of a government agency offering legal services for children. It was hard to make contact with them, however, and the mother tried calling several times but was unable to secure an advocate. She would occasionally call in times of crisis (e.g., his running away for days, which required calling local detectives, police, radio stations, and posting notices). Once the immediate crisis was resolved, the impetus to obtain further assistance subsided. Finally, following an arrest, a lawyer was located who strongly began advocating to secure appropriate services for him, including placement in a residential school.

Francisco's case is particularly poignant, because it affected his whole family and disrupted their lives for many years. His parents, and particularly his mother, felt very overwhelmed and powerless in dealing with their son, in that he could express remorse and promise not to engage in undesirable behaviors (such as stealing, molesting his sisters, or running away) but would persist in these behaviors anyway. (He would sometimes steal even when he had money in his pocket.) The issue was compounded by a lack of trained professionals competent in dealing with Hispanic minorities with traumatic brain injury (TBI; Cavallo & Saucedo, 1995; Pontón, Gonzalez, & Mares, 1997; Armengol, 1999).

Neuropsychological assessment demonstrated clearly that it was within his power to inhibit a response while an authority figure was present but not when that person was absent. (Goleman, 1995, cited a study by Mischel demonstrating this behavior in children who later develop significant problems with impulsivity and behavioral self-regulation.)

Raúl

Raúl is a 10-year-old Cuban American child, born to a successful businessman and his college-educated wife, who takes care of the house, Raúl, and his 7-year-old brother. Raúl's delivery was complicated by having the umbilical cord wrapped around his neck. He was "blue" and had to be kept in the hospital for a week. Raúl, unlike his younger brother, was fussy and difficult to appease. Developmental milestones were delayed in that Raúl did not speak until age 2, and then it became apparent that he had a stutter. Toilet training was slow and he continues to wet his bed. He is easily startled and fearful. Fine motor coordination problems (poor handwriting) have been addressed with occupational therapy. Raúl prefers to play alone or with younger children. He is able to make friends readily but does not maintain them; he is easily frustrated when engaged in group play (he may strike out on occasion). He was referred for an evaluation by the director of a summer camp in New England.

Raúl attends a bilingual school in Florida, but dislikes it. In preschool and Kindergarten he was considered disobedient, tending to leave the classroom and failing to return. Academic performance has been variable, most often determined by whether a teacher connects with him. Most recent teachers' perceptions of him were generally unfavorable, ranging from his being disobedient and inattentive, to immature and arrogant; only 30% described him as doing well academically and presenting no disciplinary problems. Reported undesirable behaviors include talking nonstop, tardiness, sullen withdrawal, singing, drumming on the desktop, echolalia, yelling, and threats. His mother has to work with him in order for him to complete his homework. She indicates that he learns when "he puts his mind to it," sees him as having problems with persistence, and feels he is not a bad child; he has many strengths such as intelligence, personal independence, self-sufficiency, ability to handle responsibility, and caring for his brother. Areas of difficulty per his mother are hiding feelings, impulsivity, overreacting when faced with a problem or when people raise their voice at him, immaturity, inability to compromise for the sake of politeness (if he feels he is right), and responding forcefully to teachers if he disagrees. A psychotherapist worked with Raúl to increase self-esteem and explore interpersonal difficulties, and with his mother to address limit setting and encouraging responsible behavior. Although some people who have followed him have noticed increased maturity, the bulk of his problems have persisted. Raúl's mother was particularly concerned about his ability to attend college (some teachers have expressed doubts), and the impact of his difficulties on self-esteem. A clinical psychologist who had evaluated him in Florida indicated that he met criteria for attention deficit hyperactivity disorder (ADHD). His mother has approached her pediatrician in the hopes that he would prescribe Ritalin. The pediatrician, however, has been reluctant to do so.

Raúl was evaluated by this writer. The child was very polite, alert, and cooperative, engaging in sessions of several hours duration. He exhibited marked motor restlessness (moving legs, fidgeting with his fingers, and talking through tasks), which disappeared when engaged in a challenging task. He occasionally let out a four-letter word, which he appeared unable to inhibit; this was out of character with his respectful stance. Testing revealed excellent attentional abilities when the task was demanding (including those requiring divided attention), but some difficulty persisting on more repetitive tasks. He scored in the superior range of intellectual ability, and memory was within normal limits. Some compromise in organization, pragmatic aspects of problem solving (including lack of flexibility), and to a mild degree visuospatial processing were evident. For an understanding of Raúl's presentation, it was important to obtain data from the summer camp director. He perceived Raúl to be very bright and bored with age-appropriate activities, and he noticed time management difficulties (e.g., while dressing) that resulted in tardiness and that improved with external limits; Raúl also engaged in ritualistic food arrangement and selection (also time consuming). He "collected" all sorts of items found on walks, and had a hard time accommodating to arbitrary rules that made no logical sense to him. These observations, in addition to a family history of Tourette's syndrome (TS) in a close relative, suggested that Raúl's problem was more than typical ADHD. Given Raúl's behavioral presentation, the possibilities of compulsive and tic disorders were entertained. A significant degree of overlap is often found in Tourette's and obsessive compulsive disorder (OCD), and a greater prevalence of the latter in first-degree family members has been documented (Baron et al., 1995). Bornstein, Carrol, and King (1985) found that both groups presented with difficulties in shifting cognitive set, visuospatial functions, and praxis. Raúl's neuropsychological profile revealed visuospatial and visuomotor difficulties.

A neurological examination was recommended. Excessive fidgeting, but no signs of frustration when having to wait, were noticed during the examination. Raúl was diagnosed with ADHD and possible Tourette's syndrome with mild compulsive features. A medication trial was recommended, with a warning that typical stimulant medication to treat attentional disorders were contraindicated because they tend to aggravate tics and may aggravate anxiety associated with compulsive tendencies.

Raúl's case is of interest in that despite having all social and economic advantages, the appropriate intervention was not available to him. In Raúl's case, it was extremely important that he be educated regarding Tourette's disorder (which was not too difficult, given that the condition was known in the family) and OCD. This would provide him a better rationale of his aberrant behaviors (for him, in particular, knowing "why" was extremely important), making him more amenable to therapeutic intervention and an active participant in his treatment. Educating his teachers and the professionals was also important. An unexpected finding was the theory held by his paternal grandmother regarding the nature of his difficulties: She felt that the fact that his father's brother died around the time Raúl was conceived was reflected in his restlessness, this representing the lost uncle that suffered from periodic convulsions. The grandmother exerted considerable influence in the family, and her views, which contrasted with more biological views held by her daughter-in-law, were a source of discord.

TREATING BEHAVIORAL PROBLEMS OF ORGANIC ORIGIN

Psychological approaches to dealing with behavioral and social skills problems in children and adolescents have been overwhelmingly behavioral in orientation. Pharmacological treatment has also been used as a way of facilitating behavior control. Although the latter is often a key component of interventions, in-depth discussion of it is beyond the scope of this chapter. The reader is encouraged to consult Silver and Yudofsky (1997), and Silver, Yudofsky, and Hales (1994), for reviews of this topic.

The treatment of behavioral and social dysfunction in children has been a long-standing focus of psychologists devoted to behavior therapy and applied behavioral analysis. Intervention models have spanned the gamut of levels of behavioral analysis, from the respondent to the more cognitive behavioral modes. Very effective interventions have been developed with large populations of neurologically impaired children, typically those with severe behavioral and cognitive limitations (e.g., the approaches to autism by Lovaas, 1987). This focus on the most impaired populations (those for whom other forms of psychotherapy did not have much to offer) was perhaps a historical necessity.

Generally, traditional operant and respondent behavioral paradigms proved sufficient to address and explain behavioral problems faced by clinical populations being served by many behaviorists. There was no pressing need to be concerned with those "black box" intervening variables that Skinner and his followers did not consider relevant for their stimulus–response analysis of learning and behavior.

Later, other voices began acknowledging the role of social (Bandura, 1969) and cognitive (e.g., Beck, 1970; Craighead, Kazdin, & Mahoney, 1976; Meichenbaum, 1974) variables in learning and behavior, broadening the range of interventions, and thus allowing behavior therapy to tackle a greater number of problems. Despite the interest in cognitive variables, cognitive limitations were not taken into account as a moderating variable in designing, implementing, and modifying behavioral interventions.

To a neuropsychologist, it is crystal clear that if children have lost the capacity to self-direct behavior, then they cannot be expected to profit from self-reinforcement. As described earlier, Francisco's case clearly illustrates this: He understood the nature of undesirable behaviors (e.g., stealing) and the attendant punishment, but his behavior was not governed by this understanding. He was unable to inhibit a "pull" to a desired stimulus by generating and mentally comparing two courses of action and selecting the most appropriate one (this is considered the hallmark of "executive abilities," and in Luria's model the highest expression of the third functional unit—planning, comparing, and modifying motor programs). Only the presence of concrete reminders of "social restraint" (e.g., his mother, brother, a teacher keeping an eye on him) could prevent him from engaging in antisocial behavior most of the time. An abstract principle, such as "honesty," even if he were capable of generating it, or even a remote negative consequence of behavior (i.e., one that was not immediately present), lacked the force to inhibit a prepotent, more strongly cued response. Mischel (1990, cited in Goleman, 1995) with his "marshmallow studies" looked at the developmental progression of this self-inhibitory capacity, and individual differences in this ability as denoting differential social intelligence.

Meichenbaum's (1974) work is a direct application of Luria's principles. In his work with hyperactive children, Meichenbaum acknowledged that for these children thought was not directing action; in other words, executive functions were weak and needed to be remedied. More and more, attention deficit hyperactivity disorder (ADHD) is recognized as an executive function disorder (e.g., Pennington, 1991). Unfortunately, the *DSM–IV* does not reflect this, which leads to frequent misclassifications of individuals with other presentations (e.g., bipolar disorder and obsessive compulsive disorder, as in Raúl's case).

As Luria argued, language plays a paramount role in regulating behavior. Using this premise, Meichenbaum developed his self-instructional training approach (sometimes known as "stop, look, and think" techniques), which involves bringing behavior under the control initially of overt speech, and later of thought (covert speech). Kirby and Grimley (1986) demonstrated the efficacy of such interventions even at 1-year follow-up.

They cautioned that "people who are not thoroughly familiar with cognitive-behavior theory do not readily learn to successfully implement cognitive-behavior treatment" (p. 107), and they ascribed their success in part to the thorough training of their staff.

More approaches of this kind need to be developed to better address the needs of children who, because of developmental or acquired reasons, have unusual or compromised cognitive abilities that manifest themselves, directly or indirectly, in behavioral and interpersonal dysfunction. Other useful approaches have been developed (e.g., Blackerby, 1988; McNeill Horton & Sauter, 1984) that can be applied to treating organic behavioral disorders, provided they are adapted or selected to incorporate the cognitive strengths and weaknesses of a specific child. A recent article by Kazdin (1993) is notable for its attempt at taking into account in its behavior therapy formulations, developmental factors, and dual diagnosis considerations. The rest of this section provides a few examples of ways behavior modification techniques and neuropsychological data can be intertwined to attain more effective interventions.

Memory Limitations

Behavioral interventions, predicated as they are on learning theory are, not surprisingly, affected by the child's learning capacity. Although this is well known in the experimental animal literature, the natural corollary to human clinical applications has not followed. This is not surprising, again, due to the virtually nonexistent cross-fertilization of these fields, and the sparse body of literature on memory disorders of childhood. Three types of memory impairment and their implications for designing, selecting, and implementing behavior modification strategies are discussed.

Limbic Lesions.   Memory becomes a paramount issue with specific brain dysfunction that affects even the most basic forms of associative learning. An extreme example of structural brain damage that impairs learning is the Kluver–Bucy syndrome. This disorder involves bilateral destruction of the amygdala and hippocampus, essential in the process of learning. The animal literature indicates that lesions in these areas result, among other things, in an inability to discriminate between edible and inedible substances; the presence of this syndrome in humans has also been documented in a few case studies (Lilly, Cummings, Benson, & Frankel, 1983). Because of destruction of basic areas of learning, even attempts at operant conditioning are unsuccessful. Environmental constraints have to be relied on for their care.

Frontal Amnesias.   Memory dysfunction in itself, when marked, can lead to behavioral disruption. Individuals who lack an ongoing record of their activities become quite angry, oppositional, and at times, violent when faced by other individuals with information about a past event that they do not recall or even recognize. A late adolescent seen at a long-term care facility presented with such a profile following a traumatic head injury. He was able to learn new behavior through respondent and operant conditioning techniques, but learning that required intentional self-direction, or consciousness, yielded very limited or no success. In this case, routines were established for him. He was also trained via methods such as vanishing cues, in the use of organizers, along with hourly reminders via an alarm watch, which prompted him to look for what he was to do next.

Encoding Limitations.   Often memory disorders are secondary to limitations in short-term (working) memory, particularly where mental manipulation of information is required. Because information is passively attended to, it is not easily remembered. These individuals respond well to strategies that highlight the saliency of some events, or to a ready-made structure (which acts as an information organization device). Some widely utilized behavioral interventions, such as token economies (Kazdin, 1977), self-monitoring (Goldiamond, 1965), and behavioral contracting, can be very helpful in this regard. Those interventions have been used successfully with a number of individuals with substantial memory compromise.

Language Capacities

Language problems can interfere with social relations for various reasons. These children, being less adept at verbal expression, may be more likely to act out their feelings, or to shy away from interaction. A child who chooses not to speak when talked to can be viewed as shy, or worse, oppositional. Verbally loaded directives at times may not be understood or may be disregarded by a language-impaired child, and may be misinterpreted as disobedience.

One such child seen by this author in psychotherapy touchingly illustrated this point. A bright 12-year-old girl with academic and behavioral difficulties had particular problems relating to her parents; much of their conflict revolved around disciplinary issues. Both parents and child were very eager to address their discord, and were baffled and exasperated by each other. At one time, the tearful girl confided: "My dad gets mad at me, and tells me to mind my own business . . . how do you mind your own business?" Clearly, she was unable to determine how this abstract command translated into specific action. No behavioral intervention (reward, behavioral cost, etc.) can be effective if the desired specific behavior (beyond the proverbial "being good") was not clearly communicated. Whereas most children of her age could be expected to understand this directive, for her the command was too abstract. Problems with language are particularly likely to arise in bilingual (e.g., Hispanic) children, for whom language delays are not uncommon (Schiff-Myers, Djukic, McGovern-Lawler, & Pérez, 1993).

It is important to determine the level of cognitive and linguistic ability of a child before specific incentive behavioral strategies are put into place to address a behavioral or social problem. It may be that in addition to reinforcers, instructions must be modified, the children may require special therapies to deal with language disabilities, or alternative ways of addressing their limitations must be sought so that the children do not resort to physical demonstrations of frustration and anxiety.

Nonverbal Reasoning and Communication

Some children, rather than having difficulty with language and word skills, appear to have difficulties with the nonverbal aspects of communication and understanding. Imagine a child who responds to the literal meaning of what others tell him, rather than interpreting it by the tone of voice in which it is said. Such children may have difficulty understanding when something is being said sarcastically or ironically and may fail to place the statement in the context of the overall social situation to infer the appropriate meaning.

Interpreting social cues, prosody, novel juxtapositions of ideas (as in jokes or puns), and being able to create context and take perspective are functions that have systematically been found to be subserved by the right hemisphere (e.g., Heilman & Satz, 1983; Ross, 1981). Their contribution, when deficient, to behavioral, academic, and especially social problems, has only recently begun to be a focus of interest. Interventions to address them are virtually nonexistent.

The study of a developmental "nonverbal learning disability" and its adult presentation began in the early 1980s (e.g., Denckla, 1983; Strang & Rourke, 1985; D. Tranel, Hall, Olson, & M. M. Tranel, 1987; Weintraub & Mesulam, 1983). Writing, spatial, mathematical, and social competency deficits were described as components of this type of disability. Because of socially awkward presentations and at times difficulty with affective regulation, these individuals have tended to receive other psychiatric diagnoses (e.g., schizotypal, schizoaffective, bipolar, etc.).

Asperger (1944, cited in Baron et al., 1995) first described individuals who presented with communication difficulties, largely due to narrow and repetitive interests, rigidity and concreteness, and deficient processing of nonverbal aspects of language. Eventually, the syndrome was named after this psychiatrist. The question of whether a more profound deficit in communication (Autism) and Asperger's syndrome overlap has been debated, with views for and against it. The *DSM–IV* (1994) classifies both as part of a continuum: pervasive developmental disorders.

On the other hand, there are also questions regarding whether spatial/mathematical disabilities must co-occur with social disabilities, or whether they are dissociable. In other words, are there separate neural mechanisms underlying spatial/mathematical and social abilities? Rourke (1989) viewed white matter, right hemisphere dysfunction, interfering with intermodal integration of information as underlying both, and Pennington (1991) offered preliminary evidence from literature and clinical cases of his own to support a dissociation.

Children who present with deficits in these areas are often compromised in synthetic reasoning, and engage in a methodical step-by-step analysis of information, giving the impression of being slow, not very bright, and unable to "get the point"; these are the children who "miss the forest for the trees." This often results in their being out of step with their peers and being ridiculed; avoidance or, at times, aggression are the consequences of the inability to negotiate social exchanges.

Training in social skills has so far been the most readily acknowledged way of addressing these problems (Rogers & Lewis, 1989). Behaviorists have been addressing such problems without necessarily recognizing a population with specific learning disorders in social cognition. Such interventions have included assertiveness and social skills training (Wolpe & Lazarus, 1966; Zigler & Phillips, 1961).

Teaching a deficient skill step-by-step to individuals who are unable to perform the inductive nonverbal cognitive operations to abstract the rules of social exchange may result in slight improved social functioning, but overall is not very effective (Voeller, 1997). Clinically, there is a problem because by the time the child has figured out what is going on, the response is often too late or mistimed.

It is clear, however, that early recognition of this problem is critical, as once patterns have been established, and worse, a child has acquired a social persona (the expectations others have of that child)—which among other children may be "nerd," "class clown," "retard," "idiot," and so on—it is harder to undo those already established interactional patterns. Even if the child's behavior changes, the changes are preempted and discounted by the preexisting expectations of others.

Other issues remain to be explored in the treatment of deficient social cognition, such as making the algorithms of social communications even more explicit, through the development of "metacoping" strategies to utilize when none of the algorithms seem to apply to a specific situation. Recognizing the existence of interpersonal difficulties as re-sulting from a neuropsychological condition (i.e., developing a "theory of mind"), seems in itself as important as a metacognitive strategy that can be very powerful in self-analysis and behavior change. The now famous Temple Grandin is a powerful example of this principle. In her book *Thinking in Pictures* (1995), she described her acquisition of "socially acceptable" habits (such as using deodorant and dressing more appropriately) through direct intervention from a trusted supervisor at her work. In her case, social modeling was not enough to move her into insight, but direct teaching of "principles" resulted in an understanding on her part of socially sanctioned behavior. (This is not unlike the experience of an anthropologist amidst another cultural group. Sacks' choice of the title *An Anthropologist in Mars* (1995)—for a book featuring Grandin as one case example of neuropsychological dysfunction—is felicitous indeed.)

For many Hispanic émigrés, the experience of dealing with cultural values and expec-tations different from their own, social exchanges compounded by CNS dysfunction may in some ways feel as removed and incomprehensible as they appear to individuals with social disabilities.

Executive Functions

Problems with behavioral initiation, planning, feedback utilization, sustained effort, and set maintenance are common to a variety of structural, genetic, and metabolic disruptions to the brain. Deficits in this area of functioning invariably lead to altered behavior, either active (aggression, disinhibition, impulsivity) or passive (lack of insight or drive, abulia, anhedonia).

Reconsider Raúl's case. His behavior, without the assistance of a more in-depth analy-sis, had been labeled as characteristic of a child with attention deficit hyperactivity dis-order, with oppositional features. A more in-depth neuropsychological evaluation, how-ever, revealed the presentation to be better classified as an obsessive compulsive disorder. It is not only that Raúl was disinterested in many classes or unable to persist at homework activities, he also had difficulty with teachers because of an inability to accommodate to "arbitrary" rules, which is an indication of cognitive rigidity and inability to de-center. In addition, his rigidity was evident in the inordinate amount of time it took him to eat or dress because his shoes had to be tied in a certain way, or a sandwich had to be prepared in a specific sequence.

Because of inhibitory deficits, Raúl's case can be seen as a problem in executive func-tions, involving prefrontal and connected subcortical structures. The case of obsessive compulsive disorder is seen as a variant of Tourette's, with involvement of the basal ganglia and their prefrontal connections (Pennington, 1991). In addition, however, his difficulties with visuospatial functions and perspective taking suggest frontoparietal in-volvement. Understanding how each function (social, spatial, and executive abilities) is involved in Raúl's case remains a challenge for those treating him, and for the field of pediatric neuropsychology in general.

Pennington (1991) summarized the reigning uncertainty in the field regarding con-structs such as ADHD, autism, Asperger's, and executive dysfunction as follows:

> Current evidence supports the view that the primary underlying behavioral deficit in autism is in the domain of early social cognition and more specifically in the area of intersubjectivity or theory of mind—the understanding that people have mental states and that communica-tion requires bringing mental states into coordination. However, recent results indicate a

possibly related primary deficit in executive functions. Moreover, deficits in theory of mind do not appear to be primary in Asperger's syndrome, whereas executive deficits do. Thus, across both Autism and Asperger's syndrome, executive function deficits appear to be more central. (p. 146)

SOCIOCULTURAL ISSUES IN THERAPY AND REHABILITATION

For the past 20 years, the human services field has slowly begun to acknowledge the need to take into account ethnic and socioeconomic factors when delivering services to individuals.

The issues, with respect to addressing social and behavioral disorders, range from what is considered problematic behavior in a particular subgroup, to explanations for the causes of the problem behavior, to willingness on the part of parents and teachers to implement certain interventions, and to the selection of reinforcers (Rogler, Malgady, Constantino, & Blementhal, 1987). Forehand and Kotchick (1996) warned that lack of awareness of cultural values could result in failures in parent training programs. They provided various examples of how cultural factors may determine the choice of behavioral interventions, as well as excellent, tangible examples of how a cross-cultural perspective can have a significant impact on the implementation of behavior therapy principles. They thus urged that research be conducted to test these assumptions in order to arrive at outcome-based guidelines for a culture-sensitive behavior therapy.

The role of discipline differs in Asian American and Native American families, as the former believes in strict discipline and the latter in little discipline. Although time-out may be equally effective in these two cultural groups, parents from the two groups may vary in their perceived need and willingness to use time-out as a disciplinary procedure. Second, respect is more important among many cultures, including Latinos, than is the highly valued European American concept of assertiveness (P. A. Hayes, 1995; Zayas & Solari, 1994). Thus, a focus on how reinforcement of appropriate cultural behavior can enhance children's self-respect (rather than punishing their nondeviant behavior) may increase parental cooperation in therapy. Furthermore, "as assertiveness is not highly valued even among parents, reinforcement and ignoring may be parenting skills more readily accepted than time-out" (Forehand & Kotchick, 1996, p. 197).

Language becomes quite important when implementing behavioral strategies with Hispanics; this can make the difference as to whether a client will "buy into" an intervention (Comas-Díaz, 1993). Words convey concepts, some of which will be more culture-syntonic, thereby creating positive or negative expectations. This is well known to marketers, and clinicians are beginning to pay heed to such wisdom by culturally adapting extant interventions to Hispanics when introducing behavioral strategies, or other psychotherapeutic interventions. An example is provided by Organista and Muñoz, 1996) with respect to difficulties encountered by Hispanics when presented with cognitive interventions such as Albert Ellis' ABCD. Introducing concepts such as "helpful" and "unhelpful" to describe adaptive versus maladaptive thoughts is more consistent with Hispanics' views of behavior, as opposed to a less meaningful "negative–positive" dimension.

In addition to culture, the impact of economic factors on parenting has been recognized. A study by Smith and Krohn (1995), for instance, found that among a high-risk youth sample, whereas family factors (e.g., parent–child involvement and attachment, parental control) were most important in constraining delinquency among Hispanic adolescents, economic hardship was the most important influence on those family factors, much more so than coming from a single-parent household. A similar finding is reported by Elder, Eccles, Ardelt, and Lord (1995) among inner-city Black families:

> Low income and unstable work/income enhance the risk of emotional distress and beliefs of parental ineffectiveness by increasing economic pressure; compared with White parents, a sense of parental efficacy among African American parents is more predictive of child management strategies that enhance developmental opportunities for children and minimize behavioral risk." (p. 771)

Dumas (1986) found that involvement in treatment and outcome was almost exclusively a function of socioeconomic variables (low income, lack of education, large family size, inadequate housing, and unemployment). Given the trend toward increasing disparity between Hispanic families in the United States and other ethnic groups (U.S. Bureau of the Census, 1998), the implications for Hispanic children are worth serious consideration.

CONCLUSIONS

This chapter has reviewed key factors in the challenging task of developing appropriate intervention strategies for Hispanic children with behavioral and social disorders of organic origin. It has been argued that in order to develop meaningful and effective treatment, it is necessary to gear the interventions to the neuropsychological level of functioning demonstrated by the child. This requires an understanding of neuropsychological and behavioral principles. Finally, when dealing with any specific cultural/linguistic group, it is necessary to make interventions accessible to the families, using language and concepts that are culture-syntonic and not mere translations of interventions developed for a different population. It is hoped that the analysis undertaken here will serve as a blueprint to those currently facing the task of providing clinical services to this population. Furthermore, addressing the effect of socioeconomic stressors on the implementation of cognitive and behavioral treatment is critical.

REFERENCES

American Psychiatric Association. (1994). *Diagnostic and statistical manual of mental disorders* (4th ed.). Washington, DC: American Psychiatric Association.

Armengol, C. G. (1999). A multi-modal support group with Hispanic traumatic brain injury (TBI) survivors. *Journal of Head Trauma Rehabilitation, 14,* 233–246.

Bandura, A. (1969). *Principles of behavior modification.* New York: Holt, Rinehart & Winston.

Baron, I. S., Fennell, E. B., & Voeller, K.K.S. (1995). *Pediatric neuropsychology in the medical setting.* New York: Oxford University Press.

Beck, A. T. (1970). Cognitive therapy: Nature and relation to behavior therapy. *Behavior Therapy, 1,* 184–200.

Blackerby, W. F. (1988). Practical token economies. *Journal of Head Trauma Rehabilitation, 3*(3), 33–45.

Bornstein, R. A., Carrol, A., & King, G. (1985). Relationship of age to neuropsychological deficits in Tourette's syndrome. *Journal of Developmental and Behavioral Pediatrics, 6,* 286–286.

Brown, G., Chadwick, O., Shaffer, D., Rutter, M., & Traub, M. (1981). A prospective study of children with head injuries: III. Psychiatric sequelae. *Psychology & Medicine, 11,* 63–78.

Cavallo, M. M., & Saucedo, C. (1995). Traumatic brain injury in families from culturally diverse populations. *Journal of Head Trauma Rehabilitation, 10*(2), 66–77.

Comas-Díaz, L. (1993). Latino communities: Psychological implications. In D. R. Atkinson, G. Morten, &

D. W. Sue (Eds.), *Counseling American minorities: A cross-cultural perspective*. Madison, WI: Brown and Benchmark.

Cowan, L. D., Bodensteiner, J. B., Leviton, A., & Doherty, L. (1989) Prevalence of the epilepsies in children and adolescents. *Epilepsia, 30,* 94–106.

Craighead, W. E., Kazdin, A. E., & Mahoney, M. J. (1976). *Behavior modification: Principles, issues, and applications*. Boston: Houghton Mifflin.

Denckla, M. (1983). The neuropsychology of social-emotional learning disabilities. *Archives of Neurology, 40,* 461–462.

Dennis, M. (1988). Language and the young damaged brain. In T. Boll & B. K. Bryant (Eds.), *Clinical neuropsychology and brain function: Research, measurement and practice* (pp. 87–128). Washington, DC: American Psychological Association.

Diamond, A. (1995, February). *Frontal lobe involvement in cognitive changes during early development*. Symposium presentation, International Neuropsychological Society, Seattle, WA.

Diamond, A. (1990). The development and neural bases of higher cognitive functions. *Annals of the New York Academy of Sciences, 608,* 267–317.

Dinklage, D. (1994). Neurodevelopmental disorders and psychotherapeutic interventions with children. In J. M. Ellison, C. S. Weinstein, & T. Hodel-Malinofsky (Eds.), *The psychotherapist's guide to neuropsychiatry* (pp. 145–174). Washington, DC: American Psychiatric Press.

Dumas, J. E. (1986). Parental perception and treatment outcome in families of aggressive children: A causal model. *Behavior Therapy, 17,* 420–432.

Eide, P. K., & Tysnes, O. B. (1992). Early and late outcome in head injury patients with radiological evidence of brain damage. *Acta Neurologica Scandinavica, 86,* 194.

Elder, G. H., Jr., Eccles, J. S., Ardelt, M., & Lord, S. (1995). Inner-city parents under economic pressure: Perspectives on the strategies of parenting. *Journal of Marriage and the Family, 57,* 771–784.

Ewing-Cobbs, L., Fletcher, J. M., & Levin, H. S. (1986). Neurobehavioral sequelae following head injury in children: Educational implications. *Journal of Head Trauma Rehabilitation, 1*(4), 57–65.

Fenichel, G. M. (1988). *Clinical pediatric neurology*. Philadelphia: Saunders.

Fletcher, J. M., Miner, M. E., & Ewing-Cobbs, L. (1987). Age and recovery from head injury in children: Developmental issues. In H. S. Levin, J. Grafman, & H. M. Eisenberg (Eds.), *Neurobehavioral recovery from head injury* (pp. 279–291). New York: Oxford University Press.

Forehand, R., & Kotchick, B. A. (1996) Cultural diversity: A wake-up call for parent training. *Behavior Therapy, 27,* 187–206.

Gerstadt, C. L., Hong, Y. J., & Diamond, A. (1994). Relationship between cognition and action: Performance of children 3½–7 years old on a Stroop-like day–night test. *Cognition, 53*(2), 129–153.

Goldiamond, I. (1965). Self-control procedures in behavioral problems. *Psychological Reports, 17,* 105–126.

Goleman, D. (1995). *Emotional intelligence: Why it can matter more than IQ*. New York: Bantam Books.

Grandin, T. (1995). *Thinking in pictures*. New York: Doubleday.

Hayes, P. A. (1995). Multicultural applications in cognitive-behavior therapy. *Professional Psychology: Research and Practice, 26,* 309–315.

Hayes, H.R.M., & Jackson, R. H. (1989). The incidence and prevention of head injuries. In D. A. Johnson, D. Uttley, & M. Wyke (Eds.), *Children's head injury: Who cares?* (pp. 183–193). London: Taylor & Francis.

Heilman, K. M., & Satz, P. (1983). *Neuropsychology of human emotion*. New York: Guilford.

Kaplan, E. (1983). Achievement and process revisited. In S. Wapner & B. Kaplan (Eds.), *Toward a holistic developmental psychology* (pp. 143–156). Hillsdale, NJ: Lawrence Erlbaum Associates.

Kaplan, E. (1988). A process approach to neuropsychological assessment. In T. Boll & B. K. Bryant (Eds.), *Clinical neuropsychology and brain function: Research, measurement and practice* (pp. 127–167). Washington, DC: American Psychological Association.

Kazdin, A. E. (1977). *The token economy*. New York: Plenum.

Kazdin, A. E. (1993). Tratamientos conductuales y cognitivos de la conducta antisocial en niños: Avances de la investigacíon [Behavioral and cognitive interventions for antisocial behavior in children: Advances in research]. *Psicología Conductual, 1*(1), 111–144.

Kirby, E. A., & Grimley, L. K. (1986). *Understanding and treating attention deficit disorder*. New York: Pergamon.

Kraus, J. F., Fife, D., & Conroy, C. (1987). Pediatric head injuries: The nature, clinical course and early outcomes in a defined United States population. *Pediatrics, 79,* 501.

Lewis, D. O. (1994). Etiology of aggressive conduct disorders: Neuropsychiatric and family contributions. *Child and Adolescent Psychiatric Clinics of North America, 3*(2), 303–319.

Lezak, M. (1995). *Neuropsychological assessment* (3rd ed.). New York: Oxford University Press.

Lilly, R., Cummings, J. L., Benson, D. F., & Frankel, M. (1983). The human Kluver–Bucy syndrome. *Neurology, 30,* 1231–1232.

Lishman, W. A. (1998). *Organic psychiatry: The psychological consequences of cerebral disorder* (3rd ed.). Oxford: Blackwell Scientific.

Lovaas, O. J. (1987). Behavioral treatment and normal educational and intellectual functioning in young autistic children. *Journal of Consulting and Clinical Psychology, 55,* 3–9.

Luria, A. R. (1973). *The working brain.* New York: Basic Books.

Meichenbaum, D. (1974). *Cognitive behavior modification.* Morristown, NJ: General Learning Press.

Middleton, J. (1989). Learning and behaviour change. In D. A. Johnson, D. Uttley, & M. Wyke (Eds.), *Children's head injury: Who cares?* (pp. 121–133). London: Taylor & Francis.

MacNeill Horton, A., Jr., & Sautter, S. W. (1986). Behavioral neuropsychology: Behavioral treatment for the brain-injured. In D. Wedding, A. MacNeill Horton, & J. Webster (Eds.), *The neuro-psychology handbook* (pp. 259–277). New York: Springer.

Organista, K. C., & Muñoz, R. F. (1996). Cognitive behavioral therapy with latinos. *Cognitive and Behavioral Practice, 3*(2), 255–270.

Pennington, B. F. (1991). *Diagnosing learning disorders: A neuropsychological framework.* New York: Guilford.

Pontón, M. O., González, J., & Mares, M. (1997). Rehabilitating brain damage in Hispanics. In J. León-Carrión (Ed.), *Neuropsychological rehabilitation: Fundamentals, innovations and directions* (pp. 513–530). Delray Beach, FL: St. Lucie Press.

Quay, H. C. (1979). Classification. In H. C. Quay & J. S. Werry (Eds.), *Psychopathological disorders in childhood* (2nd ed., pp. 1–42). New York: Wiley.

Rivara, F. P., & Mueller, B. A. (1987). The epidemiology and causes of childhood injuries. *Journal of Social Issues, 43,* 13–31.

Rogers, S. J., & Lewis, H. (1989). An effective day treatment model for young children with pervasive developmental disorder. *Journal of the American Academy of Child and Adolescent Psychiatry, 28,* 207–214.

Rogler, L. H., Malgady, R. G., Constantino, G., & Blementhal, R. (1987). What do culturally sensitive mental health services mean? *American Psychologist, 42*(6), 565–570.

Rosenberg, M. S., Wilson, R., Maheady, L., & Sindelar, P. T. (1997). *Educating students with behavior disorders.* Needham Heights, MA: Allyn & Bacon.

Ross, E. D. (1981). The aprosodias: Functional-anatomic organization of the affective components of language in the right hemisphere. *Archives of Neurology, 38,* 561–589.

Rourke, B. P. (1989). *Nonverbal learning disabilities: The syndrome and the model.* New York: Guilford.

Sacks, O. (1995). *An anthropologist on Mars: Seven paradoxical tales.* New York: Random House.

Schiff-Myers, N. B., Djukic, J., McGovern-Lawler, J., & Pérez, D. (1993). Assessment considerations in the evaluation of second-language learners: A case study. *Exceptional Children, 60*(3), 237–248.

Silver, J. M., & Yudofsky, S. C. (1997). Violence and the brain. In T. E. Feinberg & M. J. Farah (Eds.), *Behavioral neurology and neuropsychology* (pp. 711–717). New York: McGraw-Hill.

Silver, J. M., Hales, R. E., & Yudofsky, S. C. (1994). *Neuropsychiatry of traumatic brain injury.* Washington, DC: American Psychiatric Press.

Smith, C., & Krohn, M. D. (1995) Delinquency and family life among male adolescents. *Journal of Youth and Adolescence, 24*(1), 69–93.

Sohlberg, M. M., & Mateer, C. A. (1989). *Introduction to cognitive rehabilitation.* New York: Guilford.

Spreen, O., Risser, A. H., & Edgell, D. (1995). *Developmental neuropsychology.* New York: Oxford University Press.

Strang, J. D., & Rourke, B. P. (1985). Arithmetic disability subtypes: The neuro-psychological significance of specific arithmetic impairments in childhood. In B. P. Rourke (Ed.), *Neuropsychology of learning disabilities: Essentials of subtype analysis* (pp. 167–183). New York: Guilford.

Tranel, D., Hall, L. E., Olson, S., & Tranel, M. M. (1987). Evidence for a right-hemisphere developmental learning disability. *Developmental Neuropsychology, 3,* 113–117.

U.S. Bureau of the Census. (1998). The Hispanic population. *Population Profile of the United States: 1997* (pp. 44–45). Series P23-194. Washington, DC: U.S. Government Printing Office.

Voeller, K.K.S. (1997). Social and emotional learning disabilities. In T. E. Feinberg & M. J. Farah (Eds.), *Behavioral neurology and neuropsychology* (pp. 795–801). New York: McGraw-Hill.

Walsh, K. (1994). *Neuropsychology: A clinical approach.* Edinburgh: Churchill Livingston.

Weintraub, S., & Mesulam, M. M. (1983). Developmental learning disabilities of the right hemisphere: Emotional, interpersonal, and cognitive components. *Archives of Neurology, 40,* 463–468.

Wolpe, J., & Lazarus, A. A. (1966). *Behavior therapy techniques.* New York: Pergamon.

Wood, F. H., & Zabel, R. H. (1978). Making sense of reports on the incidence of behavior disorders/emotional disturbance in school-aged populations. *Psychology in the Schools, 15,* 45–51.

Zayas, L. H., & Solari, F. (1994). Early childhood socialization in hispanic families: Context, culture, and practice implications. *Professional Psychology: Research and Practice. 25*(3), 200–206.

Zigler, E., & Phillips, L. (1961). Social competence and outcome in psychiatric disorder. *Journal of Abnormal and Social Psychology, 63,* 264–271.

Zúñiga, M. E. (1992). Families with Latino roots. In E. W. Lynch & M. J. Harrison (Eds.), *Developing crosscultural competence: A guide for working with young children and their families* (pp. 209–250). Baltimore: Paul H. Brookes.

11

Neurobehavioral and Neuropsychological Manifestations of HIV-1 Infection: Assessment Considerations with Hispanic Populations

ANTOLIN M. LLORENTE
Baylor College of Medicine
University of California, Los Angeles School of Medicine

CHRISTINE M. LoPRESTI
University of California, Los Angeles School of Medicine

JOEL K. LEVY
FRANCISCO FERNANDEZ
Baylor College of Medicine

Neuropsychological and neurobehavioral manifestations associated with human immun-odeficiency virus (HIV-1) infection and factors relevant to their assessment in Hispanic populations warrant special consideration in a handbook of this nature. This unique merit is partly the result of the increasing incidence and cumulative prevalence of this infectious disease in this population in the United States and abroad, particularly for Hispanic women and children (Centers for Disease Control and Prevention, 1996; Mann, Tarantola, & Netter, 1992; World Health Organization, 1996). The Hispanic population in the United States has recently increased to become the fifth largest Spanish-speaking population in the world (approximately 25 million individuals) after Mexico, Spain, Argentina, and Colombia (U.S. Bureau of the Census, 1993), yet the current availability of neuropsychological tests and procedures in Spanish from which reliable and valid inferences can be drawn is extremely limited (Pontón et al., 1996). The lack of adequate assessment instruments and normative data for Hispanics is of particular concern because of the multitude of ways in which HIV affects the central nervous system (CNS) of adults (I. Grant et al., 1987; McArthur, 1994; Navia, Jordan, & Price, 1986; Snider et al., 1983) and children (Belman, 1990; Epstein et al., 1986; Falloon, Eddy, Wiener, & Pizzo, 1989; Pizzo & Wilfert, 1994) and their neuropsychological and neurobehavioral functions (Bayés, 1995; Brouwers, Belman, & Epstein, 1991, 1994; Brouwers, Moss, Wolters, Eddy, & Pizzo, 1989; Levy & Fernandez, 1997; Llorente, LoPresti, & Satz, 1997;

Llorente et al., 1998; Navia, Jordan, & Price, 1986; Tross et al., 1988; Van Gorp, Miller, Satz, & Visscher, 1989). Therefore, a chapter dedicated to the neurocognitve effects of HIV infection spectrum disease and assessment issues in Hispanic populations is sufficiently justified.

The chapter begins with a review of basic concepts in HIV and acquired immunodeficiency syndrome (AIDS) in an attempt to provide the reader with a rudimentary understanding of the relevant terminology and diagnostic nomenclature. Subsequently, U.S. and worldwide epidemiological data are presented, which depict the pandemic nature of this disease, particularly as it applies to Hispanic populations. Neuropathological and other medical concomitants associated with HIV infection are briefly reviewed and precede a discussion of behavioral and neuropsychological manifestations of HIV and AIDS. Finally, cross-cultural factors and other considerations relevant to HIV and Hispanic populations are addressed, followed by recommended assessment procedures and sources of relevant normative data. The treatment of HIV-related neurobehavioral and neuropsychological problems are beyond the scope of this chapter. In this regard, the reader is referred to Buckingham and van Gorp (1988); D. Grant (1988); M. H. Harris (1992); Levy and Fernandez (1997); Wolters, Brouwers, Moss, and Pizzo (1994); Wiener and Septimus (1994); and Wolters et al. (1990, 1991).

BASIC CONCEPTS, TERMINOLOGY, AND DIAGNOSTIC NOMENCLATURE

Infants passively acquire maternal antibodies in-utero through placental transmission, including the anti-HIV IgG antibody, which persists at least throughout the first year of life (Koup & Wilson, 1994). Virtually all infants born to HIV-positive mothers will test antibody positive for the virus at birth but may in actuality not be infected. Therefore, the use of existing diagnostic assays for the presence of HIV antibodies, indirectly suggesting the presence of the HIV retrovirus, routinely employed with adults are inadequate for diagnosing newborns of HIV-positive mothers (Hansen & Shearer, 1994). Pediatric diagnosis using antibody assays alone, without clinical presentations of the disease, is generally not made until age 15 to 18 months. At this age, it is believed that the child's own immune system is being probed (Prober & Gershon, 1991).

Currently, the most sensitive procedures for detecting HIV infection in babies born to HIV-positive mothers are the polymerase chain reaction (PCR) and virus culture assays (Burgard, Mayaux, & Blanche, 1992; Krivine et al., 1992). Use of these assays is accurate in from 30% to 50% of infants tested at birth and nearly 100% of infected newborns 3 to 6 months postdelivery. The standard p24-antigen assay is less sensitive than PCR and virus cultures, especially when HIV antibody levels are very high. However, recent modifications of this procedure (Hansen & Shearer, 1994) have increased its sensitivity in diagnosing infected infants born to HIV-positive mothers. Enzyme linked immunosorbent assay (ELISA) followed by Western blotting (Sarngadharan, Popvic, Bruch, Shupbach, & Gallo, 1984) is the most common existing procedure for detecting the presence of HIV antibodies in late childhood, adolescence, and adulthood.

Beyond issues associated with HIV virus detection in children, there are important concepts in the HIV literature that require special consideration. These include the notions of vertical versus horizontal viral transmission, age at onset of symptomatic disease, HIV diagnostic criteria, and stages of disease involvement in adolescence/adulthood.

HIV infection can be transmitted from an HIV-positive mother to her child while in-utero through the placental barrier (cf. Sprecher, Soumenkoff, Puissant, & Degueldre, 1986), during intrapartum as a result of contact with blood or other body products (Friedland & Klein, 1987), and after birth through breast feeding (de Martino, 1994; Rogers, 1989). Regardless of the particular medium of retroviral transfer, HIV-positive mother-to-child viral passage is considered a form of *vertical transmission*.

In contrast, viral transmission through blood or blood-related products associated with the treatment of medical disorders (e.g., von Willerbrand's disease), through the use of infected needles as a result of occupational accidents or intravenous drug use, or through the exchange of body fluids as a result of sexual activity is considered *horizontal transmission* by definition. The distinction between vertical and horizontal transmission is not only important from a pedagogical and scientific viewpoint, it has significant clinical importance because the disease process tends to express itself in different fashions in children afflicted through these two distinct routes of transmission (Brouwers, Moss, Wolters, & Schmitt, 1994). According to Brouwers, Moss, et al. (1994), vertical versus horizontal transmission also has significant gender- and age-related consequences in children. With regard to gender, males have a greater likelihood of becoming infected via horizontal transmission because they are prone to suffer from a greater number of diseases necessitating treatment with blood products (males relative to females have a higher prevalence of diseases—e.g., hemophilia A [an X-linked recessive hemophilia] requiring the use of blood products). In terms of age-related differences in children as it applies to route of transmission, horizontally transmitted HIV in the United States is most likely to have occurred for boys who were at least 10 years old by 1995 and thus would have been infected before the advent of available and reliable procedures to detect the presence of HIV antibodies in the blood supply. In other words, children born since 1985 primarily acquired HIV vertically rather than horizontally, because unsafe blood products have been virtually eliminated from blood supplies.

With regard to the onset of symptomatic disease, in vertically infected children, investigators have discovered two distinguishable subgroups (Auger et al., 1988; DePaula et al., 1991). According to Auger et al. (1988), in a study examining the incubation period for pediatric AIDS in New York, one group exhibited early symptomatic disease expression in infancy marked by an approximate median age of AIDS onset at 4.1 months and associated brief survival periods. A second group of children had a median incubation period of 6.1 years, with greater periods of survival. In contrast, the time lapse between infection and onset of symptomatology in children infected through blood transfusions was greater (Rogers et al., 1987) relative to vertically infected children. With regard to these varying periods of incubation, Oxtoby (1994) reported that the median age at which AIDS is diagnosed in perinatally infected children was 12 months, whereas the distribution of age at AIDS diagnosis is negatively skewed, with the majority of children under age 2 and a small number as late as age 13. In summary, from a prognostic viewpoint, age at onset of symptomatic disease plays a major role in predicting length of survival in certain infants and young children.

Although viral load, strain(s), and age at onset of symptomatic disease each have been hypothesized to play a major role in incubation periods in infancy and childhood, the variability in onset of symptoms and course of illness are not yet well understood. Recent efforts on this front have revealed interesting and promising results. For example, Bryson at al. (1993) presented the first data examining *timing* of vertical transmission (in-utero vs. intrapartum) to help explain the developmental course of the disease. In this prospective study of 74 mother–infant pairs, 22 (28%) seropositive mothers transmitted the virus to their newborns. The median time to onset of AIDS-defining symptoms was significantly earlier in the group infected in-utero (6 weeks) as compared with the group infected in the intrapartum period (86 weeks).

The Centers for Disease Control and Prevention (CDC) updated the pediatric classification scheme in 1994 describing the spectrum of HIV disease (CDC, 1994). Diagnosis of HIV in children less than age 13 is based on infection, immunologic, and clinical status. The three infection diagnostic groups are "HIV infected, perinatally exposed (E), and seroreverter (SR)." Children are diagnosed as HIV infected under the following conditions: a child is younger than 18 months and is born to an HIV-positive mother and (a) has had positive laboratory results on two HIV detection tests, or (b) has an AIDS-defining illness based on the 1987 CDC surveillance case definition. A child age 18 months or older is diagnosed as infected if either born to an HIV-positive mother or infected through any route of transmission and has repeatedly tested HIV-positive by antibody tests. A perinatally exposed child is one who is under age 18 months and is HIV seropositive by antibody tests, or is born to an HIV-positive mother but has unknown antibody status. A seroreverter is a child born to an HIV-positive mother but who is antibody negative, has no laboratory evidence of viral infection, and has not had an AIDS-defining illness.

Children who are infected or perinatally exposed based on the aforementioned CDC criteria are further classified according to both immunologic and clinical status. Immunologic categories are established on both age and level of immunosuppression and are based on CD4+ counts and percent of total lymphocytes (Table 11.1). Categorically, they range from "no evidence of suppression to severe suppression." Clinical categories are based on the presence and severity of symptomatology and range from asymptomatic to severe signs and symptoms (CDC, 1994).

In adults, HIV is most commonly transmitted via horizontal transmission. Progression of HIV to AIDS varies significantly with clinical symptoms rarely appearing earlier than 2 years postinfection and the majority of individuals remain symptom free for several years. Nair and Schwartz (1994) noted that the natural and clinical history of HIV in adults is characterized by three phases. The initial phase is marked by a period of acute illness involving nonspecific symptoms similar to those seen in a common cold (cf. Tindell et al., 1988). The initial stage is followed by a phase characterized by a lack of symptoms with average duration of approximately 7 years, followed by the full-blown disease stage (AIDS).

TABLE 11.1

CDC Immunologic Classification System for Human Immunodeficiency Virus Infection in Infancy and Childhood

| | Age-Specific CD4+ T-lymphocyte Count Categories | | | | | |
| | < 12 months | | 1–5 years | | 6–12 years | |
Immunologic Category	T-cells/μL	(%)	T-cells/μL	(%)	T-cells/μL	(%)
No evidence of suppression	≥1,500	(≥25)	≥1000	(≥25)	≥500	(≥25)
Evidence of moderate suppression	750–1,499	(15–24)	500–999	(15–24)	200–499	(15–24)
Severe suppression	<750	(<15)	<500	(<15)	<200	(<15)

Note: Adapted from Centers for Disease Control (1994).

TABLE 11.2

CDC Immunologic Classification System for Human Immunodeficiency Virus Infection
in Adulthood and Adolescence

Immunologic Category	CD4+ T-lymphocyte Count Categories		
	≥ 500 T-cells/µL	200–499 T-cells/µL	< 200 T-cells/µL*
Asymptomatic (A), Acute HIV	A1	A2	A3
Symptomatic (B), Not (A) or (C) Status	B1	B2	B3
AIDS-defining Conditions (C)	C1	C2	C3

Note: Adapted from Centers for Disease Control (1993).
* Indicates AIDS-defining CD4+ count

According to Rottenburg et al. (1987), after 10 years of initial infection, approximately one half of a group of HIV infected individuals will acquire AIDS (recent advances in HIV treatment—e.g., prophylactic treatment—may increase the incubation period of this infectious disease).

With regard to adolescents and adults, two immunologic classification systems describing the progressive stages of HIV infection are currently in use, namely the Walter Reed (WR; Redfield, Wright, & Tramont, 1986) and the Centers for Disease Control and Prevention (1993) classifications, the latter being the most commonly used in the United States. These nosologic systems use CD4+ lymphocyte counts (e.g., CDC, 1993: ≥ 500/µL, 200–499/µL, < 200/µL) and three clinical levels of symptomatology (Category A, asymptomatic; Category B, minor opportunistic infections and symptoms; and Category C, AIDS-defining conditions) (Table 11.2) as the basis for categorization. Classification and definition of HIV-related neurological manifestations are based on the American Academy of Neurology nomenclature and vary from the earliest level of cognitive impairment now termed HIV-1-Associated Minor Cognitive/Motor Disorder to HIV-1-Associated Dementia (American Academy of Neurology Task Force, 1991).

The populations of children, adolescents, and adults infected with HIV are quite heterogeneous. The heterogeneity of neurocognitive profiles may be a consequence of characteristics of the virus (viral strain, virus load, etc.) and/or environmental and host-related factors (drug use; education; onset of symptomatic disease; SES, Pérez-Arce, 1994; transmission mode; quality of treatment; etc.; Fama, Pace, Tiempiero, & Bornstein, 1992; Satz et al., 1993; cf. Satz, 1993).

HIV EPIDEMIOLOGY AND ITS IMPACT ON HISPANIC POPULATIONS: U.S AND WORLDWIDE SUMMARY

The population of HIV-infected children and adults has grown dramatically in the United States. As of June 1996, 7,296 children under age 13 had been diagnosed with AIDS, accounting for 1.3% of the total number of reported AIDS cases in the United States, including territories outside the mainland. Adults and adolescents (540,806) accounted for the remainder of cases reported. In the age 24 to 44 group, AIDS is now the leading cause of death in men and the third leading cause of death in women (CDC, 1996). Infant and childhood mortality resulting from AIDS has also experienced a dramatic increase worldwide (Mann et al., 1992; Novello, Wise, Willoughby, & Pizzo, 1989). This rise in the number of cases and deaths, whether the result of better surveillance techniques or the rapid spread of the disease, has led to enormous social and economic consequences (Mann et al., 1992). Kranczer (1995) further noted that HIV infection has contributed to the first known reduction in average life expectancy in the United States.

Five states have accounted for over half of the pediatric and adult/adolescent AIDS cases reported in the United States: New York, California, Florida, Texas, and New Jersey. New York has reported the largest percentage of both children (25%) and adults/adolescents (19%) with AIDS in the country (CDC, 1996). Through June 1996, Hispanics (17%) and African Americans (31%) accounted for almost half of the 462,152 male adult/adolescent AIDS cases, although these populations comprise only 10% and 13%, respectively, of the population nationwide (CDC, 1996). Most of the remaining cases were White males (51%). Sexual contact with other males and injecting drug use were the risk factors associated with 89% of AIDS cases in adult and adolescent males. The pattern of exposure to HIV, however, varied within racial/ethnic groups. Roughly equal proportions of Hispanic and African American males were infected through sex with males as were infected through injecting drug use, whereas the vast majority (81% to 94%) of males in all other groups were infected through sex with other males (CDC, 1996).

Females account for 15% of all adult/adolescent AIDS cases in the United States. As with males, selective minority groups are disproportionally affected, with Hispanic and African American women accounting for 20% and 55%, respectively, and White women for 24% of reported AIDS cases (CDC, 1996). The fastest growing mode of HIV transmission in adult/adolescent females across all racial/ethnic groups is heterosexual contact, with most of these women becoming infected via sexual activity with males who inject drugs. From July 1995 through June 1996, 40% of females were exposed to HIV through sex with males and 36% were infected through their own intravenous drug use. Cumulative statistics indicate that Hispanic females accounted for the greatest proportion (45%) of women infected through heterosexual contact, as compared with African American (35%) and White (38%) women (CDC, 1996).

In the United States, 90% of children with AIDS were vertically infected. Forty-four percent of their mothers acquired HIV through injecting drug use or sexual contact with an injecting drug user (CDC, 1996). This rise in vertically infected cases probably reflects the increasing number of infected women and the relative decreases in other methods of transmission, including infection from blood and blood products (Andiman & Modlin, 1991). For this reason, vertical transmission can be expected to account for virtually all cases of pediatric HIV infection in the future. Because most children are exposed to HIV through their mothers, the disproportionate impact on selective minority groups observed in women is also reflected in the distribution of children with AIDS. Through June 1996, 81% of pediatric AIDS cases were accounted for by Hispanic and African American children (23% and 58%, respectively), and White children comprised 18% of the cases. Among both pediatric and adult/adolescent cases, less than 1% of cases were accounted for by Asian/Pacific Islanders and American Indian/Alaskan Natives (CDC, 1996).

Although epidemiological data from the United States are informative, these figures misrepresent the magnitude of the epidemic in Hispanic and other minority groups in terms of worldwide prevalence. Since the late 1970s to early 1980s, approximately 25.5 million adults and more than 2.4 million children are estimated to have been infected with HIV. It is estimated that approximately 21 million adults and 800,000 children are currently living with HIV/AIDS, with Sub-Saharan Africa accounting for more than half of the cases, followed in descending order of prevalence by South and South East Asia,

TABLE 11.3
Worldwide Epidemiological Data (Adults and Children)—
HIV Seroprevalence Estimate in Total Number of Cases

Region	Estimated Number of Cases
Sub-Saharan Africa	14,000,000
South & South-East Asia	4,800,000
Latin American & the Caribbean	1,600,000
North America	780,000
Western Europe	470,000
North Africa & the Middle East	200,000
East Asia & the Pacific	35,000
Eastern Europe & Central Asia	30,000
Australia	13,000

Note: Adapted from the World Health Organization (1996).

Latin American and the Caribbean, North America, Western Europe, North Africa and the Middle East, East Asia and the Pacific, Eastern Europe and Central Asia, and Australia (Table 11.3) (WHO, 1996). These data clearly demonstrate that areas highly populated with ethnic minority individuals have been substantially impacted by this disease.

Prior to embarking on a survey of the clinicopathological manifestations of HIV infection, the reader should be cognizant that the majority of studies reported here may not have incorporated Hispanics as part of their investigation. Although there is no particular reason to suspect that underlying neuropathology would differ as a function of ethnicity, it should be noted that certain variables capable of moderating medical factors could very well limit the applicability of these investigations as they relate to Hispanics (even general disease progression differs across ethnic groups, which is probably the result of access to insurance and medical treatment, quality of medical care [cf. Tuckson, 1994], and/or cultural stigma associated with this infectious disease in conjunction with physiological factors of the host).

CLINICOPATHOLOGICAL FINDINGS ASSOCIATED WITH CNS HIV-1 INFECTION

Ample evidence (Brouwers et al., 1994; Gottlieb et al., 1981; I. Grant et al., 1987; Ho et al., 1985; Koenig et al., 1986; Navia, Cho, Petito, & Price, 1986; Navia, Jordan, et al., 1986; Pang et al., 1990; Resnick, Berger, Shapshak, & Tourtellete, 1988; Snider et al., 1983) from multiple research fields (cognitive, neuroimaging, neuropathology, etc.) suggests that the human immunodeficiency virus invades the CNS of adults and children. The invasion occurs shortly after initial systemic infection, eventually causing dramatic behavioral, cognitive, and neuropathological disturbances in a large number of infected individuals (Belman, 1990; Belman et al., 1984; McArthur, 1994).

Neurological Findings

Evidence in Children. HIV-related neurological manifestations experienced by children vary substantially. Some children exhibit mild alterations in cognition and motor skills. More severe expressions of the disease are manifested through childhood encepha-lopathy capable of causing substantial deviations from normal development (Sharer et al., 1986; Ultmannn et al., 1987). Belman et al. (1988) and Belman (1990) described two forms of encephalopathy, namely progressive and static HIV-related encephalopathy. *Progressive encephalopathy* is subcategorized into two different types (*Subacute and Plateau*) to describe the distinct rates of disease progression observed in infants and children. Sub-acute progressive encephalopathy, most commonly seen in infants and young children (Belman et al., 1988), is the most crippling neurological expression of HIV infection. It is marked by a gradual and progressive decline across most domains of neurological func-tioning. Its greatest impact is observed in overall cognition, expressive functions includ-ing motor and language skills, and adaptive functioning in preschool age children, or loss of already attained developmental milestones in infants and younger children with lack of further development usually leading to death (Epstein et al., 1985). Subacute encepha-lopathy causes serious CNS debilitation, including profound cerebral atrophy and micro-cephaly (acquired as a result of lack of continued CNS development; Epstein et al., 1985, 1986; see also DeCarli et al., 1991). In contrast, plateau encephalopathy is often ob-served in infants and young children who fail to acquire new developmental milestones, or acquire them very slowly. Unlike youngsters experiencing progressive subacute en-cephalopathy, children suffering from plateau encephalitis typically do not display losses from previously acquired levels of functioning (Belman et al., 1989). Belman (1990) reported that these children suffer from motor deficits as well as declines in overall intel-lectual functioning.

Static encephalopathy is characterized by continued acquisition of skills at rates below expected levels of normal development but commensurate with their level of functioning. Furthermore, the delays observed during static encephalopathy longitudinally remain rel-atively stable over time from initial levels of functioning (Belman et al., 1985; Brouwers, Moss, et al., 1994; Epstein et al., 1986; Epstein, Sharer, & Goudsmit, 1988). The grad-ual decline or lack of gains in development observed during progressive encephalopathy is not seen in children with static encephalopathy. The American Academy of Neurology recently combined the various categorizations of HIV-related encephalopathy under one category termed HIV-associated encephalopathy of childhood (American Academy of Neurology AIDS Task Force, 1991). Some researchers (Brouwers, Belman, & Epstein, 1994) argued that the singular categorization fails to account for the different neurolog-ical presentations associated with the various types of encephalopathy, contending that Belman et al.'s (1988) classification better characterizes the various courses of progres-sion observed during each of the three types of childhood encephalopathy.

Although the actual frequency of these disorders is not high relative to adults, other neurological diseases associated with an immunodeficient state secondary to HIV infec-tion have also been observed in children (Belman, 1990), including opportunistic infec-tions and other CNS complications (e.g., neoplasia), typically in children who have devel-oped encephalopathy (Belman, 1990). For example, neoplasms have been documented in the literature, primary CNS lymphoma being the most common (Belman, 1990; Epstein et al., 1988). Neoplasia have been observed in children between age 6 months and 10 years, but occur chiefly after the first birthday (Epstein et al., 1988). Their most prominent locations are in the basal ganglia and areas surrounding the third ventricle (Belman, 1990). Secondary CNS lymphomas also have been noted (Dickson et al., 1989) as well as cerebrovascular complications, including infarctions (Belman, 1990; Frank, Lim, & Kahn, 1989) and strokes (Park et al., 1988). Although there is a great deal of consensus regarding the infrequency of CNS opportunistic infections in children (Epstein et al., 1988), they have been nonetheless reported in the neurological literature (Belman et al., 1988; Dickson et al., 1989). Of these, bacterial meningitis, candida meningitis, and acquired cytomegalovirus (CMV) have been the most common. In contrast, HIV-related CNS toxoplasmosis, commonly observed in adults (McArthur, 1994), has rarely been reported in children (Belman, 1990; Nicholas, 1994).

Evidence in Adults.   In adulthood, the spectrum of neurological problems varies from a lack of neurological symptoms in most HIV-positive asymptomatic patients (Heaton et al., 1995) to HIV-related dementia in late-stage disease (McArthur, 1994; Navia et al., 1986). In some cases, primary neurological symptoms, including neuropathies, have been observed in the absence of constitutional symptoms in asymptomatic patients (McArthur, 1994). Acute aseptic meningitis also has been reported as a primary neurological problem in a number of patients (Cooper et al., 1985). Although motoric and myelopathic disturbances have been found to commonly occur as a result of HIV-1 infection, the most compromising primary neurological sequelae associated with this infectious disease is HIV-1–related dementia secondary to HIV encephalopathy (Navia et al., 1986) with a clinical presentation marked by cognitive slowing, depression, and memory loss (Navia et al., 1986; Navia, Cho, et al., 1986) similar to symptoms ascribed to the subcortical dementias described by Cummings and Benson (1983; cf. Filley, 1996). Within an HIV-1-related dementing state, several clinical stages of impairment have been postulated from mild to end stage (Price & Brew, 1988).

Secondary CNS neuropathology, including opportunistic infections (cytomegalovirus, CMV; Progressive Multifocal Leukoencephalopathy, PML; toxoplasmosis; cryptococcal meningitis; etc.), malignancies (Kaposi's sarcoma) and neoplasms (lymphoma) have been commonly reported in adults with AIDS. Of these potential complications, cerebral toxoplasmosis caused by *Toxoplasma gondii* and cerebral cryptococcal meningitis (caused by *Cryptococcus neoformans*) are the most prevalent nonviral forms of CNS infections observed (Bredesen, Levy, & Rosenblum, 1988; Levy & Fernandez, 1997), whereas PML (Fong et al., 1995; J. K. Miller et al., 1982) and acquired CMV (Bredesen et al., 1988) are the most common secondary coexisting viral infections. Non-Hodgkin's lymphoma is the primary CNS neoplastic manifestation associated with AIDS (Bredesen et al., 1988). Cerebrovascular problems may result from viral or bacterial vasculitis (Brightbill, Ihmeidan, Post, Berger, & Katz, 1995) or from cerebral infarcts secondary to nonbacterial thrombotic endocarditis (Bredesen et al., 1988). These complications may occur at any time due to immune compromise, but they are usually associated with late-stage HIV disease (CD4+ counts of less than 200 per cubic millimeter). They may initially present as a focal or diffuse process. In addition, they may at first present as a cognitive or affective disturbance (Levy & Fernandez, 1997).

Findings from Neuroimaging Studies

Evidence in Children.   Several investigators have found abnormalities in the brains of HIV infected children (Tardieu, 1991) using various neuroradiological procedures. Belman et al. (1985) noted cerebral atrophy of varying degrees, marked by cortical atrophy with dilation of the ventricular system and calcifications of the basal ganglia and frontal white matter in an 8-month-old with AIDS, using Computed Tomography (CT). These abnormalities were again observed longitudinally at ages 18 and 21 months. CT studies conducted by Belman et al. (1988) also found cortical atrophy and white matter abnormalities (basal ganglia [bilaterally] and frontal calcifications) in children with AIDS or AIDS Related Complex (ARC). In addition, 16 of 17 participants who were longitudinally evaluated in the study showed progressive levels of atrophy. These results were substantiated by DeCarli, Civitello, Brouwers, and Pizzo (1993). They found bilateral symmetrical calcification of the basal ganglia and frontal white matter calcification on CT in 100 children with symptomatic HIV infection. Furthermore, a recent study reported a significant relation between white matter abnormalities on CT and neuropsychological functioning. With children matched on level of cortical atrophy, Brouwers et al. (1995) found greater cognitive dysfunction in the group with white matter abnormalities relative to the children with no cerebral calcifications. Studies using Magnetic Resonance Imaging (MRI) also have revealed CNS abnormalities associated with pediatric HIV infection. Belman et al. (1986) detected decreased and increased signal intensities on T1- and T2-weighted images, respectively, as a result of bilateral white matter atrophy in the basal ganglia and cerebral atrophy in a 10-year-old male. Similar results using T2-weighted imaging were evidenced by other investigators (cf. Epstein et al., 1986). A study examining cerebral metabolism through the use of Positron Emission Tomography (PET) have supported the findings obtained with the structural neuroradiological techniques described earlier. Pizzo et al. (1988), while conducting a study assessing the effects of AZT pharmacotherapy, reported diffuse cortical, focal right frontal, and right superior temporal hypometabolism prior to treatment in an 11-year-old male with HIV-1 infection.

Evidence in Adults.   Structural (qualitative and quantitative) and functional neuroimaging procedures have revealed abnormalities most likely associated with HIV-spectrum disease in adults (Dooneief et al., 1992; Flowers et al., 1990; Sacktor et al., 1995). In fact, as early as 1983, Whelan et al. (1983) reported remarkable cerebral manifestations associated with AIDS using computed tomography (CT). In another study employing CT, Post et al. (1988) reported cortical atrophy and ventricular enlargement in 95% and 61%, respectively, of a sample of 21 patients with HIV encephalitis. H. S. Levin et al. (1990) reported structural (CT) abnormalities marked by small focal lesions (<1cm) in 25% of their symptomatic HIV-positive group (CDC II-IV). In addition, these investigators observed the presence of brain atrophy, particularly in their CDC IV group relative to the other diagnostic groups. Equally important, a significant relation was found between atrophy as measured by the CT and psychomotor retardation appraised using neuropsychological procedures (reaction time, RT). More recently, Post, Berger, and Quencer (1991) used qualitative MRI methods and found abnormalities in 13% of the asymptomatic participants and 46% of the symptomatic subjects in a sample of 119 HIV-positive patients. In particular, this study revealed white matter lesions present in the neurologically symptomatic group that were larger and more numerous relative to those found in the asymptomatic group. It is interesting to note that several factors, including drug use and a history of head injury, were not correlated with the abnormalities found in these patients, but a correlation was found between decreased CD4+ count and cortical atrophy. A quantitative (morphometric) MRI study (Jernigan et al., 1993) revealed the presence of brain volume loss associated with HIV infection in the HIV-positive symptomatic group but not in the asymptomatic group employed in their investigation. This study also revealed that a large amount of the volume loss in the symptomatic seropositive group was the result of white matter loss, despite the fact that the subjects were free of clinical (neurological) signs. Cerebral gray matter losses were also reported as part of this investigation.

Finally, similar to the results obtained by Belman et al. (1986) with children, Aylward et al. (1993) reported the presence of atrophy in basal ganglia structures in adults with HIV dementia using quantitative MRI procedures. With regard to functional imaging, Rottenberg et al. (1987) used resting state PET (flurodeoxyglucose, FDG) to study glucose metabolism in a group of 12 patients diagnosed with AIDS Dementia Complex and a group of 18 HIV-negative controls. The results of that study revealed evidence for increased thalamic and basal ganglia metabolic activity in patients with mild HIV-related encephalopathy relative to controls. In contrast, the remaining patients with more advanced dementia exhibited both decreased cortical and subcortical metabolism when compared to controls. Similarly, van Gorp and his colleagues (1992) investigated resting state cerebral glucose metabolism through PET with 17 AIDS patients diagnosed with and without dementia using Sidtis and Price's (1990) AIDS Dementia Rating Scale and a group of 14 uninfected individuals. Only thalamic and basal ganglia metabolism differed significantly between the AIDS group and controls, the former exhibiting hypermetabolism as had been the case in the study by Rottenberg et al. (1987). Perfusion defects have also been found in HIV-positive, relative to HIV-negative, adults using SPECT (Krammer & Sanger, 1990; La France et al., 1988). Altogether, neuroimaging studies with adults and children have revealed that both CT and MRI are capable of detecting atrophy and ring enhancing lesions as well as certain aspects of white matter compromise. Whereas MRI has been proven to be superior in detecting focal signal intensities in grey and white matter areas using T2-weighted procedures (Dooneief et al., 1992), it has not been found useful in detecting structural correlates of asymptomatic infection (M.J.D. Post et al., 1991). PET, SPECT, and magnetic resonance spectroscopy (MRS) have been able to capture regional functional abnormalities reflecting metabolism, brain perfusion, and biochemical function, respectively.

Electroencephalographic Correlates

Given the abnormalities observed in the CNS using other functional diagnostic procedures (e.g., imaging), positive findings from electroencephalographic (EEG) studies with HIV-positive adults and children are not surprising. Abnormalities on this functional modality are most commonly present during the late stages of the disease.

Evidence in Children.   In a study conducted by Belman et al. (1985) with six children with AIDS, five of the six displayed EEG abnormalities consistent with the imaging results. Three of the five showed mild diffuse slowing, and the other two displayed moderate diffuse slowing. Four of the six also displayed abnormalities in brain stem evoked potential (BAEP) marked by abnormal rate function ($n = 1$) and prolongation ($n = 3$) of the I-V interwave latency. Other pediatric studies have found similar abnormalities (Ultmann et al., 1985).

Evidence in Adults.   EEG abnormalities in adults also have been reported in the literature (Darko et al., 1995; Gazbuda, Levy, & Chiappa, 1988; Leuchter, Newton, van Gorp, & E. Miller, 1989). As early as 1986, Navia, Cho, Petito et al. (1986) noted the presence of diffuse slowing in the late stages of HIV-related dementia. Leuchter and his colleagues studied a group of 28 individuals with AIDS and 56 HIV-negative controls using quantitative EEG coherence. Subjects with AIDS exhibited significantly higher EEG coherence in the 6–10 Hz band relative to the seronegative controls. Although

EEG investigations have demonstrated increased abnormalities in the EEG traces of individuals with significant impairments (e.g., AIDS), Nuwer et al. (1992) noted the absence of increased abnormalities in asymptomatic HIV-positive subjects during their large prospective investigation. In a similar vein, McArthur (1987) noted that in less advanced stages of dementia, the EEG traces can be normal in up to 50% of that population of patients. Most recently, using sleep EEG paradigms, Darko et al. (1995) demonstrated sleep disturbances associated with HIV infection (see also Wiegand, Möller, Schreiber, Krieg, & Holsboer, 1991).

Neuropathological Features

Evidence in Children. Measurable neuropathology has been observed in microscopic and gross specimens of the brain and spinal cord. Several investigators reported abnormalities in the brains of children diagnosed with HIV as early as 1985. Sharer, Cho, and Epstein (1985) conducted autopsies on 11 children infected with HIV. The results of these autopsies revealed diminished gross brain weight for their respective age, inflammatory cell infiltrates, multinucleated cells and multinucleated giant cells, cerebrovascular calcification, vascular and perivascular calcification, and white matter changes. In addition, inflammatory and vascular lesions were most pronounced in the basal ganglia and pons (Sharer et al., 1985). Similar results have been obtained by subsequent investigators (Belman et al., 1988; Epstein et al., 1988). The investigation by Epstein and his colleagues (1988) revealed diminished brain weight for age under gross examination in the children who had died of AIDS-related progressive encephalopathy. Microscopic examination indicated the presence of inflammatory cell infiltrates, multinucleated giant cells, white matter changes, and vascular calcification supporting earlier reports by Sharer et al. (1985). On autopsy, Sharer et al. (1990) found nine spinal cords with inflammatory cell infiltrates and six spinal cords with multinucleated cells as part of a study with 18 children (16 spinal cords were autopsied) who died as a result of HIV-1 infection. They also identified myelin pallor in the cortico-spinal tracts in nearly half of the cases, consistent with previous studies (e.g., Dickson et al., 1989). Several studies have identified viral particles or HIV-related antigen in the multinucleated cells and other cells (Epstein et al., 1985; Koenig et al., 1986). As discussed earlier, it appears that the neuropathological effects of HIV infection on the developing brain are so devastating that they often can be detected under gross examination.

Evidence in Adults. Price and his colleagues (Brew, Sidtis, Petito, & Price, 1988; Navia, Cho, et al., 1986) initially noted substantial atrophy marked by ventricular enlargement, involvement of the white matter and subcortical structures, as well as vacuolar myelopathy of the spinal cord in individuals with AIDS. Vinters, Tomiyasu, and Anders (1989) found neuropathological abnormalities in from 70% to 90% of the brains of adult subjects with AIDS. Among their various findings, diffuse pallor of the white matter was the most common abnormality found. The subcortical structures most frequently reported as showing involvement include the basal ganglia, thalamus, and the temporal-limbic centers. In contrast to the data supporting the presence of subcortical grey matter and white matter abnormalities, Wiley et al. (1991) and other researchers (cf. Everall, Luthert, & Lantos, 1991, 1993) documented the presence of neuronal loss in cortical areas as well. Using quantitative histological analysis, this group of investigators (Masliah et al., 1992) noted losses of neocortical dendritric areas of up to 40% and correlated with levels of HIV gp41 immunoreactivity (Masliah et al., 1992). More recent studies conducting extensive reviews of autopsy data of individuals diagnosed with AIDS continue to support these findings (Masliah, Ge, Achim, & Wiley, 1995).

Neuropathological differences emerge when comparing adults and children that may be associated with developmental factors. Although similar findings have been observed in both groups, white matter pallor is difficult to identify in children relative to adults and periventricular infiltrates and multinucleated giant cells are common in both (McArthur, 1994).

Other CNS Correlates

Other abnormalities thought to be the result of HIV-1 infection have been identified in various CNS biological markers. Cerebral spinal fluid (CSF) has been one such marker targeted (Brew et al., 1992; Brouwers et al., 1993; Carrieri, Indaco, Maioino, & Buscaino, 1992; Epstein et al., 1987; McArthur et al., 1992).

Evidence in Children.   Brouwers et al. (1993) found a high correlation between CSF levels of quinolinic acid (QUIN) and degree of encephalopathy in 40 children with HIV infection relative to 16 controls. In addition, this study revealed decreasing levels of overall mental abilities (Bayley scales, MDI; McCarthy scales, GCI; and WISC–R, FSIQ) to be associated with increasing levels of QUIN. Similarly, in a study assessing levels of serum tumor necrosis factor alpha (TNF α), Mintz (1989) found elevated levels of this marker related to progressive encephalopathy in children with AIDS. Tardieu et al. (1989), using antigen capture assays specific to HIV-1-p24, also found detectable levels of this marker in the CSF of children. In the same year, Hutto et al. (1989) reported abnormalities in the CSF of children infected with HIV.

Evidence in Adults.   Investigations examining CSF composition (Heyes et al., 1991) also have detected elevated levels of QUIN in HIV-infected adults. In fact, A. Martin et al. (1992) reported significant correlations between elevated CSF excitotoxic quinolinic acid and decreased motor performance. Resnick et al. (1985) and Resnick et al. (1988) were able to isolate HIV in the cerebrospinal fluid of infected adult subjects. More important, CSF β-2 microglobulin absolute levels and CSF/serum ratios have exhibited some specificity in discriminating between HIV-1-Associated Dementia and multiple sclerosis or other CNS disorders (Carrieri et al., 1992).

NEUROBEHAVIORAL, NEUROPSYCHOLOGICAL, AND NEUROPSYCHIATRIC FINDINGS IN HIV-1 DISEASE

Neurobehavioral, neuropsychiatric, and neuropsychological (NP) sequelae as a result of HIV infection have been frequently reported in the literature (Brouwers et al., 1994; Cohen et al., 1991; Diamond et al., 1987; Fernandez, 1988; Fowler, 1994; I. Grant & Martin, 1994; B. E. Levin, Berger, Didona, & Duncan, 1992; Levy & Fernandez, 1997; Llorente et al., 1997, 1998; McArthur et al., 1989; E. N. Miller et al., 1990; Navia et al., 1986; Perdices & Cooper, 1989; van Gorp et al., 1989). Therefore, the remainder of this chapter reviews behavioral and neuropsychological correlates associated with this infectious disease and their assessment in Hispanic populations. Although an attempt will be made to integrate the clinicopathological findings presented earlier with the neuro-psychological literature, thus describing the brain–behavior relations associated with this disease, the reader is cautioned regarding the scarce number of studies addressing the impact of HIV on cognition that have included Hispanics.

Overall Intellectual Functioning

Several studies have found impairments in overall levels of cognitive abilities as a result of HIV infection in children and adults. A lowering in overall intellectual functioning in children to within the Borderline and Mild Mental Retardation range has been reported by several researchers (Boivin, 1995; Brouwers et al., 1991; see Fowler, 1994, for review). In adults, van Gorp et al. (1989) reported data noting lower WAIS–R (Wechsler, 1981) Full Scale and Verbal IQ scores in a group of symptomatic HIV-positive subjects in the United States, some of which were of Hispanic descent albeit fully fluent in English, rela-tive to a group of HIV-negative controls. Similar findings were reported by Rubinow, Berettini, Brouwers, and Lane (1988) for the WAIS–R Full Scale IQ score. In general, however, no differences in measures of global intellectual functioning have been found between asymptomatic HIV-positive subjects and HIV-negative controls (McAllister et al., 1992; Y. Stern et al., 1991) even in studies that examined a significant number of His-panics (e.g., see McArthur et al., 1989, and Miller et al., 1990, for an investigation [MACS] evaluating the natural history of HIV infection in men where 3% of their cohort were Hispanics).

In summary, it appears that HIV infection may be capable of causing impairments in the overall cognitive abilities of some children and adults regardless of ethnicity. The degree of intellectual impact in some patients is consistent with the magnitude of neuro-pathology sometimes observed in this disease process. Specifically, neuropathological findings, including HIV-related cerebral atrophy and acquired microcephaly in the case of some infants and children and opportunistic diseases in the case of adults, should be noted. These debilitating CNS insults are quite capable of accounting for the global dampening in intellectual functioning observed in some of these patients, particularly during the late stage of the disease process (Heaton et al., 1995).

Attention and Concentration

Evidence in Children. A study with children (Brouwers et al., 1989) examined the effects of viral involvement on attentional processes by looking at the WISC–R (Wechsler, 1974) Freedom from Distractibility factor (Kaufman, 1975). The results from this inves-tigation revealed that HIV-positive children experienced "relative weaknesses" on this factor. However, Brouwers et al. (1994) cautioned that these deficits could very well have been the result of other factors not related to HIV involvement per se, such as potential confounds (e.g., the high base rates of attention difficulties in children for this age group in the general population). Furthermore, although behavioral assessment has revealed that these children may indeed suffer from attentional deficits (Hittleman et al., 1991), the children studied in these investigations were quite young. In another investigation using cluster analytic procedures, one group of symptomatic HIV-infected children revealed a cluster that could be identified as a result of attention deficits (Brouwers et al., 1992). Although further studies need to be conducted with children infected with the human immunodeficiency virus to determine whether the attention deficits observed during neuropsychological testing are the result of the disease process versus other etiologies (diseases in general; cf. Tarter, Edwards, & van Thiel, 1988; Routh, 1988), given the fragile nature of these processes (Lezak, 1978), the probability is high that these mechanisms may be indeed compromised by this infectious disease. In addition, from a brain–behavior perspective, during severe expressions of the disease in children, white matter involvement has been identified as a neuropathological hallmark of HIV, especially calcifications in the pons (Sharer et al., 1985). Therefore, it is possible that HIV affects ascending pathways from the reticular activating system or other substrates involving attention mechanisms responsible for the deficits observed in this domain.

Evidence in Adults.   Disturbances in attention and concentration represent a hallmark manifestation of this disease in adults (Butters et al., 1990; Heaton et al., 1995; Levy & Fernandez, 1997; E. N. Miller et al., 1990; Navia et al., 1986; Y. Stern et al., 1991), particularly as they relate to attentional mechanisms such as complex divided and sustained attention as measured by the Paced Auditory Serial Addition Test (PASAT; Gronwall, 1977) during late disease stages (I. Grant et al., 1987; van Gorp et al., 1989). Some investigators, however, have reported deficits in complex attentional skills even during the asymptomatic stage of HIV disease, although usually identifying subtle differences on variables such as reaction time, which may have little clinical significance (see Y. Stern et al., 1990). In contrast to deficits found on tasks requiring complex attentional processes, results from procedures capable of measuring simple attention (e.g., WAIS–R, Digit Span; Wechsler, 1981) have not revealed impairment in either asymptomatic or symptomatic adults (E. N. Miller et al., 1990; van Gorp et al., 1989). Similar results have been noted in studies that included Hispanics. For example, deficits in simple attention span were not observed in the controlled investigation that utilized "ethnicity" (Hispanics) as a research variable by Levin and her colleagues (B. E. Levin et al., 1992). Although a study (Klusman et al., 1991) examining attentional processes in military personnel (including Hispanics as part of their "mixed" ethnic group) found significant differences in the WAIS–R, Digit Span subtest, particularly Digits Backward, these differences did not apply to the "mixed" groups of subjects. In summary, simple attentional processes appear to be spared in both asymptomatic and symptomatic groups, with deficits in complex attentional mechanisms, such as divided and sustained attention, most commonly observed in late-stage HIV disease. As was the case with children, alterations in attention and concentration should be interpreted with care in adult populations as neuropsychiatric disturbances (e.g., anxiety and depression), commonly observed during HIV infection (Fernandez, 1989), could account for a portion of the attentional deficits attributed to primary concentration/attention mechanisms (van Gorp et al., 1993).

Learning and Memory

Evidence in Children.   Infection with HIV may cause direct memory deficits (Bellman et al., 1988; Diamond, 1989; Levenson et al., 1992) in children. Boivin et al. (1995) reported deficits in verbal and visual memory in a group of children of color, age 2 and older in Africa. Specifically, HIV-positive participants, relative to controls and HIV-negative children born to infected mothers, obtained significantly lower levels of performance on the K–ABC (Kaufman & Kaufman, 1983) Immediate Recall and Spatial Memory subtests (these measures assess, among other functions, immediate verbal and visual recall, respectively). Significant differences were also observed on another measure of visual immediate recall (K–ABC, Hand Movements). In summary, although it is difficult to define what constitutes memory in very young children, it appears that HIV infection may not only cause disturbances in attentional mechanisms, but may significantly impact verbal and visuospatial memory functions in childhood.

Evidence in Adults. Although conflicting results have been reported in the litera-ture regarding the extent of verbal and visual memory difficulties in adults (van Gorp et al., 1993), different aspects of these abilities have been observed to undergo compromise during HIV-1 infection. Janssen et al. (1989) reported that a group of symptomatic HIV seropositive subjects performed worse than seronegative controls on the Wechsler Mem-ory Scale (Wechsler, 1987), recall of passages (Logical Prose subtest). E. N. Miller et al. (1990) found symptomatic seropositive subjects to perform worse on the Rey Auditory Verbal Learning Test (Rey, 1964) relative to seronegative controls (see Harris, Cullum, and Puente, 1995, with regard to the effects of bilingualism on verbal learning tasks). Although somewhat against expectations due to their asymptomatic state, Wilkie et al. (1990) found a group of infected participants to perform significantly lower relative to controls on a task assessing delayed recall of passages, whereas B. E. Levin et al. (1992) found Hispanic infected participants to perform lower than noninfected, non-Hispanic subjects on a list learning task (California Verbal Learning Test, Trial 5; Delis, Kramer, & Kaplan, 1987).

With regard to visual memory, several investigations have noted impairments in per-formance in groups of HIV symptomatic subjects relative to seronegative controls on various measures assessing this domain. For example, van Gorp et al. (1989) and Ollo and Pass (1988) reported significantly lower recall on the Wechsler Memory Scales (WMS–R), Visual Reproduction subtest, and on the delayed recall portion of the Rey–Osterrieth Complex Figure (Rey, 1941) on the part of symptomatic HIV seropositive subjects rela-tive to seronegative controls. Despite the unfortunate fact that their study did not use a control group, Klusman et al. (1991) found lower performance on the WMS–R, Visual Reproduction Subtest (Immediate recall), in their "mixed" asymptomatic group (10% of whom were Hispanics) relative to their group of White asymptomatic subjects (see Ardila, M. Roselli, & Rosas, 1989, for a discussion on the effects of illiteracy on visual-spatial and memory skills). Overall, the aforementioned findings combined (children and adults) buttress a hypothesis suggesting that memory compromises may be a manifestation of HIV infection (Ryan, Paolo, & Skrade, 1992).

Language and Auditory Processing

Evidence in Children. Declines and deficits in language, specifically expressive lan-guage skills and auditory processing, associated with HIV infection have been reported in the literature in children (Bellman et al., 1985; Wolters et al., 1994). Language-related deficits in infancy and childhood are to a certain extent modulated by the mode of viral transmission in conjunction with the degree of disease progression and age of the child. A vertically infected infant who suffers from progressive encephalopathy will display delays in acquiring and developing language, whereas an older child who becomes infected with HIV horizontally may eventually develop regression or complete loss of speech, slurred speech (probably confounded with oral-motor difficulties), as well as regression in other language skills from previous levels of functioning.

Although deficits in both receptive and expressive language have been reported in the pediatric literature (see Epstein et al., 1986), the majority of insult occurs in the expressive domain with relatively spared receptive skills (Brouwers, Moss, et al., 1994). Data-based evidence for this observation was also reported by Wolters and her associates (1994). They demonstrated, as part of a study of adaptive functioning using the Vineland Adaptive Behavior Scales (Sparrow, Balla, & Ciccheti, 1984), that expressive skills underwent greater insult relative to receptive abilities.

Evidence in Adults.   In contrast to findings in the pediatric literature, language functions have largely been found to be spared in adulthood using a variety of tasks such as confrontation naming (Boston Naming Test; Kaplan, Goodglass, & Weintraub, 1983), word list generation (controlled oral-word fluency test), and vocabulary tests (WAIS–R), even when comparing symptomatic HIV-positive subjects to seronegative controls (E. N. Miller et al., 1990; Y. Stern et al., 1989; Tross et al., 1988; van Gorp et al., 1989). Two investigations, however, yielded results indicating language impairments. Differences in the WAIS–R Vocabulary subtest were found between asymptomatic HIV-positive subjects and controls (Heaton el al., 1995) and between symptomatic seropositive subjects and controls (Heaton et al., 1995; Saykin et al., 1988), as well as between symptomatic seropositive subjects relative to controls on a word list generation test. Levin and her colleagues (1992) also found language differences not only as a result of sero-status (asymptomatic seropositive subjects performed poorer on these measures relative to seronegative controls) but secondary to ethnicity (Hispanics scored lower than non-Hispanics) on the Boston Naming Test, Controlled Oral-Word Fluency Test (Food), and WAIS–R Vocabulary subtest.

A comparison of results for this domain between adults and children is important because it provides clues regarding putative developmental effects of the disease process. A contrast between adults and children suggests that language skills in childhood are more compromised relative to adulthood during HIV infection. The difference between these two age groups may be associated with the nature of these skills in children. Language skills, which are in "ascendency" during infancy and early childhood, may be more vulnerable to insult and disruption, making them more vulnerable and prime targets to the effects of this infectious disease (see Ewing-Cobbs, Fletcher, H. S. Levin & Landry, 1985; see also Laosa, 1984, who discussed the effects of home language influences on performance on measures of cognitive abilities applicable to Hispanic populations).

Motor, Psychomotor, Speeded Functions, and Executive Skills

Evidence in Children.   Given the striking and profound involvement observed in the basal ganglia complex observed with neuroradiological and neuropathological techniques in children with HIV infection and AIDS, specifically calcific vasculopathy and inflammatory CNS diseases, it is not surprising to detect motor deficits in these children during developmental evaluation. As a result, gross and fine motor delays are prominent in symptomatic immunosupressed infants and older children and are often some of the most frequent aspects of functioning to fall prey to the disease process (Fowler, 1994; Hittleman et al., 1990, 1991; Ultmann, 1985). Specifically, infants display muscle tone abnormalities as well as delays across all other aspects of this domain. Even seemingly unaffected asymptomatic HIV-positive children less than age 2 have been observed to suffer from motor delays (Boivin et al., 1995). Older children, including preschoolers and school-age children, also display abnormalities in this domain, initially marked by disturbances in gait and balance (Brouwers, Moss, et al., 1994). However, according to Fowler (1994), in contrast to infants and toddlers, older children and adolescents tend to only suffer from mild neurologic impairments, including motor dysfunction (e.g., fine motor tremor) until the latter stages of the disease process. In more severe cases, the ability to ambulate is lost due to pronounced gross motor deficits in the lower extremities, most likely associated with neuropathological processes affecting the basal ganglia complex. Brouwers, Moss, et al. (1994) reported, as might be expected, that more serious deficits in this domain may be observed, including spastic quadriparesis and pyramidal tract signs, with greater levels of CNS involvement such as progressive encephalopathy (cf. Belman et al., 1988).

In summary, pronounced delays in motor functioning are evidenced in symptomatic immunocompromised infants and older children, including motor tone abnormalities and other motor delays, with greater arrest in development correlated with increasing levels of disease involvement, particularly progressive encephalopathy. Even seemingly unaffected HIV-positive asymptomatic infants may display mild delays in this domain. Although rare, due to the low incidence of these diseases in children, abrupt onset of motor difficulties, different from those already described, are sometimes seen in those with acquired opportunistic diseases (e.g., lymphoma) as a result of their immunocompromised condition.

Evidence in Adults. Navia, Jordan, and Price (1986) considered motor difficulties to be one of the hallmark symptoms of the AIDS Dementia Complex, and gross motor impairment is commonly found in late stages of HIV dementia. Results on neuropsychological indices of fine motor skills, however, have been mixed. Motor speed (finger tapping) and fine motor coordination as measured by the Grooved Pegboard (Kløve, 1963) failed to show impairments in groups of symptomatic HIV-positive research participants in studies conducted by Claypoole et al. (1990), Franzblau et al. (1991), and Y. Stern, Sano, Williams, and Gorman (1989). In contrast, relative to controls, symptomatic HIV seropositive subjects displayed slower performance on the Grooved Pegboard Test in investigations conducted by E. N. Miller et al. (1990) and Tross et al. (1988). Klusman et al. (1991) also found motor and psychomotor differences between their groups of Whites and Mixed participants, including Hispanics on finger tapping asymmetry. Therefore, it is evident that at least a subsample of HIV-infected individuals display fine motor impairment, particularly during the advanced stages of the disease, and in some cases during early mildly symptomatic stages (CDC Group A; Heaton et al., 1995; Levy & Fernandez, in press), and these difficulties do indeed represent one of the cardinal abnormalities observed in HIV infection in adulthood (Butters et al., 1990; Navia et al., 1986; Selnes & E. N. Miller, 1994).

Combined with these motor difficulties, slowing of information processing (Hart, Wade, Klinger, & Levenson, 1990; Llorente et al., 1998; E. M. Martin et al., 1992), even after controlling for the effects of peripheral neuropathy (Llorente et al., 1998), slowed psychomotor speed (Perdices et al., 1989; Selnes & E. N. Miller, 1994), and impaired cognitive flexibility (e.g., Martin, Robertson, et al., 1992) are also considered chief signs of HIV-related cognitive impairments in adulthood. As was the case with children (Brouwers et al., 1994), it is interesting to note that the majority of these skills are either higher order skills or expressive abilities in nature. Although the findings have been more equivocal (cf. Y. Stern et al., 1989), executive skills in adults have been shown in some investigations to be impaired in seropositive subjects relative to controls on tasks including the Wisconsin Card Sorting Test (Heaton, 1981) and Trails B (Claypoole et al., 1990; I. Grant et al., 1987; Klusman et al., 1991).

Adaptive, Behavioral, and Neuropsychiatric Manifestations

Evidence in Children. Other areas of psychological functioning have been shown to undergo dramatic alterations associated with adult and pediatric HIV infection and/or treatment thereof (Bayés, 1995; Brouwers, Moss, et al., 1994; Fernandez, 1988; Fernandez, Levy, & Pirozzolo, 1988; Perry, 1990). These disturbances may be capable of further impacting neuropsychological performance. For example, indirect effects (Brouwers, Moss, et al., 1994) associated with environmental factors and stressors, coupled with host variables (e.g., psychological resources, coping strategies; see Satz's, 1993, threshold theory for adults in this regard), synergistically operating with the disease process (e.g., undergoing multiple medical procedures and hospitalizations as part of radiation treatment for an opportunistic disease; see Tarter, Edwards, & van Thiel, 1988, and Routh, 1988), may impact on the child's overall level of functioning. These behavioral and adaptive factors play a major role in the way that HIV symptoms exhibit themselves from patient to patient and must be taken into consideration when evaluating a patient, performing research with these populations, or providing rehabilitative interventions. Similarly, a large portion of Hispanic children infected with the human immunodeficiency virus, whether in the United States or abroad, come from low SES backgrounds (Tuckson, 1994) for which there is sometimes little normative data or for which inferences made on the data available would be invalid for the purposes at hand or the population under investigation. For this reason, caution must be exercised when interpreting neuropsychological findings, in light of these potential confounds, because children with HIV infection tend to display augmented behavioral disturbances (Ultman et al., 1985).

Evidence in Adults. Mood and anxiety disorders have been assessed in adult individuals with HIV infection and appear to be the most common of all neuropsychiatric disorders to affect this population. Fernandez (1988), Fernandez et al. (1988), and Levy and Fernandez (1997) reported elevations on measures assessing these domains. E. N. Miller et al. (1990) reported elevations on the CES-D (Radloff, 1977) in their group of symptomatic patients relative to controls (MACS) of which approximately 3% of the sample were of Hispanic origin, some of whom were bilingual. Van Gorp and his colleagues (1990) also reported elevations on the Beck Depression Inventory (BDI; Beck, 1987) and on Scale 2 of the MMPI–168 (Overall & Gomez-Mont, 1974) in a group of clinically referred symptomatic seropositive individuals relative to controls. Although equivocal findings were reported by several investigators in the literature (Janssen et al., 1989; van Gorp et al., 1989), a recent report by Heaton and his colleagues (1995) noted significant elevations on the Hamilton Anxiety and Depression Scales (Hamilton, 1967) and the BDI in their HIV-positive group relative to controls. However, several studies failed to find a significant relation between mood dysfunction and cognitive compromise (cf. van Gorp et al., 1989, 1990).

SPECIAL CONSIDERATIONS FOR RESEARCH AND CLINICAL EVALUATIONS WITH HISPANIC POPULATIONS

A number of researchers (Bornstein, 1994; Brouwers, Moss, et al., 1994; Butters et al., 1990; Selnes & E. N. Miller, 1994) have addressed critical methodological issues associated with the NP assessment of HIV infection in adulthood and childhood, which also apply to research and clinical interventions with Hispanic populations. Butters and his colleagues (1990) alluded to the need to assess a broad set of functions typically affected by prototypical subcortical dementias (e.g., Supranuclear Palsy) as described by Cummings and Benson (1983). To this end, they recommended procedures that would assess attention, executive skills (abstraction), language, memory (verbal and visual), motor abilities, psychomotor speed and speed of processing, and visuospatial/visuoperceptive skills. Bornstein (1994) discussed the importance of variables such as adequate sample size, the need for repeated assessment, and issues associated with impairment and exclusion criteria. Selnes and E. N. Miller (1994) also addressed important methodological concerns, including the need for comprehensive assessment while simultaneously attending to issues associated with fatigue in individuals with HIV, the need for longitudinal assessment, the assessment of a wide range of impairments, and the robustness of neuropsychological tests to serial repetition. LoPresti, Llorente, Guzzard, and Brumm (1998) noted the need to be cautious about attributing neurologically based neuropsychological impairments to personality variables when conducting research.

Methodological issues relevant to longitudinal assessment of HIV infected infants and children also must be considered. Brouwers et al. (1991) discussed the importance of using a comprehensive test battery with interim monitoring using a smaller number of tests to ensure that treatment effects and/or disease progression are monitored while at the same time minimizing practice effects. Despite the fact that HIV-positive Hispanic children displayed similar characteristics relative to White samples (Brouwers, personal communication) during a study in the United States as part of the AIDS Clinical Trials Group 128 (see Brady et al., 1996), Brouwers et al. (1991) highlighted the need to interpret serial assessments within the context of normal developmental growth, possible AIDS-related deterioration, and sociocultural factors. In addition, they provided suggestions for modifying testing procedures to accommodate chronically ill children who are functioning below age level (commonly seen in children with progressive encephalopathy) or have other handicapping conditions.

General cross-cultural issues unique to the assessment of neurobehavioral disorders in Hispanics addressed in this handbook (see chap. 1), and as expounded by other investigators (Ardilla, N. M. Rosselli, & Puente, 1994; Pontón & Ardila, 1999; Pontón & Herrera, 1993), should be strongly considered. At the very least, an assessment posture should be adopted addressing level of acculturation (G. Marín & B. V. Marín, 1991; R. A. Stern et al., 1992), problems posed by language issues including bilingualism (Harris et al., 1995; Laosa, 1984; G. Marín & B. V. Marín, 1991), SES (Pérez-Arce, 1994), level of education (Ardilla et al., 1994), examiner characteristics, and other factors capable of modulating these variables (see Llorente, Pontón, Taussig, & Satz, 1999, for a discussion of the impact of American immigration patterns on the acquisition and application of normative data with Hispanic populations). When conducting assessments with Hispanic toddlers and preschool children from families whose primary language is Spanish, problems with rapport may occur when the evaluation is conducted through an interpreter (cf. Likely, 1987, for this topic in general) or when the clinician is unfamiliar with sociocultural issues relevant to this population. A nonstandardized administration is often conducted, translating items into Spanish, which then further limits the inferences that can be made from test results. Even when administering tests and procedures in English, level of acculturation is one factor that influences the degree to which valid and reliable interpretations can be made. For example, children from primarily Spanish-speaking families often demonstrate increased familiarity with the English language after enrolling in school. Improvements noted on subsequent evaluations, rather than indicating beneficial response to treatment, may simply reflect greater understanding and expression of the English language, and for children who have not attended preschool settings, a greater comfort level with elements of the evaluation, such as sitting at a child's table and attending in a sustained manner to activities presented by the examiner. The lack of neuropsychological measures developed and standardized on Hispanic children and adults and the dearth of appropriate normative data are also major obstacles that greatly limit the validity of inferences that can be made from test results.

With regard to specific assessment procedures to be employed with this population, a recommended list of procedures and normative data sets from studies that have included Hispanics (infants, children, adolescents, and adults) infected with HIV (Table 11.4) is provided for consideration. Although these instruments have been chosen to capture cardinal symptoms associated with HIV infection (cf. Butters et al., 1990; Selnes et al., 1991;

TABLE 11.4

Recommended Procedures to Be Used in the Assessment of HIV-Related
Neuropsychological Impairments with Hispanic Populations

Procedure(s)	Comparison Group/Normative Data[0]
INFANTS	
Bayley Scales of Infant Development, 1st Edition[1,2] (Mental and Motor Developmental Indices)	Manual
Clinical Interview	N/A
Minnesota Child Development Inventory[1,2]	Manual
Vineland Adaptive Behavior Scales[1,2] Spanish edition	Manual
PRESCHOOLERS AND SCHOOL-AGE CHILDREN[3]	
Bruininks–Oseretsky Test of Motor Proficiency[2]	Manual
Child Behavior Checklist (CBCL)[1,2]	Manual
Children's Color Trails[1,2]	Williams et al. (1995)
Clinical Evaluation of Language Fundamentals (CELF–R)[2] Spanish Edition	Manual
Clinical Interview	N/A
Conners' Rating Scales[1,2]	Manual
Developmental Test of Visual-Motor Integration (VMI)[2]	Manual
Escala de Inteligencia Wechsler para Niños–Revised (EIWN-R)	Manual (Wechsler, 1982) (Martin, 1977)
Expressive One-Word Picture Vocabulary Test–Revised[2] (Spanish Translation)	Manual
Grip Strength Test[2]	Manual
Grooved Pegboard Test[2]	Manual
Luria Alternating Movements Task (informal)[2]	N/A
Peabody Picture Vocabulary Test–Revised (PPVT–R)[2] (Adaptación Hispanoamericana)	Manual
Vineland Adaptive Behavior Scales[1,2]	Manual
Wechsler Intelligence Scale for Children–Revised (WISC–R)[2]	Manual
Woodcock-Johnson (Achievement)–Spanish Adaptation	Manual

Continued

TABLE 11.4 (*Continued*)

Procedure(s)	Comparison Group/Normative Data[0]
ADULTS[4]	
Boston Naming Test (BNT)	B. E. Levin et al. (1992)
BNT-WHO-UCLA	Pontón et al. (1996)
CALCAP	MACS
California Verbal Learning Test (Trial 5)	B. E. Levin et al. (1992)
CES–D	MACS
Escala de Inteligencia Wechsler para Adultos–Revised[2] (EIWA-R)	Manual
Judgement of Line Orientation[1]	B. E. Levin et al. (1992)
MMPI/MMPI–2 (Spanish Version)	Publisher
Rey Auditory Verbal Learning Test[1]	Klusman et al. (1991)[5]
	MACS
Rey–Osterrieth Complex Figure	B. E. Levin et al. (1992)
	MACS
	Pontón et al. (1996)
Stroop Interference Test[1]	Klusman et al. (1991)
	MACS
Symbol Digit Modalities Test[1]	Klusman et al. (1991)
	MACS
Trails A & B[1]	Klusman et al. (1991)
	MACS
Verbal Fluency Test	Klusman et al (1991)
	B. E. Levin et al. (1992)
	MACS
	Pontón et al. (1996)
Wechsler Adult Intelligence Scale–Revised (WAIS–R)	Manual
	B. E. Levin et al. (1992)
	MACS
Wisconsin Card Sorting Test	Manual
	B. E. Levin et al. (1992)
WHO–UCLA Auditory Verbal Learning Test[2] (Spanish Version)	Pontón et al. (1996)
WMS–R	Klusman et al. (1992)
	B. E. Levin et al. (1992)
	MACS

[0]Some data labeled here as normative data are actual data from investigations and not from studies used to standardized the tests shown with Hispanic populations.

[1]Spanish version or adaptation of test available.

[2]No normative data available for Hispanics with HIV from manual; normative data may be available from study.

[3]Due to declines from previously attained milestones, assessment of these children may require the administration of tests and procedures primarily used during infancy and early childhood.

[4]See Silberstein et al. (1987) for data in a group of asymptomatic individuals undergoing drug treatment.

[5]Study sample composed of military personnel only.

Selnes & E. N. Miller, 1994), while addressing many of the methodological issues previously discussed, they are by no means all-inclusive. Albeit restricted to selected groups of Hispanics, the normative or research data presented have in some cases included this minority group as part of their sample unless noted otherwise.

Although Table 11.4 provides useful information, it also illustrates the scarce number of investigations that have employed Hispanics while assessing the effects of HIV. For this reason, little is known about the impact of the virus on neuropsychological functioning in Hispanic adults or children, particularly Spanish-speakers. Research studies have yet to determine whether behavior, cognition, and mood are differentially affected in this population, relative to the pattern of impairment documented in White individuals, who comprise most study samples. The difficulties that arise in conducting clinical evaluations with Hispanics, and in appropriately interpreting the results from such assessments, also have unfortunately contributed to the routine exclusion of this population from research studies. Barriers include sociocultural factors that may limit the effectiveness of community outreach efforts and subject recruitment for studies, or contribute to subject attrition. Other factors, such as the limited availability of appropriate measures and the linguistic variability of Hispanics, with individuals either bilingual or solely Spanish or English speaking, add to the difficulty investigators have faced in attempting to investigate the effects of HIV in this population.

CONCLUSIONS

The study of the neuropsychological effects of HIV in Hispanic adults and children warrant unique consideration. This special merit is derived from the documented effects of HIV on the CNS in conjunction with the epidemic nature of this disease worldwide and its impact on persons of color, particularly Hispanic women and children. Clinicopathological correlates and neuropsychological sequelae clearly indicated the proclivity of the virus to enter and infect the CNS early in the disease process, exhibiting minor if any manifestation during the asymptomatic stage but more dramatic sequelae subsequent to the development of constitutional symptomatology or a significant immunocompromised state. At its most pernicious expression, neuropsychological findings suggest that HIV is capable of producing significant encephalopathy in infants and children while mimicking normal aging or subcortical dementias predominantly infringing on speeded functions during adulthood. Although moderate strides have been made in understanding the effects of HIV infection on the brain since the initial reports of AIDS in the early 1980s, further research needs to be conducted, particularly with Hispanic populations, in an attempt to elucidate in more detail the complex manifestations of this infectious disease on the CNS and its subsequent impact on behavior.

ACKNOWLEDGMENTS

Portions of this chapter were supported in part by a grant from the UCLA CIRID-Fogarty AIDS International Foundation to Antolin M. Llorente. The authors wish to express their sincere thanks to Eric N. Miller Ph.D., Department of Psychiatry and Biobehavioral Sciences, University of California, Los Angeles, for his thoughtful comments and suggestions.

REFERENCES

American Academy of Neurology AIDS Task Force. (1991). Nomenclature and research case definition for neurologic manifestations of human immunodeficiency virus-type 1 infection. *Annals of Neurology, 41,* 778–785.

Andiman, W. A., & Modlin, J. F. (1991). Vertical transmission. In P. A. Pizzo & K. M. Wilfert (Eds.), *Pediatric AIDS: The challenge of HIV infection in infant, children, and adolescents* (pp. 140–155). Baltimore: Williams & Wilkins.

Ardilla, A., Rosselli, M., & Rosas, P. (1989). Neuropsychological assessment of illiterates: Visuospatial and memory abilities. *Brain and Cognition, 11,* 147–166.

Ardilla, A., Rosselli, N. M., & Puente, A. E. (1994). *Neuropsychological evaluation of the Spanish speaker.* New York: Plenum.

Auger, I., Thomas, P., De Gruttola, V., Morse, D., Moore, D., Williams, R., Truman, B., & Lawrence, C. E. (1988). Incubation periods for pediatric AIDS patients. *Nature, 336,* 575–577.

Aylward, E. H., Henderer, J. D., McArthur, J. C., Brettschneider, P. D., Barta, P.E., & Pearlson, G. D. (1993). Reduced basal ganglia atrophy in HIV-1 associated dementia complex: Results from quantitative neuroimaging. *Neurology, 43,* 2099–2104.

Bayés, R. (1995). *Sida y psicología.* Barcelona: Martínez Roca.

Beck, A. T. (1987). *Beck Depression Inventory: Manual.* San Antonio, TX: The Psychological Corporation.

Belman, A., Diamond, G., Park, Y., Nozyce, M., Douglas, C., Cabot, T., Bernstein, L., & Rubinstein, A. (1989). Perinatal HIV infection: A prospective longitudinal study of the initial CNS signs. *Neurology, 39* (Suppl. 1), 278–279. (Abstract).

Belman, A. L. (1990). AIDS and pediatric neurology. *Neurology Clinics, 8,* 571–603.

Belman, A. L., Diamond, G., Dickson, D., Horoupian, D., Liena, J., Lantos, G., & Rubinstein, A. (1988). Pediatric acquired immunodeficiency syndrome. *American Journal of Diseases of Children, 142,* 29–35.

Belman, A. L., Lantos, G., Horoupian, D., Novick, B. E., Ultmann, M. H., Dickson, D. W., & Rubinstein, A. (1986). AIDS: Calcification of the basal ganglia in infants and children. *Neurology, 36,* 1192–1199.

Belman, A. L., Novick, B., Ultmann, M. H., Spiro, A. J., Rubinstein, A., Horoupian, D. S., & Cohen, H. (1984). Neurologic complications in children with AIDS. *Annals of Neurology, 16,* 414. (Abstract).

Belman, A. L., Ultmann, M. H., Horoupian, D., Novick, B., Spiro, A. J., Rubinstein, A., Kurtzbert, D., & Cone-Wesson, B. (1985). Neurological complications in infants and children with acquired immune deficiency syndrome. *Annals of Neurology, 18,* 560–566.

Boivin, M. J., Green, S.D.R., Davies, A. G., Giordani, B., Mokili, J.K.L., & Cutting, W.A.M. (1995). A preliminary evaluation of the cognitive and motor effects of pediatric HIV infection in Zairian children. *Health Psychology, 14*(1), 13–21.

Bornstein, R. A. (1994). Methodological and conceptual issues in the study of cognitive change in HIV infection. In I. Grant & A. Martin (Eds.), *Neuropsychology of HIV infection* (pp. 146–160). New York: Oxford University Press.

Brady, M. T., McGrath, N., Brouwers, P., Gelber, R., Fowler, M. G., Yogev, R., Hutton, N., Bryson, Y. J., Mitchell, C. D., Fikrig, S., Borkowsky, W., Jimenez, E., McSherry, G., Rubinstein, A., Wilfert, C. M., McIntosh, K., Elkins, M. M., & Weintrub, P. S. (1996). Randomized study of the tolerance and efficacy of high-versus low-dose zidovudine in human immunodeficiency virus-infected children with mild to moderate symptoms (AIDS Clinical Trials Group 128). *The Journal of Infectious Diseases, 173,* 1097–1106.

Bredesen, D. E., Levy, R. M., & Rosenblum, M. L. (1988). The neurology of human immunodeficiency virus infection. *Quarterly Journal of Medicine, 68,* 665–677.

Brew, B. J., Bhalla, R. B., Paul, M., Sidtis, J. J., Keilp, J. J., Sadler, A. E., Gallardo, H., McArthur, J. C., Schwartz, M. K., & Price, R. W. (1992). Cerebrospinal fluid β2 microglobulin in patients infected with AIDS dementia complex: An expanded series including response to zidovudine treatment. *AIDS, 6,* 461–465.

Brew, B. J., Sidtis, J. J., Petito, C. K., & Price, R. W. (1988). The neurologic complications of AIDS and human immunodeficiency virus infection. In F. Plum (Ed.), *Advances in contemporary neurology* (pp. 1–49). Philadelphia: Davis.

Brightbill, T. C., Ihmeidan, I. H., Post, M.J.D., Berger, J. R., & Katz, D. A. (1995). Neurosyphilis in HIV-positive and HIV-negative patients. Neuroimaging findings. *American Journal of Neuroradiology, 16,* 703–711.

Brouwers, P., Belman, A. L., & Epstein, L. G. (1991). Central nervous system involvement: Manifestations and evaluation. In P. A. Pizzo & K. M. Wilfert (Eds.), *Pediatric AIDS: The challenge of HIV infection in infants, children, and adolescents* (pp. 318–335). Baltimore: Williams & Wilkins.

Brouwers, P., Belman, A. L., & Epstein, L. (1994). Central nervous system involvement: Manifestations, evaluation, and pathogenesis. In P. A. Pizzo & K. M. Wilfert (Eds.), *Pediatric AIDS: The challenge of HIV infection in infants, children, and adolescents* (2nd ed., pp. 433–455). Baltimore: Williams & Wilkins.

Brouwers, P., DeCarli, C., Civitello, L., Moss, H., Wolters, P., & Pizzo, P. (1995). Correlation between computed tomographic brain scan abnormalities and neuropsychological function in children with symptomatic human immunodeficiency virus disease. *Archives of Neurology, 52*, 39–44.

Brouwers, P., Heyes, M., Moss, H., Wolters, P., Poplack, D., Markey, S., & Pizzo, P. (1993). Quinolinic acid in the cerebrospinal fluid of children with symptomatic HIV-disease: Relationships to clinical status and therapeutic response. *Journal of Infectious Diseases, 168*, 1380–1386.

Brouwers, P., Moss, H., Wolters, P., Eddy, J., & Pizzo, P. (1989). Neuropsychological profile of children with symptomatic HIV infection prior to antiretroviral therapy. *Proceedings from the V International Conference on AIDS, 1*, 316. (Abstract).

Brouwers, P., Moss, H., Wolters, P., el-Amin, D., Tassone, E., & Pizzo, P. (1992). Neurobehavioral typology of school-age children with symptomatic HIV disease. *Journal of Clinical and Experimental Neuropsychology, 14*, 113. (Abstract).

Brouwers, P., Moss, H., Wolters, P., & Schmitt, F. A. (1994). Developmental deficits and behavioral change in pediatric AIDS. In I. Grant & A. Martin (Eds.), *Neuropsychology of HIV infection* (pp. 310–338). New York: Oxford University Press.

Bryson, Y., Dillon, M., Garratty, E., Dickover, M., Keller, A., & Deveikis, A. (1993). The role of timing of HIV maternal–fetal transmission (in-utero vs. intrapartum) and HIV phenotype on onset of symptoms in vertically infected infants (Abstract WS-C10-2). *Proceedings from the IXth International Conference on AIDS/IV STD, World Congress (Berlin)*. London: Wellcome Foundation.

Buckingham, S., & van Gorp, W. (1988). AIDS-dementia complex: Implications for practice. *Social Casework: The Journal of Contemporary Social Work, 69*, 371–375.

Burgard, M., Mayaux, J., & Blanche, S. (1992). The use of viral culture and p24 antigen testing to diagnose human immunodeficiency virus in neonates. *New England Journal of Medicine, 327*, 1192–1197.

Butters, N., Grant, I., Haxby, J., Fudd, L. L., Martin, A., McClelland, J., Pequegnat, W., Schacter, D., & Stover, E. (1990). Assessment of AIDS-related cognitive changes: Recommendations of the NIMH workshop on neuropsychological assessment approaches. *Journal of Clinical and Experimental Neuropsychology, 12*, 963–978.

Carrieri, P. B., Indaco, A., Maiorino, A., & Buscaino, G. A. (1992). Cerebrospinal fluid beta-2-microglobulin in multiple sclerosis and AIDS dementia complex. *Neurological Research, 14*, 282–283.

Centers for Disease Control and Prevention (1993). *HIV/AIDS Surveillance Report, 5*, 1–19.

Centers for Disease Control and Prevention. (1994). Revised classification system for human immunodeficiency virus (HIV) infection in children less than 13 years of age. *Morbidity and Mortality Weekly, 43*, 1–10.

Centers for Disease Control and Prevention. (1996). *HIV/AIDS Surveillance Report, 8*(1), 1–33.

Claypoole, K., Townes, B., Collier, A., Combs, R., Longstreth, W., Cohen, W., Marra, C., Gerlach, R., Maravilla, K., Bahls, F., White, D., Murphy, V., Maxwell, C., & Handsfield, H. (1990, February). *Neuropsychological aspects of early HIV infection*. Presented at the 18th annual International Neuropsychological Society Conference, Orlando, FL.

Cohen, S., Mundy, T., Karrassik, B., Lieb, L., Ludwig, D., & Ward, J. (1991). Neuropsychological functioning in human immunodeficiency virus type 1 seropositive children infected through neonatal blood transfusion. *Pediatrics, 88*, 58–68.

Cooper, D. A., Gold, J., Mclean, P., Donovan, B., Finlayson, R., Barnes, T. G., Michelmore, H. M., Brooke, P., & Penny, R. (1985). Acute AIDS retrovirus infection: Definition of a clinical illness associated with seroconversion. *Lancet, 1*, 537–540.

Cummings, J. L., & Benson, D. F. (1983). *Dementia: A clinical approach*. Boston: Butterworth's.

Darko, D. F., Miller, J. C., Gallen, C., White, J., Koziol, J., Brown, S. J., Hayduk, R., Atkinson, J. H., & Assmus, J. (1995). Sleep encephalogram delta-frequency amplitude, night plasma levels of tumor necrosis factor α, and human immunodeficiency virus infection. *Proceedings of the National Academy of Science, 92*, 12080–12084.

DeCarli, C., Civitello, L. A., Brouwers, P., & Pizzo, P. A. (1993). The prevalence of Computed Axial Tomographic abnormalities of the cerebrum in 100 consecutive children symptomatic with the HIV. *Annals of Neurology, 34*, 198–205.

DeCarli, C., Fugate, L., Falloon, J., Eddy, J., Katz, D. A., Friedland, R. P., Rapoport, S. I., Brouwers, P., &

Pizzo, P. A. (1991). Brain growth and cognitive improvement in children with human immune deficiency virus-induced encephalopathy after six months of continuous infusion azidothymidine therapy. *Journal of Acquired Immune Deficiency Syndromes, 4,* 585–592.

Delis, D. C., Kramer, J. H., & Kaplan, E. (1987). *California Verbal Learning Test: Adult Version Manual.* San Antonio, TX: The Psychological Corporation.

de Martino, M. (1994). Human Immunodeficiency Virus type 1 infection and breast milk. *Acta Paediatrica Supplement, 400,* 51–58.

DePaula, M., Queiroz, W., Llan, Y., Rodriguez-Taveras, C., Janini, M., & Soraggi, N. (1991). Pediatric AIDS: Differentials in survival. *Proceedings of the VII International Conference on AIDS, 2,* 190. (Abstract).

Diamond, G. W. (1989). Developmental problems in children with HIV infection. *Mental Retardation, 27,* 213–217.

Diamond, G. W., Kaufman, J., Belman, A. L., Cohen, L., Cohen, H. J., & Rubinstein, A. (1987). Characterization of cognitive functioning in a subgroup of children with congenital HIV infection. *Archives of Clinical Neuropsychology, 2,* 245–256.

Dickson, D. W., Belman, A. L., Park, Y. D., Wiley, C., Horoupian, D. S., Llena, J., Kure, K., Lyman, W. D., Morecki, R., & Mitsudo, S. (1989). Central nervous system pathology in pediatric AIDS: An autopsy study. *Acta Pathologica Microbiologica, et Immunologica Scandinavica (Suppl.), 8,* 40–57.

Dooneief, G., Bello, J., Todak, G., Mun, J. K., Marder, K., Malouf, R., Gorman, J., Hilal, S., Stern, Y., & Mayeux, R. (1992). A prospective controlled study of magnetic resonance imaging of the brain in gay men and parental drug users with human immunodeficiency virus infection. *Archives of Neurology, 49,* 38–43.

Epstein, L. G., Goudsmit, J., Paul, D. S., Morrison, S. H., Connor, E. M., Oleske, J. M., & Holland, B. (1987). Expression of human immunodeficiency virus in cerebrospinal fluid of children with progressive encephalopathy. *Annals of Neurology, 21,* 397–401.

Epstein, L. G., Sharer, L. R., & Goudsmit, J. (1988). Neurological and neuropathological features of human immunodeficiency virus infection in children. *Annals of Neurology, 23*(Suppl.), S19–S23.

Epstein, L. G., Sharer, L. R., Joshi, V. V., Fogas, M. M., Koenigsberger, M. R., & Oleske, J. M. (1985). Progressive encephalopathy in children with acquired immune deficiency syndrome. *Annals of Neurology, 17,* 488–496.

Epstein, L. G., Sharer, L. R., Oleske, J. M., Connor, E. M., Goudsmit, J., Bagdon, L., Robert-Guroff, M., & Koenigsberger, M. R. (1986). Neurologic manifestations of human immunodeficiency virus infection in children. *Pediatrics, 78,* 678–687.

Everall, I., Luthert, P. J., & Lantos, P. L. (1991). Neuronal loss in the frontal cortex in HIV infection. *Lancet, 337,* 1119–1121.

Everall, I., Luthert, P. J., & Lantos, P. L. (1993). A review of neuronal damage in human immunodeficiency virus infection: Its assessment, possible mechanism and relationship to dementia. *Journal of Neuropathology and Experimental Neurology, 52,* 561–566.

Ewing-Cobbs, L., Fletcher, J. M., Levin, H. S., & Landry, S. H. (1985). Language disorders after pediatric head injury. In J. Darby (Ed.), *Speech and language evaluation* (pp. 97–111). New York: Academic Press.

Falloon, J., Eddy., J., Wiener, L., & Pizzo, P. A. (1989). Human immunodeficiency virus infection in children. *Journal of Pediatrics, 114,* 1–30.

Fama, R., Pace, P. L., Timpiero, A. M., & Bornstein, R. A. (1992). Effects of alcohol and drug use on neuropsychological performance in HIV asymptomatic individuals. *Journal of Clinical and Experimental Neuropsychology, 14,* 79.

Fernandez, F. (1988). Psychiatric complications in HIV-related illnesses. *American Psychiatric Association AIDS primer.* Washington, DC: American Psychiatric Association Press.

Fernandez, F. (1989). Anxiety and the neuropsychiatry of AIDS. *Journal of Clinical Psychiatry, 50*(Suppl.), 9–14.

Fernandez, F., Adams, F., Levy, J. K., Holmes, V. F., Neidhart, M., & Mansell, P. W. (1988). Cognitive impairment due to AIDS-related complex and its response to psychostimulants. *Psychosomatics, 29,* 38–46.

Fernandez, F., Levy, J. K., & Pirozzolo, F. J. (1989, June). *Neuropsychological and immunological abnormalities in advanced HIV infection.* Paper presented at the Fifth International Conference on AIDS, Montreal, Canada.

Filley, C. M. (1996). Neurobehavioral aspects of cerebral white matter disorders. In B. S. Fogel, R. S. Schiffer, & S. M. Rao (Eds.), *Neuropsychiatry: A comprehensive textbook* (pp. 913–933). Baltimore: Williams & Wilkins.

Flowers, C. H., Mafee, M. F., Crowell, R., Raofi, B., Arnold, P., Dobben, G., & Wycliffe, N. (1990). Encephalopathy in AIDS patients: Evaluation with MR imaging. *American Journal of Neuroradiology, 11,* 1235–1245.

Fong, I. W., & Toma, E. (1995). The natural history of progressive multifocal leukoencephalopathy in patients with AIDS. *Clinical Infectious Diseases, 20,* 1305–1310.

Fowler, M. G. (1994). Pediatric HIV infection: Neurologic and neuropsychological findings. *Acta Paediatrica Supplement, 400,* 59–62.

Frank, K. Y., Lim, W., & Kahn, E. (1989). Multiple ischemic infarcts in children with AIDS, varicella zoster infection and cerebral vasculitis. *Pediatric Neurology, 5,* 64–67.

Franzblau, A., Letz, R., Hershman, D., Mason, P., Wallace, J. I., & Bekesi, G. (1991). Quantitative neurologic and neurobehavioral testing of persons infected with human immunodeficiency virus type 1. *Archives of Neurology, 48,* 263–268.

Friedland, G., & Klein, R. (1987). Transmission of the human immunodeficiency virus. *New England Journal of Medicine, 317,* 1125–1135.

Gazbuda, D. H., Levy, S. R., & Chiappa, K. H. (1988). Electroencephalography in AIDS and AIDS-related complex. *Clinical Electroencephalography, 19,* 1–6.

Gottlieb, M., Schroff, R., Schanker, H., Weisman, J., Fan, P., Wolf, R., & Saxon, A. (1981). *Pneumocystis Carinii* pneumonia and mucosal candidiasis in previously healthy homosexual men: Evidence of a newly acquired cellular immunodeficiency. *New England Journal of Medicine, 305,* 1425–1430.

Grant, D. (1988). Support groups for youth with the AIDS virus. *International Journal of Group Psychotherapy, 38,* 237–250.

Grant, I., Atkinson, J. H., Hesselink, J. R., Kennedy, C. J., Richman, D. D., Spector, S. A., & McCutchan, J. A. (1987). Evidence for early central nervous system involvement in the acquired immunodeficiency syndrome (AIDS) and other human immunodeficiency virus (HIV) infections. *Annals of Internal Medicine, 107,* 828–836.

Grant, I., & Martin, A. (1994). Introduction: Neurocognitive disorders associated with HIV-1 infection. In I. Grant & A. Martin (Eds.), *Neuropsychology of HIV infection* (pp. 3–19). New York: Oxford University Press.

Gronwall, D.M.A. (1977). Paced Auditory Serial-Additions Task: A measure of recovery from concussion. *Perceptual and Motor Skills, 44,* 367–373.

Hamilton, M. (1967). Development of rating scale for primary depressive illness. *British Journal of Social and Clinical Psychology, 6,* 278–296.

Hansen, I. C., & Shearer, W. T. (1994). Diagnosis of HIV infection. *Seminars in Pediatric Infectious Diseases, 5*(4), 266–271.

Harris, M. H. (1992). Habilitative and rehabilitative needs of children with HIV infection. In A. C. Crocker, H. J. Cohen, & T. A. Kastner (Eds.), *HIV infection and developmental disabilities: A resource for service providers* (pp. 85–94). Baltimore: Brookes.

Harris, J. G., Cullum, C. M., & Puente, A. E. (1995). Effects of bilingualism on verbal learning and memory in Hispanic adults. *Journal of the International Neuropsychological Society, 1,* 10–16.

Hart, R. P., Wade, J. B., Klinger, R. L., & Levenson, J. L. (1990). Slowed information processing as an early cognitive change associated with AIDS and ARC. *Journal of Clinical and Experimental Neuropsychology, 12,* 72.

Heaton, R. K. (1981). *Wisconsin Card Sorting Test Manual.* Odessa, FL: Psychological Assessment Resources.

Heaton, R. K., Grant, I., Butters, N., White, D. A., Kirson, D., Atkinson, J. H., McCutchan, J. A., Taylor, M. J., Kelly, M. D., Ellis, R. J., Wolfson, T., Velin, R., Marcotte, T. D., Hesselink, T. L., Jernigan, J., Chandler, J., Wallace, M., Abramson, I., & the HNRC Group. (1995). The HNRC 500-neuropsychology of HIV infection at different disease stages. *Journal of the International Neuropsychological Society, 1,* 231–251.

Heyes, M. P., Brew, B. J., Martin, A., Price, R. W., Salazar, A. M., & Sidtis, J. J. (1991). Quinolinic acid in cerebrospinal fluid and serum in HIV-1 infection: Relationship to clinical neurological status. *Annals of Neurology, 29,* 202–209.

Hittleman, J., Willoughby, A., Mendez, H., Nelson, N., Gong, J., Holman, S., Muez, L., Goedert, J., & Landesman, S. (1990). Neurodevelopmental outcome of perinatally-acquired HIV infection on the first 15 months of life. *Proceedings from the VI International Conference on AIDS, 3,* 130. (Abstract).

Hittleman, J., Willoughby, A., Mendez, H., Nelson, N., Gong, J., Mendez, H., Holman, S., Muez, L., Goedert., J., & Landesman, S. (1991). Neurodevelopmental outcome of perinatally-acquired HIV infection on the first 24 months of life. *Proceedings from the VI International Conference on AIDS, 1,* 65. (Abstract).

Ho, D. D., Rota, T. R., Schooley, R. T., Kaplan, J. C., Allan, J. D., Groopman, J. E., Resnick, L., Felsenstein, D., Andrews, C. A., & Hirsch, M. S. (1985). Isolation of HTLV–III from cerebrospinal fluid and neural tissues of patients with neurologic syndromes related to the acquired immunodeficiency syndrome. *New England Journal of Medicine, 313,* 1493–1497.

Hutto, C., Scott, G. B., Parks, E. S., Fischl, M., & Parks, W. P. (1989, June). *Cerebrospinal fluid (CSF) studies in adults and pediatric HIV infections.* Paper presented at the Third International Conference on AIDS, Washington, DC.

Janssen, R., Saykin, J., Cannon, L., Campbell, J., Pinsky, P. F., Hessol, N., O'Malley, P. M., Lifson, A. R., Doll, L. S., Rutherford, G. N., & Kaplan, J. (1989). Neurological and neuropsychological manifestations of human immunodeficiency virus (HIV-1) infection: Association with AIDS-related complex but not asymptomatic HIV-1 infection. *Annals of Neurology, 26,* 592–600.

Jernigan, T.T.L., Archibald, S., Hesselink, J. R., Atkinson, J. H., Velin, R. A., McCutchan, J. A., Chandler, J., & Grant, I. (1993). Magnetic resonance imaging morphometric analysis of cerebral volume loss in human immunodeficiency virus. The HNRC group. *Archives of Neurology, 50,* 250–255.

Kaplan, E. F., Goodglass, H., & Weintraub, S. (1983). *The Boston Naming Test* (2nd ed.). Philadelphia, PA: Lea & Febiger.

Kaufman, A. S. (1975). Factor analysis of the WISC–R at 11 age levels between 6½ and 16½ years. *Journal of Consulting and Clinical Psychology, 43,* 135–147.

Kaufman, A. S., & Kaufman, N. L. (1983). *K-ABC: Kaufman Assessment Battery for children.* Circle Pines, MN: American Guidance Service.

Kløve, H. (1963). Clinical neuropsychology. In F. M. Foster (Ed.), *The medical clinics of North America.* New York: Saunders.

Klusman, L. E., Moulton, J. K., Hornbostel, L. K., Picano, J. J., & Beattie, M. T. (1991). Neuropsychological abnormalities in asymptomatic HIV seropositive military personnel. *Journal of Neuropsychiatry, 3,* 422–428.

Koenig, S., Gendelman, H. E., Orenstein, J., Dal Canto, M. C., Pezeshkpour, G. H., Yungbluth, M., Janotta, F., Aksamit, A., Martin, M. A., & Fauci, A. S. (1986). Detection of AIDS virus in macrophages in brain tissue from AIDS patients with encephalopathy. *Science, 233,* 1089–1093.

Koup, R. A., & Wilson, C. B. (1994). Clinical immunology of HIV infected children. In P. A. Pizzo & K. M. Wilfert (Eds.), *Pediatric AIDS: The challenge of HIV infection in infants, children, and adolescents* (pp. 129–157). Baltimore: Williams & Wilkins.

Kramer, E. L., & Sanger, J. J. (1990). Brain imaging in acquired immunodeficiency syndrome dementia complex. *Seminars in Nuclear Medicine, 20,* 353–363.

Kranczer, S. (1995). U.S. longevity unchanged. *Statistical Bulletin, 76,* 12–20.

Krivine, A., Firtion, G., Cao, L., Francoual, C., Henrion, R., & Lebon, P. (1992). HIV replication during the first weeks of life. *Lancet, 339,* 1187–1189.

Likely, J. J. (1987). Forensic psychological evaluations through an interpreter: Legal and ethical issues. *American Journal of Forensic Psychology, 5,* 29–43.

LaFrance, N., Pearlson, G., Shaerf, F., McArthur, J., Polk, B., Links, J., Bascom, M., Knowles, M., & Galen, S. (1988). I-123 IMP-SPECT in HIV-related dementia. *Advances in Functional Neuroimaging, Fall,* 9–15.

Laosa, L. M. (1984). Ethnic, socioeconomic and home language influences upon early performance on measures of abilities. *Journal of Educational Psychology, 76,* 1178–1198.

Leuchter, A., Newton, T., van Gorp, W., & Miller, E. (1989, May). *Early detection of HIV effects on brain function.* Paper presented at the 142nd annual meeting of the American Psychiatric Association, San Francisco, CA.

Levenson, R. L., Jr., Mellins, C. A., Zawadzki, R., Kairam, R., & Stein, Z. (1992). Cognitive assessment of human immunodeficiency virus-exposed children. *American Journal of Diseases in Children, 146,* 1479–1883.

Levin, B. E., Berger, J. R., Didona, T., & Duncan, R. (1992). Cognitive function in asymptomatic HIV-1 infection: The effects of age, education, ethnicity, and depression. *Neuropsychology, 6,* 303–313.

Levin, H. S., Williams, D. H., Borucki, M. J., Hillman, G. R., Williams, M. B., Guinto, F. C., Amparo, E. G., Crow, W. N., & Pollard, R. B. (1990). Magnetic resonance imaging and neuropsychological findings in human immunodeficiency virus infection. *Journal of Acquired Immune Deficiency Syndrome, 3,* 757–762.

Levy, J. K., & Fernandez, F. (1997). Human immunodeficiency virus infection of the Central Nervous System: Implications for neuropsychiatry. In S. C. Yudofsky & R. E. Hales (Eds.), *Textbook of neuropsychiatry* (3rd. ed., pp. 663–692). Washington, DC: American Psychiatic Press.

Lezak, M. D. (1978). Subtle sequelae of brain damage: Perplexity, distractibility, and fatigue. *American Journal of Physical Medicine, 57,* 9–15.

Llorente, A. M., LoPresti, C. E., & Satz, P. (1997). Neuropsychological and neurobehavioral sequelae associated with pediatric HIV infection. In C. R. Reynolds & E. Fletcher-Janzen (Eds.), *Handbook of clinical child neuropsychology* (2nd. ed., pp. 634–650). New York: Plenum.

Llorente, A. M., Miller, E. N., D'Elia, L. F., Selnes, O. A., Wesch, J., Becker, J. T., & Satz, P. (1998). *Slowed Information Processing in HIV-1 disease, 20,* 60–72.

Llorente, A. M., Pontón, M. O., Taussig, I. M., & Satz, P. (1999). Patterns of American immigration and their influence on the acquisition of neuropsychological norms for Hispanics. *Archives of Clinical Neuropsychology, 14,* 603–614.

LoPresti, C. M., Llorente, A. M., Guzzard, C. R., & Brumm, V. L. (1988, August). Neuropsychological functioning of HIV+ women: Consultation with community-based organizations. Poster presented at the 106th Annual Meeting of the American Psychological Association, Chicago, IL.

Mann, J. M., Tarantola, D. M., & Netter, T. W. (1992). *AIDS in the world.* Cambridge: Harvard University Press.

Marín, G., & Marín, B. V. (1991). *Research with Hispanic populations.* Newbury Park, CA: Sage.

Martin, A., Heyes, M. P., Salazar, A. M., Kampen, M. S., Williams, J., Law, W. A., Coats, M. F., & Markey, S. P. (1992). Progressive slowing of reaction time and increasing cerebrospinal fluid concentrations of quinolinic acid in HIV-infected individuals. *Journal of Neuropsychiatry and Clinical Neuroscience, 4,* 270–279.

Martin, E. M., Robertson, L. C., Edelstein, H. E., Jagust, W. J., Sorensen, D. J., San Giovanni, D., & Chirurgi, V. A. (1992). Performance of patients with early HIV-1 infection on the Stroop Task. *Journal of Clinical and Experimental Neuropsychology, 14*(5), 857–868.

Martin, P. C. (1977). *A Spanish translation, adaptation, and standardization of the Wechsler Intelligence Scale for Children–Revised.* Unpublished doctoral dissertation, University of Miami, FL.

Masliah, E., Achim, C. L., Ge, N., DeTeresa, R., Terry, R. D., & Wiley, C. A. (1992). Spectrum of human immunodeficiency virus associated neocortical damage. *Annals of Neurology, 32,* 321–329.

Masliah, E., Ge, N., Achim, C. L., & Wiley, C. A. (1995). Differential vulnerability of calbindin-immunoreactive neurons in HIV encephalitis. *Journal of Neuropathology and Experimental Neurology, 54,* 350–357.

McAllister, R. H., Herns, M. V., Harrison, M. J. G., Newman, S. P., Connolly, S., Fowler, C. J., Fell, M., Durrance, P., Manji, H., & Kendall, B. E. (1992). Neurologic and neuropsychologic performance in HIV seropositive men without symptoms. *Journal of Neurology, Neurosurgery and Psychiatry, 55,* 143–148.

McArthur, J. C. (1987). Neurologic manifestations of AIDS. *Medicine (Baltimore), 66,* 407–437.

McArthur, J. C. (1994). Neurological and neuropathological manifestations of HIV infection. In I. Grant & A. Martin (Eds.), *Neuropsychology of HIV infection* (pp. 56–107). New York: Oxford University Press.

McArthur, J. C., Cohen, B. A., Selnes, O. A., Kumar, A. J., Cooper, K., McArthur, J. H., Soucy, G., Cornblath, D. R., Chmiel, J. S., & Wang, M. C. (1989). Low prevalence of neurological and neuropsychological abnormalities in otherwise healthy HIV-1-infected individuals: Results from the Multicenter AIDS Cohort Study. *Annals of Neurology, 26,* 601–611.

McArthur, J. C., Nance-Sproon, T. E., Griffin, D. E., Hoover, D., Selnes, O. A., Miller, E. N., Margolick, J. B., Cohen, B. A., Forzadegon, H., & Saah, A. (1992). The diagnostic utility of elevation in cerebral spinal fluid β2-microglobulin in HIV-1 dementia. *Neurology, 42,* 1707–1712.

Miller, E. N., Selnes, O. A., McArthur, J. C., Satz, P., Becker, J. T., Cohen, B. A. Sheridan, K., Machado, A. M., van Gorp, W. G., & Visscher, B. (1990). Neuropsychological performance in HIV-1 infected homosexual men: The Multicenter AIDS Cohort Study (MACS). *Neurology, 40,* 197–203.

Miller, J. R., Barrett, R. E., Britton, C. B., Tapper, M. L, Bahr, G. S., Bruno, P. J., Marquardt, M. D., Hays, A. P., McMurty, J. G., III, Weissman, J. B., & Bruno, M. S. (1982). Progressive multifocal leukoencephalopathy in a male homosexual with T-cell immune deficiency. *New England Journal of Medicine, 307,* 1436–1438.

Mintz, M. (1989). Elevated serum levels of tumor necrosis factor associated with progressive encephalopathy in children with acquired immunodeficiency syndrome. *American Journal of Diseases of Children, 143,* 771–774.

Nair, M.P.N., & Schwartz, S. A. (1994). Immunopathogenesis of HIV infections: CNS-immune interactions. In I. Grant & A. Martin (Eds.), *Neuropsychology of HIV infection* (pp. 41–55). New York: Oxford University Press.

Navia, B., Cho, E. S., Petito, C. K., & Price, R. W. (1986). The AIDS dementia complex: II. Neuropathology. *Annals of Neurology, 19,* 525–535.

Navia, B., Jordan, B., & Price, R. (1986). The AIDS dementia complex: I. Clinical features. *Annals of Neurology, 19,* 517–524.

Nicholas, S. W. (1994). The opportunistic and bacterial infections associated with pediatric Human Immunodeficiency virus disease. *Acta Paediatrica Supplement, 400,* 46–50.

Novello, A. C., Wise, P. H., Willoughby, A., & Pizzo, P. A. (1989). Final report of the United States Department of Health and Human Services Secretary's Work Group on pediatric human immunodeficiency virus infection disease: Content and implications. *Pediatrics, 84,* 547–555.

Nuwer, M. R., Miller, E. N., Visscher, B. R., Niedermeyer, E., Packwood, J. W., Carlson, L. G., Satz, P.,

Jankel, W., & McArthur, J. C. (1992). Asymptomatic HIV infection does not cause EEG abnormalities: Results form the Multicenter AIDS Cohort study (MACS). *Neurology, 42,* 1214–1219.

Ollo, C., & Pass, H. (1988, February). *Neuropsychological performance in HIV disease. Effect of depression and chronic CNS infection.* Paper presented at the 16th annual meeting of the International Neuropsychological Society, New Orleans, LA.

Overall, J. E., & Gomez-Mont, F. (1974). The MMPI-168 for psychiatric screening. *Educational and Psychological Measurement, 34,* 315–319.

Oxtoby, M. J. (1994). Vertically acquired HIV infection in the United States. In P. A. Pizzo and C. M. Wilfert, (Eds.), *Pediatric AIDS: The challenge of HIV infection in infants, children, and adolescents* (2nd ed., pp. 3–20). Baltimore: Williams & Wilkins.

Pang, S., Koyanagi, Y., Miles, S., Wiley, C., Vinters, H., & Chen, I. (1990). High levels of unintegrated HIV-1 DNA in brain tissue of AIDS dementia patients. *Nature, 343,* 85–89.

Park, Y., Belman, A., Dickson, D., Llena, J., Josephina, F., Lantos, G., Diamond, G., Bernstein, L., & Rubinstein, A. (1988). Stroke in pediatric AIDS. *Annals of Neurology, 24,* 279. (Abstract).

Perdices, M., & Cooper, D. (1989). Simple and choice reaction time in patients with human immunodeficiency virus infection. *Annals of Neurology, 25,* 460–467.

Pérez-Arce, P. (1994). The role of culture and SES on cognition. *The Clinical Neuropsychologist, 8,* 350.

Perry, S. W. (1990). Organic mental disorders caused by HIV. Update on early diagnosis and treatment. *American Journal of Psychiatry, 147,* 696–710.

Pizzo, P. A., & Wilfert, C. M. (Eds.). (1994). *Pediatric AIDS: The challenge of HIV infection in infants, children, and adolescents* (2nd ed.). Baltimore: Williams & Wilkins.

Pizzo, P., Eddy, J., Falloon, J., Balis, F., Murphy, R., Moss, H., Wolters, P., Brouwers, P., Jarosinski, P., Rubin, M., Broder, S., Yarchoan, R., Brunetti, A., Maha, M., Nusinoff Lehrman, S., & Poplack, D. (1988). Effect of continuous intravenous infusion of zidovudine (AZT) in children with symptomatic HIV infection. *New England Journal of Medicine, 319,* 889–896.

Pontón, M. O., & Ardila, A. (1999). The future of Hispanic neuropsychology in the U.S. *Archives of Neuropsychology, 14,* 565–580.

Pontón, M. O., & Herrera, L. (1993). The state of the art in cross-cultural neuropsychology: I. Salient Issues. *Journal of Clinical and Experimental Neuropsychology, 15,* 18.

Pontón, M. O., Satz, P., Herrera, L., Ortiz, F., Urrutia, C. P., Young, R., D'Elia. L., Furst, C. J., & Namerow, N. (1996). Normative data stratified by age and education for the Neuropsychological Screening Battery for Hispanics (NeSBHIS): Initial Report. *Journal of the International Neuropsychological Society, 2,* 96–104.

Post, M.J.D., Berger, J. R., & Quencer, R. M. (1991). Asymptomatic and neurologically symptomatic HIV-seropositive individuals: Prospective evaluation with cranial MR imaging. *Radiology, 178,* 131–139.

Post, M., Tate, L., Quencer, R., Hensley, G., Berger, J., Sheremata, W., & Maul, G. (1988). CT, MR, and pathology in HIV encephalitis and meningitis. *American Journal of Radiology, 151,* 373–380.

Price, R. W., & Brew, B. J. (1988). The AIDS dementia complex. *Journal of Infectious Diseases, 158,* 1079–1083.

Prober, C., & Gershon, A. (1991). Medical management of newborns and infants born to seropositive mothers. In P. A. Pizzo & C. M. Wilfert (Eds.), *Pediatric AIDS: The challenge of HIV infection in infants, children, and adolescents* (pp. 516–530). Baltimore: Williams & Wilkins.

Radloff, L. S. (1977). The CES-D scale: A self-report depression scale for research in the general population. *Applied Psychological Measurement, 1,* 385–401.

Redfield, R. R., Wright, D. G., & Tramont, E. C. (1986). The Walter Reed staging classification of HTLV-III/LAV infection. *New England Journal of Medicine, 314,* 131–132.

Resnick, L., diMarzio-Veronese, F., Schüpback, J., Tourtellete, W. W. , Ho, D., Müller, F., Shapshak, P., Vogt, M., Groopman, J. E., & Markham, P. D. (1985). Intra-blood-brain-barrier synthesis of HTLV-III specific IgG in patients with neurological symptoms associated with AIDS or ARC. *New England Journal of Medicine, 313,* 1498–1504.

Resnick, L., Berger, J. R., Shapshak, P., & Tourtellote, W. W. (1988). Early penetration of blood-brain barrier by HIV. *Neurology, 38,* 9–14.

Rey, A. (1941). L'examen psychologique dans les cas d'encéphalopathie traumatique [Psychological examination in cases of traumatic encephalopathy]. *Archives de Psychologie, 28,* 286–340.

Rey, A. (1964). *L'examen clinique au psychologie* [The clinical examination in psychology]. Paris: Press Universitaire de France.

Rogers, M. F. (1989). Modes, rates, and risk factors for perinatal transmission of HIV. *Proceedings of the V International Conference on AIDS, 1,* 199. (Abstract T.B.O.19).

Rogers, M. F., Thomas, P. A., Starcher, E. T., Noa, M. C., Bush, T. J., & Jaffe, J. W. (1987). Acquired immuno-deficiency syndrome in children: Report of the Center for Disease Control National Surveillance, 1982 to 1985. *Pediatrics, 79,* 1008–1014.

Rottenberg, D., Moeller, J., Sidtis, J., Navia, B., Dhawan, V., Ginos, Z., & Price, R. (1987). The metabolic pathology of the AIDS dementia complex. *Annals of Neurology, 22,* 700–706.

Routh, D.K. (Ed.)(1988). *Handbook of pediatric psychology.* New York: Guilford.

Rubinow, D., Berettini, C., Brouwers, P., & Lane, H. (1988). Neuropsychiatric consequences of AIDS. *Annals of Neurology, 23* (Suppl.), S24–S26.

Ryan, J. J., Paolo, A. M., & Skrade, M. (1992). Rey Auditory Verbal Learning Test performance of a federal corrections sample with acquired immunodeficiency syndrome. *International Journal of Neuroscience, 64,* 177–181.

Sacktor, N., van Heertum, R. L., Dooneief, G., Gorman, J., Khandji, A., Marder, K., Nour, R., Todak, G., Stern, Y., & Mayeux, R. (1995). A comparison of cerebral SPECT abnormalities in HIV-positive homosexual men with and without cognitive impairment. *Archives of Neurology, 52,* 1170–1173.

Sarngadharan, M. G., Popovic, M., Bruch, L., Shupbach, J., & Gallo, R. C. (1984). Antibodies reactive with human T-lymphotropic retroviruses (HTLV-III) in the serum of patients with AIDS. *Science, 224,* 506–508.

Satz, P. (1993). Brain reserve capacity on symptom onset after brain injury: A formulation and review of evidence for threshold theory. *Neuropsychology, 7,* 273–295.

Satz, P., Morganstern, H., Miller, E. N., D'Elia, L. F., van Gorp, W., & Visscher, B. (1993). Low education as a possible risk factor for cognitive abnormalities in HIV-1: Findings from the Multicenter AIDS Cohort Study (MACS). *Journal of Acquired Immune Deficiency Syndrome, 6,* 503–511.

Saykin, A., Janssen, R., Sphren, G., Kaplan, J., Spira, T., & Weller, P. (1988). Neuropsychological dysfunction in HIV-infection: Characterization in a lymphadenopathy cohort. *International Journal of Clinical Neuropsychology, 10,* 81–95.

Selnes, O. A., Jacobson, L., Machado, A. M., Becker, J. T., Wesch, J., Miller, E. N. et al. (1991). Normative data for a brief neuropsychological screening battery. Multicenter AIDS Cohort Study. *Perceptual and Motor Skills, 73,* 539–550.

Selnes, O. A., & Miller, E. N. (1994). Development of a screening battery for HIV-related cognitive impairment: The MACS experience. In I. Grant & A. Martin (Eds.), *Neuropsychology of HIV infection* (pp. 176–187). New York: Oxford University Press.

Sharer, L., Cho, E. S., & Epstein, L. G. (1985). Multinucleated giant cells and HTLV-III in AIDS encephalopathy. *Human Pathology, 16,* 760.

Sharer, L. R., Dowling, P., Micheals, J., Cook, S., Menonna, J., Blumberg, B., & Epstein, L. (1990). Spinal cord disease in children with HIV-1 infection: A combined biological and neuropathological study. *Neuropathology of Applied Neurobiology, 16,* 317–331.

Sharer, L. R., Epstein, L. G., Cho, E., Joshi, V. V., Meyenhofer, M. F., Rankin, L. F., & Petito, C. K. (1986). Pathologic features of AIDS encephalopathy in children: Evidence for LAV/HTLV-III infection of brain. *Human Pathology, 17,* 271–284.

Sidtis, J. J., & Price, R. W. (1990). Early HIV-1 infection and the AIDS dementia complex. *Neurology, 40,* 323–326.

Silberstein, C. H., McKegney, F. P., O'Dowd, M. A., Selwin, P. A., Schoenbaum, E., Drucker, E., Feiner, C., Cox, C. P., & Friedland, G. (1987). A prospective longitudinal study of neuropsychological and psychosocial factors in asymptomatic individuals at risk for HTLV-III/LAV infection in a methadone program: Preliminary findings. *International Journal of Neuroscience, 32,* 669–676.

Snider, W., Simpson, D., Nielsen, S., Gold, J., Metroka, C., & Posner, J. (1983). Neurological complications of acquired immune deficiency syndrome: Analysis of 50 patients. *Annals of Neurology, 14,* 403–418.

Sparrow, S. S., Balla, D. A., & Cicchetti, D. V. (1984). *Vineland Adaptive Behavior Scales.* Circle Pines, MN: American Guidance Service.

Sprecher, S., Soumenkoff, G., Puissant, F., & Degueldre, M. (1986). Vertical transmission of HIV in a 15-week fetus [letter]. *Lancet, 2,* 288–289.

Stern, R. A., Singer, N. G., Silva, S. G., Rogers, J. H., Perkins, D. O., Hall, C. D., van der Horst, C. M., & Evans, D. L. (1992). Neurobehavioral functioning in a nonconfounded group of asymptomatic HIV-seropositive homosexual men. *American Journal of Psychiatry, 149,* 1099–1102.

Stern, Y., Marder, K., Bell, K., Chen, J., Dooneief, G., Goldstein, S., Mindry, D., Richards, M., Sano, M., Williams, J., Gorman, J., Ehrhardt, A., & Mayeux, R. (1991). Mulitdisciplinary baseline assessment of homosexual men with and without human immunodeficiency virus infection: III. *Neurologic and neuropsychological findings. Archives of General Psychiatry, 48,* 131–138.

Stern, Y., Sano, M., Williams, J., & Gorman, J. (1989). Neuropsychological consequences of HIV infection. *Journal of Clinical and Experimental Neuropsychology, 11,* 78.

Stern, Y., Sano, M., Morder, K., Mindrey, D., Goldstein, S., Richards, M., & Gorman, J. (1990). Subtle neuropsychological changes in HIV+ gay men. *Journal of Clinical and Experimental Neuropsychology, 12,* 48.

Tardieu, M. (1991, June). Brain imaging in pediatric HIV infection. In A. Belman & A. M. Laverda, chairs, *Pediatric HIV-1 infection: Neurological and neuropsychological aspects.* Symposium conducted at the meeting of the Neuroscience of HIV Infection: Basic and Clinical Frontiers, Padova, Italy.

Tardieu, M., Blanche, S., Duliege, A., Rouzioux, C., & Griscelli, C. (1989). Neurologic involvement and prognostic factors after materno-fetal infection. *Proceedings of the V International Conference on AIDS, 1,* 194. (Abstract).

Tarter, R.E., Edwards, K. L., & van Thiel, D. H. (1988). Perspective and rationale for neuropsychological assessment of medical disease. In R. E. Tarter, D. H. van Thiel, & K. L. Edwards (Eds.), *Medical neuropsychology: The impact of disease on behavior* (pp. 1–10). New York: Plenum.

Tindell, B., Barker, S., Donovan, B., Barnes, T., Roberts, J., Kronenberg, C., Gold, J., Penny, R., Cooper, D., & the Sidney AIDS Study Group. (1988). Characterization of the acute illness associated with human immunodeficiency virus infection. *Archives of Internal Medicine, 148,* 945–949.

Tross, S., Price, R., Navia, B., Thaler, H., Gold, J., & Sidtis, J. (1988). Neuropsychological characterization of the AIDS dementia complex: A preliminary report. *AIDS, 2,* 81–88.

Tuckson, R. (1994). Health care perceptions and needs of America's poor. In P. A. Pizzo & K. M. Wilfert (Eds.), *Pediatric AIDS: The challenge of HIV infection in infants, children, and adolescents* (2nd ed., pp. 963–973). Baltimore: Williams & Wilkins.

Ultmann, M. H., Belman, A. L., Ruff., H. A., Novick, B. E., Cone-Wesson, B., Cohen, J. J., & Rubinstein, A. (1985). Developmental abnormalities in infants and children with acquired immune deficiency syndrome (AIDS) and AIDS-related complex. *Developmental Medicine and Child Neurology, 27,* 563–571.

Ultmann, M. H., Diamond, G. W., Ruff, H. A., Belman, A. L., Novick, B. E., Rubinstein, A., & Cohen, H. J. (1987). Developmental abnormalities in children with acquired immunodeficiency syndrome (AIDS): A follow up study. *International Journal of Neuroscience, 32,* 661–667.

U.S. Bureau of the Census. (1993). 1990 census of population: Social and economic characteristics, United States (1990CP-2-1, November 1993).

van Gorp, W. G., Hinkin, C., Satz, P., Miller, E., & D'Elia, L. F. (1993). Neuropsychological Findings in HIV Infection, Encephalopathy, and Dementia. In R. W. Parks, R. F. Zec, & R. S. Wilson (Eds.), *Neuropsychology of Alzheimer's disease and other dementias* (pp. 153–185). New York: Oxford University Press.

van Gorp, W., Hinkin, C., Freeman, D., Satz, P., Weisman, J., Rothman, P., Scarsella, A., & Buckingham, S. (1990, July). *Depressed vs. non-depressed mood and its effect on neuropsychological test performance among HIV-1 seropositive individuals.* Paper presented at the conference on neurological and neuropsychological complications on HIV infection: A satellite conference to the VI international AIDS conference, Monterey, CA.

van Gorp, W., Mandelkern, M., Gee, M., Hinkin, C., Stern, C., Paz, D., Dixon, W., Evans, G., Flynn, F., Frederick, C., Ropchan, J., & Bland, W. (1992). Cerebral metabolic dysfunction in AIDS: Findings in an AIDS sample with and without dementia. *Journal of Neuropsychiatry and Clinical Neurosciences, 4,* 280–287.

van Gorp, W. G., Miller, E. N., Satz, P., & Visscher, B. (1989). Neuropsychological performance in HIV-1 immunocompromised patients: A preliminary report. *Journal of Clinical and Experimental Neuropsychology, 11,* 763–773.

Vinters, H. V., Tomiyasu, U., & Anders, K. H. (1989). Neuropathological complications of infection with the human immunodeficiency virus (HIV). *Progress in AIDS Pathology, 1,* 101–130.

Wechsler, D. (1974). *Wechsler Intelligence Scale for Children–Revised.* New York: Psychological Corporation.

Wechsler, D. (1981). *Wechsler Adult Intelligence Scale–Revised.* New York: Psychological Corporation.

Wechsler, D. (1982). *Escala de Inteligencia Wechsler para Niños–Revisada.* New York: Psychological Corporation.

Wechsler, D. (1987). *Wechsler Memory Scale–Revised.* New York: Psychological Corporation.

Whelan, M. A., Kricheff, I., Handler, M., Ho, V., Crystal, K., Gopinathan, G., & Laubenstein, L. (1983). Acquired immunodeficiency syndrome: Cerebral computed tomographic manifestations. *Radiology, 149,* 477–484.

Wiegand, M., Möller, A. A., Schreiber, W., Krieg, J. C., & Holsboer, F. (1991). Alterations of nocturnal sleep in patients with HIV infection. *Acta Neurologica Scandinavian, 83,* 141–142.

Wiener, L., & Septimus, A. (1994). Psychosocial support for child and family. In P. A. Pizzo & K. M. Wilfert

(Eds.), *Pediatric AIDS: The challenge of HIV infection in infants, children, and adolescents* (2nd ed., pp. 809–829). Baltimore: Williams & Wilkins.

Wiley, C. A., Masliah, E., Morey, M., Lemere, C., DeTeresa, R., Grafe, M., Hansen, L., & Terry, R. (1991). Neocortical damage during HIV infection. *Annals of Neurology, 29,* 651–657.

Wilkie, F. L., Eisdorfer, C., Morgan, R., Loewenstein, D. A., & Szapocznik, J. (1990). Cognition in early human immunodeficiency virus infection. *Archives of Neurology, 29,* 651–657.

Williams, J., Rickert, V., Hogan, J., Zolten, A. J., Satz, P., D'Elia, L. F., Asarnow, R. F., Zaucha, K., & Light, R. (1995). Children's Color Trails. *Archives of Clinical Neuropsychology, 10,* 211–223.

Wolters, P., Brouwers, P., Moss, H., el-Amin, D., Eddy, J., Butler, K., Husson, R., & Pizzo, P. (1990). The effect of 2'3' dideoxyinosine (ddI) on the cognitive functioning of infants and children with symptomatic HIV infection. *Proceedings of the VI International Conference on AIDS, 3,* 130 (Abstract).

Wolters, P., Brouwers, P., Moss, H., el-Amin, D., Gress, J., Butler, L., & Pizzo, P. (1991). The effect of dideoxyinosine on the cognitive functioning of children with HIV infection after 6 and 12 months of treatment. *Proceedings from the VII International Conference on AIDS, 2,* 194 (Abstract).

Wolters, P., Brouwers, P., Moss, H., & Pizzo, P. (1994). Adaptive behavior of children with symptomatic HIV infection before and after Zidovudine therapy. *Journal of Pediatric Psychology, 19,* 47–61.

World Health Organization. (1996). *Weekly Epidemiological Record, 71,* 205–212.

Neurobehavioral Disorders

JOSÉ LEÓN-CARRIÓN
University of Seville, Spain

Hispanics, that is to say, those persons who live in the United States but were born in Central or South America, along with their descendants who live with them, can suffer from the same neurological disorders as non-Hispanics living in the United States. The variation is found in the severity of incidence and especially how they cope with their illness in an environment that—in regards to language, social organization, cultural memory, interests, and motivations—is different from their own. Therefore the clinical manifestations of the neurological disorders are metasymptoms that the professionals should not misinterpret. The symptoms and complaints shown by these patients should be understood in their context; more importantly, some of the behavioral gestures, or the way they express their feelings, are not symptoms, but references to their cultural origin. When Hispanic patients with brain damage say, "May God and the Virgin help me," or they say that they speak with God to solve their problems, for example, they are not referring to delusions, but to how they live their religion. Table 12.1 shows the values to be considered when carrying out any type of neuropsychological intervention with ethnic minorities in a multicultural society.

NEUROLOGICAL DISORDERS AND MULTICULTURAL SOCIETY

Hispanics living in the United States feel they live in a multicultural society, and they come with their own culture to a country with a precise structure, where diverse ethnic and cultural minorities live. Hispanics in the United States are considered to be a minority, and therefore make up a *cultural minority* within a society where different cultures cohabitate. Therefore, their normal behavior and their behavior when ill follow a multicultural, as opposed to a monocultural, pattern. In other words, they do not act as if they were living in a monocultural society, or in a homogeneous culture, as would be the case in their country of origin.

They live more in a multicultural environment than in a cross-cultural one. A cross-cultural country does not exist; a country may only be monocultural or multicultural. When the cultures from different countries are compared from their country of origin, a cross-cultural analysis is offered. When these same cultures collectively establish themselves in another country, however, they resemble multiculturality. That is why the stud-

TABLE 12.1
Value Dimensions for Five Major Groups

| Group | Dimension* | | | | |
	Human Nature	Person–Nature Relationship	Time Focus	Relationships	Activity
Anglo-American	Evil	Mastery of Nature	Future	Individual	Doing
African American	Good/evil	Harmony with nature	Future	Individual	Doing
Asian American	Good	Subjugation to nature	Past	Lineal	Being-in-Becoming
Hispanic American	Good/evil	Subjugation to nature	Present	Lineal	Being
Native American	Good/evil	Harmony with nature	Present	Collateral	Being/Doing

Note: Reprinted from Dana (1993).

* These dimensions are subject to extreme within-group variations due to age, generation, and cultural orientation. They are used here as illustrative guidelines.

ies that interest neuropsychology with Hispanic populations are those that are multicultural. Cross-cultural studies are interesting in their general development of psychology and neuropsychology, but they are not essential for this book. It is interesting to know a Venezuelan's neuropsychological profile, but this is auxiliary knowledge, because the Venezuelan emigrant in the United States leaves a monocultural society to integrate into a multicultural society with different sociocultural rules. Furthermore, in psychology, multiculturalism is a social-intellectual movement that promotes the value of diversity as a core principal and insists that all cultural groups be treated with respect and as equals (Fowers & Richardson, 1996).

This multiculturalness obviously affects the members of each culture's health and illness. In addition, it definitively affects the way they use health services. Regarding services used and cultural competence, Dana (1993) explained it clearly:

> Mental health services in the United States were originally designed by middle-class Anglo-Americans for clients who were similar to themselves. Populations from other cultures were provided services on the basis of the belief that these clients were either highly similar to Anglo-Americans or would inevitably become more similar over time as they assimilated into the melting pot of American society. As a result these services were underutilized because they were often perceived by potential consumers as inappropriate and/or ineffective. . . . Multicultural persons have been less likely to seek services, and the services they received differed in kind and/or quality from services delivered to Anglo-Americans. (pp. 2–3)

And so, patients with brain damage in a multicultural society feel lost and abandoned if they do not find professionals with sufficient cultural competence to assist them. This cultural competence requires training and should indispensably include the knowledge of what it means to be Hispanic in the United States today (see chap. 1) and also know their values, beliefs, motivations, and social organization in the multicultural society they live in. The first step to establish the correct diagnosis, at the right time, in a patient with a neurological deficit is to understand what the patient means to say. Are clinical neuropsychologists prepared for service and research with Hispanic patients? This question is answered by Bernel and Castro (1994) when found that, although in the last years much change has occurred in clinical psychology's preparation of psychologists for work with ethnic minorities, even greater changes are needed. Also, as noted by Artiola i Fortuny and Mullaney (1997), those psychologists that want to have Hispanic clients and wish to work with them with dignity may wish to determine their level of fluency and they can do so easily by taking an advanced language proficiency examination offered by university language departments. Formal training of individuals who possess advanced native competence in all dimensions of the Spanish language needs to be encouraged, especially in geographic areas with high densities of Spanish-speakers.

Neurological disorders should be detected as early as possible so they can be treated with the greatest efficiency. It therefore requires adequate politics to facilitate multiculturality in health services. According to Miranda, Azocar, Organista, and Lieberman (1996, p. 870), "Availability and accessibility to health services are the main important reason in Latinos' general underutilization of services. Lack of insurance, time, child care, transportation, etc. . . . are instrumental barriers to health care in ethnic minorities and low socio-economic status" (see also B. Marin, G. Marin, Padilla, & de la Rocha, 1983; Norquist & Wells, 1991; Takeuchi, Leaf, & Kuro, 1988).

CEREBROVASCULAR DISORDERS

Introduction

This section is called cerebrovascular "disorders" and not cerebrovascular "accidents" because it can be proven that the causes that provoke these disorders are not accidental; in fact, the majority are predictable. It seems clear that obesity, daily alcohol intake, sodium and potassium consumption, hypertension and physical activity, among others, are all totally preventable and therefore controllable (Bornstein & Brown, 1991; Gillman, Cook, & Evans, 1995; Green & Peled, 1992; Kannel, Wolf, & Verter, 1984; Martínez, Izquierdo, & Balanzategui, 1987; Mora & Ocón, 1989; Nan, Tuomilehto, & Dowse, 1991). So, for example, according to the American Heart Association (1994), if patients take preventative measures to lower systolic arterial pressure only 2 mm Hg, this could prevent approximately 18,000 fatal heart attacks and 13,000 cerebrovascular accidents per year. A healthy diet rich in fruits and vegetables, polyunsaturated oils, balanced consumption of carbohydrates and proteins, daily physical exercise, and so on, shows that the majority of cerebrovascular disorders can be prevented, and are therefore not accidents but disorders owing to organic factors related to lifestyle. Table 12.2 shows the modifiable vascular risk factors and those that are not modifiable.

The epidemiology of the cerebrovascular disorders is varied in function of the different risk variables studied: age, gender, race, hypertension, cardiac disease, smoking, and so on. According to Thompson and Furlan (1996; see Table 12.3),

> Only recently has information regarding how stroke affects Hispanics been reported. The stroke risk for Hispanic is similar to that of non-Hispanic white in the population aged between 45 and 59 but is slightly lower in the population older than or equal to 75 years of age. Even though stroke risk is similar for Hispanic and non-Hispanic whites, there is a greater incidence of fatal strokes in younger Hispanic white (45–59 years of age). Hispanics older than 75 years, however, have a statistically lower incidence in stroke mortality compared to non-Hispanic whites. These observations have been attributed to the smaller proportion of older Hispanic whites relative to older non-Hispanic whites in their respective populations and a marginally lower stroke mortality risk. (p. 316; see Howard et al., 1994)

In regard to the prognosis, according to the American Heart Association, nearly 80% of stroke patients survive their first attack, but 10 years later the survival rate is around 50%. Only 10% of the patients can return to work normally, 80% will retain mild or severe

TABLE 12.2
Main Cardio- and Cerebrovascular Risk Factors

Not Modifiable	Modifiable
Age	Arterial hypertension
Male	Tobacco*
Postmenopause	Obesity*
Genetic factors	Hypercholesterol 2*
Heart disease	Alcohol*
Mellitus diabetes	Sedentary lifestyle*
	Left ventricle hypertrophy
	Insulin resistance
	Fibrogen
	Lipoprotein A
	Microalbuminuria

Note: Data are from Banegas (1995).
   * Easily controllable and highly preventative factors

TABLE 12.3
Risk Factors for Stroke

Risk Factor	Features
Hypertension	Increases the risk of ischemic stroke *3.1 in men* and *2.1 in women* The more elevation in blood pressure the more the risk whether systolic or diastolic +65 years old with isolated hypertension, twice the incidence of cerebral infarction
Age	Deaths caused by stroke increase with age, around 88% among > 65-year-old people Low death rate under age 45 Risk of stroke about 5% in age 55–59 Risk of stroke about 25% in age > 80
Cardiac Disease	Increase in risk of stroke Low atrial fibrillation, lowest risk of stroke (< 3% per year) Atrial fibrillation with mitrial stenosis risk increases by a factor of 17
Gender	Men higher risk of stroke-related death than women
Smoking	A factor risk of stroke, independent of age and hypertension The more cigarettes smoked, the higher the risk Risk increased 40% in men and 60% in women Risk of stroke declined rapidly with cessation of smoking returning to the risk of a non-smoker within 5 years

Note: For more detailed information, see Thompson and Furlan (1996).

disabilities, and 10% will require institutional care (Sahs, Hartman, & Aronson, 1979). The fatality rate during the first 30 days following a vascular disorder is varied and depends on the type of stroke. The 30-day case fatality rate is 46% for subarachnoid hemorrhage, and 67% for intracerebral hemorrhage. Long-term survival is also varied after surviving the first episode. According to Ozer, Materson, and Caplan (1996):

> Those patients with atherothrombotic infarction (ABI) who were free of hypertension and cardiac complications survived nearly as well at the end of the 5 years as did the general population in the same age group. For men with both cardiac morbidity and hypertension, the

cumulative 5-year survival rate was reduced from 85% to 35%. Cardiac comorbidity alone reduced the ABI 5-year survival rate in men substantially—from 69% to 41%. Hypertension alone reduced the male survival rate to 51%. For women, there was somewhat less effect; however, in the presence of both risk factors, a substantial reduction (from 70% to 55%) was seen in 5-year survival rates. For a second stroke after ABI, men experienced a 42% 5-year cumulative recurrence rate and women a 24% rate, despite a similarity in age in the two groups. (p. 3)

Main Issues

The diagnostic for cerebrovascular disorders is made after the sudden apparition of neurological and neuropsychological deficits that are suspected to be of vascular origin given its clinical characteristics. At times, the symptoms are confused with those of stroke: subdural hematoma, brain tumor, epilepsy, and even cardiac or respiratory arrest (see Fig. 12.1). It is classic to distinguish between the principal types of cerebrovascular disorders: embolism, thrombosis, hemorrhage (see Fig. 12.2), cerebral infarction, and lacunar infarction.

An *embolia* occurs when globular material or embolus of cardiac or noncardiac origin occlude a blood vessel. This normally occurs because the embolia travels through the blood vessels and when it comes across one of larger size they become "jammed" between the walls forming a plug. Therefore, the majority of times the cerebral attack is sudden. The most affected cerebral artery is the middle cerebral artery.

A *thrombosis* is, actually, the occlusion of blood vessels owing to the growth of their walls or accumulation of a thrombo or plaque, which impedes the normal and sufficient blood supply to the brain provoking neurological and neuropsychological disorders. The origins may be many and varied: arteriosclerosis, inflammatory disorder, leukemia, and so on, as well as alterations in cerebral circulation after a myocardial infarction, traumatic brain injury, and so on.

A *hemorrhage* is the massive entry of blood, normally, inside the brain: in the subarachnoid space, intraventricularly, or subdurally. These causes are also varied: hypertension, a break in aneurysm, arterial malformation, and traumatic brain injury, among others. It may be classified as intracerebral or subarachnoid hemorrhage.

A *cerebral infarction* occurs as a result of obstruction of local circulation producing a regional neural tissue death, and represent from 70% to 80% of acute strokes. An estimated 15% of cerebral infarctions are due to cardiac embolism, usually atrial fibrillation or ischemic heart disease. Others are large artery atherothrombotic infarctions and small artery lacunes, at least 20% of cerebral infarction remains unknown (Thompson & Furlan, 1996). The severity of the picture depends on the length of the hypoxic to the tissue.

A *lacunar infarction* is a vasculo-occlusive disease. In these cases, the distal branches of the artery may occlude and produce thrombosis so small that they do not show clear and specific neurological symptoms. It is very common in chronic hypertension. The most frequent locations of lacunar infarction are the putamen, caudete region, thalamus, pons, internal capsule, and cerebral white matter. There may also be symptomatic lacunar lesions producing pure motor hemiplegia, disartria, and paresthesis (see Fig. 12.2).

Neuropsychological Features of Cerebrovascular Disorders

The first thing to consider is that cerebrovascular disorders generally occur in those persons over age 45. The risk of stroke for people between age 55 and 59 is 5%, increasing to

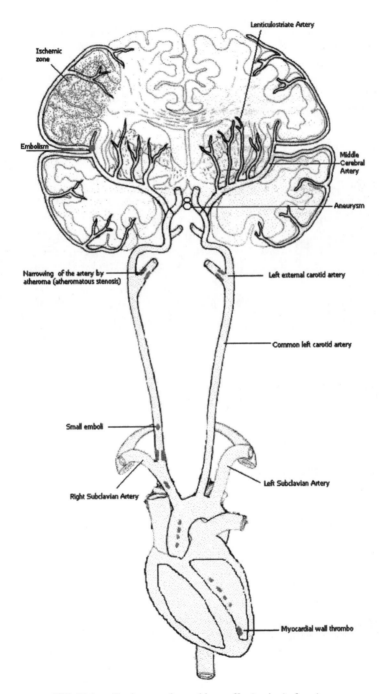

FIG. 12.1. Cerebrovascular problems affecting brain functions.

almost 25% for people between age 80 and 84. According to Thompson and Furlan (1996), "The proportion of deaths caused by stroke also increases with age, estimated at 88% among people older than age 65 years. The risk of death from stroke in young people (younger than 45 years) is low: fewer than 10 deaths per 100,000 population" (p. 309). Therefore, neurogerontological and developmental neuropsychology factors must be kept in mind. Those psychological functions affected by age, as well as those that are not, must be considered when performing the neuropsychological assessment. Another aspect to consider is the prestroke neuropsychological state of the patient. In a study being completed by a research group at the University of Seville using patients undergoing coronary bypass, it has been noted that the majority of these patients have a prior cerebral affectation accompanied by evident neuropsychological deficits. It is possible that the patient's vascular disorders have been making themselves noticeable neuropsychologically, more or less subtly, even years before the cerebrovascular disorder became evident from a neurological point of view.

Therefore, the neuropsychological aspects of cerebrovascular disorders must be considered from different views because they may affect a wide area of human psychological activity. At the same time, the importance of the areas affected is narrowly related to the patient's lifestyle and the magnitude of the lesion (Fig. 12.3).

Lesion magnitude is one of the most important factors to take into account and *localizing the lesion* gives information about the stroke mechanism as well as the nature of the

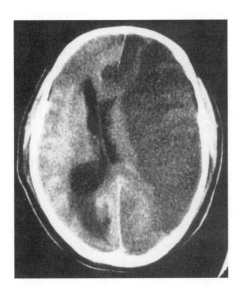

FIG. 12.2.   Patient with a massive left CVA. A significant displacement of the midline is observed along with herniation of the cingulate.

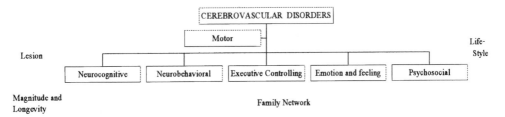

FIG. 12.3.   Neuropsychological impairment by cerebrovascular disorders.

neurological deficits associated with it (as seen in Table 12.4). Evidently, the larger the size of the lesion, the more functions are affected.

Neurocognitive deficits are commonly observed after stroke, any of which may produce, depending on the size of the lesion, disorders affecting one or various functions. As a recommendation, when an "apparently" isolated neuropsychological symptom appears, an attempt must be made for a finer and more precise evaluation because other disturbances with more subtle symptomology will probably appear. *Life style* is associated with cerebrovascular disorders not only as one of the possible trigger factors, but also as an essential factor when determining the importance that the neurological defects after stroke have for the patient. The patients' activity level and the type and number of activities in which they are involved require the use of determined and, at times, selected neuropsychological functions. When the required functions are affected by the cerebrovascular defects, the impact on patients and their surroundings is bigger.

Another factor to consider is the *family network*. The family is an important factor in Hispanic cultures. The family consists not only of a married couple and their children, but there also exists a network in which feelings and emotions have an important role. An affective network exists that affects all members of the family, that is to say, parents, children, aunts, uncles, nieces and nephews, cousins, and so on. The meaning of life in Hispanic cultures includes the whole family. Therefore, when a member of the family suffers from any problem—in this case a cerebrovascular disorder—the problem is felt by the whole family, and in general, all are willing to collaborate to help in the solution. This fact is especially important when evaluating the importance of the stroke suffered by the patient and in planning poststroke rehabilitation.

Prognostic Factors

In cerebrovascular disorders, it seems as if the sequelae are more or less established around the fourth posttrauma month. Until then, there is hope for a spontaneous recuperation. It has been proven that 500,000 people each year suffer from strokes in the United States, half die before a month is up, 40% are incapacitated due to a neurological sequelae, 10% have prolonged hospital stays, and only 10% recover sufficiently to reincorporate themselves in daily life activities. Neuropsychological rehabilitation programs are important in treating cerebrovascular disorders.

The recuperation period varies for survivors of stroke and there are no fixed periods. However, patients begin recuperation after 1 or 2 weeks. Recovery is a gradual process and may take weeks, months, or even years. The first phase of treatment is medical and treats at the same time the possible complications derived from the disorder: For example, if patients cannot swallow properly, an attempt is made to feed them with a nasogastric tube. Anticoagulants are used to present future thrombosis or clots from forming. But one important part of the treatment is the exercises that help patients improve their posture, movements, speech, and cognitive functions. It is in these situations that the neuropsychologist plays an important role (see Fig. 12.4).

Surgical revascularization procedures are being used to prevent a first or recurrent thromboembolic stroke, but there are discrepancies about the conductual benefits, as expressed by Baird (1991):

> We lack strong evidence that most patients manifest behavioral improvements after surgery. We have not identified consistent similarities among the few patients who have shown behavioral improvement after the procedures, much less formulated a strategy for identifying these

TABLE 12.4
Common Stroke Localization Patterns

1. *Large hemisphere lesions* (full middle cerebral artery territory infarcts, large putaminal ICH)
   Contralateral hemiaparesis, hemisensory loss, hemianopsia, neglect
   Decreased alertness, eyes deviated ipsilaterally, and contralateral gaze paresis
   Left lesion: global aphasia
   Right lesion: left neglect, anosognosia, motor impersistence

2. *Frontal lobe dorsolateral suprasylvian lesion* (upper division middle cerebral artery, frontal lobe hematomas)
   Contralateral hemiparesis and hemisensory loss (mostly arm, hand, face); eyes conjugatedly deviated ipsilaterally with contralateral gaze palsy
   Left lesion: Broca's aphasia
   Right lesion: left neglect, motor impersistence

3. *Temporal lobe and inferior parietal lobe lesions* (inferior division middle cerebral artery infarcts, temporal lobe hematomas)
   Contralateral hemianopia or upper quadrantanopia
   Left lesion: Wernicke type of aphasia
   Right lesion: poor drawing and copying ability; agitated delirium

4. *Medial frontal lesions* (anterior cerebral artery territory infarcts)
   Contralateral lower extremity and shoulder weakness; cortical-type sensory loss in the foot; abulia; left arm apraxia

5. *Occipital lobe lesions, unilateral* (posterior cerebral artery territory infarcts, occipital lobe hematomas)
   Contralateral hemianopia or upper or lower quadrantanopia
   Left lesion: alexia without agraphia
   Right lesion: disorientation to place

6. *Bilateral occipital lobe and temporal lobe lesions* (top of basilar embolism)
   Cortical blindness; Balint's syndrome features; prosopagnosia; achromatopsia; amnesia; agitated delirium

7. *Cerebellar lesions* (cerebellar infarcts and hemorrhages)
   Gait ataxia; dysarthia; veering and learning to ipsilateral side; ipsilateral CN VI or conjugate gaze paresis

8. *Brainstem lesions, bilateral* (basilar artery occlusion, pontine hematomas)
   Diplopia; internuclear opthalmoplegia; nystagmus; crossed motor or sensory signs (ipsilateral cranial nerve to contralateral limbs); bilateral motor, sensory, or cerebellar signs

9. *Small, deep white matter or unilateral brainstem lesions* (lacunes or atheromatous branch occlusions, small hematomas)
   Pure motor hemiparesis: weakness of contralateral face, arm, and leg with no cognitive, behavioral, sensory, or visual signs (lesions in internal capsule or pons)
   Pure sensory stroke: paresthesia or numbness of contralateral face, arm, leg, and trunk with no cognitive, behavioral, motor, or visual signs (lesion in lateral thalamus or pontine tegmentum)
   Ataxic hemiparesis: mixed contralateral paresis and ataxia with pyramidal signs (lesion in posterior limb of capsule or pons)

10. *Lateral thalamic lesions* (thalamogeniculate artery occlusions, small lateral thalamic hematomas)
    Contralateral parasthesia or numbness; contralateral hemiataxia, hemichorea, or hemidystonia

11. *Lateral medullary lesions* (intracranial vertebral artery occlusions, branch circumferential artery occlusions)
    Ipsilateral Horner's syndrome, decreased pain, and temperature loss of the face; hoarseness; palatal and laryngeal palsy; mystagmus; limb and gait ataxia; lateral pulsion of the eyes
    Contralateral loss of pain and temperature on trunk and limbs

12. *Frontal lobe, caudate nucleus, and anterolateral thalamic lesions* (small infarcts or hematomas)
    Abulia; sloppiness; poor organization; poor confrontational memory

Note: Adapted from Caplan (1994).

FIG. 12.4.   A patient training her paralyzed face muscle in a rehabilitation session using the REMIOCOR-02 computerized rehabilitation system. (Courtesy of Center for Brain Injury Rehabilitation [C.RE.CER], Seville, Spain)

patients before surgery. However, limitations in study designs available thus far and continuing technical advances by neurosurgeons and neurophysiologists suggest the need for restraint in drawing final conclusions about the possible behavioral benefits of cerebral revascularization in more precisely selected patient populations. (p. 310)

One of the most upsetting questions and for which a lack of response provokes the greatest anxiety for patients and their family is to know if once a stroke is suffered it is more probable that patients will suffer another. The answer is that no one is sure whether patients will necessarily suffer another. However, if patients do not follow some healthy behavioral rules, then it may possibly occur. But the chances are much lower if blood pressure is reduced, because this is the main source of this disorder. Therefore, hypertension should be treated and it is important to know that when the treatment is interrupted, the blood pressure may increase again and be very dangerous. It seems that aspirin prevents clotting, although the correct dose remains undiscovered. Other aspects to keep in mind are if the patient should quit smoking, lose weight if there is an excess, moderate the use of alcoholic beverages and salt, adjust diet adequately, and exercise regularly.

TRAUMATIC BRAIN INJURY

Introduction

Traumatic Brain Injury (TBI) is one of the most frequent causes of mortality and disability in the United States in people under age 45. The estimated incident rate oscillates between 160 and 375 per 100,000 persons per year (Annegers, Grabow, & Kurland,

1980; Jagger, Levine, Jane, & Rimel, 1984; Whitman, Conley-Hoganson, & Dasay, 1984). A study done in Spain by Forastero, Prieto-Lucena, and Gamero (1992) deduced that of the total number of neurotraumatology visits in a large trauma hospital, 4.7% were there for brain injury. Of these patients (81.5% men and 18.6% women), 7.3% had to be admitted to the Intensive Care Unit (ICU) due to severe brain injury. The *profile* compiled from those with severe TBI that needed to be hospitalized coincides with the majority of other European countries. So, in Spain, the candidate to suffer a severe TBI is a male, between age 20 and 40, suffering from a brain lesion as the result of a traffic accident, generally on a motorcycle on the weekend, usually in the early morning, especially Fridays and Saturdays. These patients generally show a space occupying lesion, and often some type of associated traumatic lesion. Most were under the effect of drugs or alcohol at the moment of the accident. They stay in the hospital for 20 to 30 days, and during this time, depending on the severity of the trauma suffered, they have a 20% chance of dying.

In the United States, the group at highest risk for traumatic brain injury is those between age 15 and 24 (Annegers et al., 1980; Kraus, 1992), and also especially those involved in motor vehicle crashes. Table 12.5 shows the intracranial diagnosis correlated with outcome at hospital discharge.

There is not much reliable data on the epidemiology of traumatic brain injury for Hispanics in the United States, but all the data suggest that the socioeconomic and cultural level is closely associated to risky behavior, and therefore to suffer accidents that may produce brain injury (León-Carrión, 1994). This is to say, it is the socioeconomic and cultural status responsible for the epidemiological data in brain injury, not ethnicity. In this way, regarding ethnicity and socioeconomic status, according to Kraus and McArthur (1996),

> In the United States, blacks have higher rates of brain injury and associated death than other groups; such rates appear to stem from increased exposure to firearms and higher rates of homicide. US data from 1992 demonstrated a brain contusion rate of 4.3 per 100 in whites and Hispanics compared with a rate of 4.7 per 100 in blacks. . . . Accordingly, in 1992, Hispanics and blacks in Los Angeles County were disproportionately more likely than whites to be killed in homicides or motor vehicle crashes. In the United States, individuals from the lowest income levels incur the highest numbers of injuries of all types on a per capita basis. This socioeconomic finding also was true for TBI in studies in San Diego County and Chicago. The San Diego study demonstrated that the association between injury and low socioeconomic status was not modified by race or ethnicity. Cultural differences have a profound effect on patterns of disease and death. In general, minority populations of the urban United States are often of lower socioeconomic status and have an elevated risk for injury. A relationship between ethnicity and head injury was suggested in a complex analysis of cognitive impairment in blacks, Mexican-Americans, and Whites by Molgaard et al. (pp. 441–442)

Main Types of Brain Injury

A new classification of head injury has been developed recently by L. F. Marshall, Marshall, and Klauber (1992, p. S-15). This was considered important in order to permit a more accurate description of types of injuries patients may suffer, and to assess the relation between the patterns of brain injury determined by CT and, in part, by clinical examination. The authors intended with this new classification to facilitate the identification of those patients at risk of impairment, and to provide a better prognosis of the outcome, as well as the duration of treatment. This classification is recommended because it is easy to

TABLE 12.5
Intracranial Diagnosis Correlated with Outcome at Hospital Discharge

GOS at Discharge	Diffuse Injury I (No Visible Pathology)		Diffuse Injury II		Diffuse Injury III (Swelling)		Diffuse Injury IV (Shift)		Evacuated Mass		Nonevacuated Mass		Brainstem Injury		Unknown		Total Cases	
	$N°$	%	$N°$	%	$N°$	%	$N°$	%	$N°$	%	$N°$	%	$N°$	%	$N°$	%	$N°$	%
Good	14	27.0	15	8.5	5	3.3	1	3.1	14	5.1	1	2.8	0	0	0	0	50	7.0
Moderate disability	18	34.6	46	26.0	20	13.1	1	3.1	49	17.7	3	8.3	0	0	1	5.9	138	18.5
Severe disability	10	19.2	72	40.7	41	26.8	6	18.8	72	26.1	7	19.4	1	33.3	0	0	209	28.0
Vegetative	5	9.6	20	11.3	35	22.9	6	18.8	34	12.3	6	16.7	0	0	0	0	106	14.0
Dead	5	9.6	24	13.5	52	34.0	18	56.2	107	38.8	19	52.8	2	66.7	16	94.1	243	32.5
Totals	52	100	177	100	153	100	32	100	276	100	36	100	3	100	17	100	746	100

Note: From L. F. Marshall, Gautille, and Klauber (1991).

understand and makes it simple to get an idea of the severity of the injury. This classification, along with the Glasgow Coma Scale (GCS) and other indexes of severity and prognosis, gives a clear picture of the patient's true condition.

Marshall et al. (1992) proposed five categories of abnormal CT scan types. The first is Diffuse Injury I, with no visible pathology, which is defined as an absence of intracranial pathology seen on a CT scan. The second, Diffuse Injury II, is defined as present cisterns with a midline shift of 0–5 mm and/or present lesion densities, no high or mixed density lesions > 25 cc or may include bone fragments and foreign bodies. The third is Diffuse Injury III (swelling), which shows cisterns compressed or absent with a midline shift of 0–5 mm and no high or mixed-density lesion > 25 cc. Diffuse Injury IV (shift), which is the fourth, shows a midline shift of > 5 mm, no high or mixed-density lesions > 25 cc. Finally, they defined evacuated mass lesion as any lesion that is surgically evacuated and nonevacuated mass lesion as high or mixed density lesion > 25 cc which is not surgically evacuated.

A trauma is classified as *very severe* when the patient receives a score on the GCS lower than 6; as *severe* if the score is from 7 to 9; *moderate* if the score is from 10 to 12; and *mild* if the score is over 13. According to the posttraumatic amnesia period (once awake), the TCE is very severe when it lasts more than 7 days, severe when it lasts 1 to 7 days, moderate when it lasts from 1 to 24 hours, and mild when it lasts less than an hour.

In clinical practice, the depth of coma is measured by the GCS. The GCS is an instrument used to describe the posttraumatic states with consciousness alterations. States from mild confusion that correspond to high scores on the scale to deepest coma with low GCS scores can be described using this scale. The GCS is divided into three dimensions (open eyes, verbal response, and motor response), with four levels in each. The score range oscillates between 3 (minimum score) and 15 points (maximum score); a score of 8 points or more the first days following the accident is considered a prediction of good evolution.

Brain injury produced after a brain trauma is due to some physical and physiological mechanisms that make it possible. Generally, when these types of accidents occur, there is an area directly hurt by the *blow*. It is the impact site that will be affected by a contusion or a laceration. But another area of the brain will be affected as a result of the *counter-coup*. In other words, the dynamic of the impact itself will provoke an inertial propagation in the direction of the force applied, which will produce some type of lesion, directly opposite the initial blow.

Those changes produced in the physiology and neuropsychological functioning of the brain are due fundamentally to the type of trauma suffered; it is the *primary damage* that is directly related to the impact and the magnitude of the trauma. In other words, the dynamic forces provoked by the blow itself will cause an inertial propagation in the direction of the force applied, which will produce some kind of lesion, directly on the opposite side of the initial blow (Fig. 12.5).

The changes produced in the brain's physiology and neuropsychological functioning fundamentally owe to the type of trauma received; it is the *primary damage* that is directly related to the blow and the magnitude of the trauma. But these changes also owe to the *secondary damage,* that is, as a consequence of the alterations caused previously, for example, an increase in the intracranial pressre, hemorrhages, edemas, infections, and so on. In the same way, *nonneurological alterations* can also effect the brain when a person suffers a brain trauma, water retention, and so on.

Different types of fractures may result when a blow is received on the head. Evidently, the force of the blow and its magnitude will play an important and revealing role in this

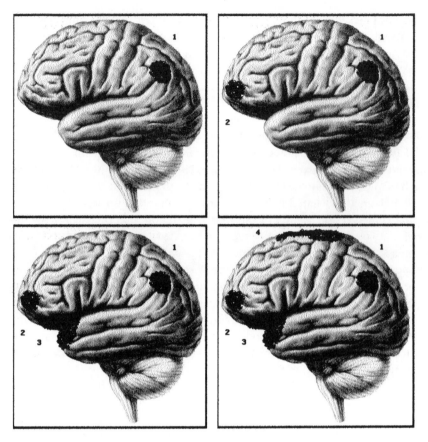

FIG. 12.5.   Mechanisms of damage to the brain surface in closed head injury. (1) Coup;
(2) Contercoup; (3) Sphenoidal Ridge; (4) Vein-Avulsion.

aspect. Results may be a simple linear fracture, a star-shaped fracture, or in the most serious cases, fractures accompanied by indentation. Traditionally, craneoencephalic trauma-
tisms are classified as open or closed.

Open brain injuries are those where the object that produces it breaks or preforates
the cranium, producing a wound and exposing the encephalic mass or leaving it in contact with air. At times, remains of the material that caused the wound may become
encrusted in the brain. Normally, those who suffer this type of damage do not lose consciousness, and sometimes they seek help or go to a hospital or center for medical attention *themselves.*

In general, from a neuropsychological viewpoint, the symptoms will be directly related
to the place or zone affected by the blow. This type of damage leaves sequelae, generally,
very localized in the region of the lesion and therefore will affect the neuropsychological
functions that depend on this zone, making these neuropsychological sequelae more predictable. In the same manner, the risk of appearance of epileptic focus, as a consequence
of the scarring of the wounds, is very high.

Closed brain injuries are those that, although still being caused by a strong blow to the
head, do not cause an exterior wound exposing the brain to the exterior. Generally, the
subjects that suffer them lose consciousness for a time lasting from a few minutes to days.

This is the type of lesion that clearly shows the effects of coup-counter-coup. This type of damage is most often suffered in the lateral area of the face and internally in the frontal and temporal lobes (Fig. 12.6).

Neuropsychological sequelae are quite varied and can affect any part of the patient's activity. Persistent deficits of memory are frequently observed, in concept-forming capacity, and in executive systems (León-Carrión & Barroso y Martín, 1997). At the same time, there may be deficits and problems in personality, agressive behavior, sexual alterations, and social and family problems. Very few return to the work or school level they had before the accident (see León-Carrión, 1994).

The *prognosis* depends on the type and extension of the lesion, the time and deepness of coma, and the period of posttraumatic amnesia. *Treatment* should begin as soon as possible and deal with rehabilitation of cognitive processes, personality, social, family, and professional life. With the proper neuropsychological rehabilitation, the recuperation can be very noticiable. There are different types of models of rehabilitation for neurobehavioral disorders (see León-Carrión, 1998b).

Traumatic brain injury can affect the psychological human process in various ways. Focal lesions are those that more easily permit the prediction of which deficits the patient may suffer because the damage is localized in a specific and known area of the brain. Diffuse lesions are those that produce neuropsychological deficits that are more difficult to determine because the interaction of the different functional brain systems produce a series of deficits that are difficult to predict and even evaluate. At any rate, TBI is capable of interfering and damaging any functional brain system.

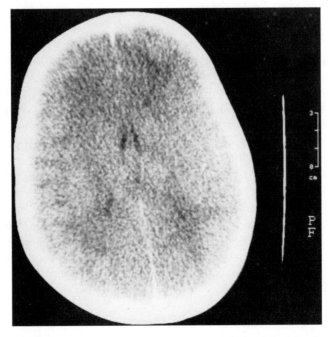

FIG. 12.6.   CT scan showing cerebral edema secondary to a traumatic brain injury. The ventricles are significantly reduced.

Prognosis Factors

In regards to the prognosis, the Traumatic Coma Bank (L. F. Marshall, Gautille, & Klauber, 1991) has provided data to know the outcome of severe closed head injury:

> The overall mortality rate for the 746 patients was 36%, determined at 6 months postinjury. As expected, the mortality rate progressively decreased from 76% in patients with a post-resuscitation GCS score of 3 to approximately 18% for patients with a GCS of 6, 7, or 8. Among the patients with nonsurgical lesions (overall mortality rate, 31%), the mortality rate was higher in those having an increased likelihood of elevated intracranial pressure as assessed by a new classification of head injury based on the computerized tomography findings. In the 276 patients undergoing craniotomy, the mortality rate was 39%. Half of the patients with acute subdural hematomas died (a substantial improvement over results in previous reports. Outcome differences between the four TCDB centers were small and were, in part, explicable by differences in patient age and the type and severity of injury. (p. S-28)

Normally, outcome after brain injury is evaluated by the Glasgow Outcome Scale (GOS). It is a measurement generally used by neurosurgeons. However, it offers many false negatives and there is no consensus that it is a good instrument for neuropsychological outcome. A study was designed by León-Carrión, Alarcón, et al. (1998) to determine how traumatic brain injury affects executive functioning, to know whether different treatments in the acute phase improve this functioning, and to check whether the severity of the neurocognitive impairment is detected by the GOS. Ability for problem solving and executive functioning within 2 years after Traumatic Brain Injury (TBI) was examined in 35 conscious survivors. Two groups were formed. One group consisted of 13 patients who needed neurosurgery. The other group was made up of 22 patients without neurosurgical treatment. All were treated in the Neurosurgical Intensive Care Unit and in the Rehabilitation Service. The following variables were registered: Secondary Lesions, GCS, CT, subacute CT, and GOS. Neuropsychological tests administered were Wisconsin Card Sorting Test (WCST) and the Tower of Hanoi/Seville. Comparing both groups' test performance (Man Whitney U), the authors found that a severe traumatic brain injury, whatever the treatment applied in the acute phase, impairs the patients' executive functioning; this impairment is related to acute pathophysiological events. The neurosurgical intervention does not improve the executive functioning. The GOS does not detect more than 25% of the patients with severe impairment. It is suggested that the Tower of Hanoi/Seville could be a good tool to evaluate the executive functioning routinely in TBI patients as outcome. It is also suggested that mild TBI patients must be referred for a complete neuropsychological examination.

Treatment of patients with brain injury should be tried as soon as the patient is accessible, in their own language and cultural context (León-Carrión, 1994; Pontón, Gonzalez, & Mares, 1997). Recently, the effectiveness of an intensive, holistic, multidisciplinary (INHOM) treatment has been shown for brain injury patients. Results show that TBI patients obtained more than 70% recovery in emotional deficits and more than 60% in the global neuropsychological recovery after completing a 6-month INHOM program (León-Carrión, Machuca, Murga, & Domínguez-Morales, 1999).

Mild Brain Injury

A significant number of people have suffered a mild brain injury throughout their lifetime. Approximately 80% of all TBI is of mild nature, and the ratio of male to female is

2:1, but it must be taken into account that from 20% to 40% of all patients with mild TBI do not seek medical attention. There is no data on mild brain injury incidence in Hispanics. It cannot be dismissed that a significant number must be considered, especially among young adults and adolescents with risky behavior patterns who use cars without being in control or taking the necessary precautions. Probably many of the Hispanics and non-Hispanics litigating in the courts for problems related to auto accidents, violent fighting, and so on, suffer some type of mild brain injury. Most can sustain a *whiplash* injury, which is a term introduced to describe an injury to the neck in rear-end automobile collisions. This is a trauma to the neck when the head is suddenly thrown backward, forward, or laterally, and immediately afterward is thrown in the opposite direction in a recoil (Berstad, Baerum, Löche, Mogstad, & Staastad, 1975; Braaf & Rosner, 1966; States, Korn, & Merengill, 1970). Neuropsychological phenomena following this kind of accident may be organically determined and caused by injury to the brain and the brainstem (Ommaya, Faas, & Yarnell, 1968), although in the subacute period, neurological examination, imaging, and clinical electrophysiological studies are unable to localize, structurally or functionally, the source of the neuropsychological dysfunction (Yarnell & Rossie, 1988).

The Mild Traumatic Brain Injury Committee of the Head Injury Interdisciplinary Special Interest Group of the American Congress of Rehabilitation Medicine (1993, p. 86) has developed a definition of criteria for *mild Traumatic Brain Injury* (mTBI). The mTBI is a traumatically induced physiological disruption of brain functions, as manifested by *at least* one of the following: (a) any period of loss of consciousness; (b) any loss of memory for events immediately before or after the accident; (c) any alteration in mental state at the time of the accident (e.g., feeling dazed, disoriented, or confused); and (d) focal neurological deficit(s) that may or may not be transient. But the severity of the injury does not exceed the following: (a) loss of consciousness of approximately 30 minutes or less; (b) after 30 minutes, an initial Glasgow Coma Scale of 13–15; and (c) posttraumatic amnesia (PTA) not greater than 24 hours.

Another more widely accepted definition of mild brain injury is related to those patients having an accident with the result of a period of unconsciousness of 20 minutes or less, a GCS of 14–15, and hospitalization not exceeding 48 hours (see Culotta, Sementilli, Gerold, & Watts, 1996). The patients may complain of physical, cognitive behavioral, social, and labor problems. Table 12.6 shows the main mild brain injury characteristics.

It seems to be clear that evidence of cognitive impairment will appear within the first days after mild TBI, or even several weeks later (Binder, 1986). Normally, the symptoms have to disappear before 6 months, otherwise another picture other than a mild brain injury must be considered. Gronwall and Wrighton (1975) implied that the effects of mild brain injuries may be cumulative. Many of these patients are labeled as hysteric when they go to the doctor because they insist on their complaints for weeks and the medical exam does not find anything to explain the complaints.

Clinical guidelines for the management of mild Traumatic Brain Injury patients are given by the American Congress of Rehabilitation Medicine (1993, p. 80):

1. Intervene immediately after injury to prevent dysfunctional scenarios.
2. Give information and education about understanding and predicting symptoms and their resolution.
3. Actively manage a gradual process of return of functioning.
4. Whenever possible, negotiate a gradual return to work with the employer.
5. Involve the patient's family or significant others.

TABLE 12.6
Mild Brain Injury Features

Causes	Include:	by being struck
		by being struck by an object
		by whiplash
	Exclude:	stroke
		anoxia
		tumor
		encephalitis
		etc.
Neuroimaging		May be normal
1. Possible Physical Symptoms		Nausea
		Vomiting
		Headache
		Quickness to fatigue
		etc.
2. Possible Cognitive Deficits		Attention
		Concentration
		Perception
		Memory
		Language
		etc.
3. Behavioral and Emotional Changes		Irritability
		Quickness to anger
		Emotional instability
		Disinhibition
		etc.

6. Provide referral or treatment for specific symptoms that do not improve spontaneously.

TOXIC ENCEPHALOPATHY BY ORGANIC SOLVENT INTOXICATION

Introduction

Some groups of workers are exposed to organic solvents, such as glue, cetone, and paints over long periods of time. During their working life, many of these workers have frequently requested sick leave and medical consultations due to subjective complaints that are difficult to assess and for which they cannot determine the cause. Recently, various studies have advised about the neurotoxic effects of prolonged exposure to organic solvents. The clearest and most obvious symptoms after various years of exposure are memory disorders, tiredness, irritability and emotional liability, changes in visual perception, and psychomotor functioning. This group of symptoms has been denominated as *neuroasthenic* or *psychoorganic syndrome*. This syndrome is not specific to organic solvent exposure alone, but can also be seen in the use of toxins such as alcohol, in organic brain disorders, and in presenile dementia. This therefore makes the clinical assessment more difficult in the majority of cases. There is a strong need for objective exams of the nervous system to complement the clinical and psychometric data.

Epidemiological data on the number of Hispanics in the United States exposed to this type of intoxication is not available, but the number is estimated to be from 1 to 3 million Latinos in working conditions that can produce serious intoxication of the central nervous system. In any case, according to Vaughan (1993b, p. 674), exposure to toxic agents is not uniformly distributed throughout the United States. Generally, members of ethnic minority and low income groups tend to be exposed more than others to increased levels of chemical and other environmental hazards, whether in the workplace or in residential settings. In the study developed by Vaughan (1993a), more than 90% of those exposed to toxic substances used in agriculture were from Mexico. Of these workers, despite knowing the risk and danger of personal exposition to pesticides and other substances, 43% did not report heightened fear or worry and 60% did not consistently use any self-protective methods to minimize the risk. Numerous studies have been carried out that show the effects different organic solvents used in the workplace may provoke. Some of the most relevant are discussed next.

Main Issues

Long-term cognitive sequelae of solvent intoxication have been studied by different authors. Three years after an accidental workplace solvent intoxication patients show residual impairment of cognitive functions (Stollery, 1996). The major residual difficulty uncovered related to the speed of processing linguistic material, with workers showing slower verification on tasks probing syntactic and semantic reasoning within the context of relatively unimpaired response execution speeds. The intoxicated workers showed difficulties with the conceptually more complex negative syntactic reasoning problems. This difficulty was also shared by solvent workers who were not involved in that accidental intoxication. Decision fatigue was also observed following prolonged responding in a continuous choice reaction time task, although the ability to mantain vigilance and concentration were unaffected. It was concluded that a single solvent intoxication can give rise to long-term cognitive sequelae in solvent workers.

House painters suspected of toxic encephalopathies, and whose Computerized Axial Tomography showed the presence of cerebral atrophy, obtained a level of cerebral blood flow 19% lower than those patients not exposed to solvents (Arlien-Soborg et al., 1982). Another study done by Maximilian and Risberg (1982) found a mean decrease of 6% in the blood flow compared to the control values. Similarly, Ørbaek et al. (1985) found a reduction in the regional cerebral blood flow in 50 painters who worked in a Swedish factory when compared with the flow of similar workers who had not been exposed. The exposed workers showed higher decreases in blood flow in the frontotemporal lobes of the brain. The higher the exposure level the workers had to solvents, the larger the decreases registered in the cerebral blood flow.

A study carried out by Risberg and Hagstadius (1983) measured the blood flow in factory painters who had been exposed to mixed organic solvents during a mean of 18 years, and a group of workers in a sugar refinery with the same characteristics that served as the control group. The results showed a significantly slight decrease in the blood flow of the exposed workers. The largest differences were found in the frontotemporal brain areas. Similarly, the more years they were exposed to solvents, the larger the flow problems. The authors concluded that the results provide evidence that exposure to organic solvents alter blood flow to the brain and the related cerebral functions. In another study, Linz et al. (1986) found a high prevalence of neurasthenic symptoms, most frequently, memory loss and personality changes in a sample of industrial painters. Other authors have pointed out that cognitive deterioration of this group may continue for years after the initial diagnosis.

All this data leads to the belief that continued exposure for workers, especially painters, to organic solvents with which they work daily can lead to brain impairment similar to organic dementias. Therefore, it can be said that continued exposure to this type of solvent without any type of protection is, in some form, a type of toxic contamination. The effects of occupational exposure to organic solvents and its consequences on the general functioning of the individual can be summed up as follows:

First of all, *subjective reactions caused by irritation of sensory organs* is observed. Among the most common complaints of this collective of workers is irritation of the eyes, nose, and throat. Besides these reactions, the subjects note fatigue, constant tiredness in the workplace as well as at home, and decrease in the quality of air breathed after exposure to these types of organic compositions (Otto et al., 1990).

Second, there are *neuropsychological* and *neurophysiological deficits*. Those subjects exposed for a prolonged period to organic solvents complain habitually of mental confusion, a weakness in daytime alertness, which has very dangerous consequences for drivers, memory deficits, persistent headaches (Anger & Johnson, 1985), and low sleep quality, to which is added determined sleep disorders of which apnea syndrome is the nocturnal pathology most prominent and attention getting, not only for its symptomology (sleep fragmentation, prolonged respiratory stops during sleep, excessive snoring and daytime sonambulance) but also for its high indexes of apparition in this working environment (Monstad, Nissen, Sulg, & Mellgran, 1987; Monstad, Mellgren, & Sulg, 1992).

There are also *inflammatory effects*. It was commented earlier on irritated areas due to prolonged exposure to organic solvents. These same areas—eyes, nose, throat—are those that show early inflammation, generating itching and prolonged feelings of pain (Koren, Devlin, House, Steingold, & Graham, 1990). Additionally, *pulmonary effects* are also observed. The majority of these subjects suffer from respiratory tract infections, chronic cough, and loud, difficult, and interrupted breathing (Molhave, Bach, & Pederson, 1986). This symptomology has been consistently proven in humans as well as in animal models (Kane, Dombroske, & Alarie, 1980).

Diagnosing Toxic Encephalopathy

In the United States, approximately 20 million people are exposed to chemical substances that affect the central nervous system (Landrigan, Kreiss, Xinteras, Feldman, & Health, 1980). These figures have called for the development of various mandates in Congress obligating research on the effects of chemical contamination not only physically, but also motivationally and behaviorally. Some authors suggest that periodic neuropsychological monitoring for those workers exposed to these substances is fundamental and the first that should be done. Neuropsychological assessment indicates how the central nervous system is affected, and the first symptoms of intoxication by organic solvents are observed by changes in mood, affectiveness, and the way information is processed, even when the toxic effects are especially directed at the neuron membranes (Silbergeld, 1983). As noted by Eskenazi and Maizlish (1988, p. 223), the neurological routines of assessment are, in any case, too general to discover subtle changes in function. Consequently, neuropsychological assessment has been used in recent years to evaluate neurotoxic effects of chemical exposure to workers.

The diagnosis of toxic encephalopathy from organic solvents is not easy and can often give false positives and false negatives. The majority of times this occurs owing to the type of instruments, techniques, and methods used during the diagnostic process not being the most appropriate; between variations in diagnostic nomenclature; and in other cases, the lack of training on the evaluator's part in the study and exploration of neuropsychological toxicity. Dumont (1989) critiqued psychiatric aspects derived from the exposition to toxins such as heavy metals, volatile solvents, and pesticides. But, be advised about the risk of incorrect diagnoses in toxic episodes, and the futility of psychiatric interventions of use. The variability of conductual answers to psychotoxic agents challenges the psychiatric nomenclature based on categories of conductual disorders. The psychopathological and psychiatric exploration should routinely include questions about exposure to toxic substances in the home and at work, include more knowledge about behavioral effects in environmental toxins, and be more prudent in the prescription of teratogenic drugs.

The possibility of help for these patients in the diagnostic procedure implies *neuropsychological assessment* in different functional areas. First of all, *intellect level* should be measured to determine the severity of cognitive loss. Impairment in language, reading, and writing may offer data for a differential diagnosis. For example, if patients conserve their writing and reading abilities, and do not paraphrase, this may be toxic encephalopathy. Memory, especially retrograde, assessment is another area to be included in the diagnostic process. If the memory disorders show up after exposure to toxins, then they do not tend to extend into other spheres such as Alzheimer's disease, making toxic encephalopathy likely. In the same way, attentional and visual-spatial skills should be assessed for their importance in determining the severity of the neurocognitive losses.

The diagnosis of chronic toxic encephalopathy depends, of course, on the amount of time exposed and the concentration of the toxic material. The diagnosis in these cases should be based fundamentally on the fact that those patients have had chronic exposure to concentrated organic solvents and expressed subjective complaints of affective and emotional or personality problems, along with memory and intelligence functioning deficits, but do not show severe neurological signs. When neurological signs are observed, a different diagnosis should be considered.

For all these reasons, the diagnosis of *toxic encephalopathy* from organic solvents should be conducted fundamentally through a specialized *neuropsychological assessment* process that should offer pertinent information to identify the three diagnostic categories for disturbances in the central nervous system included in solvents proposed by the World Health Organization (WHO, 1985), as indicated in Table 12.7.

A pilot study on neuropsychological rehabilitation of patients with solvent-induced toxic encephalopathy was done by Ørbaek, Hagstadius, Lindgren, and Abjörnsson (1992). The neuropsychological intervention comprised crisis therapy, information about the disease, and cognitive training. As a result of the intervention, patients experienced substantial improvement in their daily life and family relations. Their affective symptoms decreased and their verbal memory improved. Regional cerebral blood flow (rCBF) measurements showed training-dependent changes of functional activity related to change in memory strategy. This rCBf change had disappeared 6 months later, however, suggesting that the duration of intervention needs to be extended in order for use of the learned memory techniques to become automatic. It was concluded that neuropsychological rehabilitation is effective and should be made available to patients with chronic toxic encephalopathy.

TABLE 12.7
Diagnostic Categories, Symptomology, and Severity of the Neurotoxic Syndromes
Induced by Organic Solvents

Diagnostic Category	Definition of Tables	Severity
Type I Solvent Intoxication	*Neurasthenic* or *psychoorganic syndrome*, which includes fatigue, depression, and episodes of anxiety. No deficits show in the neuro-psychological tests. Reversible if exposure to toxic is discontinued. Also called *affective organic syndrome*.	Minimum
Type II Solvent Intoxication	*Moderate toxic encephalopathy* includes emotional, mood, and behavior disorders, fatigue, motivation-related problems, and problems controlling impulses.	Moderate
Type II B Solvent Intoxication	*Moderate toxic encephalopathy*, including intellectual disorders, or problems in the cognitive sphere easily detectable through neuro-psychological tests, such as alterations in memory, learning and concentration, and psychomotor functioning, among others.	Moderate
Type III Solvent Intoxication	*Chronic or severe toxic encephalopathy* showing neuropsychological deterioration in intelligence and general emotions, which occur after many years of toxic exposure. May meet the criteria for toxic dementia.	Severe

CENTRAL NERVOUS SYSTEM NEOPLASMS

Introduction

Most of the causes of nervous system tumors are yet unknown, but in the United States in 1995, around 13,300 people died from primary nervous system tumors, and around 17,200 were newly diagnosed with one of these tumors (Preston-Martin, 1996); and, the incidence of mortal subtypes has increased in the last decades (Greig, Ries, & Yanick, 1990). Meningiomas are the most commom benign brain tumors, accounting for from 15% to 20% of intracraneal tumors (2.7 per 100,000 population) tending to occur late in life, and is increasing in patients with carcinoma of breast (Rubinstain, Schein, & Reichental, 1989). Epidemiologic studies have suggested increased brain tumor risk for different occupational groups. Most of these groups had the opportunity for multiple chemical exposures, including a variety of organic solvents. But narrowing the list of substances that may be linked to excess brain tumor risk in humans is difficult, and no firm conclusions can be drawn regarding the role of any of the chemicals in the etiology of brain tumors (see Thomas, 1994).

Incidence of brain tumors in Hispanics is not well known. Table 12.8 shows the annual incidence rates (per 100,000) by major primary brain tumors by gender and ethnic group, according to the Cancer Surveillance Projects, in Los Angeles County from 1972 to 1992.

According to Preston-Martin (1996),

In general, rates amongst whites in Canada, the United States, Europe, the United Kingdom, and Australia are relatively similar, although rates are lower in certain Eastern European countries and former Soviet republics (Russia, Belarus, and Krygystan). Rates are lowest in Asian populations in Japan, India, and among Chinese in Singapore. Rates are also lower in Puerto Rico, Costa Rica, and Brazil. Among each racial group, rates are usually higher in migrant populations than in native populations that remain in the continent of origin. These

TABLE 12.8
Average Annual Incidence Rates of Tumor in Different Ethnic Groups
(per 100,000).

	Gliomas	Meningiomas	Nerve Sheath Tumors
Male			
Other Whites	6.5	1.7	0.8
All Races	5.5	1.6	0.6
Spanish-surnamed	**4.4**	**1.4**	**0.3**
Black	4.0	2.2	0.2
Filipino	2.4	2.0	0.7
Chinese	2.3	0.6	0.3
Japanese	2.1	0.6	0.6
Other races	1.5	0.9	0.3
Korean	2.4	0.4	0.0
Female			
Other Whites	4.3	2.8	0.8
All races	3.7	2.7	0.7
Black	2.6	3.2	0.2
Spanish-surnamed	**3.1**	**2.6**	**0.4**
Korean	1.9	1.4	0.4
Filipino	1.7	2.3	0.4
Chinese	1.4	1.8	0.4
Other races	1.5	1.6	0.7
Japanese	1.1	1.4	0.7

Note: Data courtesy of the Cancer Surveillance Project.

differences between migrant and native populations suggest that some change in lifestyle may be occurring in migrant populations that places them at higher risk for brain tumors, although an increase in diagnostic efficiency may explain partially some of these differences. (p. 278)

Main Issues

Tumors are classified depending on where they appear and the histology (Table 12.9). In the same way, they can be classified as *primary* when they grow forming part of the central nervous system itself and *secondary* when they originate outside the nervous system and make metastasis within it. Brain tumors have specific characteristics that differentiate them from other tumors that evolve outside the nervous system. First of all, the brain is enclosed in a nonexpansive protective box, the cranium. And so all that grows abnormally within the brain occupies a volume that does not correspond to it and therefore grows and increases the intracranial pressure, producing neurological deficits that acquire importance depending on the type and growth of the tumor (Fig. 12.7).

Another thing to keep in mind is that the tumor originating in the central nervous system rarely forms metastasis outside. At the same time, the tumors can be filtered or encapsuled. *Filtered* or *intracerebral tumors* are those that penetrate and are not clearly limited to the tissue around them. They originate from glial cells. *Encapsuled* or *extracerebral tumors* generally originate in the cranium (osteomas, sarcomas, and hemangiomas), in the meninges (meningiomas), or in the brain nerves (neuromas) among others; the clinical and behavioral effects appear consequently from the mechanic oppression executed on the brain structures. The symptoms produced by brain tumors depend on where they are

TABLE 12.9
Anatomic and Pathologic Classification of Tumors of the CNS

Location	Histologic Type
Brain	Gliomas
Cranial nerve	—Astrocytoma
Cerebral meninges	—Glioblastoma multiforme
Spinal cord	—Ependymoma
Spinal meminges	—Primitive neuroectodermal tumor
	—Oligodendroglioma
	—Other gliomas
	Meningioma
	Nerve sheath tumors
	Other
	Unspecified
	No microscopic confirmation

located, but in general, tend to cause headaches, nausea and vomiting, language disturbances, loss of vision, focal weakness, sensory disturbances, and so on. When facing the possibility of a brain tumor, a differential diagnostic should always be performed with those symptoms that may be confused with other symptomologies: strokes, brain abscess, metastatic tumors, vascular malfunctions, among others. The diagnosis should be confirmed, in any case, by CAT scans or magnetic resonance imaging (MRI); and a biopsy to know the exact tissue type and grade of malignancy.

Neuropsychological Consequences of Brain Tumors

As tumors may appear in any part of the brain, it seems advisable to note which are the more frequent neuropsychological sequelae according to the lobe where the tumor develops.

Tumors that develop in the *frontal lobe* produce basically an alteration in the capacity of the patients to plan, control, and organize behavior. Evidently, the seriousness lies in the tumor's magnitude. These patients may generally show a lack of spontaneity, inertia, and general loss of mental efficiency. In some cases, language may be affected, in any of its forms. Emotional sequelae include irritability, euphoria, depression, and apathy. Disinhibition and difficulties in recognizing contextually or actually denying the illness are especially noticeable. Tumors in the *parietal lobe* have sequelae basically associated with the sensation of touch, leading patients to complain that they cannot remember things through touch, localize parts of the body, or identify the objects they touch (Golden, 1981). At the same time, Gerstmann's syndrome may appear. Disforia can be observed when the tumor is found in the dominant hemisphere. When found in the nondominant hemisphere, disorders of body image and the ability to realize it are found. Depressions, as sequelae of these disorders, are not rare.

Tumors found in the *temporal lobe* are those that may produce a greater number of mental disorders. Almost half of these types of patients develop epilepsy; those symptoms associated with epilepsy are the most obvious. Frontotemporal tumors associated with the nondominant hemisphere may be permanent while not "showing themselves" until very advanced and great in size. In these cases, early neuropsychological assessment in those patients suspected of tumors of this type are fundamental. Intellectual and cognitive dis-

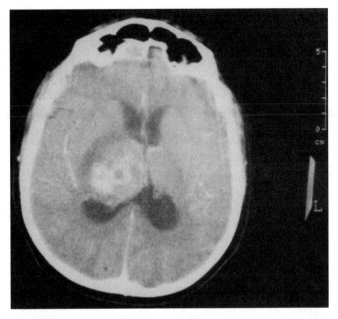

FIG. 12.7. Patient with a right thalamic tumor, showing significant mass effect and resulting in hydrocephalus.

orders can be very strong. Language, memory, and auditive disorders, apathy and indifference or, on the other hand, euphoria, mood swings, and affective disorders can be seen as sequelae of this type of tumor.

Occipital tumors are fundamentally related to visuospatial aspects, scotoma, and visual agnosia. *Corpus callosum tumors* produce a great number of cognitive and behavioral deficits, possibly due to the implication of the corpus callosum with the nearby structures. The principal disorders are associated with interhemispherical coordination. When produced in the frontal part, before any other symptoms are evident, rapid mental deterioration may be noted, beginning, generally, with memory problems and personality changes.

There are various ways of treating brain tumors. *Treatment* depends basically on the type of tumor and its location. *Surgical resection* is an attempt to remove the tumor if it is accessible. The instruments used for this are surgical laser, ultrasonic vacuum, and stereotaxic apparatus. Tumors can also be removed partially, leaving other treatments (radiology, chemotherapy) to be applied.

Radiotherapy is an important component of treatment for malignant gliomas, although long-term results obtained continue to be disappointing. Best results have been obtained in those patients treated with innovative techniques, such as bracytherapy or radiosurgery, in addition to surgery and standard radiotherapy and chemotherapy. It seems that focal irradiation of benign tumors and metastases appear to offer advantages over more conventional therapies. A better understanding of the biology of brain tumors is necessary in order to direct selective treatment at both gross and microscopic disease while sparing the surrounding normal brain in order to improve survival and quality of life in these patients (see Shrieve & Loeffler, 1995).

Chemotherapy plays a role in the treatment of patients with brain tumors and although some modest benefits can be observed in patients with malignant gliomas, overall progress in the treatment of these tumors has been disappointing, and the efficacy in the management of brain metastases has not been demonstrated. Problems that remain unsolved are related to the improvement of drug delivery and overcoming drug resistance, and, in others, problems of toxicity (see Conrad, Milosavljevic, & Yung, 1995).

NEUROPSYCHOLOGICAL ASSESSMENT FOR HISPANIC POPULATIONS

Neuropsychological assessment is a process that must be directed to find out which are the principal affectations derived from the neurological disorders suffered. Different test batteries may be used to help clinical diagnosis in neuropsychology. The following briefly describes a neuropsychological test battery that can be used for qualitative and quantitative evaluation of patients with neurobehavioral disorders.

The Computerized Seville Neuropsychological Test-Battery (BNS) originates from a series of tasks classically used in neuropsychological assessment. The battery is structured in various computerized sections that allow a study of the subject's cognitive and behavioral functioning. Within this assessment process, it centers mainly on the assessment of attention, vigilance, inattention, perception, neurocognitive interference, reasoning, problem solving, and executive functions (see León-Carrión, 1997). Another part assesses the memory processes of learning, and yet another the emotional changes produced by neurological deficits. There is a version in Spanish and another in English.

The first of the sections centers on the *assessment of attentional mechanisms* in their alert tonic and phasic components. It is a computerized version of the conditioned letter cancellation tests. The last of the attentional components evaluated is tachistoscopic attention, through which it is possible to evaluate the deficits from hemianopsia and quadrantanopsia.

The second of the sections is the one that most directly assesses the functions associated with the frontal lobe, this being a classically used problem-solving task like the *Tower of Hanoi;* in the BNS, the adaptation implies a modification of this, resulting in the "Seville" version of the Tower of Hanoi. This modification consists of not telling the subject all of the necessary information to correctly solve the problem, so the subject has to organize a plan to solve the task. That is, the information given to the subjects is not very structured, leaving the subject to structure it because this is the type of task where frontal lesion patients tend to have the most difficulty.

The next section centers on *assessment of neurocognitive interference* in attentional and perceptive processes. In this case, a computerized version of the Stroop Effect was used, which allows control of reaction time, as well as the number and type of mistakes made by the subject, storing all of the information in the computer so it can be used in a later quantitative and qualitative analysis of the subject's execution.

According to Pérez Gil and Machuca (1999), the subtests of Conditioned Simple Attention and Taquistoscopic Attention are the most effective tests for differentiating among patients with slight, moderate, or severe brain injury. The discriminating function of the subtest Tower of Hanoi/Seville is the best for classifying patients with brain injury according to the Glasgow Coma Scale (GCS). Finally, these authors affirmed in their study that the BNS is a sensitive instrument for assessing the consequences of traumatic brain injury. The BNS is shown to be very effective as an assessment instrument for children with learning problems.

Memory Examination and Learning Processes
(Luria's Memory Words–Revised)

This is a computerized version of the Luria's Memory Words–Revised, a task that allows an exhaustive assessment of memory and learning processes through an exam of the subject's verbal memory in semantic components. Among the memory aspects to be evaluated are the volume of memory, memory contamination, awareness of memory deficits, mnesic gain, memory consolidation, learning indexes, as well as the effects of primacy and recency. Memory volume is understood as the amount of information the patient is able to remember at a certain time, excluding fabulated or repeated information, which would be what forms mnesic contamination and would occupy a part of the subject's memory volume. Mnesic gain refers to the increase of retained information the patient obtains through repeated presentation of information. Consolidated information is that which the subject is able to maintain during the duration of the task. Finally, the effects of primacy and recency are obtained, referring to the part of the material the subject retains most easily whether it be the initial or final part, respectively. In addition, an evaluation of the learning processes used by the subject to memorize information is done, the test offering three indexes of learning referring to different types of learning curves that the subject develops, which can be a normal curve, a rigid curve, and an extenuation curve. The test allows a quantitative evaluation and when required the interpretation can be done qualitatively, according to the data, norms, and theories collected in the manual of the test.

The test's manual offers data of the memory indexes in relation to the anatomic and functional neuroimages.

Neurologically Related Changes in Personality Inventory
(NECHAPI)

The Neurologically Related Changes in Personality Inventory is conceived as an assessment instrument specifically designed to evaluate the emotional changes most frequently observed in patients with brain injury. Evaluations done by some of the patient's family members on each of the five factors analyzed in the test are collected. The family member or significant other is asked to evaluate patients on a scale of 5 points on each of the 40 items of the inventory in relation to how patients were before suffering brain injury and how they behave in those same items after the brain injury. This will allow making a direct comparison on the change suffered by the patient. For this, the inventory presents a series of values and normative data that can be taken as reference scores to give or not give significance to the alterations studied (León-Carrión, 1998a).

The five factors on which the evaluation is done are obtained from a factorial analysis on the complaints most frequently presented by the patients and their family members after brain injury. The dimensions assessed with this test are Anger, Sensation Seeking, Emotional Vulnerability, Sociability, and Motivation.

NECHAPI allows monitoring the patient's personality changes owing to pharmacological and/or neuropsychological treatment, as well as know the self-awareness patients present on their own limitations when comparing the results of the self-applied version with those obtained when administering it to some of their surrounding members. It is an excellent instrument for monitoring the effects drugs and treatment have on neurological patients that can be repeated as many times as necessary.

CONCLUSIONS

The main neurobehavioral disorders in Hispanic patients are traumatic brain injuries, cerebrovascular disorders, toxic encephalopathies, and brain tumors. Hispanic patients living in the United States experience and cope with their neurological disorders within a multicultural society. The difference of culture and the design of the mental health services cause Hispanics to under-use health services. Nevertheless, neurological disorders need to be detected as early as possible. Diagnosis and treatment should be addressed by competent, specialized, Spanish-speaking doctors, who are well trained in the Hispanic culture.

REFERENCES

American Congress of Rehabilitation Medicine. (1993). Definition of mild traumatic brain injury. *Journal of Head Trauma, 8*(3), 86–87.

American Heart Association. (1994). *Heart and Stroke facts;* 1994 statistical supplement.

Anger, K., & Johnson, B. (1985). Chemicals affecting behavior. In J. O'Donoghue (Ed.), *Neurotoxicity of industrial and commercial chemicals* (Vol. 1, pp. 52–148). Boca Raton, FL: CRC Press.

Annegers, J. F., Grabow, J. D., & Kurland, L. T. (1980). Seizures after head trauma: A population study. *Neurology, 30,* 683–689.

Arlien-Soborg, P., Henriksen, L., Gade, A., Gyldensted, C., Paulson, Ob. (1982). Cerebral blood flow in chronic toxic encephalopathy in house painters exposed to organic solvents. *Acta Neurologica Scandinavica, 66,* 34–41.

Artiola i Fortuny, L., & Mullaney, H. A. (1997). Neuropsychology with Spanish speakers: Language use and proficiency issues for test development. *Journal of Clinical and Experimental Neuropsycholgy, 19*(4), 615–622.

Baird, A. D. (1991). Behavioral correlates of cerebral revascularización. In R. A. Bornstein & G. Brown (Eds.), *Neurobehavioral aspects of cerebrovascular disease* (pp. 314–316). New York: Oxford University Press.

Banegas, J. R. (1995). Concepto de factor riesgo: Contribución de los principales factores de riesgo a la mortalidad cardiovascular en España [Risk factor concept: Main factors for cardiovascular risk in Spain]. In M. Luque (Ed.), *Factores de riesgo cardiovascular: Implicaciones prácticas en la clínica diaria* [*Cardiovascular risk factors: Implications for daily practice*]. Madrid: Fundación Ciencia y Medicina.

Bernal, M. E., & Castro, F. G. (1994). Are clinical psychologists prepared for service and research with ethnic minorities? Report of a decade of progress. *American Psychologist, 49*(9), 797–805.

Berstad, J. R., Baerum, B., Löche, E. A., Mogstad, D., & Staastad, H. (1975). Whiplash: Chronic organic brain syndrome without hydrocephalus ex vacuo. *Acta Neurolgica Scandinavica, 51,* 268–284.

Binder, L. M. (1986). Persisting symptoms after mild head injury: A review of the post-concussive syndrome *Journal of Clinical and Experimental Neuropsychology, 8,* 323–346.

Bornstein, A., & Brown, G. (1991). *Neurobehavioral aspects of cerebrovascular disease.* New York: Oxford University Press.

Braaf, M. M., & Rosner, S. (1966). Whiplash injury to the neck—fact or fancy? *International Surgical Digest, 46,* 176–182.

Cakmak, M. (1996). Current developments in the field of occupant protection for side impacts. In H. E. Diemath, J. Sommerauer, & K.R.H. von Wild (Eds.), *Brain protection in severe head injury. Accident prevention, rescue systems and primary care* (pp. 11–21). W. München: Zuckschwerdt verlag.

Caplan, L. R. (1994). Neurologic management plan. In M. N. Ozer, R. S. Materson, & L. R. Caplan (Eds.), *Management of persons with stroke* (pp. 61–113). St. Louis, MO: Mosby.

Christensen, A. L. (1978). *El diagnóstico neuropsicológico de Luria* [Luria's neuropsychological examination]. Madrid: Pablo del Río Editor

Conrad, C. A., Milosavljevic, V. P., & Yung, W.K.A. (1995). Advances in chemotherapy for brain tumors. *Neurology Clinic, 13*(4), 795–812.

Culotta, V. P., Sementilli, M. E., Gerold, K., & Watts, C. C. (1996). Clinipathological heterogenity in the classification of mild head injury. *Neurosurgery, 38*(2).

Dana, R. H. (1993). *Multiculture assessment perspectives for professional psychology*. Boston: Allyn & Bacon.

Desmeules, M., Mikkelsen, T., & Mao, Y. (1992). Increasing incidence of primary brain tumors: Influence of diagnostic methods. *Journal of National Cancer Institute, 84,* 442–445.

Dikmen, S., & Temkin, N. (1987). Determination of the effects of head injury and recovery in behavioral research. In H. S. Levin, J. Grafman, & H. M. Eisenberg (Eds.), *Neurobehavioral recovery from head injury* (pp. 373–387). New York: Oxford University Press.

Dikmen, S., Machamer, J., Temkin, N., & McLean, A. (1987). Neuropsychological recovery in patients with moderate to severe head injury. *Journal of Clinical and Experimental Neuropsychology, 12*(4), 507–519.

Dumont, M. (1989). Psychotoxicology: The return of the mad hatter. *Social Sciences & Medicine, 29*(9), 1077–1082.

Eskenazi, B., & Maizlish, N. (1988). *Effects occupational exposure to chemicals on neurobehavioral functioning*. New York: Plenum.

Forastero, P., Prieto-Lucena, J-R., & Gamero, A. (1992). Epidemiología de los traumatísmos craneo-encefáli-cos [Epidemiology of traumatic brain injury]. *Rehabilitación, 26*(5), 211–216.

Fowers, B. J., & Richardson, F. C. (1996). Why is multiculturalism good? *American Psychologist, 51*(6), 609–621.

Fuster, J. M. (1996). Frontal lobe lesions. In B. S. Fogel, R. B. Shiffer, & S. M. Rao (Eds.), *Neuropsychiatry* (pp. 407–414). Baltimore: Wilkens Press.

Gillman, M. W., Cook, N. R., & Evans, L. H. (1995). Relationship of alcohol intake with blood pressure in young adults. *Hypertension, 25,* 1106–1110.

Golden, C. J. (1981). The Luria–Nebraska Children's Battery: Theory and formulation. In G. W. Hynd & J. E. Obrzut (Eds.), *Neuropsychological assessment and the school-age child: Issues and procedures* (pp. 227–302). New York: Grune & Stratton.

Goodglass, H., & Kaplan, E. (1996). Assessment of cognitive deficits in the brain-injured patient. In M. S. Gazzaniga (Ed.), *Handbook of behavioral neurobiology: Vol. 2. Neuropsychology* (pp. 3–22). New York: Plenum.

Green, M. S., & Peled, I. (1992). Prevalence and control in a large cohort of occupationally active Israelis examined during 1985–1987: The Cordis study. *International Journal of Epidemiology, 2,* 995–997.

Greig, N. H., Ries, L. G., & Yanick, R. (1990). Increasing annual incidence of primary malignant brain tumors in the elderly. *Journal of the National Cancer Institute, 82,* 1621–1624.

Gronwall, D.M.A., & Wrighton, P. (1975). Cummulative effect of concussion. *Lancet, 2,* 995–997.

Howard, G., Anderson, R., Sorlie, P., Andrews, V. Backhend, E., & Burke, G. L. (1994). V *Stroke, 25*(11), 2120–2125.

Jagger, J., Levine, J. L., Jane, J. A., & Rimel, R. W. (1984). Epidemiological features in head injury in a predominantly rural population. *Journal of Trauma, 24*(1), 40–44.

Kannel, W. B., Wolf, P. A., & Verter, J. (1989). Risk factors for stroke. In R. R. Smith (Ed.), *Stroke and the extracranial vessels* (pp. 47–58). New York: Raven Press.

Kane, L., Dombroske, R., & Alarie, Y. (1980). Evaluation of sensory irritation from some common industrial solvents. *American Industrial Higyene Association Journal, 41,* 451–455.

Koren, H., Devlin, R., House, D., Steingold, S., & Graham, D. (1990). The inflammatory response of the human upper airways to volatile organic compounds (VOC). *Proceedings of the Fifth International Conference on Indoor Air Quality and Climate, Ottawa, 1,* 325–330.

Kraus, J. F. (1992). Epidemiology of head injury. In P. Cooper (Ed.), *Head injury* (3rd rev., pp. 1–25). Baltimore, MD: Williams & Williams.

Kraus, J. F., & McArthur, O. C. (1996). Epidemiology aspects of brain injury. *Neurology Clinic, 14*(2), 435–450.

Landrigan, P. J., Kreiss, K., Xinteras, C., Feldman, R. G., & Heath, C. W., Jr. (1980). Clinical epidemiology of occupational neurotoxic disease. *Neurobehavioral Toxicology, 2,* 43–48.

León-Carrión, J. (1994). *Daño cerebral: Guia para familiares y cuidadores* [*Brain injury: A guide for families and caregivers*]. Madrid/Mexico City: Siglo XXI Editores.

León-Carrión, J. (1997). Rehabilitation and assessment: Old task revisited for computerized neuropsychological assessment. In J. León-Carrión (Ed.), *Neuropsychological rehabilitation: Fundamentals, innovations, and directions.* Del Ray Beach, FL: St. Lucie Press.

León-Carrión, J. (1998a). Neurologically-related changes in personality inventory (NECHAPI): A clinical tool addressed to neurorehabilitation planning and monitoring effects of personality treatment. *Neurorehabilitation, 11,* 129–139.

León-Carrión, J. (1998b). Rehabilitation model for neurobehavioral disorders after brain injury. *Brain Injury Sources, 2*(4), 16–44.

León-Carrión, J., Alarcón, J. C., Revuelta, M., Murillo, F., Domínguez-Roldan, J. M., Domínguez-Morales, M. R., Machuca, F., Murga, M., & Forastero, P. (1998). Executive functioning as outcome in patients after traumatic brain injury. *Internal Journal of Neuroscience, 94,* 75–83.

León-Carrión, J., & Barroso y Martin, J. M. (1997). *Neuropsychology of thinking: Control and executive functioning.* Sevilla: Kronos.

León-Carrión, J., Machuca, F., Murga, M., & Domínguez-Morales, M. R. (1999). Outcome after intensive, holistic and multidisciplinary rehabilitation program for Traumatic Brain Injury. Medical-legal values. *Revista Española de Neuropsicología, 1*(2–3), 49–68.

Levin, H. S. (1989). Memory deficit after closed head injury. *Journal of Clinical and Experimental Neuropsychology, 12,* 129–153.

Linz, D. H., de Garmo, P. L., Morton, W., Wiens, A. N., Coull, B. M., & Maricle, R. (1986). Organic solvent-induced encephalopathy in industrial painters. *Journal of Occupational Medicine, 28*(2), 119–125.

Marin, B., Marin, G., Padilla, A., & De la Rocha, C. (1983). Utilization of traditional and non-traditional sources of health care among Hispanic. *Hispanic Journal of Behavioral Sciences, 5,* 65–80.

Marshall, L. F., Gautille, T., & Klauber, M. R. (1991). The outome of severe closed head injury. *Journal of Neurosurgery, 75,* S28–S36.

Marshall, L. F., Marshall, S. B., & Klauber, M. R. (1992). A new classification of head injury based on computerized tomography. *Journal of Neurosurgery, 75,* S14–S20.

Martínez, A., Izquierdo, R., & Balanzategui, I. (1987). Hipertension, obesidad, consumo de alcohol y cafeína frente a enfermedades vasculares en la Comunidad Foral de Navarra [Hypertension, obesity, alcohol consumption and caffeine in vascular diseases in Narvarre]. *Rev. Clínica Española, 180,* 25–31.

Maximilian, A. V., & Risberg, J. (1982). Regional cerebral blood flow and verbal memory after chronic exposure to organic solvents. *Brain Cognition, 1,* 196–205.

The Mild Traumatic Brain Injury Committee of the Head Injury Interdisciplinary Special Interest Group of the American Congress of Rehabilitation Medicine. (1993). Definition of mild traumatic brain injury. *Journal of Head Trauma Rehabilitation, 8*(3), 86–87.

Miranda, J., Azocar, F. Organista, K. C., Muñoz, R. F., & Lieberman, A. (1996). Recruiting and retaining low-income latinos in psychotherapy research. *Consult clin Psycholy, 64*(5), 868–874.

Molhave, L., Bach, B., & Pedersen, O. F. (1986). Human reactions to low concentrations of volatile organic compounds. *Environmental International, 12,* 167–175.

Monstad, P., Nissen, T., Sulg, Ia., & Mellgran, Si. (1987). Sleep apnoea and organic solvent exposure. *Journal of Neurology, 234,* 152–154.

Monstad, P., Mellgren, Si., & Sulg, Ia. (1992). The clinical significance of sleep apnoea in workers exposed to organic solvents: Implications for the diagnosis of organic solvent encephalopathy. *Journal of Neurology, 239,* 195–198.

Mora, J., & Ocón, J. (1989). Ejercicio físico y hipertensión arterial [Physical exercise and arterial hypertension]. *Hipertensión, 6,* 453–459.

Nan, L., Tuomilehto, J., & Dowse, G. (1991). Prevalence and medical care of hypertension in four ethnic groups in the newly-industrialized nation of Mauritius. *Journal of Hypertension, 13,* 965–970.

Norquist, G., & Wells, K. (1991). How do HMOs reduce out-patient mental health care costs? *American Journal of Psychiatry, 148,* 96–101.

Ommaya, O. K., Faas, F., & Yarnell, P. (1968). Whiplash injury and brain damage. *Journal of the American Medical Association, 204,* 285–289.

Ørbaek, P., Risberg, J., Rosen, I., Haeger-Aronsen, B., Hagstadius, S., Hjortsberg, U., Regnell, G., Rehnstrom, S., Svensson, K., & Welinder, H. (1985). Effects of long-term exposure to solvents in the paint industry. A cross-sectional epidemiologic study with clinical and laboratory methods. *Scandinavian Journal of Work and Environmental Health, 11*(2), 1–28.

Ørbaek, P., Hagstadius, S., Lindgren, N., & Agjörnsson, C. (1992). A pilot study: Neuropsychological rehabilitation of patients with solvent-induced toxic encephalopathy. *Lakartidningen, 289*(36), 2845–2846, 2851–2852.

Otto, D., Mølhave, L. , Rose, G., Hudnell, H., & House, D. (1990). Neurobehavioral and sensory irritant effects of controlled exposure to a complex mixture of volatile organic compounds. *Neurotoxicology and Teratology, 12,* 167–175.

Ozer, M. N., Materson, R. S., & Caplan, L. R. (1996). *Management of persons with stroke.* St. Louis, MO: Mosby-Year Book.

Perez-Gil, J. A., & Machuca, F. (1999). Discriminant validity of Seville Neuropsychological Test Battery (BNS) for traumatc brain injury. *Revista Españole de Neuropsicologia, 1*(1), 49–66.

Pontón, M., Gonzalez, J., & Mares, M. (1997). Rehabilitating brain damage in Hispanics. In J. León-Carrión (Ed.), *Neuropsychological rehabilitation: Fundamentals, innovations and directions* (pp. 513–529). DelRay Beach, FL: St. Lucie Press.

Preston-Martin, S. (1996). Epidemiology of primary CNS neoplasms. *Neurologic Clin, 1412,* 273–290.

Risberg, J., & Hagstadius, S. (1983). Effects on the regional cerebral blood flow of long-term exposure to organic solvents. *Acta Psychiatrica Scandinavica, 67*(303), 92–99.

Rubenstein, A. B., Schein, M., & Reichental, E. (1989). The association of carcinoma of the breast with meningioma. *Surgical Gynecology and Obstetrics, 169,* 334–336.

Sahs, A. L., Hartman, E. L., & Aronson, S. M. (1979). *Stroke: Causes, prevention, treatment, and rehabilitation.* London: Castle Publishers.

Shrieve, D. C., & Loeffler, J. S. (1995). Advances in radiation therapy for brain tumors. *Neurology Clinic, 13*(4), 773–793.

Silbergeld, E. K. (1983). Indirectly acting neurotoxins. *Acta Psychiatrica Scandinavica, 67*(303), 16–25.

States, J. D., Korn, M. W., & Merengill, J. B. (1970). The enigma of whiplash injury. *Journal of Medicine, 70,* 2971–2978.

Stollery, S. (1996). Long-term cognitive sequelae of solvent intoxication. *Neurotoxicological Teratology, 18*(4), 471–476.

Takeuchi, D., Leaf, P., & de Kuo, H. S. (1988). Ethnic differences in the perception of barriers to help-seeking. *Social Psychiatry & Psychiatric Epidemiology, 23,* 273–280.

Thomas, T. H. (1994). Primary brain tumors associated with chemical exposure. In M. L. Bleecker (Ed.), *Occupational neurology and clinical neurotoxicology* (pp. 187–206). Baltimore: Williams & Wilkins.

Thompson, D. W., & Furlan, A. J. (1996). Clinical epidemiology of stroke. *Neurology Clinic, 14*(2), 309–311.

Vaughan, E. (1993a). Chronic exposure to an environmental hazard: Risk perceptions and self-protective behavior. *Health Psychology, 12,* 74–85.

Vaughan, E. (1993b). Individual and cultural differences in adaptation to environmental risks. *American Psychology, 48*(6), 673–680.

Whitman, S., Conley-Hoganson, R., & Dasay, B. T. (1984). Comparative head trauma experiences in two socioeconomically different Chicago-area communities: A population study. *American Journal of Epidemiology, 119,* 570–580.

WHO/Nordic Council of Ministers Working Group. (1985). Organic solvents and the central nervous system. World Health Organization, Copenhagen (Environmental Health 5)

Yarnell, P. R., & Rossie, G. V. (1988). Minor whiplash head injury with major debilitation. *Brain Injury, 2,* 255–258.

Mood and Organic Personality Disorder Following Brain Injury

PETER D. PATRICK
University of Virginia

JOSÉ LEÓN-CARRIÓN
University of Seville, Spain

Personality is probably one of the most difficult to understand constructs from a neuropsychological point of view. This difficulty can be summed up fundamentally in three aspects: first, theoretical confusion; second, neuroanatomic distribution of the dimensions that make up the constructs of personality; and third, the influence cultural and educational factors have on the development of personality.

The *theoretical confusion* is evident in that different personality theories do not agree even in defining that which is understood as personality. However, in the complex field of personality studies, there is one rough statement that is generally agreed on: Each person has a personality and personality certainly exists. However, the scientific community is unable to define it. One of the most accepted definitions is that personality is the collective perceptions, emotions, cognitions, motivations, and actions of the individual that interact with various environmental situations (Cripe, 1996). So, personality must be the interactive product of these psychological structures as they interact with environment and are in turn dependent on biological, psychological, and social influences.

Although there is agreement about the existence of personality, there is no universally accepted definition. Personality is the most complex integrated product of brain functioning. Consequently, alteration to brain functioning can be reasonably understood to affect "personality," a multifactorial product. Disease or injury that alters substructures that support perceptions, emotions, cognitions, motivations, and actions that in turn affect the basic mood, temperament, and nature of the individual serve as the focus of study. Furthermore, it is reasonable to expect that neurologic events that change or alter the fundamental psychological substructures of the individual can and will be detected as quantitative and qualitative changes in the person's personality. As long as there is no operative and true agreement in the concept of personality, it is very difficult to define normal and pathological personality. Neuropsychological studies can be of great use in correcting this problem. The methodology and the accuracy neuropsychology requires may give the criterial validity needed in the theory of personality (León-Carrión, 1997c).

If there is no agreement concerning the definition of personality, then it is even more difficult to know the *neuropsychological* and *brain organization* of personality. Even if it is accepted that the subcortex structures respond to emotions, feelings, and so on, new problems arise, equivalent to technical availability. What objective, valid, and reliable methods are there for discovering *cortex function,* not just the structure? It may be argued that modern functional neuroimaging techniques are the answer. That may very well be. But there remains a serious problem in reading and interpreting these neuroimages when obtained from a particular patient. And if personality is more functional than structural neuroanatomical concept (aside from being poorly defined), then how can these neuroimages and the data obtained be joined? A doubt remains. It is probable, also, that some psychological variables associated with determined brain zones are poorly interpreted.

Finally, personality seems to be narrowly associated with factors related to *culture, education,* and *socioeconomic class.* Any attempt to obtain data on "personality neuropsychology" is, evidently, complex. In the case of this book's theme, neuropsychology with Hispanic populations, these aspects require special attention.

Therefore, if researchers want to know, study, diagnose, and treat "personality" aspects in Latinos, then the task is arduous and cannot be carried out in a simplified way. All that lies below the different socioeconomic levels related to personality is an as-of-yet-unknown world. Throughout, this chapter tries, within the limits of pages, to offer a comprehensive view of the organic personality disorders in Latinos.

SIGNIFICANT CROSS-CULTURAL ISSUES

There are important differences in social influence and patient perception that must be remembered when studying personality changes in the Hispanic patient. First of all, it must be kept in mind that they are living in a multicultural environment that causes them to express their feelings, thoughts, behaviors, emotions, and so forth, differently than they would in their country of origin. And, when attempting to express them as they would in their native country, their behavior is not congruent with their environment and so they are labeled as an ethnic minority. Therefore, multicultural and cross-cultural factors must be kept in mind when trying to understand the Hispanic person's personality. Some epidemiological factors are helpful in gaining a better understanding of these factors. According to Miranda, Azocar, Organista, Muñoz, and Lieberman (1996),

> Political and economic factors often influence immigration patters, and therefore, socioeconomic status of Latinos in the United States. Overall, Latinos have lower incomes than do non-Hispanic whites; Cubans are the most affluent and educated of Latinos in the United States, followed by Central and South Americans, Mexicans, and Puerto Ricans. In terms of poverty, only about 10% of non-Latino whites live below the poverty level, compared with 39% of Puerto Ricans, 30% of Mexican Americans, and 18% of Cuban Americans. . . . In the National Comorbidity Survey (Kessler et al., 1994) . . . Latinos were found to have a higher prevalence of current affective disorders and retire comorbidity (three or more) disorders than non-Latino whites. There were no disorders with lower prevalence rates for Latinos than those for whites. This survey provides the strongest evidence to date of significant risk for mental disorders in Latinos. This result is not surprising, given the strong inverse relationship between socioeconomic status and mental disorders that has been consistently found in epidemiological studies and the highest rates of poverty of Latinos residing in the United States.

On the other hand, Pontón (1997) commented on the *patient-specific factors* that are important for the Latino patient when evaluating and treating changes in personality following alterations in brain functioning, for example, the problem of symptom recognition and acceptance. He stated that the clinician and patient will frequently not recognize or accept changes in personality due to brain dysfunctions, because *symptom validation* fails. The Latino's symptom presentation is not accepted and this results in secondary complications of not feeling understood. Latino patients feel insulted and feel the symptoms are attributed to their culture and not the clinical entity of brain alterations. When non-Latino clinicians attempt to help or use intermediate translators, this only increases the estrangement between patient and treating clinicians. Even with the best intentions, the language and cultural barriers cannot be navigated so as to make Latino patients feel validated in their symptom presentation. Therefore, Hispanic patients are at risk for feeling invalidated.

The issue of responsibility to authority is also important. Both the patient and the treating clinician participate in what proves to be a distortion in locus of control. For example, Latinos who live within another culture may not be included in treatment planning. Latinos who are seen as unable to or unwilling to participate are excluded from active participation in their own care. This extends to the family. An old cultural segregation is acted out or the non-Latino clinician views the patient and family in a way that does not extend them a more personal involvement in treatment planning.

Family is significant in the recovery picture of all brain injured patients. However, the Latino family brings an important difference—their intransigent beliefs in roles and identity. The reversal in roles that brain disorders can have significantly challenges the family structures and functioning. For example, the father who is now dependent is unable to understand or accept the dependency. Or, the father may turn limitations and dependency into control and paternal dominance by requiring and insisting on complete care and rejecting all responsibility for self-care and achievement. Family and community roles are strong and deep within the Latino community. Family members, friends, and the patient do not easily change or accept the new roles that the brain disorders may impose on them. Old behaviors and actions remain stubborn to change and complicate recovery expectancies, participation, and long-term adjustment. As Pontón (1997) pointed out, the Latino who cannot find satisfactory change within the family is at risk for remaining in *recovery limbo*.

Another significant factor is the cultural influences of alternative treatments and care. The use of homeopathic treatments and *spiritualization of care* (*santería, limpiezas*) or views (*me embrujaron*) greatly influence how the Latino views the traditional clinician who may or may not be Latino. The nontraditional influences on understanding and recovery affect the Latino's expectations for recovery and their understanding of what must be done to promote recovery. This consequently affects motivations, cooperation, and alignment of expectations between the clinician and the patient (see Pontón, 1997).

The neurological diagnosis of personality disorders suffered by Latinos with brain injury, determined in health services, is often incorrect. Hispanic patients are incorrectly diagnosed as schizophrenic, or suffering from hallucinations, bizarre behavior, and so forth, when they refer to ancestral beliefs from the culture of origin. Patients may believe in curers (*curanderos*) or spiritualism without having any thought disorders. These beliefs are reminiscent of a magic-religious culture, where magic and religious beliefs are intertwined in a particular manner, to give order and meaning to unknown things and happenings. There is a mixture of beliefs of natural, supernatural, or superstitious origin that explain occurrences or illnesses suffered. The majority of these beliefs are irrational in this mode of classification, the world and Hispanic culture, especially among the lower socio-economic classes: They are not so irrational to them, but they fill the holes that exist in a reasoning that is not a product of a sophisticated process of education and culture. Therefore, the religious, pseudoreligous, and subcultural beliefs correspond to the "cultural axis" of diagnostic and not to the clinical or to the personality axis.

León-Carrión (1996) described an even more intricate difference for Latinos who are not living in their own country of origin. He presented the idea that Latinos who have immigrated and have either struggled with adaptation or have adapted bring an additional factor to their postneurologic event recovery. Immigrated Latinos were acting differently from their home country already. They were changed due to stresses, pressures, and challenges of immigration that were different from the home country. Once neurologically changed, they act differently, and cope and adjust differently, from either a Latino in the home country or a citizen of the country of immigration. Therefore, the immigrated Latino is coping with and adjusting to brain disorders within the context of a larger and more persistent challenge of living in a new country without the familiarity and comforts of the home country. Therefore, the Latino in the United States is attempting to cope with a neurologic struggle within the context of a much larger social struggle. The Latino's health care struggle is within the larger social struggle. This is a struggle within a struggle that makes Latinos' care different from Americans and different from citizens of their home country.

PERSONALITY IN BRAIN INJURED PATIENTS

Although it has been recognized since the early 1900s that alterations in brain functioning (Fig. 13.1) due to illness, injury, or disease can affect the person's emotional life and personality, it was not until the mid- to late 1970s that scientific interest and investigation occurred in this area. Meyer (1904), introduced the phrase "posttraumatic insanity." Then Goldstein (1942) presented probably the most compelling exploration of biosocial view of brain injury and its effects on the person. In addition, Goldstein (1952) presented a review and position paper on the interactions between brain changes and personality.

However, in the 1970s, with the increased demand for acute and postacute rehabilitation of those persons surviving catastrophic brain injury, stroke, and neurologic disease, there was a rapid growth of interest in the psychological, neurocognitive, and neurobehavioral sequelae. Lezak (1978) wrote a paper for family members in order to help them cope, manage, and understand the challenges presented by their injured survivor. Lezak developed a list of impressive descriptors that she believed are the result of neurologic injury and insult:

1. Impaired social perceptiveness
2. Impaired self-control and self-regulation
3. Stimulus-bound behavior and social dependency
4. Emotional alterations
5. Disability to profit from experience

Prigatano's work in 1986 continued to support the pursuit of knowledge regarding changes in behavior and personality characteristics following brain injury. Prigatano

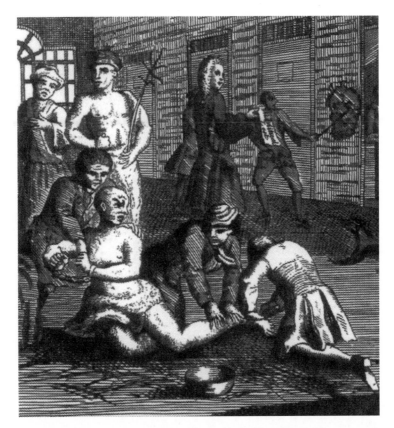

FIG. 13.1. An anonymous painting of a ward in Bethlem Hospital from approximately 1745. (Reprinted from Wellcome Institute Library, London, 1882). For centuries, temperament was thought to be immutable. Changes in behavior in other time periods were associated with magic, enchantment, devils, spells, and so on. Now it is known that these personality changes are due to changes produced in the brain functioning (see León-Carrión, 1997b).

pointed out the changes in self-awareness and insight. He presented scientific review and conceptualization of changes in self-awareness and the consequences for decision making, conduct, and community membership. Prigatano's exploration into this complex and intriguing area of self-evaluation and personal knowledge further supported in the literature the concept that following injury or illness to the brain people can change in their very nature and temperament. Not only are there changes in cognitive problem-solving skills, which had been clinically accepted and researched, but there can be a fundamental change in who the person is and can be. It was a new discovery, in the scientific world, that following brain injury the very nature of the person can change. Furthermore, this point of view, that personality can be altered, was not necessarily for the good of the person, the family, and the change in personality required attention and care. Prigatano, as did Lezak, recognized and commented on the impact of such changes on recovery and community life. In fact, the long-term effects of such changes on personality were recognized as significant complaints from family and employers and constituted the most severe long-term recovery challenges.

In the *Diagnostic and Statistical Manual–III* (APA, 1980), the classification of Organic Personality Syndrome was introduced (see Table 13.1). For the first time within the set

TABLE 13.1

DSM–III Diagnostic Criteria for Organic Personality Syndrome

A. A persistent personality disturbance, either lifelong or representing a change or accentuation of a previously characteristic trait, involving at least one of the following:
   (1) Affective instability, e.g., marked shifts from normal mood to depression, irritability, or anxiety
   (2) Recurrent outbursts of aggression or rage that are grossly out of proportion to any precipitating
       psychosocial stressors
   (3) Markedly impaired social judgement, e.g., sexual indiscretions
   (4) Marked apathy and indifference
   (5) Suspiciousness or paranoid ideation
B. There is evidence from the history, physical examination, or laboratory tests of a specific organic factor (or
   factors) judged to be etiologic related to the disturbance.
C. This diagnosis is not given to a child or adolescent if the clinical picture is limited to the features that characterize attention deficit hyperactivity disorder.
D. Not occurring exclusively during the course of Delirium, and does not meet the criteria for Dementia.

---

category of alterations to psychological, social, and mental life, there was formal recognition of a constellation of changes following brain injury that resulted in personality
alterations. This diagnostic classification was later to be included, in the *DSM–IV*, under
Personality Changes due to Medical Condition (*DSM–IV* 310.1; APA, 1994).

Silver, Hales, and Yudofsky (1994) and Fogel, Schiffer, and Rao (1996) presented an
in-depth review of changes in cognition, emotion/motivation, and personality secondary
to the effects of injury and disease on the brain. These texts provide a comprehensive
review of the scientific investigation and clinical knowledge of the state of the topic.

Also, León-Carrión (1994) addressed families and caregivers concerning aspects of
personality alterations. He explained how to cope with infantilism, emotional changes,
irritability and aggressiveness, depression, suicidal tendency, inhibition, awareness, sexual
behavior, and family and social life.

However, and despite all these reviews, pioneers, and relevant works, much remains to
be done; or better yet, this is just a beginning to an in-depth study of the new world of
organic personality disorders where multiple problems remain to be solved from the
beginning and along the way.

There is good evidence that changes in mood, conduct, and personality are among the
most disqualifying of sequelae after injury or disease to the brain. Such changes appear to
have long-lasting effects and continue to be problematic long after medicinal, sensory-
motor, and communication limitations have been addressed by traditional rehabilitation
efforts. Also, the changes to the nature of the person appear to have significant impact on
those living with the patient or those living with the patient in community (Novak,
Bergquist, Bennett, & Gouvier, 1991). Furthermore, the treatment of these conditions is
not of primary focus during acute and traditional rehabilitation. Also, the treatment of
these conditions brings together an array of professionals and technical interventions that
presently require scientific scrutiny, therapeutic trials, and improvement in diagnostic
intervention.

Not only are these conditions prevalent during initial phases of recovery, but there is
evidence that emergence of personality, mood, and emotional difficulties continue for
some time following the initial event that has altered the brain. For example, Gaultiere
and Cox (1991) discussed prevalence of delayed onset disturbance for traumatic brain
injury (TBI). They reviewed the prevalence of initial presentation of and delayed preva-

lence of affective disorders, delayed amnesia, posttraumatic epilepsy, posttraumatic psychosis, and dementia. When compared to the general population, traumatic brain injury has incidence rates of depression of five to ten factor, increased psychosis by a two to five factor, and dementia by a four to five factor.

The topics of behavior change alterations in mood and personality have to be addressed, as well as the emergence of psychiatric difficulties related to the time of onset with respect to injury and level of consciousness. "Schizophrenic-like" symptoms in some patients and the possible relation between this profile and pre-injury "constitutional predisposition" is one for discussion. Although this is not uniformly supported, there is a need to be aware and sensitive to pre-event influences on the emergence of mental status difficulties (e.g., mental health, drug/alcohol history). Also, be cautious about diagnostic stability over the time of recovery. Caution is wise in that early labels and diagnosis must be revisited and not place the patient at the risk of burden with a psychotic diagnosis that has changed (Levin, Benton, & Grossman, 1982).

It is a reality that some psychosis, depressive, and manic symptoms are present with some patients. Levin et al. (1982) attempted to outline the characteristics of patients who develop posttraumatic psychosis, concluding that the majority of disturbances to mental status and reality testing were characterized by "confabulatory and delusional themes, which were frequently fragmented, in contrast to the systematized delusions found in psychiatric patients with paranoid schizophrenia. Neurologically, the CT results are abnormal in 70% of those with posttraumatic psychosis and there is higher incident of cerebral swelling and hematomas.

In another work, León-Carrión et al. (1996) found that 48.9% of the Traumatic Brain Injury (TBI) surviving patients meet the diagnostic criteria to be categorized as depressive or suffering from clinical depressions, and about 65% of TBI-diagnosed patients with depression have suicidal tendencies, although they only represent 33.3% of the total number of patients that have suffered a severe TBI. According to Robinson and Jorge (1994), the overall frequency of major depression remained relatively stable at about 25% in the first year following TBI.

Behavioral sequelae after brain injury is also reviewed by Rosenthal, Griffith, Bond, and Miller (1983), who listed the factors contributing to the behavioral dysfunction as well as "secondary behavioral disturbances." Under the first category, Rosenthal listed the effects: (a) characteristics of the patient prior to the head injury, (b) changes in psychic traits attributable to the brain injury itself, and (c) psychological difficulties in life.

To know what Hispanic patients were like before brain injury is a complex issue that should best refer to how they behaved and adjusted their life to the multicultural environment. The patient's premorbid characteristics should not be judged by what they were like and how they behaved in the home country. In general, brain injury may fundamentally affect the functioning adaptability of the Hispanic patient.

The likelihood of vulnerability to behavioral difficulties coming into the injury in those having a high frequency of premorbid maladaptive behavior patterns. This was extended to include family disposition. Also, the effects of lesion site on behavioral sequelae correlate with frontal lobe injury, and symptoms of depression, irritability, poor frustration tolerance, and so on, are present irrespective of neuropathology of injury. The common presence of certain symptoms is well recognized. However, some of the more recent findings can shed light on assisting with a more exacting differential diagnosis. The environmental "confrontation" that takes place when the person is faced with limitations and life factors that require major adaptation must also be considered. According to Dana (1993),

It is necessary to distinguish between pathology per se, or genuine deviance, and residual deviance that may be understood only within its cultural setting. Residual deviance refers to less functional behaviors, or those problems-in-living that are not necessarily pathological but are derived from specific and unique cultural experiences. There may be no clear distinction between culture-specific pathological disorders and residual deviance or conditions that may be more adequately described as problems-in-living, so bare rates for disorders in different cultural settings are necessary. . . . There are additional problems-in-living, relevant for minority cultural groups in this country, that are not included in the current diagnostic nomenclature. These problems need to be identified for each of the major cultural groups. Some examples would include cultural confusion, damage as a result of racism by the dominant society, and deficits in skills required for functioning in the dominant society. It is necessary to distinguish between these culture-specific problems-in-living and diagnosable psychopathologies for clients in this society who do not have Anglo-American origins. (pp. 95–96)

As Secondary Behavioral Disturbances Rosenthal included denial, depression, and dependence on others. The topic of denial comments on the tendency of patients to minimize or dismiss their symptoms (see Prigatano's, 1997, conception of awareness), as a psychological manifestation that is typically confronted or reinforced by "well-meaning" family members. Although reality testing confrontation of the denial is difficult, the well-meaning approach can lead to ill-advised resumption of premorbid activities that run an even greater risk of absolute failure. For Rosenthal, in the subacute phase of recovery, depression may be viewed as a positive event, in that it signals the lessening of denial and usually reflects the patient's growing understanding and insight into the extent of the disability. Be careful, however, because this psychologistic interpretation of postbrain injury depression may not be completely correct as some of these depressions seem to have a strong biological component (see León-Carrión, 1997a). In later literature, the differentiation of reactive and primary depressions is more evident where the etiology and the solutions may include more medical intervention in order to complement the efforts of mental health recovery. The Dependence Upon Others is related to the increased demanding, egocentric, and lack in ability to delay gratification. Rosenthal underscored the effect that brain injury has on the reversal and stagnation of family roles and burden placed on family members. The brain injured person's demanding and neediness becomes a behavioral issue that impacts a number of other lives.

In an interesting work, Klonoff and Lage (1991) analyzed the "narcissistic injury" and related the "catastrophic reaction" to the anxiety of discovering the limits and changes brain injury has imposed on an individual life, a resistance to such a discovery (i.e., denial), and an impact of the narcissism on others. Novack, Bergquist, Bennett, and Gouview (1991) reviewed the results of distress on family members. They found that anxiety, not depression, is the major distress, initially. Although this improves during hospitalization, anxiety reappears 3 months later at follow-up. Interestingly, they commented that the level of anxiety did not correlate with level of disability and, in part, related to the style of coping with stress.

NEUROBIOLOGY OF MOOD AND PERSONALITY

When exploring the relation between mood, personality, and pathophysiology, several subsystems must be identified:

1. Neurochemistry of brain injury

2. Limbic system functioning
3. Limbic cortical interface
   a. Frontal-Limbic
   b. Temporal-limbic
4. Hemispheric specialization

Neurochemistry of Brain Injury

The role of chemical transmitters has been investigated and related to changes in mood and personality within and outside the brain injured population. Hayes, Jenkins, and Lyeth (1992) provided an outline of the progression from primary to secondary consequences of trauma on the neurochemical aspects of head injury. They began with the changes in neuronal depolarization (impact depolarization) and extracellular increase of potassium. They followed with the description of the neurotransmitter release (excitatory amino acid). They used as an example increase of excitatory amino acid (EAA) from the hippocampal region immediately after percussion. In addition, they reported on the increase of glutamate with immediate elevations noted and returning to base line from 2 minutes after injury to continuation of elevated levels as much as 1 hour after injury in a research model. Also, there is reported elevation of acetylcholine. The increase in acetylcholine was found in the hippocampus (74% above baseline) and in the brainstem (73% above baseline). These changes were noted even with moderate percussion. It was also found that blood–brain barrier changes allowed for increased exposure of acetylcholine to the brain, thereby contributing to the increased acetylcholine within the brain tissue.

Changes in receptor binding has also been found on the microscopic level. Changes in cholinergic and glutamatergic receptors following percussion were reported. NMDA receptor site binding was reduced from 15% to 30%. The change in postsynaptic binding was found in 5 minutes, 3 hours, and 24 hours after percussion to the cerebral cortex. In addition, muscarinic cholinergic binding was brought about in hippocampal and dentate gyrus areas at 3 hours postinjury.

Hayes, Jenkins, and Lyeth went on to describe the behavioral endpoints related to memory disturbance and motor limitations that accompany such pathophysiology. They also explored the use of antagonists to impede the excitotoxin cascade and elevate the effects of secondary insult to vital areas of functioning having to do with mood and personality. They were effective in relating the chemistry to behavioral changes in memory, cognitive, and motor activities as studied in the experimental modes.

Dixon, Taft, and Hayes (1993) concentrated on mild traumatic brain injury and reinforced the findings of depolarization and neurotransmitter excitocity, and postsynaptic receptor binding changes. They continued on and explored cholinergic mechanisms of memory dysfunction and attention limitations. These changes play out in alterations in behavioral and conduct during performance demand. Also, the cholinergic tracts have been implicated in changes in expression of affect, especially anger. Saver, Salloway, Devinsky, and Bear (1996) studied acetylcholine effects on aggression in the hypothalamus.

Further review indicates the effects of specific chemistry on an array of aggressive behaviors, including agitation and impulsivity. For example, reduced serotonin has been found to correlate with increased aggressiveness both in laboratory models and humans. In addition, Fenwick (1989) found that disturbances in central norepinephrine would lead to impulsivity and episodic violence. Aminobutyric acid, in contrast, seems to inhibit aggression and benzodiazepines, which facilitates Gamma-amino butyric acid (GABA), can decrease fighting, and reduce aggression associated with limbic lesions.

In addition to disruptions in neurotransmitter systems, alterations in neuroendocrine functioning can also contribute alterations in mood and conduct. Increased testosterone has been associated with increased aggressiveness. Also, secondary effects of stroke, trauma, and neoplasms cause changes in hypothalamic-pituitary axis that leads to endocrine changes. The disruption of hypothalamic-pituitary axis has been implicated in management of stress and depression. Studies of suicide victims found a positive relation between a positive dexamethasone suppression test and elevated plasma and urine corticosteroid levels. Also, secondary alteration in thyroid functioning due to disrupted thyroid-stimulating hormone (TSH) has been implicated in psychiatric illness such as depression.

Subcortical and Limbic Structures

The limbic system has been recognized as the "emotional brain" through research and clinical practice for quite some time. Recent knowledge has grown so as to include specific structures and axis with increased specificity in brain–behavior relations. Defining the role of specific structures is complicated by a high degree of reliance on the structures for functioning and on the neurochemistry that relates and ties together each structure's functioning with one another. Although at times individual structures are reviewed, at other times identified subsystems and the more dynamic relation between structures and their role in mood and personality are reviewed.

Specific structures that have received attention include the thalamus, hypothalamus, amygdala, hippocampus, and basal ganglia. These structures have been regularly reviewed in relations to their important connection to frontal and temporal lobe activities. The close relation of limbic structures with memory functioning adds to the importance of the structures with the recovery of emotional-behavioral sequelae. Lezak (1995) reviewed subcortical and cortical structures.

Thalamus. The thalamus is a central relay area that is important in the transfer of information from subcortical to cortical structures. In turn, the cortical connection can impose a downward influence on memory, sensory experiences, and the experiences of emotion. With its connections to orbital-frontal areas, the thalamus is able to influence the tone of motor planning.

Specifically, changes in mood and conduct are noted with alterations in thalamic functioning. The role of the thalamus as a sensory relay station and its role in memory is accompanied by the effects on the emotional capacity and responsiveness. Thalamic injury can result in apathy, lack of animation, and spontaneity. Also, emotional and personality changes have been noted in diencephalon amnesia where the interaction of memory and personality is underscored. At times, right thalamic injury has been associated with mania and lateral neglects have been noted with ipsilateral thalamic injury.

Hypothalamus. The hypothalamus has great importance in the maintenance of homeostasis, emotional temperament, and autonomic functioning. For the purposes of this discussion, the effects of emotion/motivation are of most importance. The hypothalamus is not homogeneous; instead, it consists of varied nuclei that have differential effects on the behavioral expression of emotions. For example, the stimulation of the lateral hipothalamus produces anger, and lesions in this area result in placid, docile behaviors. The medial hypothalamus, when stimulated, creates an excitable and agitated anima. When the hypothalamus loses its influences of expression by the loss of cortical influence (decortication), a series of agitated aggressive behaviors are manifest. *Sham rage* (termed by Walter Cannon in 1925) can appear suddenly and accompany increased adrenal secretions. Also, ablation of the hypothalamus during sham rage will bring sudden impulses like anger to an end. And, the hypothalamus will modulate the experience of noxious and/or pleasurable stimuli. In balance, the management of these sensations prepare and assist the body to protect. When this integrative ability is lost, then the experience of pleasure and pain can be greatly exaggerated or suppressed. There are noticeable critical signs of hypothalamic dysfunction in depression, which has led to the hypothesis that the modulation of neuroendocrine activity may be effected. The role of the hypothalamus in elementary stages of motivation and emotion are best understood in terms of its servocontrol influences and efforts to maintain checks and balances between external incentive stimuli and internal drives. The hypothalamus plays an important role in coordinating the emotional experience with the demands of the external world without compromise to the organism's homeostasis.

Amygdala. The amygdala receives multiple afferent tracts, including olfaction. In turn, the amygdala sends information on to the hypothalamus, thalamus, and cingulate gyrus. The amygdala has been suggested to relate drive-object reactions. By matching the external perceptual qualities of the object with the appropriate affective expressions, the amygdala modulates the expression of affect. Through its interconnections with the orbital-frontal area, the amygdala can influence the emotional tone of motor planning. The amygdala's role in temperament and emotional expression is evidenced by the 1937 discovery of the Kluver–Bucy syndrome where the bilaterate removal of amygdala and temporal structures produced a docile and hyper-oral animal. Damage to the amygdala is especially important in the expression of oral tendencies, hypersexuality, and tameness.

Basal Ganglia. Subcortical dementias have resulted from a number of etiological influences on cerebral white matter disorders. Initially associated with the cognitive, emotional, and movement disturbances, such as supranuclear palsy and Huntington's disease, subcortical dementia now is recognized with hypoxic ischemia, traumatic, and cerebral vascular disorders (Filley, 1996). Emotional disorders like depression, bipolar disorder, euphoria, and "emotional dysregulation" occur. The change of emotional regulation occurs in the presence of cognitive dementia. Psychosis has been reported that precedes memory and cognitive changes. The progressive failure of underlying white tracks and failure of frontal limbic integrity have been hypothesized. Cerebral white matter serves a vital function in the integration and coordination of neurobehavioral networks necessary for fluid emotional-cognitive-behavioral integration. Alterations in specific structures and/or the white matter tracks contribute to the deterioration of mood and conduct. The altered sequences of skills expresses itself in personality changes.

Limbic Cortical Interface

Temporal Lobe and Limbic Connections. The temporal lobes provide sophisticated supports to the cortical aspects of memory, auditory processing, and perception. However, it is the temporal limbic connections that draw attention. The hippocampal temporal lobe interface plays an important role in memory effects on situational comprehension and contextual awareness. The lack of temporal or situational comprehension or the loss of contextual awareness impedes behavioral selection and planning. The individual runs the risk of acting out of context. This lack of "matching behavior to situation" results in confrontations with reality and rejection by others. The awkward mismatch between behavior and situation is not an uncommon confrontation for persons suffering temporal and frontal injuries.

Three types of emotional disturbances find correlation with injury to the temporal lobes and its limbic connections. Right temporal lesions interfere with the ability to detect, comprehend, and/or express the emotional tone of verbal expressions. The prosodies, inability to detect or express emotional intonations or innuendo, can undermine social comprehension and social discourse. Another disturbance is temporal lobe seizure disorder. Manifestation of this disorder includes emotional changes, alterations in conduct, and inter-ictal sequelae. These symptoms can include a sense of depersonalization, transient visual or auditory hallucinations, fear, anger, delusions, sexual feelings, and paranoia. There can be complex motor acts and illusory phenomena. Also, with chronic temporal lobe seizures, there are characteristic obsessive-compulsive like features, hypergraphia, and examples of hyperreligiosity. Many times, the dedication to particular expressions or behaviors are justified through the reference to strong moralistic feelings and rules about right and wrong. Third, temporal lobe injury has been related to panic attacks. These are acute anxiety disorders with autonomic nervous system sequelae, such as racing heart and shortness of breath. The parahippocampal blood perfusion increases bilaterally and there is hyperperfusion on the right between panic episodes.

Frontal Limbic Structures.   The frontal lobes have been said to provide executive oversight to the integration of cognition, emotion, and motor planning. It is in the frontal lobe where thought and deed interface. Disruption to the frontal executive skills produces a dysregulation in the emotional/motivational and complex cognitive control over social conduct. This disruption in conduct is most apparent in the social transactional disturbances noted in patients with diminished frontal lobe functioning. Fuster (1996) reviewed the effect of dorsal lateral injury on prefrontal structures and the resulting disorder in the "temporal organization of behavior." This effect is believed to impact short-term memory and the development of preparatory set affecting current conduct. Planning is weakened and conduct falls to the immediate influences of environment and emotions.

Another syndrome noted in the orbitomedial prefrontal reflects the postulated connection with the limbic structures. Damasio (1994) provided an entertaining review commenting on the common knowledge that the effect emotion has on the distortions in reasoning and conduct. Acknowledging the common influence that too much emotion has, Demasio explored the equal problem of too little guidance of emotions over reasoning and social conduct. Lezak (1991) reported on the effects of volition, planning purposive action, and performance effectiveness. Hart and Jacobs indicated that the frontal limbic interfaces: (a) decide what is worth attending to and what is worst doing; (b) provide continuity and coherence to behavior across time; (c) modulate affective and interpersonal behavior so that drives are satisfied within the constraints of the internal and external environments; and (d) the frontal lobes monitor, evaluate, and adjust.

Hemispheric Asymmetry

The cerebral hemispheres demonstrate specialization for the perception and comprehension of emotional behaviors. Heilman and Bowers (1996) discussed "emotional cognition and communication" as a complex multisystem effect that impacts the person's ability to "read" and "express" emotional aspects of gestures and verbal exchange. These systems are especially attributed to the right or nondominant hemisphere. Disorders in emotional facial recognition have been recognized; however, the more specific limitation in facial emotional expressions is relevant to the social perceptiveness and situational analysis. An equally interesting finding has been that patients with damaged right hemispheres are unable to produce emotional facial expressions. The lack of animation has been found with other injuries (i.e., frontal injury), however, the inability to produce facial expressions spontaneously in naturally occurring situations has importance for the social transaction and social nature of the person.

Of equal importance is the loss of ability to detect emotional scenes. Recognition of emotionally relevant information is difficult for both right and left hemisphere patients, but may occur more frequently with right hemisphere injury due to increased likelihood of visual perceptual disturbance.

The inability to read the emotional intonations and emotional expressions of language has resulted in a series of disturbances to prosody. The aprosodic nature of a right hemisphere patient can include both the inability to convey emotional content or to comprehend emotional content. Heilman and Bowers spoke of emotions semantics or the inability to understand the type of circumstances that may be associated with an emotion. They indicated that certain brain injuries result in the loss of ability to read a situation and interpret its likely emotional intention. This has been viewed in Alzheimer's patients and diffuse or bi-hemispheric patients. Although a patient may lose the ability to read specific emotional stimuli, unless there is more diffuse or generalized injury the ability to infer an emotional semantics is intact.

Whereas the culture, language, and societal differences present great challenge and variability, the neurobiology of change is considered more the same for all people. For example, depression is probably the most ubiquitous emotional disorder following many types of brain injury or disease. The research literature for mood and behavioral changes after brain injury has greatly expanded. Longitudinal research (Robinson & Travella, 1996) indicates that following stroke, for example, both psychological reactions to limitations (Goldstein's Catastrophic Reaction) and neurogenic mood disorder (major mood disorder and dysthemia) exists. Although the prevalence of these disorders varies, Robinson and Travella indicated poststroke depression is not a transient but a long-standing disorder with a natural course somewhat less than one year for major depression and, perhaps a more viable course for minor depressions. Consistent with the dynamic occurrences in the clinical setting, Robinson and Travella concluded that some major depressions, however, last more than three years, and some minor depressions evolve into major depressions and may last for several years.

An understanding of the neurobiology and the alterations in mood or personality secondary to medical conditions is extremely important. Consideration of therapeutic resources cannot proceed until underlying medical etiologies have been considered and evaluated. Not to consider the medical aspects that contribute to the alteration of mood and personality runs the risk of misdiagnosis and more importantly the elimination of an entire source of therapeutic interventions that are in the best interest for the patient.

PERSONALITY ASSESSMENT OF THE BRAIN INJURED PATIENT

Various authors have noted that the key to success in treatment of Hispanic patients lies in an effective, accurate, and valid assessment (Dana, 1993; Padilla & Ruiz, 1973; Velásquez, 1995; Velásquez & Callahan, 1992). However, the Hispanic patient is not always given an adequate psychological or neuropsychological assessment. First of all, the majority of tests given are *translations* from English (and normally have defects in the translation) and not *adaptations* of the test. The fact that they are translations and not adaptations *invalidates* the test de facto to be used in the assessment process. Second, problems in personality (behavior, emotions, feelings, motivation, etc.) cannot be attended to if the clinician is not truly familiar with the world and environment in which the patient lives. And third, significant linguistic problems exist between the evaluator and the patient. The evaluator is generally a native English-speaker and tries to speak elemental Spanish, whereas the Latino patient uses a superficial English, therefore only communicating on a superficial level. Latino patients, when asked questions they do not understand well, tend to respond positively or what they believe to be beneficial, although it may not be true. For these reasons, it is difficult to correctly capture the normal or pathological personality of the Latino patient after TBI. Keep in mind that the personality assessment must consider the more subtle aspects in order to understand it. Therefore, it is essential to dominate the language and knowledge of the patient's world.

On the other hand, evaluators should revise their own philosophic and scientific beliefs and perceptions when evaluating a patient whose language they do not understand well and whose culture seems strange and unfamiliar to them. The neuropsychologist should understand that the personality assessment of a Latino patient is not a ritual and mechanical act; on the contrary, it is a complex process. Neuropsychologists should therefore evaluate their own aptitude for this type of assessment. Many evaluators have misconceptions about Latino patients that make an adequate neurological personality assessment difficult. Velásquez (1995, pp. 112–123) identified some of the common misconceptions regarding the psychological assessment of Hispanic clients:

1. Hispanic clients are more difficult to assess or evaluate because they are not psychologically minded.

2. Problems in the clinical assessment of Hispanic clients are similar to those found in the intelligence/educational testing of Hispanics.

3. Psychological assessment devices, whether projective or objective, often misdiagnose or misclassify Hispanic patients.

4. Issues in the psychological assessment of Hispanic clients are identical to those found in other ethnic minority groups, most notably African Americans.

5. Only Hispanic psychologists can effectively assess and treat Hispanic clients.

None of these misconceptions is actually true (see Velásquez, 1995), although they guide many neuropsychologists when they are going to plan or design the neuropsychological assessment of the Hispanic patient.

When neuropsychologists assess personality naturally, the question of "What is being evaluated?" confronts the examiner. Personality is composed of intransigent and to a less degree modifiable psychological systems supported by physical substructures. It is clear that the scientific study of personality has difficulty with the definition of the infrastructure of events called "personality."

In brain injury, the recognition that conduct and temperament has changed due to alterations in the physical substrata that supports personality leads to questions about what is being assessed:

1. Personality as it is and as it will be in the future for the person following injury?
2. Personality as it was before injury?
3. Personality as an interaction of events before and following injury?
4. personality problems as they present in the course of recovery?

On first pass, it intuitively is apparent that quantitative as well as qualitative measures must be considered in the armamentarium of tools for clinical examination. The clinical need to address these complex issues requires casting a broad net of investigation. The need for observational and actuarial investigation becomes even more important during this early stage of clinical development. This chapter hopes to emphasize the need and importance of *qualitative examination* as well as the cross-cultural sensitivity to the Hispanic. When the examination cannot meet the strict standards of standardized testing, alternative, yet equally revealing, methods must be considered in order to meet the applied problems seeking solutions in the clinical environment.

The assessment and evaluation of personality after brain injury is in a very early stage of development. There is an absence of specific tools for the job of assessing mood and personality in the brain injured patient. The presently used tools were developed and standardized on psychiatric populations. The most commonly used tests are tools that have been used in psychological testing and psychiatric diagnosis. For example, the widely used Minnesota Multiphasic Personality Inventory (MMPI) and MMPI–2 have new scales for neurological injury. However, they lack standardization. Consequently, the brain injured patient will score high on several scales but their validation is not for the subject presently measured by the scale. Instead, patients answer according to their brain injury experience and gain a "false elevation."

The majority of research and clinical activity has been to assess questions of personality during the period of recovery from brain injury. Due to clinical need and practical issues of recovery, the therapist or doctor and family are responding to problems that must be solved. The emphasis has been on identifying clinically significant traits and elements in need of care at that time (see Cripe, 1996).

In many ways, the idea of personality assessment is a misnomer. Instead, there has been a need to identify problematic behaviors, altered emotional life, and changes in temperament needing psychological care and psychiatric intervention.

Cripe's critique of the state of measurement focuses on several important observations for the clinician. The appreciation for a comprehensive definition of personality is well understood. The majority of research has been on the study of emotional disorders and personality. He was quick to state that cognition, action systems, and perceptual changes are also a part of personality functioning. The bias of studies in emotions speaks to the immediate clinical needs but is narrow in perspective. In contrast, a more comprehensive understanding of personality systems allows for the use of standard cognitive, motivation, and perceptual testing as valuable information for the description and explanation of personality. Also, the present state of the art is lacking in validation studies and standardization and norms for the population in question. This structural flaw becomes even more emphasized with cross-cultural clinical investigation.

The Hispanic patient is frequently compared to the norms of the United States, or at times to those of their home coutry. However, Latino immigrants should have their own norms since this group is not encompassed either in the norms of their home country nor those of the United States.

Another feature affecting the Latino is the mind set for test taking. As reviewed by Pontón (1997), the Latino tends to seek alternative types of treatment and explanations. How does this affect test-taking behavior and response tendencies? The Latino's response to examination alone may bias the response and elevate validation scales. Furthermore, the response to authority and sensitivity to positioning in the culture again may affect the response tendency. With the structural difficulties noted, especially for the immigrated Latino, observational tools and qualitative measures can be even more attractive and useful in determining clinical course.

There is an emerging need to advise the clinician against the idea of trying to measure "personality" as a global concept. Instead, measure for specific issues. Also, the existence of adequate standardized and normed tools is lacking. Therefore, the need for reliable observational tools that meet the standards of ecological validity are best given the present state of the art.

From the 1940s to the present day, the five principal tools for evaluating personality in Hispanic patients have been, in order of use, MMPI/MMPI–2, Thematic Apperception Test, Rorschach, Beck Depression Inventory, and Million Clinical Multiaxial Inventory. But, the use of these tests does not mean that the conditions in which they are used are necessarily totally correct.

OBSERVATIONAL TOOLS AND INVENTORIES

Personality evaluation through questionnares, self-reports, and inventories is simple in language, and the questions are very clearly stated. However, it is a fact, as noted by Artiola i Fortuny and Mullaney (1997), that

> a review of materials used with Spanish speakers in North America reveals that the Spanish language found in much of the material is of generally poor quality. Such materials include published questionnares, manuals, test instructions, test items, and test protocols included in manuscripts submitted for publication. Most prominently, egregious errors are frequently found in unpublished tests which somehow make their way into neuropsychologists' offices. (pp. 1–2)

For these reasons, "we should expect no less than the same lingüistic and methodological standards which are applied to the development of tests in English" (p. 615).

Observational tools have been developed for a number of special populations. Geriatric groups and dementia inventories, as well as Alzheimer's disease, are available. However, those are not standardized for the brain injury population. Lezak (1995) reviewed several observational tools. She stated they are "relatively brief . . . standardized and . . . provide behavioral descriptions that can amplify or humanize test data" (p. 615).

Assessment is different from diagnosis (León-Carrión, 1986, 1995). To put it simply, personality assessment is the process through which information is obtained about key aspects about the patient, and the diagnosis is the articulation and elaboration of all the data obtained in the assessment process and clinical exploration to situate the patient

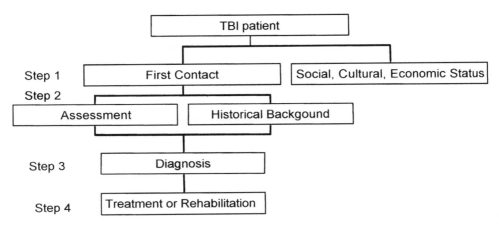

FIG. 13.2.   The four fundamental steps of the assesment, diagnostic, and treatment process.

in neurological criteria that has a concrete name or label. Figure 13.2 shows the four fundamental steps of the assessment, diagnostic, and treatment process for a personality disorder in a posttraumatic Hispanic patient.

Step 1 is the *first contact* with the traumatic brain injury (TBI) Hispanic patient. This is a very important step that should not be done carelessly and should be done by the same senior neuropsychologist that is going to do the whole assessment, diagnostic, and treatment process. This person should, under no circumstances, be substituted by an interview with the tester. At this point, the neuropsychologist should get a general idea of the principal idiosyncratic characteristics and traits of the patient's life. The social aspects in which the patient actually and actively, as well as passively, participates are to be determined here. At the same time, the cultural and multicultural level of the patient should be established. That is not only the level of education, but also the patient's cultural background, values, beliefs, motivations, and so on. At the same time, it is important to know the patient's economic status for two reasons. First, the majority of patients of a lower socio-economic class are usually misinterpreted in the psychological tests, giving a psychological profile that does not correspond to the true reality. Second, these same patients do not tend to take full advantage of those social and legal resources at their disposal. It is therefore very important after this first meeting for the neuropsychologist to design an evaluation that realistically takes into account all of the aspects mentioned.

Step 2 is the *data gathering process* relevant to the possible personality disorder shown by the patient. The process begins with gathering background, including information concerning how the patient's personality has changed from earlier behavior. It is fundamental to establish the time when this change occurred and how the person is different from when previously "normal." Once the historical background has been exposed, the assessment process begins, using tests and questionnaires. These tests, adapted to Spanish and translated so as not to permit misunderstandings, should be selected beforehand. If these tools are not available, then it is always better to use an expert qualitative assessment through an interview with the patient and family members as opposed to assessment through inadequate tests.

Step 3 is to *establish the diagnosis*, if relevant. This is when all the data obtained during the whole process (Steps 1 and 2) is compiled and a diagnosis is made if the data calls for it. The diagnosis is a label and the end of the assessment and clinical exploratory process.

For example, the depressed patient is diagnosed according to historical background and the results of the tests given.

However, there may not be any diagnosis, despite alterations in personality. In this case, for neuropsychological rehabilitation purposes, it may be interesting to get a report about the qualitative functioning of the personality of the TBI Hispanic patient. In this case, the neuropsychological report will describe all those qualitative data relevant to internal working of emotions, feelings, motivations, needs, and so on, of the patient.

Finally, in Step 4, deriving from the assessment process, a *neuropsychological treatment plan* should be determined, or in certain cases, *rehabilitation* of those aspects of personality that were found to be dysfunctional (see León-Carrión, 1995).

Promising tools include the following:

1. *Neurobehavioral Rating Scale* (NBRS; Levin, High, & Goethe, 1987). Copied from the Brief Psychiatric Rating Scale, this tool was developed with specific items for patients of traumatic brain injury. It includes specific items for planning, level of motivation, and insight and awareness. As indicated by Lezak (1995), the interrater reliability in the initial study was $r = .90$, $.88$ on two trials. Later retrials were $r = .789$ and $.76$. In a study of a French version, reliability did not reach the .05 level (Levin, Mazuak, & Vanier, 1990). The use of the NBRS is intended for the trained professional. Efforts at the University of Seville are on to explore a Spanish-speaking version of the NBRS.

2. *Portland Adaptability Inventory* (PAI; Lezak, 1987). This inventory is constructed to review items believed to sample the personal and social maladaptation that serve to prevent resumption of "normal activities." Information can be gathered from a combination of sources. Use of client, family, community, medical record, and indirect sources can be used. Initial results suggest PAI can be effective in predicting outcomes for vocational activities and rehabilitation outcomes.

3. *Neurologically Related Changes in Personality Inventory* (NECHAPI; León-Carrión, 1998). NECHAPI is in its initial phase as an observational tool with five factors: anger, sensation seeking, emotional vulnerability, sociability, and motivation. There are 40 observational items that ask for yes–no responses before and after injury. Simplified patient response is required within self-administration or interview administration (as structured interview). Also, items are developed and phrased from a culturally sensitive perspective (Spanish version). In addition, additional observations are gained from family, community members, or significant others. Analysis of items allows for clustering of responses into before–after categories and within test. Reliability awareness shows and Alpha $(\alpha) = 0, 68$ for the whole inventory. Factor 1 has an $\alpha = 0, 81$; Factor 2 = 0, 80; Factor 3 = 0, 80; Factor 4 = 0, 60; and Factor 5 = 0, 55. (See Appendix 13A and Appendix 13B.)

However, these are behavioral observations and are not to be confused with measures of psychological constructs. If observational tools are to be used, then the items must be developed from the cultural point of view and interpreted by the Spanish clinician.

4. *Rorschach.* Given the state of the art, the projective tools, Rorschach and the Holtzman ink blot tests, can serve clinicians well. These will have the least cultural bias. When administered and interpreted by the clinician from the patient's home country, observation and examination can become very useful. For example, in experience with the Rorschach and depressed and potentially suicidal patients, important and vital patient information was gained (see León-Carrión, 1996, 1997a).

To date, the body of literature regarding Rorschach and brain injury is not inclusive of cultural differences. However, the tool may represent the most culture-free approach to capturing unbiased patient responses. In reflection, the application of the ink blot tools require nonpsychoanalytic scoring and interpretation by a Hispanic (preferably home country) clinician. The use of the test scores and the application to treatment could then be opened to other then Hispanic/Spanish clinician.

During the course of clinical evaluation and measurement, the practitioner must remain focused on key questions. There are several specific questions that need to be addressed when engaging in personality testing of a brain injured patient. What questions need solutions, and will the tool used address such questions? Is the evaluation testing personality or is it interested in measurement of specific emotional and/or behavioral problems? Is a standardized assessment possible, and how can observational tools compare to the test being selected? How do the techniques to be used relate to the Latino community?

REHABILITATION, TREATMENT, AND RECOVERY

Recovery from complex behavioral disturbances, neuropsychiatric illness, and changes in personality is an extended process and requires the integration of many disciplines, Mental health, psychiatry, and neuropsychology all work together to effect changes that will support a successful recovery. Measurements of success must go beyond assessing the reduction in symptoms. Instead, assessing successful recovery must include measures of how the patient is able to live in real-life situations. The patient's home environment, the level of productivity, the extent of social life, and the abilities to care for and protect oneself are the ultimate measures of success. Although this is very difficult and treatment of complex behavioral, personality problems is challenging, the real test or measure of success in "how the patient is able to live outside of a clinical environment." It is only at this level of success that all the efforts, investment of time, and resources can be seen as worthwhile (see León-Carrión, 1998).

Phinney (1996) helped to focus exactly on the issue of managing differences. Phinney helped with operational definition of terms that can help make a difference in the midst of differences. Phinney spoke of the need to understand psychological implications of "ethnicity." In this clinical world, this is a very important issue. What difference does the patient's ethnic background make in test taking, response to therapy, and outcomes? Phinney stated that "ethnicity is a complex multidimensional construct that, by itself, explains little. . . . It is necessary to identify and assess those aspects of ethnicity that may have an impact on outcomes of interest" (p. 9). Phinney went on to identify three areas of importance: cultural norms and values; the strength, salience, and meaning of ethnic identity; and the experiences and attitudes associated with minority status.

This may serve as a beginning point of investigation as to the effects of cultural, linguistic, and ethnic influence on neuropsychological recovery. It is important to recognize that this requires investigation beyond the patient into the family unit, the collective community experience, and the cultural identity of a people as a whole. It is within this context of understanding that the patient's diagnosis, response to therapy, and determination of successful outcome only can have meaning.

There is a modest group of research that is specific to the brain injured patient as to how symptom manifestation is expressed. For example, Prigatano and Leatham (1993) explored the relation between the expression of the neurologic symptom of anosagnosia and the psychogenic symptom of denial across cultures. Prigatano found that TBI in the United States underestimated emotional and social difficulties but no self-care skills.

In the review of the literature, treatment for personality problems actually is the treatment not of personality but of a specific subgroup of problems. Treatment of personality tends to address emotional dysregulation, cognitive disorders, conduct disorders, and self-care/protection.

Emotional Dysregulation	Cognitive Disorders	Conduct Disorder	Self-Care/ Protection
Mood disorders	Thought disorders	Impulse disorders	Frontal lobe dysfunction
Depression	Paranoia	Aggression	Executive disorders
Mania		Hypersexuality	Social competency
Amotivation		Kleptomania	
		Non-compliance	

Treatment approaches generally have evolved from specific lines of research and individual interests. Again, there has been little or no reference to cross-cultural influences and effects. Until there can be more exact determination of treatment efficacy within and between cultures, there may be more value in considerations of clinical roles and duties during the use of existing tools.

As therapeutics used move from the more medical to the more sociocentric, the issues and factors outlined will require additional attention. The use of medications may be more uniform across populations, however, group membership, and prosocialization efforts must be sensitive to the elements outlined in ethnic appreciation.

Medical Treatment

Initial efforts to treat mood and personality changes must include the comprehensive consideration of medical conditions that could be at the foundation of such a clinical presentation. For example, it is not unusual for diabetics to have alterations in behavior during either elevated or reduced blood sugars. Following traumatic injury and with some strokes and tumors, diabetis insipidis is common. Another example would be liver dysfunction or kidney disease. Therefore, the medical basis of conduct should be considered. There are a number of medical conditions that can affect mood and conduct (see Table 13.2).

The medical consideration must include the examination and diagnosis of neuro-endocrine limitations. The integrity of the hypothalamic-pituitary axis plays an important role in maintenance of energy, management of stress, and mood. Hypothalamic lesions can present as mental or behavioral disorders. This could include disturbance with aggression, hyperphagia, and the picture of dementia. Primary and secondary thyroid disease can be expressed in depression, poor memory, anxiety, insomnia, irritability, difficulty with concentration, paranoia, or lethargy. Therefore, it is important that medical conditions be ruled out and that, when possible, medical care be available to treat any primary medical condition that is effecting mental status.

Medication Treatments

Of most importance in treating mood and personality disturbance is the role of medications. Pharmacology has be developed to where "corrective" intervention is possible. Unlike the past when symptoms were medicated, there is now the opportunity to make "corrective" use of pharmacology. The use of neuroleptics can now be replaced or com-

TABLE 13.2
Medical Conditions Affecting Mood and Conduct

Generalized System Failures or Involvement

1. Specific or generalized infection and/or sepsis
2. Organ system involvement (i.e., liver, kidney, cardiovascular disease
   Hepatitis
   Urmic toxicity
   Multi-infarct dementia)
3. Endocrine disorder: (i.e., diabetes, thyroid disorder, Addison's disease)
4. Toxic conditions: (i.e., lead poisoning, carbon monoxide)
5. Hypoxic or anoxic episode
6. Nutritional insufficiencies
7. Sleep disturbances (i.e., REM deprivation)

Degenerative Disorders

1. Demylenating disease: multiple sclerosis
2. Alzheimer dementia
3. Picks, huntington's chorea
4. Diffuse axonal injury

Iatrogenic Disorders

1. Medication side effects: (i.e., benzodiazepine and memory disturbance, SSRI* and hypomania)
2. Drug interactions (i.e., polypharmacy, either multiple psychoactive or interactions with medical agents)

* SSRI = serotonin selective reuptake inhibitor.

plemented by the use of additional medications that assist with adjusting the chemistry of the brain (see Table 13.3).

Mental Health Treatments

Mental health intervention can be considered under the headings of psychotherapy and behavior management. Historically, the use of counseling or psychotherapy was disappointing in attempts to confront disturbances in mood and personality. Clinicians would struggle with the individual who did not possess the cognitive, perceptual, or motivational skills necessary to participate in psychotherapy. Patients were not able to benefit from therapy because they lacked the very skills necessary to use and participate in treatment. It was the lack of these skills—such as self-awareness, social perceptiveness, and emotional management—that were both the problem and the skills necessary to participate in productive therapy. However, more recent reviews have been able to point a new way and use of psychotherapy with the brain injured patient.

Prigatano (1991) focused on psychotherapeutic interventions after traumatic brain injury. An article called "Disordered Mind, Wounded Soul: The Emerging Role of Psychotherapy in Rehabilitation After Brain Injury" tackled the difficult chore of reestablishing a sense of meaning after brain injury. Listing the deterioration in personality over years and the increasing burden on family, Prigatano commented that failure to address the residual cognitive and personality problems of TBI people often causes their psychosocial adjustment to deteriorate. He presented several assumptions: First, self-awareness has a neuropsychological substrata. The therapist must remember that self and social

TABLE 13.3
Medications and Target Disorders in a Brain Injury Population
(Reviewed From Fogel, Shiffer, & Rao, 1996)

Thought Disorders of Systematized Delusions with or without Hallucinations

---

1. Neuroleptics: Prescriptions according to sensitivity of patient to extrapyramidal side effects (EPS), and sensitivity to clouding of sensorium (increased confusion, delirium), or sensitivity to medical effects (i.e., orthostatic hypotension) and presence of medical comorbidity.
   a. Atypical neuroleptics, Respiridol and Clozapine due to reduced EPS and effects on "negative symptoms." However, cautions due to multiple system side effects.
   b. Traditional neuroleptics: Haldol, Mellaril

Agitation and Aggression

The use of medications to corrects and/or manage aggression during recovery:
Acute Phase—
1. Neuroleptics when aggression is accompanied by psychotic symptoms
2. Benzodiazepines during abbreviated periods (i. e., lorazepam)
3. Beta blockers (i.e., propranolol, clonodine)
Chronic Phase—
1. Antiseizure medications
2. Lithium for manic-like patients
3. Propranolol and clonidine

Anxiety Disorders

---

1. Benzodiazepines especially for patients with hyperarousal
2. Buspirone especially for patinets with cognitive symptoms
3. Neuroleptics for anxiety with accompanying paranoid thought disorder
4. Lithium for patients with hypomania
5. SSRIs for patients with OCD factors

Depression

Depression with biological indicators
1. Tricyclic medications with sensitivity to patients vulnerability to side effects
2. Seratonin re-uptake blockers
3. Trazodone and Nefazodone
4. Psychostimulants

Apathy and Amotivation

---

1. Psychostimulants
2. Dopamine agonists

---

awareness can be impaired on a neurological basis. Second, as the therapist becomes more familiar with the patient, the therapist must consider the patient's neuropathological changes as well as psychodynamics. Third, the therapist must provide information in a manner the patient can handle and not be overwhelmed. Prigatano believed the psychotherapist must focus on problems that interfere with the patient's ability to maintain a productive lifestyle. Also, research must focus on how to measure when the psychotherapist has attained goal (Prigatano, 1997).

Jacobs provided a step-by-step approach to the use of well-grounded approaches and the use of learning theory on altered conduct following brain injury. Inclusive of association learning and reinforcement scheduling, Jacobs provided a structured approach to these complex problems. He included a review of selective use of contingencies and behavioral contracting.

In more recent works, Jacobs (1993) expanded upon his behavioral analysis offering and described the impact of systematized interventions beyond the issues of stimulus and response. He acknowledged that behavioral techniques originated from early learning theorists who wanted to document how environmental influences could affect learning and personality. Jacobs concluded that the role of behavior analysis and intervention for brain injured patients is to make the environment more salient for the client by accommodating their unique perceptual and cognitive abilities. This is to emphasize the important effect of environment on mood and personality for persons recovering from brain injury.

Jacobs (1993) presented an array of new and innovating methods for the application of known behavioral approaches. Jacobs included the use of behavior intervention in home and community. He included an article on "functional analysis," wherein complex environmental determinants of "severe behaviors" are captured for care and treatment. Of particular interest is the article "Natural-setting Behavioral Management of Individuals with Traumatic Brain Injury, Results of a Three-Year Caregiver Training Program," which Carnevales described as a training method for caregivers as they address "target behaviors" in a home environment. For it is in the successful care and treatment of mood and personality problems in real-life settings that becomes the fundamental challenge for all types of treatment. The real satisfaction must come in the community where individuals will be required to qualify themselves to take the challenges of daily responsibility.

Patrick and Hebda (1997) described the ultimate importance of "pro-socialization" of aggressive clients during the recovery from brain injury. They proposed that until the final phase of socialization is completed, treatment remains partial and short of the applied goal. In their presentation, the parallel influences of medications and psychological intervention lead inextricably to group membership and role definition in the home community.

The need for social discourse skills and a repertoire of interpersonal skills become uniquely important in the patient's reintegration. It is in the re-entry to life's daily events that success is determined and not in the sheer measurement of symptom reductions. Patrick and Hebda proposed a stepwise integration of multiple influences, all of which are neccessary in the treatment of complex emotional and personality problems.

In short, Table 13.4 shows complementary treatment interventions for complex mood and personality disorders following brain injury.

TABLE 13.4
Complementary Treatment Interventions for Complex Mood and Personality Disorders
Following Brain Injury

Biological	Psychological	Sociocentric
Physical/medical systems	Behavioral tolerances	Group membership skills
Chemical integrity of the brain	Tolerance for change	Codes of conduct
Biological supports for learning/thinking and feeling	Cognitive/perceptual skills	Role development within idiosyncratic systems
	Emotional management skills	Social inclusiveness
	Social discourse skills	Social identity at home, work, school, and play

CONCLUSIONS

Personality disorders are evident and present after traumatic brain injury. From a neuro-psychological point of view, the difficulties appear when an attempt is made to assess, eval-uate, and treat these orders. The effects of brain injury on personality can be observed from a clinical as well as a functional point of view. From the clinical perspective, the patient may show early or delayed affective disorders, episodes of psychosis, anxiety, and/or conduct disturbance. From the personal perspective, the individual may report diffi-culties expressing emotions, mood dysregulation, alterations in sexual desire and per-formance, family adjustment problems, aggressiveness, and so on. All of these aspects, and others, should be assessed within the context of the physical, psychological, and social uniqueness of the individual.

The neuropsychologist should have a broad perspective, training, and understanding of the complex disturbances in personality and mood. Also, it is best that the neuro-psychologist is matched in terms of language, culture, and social experiences. Enlistment of less well-matched clinicians is acceptable when preceded by a complex evaluation and knowledgable treatment plan prepared by a clinician of cultural likeness and similarity.

Scientific knowledge of mood and personality disorders following brain injury has advanced; however, the cross-cultural nuances and sensitivities that explain the idiosyn-cracies of the patient fall below present scientific capabilities. Presently, tools for evalua-tion, treatment programs, and outcome determinants are synonomous with the clinical expertise and knowledge of the clinician. Care, caution, and sensitivity to the job ahead is important in avoiding false diagnosis, misattribution of cause–effect, and unsuccessful treatment intervention.

The neuropsychologist has always felt the clinical burden to know and comment on the multiple clinical factors, ranging from the neurology of the case to the sociocentric specialness of each patient. This clinical task is heightened when caring for the neuro-logically injured Hispanic person who is struggling with a medical condition within the context of an already existing social struggle. The pride, uniqueness, and vitality of the Hispanic culture, experience, and struggle will all interact with the biomedical variables of the case.

At the same time, however, the neuropsychologist should be careful. Psychopharma-cals notably affect the patient's behavior and personality. Possibly, when neuropsycholo-gists see the patient, they are under the effects of a psychopharmacal. In these cases, it is very important, especially in assessment, to know beforehand the effects of the medica-tion on this particular patient and, if possible, assess and evaluate the patient when drug free. Medication is a powerful weapon that, according to experience, noticeably affects patients with brain injury. Therefore, much care and research needs to be taken respect-ing the medication patients need to be or are taking.

The challenge of caring for the Hispanic patient within the context of a foreign envi-ronment is among the most challenging of the neuropsychologist's task. For it is on the knowledge of the interactions between biological, psychological, and social factors that the understanding, treatment, outcomes, and success for the individuals and their family will depend.

Personality disorders are evident and present after a traumatic brain injury. From a neuropsychological viewpoint, the difficulties appear when an attempt is made to assess, evaluate, and treat such disorders. The effects of brain injury on personality can be observed from a clinical as well as a functional point of view. From the clinical, the patient may show, in early or delayed stages, affective disorders, episodes of psychosis, anxiety disorders, and so on. And from the personal functioning point of view, the patient may have difficulties expressing emotions, mood regulation, sexual desire and competence, family adjustment, aggressiveness, and so on. So the neuropsychologist should speak the language well, as well as be very familiar with cultural values. The neuropsychological rehabilitation should follow a complete analysis of the evaluation process to be followed by the patient, and carried out with maximum respect and efficiency.

APPENDIX 13A

<u>*NEUROLOGICALLY-RELATED CHANGES IN PERSONALITY INVENTORY (NECHAPI)*</u>

José León-Carrión
University of Seville, Spain
Center for Brain Injury Rehabilitation (C.RE.CER)

(APPENDIX)

NAME:_____   DATE : ____ / ____ / ____

AGE: ____   EDUCATIONAL LEVEL:_____   SEX:____   MARITAL STATUS:_____

A B C D (1)

	LESS				MORE
1.-Is usually a hot blooded person	1	2	3	4	5
2.-Usually experiences everything very intensely	1	2	3	4	5
3.-Is difficult to calm down when he/she gets excited	1	2	3	4	5
4.-Has very strong emotions	1	2	3	4	5
5.-Sometimes behaves in a very cruel way	1	2	3	4	5
6.-Gets upset easily	1	2	3	4	5
7.-Is a violent person	1	2	3	4	5
8.-Normally engages in dangerous behavior	1	2	3	4	5
9.-Is usually in control of him/herself and his/her behavior	1	2	3	4	5
10.-Is easily annoyed	1	2	3	4	5
11.-Is a vulnerable person	1	2	3	4	5
12.-Is a very sensitive person	1	2	3	4	5
13.-Gets in a lot of trouble	1	2	3	4	5
14.-Is not afraid of anything	1	2	3	4	5
15.-Has a lot of friends	1	2	3	4	5
16.-Is involved in a lot of social activities	1	2	3	4	5
17.-In my opinion, drinks more than he/she should	1	2	3	4	5

	LESS				MORE
18.-Probably takes drugs sometimes	1	2	3	4	5
19.-Likes to make other people suffer	1	2	3	4	5
20.-Is always on the lookout for new emotional experiences	1	2	3	4	5
21.-Is fickle	1	2	3	4	5
22.-Doesn´t offer explanations for what he/she does	1	2	3	4	5
23.-Is definitely shy	1	2	3	4	5
24.-Usually feels guilty about insignificant things	1	2	3	4	5
25.-Could be described as being on the sadistic side	1	2	3	4	5
26.-Does things as if he/she were fearless or unaware of danger	1	2	3	4	5
27.-Is always open to new experiences	1	2	3	4	5
28.-Is always looking for new sensations	1	2	3	4	5
29.-Never takes into account how his/her actions may have made other people feel	1	2	3	4	5
30.-Is not interested in very many things	1	2	3	4	5
31.-Is a hostile person	1	2	3	4	5
32.-Is a frustrated person	1	2	3	4	5
33.-Is a very negative person	1	2	3	4	5
34.- Is a depressive person	1	2	3	4	5
35.-Is capable of committing suicide	1	2	3	4	5
36.-Enjoys sex a lot	1	2	3	4	5
37.-Probably wouldn´t mind any kind of sexual experience, no matter how strange	1	2	3	4	5
38.-Has a lot of sexual experience	1	2	3	4	5
39.-Is easily angered	1	2	3	4	5
40.-Has a strong desire to live	1	2	3	4	5

(1)

A: Family members that live with the patient.
B: Girl / boyfriend; committed relationship
C: Close friends
D: Neighbors, acquaintances, other: please specify.................

Fixed Graphic 1b.

APPENDIX 13B

INVENTARIO DE CAMBIOS DE PERSONALIDAD NEUROLÓGICOS
José León-Carrión

NOMBRE:————————————————— FECHA :——/——/——

EDAD: ——— EDUCACION:——— SEXO:——— ESTADO CIVIL:———

	POCO	MEDIO	MUCHO		
1.- Normalmente es una persona pasional	1	2	3	4	5
2.- Normalmente vive todo con intensidad	1	2	3	4	5
3.- Cuando se emociona es difícil calmarle	1	2	3	4	5
4.- Tiene emociones muy intensas	1	2	3	4	5
5.- A veces se comporta de un modo realmente cruel	1	2	3	4	5
6.- Se angustia fácilmente	1	2	3	4	5
7.- Es una persona violenta	1	2	3	4	5
8.- Normalmente tiene conductas peligrosas	1	2	3	4	5
9.- Normalmente tiene buen control sobre sí mismo y su conducta	1	2	3	4	5
10.- Más bien puede decir que es una persona arisca	1	2	3	4	5
11.- Es una persona vulnerable	1	2	3	4	5
12.- Sin lugar a dudas es una persona muy emotiva	1	2	3	4	5
13.- Es una persona que se mete en muchos líos	1	2	3	4	5
14.- No tiene miedo a nada	1	2	3	4	5
15.- Es una persona que tiene muchos amigos	1	2	3	4	5
16.- Participa en muchas actividades sociales	1	2	3	4	5
17.- Yo creo que bebe más de lo que debiera	1	2	3	4	5
18.- Seguro que de vez en cuando toma drogas	1	2	3	4	5
19.- Le gusta castigar a los demás	1	2	3	4	5
20.- Siempre está buscando emociones nuevas	1	2	3	4	5

	POCO MEDIO MUCHO		
21.- Es una persona caprichosa	1 2 3 4 5		
22.- Es una persona que da pocas explicaciones	1 2 3 4 5		
23.- Definitivamente es una persona vergonzosa	1 2 3 4 5		
24.- Normalmente se siente culpable por cosas o hechos insignificantes	1 2 3 4 5		
25.- Se puede decir que es más bien sádico	1 2 3 4 5		
26.- Hace cosas como si no tuviera miedo, o no fuera consciente del peligro	1 2 3 4 5		
27.- Es una persona que está siempre abierta a nuevas experiencias	1 2 3 4 5		
28.- Siempre está buscando nuevas sensaciones	1 2 3 4 5		
29.- Nunca tiene en cuenta, cuando hace algo, como le sienta lo que ha hecho a los demás	1 2 3 4 5		
30.- Es una persona a la que le interesan pocas cosas	1 2 3 4 5		
31.- Es una persona hostil	1 2 3 4 5		
32.- Es una persona frustrada	1 2 3 4 5		
33.- Es una persona muy negativa	1 2 3 4 5		
34.- Es más bien una persona depresiva	1 2 3 4 5		
35.- Tiene valor suficiente para suicidarse	1 2 3 4 5		
36.- Le gusta mucho el sexo	1 2 3 4 5		
37.- Seguro que no le importa tener cualquier tipo de experiencia sexual, por rara que sea	1 2 3 4 5		
38.- Tiene mucha experiencia sexual	1 2 3 4 5		
39.- Se enfada rápidamente	1 2 3 4 5		
40.- Tiene muchas ganas de vivir	1 2 3 4 5		

A: Familiares directos que conviven con el paciente.
B: Novio/a, pareja estable.
C: Amigos habituales
D: Vecinos, conocidos y otros: especificar ....

REFERENCES

American Psychiatric Association. (1980). *Diagnostic and statistical manual of mental disorders* (3rd ed.). Washington, DC: Author.

American Psychiatric Association. (1994). *Diagnostic and statistical manual of mental disorders* (4th ed.). Washington, DC: Author.

Artiola i Fortuny, L., & Mullaney, H. A. (1997). Neuropsychology with Spanish-speakers: Language and proficiency issues for test development. *Journal of Clinical and Experimental Neuropsychology, 19*(1), 1–9.

Cripe, L. I. (1996). Personality assessment of brain injury patients. In M. Maurish & J. Moses, (Eds.), *Theoretical foundations of clinical neuropsychology for clinical practicioners.* Hillsdale, NJ: Lawrence Erlbaum Associates.

Damasio, A. R. (1994). *Descartes's error: Emotion, reason and human brain.* York: Grosset/Putnam.

Dana, R. H. (1993). *Multiculture assessment perspectives for professional psychology.* Boston: Allyn & Bacon.

Dixon, C. E., Taft, W. C., & Hayes, R. L. (1993). Mechanisms of mild traumatic brain injury. *Journal of Head Trauma Rehabilitation, 3,* 1–12.

Fenwick, P. (1989). Dyscontrol. In E. H. Rehnolds & R. M. Trimble (Eds.), *Between neurology and psychiatry.* London: Churchill.

Filley, C. M. (1996). Neurobeahvioral aspects of cerebral white matter injury. In B. S. Fogel, R. B. Shiffer, & S. M. Rao, (Eds.), *Neuropsychiatry* (pp. 913–934). Baltimore: Wilkens Press.

Fogel, B. S., Shiffer, R. B., & Rao, S. M. (1996). *Neuropsychiatry.* Baltimore: Wilkens Press.

Fuster, J. M. (1996). Frontal lobe lesions. In B. S. Fogel, R. B. Shiffer, & S. M. Rao, (Eds.), *Neuropsychiatry* (pp. 407–414). Baltimore: Wilkens Press.

Gaultiere, T., & Cox, D. R. (1991). The delayed neurosequelae of brain injury. *Brain Injury, 5,* 219.

Goldstein, K. (1942). *Aftereffects of brain injuries in war: Their examination and treatment.* New York: Grune & Stratton.

Goldstein, K. (1952). The effect of brain damage in personality. *Psychiatry, 15,* 245–260.

Hayes, R. L., Jenkins, L. W., & Leyth, B. G. (1992). Neurotransmitter-mediated mechanisms of traumatic brain injury. *Journal of Neurotrauma, 9,* 5173–5187.

Heilman, K. M., & Bowers, D. (1996). Emotional disorders associated with brain dysfunction. In B. S. Fogel, R. B. Shiffer, & S. M. Rao, (Eds.), *Neuropsychiatry* (pp. 401–406). Baltimore: Wilkens Press.

Jacobs, H. E. (1993). *Behavioral analysis guidelines and brain injury rehabilitation: People, principles and programs,* Gaithesburg, MD: Aspen.

Klonoff, P. S., & Lage, G. A. (1991). Narcissistic injury in patients with traumatic brain injury. *Journal of Head Trauma Rehabilitation, 21.*

León-Carrión, J. (1986). *Diagnóstico clínico en psicología* [*Clinical diagnosis in psychology*]. Seville, Spain: Alfar Ed.

León-Carrión, J. (1994). *Daño cerebral: Guia para familiares y cuidadores* [*Brain injury: A guide for families and caregivers*]. Madrid/Mexico City: Siglo XXI.

León-Carrión, J. (1995). *Manual de neuropsicología humana* [*Handbook of human neuropsychology*]. Madrid: Siglo XXI.

León-Carrión, J. (1996). *Neuropsychology master degree: Seminars.* University of Seville, Spain.

León-Carrión, J., Serdio, M. L., Murillo, F., Dominguez-Roldan, J. M., Dominguez-Morales, M. R., & Barroso y Martin, J. M. (1996, November). *Depression and suicide after brain injury: Notes for rehabilitation.* Paper presented at the National Head Injury Association Meeting, Dallas, TX.

León-Carrión, J. (1997a). An approach to the treatment of affective disorders and suicide tendencies after TBI. In J. León-Carrión (Ed.), *Neuropsychological rehabilitation: Fundamentals, innovations and directions* (pp. 415–430). DelRay Beach, FL: St. Lucie Press.

León-Carrión, J. (1997b). A historical view of neuropsychological rehabilitation: The search for human dignity. In J. León-Carrión (Ed.), *Neuropsychological rehabilitation: Fundamentals, innovations and directions* (pp. 3–40). DelRay Beach, FL: St. Lucie Press.

León-Carrión, J. (1997c). *Sleep questionnare for brain injury.* Madrid/Seville, Spain: Center for Brain Injury Rehabilitation.

Levin, H. S., High, W. M., & Goeth, K. E. (1987). The Neurobehavioral Rating Scale assessment of the behavioral sequelae of head injury by the clinician. *Journal of Neurology, Neurosurgery, and Psychiatry, 50,* 183–193.

Levin, H. S., Benton, L. A., & Grossman, R. G. (1982). *Neurobehavioral consequences of closed head injury.* New York: Oxford Press.

Levin, H. S., Mazaux, J. M., & Vanier, M. (1990). Évaluation des troubles neuropsychologiques et comportamentaux des traumatises crâniens par le clinicien: Proposition d'une échelle neurocomportamentale et premier résultats de sa version française. *Annales de Readaptation et de Médicine Physique, 33,* 35–40.

Lezak, M. (1978). Living with the characterologically altered brain injured person. *Journal of Clinical Psychiatry, 36,* 56.

Lezak, M. (1987). Making neuropsychological assessment relevant to head injury. In H. S. Levin, J. Grafman, & H. M. Eisenberg (Eds.), *Neurobehavioral recovery from head injury* (pp. 116–128). New York: Oxford University Press.

Lezak, M. D. (1991). Emotional impact of cognitive inefficiencies in mild head trauma. *Journal of Clinical and Experimental Neuropsychology, 13,* 23 (Abstract).

Lezak, M. (1995). *Neuropsychological assessment* (3rd ed.). New York: New York University Press.

Meyer, E. (1904). The anatomical facts and clinical varieties of trauma. *American Journal of Insanity, 60,* 37.

Miranda, J. Azocar, F., Organista, K. C., Nuñoz, R. F., & Lieberman, A. (1996). Recruiting and retaining low-income Latinos in psychotherapy research. *Consulting Clinical Psychology, 64*(5), 864–874.

Novak, T. A., Bergquist, T. F., Bennett, G., & Gouvier, W. D. (1991). Distress following severe head injury. *Journal of Head Trauma Rehabilitation 4,* 69.

Padilla, A. M., & Ruiz, R. A. (1973). *Latino mental health: A review of literature* (DHEW Pub. No. ADM 74-113) Washington, DC: U.S. Government Printing Office.

Patrick, P., & Hebda, D. (1997). Management of agression. In J. León-Carrión (Ed.), *Neuropsychological rehabilitation: Fundamentals, innovations and directions* (pp. 431–452). DelRay Beach, FL: St. Lucie Press.

Phinney, J. S. (1996). When we talk about American ethnic groups, what do we mean? *American Psychologist, 51*(9), 9.

Pontón, M. (1997). Rehabilitating brain damage in Hispanics. In J. León-Carrión (Ed.), *Neuropsychological rehabilitation: Fundamentals, innovations and directions* (pp. 513–530). DelRay Beach, FL: St. Lucie Press.

Prigatano, G. (1997). The problem of impaired self-awareness in neuropsychological rehabilitation. In J. León-Carrión (Ed.), *Neuropsychological rehabilitation: Fundamentals, innovations and directions* (pp. 301–312). DelRay Beach, FL: St. Lucie Press.

Prigatano, G. P. (1991). Disordered mind, wounded soul: The emerging role of psychotherapy in rehabilitation after brain injury. *Journal of Head Trauma Rehabilitation, 6,* 1–10.

Prigatano, G. P. (1986). *Neuropsychological rehabilitation after brain injury.* Baltimore: Johns Hopkins University Press.

Prigatano, G. P., & Leathem, J. M. (1993). Awareness of behavioral limitations after traumatic brain injury: A cross-cultural study of New Zealand Maoris and non-Maoris. *Clinical Neuropsychologist, 7*(2), 123–135.

Robinson, R. G., & Travella, J. I. (1996). Neuropsychiatry of mood disorders. In B. S. Fogel, R. B. Shiffer, S. M., Rao (Eds.), *Neuropsychiatry* (pp. 287–306). Baltimore: Wilkens Press.

Robinson, R. G., & Jorge, R. (1994). Mood disorders. In J. M. Silver, S. C. Yudofsky, & R. E. Hales (Eds.), *Neuropsychiatry of traumatic brain injury* (pp. 219–250). Washington, DC: American Psychiatric Press.

Rosenthal, M., Griffith, E. R., Bond, M. R., & Miller, J. D. (Eds.). (1983). *Rehabilitation of the brain injured adult.* Philadelphia: Davis.

Saver, J. L, Salloway, S. P., Devinsky, O., & Bear, D. M. (1996). Neuropsychiatry of agression. In B. S. Fogel, R. B. Shiffer, S. M., Rao (Eds.), *Neuropsychiatry* (pp. 523–548). Baltimore: Wilkens Press.

Silver, J., Hales, R., & Yudofsky, S. (1994). *Neuropsychiatry of Traumatic Brain Injury.* Washington, DC: American Psychatric Association.

Velázquez, R. J. (1995). Personality assesment of Hispanic clients. In J. N. Butcher (Ed.), *Clinical personality assesment* (pp. 120–139). New York: Oxford University Press.

Velázquez, R. J., & Callahan, W. J. (1992). Psychological testing of Hispanic Americans in clinical setting: Overview and issues. In J.M.K. Geisinger (Ed.), *Psychological testing of Hispanics* (pp. 253–265). Washington, DC. American Psychological Association.

Rehabilitation of Brain Injury Among Hispanic Patients

Marcel O. Pontón
Harbor–UCLA Medical Center

Ines Monguió
Private Practice, Ventura, CA

This chapter focuses on a conceptualization of how cultural issues impact the recovery of head injured Hispanic patients. This discussion, like many others in this book, is limited by factors that preclude absolute generalizations. Of note, the following observations are clinical in nature and relate to a mostly rural, low socioeconomic status, SES, low acculturation, immigrant Hispanic population. As such, these impressions may or may not be valid in approaching the well-educated, upper SES Hispanic immigrant from major urban centers in Latin America who resides in New York, for instance. Nor may it be appropriate for the second or third generation Hispanic who is monolingual English speaking and totally integrated into the U.S. culture. However, the issues presented provide a framework for understanding the areas of clinical interaction that typically evolve into sources of conflict within rehabilitative settings.

CONFLICT

Conflict in rehabilitation can be plentiful and expected. Multiple concerns are at stake, and opinions about the direction and effectiveness of treatment dominate the rehabilitation process. As a result, patients can find themselves in conflict with the very people who should care for their recovery: family and/or caretakers, treating doctors, therapists, house staff, case managers, lawyers, and so on. These conflicts are potentiated by differences in cultural and linguistic backgrounds between patients and those who treat them. For the purposes of this chapter, conflict is discussed within the context of cultural differences between Hispanic patients and their non-Hispanic treaters.

What Culture Is Your Brain?

Brain injured patients, like any other patient, bring into their recovery characteristics of premorbid personality, as well as their worldview (e.g., explanations, beliefs, and expectations of reality). How patients understand their condition will affect the options they perceive as available for their recovery (Ware & Kleinman, 1992).

Culture provides the metaphors by which to understand reality (Guarnaccia & Rodriguez, 1996). Culture also constricts the available choices of behavior through implicit or explicit rules that strengthen or extinguish certain courses of action (Syme, 1984; Ware & Kleinman, 1992). Issues of illness and health, available resources, and the values that allow individuals to form priorities depend on the cultural patterns to which they are exposed early in life, and that they later integrate as their own (see chap. 2 in this volume). Hispanic culture, in general, submits the needs and expressions of the individual to those of the group, be it the family or larger units (Mirowsky & Ross, 1984; Padilla, 1995; Ramirez, 1983). There is an important clinical implication of this cultural issue: Few Hispanics will make their needs or feelings known "assertively" if there is any chance that someone else in the family may be inconvenienced by this expression (Cohen, 1985). In the absence of a legitimate catharsis for those emotions, the option of choice is *somatization*. There appears to be a preponderance of somatizers among Hispanics (Escobar, 1987; Young, 1987). This does not mean, however, that somatization is exclusive of the Hispanic culture or that all Hispanics are somatizers. However, Hispanic patients tend to repress emotions that are considered negative within the culture, thus increasing the likelihood of psychological factors affecting physical conditions (i.e., recovery from a head injury; Gaw, 1993).

This difference in worldview and expectation of the provider–patient relationship can result in several forms of conflict between the patient and the doctor, the doctor and the patient, and the patient and the rehabilitation center.

Patient–Doctor Conflict

Because Hispanics are more likely to express psychological distress in terms of physical illness (Escobar, 1987), symptoms of anxiety and depression will be reported in terms of "being sick" with a clear admission of the physical aspects of the diagnoses but with denial of the emotional symptomatology. When reported to the clinician, patients expect that they will alleviate and "cure" all of the symptoms of distress via medication. Clinicians unfamiliar with these cultural expectations may respond to the patient from their own set of expectations that stress personal responsibility to change lifestyle and maintain health. More often than not, this advice will be received by the patient with critical distrust of the doctor. It is typical to hear patients say, for instance, "¿Qué clase de médico es este que ni si quiera me da medicinas?" ["What kind of a doctor is he if can't even prescribe medication?]

Whether the patient goes to a physician or to a *curandero* (folk healer), the assumptions about successful intervention will be the same; namely, the provider should be actively "doing something unto" the patient. The clinician should do something that results in the patient's improvement and cure. In many a Hispanic mind, a "good doctor" has an abundance of medication (whether they be in the form of pills, potions, herbs, or salves) and is willing to dispense them generously. Otherwise, friction and conflict with the patient can be expected.

Doctor–Patient Conflict

It is no surprise that clinicians working with this population can become frustrated, angry, suspicious of the patient's motives, and easily exasperated by demands and expectations so foreign to their regular experience. Then, it is the clinician who complains, although in a more sophisticated fashion.

Clinicians expect patients to be succinct, precise, and thorough while reporting their history, their symptoms, and their progress through treatment. However, clinicians soon become keenly aware of two elements that frustrate their expectations: First, the patient is likely to report symptoms in vague, colloquial terms. This requires the doctor to spend considerable time clarifying information to avoid misunderstandings and to reflect those symptoms accurately. Second, if patients become frustrated with the questioning, they are likely to give minimal information to the clinician, or give only the information that, in the patients' understanding, the clinician "wants to hear." When the doctor attempts to clarify in detail the answers given by patients, they may become annoyed at the questioning, as if they are going through an interrogation rather than an interview. "Resistance," or "guardedness," is a common description of this interaction.

Consider the response of patient R.A. to detailed questions about his accident:

> Doctor, I think it is so stupid when *other* doctors ask me to tell them how long I lost consciousness. If I passed out, how am I supposed to know what time it was. Also, these stupid doctors don't understand that I had just been thrown by an explosion. You think that when I woke up I was going to look at my watch? I ran away! That makes me angry when they ask me about loss of consciousness.

Clinicians can interpret the previous statement in different ways. The most negative, and often the first to be considered, may attribute ill intentions to the patient. Thus, he will be perceived as unwilling to provide details of the accident because of exaggeration, confabulation, or outright malingering. The most positive, and the least considered, interpretation of the response may be to listen to his distress and to take the patient's perspective. In particular, the very detailed questioning of his accident by numerous other physicians has become quite meaningless to the patient's situation. R.A. needs to convey the larger picture of his distress, not minutiae about the accident. He needs to be heard, not questioned. The doctor needs information, not attitude. This conflict cannot be resolved productively by forcing the patient to conform to the doctor's expectations. Understanding his position conveys respect to the patient. A Hispanic patient who feels respected will convey all the information the doctor needs.

There is yet a third, or "in-between," way of dealing with R.A.'s response: the clinician should listen empathically to his complaints and redirect questioning with a pedagogic approach. In fact, the importance of loss of consciousness in classifying the type of injury and its role as a predictor of recovery were presented to the patient in a relevant and comprehensive manner. He understood not only why this information was important to the evaluation, but also that he could learn as much about his injury as the neuropsychologist conducting the evaluation. Doctor–patient conflict can be averted in most situations through good "bed manners" and by conveying respect to the patient.

Patient–Procedure Conflict

Another area of conflict with this population pertains to the results of therapeutic interventions. Clinicians expect their interventions to be effective. If they do not work, generally, then it is the patient's motivation or effort that is questioned well before the treatment modality or the clinician's ability to work with this population are reexamined. As a result, clinicians communicate their "concern" to other providers in the treatment team that patients may be exaggerating when they report in vague but persistent terms that "everything hurts." As proof, clinicians report that when patients are asked to specifically rate the level of pain on a scale of 1 to 10, for instance, they are unable to do so. Lack of genuineness in the patient's motivation can then easily explain why treatment has not progressed as smoothly as with other patients who had similar injuries. Malingering, premorbid personality problems, or other pathology intrinsic to that patient are diagnosed, thus placing the patient in a lose–lose situation. However, before such conclusions are reached, clinicians should be vigilant about the ecological validity of their interventions, as well as the cultural sensitivity of their approach. Overpathologizing of a culturally different person is a clear sign that miscommunication rather than clinical judgment is dominating the therapeutic process.

Patient–Rehabilitation Center Conflict

Another source of conflict can be found in the interaction of the patient with the rehabilitation center. The model of rehabilitation commonly used in the United States assumes the patient to be an integral part of the team (Janis, 1983). The average rural immigrant Hispanic patient may become confused by his inclusion in the team as a decision-maker. Rather, these patients likely expect the treatment team, as the experts, to set the treatment goals, dictate the frequency of therapy, tell them where to go for appointments, and to solve problems that arise. Some Hispanic patients wonder aloud why their opinion is being sought. One patient replied when asked about alternative goals: "If you don't know, how am I supposed to know? You are the people with the education. You decide." Interacting with Latino patients or their family in an open, egalitarian fashion that is the norm in most rehabilitation settings can confuse some patients. It is usually more effective to give clear and consistent information to patients regarding the expectations for their participation and for the outcome of the various therapies. This may require more organization, effort, and focus of the individuals in the treatment team, but the resulting increased cooperation from patients certainly would make up for the added effort.

As patients are reintegrated into the community, it is not uncommon for Hispanic patients to resist suggestions that require taking charge of changing their lifestyle. "Poor" followthrough is commonly seen during this stage of rehabilitation. Success is mixed when a therapist recommends or expects the patient to continue therapeutic exercises at home, particularly if these exercises are not of a physical nature. The Hispanic patient will likely resist recommendations (or orders) to change his approach to activities of daily living to compensate for his impairment. Because treatment is something that "happens" to patients at the hands of the experts, it is likely that Hispanic patients will resist incorporating things that they have learned in therapy into their daily life, when the structure in their life (outside the treatment center) for the implementation of such strategies is absent. Moreover, it is obvious that many of the activities that patients learn during their retraining may have little ecological validity.

Case M.A.   M.A. was 42 years old when he sustained a traumatic head injury, with a Glasgow Coma Scale (GCS) of 10 and positive loss of consciousness of 3 days. He was married with three children. Two months postinjury he had moderate deficits in visuospatial functions, memory, and attention. He presented with weakness and paresthesias on his left upper extremity. Details of his history revealed that he began working in Mexico at age 6 helping his father on the farm. He attended school sporadically for 2 years, barely learning to read and write. He could do only simple arithmetic operations. At age 8, his father pulled him out of school completely because he was needed in the field. Since emigrating to the United States, he has had several manual labor jobs.

In rehabilitation, the speech therapist was frustrated with him because he was seen as unmotivated to participate. He gave up easily on therapy tasks. Physical therapy, however, reported no problems with him. Occupational therapy (OT) described him initially as a motivated and engaged patient. As OT progressed from dressing and upper extremity strengthening to broader activities of daily living, the patient's cooperation and motivation decreased until he became oppositional and argumentative. M.A. refused to participate in recreational therapy.

When transferred to a transitional living center, M.A. continued working at physical therapy, but neglected speech and occupational therapies. During psychotherapy, issues of pertinence to the patient were clarified in different treatment modalities. M.A. understood cognitive and occupational therapy to be irrelevant for him. Paper-and-pencil tests were meaningless. Keeping a diary of events and activities was alien to him, and participation in shopping and meal preparation was considered unnecessary by M.A., who never engaged in this behavior premorbidly. The patient's only goal for recovery was his return to gainful employment, and because none of these interventions addressed this priority, many of the therapists were perceived by him as wasting his time.

Intervention was two-pronged: First, M.A. was educated regarding the specific deficits that each therapy addressed. He was helped to break down his goals into manageable units, and was instructed on problem-solving strategies to achieve those goals. Other therapists were urged to design tasks that were ecologically meaningful to the patient. For example, gardening tools were placed around the horticulture lot, first in the presence of the patient and then without his knowing beforehand where the tools were located. If the patient was aware of where the tools were located, increasingly longer periods of time were required before having M.A. retrieve all of the items. Initially, the patient used a checklist to complete the task. Then, as he demonstrated improvement in his memory for the location of the tools, the list was withdrawn. Visual scanning treatment was done with tools, pipes, nuts, and bolts. Once the patient realized the practical benefits of therapy, he was taught to use a hand-held calculator to help him with money management and banking. He was also taught to use a calculator to calculate his pay. Cooperation improved and remained good until discharge.

The aforementined case illustrates how ecologically valid interventions can narrow the divide between the patient's and the treatment team's expectations of recovery. However, differing expectations are only one source of conflict.

Diet. An important, yet easily neglected, source of conflict between the patient and the rehabilitation center is diet. Simple as it may sound, maintaining dietary habits is crucial to a person's sense of well-being. Eating unappetizing foods is low in anyone's priority list, more so when the person is in the process of rehabilitation. One frustrated patient complained bluntly: "How am I supposed to get better with this food? They don't care about my health." Hospital and institutional settings have long ago abdicated their claim to palatable gastronomy. Requiring it from rehabilitation centers may not only upset third-party payors; in some cases, it may be unreasonable. Patients who repeatedly complain about the taste of their food may be suffering from anosmia or ageusia and will not enjoy any food regardless of its familiarity. However, there are some basic allowances that can be made in the menu preparation and planning that should include "ethnic food."

This can be done with the assistance of the family, who can recommend food items, or can prepare them for the patient, as needed. Legend has it that Hispanic food can expedite recovery of many a patient, making it highly cost-effective. Its inclusion in the menu of the rehabilitation center ought to be considered.

Language.   The most obvious, yet systematically neglected, issue in the interaction of the Hispanic patient with the rehabilitation center is that of *language*. Most large hospitals that serve Hispanic patients will have personnel with varying degrees of bilingualism who interact with the patient. However, it will be rare when the bilingual employee has exclusively the role of a translator. Frequently, family or friends are asked to translate, and sometimes even housekeeping personnel are asked to help with the evaluation or the treatment of the patient. This is never appropriate (LaCalle, 1987). In the first place, housekeeping personnel or the family of the injured patient most likely lack the vocabulary and intellectual sophistication to be able to understand, much less translate, the complicated issues involved in rehabilitation. Second, the clinician cannot control dynamics between the translator and the patient. When a member of the treatment team tells the 45-year-old male patient through his 13-year-old daughter that he needs to change his behavior or his lifestyle, it will likely result in more resistance from the patient to the suggestion. The dynamics of a 13-year-old girl telling her father to change will taint how the recommendation is received. Furthermore, the clinician will never know the tone of the recommendation as translated by the daughter.

A patient who presented with aphasia was being treated by several "bilingual" therapists. When problems arose with the occupational therapist, it became clear to the neuropsychologist that she was approaching this aphasic patient using agrammatical Spanish, imprecise vocabulary, and incorrect pronunciation. The speech therapist was an American with good command of conversational Spanish, but with frequent errors in verbal tenses and prepositions. The goal of returning the patient to premorbid levels of language functioning could never be adequately accomplished under these circumstances.

Finally, there are the professional interpreters. LaCalle (1987) indicated that there are several levels of interaction between the professional interpreter and the clinician and between the professional interpreter and the patient that can clearly affect the nature of the therapeutic or assessment process.

In addition to LaCalle's concerns, the clinician should be aware of the actual ability of the interpreter. Not everyone who works for an agency is certified or has a high level of proficiency in Spanish necessarily. Consider the following real-life interaction that took place in a case conference:

Nurse case manager (in English):   We would like you to know that you can return to work whenever you feel ready. Your employer has agreed to take you back on a modified job situation. You will begin with a few hours, and as you build endurance, you can increase the number of hours that you spend at the work site. You will continue to receive your benefits until you return on a full-time basis.

Interpreter sent by an agency (English into Spanish):   She says more or less [*sic*] that you have to go back to work, it is the best thing for you, otherwise they will cut your benefits.

Patient (in Spanish):   How can I go back to work if I am not ready? I do not feel I am ready to face the stress of eight hours of work.

Interpreter (to Patient):   It is in your best interest to return to work.

Patient: I am not ready to go back right now.

Nurse [to Interpreter]:   What is the patient saying?

Interpreter: He simply does not want to go back to work. I told him, but he says no way.

Nurse [in English to Patient]: We know you are not ready to do what you did before the accident. You will start with work-hardening and then gradually build up the hours. Your employer is willing to give you all the time you need in the modified position. There's no pressure of starting full-time or to do work that goes against your restrictions. The law requires your employer to provide modified work or else send you to vocational rehabilitation. Right now you have the option of modified work. Do you understand that Mr. R.?

Interpreter [to Patient]: She says more or less that you have to go back to work, that's the law. They will give you new work, but you have to go back.

Patient [to Interpreter]: They don't care how I feel. They just want me to work. No way I can do that the way I feel now. I am not doing anything until I feel better.

The first author took it upon himself to rectify the misunderstandings in this dialog and throughout the case conference. It is of concern, however, how easily good intentions by all parties might derail into mutual suspicion because of the vast language gap, even in the presence of a "professional" interpreter. The reader is referred to Melendez (chap. 15, this volume) to address the issue of handling interpreters.

In summary, a large part of providing a successful rehabilitation experience is to be aware of all the potential sources of conflict and to address them with cultural sensitivity where possible, or better yet, to prevent them having adequate personnel to treat the Hispanic patient.

LOCUS OF CONTROL

In discussing the conflicts that emerge from differing expectations between a Hispanic patient and his caregivers, the astute clinician can glean that how the parties address locus of control accounts for a large proportion of those conflicts. In the majority culture of the United States, an internal locus of control that emphasizes autonomy, personal responsibility, self-direction, and control over the internal and external environment is encouraged and promoted as socially desirable (Connors, 1995; Powers & Rossman, 1984; Smith, 1985; Turner, 1996; Yum, 1988) In contrast, Hispanic culture values an external locus of control (Mirowsky & Ross, 1984). As part of their worldview, Hispanics generally believe that agents outside of the individual are more powerful and control the individual. These external forces may be the doctor, God, or fate.

The Doctor Is in Control

In rehabilitation, the patient perceives the treating doctor to be in control. Passivity exhibited by the patient does not necessarily mean lack of cooperation or a "lack of initiation" syndrome. Rather, it may simply mean that the patient is allowing the clinicians to do their job by being in charge of the recovery process. If the patient's expectations are respected, the clinician can intervene to promote the patient's recovery by prescribing specific activities/behaviors that enhance rehabilitation.

This "trust" on the power of external agents to produce a change in the patient makes confusion and anger the responses of choice when benzodiazepines are reduced or discontinued in the management of posttraumatic vertigo, or when opiate pain medication is no longer prescribed to treat posttraumatic headaches. As far as the Hispanic patient is concerned, it is the physician's duty to alleviate symptoms and to "cure."

The neuropsychologist can meet the patient's expectations, yet function therapeutically by:

1. Mediating between the patient and the clinician prescribing the medication through appropriate consultation.
2. Educating the patient on the role of medication and secondary effects.
3. Validating the experience of the patient to enhance their trust in the treating team.
4. Using cognitive reframing strategies to help patients communicate their needs effectively to caregivers so they can better serve them.

God Is in Control

The following are verbatim statements from patients regarding their perspective on recovery:

> I put my trust in God and in my doctors, and, as long as I keep faith, everything will be all right.
> —G.G.

> If God wanted me to feel better (or return to work, reduce pain, etc.) he would have intervened already.
> —A.E.

Among the external forces that control life, none is more frequently alluded to than God. Chapter 2 in this book addressed the importance of religion within Hispanic culture. To avoid redundancy, this section briefly discusses the attributions made to God as an agent in recovery.

Beliefs in miracles based on religious faith are abundant and will conflict with the patients' ability to accept and adapt to permanent changes in their cognitive and physical status. Many may view acceptance and subsequent adaptation as a loss of hope and a lack of faith, which is "sinful." Once they accept the limits of medicine to significantly impact their condition, they often count on faith, the intervention of the Virgin Mary, or a miracle from God Himself to produce the desired improvement. Other patients may accept their condition in a fatalistic manner, explaining to doctors and therapists that God's plans are mysterious, and they must accept their condition without fighting it. In this view, accepting fate guarantees special rewards in the afterlife.

On the one hand, fatalistic acceptance likely serves to protect the patient from depression and anxiety. On the other hand, this same coping mechanism can interfere with the patients' effort in treatment to regain their functional ability.

To assist patients caught in this process, the neuropsychologist has several options:

1. Enlist the assistance of a priest or pastor, whenever appropriate, to address the spiritual concerns the patient has regarding treatment or postinjury adjustment.
2. A prominent and respected member of the community or the family may also be useful to motivate the patient to cooperate with rehabilitation efforts.
3. Above all, the clinician must proceed with respect for the client's spiritual perspective.
4. A good source of information on this issue is McMinn (1996).

Clarifying for a patient who is in control of different areas of his or her recovery can have multiple benefits. However, movement in this dimension is affected by the patient's expectations, deficits, and background.

DEVELOPMENTAL ISSUES

The literature indicates that premorbid levels of functioning play an important role in the recovery process. Socioeconomic status (SES) has gained attention, as it is intertwined with other factors such as education and access to health care (Gordon, 1995; MacNiven & Finlayson, 1996; Rodríguez, 1983). Clinically, it makes intuitive sense that the patients' resources and coping ability prior to the injury will affect their ability to recover from the injury. There is a large proportion of day laborers and blue-collar workers within the Hispanic community who suffer head injuries. Many of them come from low SES backgrounds. Most grew up in conditions of economic deprivation and poverty that forced them to work in their late childhood or early adolescence. The absence of clear developmental transitions from childhood into adolescence and then into adulthood, likely impact negatively the emergence of adequate coping skills (Houston, Fox, & Forber, 1984).

Stages and Coping Skills

Children use different coping skills than adults (Aldwin & Sutton, 1998; Palmer, 1970; Zeitlin & Williamson, 1994). In the United States and other industrial countries, individuals usually have up to late adolescence or early adulthood to leisurely develop coping mechanisms and resources, problem-solving strategies, values, and goals that will take them into maturity. However, many Hispanic patients from a low SES background may never have had a time to develop mature coping mechanisms. Commonly, patients who began to work early in life were required to contribute financially to the family and to behave "like grown ups." In the face of such demands, defenses such as denial, somatization, and repression were the only legitimate responses. The opportunities to have experiences leading to the development of varied mature coping resources often fail to materialize.

Many Hispanics with these developmental characteristics adjust to the demands of adult life in rigid, inflexible styles that may be appropriate when life offers few options or challenges. When under stress, individuals tend to return to behaviors that were successful in a former situation (Houston, 1969; Prieto-Bayard, 1993). Brain injury and the subsequent recovery process offer the patient many sources of stress, both internal and external. A Hispanic patient with a limited number of coping skills may revert to patterns of behaviors that were successful in the past to manage stressful situations. Because many of these patients had forceful transitions from childhood into adulthood, they had limited opportunities to acquire sophisticated coping skills. Therefore, in the presence of trauma, they will tend to regress to an immature style of denial and passivity.

For these patients, the stress of adaptation to postinjury, chronic pain, loss of finances, and the distress that brain injury symptoms bring into the individual and the family are handled in a very childlike manner. These patients are often described as whining, oppositional, lacking in motivation, and uncooperative.

Case J.G. J.G. was 52 years old when he suffered a mild brain injury after falling backward from the back of a truck, striking his occiput against the pavement. The symptoms included posttraumatic cephalgia, vestibular disturbance, and cervical pain. Cognitive symptoms included visuospatial and verbal memory impairment, decreased speed of processing, significant deficits in attention in all modalities, and executive problems. He was not identified as a head injury patient until 5 months after the accident. J.G. was referred to the second author for an evaluation. Initially, the patient was confused, afraid, and moderately depressed. The patient was referred to a comprehensive neurocognitive rehabilitation program, with multidisciplinary treatment (speech, physical, and occupational therapies; psychotherapy; and cognitive retraining). The patient was thought to have reached a plateau in his recovery 9 months into treatment. However, when J.G. failed to return to premorbid levels of functioning, he became morose, angry, and oppositional. He began refusing physical therapy because his upper back discomfort was not responding to treatment as he expected. He refused to do vestibular retraining because the exercises made him feel sick. Eventually he began refusing occupational therapy because the therapist expected him to "work" while in a state of malaise. He was eventually discharged and underwent vocational rehabilitation.

When J.G. was seen for neuropsychological reevaluation at 3 years postinjury, he had become passive, failed to maintain any of the jobs that were found for him, stopped volunteer activities, and spent most of his time at home ordering his wife about. He defined himself as "ill" and systematically declined the neuropsychologist's suggestions for treatment as inadequate for his condition.

J.G. had regressed into a coping style that had been effective in his childhood or adolescence: oppositional attitude and passive resistance. During the initial stages of treatment, he was suffering from severe headaches, memory problems, visuospatial disturbance, and vestibular symptoms, and he felt protected and cared for by the treatment team. As his condition stabilized and some of the symptoms were not going into remission, he began exhibiting anger toward the treatment team, dismissed treatment as useless, and began resisting any form of therapy. These symptoms, at 3 years postinjury, could not be accounted for by the focus or mechanism of injury, nor by the nature of his injury. Instead, his passive resistance, tantrums, and oppositional behavior were immature and reflective of the patient's early style of coping: the only one readily available to him in the face of conflict.

Clinicians working with this population may find a pedagogical approach useful, particularly when addressing coping styles. The process of reeducation requires resourcefulness and structure, so that the patient "buys into" the focus of treatment.

GENDER ISSUES

Latina patients who come from rural, undereducated, and economically disadvantaged backgrounds have unique issues and needs that ought to be considered in their own right. These issues pertain to gender roles and self-esteem.

Latinas have characteristics and needs that may need to be considered at the time of enhancing the effectiveness of a brain injury rehabilitation program (Comas-Diaz, 1989; Copeland & Hees, 1995; Miranda & Castro, 1985; Vargas-Willis & Cervantes, 1987). In addition to nonassertiveness and somatization tendencies that are general characteristics within the subculture of low SES Hispanic patients, there are gender-specific factors. Their culture places more value on attending to preserving the needs of the family than of the individual (Healey, 1997), and the female is expected to center her life in the family. Self-esteem is usually low among Latinas in the United States (Flaskerud & Uman,

1996). Within their communities, women are respected as mothers, and some matriarchs are very powerful influences in the family. But ascendancy is not over executive issues, rather it is over emotional ones (Amaro & Russo, 1987; Bakan, 1966; Espin, 1987; Padilla, 1995). Their influence, however, is dependent on the allegiance of children and extended family. In the United States, these women often find themselves excised from their traditional source of support and self-esteem. They may be doubly handicapped as minorities and as females (Healey, 1997). After a brain injury, the Hispanic female patient may be even more conflicted than males about the expectations of the dominant culture with regard to her role as a patient. They may have never been overtly involved or recognized as an important contributor to the decision making in the family. Taking charge of decisions regarding their own treatment could prove overwhelming.

Ideally, the males involved in her rehabilitation will treat the Hispanic female respectfully while being supportive in handling the factors in treatment. Female treatment personnel will be supportive and comfortable with communications high in affect (D. O'Hair, M. J. O'Hair, & Southward, 1987). The study of brain-injured Latinas and their recovery is an area that needs much elucidation from an empirical perspective.

CONCLUSIONS

Therapeutic interventions for individuals outside of one's culture represent a significant challenge to the flexibility and creativity of any clinician. When the population is as heterogeneous as the Hispanic population, it behooves clinicians involved in their treatment to become familiar with cultural characteristics of this group, and how they impact the rehabilitation process. Whereas patients from different countries of origin may have their own idiosyncratic customs and belief systems, poor, rural, undereducated recent immigrants share characteristics that can result in conflict during their rehabilitation from brain injury. Although broad generalizations are inadequate, this chapter has discussed what are believed to be the most common sources of conflict between the patient and the clinician, and between the patient and treatment center. Locus of control, developmental issues, and gender roles were also discussed as variables impacting the recovery process.

Issues of cultural and religious beliefs, gender expectations, understanding of illness and recovery, and the interaction of these factors with variables belonging to the individuals in the treatment team were presented in this chapter, based on clinical experience of the authors. Literature on these issues is scarce, yet their relevance is critical. The rehabilitation community is encouraged to pursue some of these issues through research and case reports, to enrich the knowledge in the field, and to contribute to an understanding of this population.

REFERENCES

Aldwin, C., & Sutton, K. J. (1998). A developmental perspective of posttraumatic growth. In R. Tedeschi & C. Park (Eds.), *Posttraumatic growth: Positive changes in the aftermath of crisis* (pp. 46–63). Hillsdale, NJ: Lawrence Earlbaum Associates.

Amaro, H., & Russo, N. F. (1987). Hispanic women and mental health: An overview of contemporary issues in research and practice. Special issue: Hispanic women and mental health. *Psychology of Women Quarterly, 11,* 393–407.

Bakan, D. (1966). *The duality of human existence: Isolation and communion in western man.* Boston: Beacon Press.

Cohen, L. M. (1985). "Controlarse" and the problem of life among Latino immigrants. In W. A. Vega & M. R. Miranda (Eds.) *Stress and Hispanic mental health: Relating research to service delivery* (pp. 202–218). Rockville, MD: National Institute of Mental Health.

Comas-Diaz, L. (1989). Culturally relevant issues and treatment implications for Hispanics. In D. Koslow & E. Pathy Salett (Eds.), *Crossing cultures in mental health* (pp. 31–48). Washington, DC: SIETAR International.

Connors, M. (1995). Locus of control. *Therapeutic care and Education, 4,* 16–26.

Copeland, E., & Hees, R. S. (1995). Differences in young adolescents' coping strategies based on gender and ethnicity. *Journal of Early Adolescence, 15,* 203–219.

Escobar, J. I. (1987). Cross-cultural aspects of the somatization traits. *Hospital and Community Psychiatry, 38,* 174–180.

Espin, O. M. (1987). Psychological impact of migration on Latinas: Implications for psychotherapeutic practice. Special issue: Hispanic women and mental health. *Psychology of Women Quarterly, 11,* 489–503.

Flaskerud, J., & Uman, G. (1996). Acculturation and its effect on self-esteem among immigrant Latina women. *Behavioral Medicine, 22,* 123–133.

Gaw, A. C. (Ed.). (1993). *Culture, ethnicity, and mental illness.* Washington, DC: American Psychiatric Press.

Gordon, A. K. (1995). Deterrents to access and service for Blacks and Hispanics: The Medicare Hospice Benefit, healthcare utilization, and cultural barriers. Special Issue: Hospice care and cultural diversity. *Hospice Journal, 10,* 65–83.

Guarnaccia, P. J., & Rodriguez, O. (1996). Concepts of culture and their role in the development of culturally competent mental health services. *Hispanic Journal of Behavioral Sciences, 18,* 419–443.

Healey, J. F. (1997). *Race, ethnicity, and gender in the United States.* Thousand Oaks, CA: Pine Forge Press.

Houston, B. K., (1969). *American Psychological Association Proceedings, 4.*

Houston, B. K., Fox, J. E., & Forber, L. (1984). Trait anxiety and children's state anxiety, cognitive behavior, and performance under stress. *Cognitive Therapy and Research, 8,* 631–641.

Janis, I. L. (1984). The patient as decision maker. In W. D. Gentry (Ed.), *Handbook of behavioral medicine.* New York: Guilford.

LaCalle, J. J. (1987). Forensic psychological evaluations through an interpreter: Legal and ethical issues. *American Journal of Forensic Psychology, 5,* 29–43.

MacNiven, E., & Finlayson, M. A. (1996). The interplay between emotional and cognitive recovery after closed head injury. *Brain Injury, 7*(3), 241–246.

McMinn, M. R. (1996). *Psychology, theology, and spirituality in Christian counseling.* Wheaton, IL: Tyndale.

Miranda, M., & Castro, F. (1985). *A conceptual model for clinical research on stress and mental health status: From theory to assessment.* In W. Vega & M. Miranda (Eds.), *Stress and Hispanic mental health: Relating research to service delivery* (pp. 174–201). Rockville, MD: National Institute of Mental Health.

Mirowsky, J., & Ross, C.E. (1984). Mexican culture and its emotional contradictions. *Journal of Health and Social Behavior, 25,* 2–13.

O'Hair, D., O'Hair, M. J., & Southward, G. M. (1987). Physician communication and patient compliance. *Journal of Compliance in Health Care, 2,* 125–129.

Padilla, A. M. (Ed.). (1995). *Hispanic psychology: Critical issues in theory and research.* Thousand Oaks, CA: Sage.

Palmer, J. O. (1970). *The psychological assessment of children.* New York: Wiley.

Powers, S., & Rossman, M. H. (1984). Attributions for success and failure among Anglo, Black, Hispanic, and Native American community college students. *Journal of Psychology, 117*(1), 27–31.

Prieto-Bayard, M. (1993). Psychosocial predictors of coping among Spanish-speaking mothers with retarded children. *Journal of Community Psychology, 21,* 300–308.

Ramirez, M., III. (1983). *Psychology of the Americas: Mestizo perspectives on personality and mental health.* New York: Pergamon.

Rodríguez, J. (1983). Factors influencing health practices. *Journal of School Health, 53,* 136–139.

Smith, E. M. (1985). Ethnic minorities: Life stress, social support, and mental health issues. Special Issue: Cross-cultural counseling. *Counseling Psychologist, 13*(4), 537–579.

Syme, L. S. (1984). Sociocultural factors and disease etiology. In W. D. Gentry (Ed.), *Handbook of behavioral medicine.* New York: Guilford.

Turner, D. C. (1996). The role of culture in chronic illness. *American Behavioral Scientist, 39*(6), 717–728.

Vargas-Willis, G., & Cervantes, R. C. (1987). Consideration of psychosocial stress in the treatment of the Latina immigrant. *Hispanic Journal of Behavioral Sciences, 9,* 315–329.

Ware, N. C., & Kleinman, A. (1992). Culture and somatic experience: The social course of illness in neurasthenia and chronic fatigue syndrome. *Psychosomatic Medicine, 54,* 546–560.

Young, D. M. (1997). Depression. In W. Tseng & J. Streltzer (Eds.), *Culture and psychopathology* (pp. 28–45). New York: Brunner/Mazel.

Yum, J. O. (1988). Locus of control and communication patterns of immigrants. In Y. Y. Kim & W. B. Gudykunst (Eds.), *International and intercultural communication annual, 1987* (Vol. 11, pp. 191–211). Newbury Park, CA: Sage.

Zeitlin, S., & Williamson, G. G. (1994). *Coping in young children: Early intervention practices to enhance adaptive behavior and resilience.* Baltimore: Paul H. Brookes.

Forensic Assessment of Hispanics

FERNANDO MELENDEZ
Private Practice, San Diego, CA

Neuropsychological practitioners are called on, with increasing frequency, to examine and render opinions about the status of the cognitive functioning and the neuropsychological status of Hispanic subjects. There are some fundamental problems involved in such assignments, and this chapter briefly addresses the more salient difficulties attendant to such evaluations, and in some cases offers ways of minimizing the systematic errors and distortions that may occur when examining Hispanics.

Even though the term *Hispanic* is considered to be culturally overinclusive, it is linguistically limited to those people whose primary language is Spanish and it is used in that manner here. A native of Spain is just as Hispanic as a native of Paraguay, who is as Hispanic as one hailing from the Galapagos or Tijuana. The cultures will certainly be significantly different between such people (at least on the surface), but the language will be fundamentally similar in grammar and structure. The phonics (accents) will vary and be different from one another, but no more than they are between a Southern U.S. accent and one from Brooklyn, New York.

As noted in the introduction to this book, Hispanics are ethnically diverse. The main groups are composed by those with primarily European bloodlines, those who trace their origin to Africa, the descendants of indigenous populations, and those who are a mixture of all of these groups. Additional waves of immigrants from Asian countries add to the ethnic mixture. Hispanics are educationally diverse, ranging from illiterates to professionals with doctoral degrees. Although predominantly Catholic, Hispanic religious preferences are wide ranging and include all the major world religions.

This chapter focuses on the more difficult issues involving the examination of Hispanics in a U.S. setting. Obviously, a well-educated individual with flawless command of the English language, who happens to be Hispanic, may not represent a particular problem when evaluated neuropsychologically. However, a Hispanic with a minimal education, low socioeconomic level, and no knowledge of English represents a true assessment challenge when the question is whether or not this person has suffered brain impairment following a head injury. The tools and the way of doing things in the United States do not readily accommodate to such a person.

Although *forensic assessment* should be no different from *clinical assessment,* in that they each should reflect an objectively derived description of the neuropsychological status of an individual, in reality forensic and clinical assessments demand different ways of gathering neuropsychological data and of presenting them. Forensic assessments are subject to challenge in an open court, whereas clinical assessments are rarely challenged, at least openly. The results and conclusions derived from a clinical examination may or may not be accepted by other professionals, but in a nonforensic case, neuropsychologists will rarely be asked to "prove" their opinions in an adversarial manner. The chapter is divided into two major sections: the gathering of data and the reaching of neuropsychological conclusions involving Hispanic subjects, and the presentation of these data to the jury in a convincing manner despite the challenges of the adversarial parties.

Clinical assessments can easily become forensic as a result of legal actions taken after the neuropsychological study, and all pertinent records about the case may then be subpoenaed. At that point, the clinician may wish the report had been prepared in such a way that it would be easily defensible in court; it is not a bad idea to write assessment reports so that every sentence can be reasonably defended publicly.

If the Hispanic client speaks only Spanish, or an amalgamation of Spanish and English (known as Spanglish), it is critical that the examiner be a native speaker of Spanish with a good knowledge of English, because problems with the assessment will be serious enough that no additional burden need be introduced into the equation (LaCalle, 1987). The use of translators should be avoided whenever possible, because such a practice invalidates the tests being administered. If a translator is to be used, certain procedures to safeguard as much of the validity of the testing as possible should be implemented, as described later in this chapter. Clinicians who possess only a working knowledge of Spanish should never attempt to examine a monolingual Hispanic patient, for the same reason that anyone with high school level Mandarin should not attempt to examine a Chinese subject. Unfortunately, some practitioners overrate their knowledge of the language and attempt assessments in Spanish despite their limited ability to communicate in that language. Such assessments, which violate the American Psychological Association (APA) code of ethics (APA, 1990), add unnecessary complexity to the obtaining of solid neuropsychological test data on which to base neuropsychological inferences.

NEUROPSYCHOLOGICAL ISSUES

Neuropsychological methodology is inferential in nature and its accuracy is dependent on the accuracy with which the psychological test data has been obtained (Lezak, 1995). Reitan (1986) outlined the four inferential methods used by neuropsychologists in order to draw conclusions about the condition of an individual's brain; one or more of these four inferential methods apply to any attempts at determining the brain's condition through the use of psychological tests, regardless of the authorship of those tests: level of performance, patterns and relations among test results, pathognomonic signs, and the comparison between the right versus the left side of the body. Reitan insisted, correctly, that a proper neuropsychological battery should be composed of a sufficient variety of test instruments so that all four methods of making inferences about the status of the human brain are sampled by the tests.

Levels of Performance

This inferential method is based on the fact that an injury to the brain may reduce the capacity to respond accurately to test demands and, therefore, may cause a reduction in the level of performance at which an individual functions. In order to use this method, clinicians must either know, or be able to reasonably assume, the level of performance of the individual before the potential brain injury took place. There are various ways of making reasonable determinations of such pre-injury levels of functioning when dealing with U.S. natives (Barona, Reynolds, & Chastain, 1984; Blair & Spreen, 1989; Wilson, Rosenbaum, & Brown, 1979), but such methods work poorly or not at all with Hispanics. This difficulty results because there are no reliable data about the intellectual functioning of Hispanics in general, and especially of those who have demographic characteristics that include poor or nonexistent schooling in their native countries; who have migrated under harsh and impoverished conditions by unrooting their personal, familial, and social lives; and who are now functioning in primitive sociocultural environments that are neither typical of their own country or of the United States, but represents a jury-rigged combination of both. When these individuals are tested, their scores often cluster at the borderline ranges of intellectual functioning. The issue of loss of function can rarely be raised from previous levels because the band of scores in which a significant loss would be noticed is too narrow to permit such inferences. The performance of an individual with university education who is currently scoring at the borderline retarded range fairly invites the hypothesis of loss of function; but a person with little or no education, whose life work has been at the unskilled level, and who is now scoring at the borderline retarded range cannot readily give support, through test results, to a hypothesis of loss of function.

Likewise, analysis of the levels of performance based on looking at the results of those tests that are especially sensitive to brain injuries and comparing them to those resistant to such injuries does not work well when all the test results are low. As a rule, tests based on knowledge of language that are untimed are more resistant to the effects of injuries than those involving speed and quickness of perception. Unfortunately, people with initially poor language skills (e.g., low scores on tests of vocabulary) often produce test results that do not suggest that a loss of function has taken place because of the clustering of scores at the lower end of the distribution.

Patterns and Relations Among Test Results

The second inferential method requires that the person making the analysis of test results look at those functions that generally are dependent on the integrity of one or the other hemisphere, or of specific regions within each hemisphere. This methodology is based on the empirical knowledge of the functional organization of the brain and the specific areas whose integrity are the most sensitive to the various aspects of the tests administered. There is, of course, no evidence that the brain of Hispanics is organized differently than those of any other ethnic group (Ardila, Roselli, & Puente, 1993). Damage to the left hemisphere will generally produce disorders of speech and damage to the right will generally impair visuospatial performances.

There are problems when applying this methodology to Hispanic patients because there are no standardized tests to make the necessary inferences about whether or not a low performance reflects biological impairment. In a broad sense, and in cases involving clear insults such as strokes, the patterns of test results and their relation to brain structures hold well; but, in those frequent cases in which the neuropsychological assessment is aimed at examining whether or not subtle changes in the integrity of the brain have taken place after a relatively minor injury, such as a mild concussion, there are no instruments to make supportable inferences about the nature, extent, or localization of such changes. Indeed, there is no empirical evidence that the tests available in English and adapted, translated, or otherwise used with Hispanics actually measure the same constructs; or, if they do, it is unknown whether they measure them to the same extent or accuracy when used cross-culturally (Ardila et al., 1993; Artiola i Fortuny, 1996).

Pathognomonic Signs

Rather than rely on a patient's level of performance on a variety of tests, the pathognomonic sign approach judges responses and task results in terms of whether or not they suggest brain pathology. It searches for "signs" of brain pathology in the performances of the subjects, looking for those performances typically produced only (or primarily) by people with injured or defective brains. Performance results that show, for instance, a consistent weakness of execution on the left side of drawings, with few or no disturbances on the right side, are produced nearly exclusively by patients with injuries to the right cerebral hemisphere, often to the right temporoparietal area specifically. Although pathognomonic findings carry considerable diagnostic weight when present, their absence in no way rules out brain impairment.

In examining a Hispanic subject, the psychologist should weigh his battery heavily with tests that search for known pathognomonic signs. These tests must involve relatively simple performances, such as copying the geometrical figures in the Reitan-Iniana Aphasia Screening Test, copying three-dimensional cube drawings (Necker and Double Necker designs), or executing the simple Bender–Gestalt figures.

Comparison of the Right and Left Sides of the Body

In this inferential approach, the body is allowed to be the subject of a controlled experiment: by comparing the specific scores obtained with the right hand (for example) with those obtained with the left hand, inferences can be drawn about the functional integrity of one side or another, and by extension, of one hemisphere or the other. In a typical neuropsychological battery, the speed of tapping with the right index finger is compared to the speed of the left index finger. The empirically derived speeds expected for the preferred hand are known and the nonpreferred hand will usually show a 10% slower speed than the right (Spreen & Strauss, 1991). When additional measurements of sensation, perception, and speed are added to the examination, it is possible to see if one side of the body appears to be out of synchrony with the other, and thus a hypothesis can be fashioned concerning the condition of the underlying hemisphere responsible for each side. Whereas this method is extremely useful, it is subject to distortions; for one, peripheral disturbances of a limb may interfere with normal functioning in measurements of strength, sensitivity, speed, and coordination; in addition, some workers may be engaged in occupations that demand constant use of one hand, or arm, and not the other, thus breaking the expected rate of differences between hands.

In summary, the four inferential methods suggested by Reitan (1986) are a model of how inferential decisions are made in reaching neuropsychological conclusions about individuals; however, when evaluating Hispanic subjects, the value of those methods are different than when dealing with U.S. natives: Drawing inferences from the *level of performance* data is problematic because the range of such data is constricted and generally lower in Hispanics than in U.S. natives. The *pattern of test results* is also a weaker inferential method with Hispanics, not because their brains are differently organized, but because the testing instruments used are less capable of supporting localization inferences. The use of *pathognomonic signs* remains as highly desirable and convincing when examining Hispanics as when examining U.S. natives. Little or no cultural distortions should be expected as a result of inferences based on this approach. Likewise, the comparisons between the performances of each side of the body are essentially biological measures without cultural or ethnic distortions.

TEST ISSUES

Elsewhere in this book, there is a presentation dealing with the scarcity of tests that have been standardized with Hispanic populations (see Pontón, chap. 3, this volume, which discusses research and assessment issues). The question for the clinician is what to do about the selection of a battery that will be useful in obtaining a clear neuropsychological picture of Hispanics. The current state of affairs is that although many tests have been translated into Spanish, not a single neuropsychological test battery has been standardized on people whose demographics reflect the characteristics of migrant Hispanic populations in the United States. Several efforts have reached the talking stages and then were abandoned; other have progressed as far as starting field tests and then were abandoned. It seems that a standardization project for a neuropsychological battery to be used on Hispanic populations in the United States is far too large an undertaking for a dissertation theme, and there is a lack of interest on the side of the large test publication and manufacturing companies to engage in such a huge and expensive undertaking on the speculation of being able to make it financially viable.

Pontón et al. (1996) offered hope that such tests soon will be available. It is too early to determine if those norms will hold with different Hispanic populations or whether they will be useful as neuropsychological tools when the battery is used to differentiate carefully selected normals from well-diagnosed brain injured Hispanic patients.

This volume presents a discussion of additional tests and test batteries for Hispanics, but the reality is that many neuropsychologists, out of necessity and over the years, have developed their own techniques for examining Hispanics. These nonpublished, nonstandardized assessment procedures are a source of concern. They represent serious clinical, forensic, and ethical problems, even when used as wisely and cautiously as possible.

My experience, perhaps not typical but certainly illustrative of the use of nonstandardized testing procedures, was as follows: Soon after I started a private practice in Coral Gables, Florida, in 1980, the infamous Mariel "boat lift" took place, in which thousands of native Cubans, who left or were expelled from their island country through the port of Mariel, landed in South Florida. Among them were many people who had been plucked from prisons and medical institutions and sent along to the United States for being unwanted burdens on the Cuban economy. At that time, it was common for Spanish-speaking psychologists to use the Escala de Inteligencia Wechsler para Adultos (EIWA), a standardized version of the Wechsler Adult Intelligence Scale (WAIS) that had been translated and normed in Puerto Rico (Wechsler, 1955). This instrument contained many problems and, among others, there was the fact that it yielded highly inflated IQ figures (Melendez, 1994). As a consequence, immigrants who were clearly intellectually defective (e.g., due to chromosomal abnormalities) were scoring in the low average and average ranges of intellectual functioning and thus rendered ineligible for the specific government benefits reserved for those with lower IQ scores. The situation demanded that a test be developed that would reasonably reflect the intellectual level of these individuals. To that effect, several Spanish-speaking psychologists met in order to work out a modification of the WAIS–R that substituted U.S. cultural questions with questions containing reasonably universal Hispanic content; and, in one instance, that meant replacing one entire subtest (Vocabulary) with items whose definitions would reflect a progressive increase in their difficulty—something a direct translation of the vocabulary words did not achieve. The result of these efforts was an instrument that could be administered immediately and had fair face validity; it produced profiles in which the subtest score results, using U.S. values, were normally clustered, and in which the summary scores (IQs) appeared to reflect what could reasonably be expected from people with the history and background of the individuals taking the test.

I suspect that similar stories exist about other unstandardized tests and test batteries that are being used with Hispanic populations. This does not mean, however, that the responsibility to produce as accurate a profile as possible and that will conform to ethical standards should ever be abrogated. In cases in which a nonstandardized test or group of tests is used, the psychologist should mention this in the report; further, the psychologist is bound to continue to seek the best and most accurate means of conducting tests, and to use them as they appear in the market.

From a practical standpoint, the psychologist should furnish sufficient information about the testing so that those reading the report may be able to adjust their thinking to the circumstances of the examination. For instance, before the current translation to the Minnesota Multiphasic Personality Inventory (MMPI–2) had been published by the University of Minnesota, the following disclosure paragraph was included in a report I reviewed:

> The reader should be aware that the translations of the tests used in the examination of Mr. _____ have not been standardized on a Spanish-speaking population. The translations of most of the tests were made by the examiner, who has had them in use for many years; some have been published. The MMPI–2 translation incorporates those questions from the earlier version which had been translated and made public previously, and which were used again in the MMPI-2. The data obtained in the examination of Mr. _____ have normal internal consistency and reasonably reflect the socioeconomic background of the patient. While it is possible that administering the test in Spanish significantly affected or systematically distorted the conclusions that can be derived from those data, the results appear to argue against such distortions.

The Spanish translation of the MMPI–2 was published in 1993. Note that this translation has not been normed or standardized on a Hispanic population. The entire MMPI–2 English version contained 35 males and 38 females defined as having a Hispanic ethnic origin (Greene, 1991).

From a forensic standpoint, the use of nonstandardized tests presents a problem to psychologists only if they have not been forthright in explaining how they went about examining the patient. If in the report it is made clear how the examination was conducted and what tests were used, then there is little to worry about at the time of the trial: Juries are quite capable of understanding the limitations of making assessments of Hispanic patients when proper testing instruments are not available. They will not reject such findings if the psychologists appear truthful but cautionary about their results.

LANGUAGE ISSUES

In forensic as well as clinical settings, the issue of the capacity of the psychologist and the patient to communicate clearly is, or should be, paramount (Lopez, 1997). Such communication has to be based on a thorough knowledge of Spanish, as well as an understanding of the cultural factors in which such language is embedded. Unfortunately, learning Spanish appears to the beginning student as an "easy" task; people with just a smattering of the language often feel competent enough to conduct a psychological examination in it, or even to do therapy in Spanish. Such behavior is proscribed by ethics and by common sense, and yet it happens with remarkable frequency. Even more common is the use of translators to interpret back and forth while the psychologist interviews and tests the patient. This remarkable fact of testing through a translator is likely to cause the destruction of a test's validity by changing the manner in which the test is administered, among other disruptions. This violation of standards should be of monumental importance, yet it is systematically ignored by many practitioners. And, when they are reminded of what they are doing to the usefulness of a test, they are taken aback, as if it were certainly not their intention to tamper with a test's utility in that way.

Reality, however, dictates that translators will continue to be employed despite their use being less than ideal. There are, however, some methods of minimizing the potentially distorting effects on the test results caused by using translators (these methods are discussed later).

CULTURAL ISSUES

Although a huge variety of cultural norms and habits exist among the U.S. Hispanic population, depending on their nation of origin and the location of where they settled in the United States, some broad statements about the underlying Hispanic culture vis-à-vis disease and injuries are worth mentioning here, because they have a clear and potentially devastating effect on the forensic aspects of neuropsychology. One of the important cultural premises is that physical pain, organic diseases, and injuries are quite acceptable (indeed, expected) in the low socioeconomic levels of Hispanic cultures. Depending on their severity, these conditions may well incapacitate a person and render them unable to work; this, in turn, will exempt them from having to provide for their family.

"Mental" problems are something else altogether at the low socioeconomic levels in Hispanic cultures. When a person exhibits clearly bizarre or dangerous behavior that might result in hurting themselves or others, they are declared insane. Often this leads to their being locked up in dismal asylums for the insane, for their own or other's safety. This condition casts an onus on the family and marks them (and often their near relatives) as tainted with madness; and this, in turn, diminishes the social status and marriage prospects of the extended family. Madness is a condition that must be avoided at all costs, and thus claiming mental factors as reasons for not being able to work and support a family is not commonly seen among Hispanics. The notion that a man suffering from severe depression might legitimately be incapacitated from leaving his bed or from putting in a good day's work is absolutely foreign and extraordinary at the lower levels of Hispanic cultures.

Disorders that manifest without observable incapacities are considered, at best, fancy ways of showing fundamental laziness. This "either/or" concept of mental health (either you are crazy and must be locked up, or you are not and should be at work) has definite behavioral consequences in the presentation of signs and symptoms following an injury. It has been noted, therefore, that Hispanics tend to exaggerate (or even create) their physical complaints when they seek legal or medical help from society (DuAlba & Scott, 1993; Koss, 1990; Pontón, Gonzalez, & Mares, 1997).

The aforementioned cultural stance about mental health is but one of the many pressures that bear on this group to overemphasize their physical ills; other reasons for exaggerating illness include the linguistic difficulty that a person may encounter in giving expression to matters involving emotional or spiritual distress, compared to the relatively ease with which physical ailments can be conveyed and communicated; thus, because pain is easily expressed and understood, it becomes a substitute for emotional anguish or depression that Hispanics find difficult to conceptualize and convey in their own language, never mind in English (Kolody, Vegg, Meinhardt, & Bensussen, 1986).

Still other pressures to exaggerate derive from the past experiences that many Hispanics have had in dealing with the dominant U.S. culture and with non-Spanish-speaking people: Many Hispanics recall that when they were not understood linguistically, they were likely to be demeaned culturally. Immigrants, in general, know (or suspect) that they might very well be pushed aside, or even laughed at, when the people in power do not understand their language or their culture. In all fairness, many have been treated worse in their own countries, where lack of education and of social standing are even more starkly defined than in U.S. culture, and where there is a high price to pay for lack of power and influence. In any event, when trying to express a physical complaint to someone who appears to misunderstand the Hispanic patient and the nature of the complaints (and this misunderstanding always seems to be in the direction of judging that the ailment does not require their immediate and intense attention), it stands to reason that Hispanics will exaggerate and elaborate what ails them, just for good measure and in an effort capture and maintain the interest of the care giver.

Related to the previous point is the issue of exaggeration of symptoms as a simple plea for help by people who have little sophistication in the ability to understand their own bodies and to articulate the nature of their own discomfort (Pontón et al., 1997). Finally, the exaggeration or creation of symptoms may have its origin in the same factors and variables that they have for members of the dominant culture: There are some characterological determinants that may lead to such behavior, there are varieties of somatization disorders that also lead to the exaggeration or creation of symptoms, and finally there are some Hispanics that engage in plain deception of others in the hope of obtaining a financial gain. Forensic cases may result in the awarding of substantial money or other benefits to a person who has been injured, so it stands to reason that the nature of the injuries, their disabling consequences, and the amount of pain involved might be consciously exaggerated (or manufactured) as a means of obtaining the highest compensation possible.

In summary, then, there exist many pressures that contribute to the noted fact that Hispanics often exaggerate their physical complaints. It remains up to the sophisticated neuropsychologist to be able to tease out the various strands that might influence such exaggerations, and thus be able to present an accurate and well-balanced description of both the real and the fictitious elements in a person's complaints.

FORENSIC NEUROPSYCHOLOGY WITH HISPANIC PATIENTS

Although in recent years neuropsychology as a discipline has entered and is highly influential in the field of rehabilitation, it still remains primarily a descriptive and diagnostic discipline. It can address the question of presence or absence of brain damage or impairment; and, if such impairment is present, the neuropsychologist can show the cognitive and behavioral effects that follow from the specific brain damage. A certain amount of circular reasoning still exists in neuropsychology. For instance, a particular behavior can be attributed to the effects of brain damage, but that same behavior is often offered as "proof" of such damage. Nevertheless, neuropsychology remains the most accurate discipline in producing an integrated description of both the brain (in its healthy or damaged states) and the cognitive, behavioral, and socioeconomic changes that might ensue as a result of an injury to the brain.

For this reason, and since its early days, neuropsychology has been of great interest not only to the medical profession, but to the legal one too; for it is the neuropsychologist who can produce a clear picture of the functional effects of a brain injury, and how the consequences of this injury might affect individuals, their family life, and their capacity to participate in the labor market. This professional can document the changes in personality that may have taken place, how these changes may affect the individuals' emotional interactions with others, how people's access to a happy and fulfilling life might have been curtailed as a result of the injury, and finally, how to maximize the opportunities to make the best possible adjustment to family and society following a head injury.

The interface between the clinical neuropsychologist and the legal profession takes place primarily at three defined points, each of which generates a clear written record:

1. The *psychological report* is the written presentation of the facts of case, the circumstances of the assessment, the results of the test procedures, and their meaning. It furnishes a diagnosis and the conclusions derived from such an examination.

2. The *discovery* phase of the trial allows the attorney for the opposite side to question expert psychologists about the evidence that they are going to present to the jury. This discovery takes place in the form of a deposition, in which psychologists and their records are subpoenaed, and the psychologists answer questions under oath. The psychological records and test results are copied and made public at this point.

3. The *trial* is when a psychologist answers questions before a jury. These questions are asked both by the attorney who hired the psychologist and by the opposing attorney. The idea is to convince the jury about the validity of the psychologist's pronouncements and conclusions, on the one hand, or to attempt to minimize the statements by the psychologist if it is in the interest of the case to do so. A judge presides and makes rulings about the presentation of the evidence to the jury.

All those parts of the forensic activities by a neuropsychologist are separated by time and location, yet they obviously must have a clear unity, so that what appears in the psychological report must be substantially supported in both the deposition and at trial. Whereas certain minor adjustments of emphasis and interpretation might differ from psychological report to deposition to trial, the greater these differences the less credible the opinion of the neuropsychologist will be once the opposing attorney presents these discrepancies to the jury.

It is clear that the opinions of neuropsychologists should be well established and defensible long before they sit down to write the report; that the report should be based on carefully obtained data, which have been evaluated correctly and according to standards; and above all, that the report reveal not only those factors supporting the view that favors the party who hired the psychologist, but also those that may weaken or not be favorable to such a view. The issue of the psychologist's integrity as a conveyor of truthful and supportable facts that will clarify the matters being litigated is of paramount importance throughout the trial.

Imagine the following, involving a psychologist who examined Mr. Mendoza, a migrant from Oaxaca, Mexico, who does not speak English. The psychological report may or may not have mentioned that a translator was used.

Q: Doctor, did you examine Mr. Mendoza in Spanish?

A: No, I did not.

Q: Does Mr. Mendoza speak English?

A: No. I used a translator.

Q: What was the name of this translator?

A: I don't know. She was sent by Acme Translation Services.

Q: Did you understand what the translator said to Mr. Mendoza?

A: No. But she is a certified translator in Spanish.

Q: Did you understand what Mr. Mendoza told the translator?

A: I understand a little Spanish. But no, I did not understand everything that was said.

As the attorney proceeds, the valuable commodities of trust and credibility in the eyes of the jury with which the psychologists is anointed might easily and pointlessly be squandered.

Many of the difficulties that exist in the presentation of cases to the jury by a non-Spanish-speaking psychologist can be avoided with careful planning and the use of the best possible methods to minimize (although never eliminate) assessment errors and testing distortions. These procedures involved activities that should be implemented before, during, and after the assessment of a Hispanic.

Many psychologists are unaware of a publication issued by the Office of Ethnic and Minority Affairs of the American Psychological Association entitled *Guidelines for Providers of Psychological Services to Ethnic, Linguistic and Culturally Diverse Populations* (APA, 1991). This booklet contains the official position of the APA with regard to the interactions between psychologists and those of different linguistic and cultural backgrounds. It clearly suggests that psychologists not involve themselves in cases outside the limits of their competence. It suggests that they might seek consultation or make referrals to appropriate experts, as necessary. It specifically states: "Psychologists interact in the language requested by the client, and if this is not feasible, make an appropriate referral." (Guideline #6; www.apa.org/pi/oema/guide.html)

It is unlikely that many monolingual or Spanglish-speaking Hispanics would express a desire to be tested in a language they do not speak and they actually fear, that is, English. Yet there are few psychologists who offer them a choice. Responsible psychologists should have one or several colleagues to whom they feel comfortable referring Hispanic patients, or at least consulting with them about issues with Hispanics. This is an ethical obligation that may appear to be burdensome to neuropsychologists in private practice, who would naturally want to fill their days with revenue-producing activities rather than consulting or sending their patients elsewhere for treatment or examinations. Yet, in the final analysis, a practice engaged in the best possible care for its patients is bound to flourish rather than decay.

While licensing and other legal requirements act as an assessing and filtering agent to protect the public from improperly qualified "experts," there are no formal language qualifications or examinations necessary to practice psychology in any language. Codes of ethics generally forbid people from doing what they are unqualified to do; but leaving individual practitioners to judge their own competence in a matter of foreign languages is an invitation for disaster. The following illustrates a common linguistic/cultural problem in which an uneducated Hispanic and two highly educated U.S. lawyers (with the help of a certified translator) simply cannot communicate (verbatim from a transcript, except that the names have been changed):

Attorney 1: Mr. López, would you please state your full name and spell your full name for the record?

Witness: Antonio López

Interpreter: A-n-t-o-n-i-o L-o-p-e-z

Attorney 2: Okay. He does not know how to spell it. I should note that for the record I would like the applicant to try and spell his name.

Witness: An-to-nio.

Attorney 2: Okay. Do you know how to spell your name?

Witness: An-to-nio.

Attorney 2: Okay. For the record, I would like to point out that the applicant's answer to the question is not responsive. What he is doing is he is simply repeating very slowly each one of the syllables of his first name.

There are two problems here. In Spanish, "name" (**nombre**) refers to a person's given name. If you want a person's full name, you must ask for *nombre y apellidos* (name and surnames, of which there are two in Spanish). If one asks only for the name, the answer will likely be the person's given or Christian name, and if asked for *nombre y apellido* the response will likely be the given name and the first surname. Second, because Spanish is so phonetic, any inquiry about how to spell something will result in the pronunciation of the syllables of the word. The translation of "how do you spell . . ." is "*cómo se escribe . . .*," or "how does one write . . ." (Jarman & Russell, 1994). The verb that describes the act of spelling letter by letter does exist (*deletrear*), but this action is extremely rare in Spanish and is reserved for obscure or foreign words. So, even though Mr. López was being perfectly responsive to the questions he was being asked, Attorney 2 interpreted his verbalizations as being nonresponsive. These profound linguistic misunderstandings took place before they ever got to the substance of the deposition.

Reality indicates that the use of translators in forensic psychology will continue for the foreseeable future, and therefore some guidelines are suggested on how to minimize the damage this practice may cause in assessing a Hispanic subject and in maintaining the best possible communication between patient and psychologist despite the use of a translator.

When selecting a firm of translators, it is important to inquire about people with experience translating psychological or medical interactions. Translators who have not only a good knowledge of both languages, but of the subject matter that is being translated, can be invaluable in reducing the amount of error in neuropsychological examinations or clinical assessments. Psychologists should ask to interview various translators before selecting one. The interview should focus not only on the translators' background, but on their appearance, attitude, and social ease. A translator should be able to accept the role of being only a tool and a conduit of information rather than a player in the examination. The more discreet and self-effacing, the better. Horror stories abound about intrusive translators who insist in playing an active role in the assessment proceedings. During the meeting, the psychologist should perform an interview with as much care as if the translator was being considered for permanent employment in the psychologist's firm; this, of course, will be the case if there is a proper fit between psychologist and translator, because the psychologist is likely to insist on having the same translator for subsequent cases. Respect and deference toward the translator are important. The psychologist should develop a good knowledge of the person's name, educational history, social background, and interests.

Sometime before the examination, the psychologist should prepare a list of tests and procedures that are going to be used in the case. He should ask the translator to come in for a dry run of what the testing is going to involve. The translator should be shown into the testing room in order to become familiar with the seating arrangements and the layout of the room. Any printed material with which the translators are expected to work should be given to them at this point so that they will have time to work with the material, look up words in the dictionary, and make notes on the margins, all with the intention of producing a translation that is smooth and nondisruptive.

If the testing is going to involve equipment, as it often does in a neuropsychological assessment, the translator should be asked to handle it and become familiar with it. Special procedures, such as those involved in examining a person while blind-folded, should be conducted on the translator to make that person aware of the true nature of the examination and what it involves. Copies of the instructions to the tests should be furnished to the translator so that these instructions will flow naturally during the examination.

If translators have not had experience with psychological or psychiatric matters, then it is important that the examiner brief them on the general principles of psychological testing; on the importance of not helping the patient, directly or indirectly in any way; and on the need of avoiding nonverbal cues while the examination is in progress.

The translator should be given a briefing on the ground rules under which the examination will be conducted, with emphasis on preserving the confidentiality of the patient's verbalizations and on making the patient feel as comfortable as possible during the examination. In addition, it is important that the translator know that all material spoken in Spanish must be translated, even if it involves only a social exchange between the translator and the patient, or a casual exclamation of the patient; this translation should be automatic, without any need for the psychologist to inquire "What did he say?" It should also be understood that at no time are the patient and the translator to be left alone: The psychologist always must be present, even through such chores as reading the MMPI to the patient. The rationale for these conditions should be obvious. Every effort should be made so that the assessment of the patient resembles, as much as possible, what would happen if the examination were conducted without a translator.

It should be clear that the previous recommended procedure for a translated neuropsychological evaluation is complex and requires time. The cost of the examination will rise significantly based on the additional time spent on completing the assessment properly. But consider how the same questioning would now be different:

Q: Did you examine Mr. Mendoza in Spanish?

A: No, I did not.

Q: Does Mr. Mendoza speak English?

A: No, I used a translator.

Q: What was the name of this translator?

A: His name is Rogelio Fuentes. I selected Mr. Fuentes from a panel of Spanish translators at Acme Translation Services because he has fairly extensive experience in handling translations of a psychiatric or psychological nature. Before I allowed him to participate in the examination of Mr. Mendoza, I interviewed Mr. Fuentes about his background, familiarized him with the tests I would be administering . . .

Now the jury can correctly deduce that the psychologist exercised some care and professionalism in dealing with the matter of examining someone in Spanish. However, psychologists must clearly state that the results they obtained are still equivocal because of the use of an interpreter. Although efforts were made to decrease the amount of error in the evaluation, using an interpreter was never a part of the original standardization of the test battery. Therefore, the test performance of the patient was altered in ways not yet studied in this field. Thus, any results obtained via an interpreter are tentative at best.

The Psychological Report

Perhaps the most influential act of neuropsychologists in the exercise of their profession in the preparation and filing of a written report. This critical document should be written in clear and simple English, and describe the process of assessment, the results of the testing, and the conclusions and recommendations of the neuropsychologist.

Forensic and clinical reports are different in their emphasis: Clinical reports aim to address the medical, functional, and rehabilitative issues involved in the case. The legalistic issues surrounding the circumstances of an injury, such as neglect or intention to inflict harm, seldom carry critical weight in the clinical (in contrast to the forensic) assessment of the case.

In forensic reports, the legal circumstances attendant to an injury are important and often critical, in addition to the medical and rehabilitative ones. Clinical reports are not expected to become contentious, and forensic ones will be analyzed for weaknesses and conclusions may be disputed and fought over. Forensic reports involving Hispanics have additional and substantial ground for arguments about their validity and significance because of the elements of language and culture. Consequently, the following observations and comments about psychological reports in general, and for those involving Hispanics in particular, are offered.

Competence.   With today's excellent computer and communication techniques, there are no valid reasons to release psychological reports that are not properly formatted, organized, and presented. As a frequent reviewer of the reports of other psychologists, I have often been surprised by the apparent indifference to the physical characteristics and appearance of a psychological report, whether or not involving Hispanics.

The letterhead and signature blocks will be subject to scrutiny. The mention of "vanity" board certification on the letterhead (i.e., boards not recognized by the American Psychological Association, or obtained primarily as a result of the payment of fees, rather than through examinations) should be avoided in forensic cases. In the hands of a sharp opposing attorney, the display of empty or pretentious board certifications on a letterhead or signature block can cause irreversible damage to the credibility of a psychologist.

The content of the report should be well-organized, explicit, and written in plain English. Because it will be read primarily by people not acquainted with the arcane language of neuropsychology or medicine, it should use such language sparingly and only when it is unavoidable. If Spanish quotations are used for specific responses, then they should be clearly and carefully translated.

As many as 50% of medical and other professional reports cite the name of Hispanic patients incorrectly. In Hispanic cultures, a person's legal name is composed of three parts: the "given name" (e.g., "Antonio"), the surname of the person's father (e.g., "Pelayo"), and the surname of the person's mother (e.g., "Arango"). Thus, the person's legal name includes both his father's and his mother's surnames: Antonio Pelayo Arango. The confusion occurs because in the United States only one parental surname is used (the father's) and it is the *last* name on the list. In the previous example, English-speaking personnel, when seeing the string "Antonio Pelayo Arango" will erroneously call him Mr. Arango (using his mother's maiden name), instead of the correct Mr. Pelayo. I have also found that many Hispanics have given up correcting English-speakers about this simple problem and will accept whichever name they are called. Thus, the simple gesture of calling patients by their correct name is often ignored, and the psychologist uses whatever it says on "the papers," which unfortunately are often wrong. Simply inquiring about the correct manner of addressing the individual is often enough to solve the problem.

Forthrightness. Both parties to a report—the psychologist writing it and the patient who was examined—need to prove their forthrightness if a jury is to believe them. The opposing attorney will, directly or indirectly, challenge the presumption of truth about the claims found in the report. From the standpoint of the psychologist as an expert witness, the easiest way to lose the confidence of the jury is to take on the role of an advocate for one side (the side that hired him) and give up the detached objectivity under which the psychologist should be functioning. For instance, it is very rare that a case is purely black or white: Most often, there are problems with the way the data was obtained, with discrepancies among the various test findings, or with test results that do not support the conclusions of the report. All these irregularities need to be mentioned and accounted for in a forthright report.

In addition, the truthfulness (or lack thereof) of the patient needs to be documented. Most psychologists are trained in the variety of ways in which deception and exaggeration by a patient can be detected (Pankratz, 1988; Puente, 1991; Reitan & Wolfson, 1997). Because a neuropsychological examination is very extensive and literally contains hundreds of questions, a test–retest paradigm is often the most thorough approach to detecting deception or exaggeration on the side of the patient. What, as is often the case, if Hispanic subjects are found to be exaggerating their symptoms? The answer, of course, is that such exaggeration should be mentioned in the report; if and when it is appropriate, a reasonable explanation for this exaggeration, based on sociocultural factors, should also be stated.

What is not permissible is to "hide" information that the psychologist believes detracts from furthering the legal claim of the patient, and pretend it is not there. The psychologist is not (and never should be) an advocate for the patient. The moment that objectivity is compromised, the psychologist might as well quit: the psychologist's bias in favor of the patient will sooner or later be discovered and exposed before the jury, and no further credibility from that group need be expected.

Completeness. The forensic neuropsychological report should be complete. That is, it must be able to stand alone without the support of other documentation. The report should be able to describe the individuals and their background, the nature of the accident or the event that required the neuropsychological examination, the results of medical tests and medical history, the tests administered and each of the test results, the language and cultural issue involved in he case, and the conclusions and recommendations that can be derived from the reported data. Part of this completeness, which is especially important in forensic reports, has to do with dates: The report should include the date of the accident or injury of the individual; the date or dates in which the examination took place; and the date on which the report was written or dictated. The report should include each of the documents read as a matter of studying the facts of the case and reaching a conclusion about it.

Quite often, neuropsychological reports avoid addressing the primary question inherent in any neuropsychological referral: Is there evidence of brain damage? If so, what is the evidence? Can the damage be localized to one or another hemisphere of the brain? What are the social, cognitive, intellectual, and job-related consequences of the damage caused by the injury? All too often, reports contain strings of statements declaring the patient to have scored in the "impaired range" on tests, without further analysis of what significance such test scoring might have in the scheme of things, and without ever addressing the issue of presence or absence of brain damage.

Completeness also includes mentioning the circumstances of the neuropsychological examination. In the case of an Hispanic assessment, such disclosure would include citing the fact that some of the tests used had not been standardized for Hispanics, or for Hispanics with the demographic characteristics of the person who was tested; it would mention the use of a translator, and a warning about the effect that the use of a translator might have on the test results obtained. A failure to mention any of these things might be brought out at the time of deposition; questions may be raised at that time about the objectivity and impartiality of the examiner, especially if none of the weakening effects of using a translator has been mentioned voluntarily, and the facts appear only as a result of questioning by an opposing attorney.

The Deposition. This is a legal proceeding in which each side allows the opposing side to question their expert witness before the start of the trial. The deposition permits a legal record of the opinion of the experts to be created that can then be read to the jury in the event of the nonappearance of the expert.

During the deposition, opposing attorneys are permitted to question experts at length and vigorously, for not only are the attorneys trying to find out the mettle of the experts, they are gauging the experts' interpersonal qualities, their truthfulness, and their ability to speak clearly and convincingly; in fact, the attorneys are judging the effect the witness may have on the jury and on the outcome of the case. Often, cases are settled after a deposition, based on the fact that an expert has demonstrated such strength under fire (or such weakness) that the outcome of the case is no longer in question.

I believe that over the years attorneys have become very sophisticated about the business of neuropsychology and the weaknesses that can be found in the professional background of neuropsychologists and in their conduct of a neuropsychological examination. Faust, Ziskin, and Hiers (1991) certainly contributed to enlightening trial attorneys. In addition, this forensic sophistication has come as a result of attorneys hiring neuropsychologists to guide them through the contentions of the expert, and to help them formulate the questions that will show the expert's weaknesses. Having participated in counseling attorneys on how to question neuropsychologists, I can report that, as a rule, lawyers learn very quickly and indeed they posses an instinct to go for the jugular if the expert witness is perceived as being less than forthright with answers.

As a rule, the deposition starts by establishing the credentials of the expert as a psychologist and a neuropsychologist. The expert should be meticulously truthful about credentials, because they are often challenged during a deposition. These credentials may not be the ideal ones, but nevertheless, they should be stated openly and without apology. Neuropsychology is a recent discipline and field of inquiry. Some very senior and reputable neuropsychologists never took a formal course in human neuropsychology—it did not exist as part of the curriculum when they were in graduate school. In the following paragraphs, I quote verbatim from a deposition transcript. I have eliminated the names of the states, universities, and of the people mentioned in the deposition in order to preserve privacy, but otherwise those were the words that were spoken:

Q: Did you do an internship in a clinical neuropsychology setting?

A: At the time I graduated clinical neuropsychology settings were few and far between. The answer is negative in that regard.

Q: All right.

A: As I indicated though that—perhaps I didn't indicate—that many of the programs nowadays are very, very close to the experimental forms of activities that I underwent as a pre-doc and as a post-doc, so in a sense I was retooled in a specialty area.

Q: But you never studied clinical psychology in an academic setting in either one of your degrees, isn't that correct, either your M.A. or your Ph.D.? Never studied clinical neuropsychology in either one of those, did you?

A: I studied neuropsychology, but it was not part of the formal post-doc neuropsychology track.

It is obvious that it would be much better if this psychologist were open, forthright, and proud of his background. Regardless of how much he tries, he cannot change his educational history, and any attempt to enhance or distort it will invite disaster. In the following excerpt, the same psychologist persists in his defensiveness. It has been determined that his doctoral dissertation involved cats:

Q: Doctor, you don't treat cats in your clinical practice, do you?

A: No, I don't.

Q: Alright. What graduate courses did you take in clinical neuropsychology, if any?

A: I took a course in clinical neuropsychology.

Q: Where did you take that?

A: At the University of . . .

Q: Who taught it?

A: [name of a well-known neuropsychologist]

Q: One course, is that correct?

A: That was one course, yes. That was way back in 1975–76. There were very few available at that time.

The attorney, which is this case was relentless, proceeded to inquire about the psychologist's internship, and established that it was not one approved by the American Psychological Association; inquired about whether the psychologist had ever failed to pass a licensing examination (he had); and inquired about board certification, which the psychologist did not have. Toward the end of his questions about the psychologist's qualifications, he asked:

Q: . . . so where did you actually learn, in a classroom setting, what you are doing here in this report and the treatment you rendered to Ms. Gomez? Where did you learn to do this, in a classroom setting?

It is obvious that a person with such a weak background should not claim to be an expert in court. Anyone in that position would have trouble convincing a jury that they ever learned adequately the clinical procedures they performed in order to reach their conclusions. Had the case gone to trial (it did not), the attorney would surely have hammered before the jury the point that this individual was practicing neuropsychology having taken a single academic course on the subject. One can just imagine the problems that could have been brought up if the psychologist had examined a non-English-speaking Hispanic using a translator. Interestingly, the subject of his examination was a Hispanic female who was perfectly fluent in English, and who therefore required no translator.

Still, there was a slight problem: The neuropsychologist would not grant that one of the subject's errors (in pronouncing the word "Massachusetts") may have been caused by a very slight language difficulty that may crop up even among those whose English pronunciation is otherwise perfect. This failure to grant such a possibility (that a slight mispronunciation of Massachusetts by a Hispanic might be meaningless) reveals a lack of flexibility on the side of the neuropsychologist. This, again, is a mistake on his part, which would surely alienate a jury. The attorney, himself a Hispanic, probed the linguistic error that his client Ms. Gomez had produced:

Q: Do you take into account the fact that she comes from a Hispanic background and may have a slight accent? I know my mother says "Massa-chu-seets," and I know she is not brain damaged.

A: I did not notice any, and I think her primary, spoken language is that of English. She appears to not have an accent.

Q: So you gave her an NDS [Neuropsychological Deficit Scale] score of one?

A: Yes, I did.

Q: Contributing to the overall conclusion that she is brain damaged because she could not say "Massachusetts" right?

A: Contributing to this particular pathognomonic sign.

It is obvious this psychologist was not well prepared or fair in conducting this neuropsychological assessment. If the previous exchange had been conducted in the presence of a jury, it is likely that whatever remnants of credibility the psychologist may have retained up to that point would have vanished. By the time the deposition ended, the plaintiff's case was so weak that a quick settlement, for a fraction of the original demand, was agreed on by the attorneys.

The Trial

By the time the trial takes place, the litigating attorneys are well aware of what will transpire before the jury. Although the content of what each expert will say can be foreseen by what transpired during the deposition, the way the witness speaks to the jury and handles the questions from the attorney becomes critical. It is not enough to be well prepared: The expert should convey a sense of being at ease with his professional opinions, about the details of the case, and about his interventions. The expert should have committed to memory all the relevant details of the case (such as the dates in which the patient was examined and the diagnostic formulations made about the patient). This preparation pays off in showing to the jury that the expert was interested in the case and made a point of studying it well before coming to trial; the expert will be free of shuffling papers, and will thus be able to talk directly to the jury while answering questions. All the factors mentioned earlier about the nature of how the expert should be (competent, forthright, and complete) are even more important when actually facing the jury.

In cases involving Hispanics, only a couple of comments need to be made. They involve the composition of the jury and the emotional pitfalls that the expert may encounter.

In some regions of the country, it is a given that the jury will be composed of predominantly Hispanic people; in other regions, a Hispanic is unlikely to be found on the jury. It is a common assumption that juries will favor plaintiffs (or defendants) who look like them and share similar demographic characteristics. Thus, attorneys will attempt to keep (or remove) as many Hispanics as possible from the jury, depending on what they believe will favor the case. It may very well be that juries will be biased for or against individuals based on their ethnicity; but, a psychologist should maintain a neutral stance about such things, and leave them where they belong, that is, in the realm of the attorneys' concerns. The expert neuropsychologist should be single-minded and tenacious in the pursuit of the truth as it is revealed through his professional skills, and should not attempt to be something they are not, such as a sociologist, a physician, or an attorney.

It is an emotional pitfall for a Hispanic psychologist to become biased in favor of a Hispanic client for the reason that they both share a culture. This may be understandable, but it is also a grave mistake, for the loss of objectivity is easy enough to detect by others, and such a loss damages the case for the client and for the attorney who did the hiring. A conscious effort to maintain scientific distance and objectivity, as well as an unbiased attitude, should always be expected from the ethical neuropsychologist.

CONCLUSIONS

The neuropsychological examination of Hispanic patients is at present a daunting task fraught with difficulties that prevent such examinations, and their results, from having the same levels of accuracy and precision as those conducted on people who belong to the dominant, English-speaking, U.S. culture. The following summarizes the problems likely to be encountered in examining Hispanics:

1. In the dominant U.S. culture, it is extremely rare to find people who have not completed school through at least the eighth grade. Yet it is common to find Hispanic immigrants of presumably normal IQs who have never attended school, or who did so for only a year or two. There are no tests or norms to conduct valid examinations of the cognitive makeup of these individuals, much less to permit inferences about the status of their brain functions with the same probability of being correct as if U.S. natives with normal levels of school completion were being examined.

2. There is a lack of testing instruments with which to make assessment of Hispanics. At present, there is not a widely accepted neuropsychological test battery that has been standardized for use on Hispanic populations in the United States.

3. The existing problems with test materials and levels of education are systematically compounded and exaggerated by the use of "translators" in the examination of Hispanics. Such a use solves the language problem for the psychologist, but aggravates the source of error in the assessment. Ideally, such practice should be eliminated completely. However, if there is no possibility whatsoever for the psychologist to refer to an appropriate clinician, then the recommendations outlined here should be closely followed, and the caveats about the tentative nature of the results should be clearly stated in their report.

4. The cultural makeup of Hispanics is a source of error distinct from the problems of language, although they can often appear to be indistinguishable. Sensitivity to the different metaphorical forms that injury and disease have in the two cultures is needed in order to understand the distortions on test results produced by different acculturations.

5. Despite all these difficulties, and perhaps because of them, there is a healthy and growing interest among U.S. psychologists to find solutions to these problems; to that effect, significant research is currently under way.

An especially helpful development for U.S. psychology is the growth of clinical neuropsychology in the Spanish-speaking regions outside the United States; each of these regions must develop, or at least borrow and adapt to its use, tests and test batteries that will be responsive to the peculiar cultural differences of those regions. Once these instruments become established as useful diagnostic and rehabilitative devices, they will surely find their way to the United States to help assess the Hispanics who reside here. The day when it will be as easy and precise to examine an immigrant from Guatemala as it is to assess a native of Peoria is still distant, but things are moving in that direction.

REFERENCES

American Psychological Association. (1990). Ethical principles of psychologists. *American Psychologist, 45,* 390–395.

American Psychological Association (1991). *Guidelines for providers of psychological services to ethnic, linguistic and culturally diverse populations.* Washington, DC: APA Office of Ethnic and Minority Affairs.

Ardila, A., Roselli, M., & Puente, A. E. (1993). *Neuropsychological evaluation of the Spanish speaker.* New York: Plenum.

Artiola i Fortuni, L. (1996). [Review of the book Neuropsychological evaluation of the Spanish speaker]. *The Clinical Neuropsychologist, 10,* 229–234.

Barona, A., Reynolds, C. R., & Chastain, R. (1984). A demographically based index of premorbid intelligence for the WAIS–R. *Journal of Consulting and Clinical Psychology, 52,* 885–887.

Blair, J. R., & Spreen, O. (1989). Predicting premorbid IQ: A revision of the National Adult Reading Test. *The Clinical Neuropsychologist, 3,* 129–136.

DuAlba, L., & Scott, R. (1993). Somatization and malingering for workers' compensation applicants: A cross cultural MMPI study. *Journal of Clinical Psychology, 49,* 913–917.

Faust, D., Ziskin, J., & Hiers, J. B. (1991). *Brain damage claims: Coping with neuropsychological evidence.* Los Angeles: Law and Psychology Press.

Greene, R. L. (1991). *The MMPI–2/MMPI: An interpretive manual.* Boston: Allyn & Bacon.

Jarman, B. G., & Russell, R. (Eds.). (1994). *The Oxford Spanish dictionary.* Oxford, England: Oxford University Press.

Kolody, B., Vegg, W., Meinhardt, K., & Bensussen, G. (1986). The correspondence of health complaints and depressive symptoms among Anglos and Mexican-Americans. *Journal of Nervous and Mental Disease, 174,* 221–228.

Koss, J. (1990). Somatization and somatic complaint syndromes among Hispanics: Overview and ethnopsychological perspectives. *Transcultural Psychiatric Research Review, 27,* 5–29.

LaCalle, J. J. (1987). Forensic psychological evaluations through an interpreter: Legal and ethical issues. *American Journal of Forensic Psychology, 5,* 29–43.

Lezak, M. D. (1995). *Neuropsychological assessment* (3rd ed.). New York: Oxford University Press.

Lopez, E. C. (1997). The cognitive assessment of limited proficiency and bilingual children. In D. Flanagan & J. Genshaft (Eds.), *Contemporary intellectual assessment: Theories, tests and issues* (pp. 503–516). New York: Guilford.

Melendez, F. (1994). The Spanish version of the WAIS: Some ethical considerations. *The Clinical Neuropsychologist, 8,* 388–393.

Pankratz, L. (1988). Malingering on intellectual and neuropsychological measures. In R. Rogers (Ed.), *Clinical assessment of malingering and deception* (pp. 169–192). New York: Guilford.

Puente, A. E. (Ed.). (1991). Special issue: Forensic clinical neuropsychology. *Neuropsychology Review, 2,* 203–266.

Pontón, M. O., Satz, P., Herrera, L., Ortiz, F., Urrutia, C., Young, R., D'Elia, L., Furst, C. J., & Namerow, N. (1996). Normative data stratified by age and education for the Neuropsychological Screening Battery for Hispanics (NeSBHIS);Initial report. *Journal of the International Neuropsychological Society, 2,* 96–104.

Pontón, M. O., Gonzalez, J., & Mares, M. (1997). Rehabilitating brain damage in Hispanics. In Josá León-Carrión (Ed.), *Neuropsycholgical rehabilitation: Fundamentals, innovations and directions* (pp. 513–529). DelRay Beach, FL: St. Lucie Press.

Reitan, R. M. (1986). Theoretical and methodological bases of the Halstead-Reitan Neuropsychological Test Battery. In I. Grant & K.A. Adams (Eds.), *Neuropsychological assessment of neuropsychiatric disorders* (pp. 3–30). New York: Oxford University Press.

Reitan, R. M., & Wolfson, D. (1997). *Detection of malingering and invalid test scores.* Tucson, AZ: Neuropsychology Press.

Rogers, R. (1988). *Clinical assessment of malingering and deception.* New York: Guilford.

Spreen, O., & Strauss, E. (1991). *A compendium of neuropsychological tests.* New York: Oxford University Press.

Wechsler, D. (1955). *Manual para la escala de inteligencia Wechsler para adultos* [Manual for the Wechsler Adult Intelligence Scale]. San Antonio: The Psychological Corporation.

Wilson, R. S., Rosenbaum, G., & Brown, G. (1979). The problem of premorbid intelligence in neuropsychological assessment. *Journal of Clinical Neuropsychology, 1,* 49–53.

16

Normal and Abnormal Aging

Mónica Rosselli
Florida Atlantic University

Alfredo Ardila
Instituto Colombiano de Neuropsicologia

During the last two decades, significant emphasis has been placed on the neuropsychological research of normal and abnormal aging. Medical and technological advances have made it possible to detect diseases ahead of time. These advances have helped to increase life expectancy. The changes in life expectancy and the decline in mortality are the result of multiple factors: better living conditions, higher nutritional levels, and advances in diagnostic techniques and pharmacotherapy.

The increase in life expectancy is clearly seen among the U.S. population. In the United States, the number of people over age 65 was 11% in 1970, 12% in 1987, and it is projected to climb to 22.6% in the next 45 years (Albert & Knoefel, 1994).

The U.S. population includes different ethnic groups and this diversity is also reflected among the elderly. This ethnic diversity will increase in the United States (U.S. Census Bureau, 1996). The growth of the Hispanic population has been significant in the last decade, and it is expected to continue (Campbell, 1994). Hispanics represent approximately 10% of the U.S. population (U.S. Census Bureau, 1996). It has been estimated that by 2025, they to constitute the largest ethnic minority group in the United States (*Statistical Abstract,* 1990). Hispanics compromise 4.5% (1,390,000) of the total U.S. population over age 65 (30,780,000) (U.S. Census Bureau, 1996). The rapid growth of Hispanics coupled with the fact that life expectancy of persons living in the United States, including Hispanics, has continue to improve, has led to a growing increase in the population of Spanish-speaking elderly. The number of elderly Hispanics is expected to climb from 4% to 16% by 2050. It can be expected that the number of people with dementia will increase in the United States over the following decades.

This chapter reviews the neuropsychology of the elderly with emphasis on studies that include Latin populations living in Latin America and in the United States. It is divided into four sections. The first presents the cognitive deficits associated with normal aging, and the second considers studies on abnormal aging. The third section analyzes the neuropsychological assessment of the elderly Spanish-speaker. The final section includes possible future research directions.

COGNITIVE CHANGES DURING NORMAL AGING

Social, physical, psychological, and cognitive changes develop with age. Cognitive changes include general intelligence, visuospatial and visuomotor abilities, perception, memory, attention, and language. The variability on neuropsychological test performance tends to increase with age. Some subjects maintained high scores, whereas others demonstrated a rapid decline (Fig. 16.1). The first group represents "successful aging," and the second group represents "unsuccessful aging." The latter is composed of subjects who demonstrate a rapid decline in cognitive functions, eventually leading to a dementia of the Alzheimer type (Cummings & Benson, 1992). There is, however, a variation in the magnitude and rate of change depending on the cognitive function in question (Albert, 1994). Neuropsychological test performance tends to present a negative correlation with age, but subjects can maintain appropriate cognitive functioning even during the eighth decade of life (Mandell, Knoefel, & Albert, 1994).

General Cognitive Performance

Intelligence tests and mini-mental status examinations tests are commonly used by neuropsychologists to assess general cognitive performance among the elderly.

The term *general intelligence* is a construct that is difficult to define. Perez-Arce and Puente (1996) defined general intelligence by a set of test scores that are heavily correlated with the U.S. definition of scholastic success. Individual differences in intelligence as assessed by standardized tests relate to what individuals learn in school (Brody, 1992). The determinants of normal or abnormal may be established by the cultural group that develops the intelligence test (Ardila, 1995).

Age may be an important variable influencing IQ. Some of the intelligence subtest scores are influenced by age, and others remain relatively independent from this variable. The classical age–intelligence pattern describes nonverbal IQ as strongly influenced by age as compared to verbal IQ. Verbal subtests have been considered to measure "crystallized intelligence" (Cattell, 1963), a type of intelligence maintained with little variance over a lifetime. Through this type of intelligence, the subject expresses previous verbal learning and general knowledge (Horn, 1985; Horn & Cattell, 1966).

Nonverbal or performance subtests, on the other hand, are part of "fluid intelligence" that allows the use of current information in the solution of new problems (Cattell, 1963). This type of intelligence requires visuomotor and/or spatial skills and is very sensitive to age. Younger subjects outperform older ones in those tasks or problems that require the use of fluid intelligence. Older subjects perform well on tasks that use previous knowledge in the solution of the problem.

The classical pattern of aging with relative preservation of verbal versus nonverbal abilities has been demonstrated by many researchers (Brody, 1992; Hertzog, 1989; Mandell et al., 1994; Schaie, 1983). Although some studies have compared the performance of different cultural groups on verbal and nonverbal neuropsychological tests (Jacobs et al., 1997; Lopez & Taussig, 1991), no research has been carried out comparing patterns of aging in different cultural groups. The classical aging pattern (verbal skills preserved vs. decline on nonverbal test performance) does not seem to apply to illiterates (Finley, Ardila, & Rosselli, 1991), and may not be valid for groups different from the American and European cultures. Subject characteristics (e.g., age, education, language, and cul-

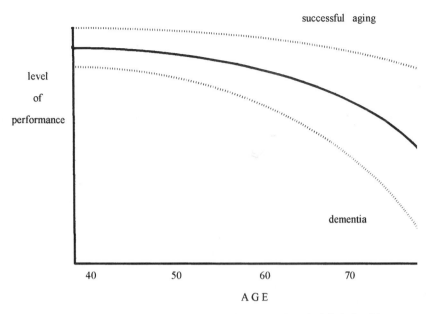

FIG. 16.1. Cognitive changes across age. The dispersions (standard deviations) in neuropsychological test scores increase with aging and groups become more heterogeneous. The higher group corresponds to the "successful aging," whereas the lower one eventually will present a dementia of the Alzheimer type.

ture) can affect performance on neuropsychological tests, and it might have an important influence over the aging pattern.

A fundamental factor influencing performance on visuomotor tests is speed. When time limits are used as part of the test, older people have a disadvantage. Age is usually associated with motor slowness, decreased speed in perceptual information processing, and increase in reaction time. Other factors, such as flexibility of thinking and meaningfulness of the test, may influence test performance as well. Flexibility of thinking presents a drop only after the seventies (Willis, Geo, Thomas, & Garry, 1988).

The most common test of intelligence in adults, independent of their ethnic origin, is the Wechsler Adult Intelligence Scale (WAIS). Two additional versions have been developed, the WAIS–R (Wechsler, 1981) and the WAIS–III (Wechsler, 1991). The original version has been adapted to Spanish (Escala de Inteligencia de Wechsler para Adultos, EIWA; Wechsler, 1968). Currently, the WAIS–III Spanish is in the developmental process. To obtain an IQ of 100 (average mean) at age 74 requires answering correctly half of the questions needed to obtain the same IQ at age 20. Due to this age effect, the WAIS–R has age correction scores. The normalization group for this battery, however, goes up only to age 74 in the English version and to age 64 in the Spanish version.

Lopez and Taussig (1991) found that the cognitive-intellectual functioning of Hispanic adults is prone to be underestimated when using the WAIS–R and overestimated when using the EIWA. In their study, the WAIS–R subtests indicated cognitive impairment in normal Spanish-speakers and the EIWA subtests indicated less cognitive impairment in Spanish-speakers with Alzheimer's disease. Jacobs et al. (1997) compared the performance of English- and Spanish-speaking elders, matched by age and level of education, on a brief neuropsychological test battery. Spanish- and English-speakers scored comparably in many of the language tests, including the Similarities subtest from the WAIS–R; Spanish-speakers scored significantly lower, however, on nonverbal reasoning and visuoperceptual skills subtests (e.g., Benton Visual Retention Test-Matching and Identities and Oddities from the Mattis Dementia Rating Scale). The authors hypothesized that the geometric nature of the stimuli on these nonverbal measures may have conferred an advantage to the English-speakers, perhaps by virtue of differences on educational emphasis or exposure.

The influence of age has also been studied in general cognitive screening tests such as the Mini-Mental Status Examination (MMSE; M. F. Folstein, S. E. Folstein, & McHugh, 1975). Ardila, Rosselli, and Puente (1994) found a mild decrease of scores associated with age across educational groups in a Spanish-speaking population from Colombia. The most significant decrease in low education subjects was observed after age 65 and in the higher educational group after age 70. No differences were found between sexes. Escobar et al. (1986) administered the MMSE to samples of the Hispanic and Anglo populations in the Los Angeles area. They found that some of the items were sensitive not only to educational level, but also to the cultural background of the subject. The Hispanic group presented a higher number of errors to questions related to the current season and to the concept of state. Seasons are not particularly relevant to orientation in the majority of the tropical and subtropical Spanish-speaking countries. The significant influence of age and education on the MMSE has also been observed in other cultural groups (Magaziner, Basset, & Hebel, 1987).

Visuospatial and Visuomotor Functions

Aging is characterized by a decline in visuospatial and visuomotor abilities (Albert, 1988; Ardila & Rosselli, 1989; La Rue, 1992). The decline on nonverbal, visuospatial tests for the elders has been parallel to the test performance of young patients with right hemisphere damage. The visuospatial difficulties are reflected in drawing and constructional tasks. It has been pointed out that figure drawing ability declines significantly with aging. Plude, Milberg, and Cerella (1986) reported that older subjects have more difficulties in drawing a cube than younger ones; this also holds true for perceiving a cube accurately. Ardila and Rosselli (1989) emphasized the important decline of nonverbal skills in normal elders from Colombia. They found that a single factor accounted for about one third (34.5%) of the variance of neuropsychological performance in 346 normal Hispanic subjects from 55 to 85 years old. Constructional, visuospatial, and visuomotor test scores were saturated by this factor. It was proposed by the authors that a visuospatial factor may represent a fundamental aging factor.

The best measure of the visuospatial aging factor in the Ardila and Rosselli (1989) study was the Rey–Osterrieth Complex Figure (ROCF). Although ROCF is frequently used as part of the neuropsychological battery in the assessment of elderly populations, research focused on the normal performance of elderly people on the ROCF has been limited. Some norms, however, are available in current literature for Spanish-speakers (e.g., Ardila et al., 1994; Ardila & Rosselli, in press; Pontón et al., 1996) and English-speakers (Spreen & Strauss, 1997). Tupler, Welsh, Yaw, and Dawson (1995) studied a group of English-speaking elderly subjects and found that ROCF performance was more closely associated with age than IQ. Age-dependent defects in the ROCF are observed not only in the copy condition, but also in the immediate and delayed recall of the figure. Scores significantly decrease after age 65 and especially after age 70 (Boone, Lasser, Hill-

Gutierrez, & Berman, 1993). A similar effect of age and education on the ROCF has been observed for both Spanish- and English-speakers.

Other visuospatial and constructional tests such as block design and object assembly show significant decline with age (M. L. Albert & Kaplan, 1980; La Rue & Markee, 1995). Low performance in block design and assembling tasks were significantly correlated in elderly subjects with slowing in reaction time (M. S. Albert, 1994). When performance on block design and drawing of tridimensional or complex figures is time dependent, score difference between younger and older subjects increases. Reaction time and motor slowness are partially responsible for the low scores on nonverbal tests among the elderly individuals (Salthouse, 1985).

It has been reported that visuospatial task performance not only depends on the subject's age, but on educational level as well. Low educational groups score significantly lower when compared to highly educated subjects. Drawing tests are school dependent (Ardila, Rosselli, & Rosas, 1989). An interaction between education and gender in visuospatial tasks has been described. In low educational level subjects, gender differences are significant in visuospatial test performance, but these gender differences disappear in higher educated groups. M. Rosselli and Ardila (1991) reported that low education Colombian females presented significantly lower scores on the ROCF when compared to high education females. No differences in the pattern of decline of visuospatial functions between males and females have been found independent from level of education. This relation between gender and educational level has been observed in different neuropsychological tests among Hispanic populations living in Latin America (e.g., Ostrosky et al., 1985; Ostrosky, Ardila, & Rosselli, 1987; M. Rosselli, Ardila, Florez, & Castro, 1990; M. Rosselli, Ardila, & Rosas, 1990) and living in the United States (Pontón et al., 1996).

Jacobs et al. (1997), found significant group differences between Spanish- and English-speakers living in the New York area in visuospatial skills. Spanish-speakers scored significantly lower when compared to English-speakers, in a multiple choice matching version of the Benton Visual Retention Test. Subjects matched a target design to the same design presented simultaneously in a four-choice multiple choice array containing the target along with the three distracters. The two cultural samples were matched by education, age, and gender. The authors proposed as a possible explanation the lack of familiarity of the Spanish-speakers with the geometric designs and the multiple choice format used for this measure.

Although it is well-known that visuospatial and constructional abilities, including drawing figures, are affected by the subject's culture (Deregowski, 1989; Pontius, 1989) and level of education (Ardila, Rosselli, & Rosas, 1989; Pontón et al., 1996), neuropsychologists do not always take this into account when performing neuropsychological evaluation. This is reflected in the limited norms available with visuospatial and constructional tests for different cultural and educational groups. In American urban society, training in drawing skills is basically provided through formal education. Then, level of schooling is a critical variable with important impact on cognitive test performance.

Memory

Senescence is associated with a decrease in memory and learning. There is a tendency to increase in forgetfulness and decrease in the capacity to store new information. This decline develops at a slow rate in normal aging, but is accelerated in abnormal aging (Cummings & Benson, 1992).

Memory is a complex and multifactorial domain of cognition (Fuster, 1993); therefore, it is not affected uniformly by age. Some aspects of memory are more affected than others. Remote memory or tertiary memory is relatively stable with age. It is preserved particularly when the events had emotional content and require verbal-cultural knowledge (La Rue, 1992). Age changes in recent memory are the most prominent. The decrease in secondary memory or long-term memory, observed in older people, may explain the recent memory defects (Miller, 1977). Secondary memory refers to acquisition, retention, and retrieval of information over intervals ranging from a few minutes to days or weeks (La Rue, 1992). This is a memory store that can contain a virtually unlimited amount of information. The greatest differences between young and old groups have been reported in secondary memory. Immediate memory, on the other hand, shows very little change with age.

Primary memory is limited in terms of the amount of information. When the information is to be retained for a substantial period of time, it must be transferred to secondary memory in order to be stored. This storage of new information is reduced with age. Although the elderly are able to encode (primary memory), their problem is in transferring it into long-term memory (secondary memory). These difficulties are true for verbal and nonverbal material (Crook et al., 1986), although they may be more pronounced for visuospatial memory (Eslinger, Pepin, & Benton, 1988). In the ROCF, for example, immediate recall scores decrease earlier in life and are more sensitive to aging effects than ROCF copy scores (Ardila & Rosselli, in press). A steady decline in the constructional/memory ratio (copy score/immediate recall score) has been observed since the 1950s.

Age decrements are greater on recall than on recognition tasks (Craik, Byrd, & Swanson, 1987), meaning that retrieval defects may contribute to secondary memory problems also (Poon, 1985). Cueing at retrieval and encoding improves the performance on memory tasks in the elderly (Craik et al., 1987; Cummings & Benson, 1992; Smith, 1980).

Normal aging is associated with a slowing in encoding (Cerella, Poon, & Fozard, 1982) and in reaction time (Ardila & Rosselli, 1986, 1992). The rate of presentation of the information to be retained may affect memory performance in the elderly. Arenberg (1982) found significant differences in the performance of younger and older adults if the memory information is presented at a high rate. These differences disappeared when the rate of presentation slowed down.

The impairment in recent memory has been associated with an age change in the use of metamemory strategies. Older people, for example, are less likely to use association strategies when learning a list of words (Albert, 1994), and therefore, required more trials than younger people to learn a list of words.

Ostrosky, Ardila, and Jaime (1998) studied memory abilities in 105 Mexican normal subjects, from 20 to 89 years old. They used five different memory tests: Wechsler Memory Scale, Serial Verbal Learning, Rey–Osterrieth Complex Figure (immediate and delayed reproduction), Corsi's blocks, and the Rivermead Behavioral Memory Test (Wilson, Cockburn, & Baddeley, 1985) as a functional scale. There was a progressive decline across ages that ranged from 4.1% and 76.6%. In all the tests, except Digits, standard deviations increased with age. About half of the tests significantly correlated with the functional memory scale.

Although the studies with Spanish-speakers have shown deficits in secondary memory with preservation of primary and remote memory, very few studies have compared neuropsychological test performance between Hispanics and other cultural groups. Jacobs et al. (1997) found significant differences in nonverbal tests between Spanish- and English-speakers living in the United States.

Attention

Attention is not an independent function (Mandell, Knoefel, & Albert, 1994). Therefore, deficits in other cognitive functions may influence performance on tests of attention. Assessment of attention includes the subject's ability to select and maintain visual and auditory attention. Digit span forward is the most commonly used test for sustained attention. There is very little effect of age over the performance on this test. There is less than one standard deviation of change between age 20 and 80 (M. S. Albert, 1994). Performance differences have consistently been found in digit span between Anglo Americans and Hispano Americans (Lopez & Taussig, 1991; Loewenstein, Arguelles, Barker, & Duara, 1993). English-speakers usually outperformed Spanish-speakers. It has been shown that subjects speaking languages in which the length of the words that express the numbers is shorter are able to repeat more digits than the subjects speaking languages with long phonetic codes (Ellis & Hennelly, 1980; Naveh-Benjamin & Ayres, 1986). Olazaran, Jacobs, and Stern (1996) suggested that this difference is the result of cultural and educational issues rather than the number of syllables. Furthermore, Spanish-speakers tend to cluster digits in everyday activities (e.g., phone numbers). Interestingly, there is a coincidence between the number of digits that an individual can repeat and phone numbers. To repeat phone numbers is an overtrained everyday task. It could be anticipated that, if instead of a digit span a multiple digit span task was used (e.g., 35, 64, 12, etc.), then Spanish-speakers would outperform English-speakers. Of course, this has to be demonstrated.

More complex attention tasks, such as the Trail Making Test, may present more significant age effects (La Rue, 1992). The majority of the attention tests influenced by age are visuomotor tasks in which reaction time is important. Most researchers agree that when tests of sustained or selective attention are controlled for reaction time and perceptual discrimination no significant differences among age groups will emerge (M. S. Albert, 1994). Ostrosky et al. (1994) studied the P300 cortical potential as a measure of speed in information processing and attention in Mexican normal elderly. They reported an average yearly increase of .38 msec in the latency and a decrease of .20 mV in the amplitude of P300. No cross-cultural comparisons were done in Ostrosky et al.'s study.

Language

Some aspects of language are particularly sensitive to aging. Vocabulary tends to increase well into the sixth decade of life, and narrative style shows complexity and sophistication with age (Obler, 1980). Syntax can be preserved, although age-related defects in comprehension of complex material can be found in elderly subjects.

The main language functions influenced by age are naming and verbal fluency. Mild naming difficulties can be observed during the seventh decade of life (Albert, Heller, & Milberg, 1987; Bayles & Kasazniak, 1987). Using the Boston Naming Test scores (Kaplan, Goodglass, & Weintraub, 1983) as a measure of lexical knowledge, a significant effect of both the age and the level of education in normal elderly subjects has been observed (LaBarge, Edwards, & Knesevich, 1986; Pontón et al., 1996; Van Gorp, Satz, Kiersch, & Henry, 1986). Verbal fluency decreases with age, particularly after age 70. M. Rosselli, Ardila, Florez, and Castro (1990) found different correlations between age and the subtests of the Boston Diagnostic Aphasia Examination in a normal population sample. The highest negative correlations were found between age and naming, and age and fluency subtests.

Some studies have analyzed the effects of age over spontaneous language. Obler (1980) studied the language production in the oral and written description of the Cookie Theft picture from the Boston Diagnostic Aphasia Examination (Goodglass & Kaplan, 1972) in normal elderly adults. Two different styles of sentence construction were found: abbreviated and elaborated. Subjects in their 60s were more likely to have fewer nouns per verb. Kemper (1987) studied the oral language production in elderly subjects between ages 50 and 90. It was noted that the mean length of utterances did not change with age, but the syntactic constructions changed. Kynette and Kemper (1986) concluded that in advanced age, syntactic processing abilities decline to the degree they are associated with increased memory and attentional demands. Ardila and Rosselli (1996) observed a reduction in spontaneous language across age groups in a Spanish-speaking sample. The amount of words used by the oldest groups (51–65 years) was only 63% of the total number of words used by the 16- to 30-year-old subjects. According to Ardila and Rosselli (1996) language changes associated with aging follow a different pattern in males and females. Whereas males presented a steady and permanent decline in spontaneous language production, evident in the 31- to 50-year-old range, spontaneous language production in females is abundant even at the 51- to 65-year-old range. Interpretation of gender differences in language decline is difficult. They can result from biological (i.e., different patterns of cerebral involution) and/or cultural factors (i.e., different gender roles in elderly, different linguistic environments, etc.). If language acquisition is influenced by gender, then it seems reasonable to hypothesize that language decline may also be affected by gender. Further, cross-cultural studies are obviously required.

Performance in language ability tests is strongly associated with the subject's educational level (Ardila, Rosselli, & Ostrosky, 1992a, 1992b; Bornstein & Suga, 1988; Heaton, Grant, & Matthews, 1986; Lantz, 1979; Ostrosky et al., 1985; Pontón et al., 1996; Rey, 1990). And this educational-level effect on language tests can even be more significant than the aging effect (Benton & Hamsher, 1978; M. Rosselli, Ardila, & Rosas, 1990). The effects of education may be so strong that, when education is controlled, there is no longer evidence of an age-related decline in verbal intelligence (Albert & Heaton, 1988). Level of education significantly correlates with IQ (Matarazzo, 1979). In Latin American countries, low educational levels are more often the result of economical limitations than academic failures, and therefore the correlation value between level of education and IQ is expected to be lower than what has been reported in more developed countries.

Few studies have compared the language test performance between Spanish- and English-speakers. No differences have been reported in repetition and naming. Differences between Spanish- and English-speakers in category fluency but not in letter fluency have been reported. Jacobs et al. (1997) found significantly lower scores in Spanish elderly living in New York city, in semantic fluency (cloth, fruits, and animals) when compared to matched English-speakers. To explain any differences, the authors suggested that the number of exemplars in each semantic category fluency test may not be comparable across languages.

COGNITIVE CHANGES DURING ABNORMAL AGING

Dementia has long been a significant topic of research in Latin American neuropsychology (Mendilaharsu & Mendilaharsu, 1978–1982). Several studies have approached the analysis of dementia in Spanish-speaking subjects. Special attention has attracted the question regarding the dementia criteria and the assessment instruments appropriate for the neuropsychological appraisal of Hispanic populations.

Dementia in Alzheimer's Disease

Donoso (1987) and colleagues in Chile have been studying the cognitive changes associated with dementia in Alzheimer's disease (AD). They pointed out that language, memory, and constructional skills are most commonly affected in the early stages of the disease. Minor naming difficulties progress toward significant language understanding defects and global language deficits. Constructional difficulties evolved into more severe spatial problems (e.g., topographical defects). Amnesia represents a central defect in AD. Recent memory defects are initially observed followed by anterograde and a progressive retrograde amnesia. The pattern of cognitive decline proposed by Donoso is coincidental with the general reports about neuropsychological evolution in AD English-speaking groups (Cummings & Benson, 1992). It represents, however, a cross-cultural corroboration that AD portrays certain fundamental clinical characteristics, beyond the immediate cultural context.

In addition to advancing age, genetic factors contribute to the development of AD. An autosomal dominant form of AD, familial AD (FAD), has been recognized (T. D. Bird et al., 1988; Kennedy et al., 1995). One of the largest families with FAD has been found in the Colombian highlands (Lopera et al., 1994). Six extended families from Antioquia (Colombia) with an autosomal dominant pattern of early onset Alzheimer's disease (EOAD)—all carrying a glutamic acid to alanine mutation at codon 280 in the presenilin 1 gene—have been analyzed. The total population within the six pedigrees now surpasses 2,500 individuals. The disease has a mean age of onset of 46.8 years and the average interval between onset and death is 8 years. The most frequent presentation was memory loss followed by behavior and personality changes and progressive loss of language ability. In the final stages, the most frequent changes were gait disturbances, seizures, and myoclonus. Other than the early onset, this clinical phenotype is indistinguishable from sporadic AD. Despite the uniform genetic basis for the disease, there was some variability in presentation and disease course among the affected individuals.

The cognitive profile of this FAD group using the CERAD neuropsychological test battery (Morris et al., 1989) revealed an impaired performance in the following areas: Verbal Fluency, Naming, MMSE, Memory of Words, Constructional Praxis, Recall of Words, Recognition of Words, Recall of Drawings, and Trail Making. Verbal fluency and naming were both impaired, but verbal fluency defects were more evident than naming deficits. Total verbal fluency scores in the FAD patients were 54% in comparison with a control group. Differences in reading words were not significant. However, memory of words differed significantly. Intrusions were frequently observed in the FAD group, but not in the controls. Constructional difficulties separated the FAD and the control group (Lopera et al., 1997). In general, these results are coincidental with other reports about FAD in other cultural groups (T. D. Bird, 1994; Kennedy et al., 1995).

In summary, some research studies have been carried out with AD among Spanish-speaking populations.

Other Dementias

Other types of dementia have been analyzed in Spanish-speaking neuropsychology. Ostrosky (Ostrosky et al., 1988, 1991) collaborated in the neuropsychological evaluation of Parkinson's disease in Mexican patients undergoing brain autograft of adrenal medullar tissue, and Pineda et al. (1988, 1995) studied the cognitive profile of the dementia associated with Parkinson's disease in Colombia. The most significant research studies about the genetics of Huntington's disease have been carried out in Venezuela (Gusella, Wexler, & Conneally, 1983). In Colombia, neuropsychological defects associated with Huntington's disease (D. Rosselli et al., 1986), and the dementia in Wilson's disease (M. Rosselli, Lorenzana, Rosselli, & Vergara, 1987) have been analyzed. Special emphasis has been placed on the reversibility of Wilson's disease dementia. Neurocysticercosis represents a relatively frequent condition in some Latin American countries, eventually resulting in global cognitive deterioration (A. Rosselli, Rosselli, Ardila, & Penagos, 1988).

The number of studies about different dementias in cross-cultural neuropsychology has been limited. Consequently, more research is needed.

NEUROPSYCHOLOGICAL ASSESSMENT

The main purpose of a geriatric neuropsychological evaluation is to detect the presence or absence of cognitive abnormalities. The use of neuropsychological tests may intend to rate cognitive improvement or decline, severity of dementia, or assist in the development of rehabilitation techniques.

Distinguishing normal and abnormal aging is a central problem in neuropsychology. Several authors (Ardila & Rosselli, 1986; Cummings & Benson, 1992; Mandell et al., 1994) have emphasized the great difficulty in discriminating normal individuals from those with mild dementia. It is difficult primarily because the cohort of elderly people is far from a homogeneous population. The boundaries of neuropsychological normality are difficult to define for a given individual and the given individual is what faces the neuropsychologist who is conducting the evaluation.

Variables Influencing Neuropsychological Test Performance

Cognitive age-dependent changes may be seen in all groups independently from their ethnic origin but must be understood within the subject's culture and the context of the life they live (McCaffrey & Puente, 1992). Cultural variables—such as linguistic factors, family values, and educational experience—may influence neuropsychological test performance. It is acknowledged that diverse cultural groups may emphasize different modes of processing information and current cognitive tests may penalize specific cultural populations (Irvine & Berry, 1988). Therefore, the profile on a standard neuropsychological battery may vary among cultures. There is a great need for instruments to assess cognitive functions in older Hispanic subjects. From 50% to 70% of U.S. Hispanics over age 60 do not speak English (Lopez-Aqueres et al., 1984). When assessing Spanish-speaking elderly, it is very important to use tests that have been normalized among the patient's cultural group. Otherwise, there is a risk of seeing abnormal aging when the changes actually correspond to the normal aging process. There appears to be strong evidence that specific cultural values have a strong impact on cognitive test performance (Perez-Arce & Puente, 1996). Many studies clearly indicate that using nonverbal tests, in and of itself does not necessarily eliminate cultural bias in the assessment of Hispanic elderly (Jacobs et al., 1997; Loewenstein et al., 1993; Lopez & Taussig, 1991).

To adapt a test to a culture does not mean simply translating the instrument, because it is also necessary to adapt it to the specific demands existing in that culture (Ardila, 1995). Differences in intellectual performance using psychometric procedures may represent in consequence an artifact of the assessment instruments. Psychological and neuropsychological tests reflect the examiners' cultural demands and their interpretation of the world. It is evident to any clinical psychologist that whenever a cross-cultural comparison is established, better scores are observed in the cultural group that is responsible for the development of the test.

Another important variable concerning the validity of the test refers to the normative data used. Most neuropsychological tests have been developed and normalized in English-speaking populations and even more, most of the standardized samples are no older than age 65. Therefore, a Spanish-speaker who is 75 years old is going to be at a greater disadvantage than a matched English-speaker when assessed with a test that has been normalized in an English-speaking sample. In addition, the pattern of cognitive decline during normal and abnormal aging is not completely coincidental in individuals with different educational backgrounds. Education level has been associated with the severity and even the duration of Alzheimer's disease (Stern et al., 1994). Cultural and educational comparisons in age-dependent cognitive changes deserve further attention from neuropsychologists.

It seems reasonable to conclude that, if appropriate instruments and fair norms are not always available, the use of functional measures represents a fairer procedure to test nondemented and demented older Hispanics in the United States, or any other minority living in an alien cultural and linguistic environment. Psychometric measures with elderly and alien groups have to be used with extreme caution. Whether one is dealing with Hispanics or any other minority or ethnic group, ecological validity is of major importance (Perez-Arce & Puente, 1996).

Spanish Geriatric Neuropsychological Tests

Several neuropsychological tests have been developed or adapted to Spanish in the last decades and have been normalized in Hispanic populations older than age 65 (e.g., Ardila, M. Rosselli, & Puente, 1994; Loewenstein, Rubert, Arguelles, & Duara, 1995; Ostrosky et al., 1999; Ostrosky et al., 1994; Pontón et al., 1996; Taussig, Henderson, & Mack, 1992).

The neuropsychological evaluation of Hispanic elderly may differ from the evaluation of other cultural groups in the use of the Spanish language and of neuropsychological tests developed and/or normalized in a Spanish population. Table 16.1 lists some neuropsychological tests that are available in Spanish. The corresponding source is indicated.

The Mini-Mental Status exam by Folstein et al. (1975) is frequently used in the assessment of Spanish-speakers. Several Spanish versions are available. Ostrosky, Ardila, and M. Rosselli (1997) developed a Spanish extended mini-mental evaluation named

TABLE 16.1
Some Geriatric Neuropsychological Tests with Norms for Spanish-Speakers

Test	Age Range	Source
General Cognitive Performance		
Neuropsi	20–100	Ostrosky et al. (1997)
MMSE	55–85	Ardila et al. (1994)
		H. R. Bird et al. (1987)
		Escobar et al. (1986)
		Gurland et al. (1992)
		Mungas et al. (1996)
		Ostrosky et al. (in press)
		Taussig et al. (1992)
EIWA	18–64	Wechsler (1968)
NeSBHIS	16–75	Pontón et al. (1996)
Raven	16–75	Pontón et al. (1996)
MDRS	60–75	Taussig et al. (1992)
Attention		
Cancellation Test	55–85	Ardila et al. (1994)
Digit Span	55–85	Ardila et al. (1994)
		Olazaran et al. (1996)
		Pontón et al. (1996)
		Loewenstein et al. (1995)
Memory		
Fuld Object Memory	70–85	Loewenstein et al. (1995)
	60–75	Taussig et al. (1992)
WHO–UCLA–AVLT	16–75	Pontón et al. (1996)
WMS	55–85	Ardila et al. (1994)
	70–85	Loewenstein et al. (1995)
	20–100	Ostrosky et al. (in press)
Serial Verbal Learn	55–85	Ardila et al. (1994)
	20–100	Ostrosky et al. (in press)
ROCF: Memory	20–85	Ardila & Rosselli (in press)
	16–75	Pontón et al. (1996)
	20–100	Ostrosky et al. (1999)
Language		
Boston Naming	55–85	Ardila et al. (1994)
	70–85	Loewenstein et al. (1995)
	16–75	Pontón et al. (1996)
Verbal Fluency	55–85	Ardila et al. (1994)
	70–85	Loewenstein et al. (1995)
	16–75	Pontón et al. (1996)
Token Test	55–85	Ardila et al. (1994)
Visuospatial and Constructional		
ROCF: Copy	20–80	Ardila & Rosselli (in press)
	55–85	Ardila et al. (1994)
	16–75	Pontón et al. (1996)
	20–100	Ostrosky et al. (in press)
Block Design	60–75	Taussig et al. (1992)
	16–75	Pontón et al. (1996)
Functional Scales		
DAFS	65–85	Loewenstein et al. (1992)

Neuropsi. The normalization of this tests among normal Mexican elderly subjects between ages 16 and 85 and AD is presented elsewhere (Ostrosky et al., 1999).

Several studies have approached the question of assessing intellectual functioning in bilingual Spanish–English populations in the United States. It has been emphasized that cultural and language bias against Spanish-speaking demented as well as nondemented patients may impact on performance on neuropsychological and functional variables (Loewenstein et al., 1992, 1993, 1995; Lopez & Taussig, 1991; Olmedo, 1981). Difficulties with the use of standard intellectual function assessment instruments developed for American English-speakers have been pointed out in a previous section. Lopez and Romero (1988) and Melendez (1994) raised serious concerns about the use of the WAIS Spanish version (EIWA) when testing Spanish populations. Lopez and Taussig (1991) emphasized the necessity to use functional measures (activities of daily living) in addition to the standard psychometric measures. According to Lopez and Taussig, the WAIS–R or the EIWA should be used depending on the specific conditions of the testee: age, level of education, proficiency in English, general cognitive functioning, and so on. Pontón et al. (1996) used the Raven Progressive Matrices as a test of reasoning or nonverbal intelligence.

Ardila, Rosselli, and Puente (1994) adapted most of the common neuropsychological tests to Spanish and administered them to a large Colombian population. Pontón et al. (1996) provided norms stratified by age, education, and gender for memory, visuospatial, concentration, psychomotor, and reasoning. Taussig et al. (1992) administered, to a sample of normal Spanish-speaking elderly and to AD patients, an extensive neuropsychological battery, plus a behavior checklist and depression inventory. Although the sample was small, the authors reported means and standard deviations.

It is important to include in the neuropsychological evaluation of the elderly a scale of functional assessment. Neurological conditions (i.e., dementia) may influence daily living skills and the degree of impairment may correlate with the severity of the neurological condition. Functional assessment includes activities of daily living (ADLs) and instrumental activities of daily living (IADLs) (Odenheimer & Minaker, 1994). ADLs include self-care skills (i.e., toileting, bathing, etc.). IADLs require planning and experience (i.e., cooking; Lawson & Brody, 1969).

Functional assessment is obtained through direct observation or by patient's or significant other's report. The detection of ADLs is easy and may not be influenced by cultural factors. The assessment of IADLs may be influence by gender, education, and culture. For example, in older Hispanics, managing money may be considered mainly a male task and cooking and cleaning may be considered mainly female responsibilities. Loewenstein et al. (1992, 1995) recommended the use of functional measures (activities of daily living) in addition to the psychometric measures. They proposed a functional battery, the Direct Assessment of Functional Status (DAFS), be used with demented and nondemented patients with different cultural and linguistic backgrounds (Loewenstein et al. 1989, 1992). Loewenstein et al. (1995) determined the extent to which various neuropsychological tests were predictive of performance on functional measures administered within the clinical setting (Loewenstein et al., 1989). Among English-speaking AD patients, Block Design and Digit Span, as well as tests of language, were among the stronger predictors of functional performance. For Spanish-speakers, Block Design, Digit Span, and the Mini-Mental Status had the highest predictive power.

In summary, there have been efforts to develop norms for elderly Spanish-speakers and better neuropsychological instruments that are more appropriate for Spanish-speaking populations. Currently, there are some norms available for Hispanic populations living in the United States and in Latin America. More research is required, however, to increase the ecological validity of the neuropsychological evaluation.

CONCLUSIONS

The population of Hispanics is increasing and the need for culturally appropriate instruments to measure cognition in this population is increasing as well. Some studies have demonstrated the significant influence of cultural factors on neuropsychological test performance. Variables that should be studied as possible factors affecting test performance are acculturation, learning opportunities, relevance of different cognitive abilities, and nonspecific factors of the testing situation. Another very important variable is the subject knowledge of more than one language. Some studies have shown that bilingual subjects may perform below monolingual subjects in some cognitive tests (Grosjean, 1989). Test performance in elderly bilingual subjects may be the aim of study of many cross-cultural neuropsychology studies. Possible differences in the aging process of the two languages should be studied. It can be anticipated that, in the near future, cross-cultural neuropsychology will develop as an important discipline and culture may become an essential variable in the test selection process for neurological patients.

Although there is no doubt that the United States will experience an increase in the size of the elderly population, the cognitive characteristics of the elderly of tomorrow are less predictable (U.S. Census Bureau, 1996). The continued study of the genetic, biochemical, and physiologic aspects of aging is going to alter the future world of the elderly. Will it be possible to prevent a large number of people from developing Alzheimer's disease? It is likely that factors such as improved health and technology will work to reduce disability among the elderly (Longino, 1994). The neuropsychologist's role is unknown, but it may be anticipated that any professional dealing with brain organization of cognitive abilities will play an important role in the development of care programs of the elderly and needs to emphasize the importance of cultural factors on these programs.

REFERENCES

Albert, M. L., & Kaplan, E. (1980). Organic implications of neuropsychological deficits in the elderly. In L. W. Poon & J. L. Fozard (Eds.), *New directions in memory and aging* (pp. 403–432). Hillsdale, NJ: Lawrence Erlbaum Associates.

Albert, M. L., & Knoefel, J. E. (Eds.). (1994). *Clinical neurology of aging.* New York: Oxford University Press.

Albert, M. S. (1994). Age-related changes in cognitive function. In M. L. Albert & J. E. Knoefel (Eds.), *Clinical neurology of aging* (pp. 314–318). New York: Oxford University Press.

Albert, M. S., & Heaton, R. K. (1988). Intelligence testing. In M. S. Albert & M. B. Moss (Eds.), *Geriatric neuropsychology* (pp. 10–32). New York: Guilford.

Albert, M. S., Heller, H. S., & Milberg, W. (1987). Changes in naming ability with age. *Psychology of Aging, 5,* 94–107.

Ardila, A. (1995). Directions of research in cross-cultural neuropsychology. *Journal of Clinical and Experimental Neuropsychology, 17,* 143–150.

Ardila, A., & Rosselli, M. (1986). *La vejez: Neuropsicologia del fenomeno de envejecimiento* [Neuropsychology of aging]. Medellin: Prensa Creativa.

Ardila, A., & Rosselli, M. (1989). Neuropsychological characteristics of normal aging. *Developmental Neuropsychology, 5,* 307–320.

Ardila, A., & Rosselli, M. (1992). *Neuropsicologia clinica* [Clinical neuropsychology]. Medellin, Colombia: Prensa Creativa.

Ardila, A., & Rosselli, M. (1996). Spontaneous language production: Age and educational effects. *International Journal of Neuroscience, 87,* 71–78.

Ardila, A., & Rosselli, M. (in press). Educational effects on the Rey–Osterrieth Complex Figure. In J. Knight & E. Kaplan (Eds.), *Handbook of Rey-Osterrieth Complex Figure usage: Clinical and research applications.*

Ardila, A., Rosselli, M., & Ostrosky, F. (1992a). Sociocultural factors in neuropsychological assessment. In A. E. Puente & R. J. McCaffrey (Eds.), *Psychobiological factors in clinical neuropsychological assessment* (pp. 181–192). New York: Plenum.

Ardila, A., Rosselli, M., & Ostrosky, F. (1992b). Socioeducational. In A. E. Puente & R. J. McCaffrey (Eds.), *Handbook of neuropsychological assessment: A biopsychosocial perspective* (pp. 181–192). New York: Plenum.

Ardila, A., Rosselli, M., & Puente, A. (1994). *Neuropsychological evaluation of the Spanish speaker.* New York: Plenum.

Ardila, A., Rosselli, M., & Rosas, P. (1989). Neuropsychological assessment in illiterates: Visuospatial and memory abilities. *Brain and Cognition, 11,* 147–166.

Arenberg, D. (1982). Change with age in problem-solving. In F.I.M. Craik & S. Trehub (Eds.), *Aging and cognitive processes* (pp. 221–236). New York: Plenum.

Bayles, K. A., & Kaszniak, A. W. (1987). Communication and cognition in normal aging and dementia. Boston: Little, Brown.

Benton, A. L., & Hamsher, K. (1978). *Multilingual Aphasia Examination.* Iowa City: University of Iowa Press.

Bird, H. R., Canino, G., Stippec, M. R., & Shrout, P. (1987). Use of the Mini-Mental State Examination in a probabilistic sample of a Hispanic population. *Journal of Nervous and Mental diseases, 175,* 731–737.

Bird, T. D. (1994). Familial Alzheimer's disease. *Annals of Neurology, 36,* 335–336.

Bird, T. D., Lampe, T. H., Nemens, E. J., Miner, G. W., Sumi, S. M., & Schelberg, G. D. (1988). Familial Alzheimer's disease in American descendants of the Volga Germans: Probable genetic founder effect. *Annals of Neurology, 23,* 25–31.

Brody, N. (1992). *Intelligence.* New York: Academic Press.

Boone, K. B., Lasser, I. M., Hill-Gutierrez, E., & Berman, N. G. (1993). Rey–Osterrieth complex figure performance in healthy, older adults: Relationship to age, education, sex, and IQ. *The Clinical Neuropsychologist, 7,* 22–28.

Bornstein, R. A., & Suga, L. J. (1988). Educational level and neuropsychological test performance in healthy elderly subjects. *Developmental Neuropsychology, 4,* 17–22.

Campbell, P. R. (1994). *Current populations reports: Population projections for states by age, sex, race, and Hispanic origin: 1993–2020.* Washington DC: U.S. Department of Commerce.

Cattell, R. B. (1963). Theory of fluid and crystalized intelligence: A critical experiment. *Journal of Educational Psychology, 54,* 1–22.

Cerella, J., Poon, L. W., & Fozard, J. L. (1982). Age and iconic read-out. *Journal of Gerontology, 37,* 197–202.

Craik, F.I.M., Byrd, M., & Swanson, J. M. (1987). Patterns of memory loss in three elderly samples. *Psychology & Aging, 2,* 79–86.

Crook, T., Bartus, R. T., Ferris, S. H., Whitehouse, P., Cohen, G. D., & Gershon, S. (1986). Age associated memory impairment: Proposed diagnostic criteria and measures of clinical change report of a National Institute of Mental Health Work Group. *Developmental Neuropsychology, 2,* 261–276.

Cummings, J. L., & Benson, D. F. (1992). *Dementia: A clinical approach* (2nd ed.). London: Butterworths.

Deregowski, J. B. (1989). Real space and represented space: Cross-cultural perspectives. *Behavioral and Brain Sciences, 12,* 51–119.

Donoso, A. (1987). *Manifestaciones clínicas y manejo de las demencias* [*Clinical manifestations and treatment of dementias*]. Santiago: Hospital Clinico de la Universidad de Chile.

Ellis, N. C., & Hennelly, R. A. (1980). A bilingual word-length effect: Implications for intelligence testing and the relative ease for mental calculations in Welsh and English. *British Journal of Psychology, 71,* 43–51.

Escobar, J. I., Burman, R., Karno, M., Forsythe, A., Landsverk, J., & Golding, J. M. (1986). Use of the Mini-Mental State Examination (MMSE) in a community population of mixed ethnicity: Cultural and linguistic artifacts. *Journal of Nervous and Mental Diseases, 174,* 607–614.

Eslinger P. J., Pepin, L., & Benton, A. L. (1988). Different patterns of visual memory errors occur with aging and dementia. *Journal of Clinical and Experimental Neuropsychology, 10,* 60–61.

Finley, G., Ardila, A., & Rosselli, M. (1991). Cognitive aging in illiterate Colombian adults: A reversal of the classical aging pattern? *InterAmerican Journal of Psychology, 25,* 103–105.

Folstein, M. F., Folstein, S. E., & McHugh, P. R. (1975). Mini-Mental State. *Journal of Psychiatric Research, 12,* 189–198.

Fuster, J. (1993). Memory cells in primate cortex and the activation of memory networks. In O. Taketoshi, L. Squire, M. E. Raichle, D. I. Perrett, & M. Fukuda (Eds.), *Brain mechanisms of perception and memory: From neuron to behavior* (pp. 426–444). New York: Oxford University Press.

Goodglass, H., & Kaplan, E. (1972). *The assessment of aphasia and related disorders.* Philadelphia: Lea & Febiger.

Grosjean, F. (1989). Neurolinguistics beware! The bilingual is not two monolinguals in one person. *Brain and Language, 36,* 3–15.

Gulard, B. L., Wilder, D. E., Cross, P., Teresi, J., & Barret, V. W. (1992). Screening scales for dementia: Toward a reconciliation of conflicting cross-cultural findings. *International Journal of Geriatric Psychiatry, 7,* 105–113.

Gussela, J. F., Wexler, N. S., & Coneally, P. M. (1983). A polymorphic DNA marker genetically linked to Huntington's disease. *Nature, 306,* 234–238.

Heaton, R. K., Grant, I., & Matthews, C. (1986). Differences in neuropsychological test performance associated with age, education and sex. In I. Grant & K. M. Adams (Eds.), *Neuropsychological assessment in neuropsychiatric disorders* (pp. 108–120). New York: Oxford University Press.

Hertzog, C. (1989). Influences of cognitive slowing on age differences in intelligence. *Developmental Psychology, 25,* 636–651.

Horn, J. L. (1985). Remodeling old models of intelligence. In B. B. Wolman (Ed.), *Handbook of intelligence: Theories, measurements and applications* (pp. 847–870). New York: Wiley.

Horn, J. L., & Cattell, R. B. (1966). Refinement and test of the theory of fluid and crystalized intelligence. *Journal of Educational Psychology, 57,* 253–270.

Irvine, S. H., & Berry, J. W. (Eds.). (1988). *Human abilities in cultural context.* Cambridge, England: Cambridge University Press.

Jacobs, D. M., Sano, M., Albert, S., Schofield, P., Dooneief, G., & Stern, Y. (1997). Cross-cultural neuropsychological assessment: A comparison of randomly selected, demographically matched cohorts of English- and Spanish-speaking older adults. *Journal of Clinical and Experimental Neuropsychology, 19*(3), 331–339.

Kaplan, E., Goodglass, H., & Weintraub, S. (1983). *The Boston Naming Test.* Philadelphia: Lea & Febiger.

Kemper, S. (1987). Syntactic complexity and elderly adults prose recall. *Experimental Aging Research, 13,* 47–52.

Kennedy, A. M., Newman, S. K., Frackowiak, V. J., Cunningham, V. J., Roques, P., Stevens, J., Neary, D., Bruton, C. J., Warrington, E., & Rossor, M. N. (1995). Chromosome 14 linked familial Alzheimer's disease. A clinico-pathological study of a single pedigree. *Brain, 118,* 185–206.

Kynette, D., & Kemper, S. (1986). Aging and the loss of grammatical forms: A cross-sectional study of language performance. *Language and Communication, 6,* 65–72.

LaBarge, E., Edwards, D., & Knesevich, J. W. (1986). Performance in normal elderly on the Boston Naming Test. *Brain and Language, 27,* 380–384.

Lantz, D. (1979). A cross-cultural comparison of communication abilities: Some effects of age, schooling, and culture. *International Journal of Psychology, 14,* 171–183.

La Rue, A. (1992). Adult development. In A. E. Puente & R. J. McCaffrey (Eds.), *Handbook of neuropsychological assessment: A biopsychosocial perspective* (pp. 81–119). New York: Plenum.

La Rue, A., & Markee, T. (1995). Clinical assessment research with older adults. Special issue: Methodological issues in psychological assessment research. *Psychological Assessment, 7,* 376–386.

Lawson, M. P., & Brody, E. M. (1969). Assessment of older people: Self-maintaining and instrumental activities of daily living. *Gerontologist, 9,* 179–186.

Loewenstein, D. A., Amigo, E., Duara, R., & Guterman, A. (1989). A new scale for the assessment of functional status in Alzheimer's disease and related disorders. *Journal of Gerontology, 4,* 114–121.

Loewenstein, D. A., Ardila, A., Rosselli, M., Hayden, S., Duara, R., Berkowitz, N., Linn-Fuentes, P., Mintzer, J., Norville, M., & Eisdorfer, C. (1992). A comparative analysis of functional status among Spanish and English-speaking patients with dementia. *Journal of Gerontology, 47,* 389–394.

Loewenstein, D. A., Arguelles, T., Barker, W. W., & Duara, R. (1993). A comparative analysis of neuropsychological test performance of Spanish-speaking and English-speaking patients with Alzheimer's disease. *Journal of Gerontology: Psychological Sciences, 48,* 142–149.

Loewenstein, D. A., Rubert, M. P., Arguelles, T., & Duara, R. (1995). Neuropsychological test performance and prediction of functional capacities among Spanish-speaking and English speaking patients with dementia. *Archives of Clinical Neuropsychology, 10,* 75–88.

Longino, C. F. (1994). Myths of an aging America. *American Demographics,* August, 36–42.

Lopera, F., Arcos, M., Madrigal, L., Kosik, K., Cornerjo, W., & Ossa, J. (1994). Demencia de tipo Alzheimer con agregacion familiar en Antioquia, Colombia [Dementia of the Alzheimer's type with familial aggregation in Antioquia, Colombia]. *Acta Neurologica Colombiana, 10,* 173–187.

Lopera, F., Ardila, A., Martinez, Al., Madrigal, L., Arango-Viana, J. C., Lemere, C., Arango-Lasprilla, J. C.,

Hincapie, L., Arcos, M., Ossa, J. E., Behrens, I. M., Norton, J., Lendon, C., Goates, A., Ruiz-Linares, A., Rosselli, M., & Kosik, K. S. (1997). Clinical features of early-onset Alzheimers disease in a large kindred within E280A presenilin 1, Colombia. *Journal of the American Medical Association, 277,* 793–799.

Lopez-Aquires, J. N., Kemp, B., Plopper, M., Staples, F. R., & Brummel-Smith, K. (1984). Health needs of the Hispanic elderly. *Journal of the American Geriatrics Society, 32,* 191–197.

Lopez, S., & Romero, A. (1988). Assessing the intellectual functioning of Spanish speaking adults: Comparisons of the EIWA and the WAIS. *Professional Psychology: Research and Practice, 19,* 263–270.

Lopez, S., & Taussig, I. M. (1991). Cognitive-intellectual functioning of Spanish-speaking impaired and non-impaired elderly: Implications for culturally sensitive assessment. *Psychological Assessment, 3,* 448–454.

Magaziner, J., Bassett, S. S., & Hebel, R. (1987) Predicting performance on the minimental state examination. *Journal of the American Geriatrics Society, 35,* 996–1000.

Mandell, A. M., Knoefel, J. E., & Albert, M. L. (1994). Mental Status Examination in the elderly. In M. L. Albert & J. E. Knoefel (Eds.), *Clinical neurology of aging* (pp. 277–313). New York: Oxford University Press.

Matarazzo, J. D. (1979). *Wechsler's measurement and appraisal of adult intelligence.* New York: Oxford University Press.

McCaffrey, R. J., & Puente, A. (1992). Overview, limitations and directions. In A. E. Puente & R. J. McCaffrey (Eds.), *Handbook of neuropsychological assessment: A biopsychosocial perspective* (pp. 511–520). New York: Plenum.

Melendez, F. (1994). The Spanish version of the WAIS: Some ethical considerations. *The Clinical Neuropsychologist, 8,* 388–393.

Mendilaharsu, C., & Mendilaharsu, S. A. (1978–1982). *Estudios neuropsicologicos* [*Neuropsychological studies*]. Montevideo: Editorial Delta.

Miller, E. (1977). *Abnormal aging: The psychology of senile dementia.* New York: Wiley.

Morris, J. C., Heyman, A., Mohs, R. C., Hughes, J. P,, van Belle, G., Fillenbaum, G., Mellits, E. D., & Clark, C. (1989). The consortium to establish a registry for Alzheimer's disease (CERAD). Part I. Clinical and neuropsychological assessment of Alzheimer's disease. *Neurology, 39,* 1159–1165.

Mungas, D., Marshall, S. C., Weldon, M., Haan, M., & Reed, B. R. (1996). Age and education correction of Mini-Mental State Examination for English and Spanish-speaking elderly. *Neurology, 46,* 700–706.

Naveh-Benjamin, M., & Ayres, T. J. (1986). Digit span, reading rate and linguistic relativity. *Quarterly Journal of Experimental Psychology, 38,* 739–751.

Obler, L. K. (1980). Narrative discourse style in the elderly. In L. K. Obler & M. L. Albert (Eds.), *Language and communication in the elderly* (pp. 75–90). Lexington, MA: Heath.

Odenheimer, G. L., & Minaker K. L. (1994). Functional assessment in geriatric Neurology. In M. L. Albert & J. E. Knoefel (Eds.), *Clinical neurology of aging* (pp. 181–189). New York: Oxford University Press.

Olazaran J., Jacobs, D., & Stern, Y. (1996). Comparative study of visual and verbal short term memory in English and Spanish speakers: Testing a linguistic hypothesis. *Journal of the International Neuropsychological Society, 2,* 105–110.

Olmedo, E. L. (1981). Testing linguistic minorities. *American Psychologist, 36,* 1078–1085.

Ostrosky, F., Ardila, A., & Jaime, R. M. (1998). Memory abilities in normal aging. *International Journal of Neuroscience, 91,* 151–162.

Ostrosky, F., Ardila, A., & Rosselli M. (1997). *Neuropsi: Un examen neuropsicologico breve en Español* [Neuropsi: A brief neuropsychological exam in Spanish]. Mexico: Bayer.

Ostrosky, F., Ardila, A. & Rosselli, M. (1999). Neuropsi: A brief neuropsychological test battery in Spanish with norms by age and educational level. *Journal of the International Neuropsychological Society, 5,* 413–433.

Ostrosky, F., Canseco, E., Quintanar, L., Navarro, E., Meneses, S., & Ardila, A. (1985). Sociocultural effects in neuropsychological assessment. *International Journal of Neuroscience, 27,* 53–66.

Ostrosky, F., & Madrazo I. (in press). *Diagnostico neuropsicologico de las enfermedades neurodegenerativas* [Neuropsychological diagnosis of neurodegenerative disorders]. Gaceta Medica Mexicana.

Ostrosky, F., Rodriguez, Y., Garcia de la Cadena C., Jaime, R., Valdes, A., Guevara, M. A., Chayo, R. & Llamosas, C. (1994). Marcadores mnesicos del envejecimiento normal y patologico [Memory markers of normal and abnormal aging]. *Revista Latina de Pensamiento y Lenguaje, 1,* 367–375.

Ostrosky-Solis, F., Madrazo, I., & Ardila, A. (1991). Autotransplante cerebral para el tratamiento de la enfermedad de Parkinson: Efectos neuropsicologicos [Brain autograft in Parkinson's disease: Neuropsychological effects]. *Revista Mexicana de Psicologia, 8,* 7–16.

Ostrosky-Solis, F., Quintanar, L., Madrazo, I., Drucker-Colin, R., Franco-Bourland, R., & Leon-Mesa, V. (1988). Neuropsychological effects of brain autograft of adrenal medullary tissue for the treatment of Parkinson's disease. *Neurology, 38,* 1442–1450.

Perez-Arce, P., & Puente, A. E. (1996). Neuropsychological assessment of ethnic minorities: The case of assessing Hispanics living in North America. In R. J. Sbordone & C. J. Long (Eds.), *Ecological validity of neuropsychological testing* (pp. 238–300). Delray Beach, FL: GR Press/St. Lucie Press.

Pineda, D., Galeano, L. M., Jasbon, H., Hoyos, L. M., & Rodriguez, J. C. (1988). Trastornos neuropsicologicos en las primeras etapas de la enfermedad de Parkinson [Neuropsychological deficits of the initial stages of Parkinson's disease]. *Acta Medica Colombiana, 13,* 21–88.

Pineda, D., Giraldo, O., & Castillo, H. (1995). Disfuncion ejecutiva en pacientes con enfermedad de Parkinson [Executive dysfunction in Parkinson's patients]. *Acta Neurological Colombiana, 11,* 17–20.

Plude, D. J., Milberg, W. P., & Cerella, J. (1986). Age differences in depicting and perceiving tridimensionality in simple line drawings. *Experimental Aging Research, 12,* 221–225.

Pontius, A. A. (1989). Color and spatial error in block design in stone age Auca: Ecological underuse of occipital-parietal system in men and of frontal lobe in women. *Brain and Cognition, 10,* 54–75.

Pontón, M., Satz, P., Herrera, L., Ortiz, F., Urrutia, C. P., Young R., D'Elia, L. F., Furst, C. J., & Namerow N. (1996). Normative data stratified by age and education for the Neuropsychological Screening Battery for Hispanics (NeSBHIS): Initial report. *Journal of the International Neuropsychological Society, 2,* 96–104.

Poon, L. W. (1985). Differences in human memory with aging. In J. E. Birren & K. W. Schaie (Eds.), *Handbook of psychology of aging* (pp. 427–462). New York: Van Nostrand Reinhold.

Rey, G. (1990). Multilingual Aphasia Examination—Spanish development and normative data. *Dissertation Abstracts International, 50,* 5892.

Rosselli, A., Rosselli, M., Ardila, A., & Penagos, B. (1988). Severe dementia associated with neurocysticercosis. International Journal of Neuroscience, 41, 87–95.

Rosselli, D., Rosselli, M., Penagos, B., & Ardila, A. (1986). Huntington's disease in Colombia: A neuropsychological analysis. *International Journal of Neuroscience, 32,* 933–942.

Rosselli, M., & Ardila, A. (1991). Rey–Osterrieth Complex Figure: Effect of age and educational level. *The Clinical Neuropsychologist, 5,* 370–376.

Rosselli, M., Ardila, A., Florez, A., & Castro, C. (1990). Normative data on the Boston Diagnostic Aphasia Examination. *Journal of Clinical and Experimental Neuropsychology, 12,* 313–322.

Rosselli, M., Ardila, A., & Rosas, P. (1990). Neuropsychological assessment in illiterates; II. Language and praxic abilities. *Brain and Cognition, 12,* 281–296.

Rosselli, M., Lorenzana, P., Rosselli, A., & Vergara, I. (1987). Wilson's disease: A reversible dementia. *Journal of Clinical and Experimental Neuropsychology, 9,* 399–406.

Salthouse, T. A. (1985). Speed of behavior and its implications for cognition. In J. E. Birren & K. W. Schaie (Eds.), *Handbook of psychology on aging* (2nd ed., pp. 400–426). New York: Van Nostrand Reinhold.

Schaie, K. W. (1983). The Seattle longitudinal study: A 21-year exploration of psychometric intelligence in adulthood. In K. W. Schaie (Ed.), *Longitudinal studies of adult psychological development* (pp. 64–135). New York: Guilford.

Smith, A. (1980). Age differences in encoding, storage and retrieval. In L. W. Poon, J. L. Fozard, L. S. Cermak, D. Aremberg, & L. W. Thompson (Eds.), *New directions in memory and aging* (pp. 23–46). Hillsdale, NJ: Lawrence Erlbaum Associates.

Spreen, O., & Strauss, E. (1997). *A compendium of neuropsychological tests.* New York: Oxford University Press.

Statistical Abstract of the United States. (1990). (110th ed.). Washington, DC: U.S. Census Bureau.

Stern, Y., Gurlamd, B., Tatemieki, T. K., Ming, X. T., Wilder, D., & Mayeux, R. (1994). Influence of education and occupation on the incidence of Alzheimer's disease. *Journal of the American Medical Association, 271,* 1004–1010.

Taussig, I. M., Henderson, V. W., & Mack, W. (1992). Spanish translation and validation of a neuropsychological battery: Performance of Spanish- and English-speaking Alzheimer's disease patients and normal comparison subjects. *Clinical Gerontologist, 11,* 95–108.

Tupler, L. A., Welsh, K. A., Yaw, A. A., & Dawson, D. V. (1995). Reliability of Rey–Osterrieth Complex figure in use with memory-impaired patients. *Journal of Clinical and Experimental Neuropsychology, 17,* 566–579.

U.S. Bureau of the Census. (1996). *Current Population Reports, Special Studies, 65+ in the United States* (pp. 23–190). Washington, DC: U.S. Government Printing Office.

Van Gorp, W. C., Satz, P., Kiersch, M. E., & Henry, R. (1986). Normative data on the Boston Naming Test for a group of older adults. *Journal of Clinical and Experimental Neuropsychology, 8,* 702–705.

Wechsler, D. (1968). *Escala de Inteligencia Wechsler para Adultos* [Wechsler Adult Intelligence Scale]. New York: Plenum.

Wechsler, D. (1981). *Wechsler Adult Intelligence Scale–Revised.* New York: Psychological Corporation.

Wechsler, D. (1991). *Wechsler Adult Intelligence Scale–III*. New York: Psychological Corporation.

Willis, L., Geo, R. A., Thomas, P., & Garry, P. J. (1988). Differential decline in cognitive function: The possible role of health status. *Developmental Neuropsychology, 4,* 23–28.

Wilson, B. A., Cockburn, J., & Baddeley, A. D. (1985). *The Rivemead Behavioral Memory Test*. London: Titchifield Thames Valley Test Co.

Dementias: Participation of Hispanic Patients in Research Programs

I. Maribel Taussig
University of Southern California

Although ethnic and racially diverse populations, especially those over age 65, are grow-ing at a very rapid rate in the United States, the awareness and level of basic knowledge regarding dementing illnesses among those ethnic groups is limited. Considering the stress and hardship cognitive dysfunction can cause to a family unit in terms of long-term care services, the need to know with certainty the prevalence and incidence of Alzhei-mer's disease (AD) and other dementing illnesses among ethnic minority groups is of paramount importance. What is the incidence and prevalence of Alzheimer's and other dementias in the Hispanic population residing in the United States? If this is not known, why? These and other pertinent questions are addressed in this chapter. At the same time, suggestions are offered based on experience and empirical research at the Spanish-Speaking Alzheimer's Disease Research Program (SSADRP) as it relates to older Hispan-ics and Alzheimer's disease.

In the past 10 years, the number of Hispanics age 65 and older has almost doubled, surpassing one million, a growth rate superior to non-Hispanics of similar age. The diver-sity of this group as it relates to heritage suggests that Mexican Americans make up the largest group of Hispanics, reaching almost 50% of its total number, followed by Cubans and Puerto Ricans (15% and 12%, respectively; U. S. Census Bureau, 1998). The remain-ing percentage is composed of Central and South American countries and Spain.

The growth trend appears to emphasize those age 80 and older, and in the next 30 years this older-old will increase drastically, in part due to a decrease in mortality rate and in part due to an increase in immigration (Taussig & Pontón, 1996). Uneasiness regard-ing older Hispanics and the validity of Census tracking linger in many researchers' minds. For example, the SSADRP at the University of Southern California found that more than 27% of the impaired population participating in the study had no health insurance of any kind, suggesting a population that had just recently arrived, or immigrated illegally with-out much of a security net, or were simply underutilizing community services. Were those with no medical coverage overlooked by the Census? If so, how can they access medical services such as in-depth medical, neurological, brain imaging, and neuropsychological evaluation associated with a differential diagnosis of dementia? Moreover, how can clini-cians know about their illness process?

As the issue of older Hispanics and Alzheimer's disease unfolds, heed a word of caution regarding the term *Hispanic*. *Hispanic* denotes an individual belonging to a group with specific attributes and similarities. In reality, Hispanics are a heterogeneous population in terms of culture and race, with complex and distinct attributes from each of the 21 Spanish-speaking countries that make up the Hispanic population in the United States (Taussig & Pontón, 1996). However, within the uniqueness of each country of origin, older Hispanics residing in the United States have a common bond, *language,* especially those age 65 and older. It is estimated that from 50% to 70% of older Hispanics residing in the United States do not speak English (Kemp, Staples, & Lopez-Aqueres, 1987), and up to 90% prefer to speak Spanish at home (U.S. Census Bureau, 1998).

Whereas the number of older Hispanics residing in the United States who suffer from Alzheimer's disease is an issue of great debate among researchers and demographers, there is a high degree of agreement about this population being at risk for dementia (Duara et al., 1996; Farrer et al., 1997; Perkins et al., 1997). For instance, this population has worked more years than other groups, they have lived a life of poverty, have received poor medical care, and may not be recipients of retirement and other financial benefits. Are they also at risk to develop a progressive or at least static dementia? After all, many Hispanic elderly have been exposed to toxic substances such as pesticides and heavy metals, or have suffered industrial accidents unreported and untreated.

Considering the financial hardship, inability to speak English, and the minimum or lack of medical insurance coverage, it is possible to misdiagnose an older Hispanic patient as suffering from a dementia. Alternatively, it is also possible to have a dementia go undetected until the person is profoundly impaired. At the same time, the family's lack of knowledge about a dementing process may keep them from reporting abnormalities in their loved ones, especially if the patient exhibits inappropriate behaviors such as a tendency to steel, hypersexuality, aggressive behaviors, or paranoid ideation.

Any clinician will find it useful to appropriate a basic, yet useful, mnemonic when working with the geriatric Hispanic patient in an effort to rule out dementia. The letters in the word *DEMENTIA* can be used to explain certain problems found in the Hispanic cultures that could be misinterpreted, at the moment of differential diagnosis:

> D = DRUGS (medication)
> E = EMOTIONS
> M = METABOLIC DISORDERS
> E = EYES AND EARS — DECREASED SENSORY STIMULI
> N = NUTRITIONAL DEFICIENCIES
> T = TRAUMAS (head and others)
> I = INFECTIONS
> A = ALCOHOLISM, ACCIDENTS

The issue of *drug* (D) abuse or misuse is often associated with self-medication due to the use of *curanderos* and/or heavy dependence on herbal therapy; a tendency to go across the border or to the country of origin to purchase familiar medications without prescription, the use of medication prescribed to other family members or to a "comadre," and the lack of proper or accessible medical care. These and other reasons may be the cause of misuse of drugs with older Hispanics residing in the United States.

Emotions (E), such as depression, when untreated may contribute to the misdiagnosis of an older Hispanic, especially when the patient is unable to express needs and feelings in English, causing the patient to somatize those emotions.

Metabolic disorders (M) such as hypothyroidism, when undetected and untreated can be a major cause of cognitive dysfunction in this vulnerable population with no or undesirable medical coverage.

Eyes and ears (E) of older adults who cannot afford annual check-ups may suffer from visual and hearing problems. This can be translated as a decline in environmental stimuli. When a person cannot speak English, cannot hear well, or cannot see properly, a neuro-psychological evaluation is a true challenge for the patient and the professional responsible for a proper differential diagnosis. Factors influencing this problems can be lack of money, lack of interest by the patient, and family negligence.

Nutritional deficiencies (N) in an older Hispanic may result because the individual is lonely and may not be eating properly. Meals on wheels, a service for the elderly homebound, attempts to meet the taste needs of the main culture—the Anglo-Saxon. Hispanic elderly often complain that such meals lack the taste and consistency they desire. Pride and inability to qualify to social programs can be some of the reasons for malnutrition.

Unreported head traumas (T)—such as falls, work-related accidents, and physical abuse—can be overlooked in older Hispanics, especially if a thorough history is overlooked. Postconcussional syndromes have their own cognitive sequelae that can lead to a misdiagnosis of dementia, or may actually precipitate a dementia in a patient.

Infections (I), such as urinary track infections, often left undetected and untreated in older adults, can cause cognitive dysfunction. For those unable to speak English or those uncomfortable talking about "private parts," these are medical problems that may not be reported and need to be addressed when dealing with older Hispanics, especially women.

Alcoholism (A), a silent problem in many cultures, deserves investigation. Love and respect for an older adult may hinder a proper diagnosis. It is imperative that when assessing an older Hispanic suspected of dementia, while being respectful and tactful, the issue of use and abuse of alcohol should be discussed with the family.

Inappropriate diagnosis and treatment, as well as ignorance regarding abnormal aging, can be sources of stress to patients and families alike and can stop families from participating in research programs or use available resources in their community. Hispanic primary caregivers responsible for older adults suffering from a progressive dementia, such as Alzheimer's disease, may be at a similar disadvantage and hardship as other groups. However, lack of financial resources in this population may hinder caregivers from paying for a proper evaluation and from obtaining the assistance required to care for a loved one with dementia. As a reflection of reality, almost 70% of the 136 subjects who participated in the SSADRP and who were diagnosed with possible Alzheimer's disease, entered the program without a diagnosis. When asked for the reasons their primary physicians gave them to seek cognitive assessment, most families were told the reason for the dementia was "old age."

Because they tend to be diagnosed rather late in their disease process, Hispanic elderly patients with Alzheimer's disease may be at higher risk than other groups. They may need 24-hour assistance in care and vigilance for their well-being. Patients are at risk when they lack medical coverage to obtain a proper differential diagnosis and treatment, but also when their primary caregiver lacks the basic knowledge regarding Alzheimer's disease and other dementias. Risk of abuse and neglect, risk of abandonment by the family, and risk of social negligence are some of the issues faced by this patient population. If it is assumed that Hispanics have a lower incidence of dementia, it is because proper efforts to reach and study this population have not been made. Not studying this population puts it at risk.

If the Hispanic population residing in the United States was better informed about aging and Alzheimer's disease, would they participate more readily in research? Professional experience reveals that a well-informed primary caregiver will have higher responsibility toward issues of research, including autopsy and more willingness to participate in general.

This issue was approached empirically. To ascertain whether Hispanic families had basic knowledge regarding Alzheimer's disease at the level of the general population, a sample of 100 Hispanic primary caregivers of demented patients was surveyed and compared to the responses obtained by Cutler survey in 1986. Cutler's survey contained 17 basic questions, with topics ranging from whether Alzheimer's disease is contagious to whether it can be diagnosed with a simple blood test. The comparison between the English-speaking sample from Cutler (1987), and the Spanish-speaking groups suggests basic differences in important areas.

In Cutler's survey, several questions were answered correctly at least 75% of the time by non-Spanish speakers. The same questions were answered correctly only 40% or less by Hispanic primary caregivers. The following is a sample of the questions where major differences were found between the two groups:

1. Older adults will develop Alzheimer's disease if they live long enough.

2. Alzheimer's disease is a form of insanity.

3. Among older adults, forgetfulness indicates the beginning of Alzheimer's.

In general, not only did Hispanic primary caregivers answer correctly less frequently than the English-speakers, but they also answered with "I don't know" more often than their English-speaking counterparts (Taussig, Harris, & Yi-Chiang, 1995).

The responses given to this survey of 100 primary caregivers suggests that, in general, Spanish-speaking caregivers of demented older adults living in the United States have a drastic knowledge gap regarding Alzheimer's disease. Looking at variables such as education and age, it was found that those with fewer years of formal education had a reduced number of correct responses, and those interviewed in English had a greater number of correct responses; gender did not yield any significant differences. The findings of this study speak loud and clear: Caregivers are in need of basic education regarding Alzheimer's disease. At present, no cure is available, so knowledge regarding this disease, including how a diagnosis is made and the importance of participating in clinical research and autopsy could be a form of empowerment for this population. At the same time, well-informed primary caregivers would most likely seek research programs for participation, and answer the needed question, "Do Hispanics suffer from dementia at the same rate as the rest of the population?"

The prevalence of dementia in adults age 65 and older is estimated at 10%, and as much as 50% for those age 85 and over. Many disorders may cause a dementia syndrome. Studies in pathological surveys with populations diagnosed as "dementia" suggest that 20% had a single diagnosis (i.e., multi-infarct dementia, alcoholic dementia, normal pressure hydrocephalus, head trauma, toxic-metabolic or infectious etiologies), 15% had a specific dementia in combination with Alzheimer's disease, and about 50% or more had a diagnosis of Alzheimer's disease. To differentiate a diagnosis of dementia is essential for optimum treatment, but keep in mind that a diagnosis is often difficult to determine while a person is alive (Chui, 1994).

To diagnose dementia, according to the *Diagnostic and Statistical Manual of Mental Disorders* (4th ed.; American Psychiatric Association, 1994), the development of multiple cognitive deficits sufficiently severe to interfere with occupational or social functioning is necessary. Memory impairment and at least apraxia, agnosia, or other disturbance in cognitive functioning must occur. Dementia is a syndrome and the etiology may differ; however, the most common cause is Alzheimer's disease.

Just as there are many theories attempting to explain the aging process, equally controversial is the understanding of the etiology of Alzheimer's disease. Although Alzheimer's disease, the most common type of dementia among older adults, was first characterized by a German neurologist named Alois Alzheimer at the beginning of this century, almost 100 years later, science is still uncertain about its specific etiology and cure.

Alzheimer's disease is not a normal part of aging, however the older individuals get the more probability they have to develop this disease. Alzheimer's can be found in individuals under age 65 (and as young as in the early forties), but the prevalence is approximately 10% in the 65 plus population. After age 65, the prevalence increases greatly in comparison to other dementias. For example, Alzheimer's doubles approximately every 4.5 years after age 65 and by age 85 almost 50% of this population suffers from it (Evans et al., 1989; Henderson & Paganini-Hill, 1995). At present and without truly counting ethnic minorities, it is estimated that from 4 to 5 million individuals are suffering from Alzheimer's disease. By 2020, the number of older adults suffering from Alzheimer's will be so large that society will be faced with a major health crisis.

Dementia of the Alzheimer's type is associated with neurofibrillary tangles in neurons of the central nervous system, neuritic plaques, as well as Beta-amyloid protein deposits (Henderson & Finch, 1989). Some of the established risk factors are age, head trauma, and family history, and at present for those not yet showing the symptoms, no test is available to predict who will develop the disease. Alzheimer's disease does not appear to discriminate among social economic status, race, or ethnicity, but the disease affects 1.5 to 3 times more women than men even after adjusting for age (Henderson, 1995).

Alzheimer's disease is associated with a cognitive decline severe enough to interfere with the ability to carry out normal daily activities, and in its earliest stage it is associated with the inability to learn and recall new information. Language disorders such as word-finding difficulty, disorientation, a tendency to get lost in familiar surroundings, and attention problems have been observed. Often these cognitive deficits are also accompanied by behavioral problems such as suspiciousness, irritability, delusions, and depression. Ultimately, Alzheimer's patients are unable to communicate, to recognize familiar people, or to care for themselves; they succumb to the disease within 5 to 15 years. Alzheimer's disease is the fourth cause of death after cardiovascular diseases, cancer, and strokes. The following summarizes its clinical presentation in the primary, secondary, and tertiary phases:

1. *Memory* problems, recent and remote, progress to grave defects in memory and the inability to learn new information, followed by global deterioration.

2. *Personality* characteristics include irritability, apathy, frustration, and paranoia, indifference, hostility, social inadequacy, flat affect.

3. *Communication* problems include disorganized content, anomia, deficient linguistic reasoning, agrammatism, global deterioration, perseveration, echolalia, and mutism.

4. *Problem solving* abilities and the capacity to deduce is affected, followed by the need for help in solving simple problems to a total inability to solve any problem.

5. *Visual spatial construction* is affected. Topographical disorientation, construction

difficulty to errors in visual perception, to global deterioration of visual spatial abilities is expected.

6. *Gait and movement,* usually normal with some extrapyramidal signals in the first stage, progress to agitation and rigidity in the advanced stage.

Early detection of Alzheimer's disease could spare families some of the anguish and confusion they experience if clinicians are able to diagnose the disease with more certainty in its earliest stages. The family can then brace emotionally to handle the disease.

Understanding how Alzheimer's symptomatology manifests itself in its earliest stage is a great concern and has been studied (see Taussig & Mack, 1992) using a sample of subjects enrolled at Alzheimer's Disease Research Center (ADRC) in the University of Southern California. The first symptoms of Alzheimer's disease among Hispanic elderly, observed by the primary caregivers, and later confirmed by autopsy in more than one third of the sample, revealed the following pattern: Twenty-nine percent of the population studied showed a decline in memory function; 24% showed a decline in activities of daily living; 13% had problems with orientation, 12% had personality changes, 7% had psychological problems, and a small percent included cognitive, behavioral, and language problems. As the disease progressed, they noticed more problems associated with activities of daily living, such as the ability to cook, drive, or keep a checkbook, followed by memory problems, disorientation, and personality changes. The finding of this study supported those of previous investigations describing memory loss as the first observable sign of AD; however, a decrease in activities of daily living was observed as a first symptom more often than previously believed. If memory loss is expected as a first symptom and family members or the patient report other problems, such as a decline in ability to carry out activities of daily living (e.g., such as cooking), inexperienced health professionals may overlook the first stage of the disease and the patient may be treated for another illness.

Language, cultural differences, and levels of formal education could have an impact in the expression and observation of early symptoms of Alzheimer's disease, thus Taussig and Mack (1995) compared Hispanic and non-Hispanic White subjects diagnosed with Alzheimer's disease for possible differences. The comparison revealed great similarities to the list of symptoms previously observed. However, in terms of the frequency and type expected in its earliest stage of the disease, two symptoms appeared to differ significantly between the two groups. White non-Hispanic caregivers observed memory loss 27% as the first symptom, whereas Hispanics observed the same symptom 47% of the time. Difficulty with activities of daily living was observed 21% versus 4% respectively. (See Table 17.1 for complete information).

If Alzheimer's disease is such a public enemy, and its symptoms are so devastating, why can there be no true estimate of the number of Hispanics suffering from this disease? The reasons for such an oversight are many, but one of the most important is *the lack of, or the small numbers of, participants in major research studies.* Until recently, ADRCs and other research programs were not forced to include this population into their studies. Other reasons that have an impact on the enrollment of subjects with Alzheimer's are associated with the slow dissemination of information regarding the impact of this disease on families in the Spanish language. The Alzheimer's Association and other entities are working very hard attempting to fulfill this gap. However, the efforts are relatively new, in comparison to the efforts put forth for the non-Hispanic population for more than 10 years. Other reasons hampering outreach and enrollment of Hispanic elderly in research studies include the following:

TABLE 17.1
Frequency of Dementia Symptoms by Ethnicity

	Frequency of Primary Symptoms: First Problem Noted	
Symptom Category	English Speaking %	Spanish Speaking %
Memory	27%	47%*
Activities of daily living	21%	4%*
Disorientation	13%	7%
Personality	13%	11%
Psychological	7%	16%
Cognition	6%	7%
Language	7%	4%
Behavioral	4%	4%
Neurological	1%	0%

Note: From "A Comparison of Spanish versus English-speaking Caregivers' Perception of Early Symptoms of Alzheimer's Disease," by I. M. Taussig and W. Mack, 1995, *American Journal of Alzheimer's Disease, September/October,* pp. 33–39.
    * Group differences significant (p < .05) after controlling for duration of illness.

1. Many Hispanic primary caregivers know very little about abnormal aging or dementias like Alzheimer's disease, and may not seek a doctor or a research program until the disease is very advanced. Seventy percent of the subjects enrolled at the SSADRP entered the program without a diagnosis.

2. The Hispanic Alzheimer's patient and the primary caregiver often are monolingual Spanish-speakers, and thus they are unable to communicate to the physician or other health professional about the cognitive changes associated with this disease.

3. By the time Hispanic older adults suffering from dementia of Alzheimer's type reach an ADRC, they may be too impaired to participate in the study, especially if neuropsychological testing is a requirement for enrollment.

4. Many older Hispanics residing in the United States suffering from cognitive deficits may be less integrated into the public health care system than non-Hispanic Whites. The inability to qualify for Medicare or Medicaid is often the result of their legal status, and thus the inability for the family or patient to pay for the expenses associated with a differential diagnosis. Without a source of reimbursement—in this instance, Medicare or Medicaid—many research centers cannot afford to enroll impaired subjects.

These and many other elements are contributing factors to the uncertainty of the estimation in the number of Hispanic elderly suffering from Alzheimer's disease in this country. Without this knowledge little can be done to provide the emotional, physical, and financial support this segment of the population so desperately needs.

To make matters worse, many health professionals often have minimum training in the area of dementias. The gradual and insidious onset of AD makes it difficult to detect, and often it is mistakenly identified as the process of normal aging or psychiatric illness. At the same time, they may be poorly informed with regard to Hispanics' multiculturalism, or their knowledge is often based on myths and misconceptions, overlooking important factors associated with the inception of dementia. Further, these professionals often lack the fluency necessary to communicate directly with the patient and the family. Instead, they rely on nonmedically trained individuals — so-called translators — in order to obtain a history of the dementing illness, complicating factors such as depression and other psychiatric illness, drug side effects, acute illness, family and work risk factors, the current functioning abilities regarding activities of daily living, as well as the present levels of cognitive functioning (e.g., neuropsychological evaluation).

Factors such as poor training in geriatrics, dementias and differential diagnosis, inability to speak the patient's language, and misconceptions regarding the patients' culture will undoubtedly lead to misdiagnosis.

Differentiating Alzheimer's disease from other dementing illness is an arduous process. The time consumed in obtaining the medical and family history, a neurological examination, the recommended blood work, brain imagining, and a complete neuropsychological evaluation, needless to say, is a very expensive proposition. If the victim of Alzheimer's disease does not fall into the "expected age category," but cognitive deficits become obvious to the family, confusion or anger toward the patient may develop — not to mention the lost chance to provide social service and psychological support.

When a person suffering from a dementing illness such as Alzheimer's disease does not meet the prescribed or expected age, and/or symptoms associated with this disease, it often can be overlooked, or misinterpreted as a psychiatric disorder. To learn about the possible differences that may exist between early and late onset of Alzheimer's disease, 391 patients meeting NINCDS–ADRDA strict criteria (McKhann et al., 1984) enrolled at the ADRC in the University of Southern California were studied. A division of early onset (under age 65) versus late onset (over age 65) were compared to ascertain whether there were differences or similarities in the expression of symptoms in the beginning stage. In this sample, 124 patients, or 32%, were classified as "early onset," and 267, or 68% were categorized as "late onset." This study revealed several important results. First, there was a greater variability in the symptoms expressed by older adults with Alzheimer's than by the younger group. From a list of 73 items (or specific symptoms), older adults utilized 53% of the entire list, whereas the younger subjects only used 38% of the total list. Second, the rank order of symptom expression also differed (see Table 17.2).

Third, there was a striking symptom in the early onset group that could be considered as a silent and diffuse symptom: the change in work behavior. Changes in work behavior can be a manifestation of impairment in memory, personality, visuospatial difficulty, judgment, and others, but only became evident through a decline in work performance.

TABLE 17.2
First Symptoms of Dementia Rank Ordered by Patients

Early Onset Sample	Late Onset Sample
1. Changes in work behavior	1. Forgetfulness
2. Forgetfulness	2. Losing, misplacing things
3. Losing, misplacing things	3. Short-term memory deficits
4. Short-term memory deficits	4. Spatial disorientation
5. Diff. managing finances	5. Repetitiveness
6. Paranoid ideation	6. Poor judgment

Although the late onset group was already retired and could not be compared with the younger group, changes in work behavior was a salient variable that deserves consideration by itself. Moreover, it is considered that 53% of the early onset sample had given up their job before retirement age, so having problems at work could be seen as a reliable symptom. Fourth, there were differences in symptom progression. For example, "cognitive problems" (e.g., poor judgment and spatial disorientation) were rarely reported as first symptoms in the early onset group and very common in late onset group (Taussig & Sanfelin, 1996).

OUTREACH TO THE COMMUNITY AND ENROLLMENT IN RESEARCH

If Hispanic elderly are to participate in Alzheimer's research, then outreach to the Hispanic primary caregivers and their families using culturally and linguistically appropriate strategies is a major necessity. Participation in research can help dispel myths while helping families to cope with difficult times and learn how to utilize available services in the community.

When a conference for primary caregivers of demented individuals is offered in the community, English-speaking caregivers, primarily Whites, seem to attend in great numbers. Since 1986, the University of Southern California–Alzheimer's Disease Research Center Consortium of Southern California, in conjunction with other entities, has provided annual presentations about Alzheimer's disease with emphasis on caregivers' needs to the general public. These conferences have been well attended, and the feedback to coordinators have been, for the most part, very positive.

When similar events are offered to the Hispanic community, a mixed review seems to follow the efforts of those willing to instruct. For example, in 1989, the first Spanish-language conference addressing Alzheimer's disease and related disorders was presented in Los Angeles County. The results of the first Spanish-language conference, as well as the many that followed, had certain themes in common: (a) the number of participants in each event was small; (b) participants, in general, were glad to attend, based on their post-conference feedback; (c) they seemed to want more information and often stayed after the presentation was over to continue their quest for information, and to interact with other conference participants; (d) they seemed to take the educational material printed in Spanish as well as the material printed in English (it seems that some younger family members are more proficient in English than Spanish); (e) they praised the speakers and thanked them profusely; (f) they wanted to know when the next event would occur in their neighborhood (Taussig & Trejo, 1992).

Personal experience working with the Spanish-speaking community in Los Angeles County alerted me to a variety of factors to keep in mind at each conference or presentation to insure success. First, I needed to be prepared to do the presentation in Spanish or English, and at times, the two languages needed to be used simultaneously. Second, the written materials appeared to be more popular if they were in short form (i.e., pamphlets), although lengthier and more materials were also taken, especially if they were free of charge. For those unable to read, the material was taken and someone at home read it for them. Keeping in mind that literacy and the Hispanic population falls in a wide spectrum, educational materials should be offered in simplistic and short, as well as lengthier and more explicit, form. These will accommodate this heterogeneous population.

In general, keeping in mind the following rules can in many instances insure the success of outreach and the enrollment of Hispanic elderly suffering from Alzheimer's disease in research programs:

1. Offer monthly presentations to different neighborhoods such as senior centers, churches, clinics, etc.

2. Provide elder care when possible. It is difficult to have someone caring for a demented older adult when the primary caregiver needs to attend an event, especially when the event is during the day (Connell & Gibson, 1997).

3. Offer enrollment to those not having proper medical coverage (by asking for more money to the funding source). This is a reality that cannot be ignored.

4. Offer transportation. Many Hispanic older adults, who are the primary caregiver and key person for participation in research, are women with no means of transportation.

5. Insure that the lecturer is fluent in Spanish and conformable doing public speaking. If a presenter barely can express the content of the talk in Spanish, then the participants may feel discomfort asking pertinent questions.

6. Make sure that after a presentation, the person working the telephone number provided is able to speak Spanish. Often the person in charge of outreach is also the person behind the phone and all the other duties in a Spanish program.

7. Do not hesitate to educate the participants of a conference or talk concerning the importance of participating in the autopsy program. Religion preference is not necessarily a detour for participation. When Hispanic families are well informed, they are as afraid as the rest of the population to develop Alzheimer's due to genetic links.

8. Develop a trusting relationship with the primary caregiver so issues of inappropriate, embarrassment, or shameful behaviors can be shared, as well as the possible fact of illegal status and fear of deportation.

SPECIFIC CONSIDERATIONS FOR EVALUATION OF ELDERLY HISPANIC PATIENTS

The issues regarding neuropsychological testing with Hispanics in general apply specifically to this age group, however, because those procedures are discussed elsewhere in this book, they are not revisited here.

A neuropsychological evaluation of an elderly patient performed by a neuropsychologist, or other professional, has two purposes: first, to obtain baseline information regarding the cognitive functioning of a patient in a standardized manner, and second, to clarify the presence and extent of possible cognitive impairments that require clinical attention. At this point, appropriate referrals—to an ADRC, to a day care, or to the Alzheimer's Association—are usually made.

Whether you are going to conduct a brief bedside screening or a more comprehensive examination, there are several factors to consider before cognitive evaluation begins. Some of these factors are applicable to any population, and some are more consistent and necessary to Hispanic older adults residing in the United States:

1. Conduct a careful evaluation of the patient's language ability and education attainment. This can be obtained by interviewing family members regarding the patient's high-

est level of education, the type of work done outside the home, and the ability to read and write previous to the cognitive decline.

2. Make sure the person in charge of evaluating the patient is fluent in Spanish and English. Insure that no translators will be used in the evaluation. If the patient cannot comprehend the tester, he or she may give the wrong answer; ascertain whether you are using the appropriate language before labeling a patient with cognitive deficits.

3. Have tests available in both Spanish and English, because a person with a Hispanic surname might be monolingual Spanish, monolingual English, or completely fluent in both languages.

4. Make sure no family member is allowed in the evaluation room. And never use a family member as a translator, because the translation can help or hinder the evaluation. Some family members out of love, respect, or pity, may "fix" the answers to give the impression of normalcy, whereas others, overburdened with the care of the patient and ashamed of such feelings, may exaggerate the answers in a negative or erroneous way as to suggest more cognitive impairment and receive some social support (Taussig, Mack, & Henderson, 1996).

5. The room in which the evaluation is performed should be well illuminated and without distracters such as telephones ringing, calendars, or people walking by as the evaluation is in progress.

6. Ascertain whether the patient requires glasses or hearing aids (note that older Hispanics due to poor financial means may not have them).

7. Older Hispanics unaccustomed to being tested with pencil-and-paper tasks may feel uncomfortable when others are observing their performance. These type of tasks may also cause great discomfort and embarrassment to older Hispanics who never attended school. Thus, a tendency to state "I can't or I don't know" may occur with great frequency, and can be interpreted as unable.

In general, as with any older adult suspected of dementia, develop a sense of trust and rapport before a neuropsychological evaluation starts. But because of the heterogeneity of the Hispanic group, ascertain the "preferred" language of patients, whether they have rural or urban background, including years of formal education, and when possible, remove family members from the room, because there is a tendency to answer for the patient (Olin, Pawluczyk, Kaufman, & Taussig, 1997).

REFERENCES

American Psychiatric Association. (1994). *Diagnostic and statistical manual of mental disorders* (4th ed.) Washington, DC: Author.

Chui, H. (1994). *Differential diagnosis of Alzheimer's disease.* Tape developed for the Los Angeles Area Alzheimer's Outreach Program, UCLA.

Connell, C. M., & Gibson, G. D. (1997). Racial, ethnic, and cultural differences in dementia caregiving: Review and analysis. *Gerontologist, 37*(3), 355–364.

Cutler, N. E. (1987). Someone I know has Alzheimer's. A statistical portrait from the first national opinion survey of Alzheimer's disease. *American Journal of Alzheimer's Care and Related Disorders and Research,* November/December, 21–25.

Duara, R., Barker, W. W., Lopez-Alberola, R., Loewenstein, D. A., Grau, L. B., Gilchrist, D., Sevush, S., & St. George-Hyslop, S. (1996). Alzheimer's disease: Interaction of apolipoprotein E genotype, family history of dementia, gender, education, ethnicity, and age of onset. *Neurology, 46*(6), 1575–1579.

Evans, D. A., Funkenstein, H., Albert, M. S., Scherr, P. A., Cook, N. R., Chown, M. J., Hebert, L. E., Hennekens, C. H., & Taylor, J. O. (1989). Prevalence of Alzheimer's disease in a community population of elder persons. *Journal of the American Medical Association, 262,* 2551–2556.

Farrer, L. A, Cupples, L. A, Haines, J. L., Hyman, B., Kukull, W. A., Mayeux, R., Myers, R. H., Pericak-Vance, M. A., Risch, N., & van Duijn, C. M. (1997). Effects of age, sex, and ethnicity on the association between apolipoprotein E genotype and Alzheimer disease. A meta-analysis. APOE and Alzheimer Disease Meta Analysis Consortium. *Journal of the American Medical Association, 278*(16), 1349–1356.

Henderson, V. W. (1995). Alzheimer's disease in women: Is there a role for estrogen replacement therapy? *Menopause Management, 4*(6), 10–13.

Henderson, V. W., & Finch, C. E. (1989). The neurobiology of Alzheimer's disease. *Journal of Neurosurgery, 70,* 335–353.

Henderson, V. W., & Paganini-Hill, A. (1995). Estrogen and Alzheimer's disease. In R. Asch & J. Studd (Eds.), *Progress in reproductive medicine* (Vol. 2, pp. 185–193). New York: Parthenon.

Kemp, B. J., Staples, F., & Lopez-Aqueres, W. (1987). Epidemiology of depression and dysphoria in an elderly Hispanic population: Prevalence and correlates. *Journal of the American Geriatrics Society, 35*(10), 920–926.

McKhann, G., Drachman, D., Folstein, M., Katzman, R., Price, D., & Stadlan, E. M. (1984). Clinical diagnosis of Alzheimer's disease: Report of the NINCDS–ADRDA Work Group under the auspices of Department of Health and Human Services Task Force on Alzheimer's Disease. *Neurology, 34*(7), 939–944.

Olin, J. T., Pawluczyk, S., Kaufman, G. T., & Taussig, I. M. (1997). A comparative analysis of Spanish- and English-speaking Alzheimer's disease patients: Eligibility and interest in clinical drug trials. *Journal of Clinical Geropsychology, 3*(3), 183–190.

Perkins, P., Annegers, J. F., Doody, R., Cooke, N., Aday, L., & Vernon, S. W. (1997). Incidence and prevalence of dementia in a multiethnic cohort of municipal retirees. *Neurology, 49*(1), 44–50.

Taussig, I. M., Harris, J. M., & Chiang, Y. C. (1995, March). *Basic knowledge of Alzheimer's disease: A survey of Hispanic primary caregivers of demented older adults and its implications for educational interventions.* Paper presented at the American Society on Aging Annual Conference, Atlanta, Georgia.

Taussig, I. M., Henderson, V. W., & Mack, W. (1992). Spanish translation and validation of a neuropsychological battery: Performance of Spanish- and English-speaking Alzheimer's disease patients and normal comparison subjects. *Clinical Gerontologist, 2*(3/4), 95–107.

Taussig, I. M., & Mack, W. (1992). Caregiver's observations and report of early symptoms of Alzheimer's disease. *American Journal of Alzheimer's Care and Related Disorders and Research,* March/April, 28–34.

Taussig, I. M., & Mack, W. (1995). A comparison of Spanish versus English-speaking caregivers' perception of early symptoms of Alzheimer's disease. *American Journal of Alzheimer's Disease,* September/October, 33–39.

Taussig, I. M., Mack, W. J., & Henderson, V. W. (1996). Concurrent validity of Spanish-language versions of the Mini-Mental State Examination, Mental Status Questionnaire, Information-Memory-Concentration Test, and Orientation-Memory-Concentration Test: Alzheimer's disease. *Journal of the International Neuropsychological Society, 2*(4), 286–298.

Taussig, I. M., & Pontón, M. O. (1996). Issues in Neuropsychological assessment for Hispanic older adults: Culture and linguistic factors. In G. Yeo & D. Gallagher-Thompson (Eds.), *Ethnicity and the dementias* (pp. 47–58). New York: Taylor and Francis.

Taussig, I. M., & Sanfelin, M. C. (1996). First symptoms of Alzheimer's disease: A comparison between early and late onset and its implications for diagnosis. *Journal of the International Neuropsychological Society, 2*(3), 195.

Taussig, I. M., & Trejo, L. (1992). Outreach to Spanish-speaking caregivers of persons with memory impairment: A brief report. *Clinical Gerontologist, 2*(3/4), 183–189.

U.S. Census Bureau. (1998, September 29). *Statistical Abstract of the United States: 1998.* http://www.census.gov/prod/3/98pubs/98statab/sasec1.pdf.

Author Index

Subject Index